BUSINESS LAW IN EUROPE

BUSINESS LAW IN EUROPE

Legal, tax and labour aspects of business operations in the ten European Community countries and Switzerland

Edited by Maarten J. Ellis
and Paul M. Storm

Prepared under the auspices of the Association européenne d'études juridiques et fiscales by:

Paul M. Storm, Benno H. ter Kuile, Maarten J. Ellis, Bernard C. Dubois, W. Hallemeesch, M. Denys, Hans Lindegaard, Eskil Trolle, Maurice Letulle, Claude Lucas de Leyssac, Denis de Ricci, Jacques Tuot, Wolfgang Rosener, Dimitri C. Lambadarios, George N. Stathopoulos, Criton Anastassopoulos, John N. Ross, Richard Rice, Giovanni M. Ughi, Jacques Loesch, Peter Forstmoser, Walter Meier, N. Fox Bassett

Springer Science+Business Media, B.V.

Library of Congress Cataloging in Publication Data
Main entry under title:

Business law in Europe

Bibliography: p.
Includes index.
1. Business enterprises--European economic Community countries. 2. Taxation--Law and legislation--European Economic Community countries. 3. Labor laws and legislation--European Economic Community countries. 4. Business enterprises--Switzerland. 5. Taxation--Law and legislation--Switzerland. 6. Labor laws and legislation--Switzerland. I. Aalders, C. A. V. II. Association européenne d'études juridiques et fiscales.

Law 346.4'07 81-20736
344.067 AACR2

ISBN 978-94-017-4360-0 ISBN 978-94-017-4358-7 (eBook)
DOI 10.1007/978-94-017-4358-7

D/1982/2664/18

Originally published by Kluwer, Deventer, The Netherlands in 1982
Softcover reprint of the hardcover 1st edition 1982

General Contents

Introduction

This book is intended to serve as a guide to businessmen and their advisers, either from outside the Common Market or from within, who seek basic information on questions in three main fields: company law and related legal matters, taxation, and labour law. For those who wish to establish an enterprise or form a holding or financing company in one of the Member States of the Common Market (including Greece, of course) or Switzerland this guide offers a unique opportunity to compare conditions in the various countries in the three fields. This is facilitated by the strict adherence to one format for each national chapter. Those who are already present in one or more of the eleven countries will find a global answer to a number of practical questions that may arise. For detailed answers the local lawyer or other consultant remains indispensable.

The format is based on two different approaches the foreign investor may take: either he 'goes it alone', by way of establishing a branch, setting up a subsidiary or taking over an existing company, or he joins forces with another investor from within the host country or from outside. In the latter event there are a number of legal forms (jointly owned company, partnership, etc.) which may be used.

Company law, taxation and labour law in the Member States of the Common Market have over the last few years acquired an additional, common dimension. In each of these fields the European Communities have been and still are harmonizing the national law systems, and are even creating entirely new law. This fact alone justifies a full opening chapter on the European developments in these fields. But there is more to this. Since the laws of the Member States have been or will soon be 'harmonized' on quite a number of points, the editors have been able to deal with these points in the 'European' chapter rather than in each national chapter. Only to the extent the implementation of EEC-Directives has given rise to peculiarities in some Member State has special mention been made of the law covered by the Directives. This should be kept in mind when one reads the national chapters.

The authors of several chapters of this book are greatly indebted to Nicholas Paines, barrister in London and son of one of our members, for his assistance in translation and his useful comments.

With some minor exceptions, in particular with respect to the Luxembourg chapter and to the section on labour aspects in the Greek chapter, the book reflects the laws in effect as of January 1, 1982.

Association européenne d'études juridiques et fiscales, Paris, January 1982.

Contents

NATIONAL CHAPTERS

The National chapters roughly follow the format set out below:

I. INTRODUCTION

II. THE LEGAL FRAMEWORK
A. *The Vehicle*
1. The wholly-owned enterprise
1.a. The branch
1.a.(i) Establishment
1.a.(ii) Organization
- management, representation
- liability
- accounts and auditing requirements
- publication of accounts.

1.b. The subsidiary
1.b.(i) Establishment
1.b.(ii) Organization
- capital, shares, transfer
- management, representation
- shareholders meetings
- liability
- accounts and auditing requirements
- publication of accounts
- groups of companies

1.b.(iii) Checklist for establishing a subsidiary
1.c. Other forms
2. The joint venture
2.a. The jointly-owned company
2.a.(i) Shareholders' agreements
2.a.(ii) Minority rights
2.b. Consortia
2.c. Other

B. *External Controls*
   1. Exchange controls
   2. Merger controls
   3. Competition
   4. Environmental controls
   5. State monopolies
   6. Others

III. TAXATION
   A. *Corporation Tax*
      1. Entities subject to tax
      2. Computation of profits
      2.a. Income
      2.b. Capital gains/losses
      2.c. Exemptions, deductions, rebates
      3. Rates of tax
      4. Tax credits
      5. Timing of payments
      6. Review and appeal

   B. *Withholding Taxes on Dividends, Interest, Royalties*
      1. Income categories subject to withholding tax
      2. Computation of income
      3. Rates
      4. Effect of tax treaties

   C. *Registration and Stamp Duties*

   D. *Individual Taxation*
      1. Persons subject to tax
      2. Computation of income
      2.a. Income
      2.b. Capital gains
      2.c. Exemptions, deductions, rebates
      3. Rates of tax
      4. Succession duties

   E. *Indirect Taxation*

   F. *Incentives*

   G. *Social Security Premiums*

   H. *Other*

   I. *Double Taxation Treaties*

   J. *Schedule of Withholding Taxes*

FEDERAL REPUBLIC OF GERMANY (INCLUDING WEST BERLIN)

GREECE

IRELAND

ITALY

LUXEMBOURG

THE NETHERLANDS

Some Terms and Abbreviations

Although we are well aware of the impossibility of adequately translating many legal terms into English we have endeavoured to achieve some uniformity of terminology throughout this book. To this end we have generally followed the terminology of the English versions of official documents of the EC. The English and Irish authors have of course used their own terms. For an explanation of some terms of European law we refer to the chapter on Some Observations on the Law of the European Communities. A short explanation of some of the other terms may be useful.

- **Enterprise** = undertaking or business
- **Public company** is used for the equivalent of *société anonyme (SA), Aktiengesellschaft (AG), naamloze vennootschap (NV), società per azioni (SpA), Aktieselskab (A/S),* the English plc, *anonymos etairia (AE)*
- **Private company** is used for the equivalent of *société à responsabilité limitée (sàrl), Gesellschaft mit beschränkter Haftung (GmbH),* the Dutch *besloten vennootschap (BV)*, the Belgian *société de personnes à responsabilité limitée (sprl)* or *personenvennootschap met beperkte aansprakelijkheid (pvba), società a responsabilità limitata (sarl), Anpartsselskab (ApS), etairia periorismenis efthinis (EPE)*
- **Partnership limited by shares** is used for the equivalent of *société en commandite par actions (SCA), Kommanditgesellschaft auf Aktien (KGaA), commanditaire vennootschap op aandelen* (in Belgium), *società in accomandita per azioni, Kommandit-Aktieselskab.*
- **Limited partnership** is used for the equivalent of *société en commandite simple, Kommanditgesellschaft (KG), commanditaire vennootschap (CV), società in accomandita semplice, Kommanditselskab, eterorrythmos etairia (EE)*
- **General partnership** is used for the equivalent of *société en nom collectif, offene Handelsgesellschaft (OHG), vennootschap onder firma (vof), società in nome collettivo, omorythmos etairia (OE)*
- **Group of companies** – the German *Konzern* (which may include entities other than companies)
- **Dominant enterprise** – the dominant (controlling) enterprise in a group of companies
- **Dependent enterprise** – the dependent (controlled) enterprise in a group of companies
- **Seat** – to some extent the equivalent of the British registered office
- **Statutes** – the equivalent of British Articles of Association

- **Board (of Directors)** – when there is a single Board
- **Director** – member of a single Board
- **Managing Board** – Board of management, the members are executives
- **Member of the Managing Board** (not: Managing Director)
- **Managing Director** – Director of *GmbH, sàrl* or *pvba*
- **Supervisory Board** – *Aufsichtsrat, raad van commissarissen, conseil de surveillance* (Board of non-executive Directors)
- **Trade Register** – *Registre du commerce, Handelsregister*
- **Works Council** – *Conseil d'entreprise, Betriebsrat, ondernemingsraad*

Abbreviations

AG – Aktiengesellschaft
ApS – Anpartsselskab
A/S – Aktieselskab
BV – besloten vennootschap
CV – commanditaire vennootschap
EC – European Communities
ECR – Official reports of cases before the European Court of Justice
EE – eterorrythmos etairia
EEC – European Economic Community
EP – European Parliament
EPE – etairia periorismenis efthinis
ESC – Economic and Social Committee (of the European Communities)
EUA – European unit of account
GmbH – Gesellschaft mit beschränkter Haftung
KG – Kommanditgesellschaft
KGaA – Kommanditgesellschaft auf Aktien
K/S – Kommanditselskab
NV – naamloze vennootschap
OE – omorythmos etairia
OHG – offene Handelsgesellschaft
OJ – Official Journal of the European Communities
plc – public limited company
pvba – personenvennootschap met beperkte aansprakelijkheid
SA – société anonyme
sarl – società a responsabilità limitata
sàrl – société à responsabilité limitée
SCA – société en commandite par actions
SpA – società per azioni
Sprl – société de personnes à responsabilité limitée
vof – vennootschap onder firma

Some Observations on the Law of the European Communities

I. GENERAL OBSERVATIONS

Paul M. Storm
Member of the Rotterdam Bar

1. The first three chapters of this book are devoted to the law of the European Communities. Reading these chapters requires some basic knowledge of certain concepts of this law. In this chapter an attempt will be made to give some basic information to those who have no knowledge at all of the legal aspects of the EC. Of course this information will be incomplete and by that very fact to some extent misleading. However, the editors felt the reader might be better served with some sketchy information than with none at all.

2. European integration is based on three Treaties instituting the European Coal and Steel Community (ECSC), the European Economic Community (EEC), and the European Atomic Energy Community (Euratom) respectively. The EEC Treaty is the more general one, the other two are limited to specific sectors of the economy. The institutions created by those Treaties, the European Parliament (officially 'Assembly'), the Council, the Commission, and the Court of Justice, have been made common to all three Treaties. In the context of this book, only the EEC Treaty is relevant. Therefore, it is only to this Treaty that reference will be made.

3. The aims of the EEC are of an economic and political nature, for example to promote throughout the Community a harmonious development of economic activities. The Treaty mentions two means to attain these aims:
- the establishment of a Common Market, and
- the progressive approximation of the economic policies of the Member States.

4. The establishment of a Common Market comprises four elements:
- the free movement of goods;
- the free movement of persons;
- freedom of establishment and freedom to supply services; and
- the free movement of capital.

The realization of these 'four freedoms' must be supplemented by the approximation of national laws in many areas. Such approximation may also be required for the proper functioning of the Common Market, now it has been established. In addition, differences between national laws may distort the conditions of competition between enterprises and persons in different Member States. The elimination of these differences may to some extent be achieved by the approximation (usually called 'harmonization') of national laws. Harmonization is effected on the basis of 'Directives' adopted by the Council of the EC. The concept of 'Directive' will be dealt with in item 13 *infra*.

5. Both the establishment and the functioning of the Common Market could be seriously impaired by obstacles to free competition. This is why the Treaty contains rules for the protection of competition, which give the Community institutions, in particular the Commission, extensive powers to adopt Regulations[1] and to formulate Decisions.[1] Competition is one of the areas in which the Community could develop its own policy and it cannot be denied that it has readily taken the opportunity. So much has been written about this subject and it is so comprehensive that the editors of this book have decided not to include it, except for a short exposé of the impact of European competition law and policy on joint ventures, an important phenomenon in the context of this book. See Section II of this Chapter.

6. The 'progressive approximation of the economic policies of the Member States' cannot be considered separately from the social policy of the Member States. This policy is of course primarily concerned with employment, wages and social security, but also with all other employment conditions. It is in respect of such conditions that a number of Directives have been adopted. Some of these are dealt with in the Chapter on European Social Law. In addition, Article 119 of the EEC Treaty provides for equal pay for men and women. This provision has given rise to important case-law of the European Court of Justice (see item 8 *infra*).

7. The aforegoing shows that there are *various sources of Community law*. To begin with, there is the Treaty. Then there are the various acts of the Community institutions as provided in Article 189 of the EEC Treaty (Regulations, Directives, Decisions, Recommendations and Opinions).[2] In addition, there are international conventions by which the Community is bound. Last but not least there is the case-law of the Court of Justice which is essential for the development of Community law and, indeed, for the whole process of integration. It is the Court which has pointed out that the Community constitutes a *new legal order* for the benefit of which the States have limited their sovereign rights, albeit within limited fields, and the subjects of which are not

1. These concepts will be dealt with in items 12 and 14 *infra*.
2. In addition to these official acts there are 'programmes', 'declarations', 'resolutions', etc. adopted by the European Council (Heads of Government and Foreign Ministers of the Member States and President and Vice-President of the Commission), 'the representatives of the Member States in Council' or simply the representatives of the governments. These measures are taken without the procedures of the Treaty being observed and cannot be reviewed by the Court of Justice, but are nevertheless in fact often very important instruments laying down Community policies.

only the Member States as such but also their nationals. The Treaty is more than the traditional convention which merely creates mutual obligations between the contracting states. In this new legal order a very prominent role is played by general principles of law, including fundamental human rights, as well as by the so-called 'secondary Community law', that is the law created by the Community institutions. Another characteristic of Community law is the extensive organisational and procedural provisions which have been made to supplement, elaborate, amend, apply and enforce it.

8. Certain provisions of the EEC Treaty have *direct effect*. This means that they are capable of creating individual rights which national courts must protect. These provisions include, among many others, Article 48 (free movement of workers), 52 and 53 (freedom of establishment) and 59 and 62 (freedom to supply services), all derivatives of Article 7 which lays down one of the Treaty's fundamental principles, the prohibition of discrimination based on nationality, Articles 85 and 86 (competition) and Article 119 (see item 6 *supra*). In most cases the provision which has direct effect is clearly addressed to the Member States and consequently the individual rights which form the other side of the obligations imposed upon the States can be relied upon only against the States. This is the so-called 'vertical direct effect'. However, in a number of cases the Court of Justice has given 'horizontal direct effect' (i.e. effect as between individuals or firms) to Treaty provisions which were addressed to the Member States. Thus the Court decided that the prohibition of discrimination laid down in Articles 7, 48 and 59 applies not only to governmental agencies but also to collective labour agreements and other collective arrangements for the supply of services[3], so that a cyclist and a soccer player could invoke this prohibition against their associations who discriminated against nationals of other Member States. As to Article 119, the Court decided that the prohibition of discrimination between male and female employees did not only apply to government acts but also to all collective labour agreements and even to contracts between individuals.[4] It should be noted, however, that the Court has so far only recognized horizontal direct effect of provisions which it characterized as principles of Community law.

9. In order to have vertical direct effect, a provision of Community law (including the secondary law) must in principle meet several conditions:
- it must contain a clearly defined obligation of a Member State;
- it must not be subject to any condition;
- no implementing act of the Community institutions or of the Member State is required to make the obligation capable of being met; and
- no discretion must have been left to the Member State in deciding how to meet the obligation.

In principle, corresponding conditions apply for horizontal direct effect.

3. Cases 36-74 (Walrave and Koch/UCI and KNWU), ECR '74, p. 1405 and 13-76 (Donà/Mantero), ECR '76, p. 1333.
4. Case 43-75 (Defrenne/Sabena), ECR '76, p. 455.

10. In numerous decisions the Court of Justice has affirmed the *priority of Community law over national law*. This means that national courts must not apply any provision of national law which conflicts with any provision of the Treaty or of secondary Community law, irrespective of whether the national law dates from before or after the Community law provision. In this connection, Article 177 of the EEC Treaty, on preliminary rulings, is of vital importance, as will be set out in item 18 *infra*.

11. As stated above, Article 189 of the EEC Treaty provides for four instruments in which secondary Community law may be laid down. This does not mean that the Community institutions are free to choose which instrument to use to cover a specific subject. In most cases the Treaty sets this out precisely. In fact, the institutions have no power to adopt any Regulations or Directives unless in a specific field it has been expressly vested in them by the Treaty.

12. The *Regulation* is the most far-reaching instrument. It has general application, is binding in its entirety, and is directly applicable in each Member State. Unless expressly stated otherwise, it does not require any national measure to become binding upon everyone in the Community. In principle, it has *direct effect* as set out in items 8 and 9 *supra*. The Regulation is the instrument most provided for in the context of common policies (such as agriculture and competition), but it is also mentioned in the Chapter on the free movement of workers (see the Chapter on European Social Law).

13. The *Directive* is the most interesting instrument in the context of this book, since harmonization in the fields of company law, taxation and social law is exclusively effected by way of Directives.
Directives are always addressed to the Member States and they are binding upon them as to the result to be achieved, while the determination of the form and means by which the result is to be achieved remains within the competence of the Member States. Thus Member States may decide whether to implement the rules of a Directive by legislative or administrative acts. In practice, Directives are often rather detailed, thus leaving the States little freedom. Some provisions of Directives meet the conditions referred to in item 9 *supra* and have therefore been held to have direct effect.
In addition, national courts must see to it that the national legislator has not exceeded his discretion in implementing a Directive, and must not apply the implementing act to the extent that he may have done so.[5] As long as a Member State fails to implement a Directive, existing national law which is in conflict with the Directive must not be applied as against individuals or firms who act in accordance with the Directive.[6]
Up to July 1981 the Court of Justice had not yet had an opportunity to decide whether a Directive could produce horizontal direct effect. One could imagine that this would be the case with some Directives on Social Law which

5. Cases 51/76 (VNO), ECR '77, p. 113 and 38/77 (Enka), ECR '77, p. 2203.
6. Case 148/78 (Ratti), ECR '79, p. 1629.

elaborate certain fundamental principles laid down in the Treaty. It would be more difficult to accept such effect in the case of Directives on Company Law. In most cases the cohesion of all the provisions of such a Directive would oppose the recognition of such effect of one or more isolated provisions.

14. *Decisions* may be addressed to one or more Member States or to one or more legal or natural persons. They are binding in every respect on the addressees named therein. In the context of this book Decisions are of little importance since they are not used for the harmonization of national laws.

15. *Recommendations* and *Opinions* have no binding force. They cannot be reviewed by the Court of Justice, and are seldom formulated by any of the Community institutions in the fields covered by this book. For an exception, see the Chapter on European Company Law, item 77 (g).

16. Regulations may be adopted by the Council or by the Commission, depending upon the Treaty. If they are adopted by the Council they must have been proposed by the Commission and the Council must have consulted the European Parliament and the Economic and Social Committee.
As to the adoption of Directives, reference is made to items 6 to 9 of the Chapter on European Company Law.

17. The role of the *Court of Justice* in maintaining, interpreting and developing Community law cannot be overestimated. The Court acts in quite a number of capacities, including that of administrative court, reviewing the legality of Community acts and adjudicating claims for damages caused by wrongful Community acts. In the context of this book, two capacities should be mentioned in particular.

18. First and foremost, *Article 177* of the EEC Treaty entrusts the Court with the task of giving *preliminary rulings*, at the request of national courts, on the interpretation of the Treaty and the validity and interpretation of acts of the Community institutions. A request to that effect *may* be made by any court or tribunal of a Member State before which such a question is raised, if it considers that a decision on the question is necessary to enable it to give judgment. However, if such a question is raised in a case before a national court from whose judgments no appeal lies, that court *must* refer the question to the Court of Justice.
Thus the Court has given a large number of preliminary rulings which have had a profound impact on the business community within the EC. These rulings are the result of a certain team-work between the national courts and the Court of Justice. The latter does not act, at least not in this capacity, as a court of appeals or a 'cour de cassation', but only as the body with final authority which gives answers to certain questions of Community law which may have been raised in a dispute between individuals not necessarily seeming at first sight to have anything to do with the Community. It follows from the aforegoing that the national courts also play an important part in the application of Community law. It is in these courts that the great majority of litigation involving Community law takes place.

The interpretation of acts of the Community institutions includes the interpretation of Directives. Persons whose rights or interests are affected by a national law implementing a Directive, or even by a State's failure to implement it, can turn to their national courts in order to get a decision prohibiting the application of their national law to the extent it is in conflict with the Directive. If, in deciding whether there is such a conflict, a national court is faced with a question concerning the interpretation of the Directive, it may (or must) refer the question to the Court of Justice. Proceedings before the Court are relatively speedy: a preliminary ruling is usually given within 12 months, in which period the parties to the litigation, the Commission, the Council and all the Member States are given an opportunity to submit their observations to the Court.

19. The other capacity in which the Court acts and which should be highlighted here finds its origin in *Article 169* of the EEC Treaty. According to this provision the Commission shall, if it considers that a *Member State has failed to fulfil any of its obligations under the Treaty*, give a 'reasoned opinion' on the matter after giving such a State the opportunity to submit its observations. If the Member State does not comply with the terms of the opinion within the period laid down by the Commission, the latter may refer the matter to the Court of Justice. The other Member States may do the same (but in practice seldom do) after having referred the matter to the Commission without the desired effect (Article 170). If the Court finds that the Member State has failed to fulfil its obligations under the Treaty, the Member State will have to take the measures required for the implementation of the Court's judgment. If it does not do so, the other Member States may take reprisals, as long as these do not violate Community law.
These procedures are mentioned here with a view to the fact that the Member States often fail to implement harmonization Directives within the prescribed time. The Commission has in fact initiated many proceedings based on Article 169. This action has in nearly all cases been successful in that the Member State concerned either complied before the Court gave its decision or did so fairly soon afterwards.

20. In concluding this brief survey mention should be made of a *source of semi-Community law*, the Conventions between the Member States based on Article 220 of the EEC Treaty or in some other way connected with the EC.

21. The most important Convention in this respect is the *Convention of 27th September 1968 on Jurisdiction and Enforcement of Judgments in Civil and Commercial Matters.* When it came into force between the six original Member States on 1st Februari 1973 it effectively abolished the frontiers between these States as far as the jurisdiction of national courts and the recognition and enforcement of their decisions on the said matters are concerned. The impact of the Convention is felt increasingly by practising lawyers in the original Member States. Meanwhile, on 9th October 1978 a *Convention of Accession* of Denmark, Ireland and the UK to the Convention was signed, but in January 1982 it looked as if this Convention would not enter into force until 1983 or 1984. The Convention of Accession contains quite a number of amendments to the original Convention.

22. The Convention is based on Article 220 of the EEC Treaty which requires the Member States to negotiate Conventions on various subjects (see also item 78 of the Chapter on European Company Law) including the subject of this Convention. These Conventions are being negotiated within the framework of the EC institutions and the Commission has taken the initiative for the negotiations. In principle, the Conventions are of the same nature as any other international Treaty. However, it is intended that endeavours be made at a Community level to ensure as effective and uniform an application of their provisions as possible. This intention is effectuated differently in the two Conventions based on Article 220 which have hitherto been signed.

23. A Protocol[7] to the Convention on the Mutual Recognition of Companies and Legal Persons (which has not entered into force, see item III. A of the Chapter on European Company Law) gives the Court of Justice competence to give preliminary rulings in exactly the same manner as Article 177 does. However, a Protocol[8] to the Convention on Jurisdiction etc., while providing that the highest courts must request the Court to give a preliminary ruling if they consider a decision on a question of Community law necessary to enable them to give judgment, gives the competence to request such a ruling only to national courts sitting in an appellate capacity, thereby excluding all courts of first instance. In addition, the 'competent authority' of each Member State may request a preliminary ruling if judgments given by courts of their State conflict with the interpretation given either by the Court of Justice or by one of the courts of another Member State, but only if its judgment has become *res judicata*. The Court's response will therefore not effect those judgments.

24. With a view to continuing in the field of private international law the work of unification of law which has already been done within the Community, in particular in the field of jurisdiction and enforcement of judgments, the *Convention on the Law Applicable to Contractual Obligations*[9] was opened for signature on 19th June 1980. On that date it was signed by seven Member States and Denmark signed it later, but the UK had not done so yet in January 1982. This Convention lays down a set of uniform rules of private international law relating to the law applicable to obligations arising under most commercial contracts.

Unfortunately, the States could not agree on conferring jurisdiction on the Court of Justice for the interpretation of this Convention. It looks as if the Convention will not be ratified by all Member States until agreement on this matter has been reached. Without such agreement the Convention, which is not provided for in the EEC Treaty, could hardly be said to belong to even the body of semi-Community law.[10]

7. The Protocol was signed on 3-6-71; see for the text M.R. Mok in 8 *CML Rev.* 1971, p. 495 and *Supplement* 4/71 *to Bulletin EC* 7-1971.
8. Protocol of the same date, see also OJ nr. L 304, 30-10-78, p. 36.
9. OJ nr. 266, 9-10-80, p. 1.
10. Cf. the very critical Opinion (80/383/EEC) dated 17-3-80 of the Commission published in OJ nr. L 94, 11-4-80, p. 39.

25. As for the *Convention on the Mutual Recognition of Companies and Legal Persons*, the *draft Convention on International Mergers of Public Companies* and the plans for a Convention on the maintenance of legal personality of companies in the event of a *transfer of seat* from one Member State to another, reference is made to item III of the Chapter on European Company Law.[11]

II. JOINT VENTURES AND EEC COMPETITION LAW

Benno H. ter Kuile
Member of the Bar of the Hague

1. Nowadays, the existence of the Common Market may affect the decision on the establishment of an enterprise in a Member State of the European Communities. This may also and more particularly apply to the establishment of an enterprise which already is or will become part of a group of companies, the central management of which is located outside the European Communities. For various reasons companies located outside the EC may wish to set up an establishment within the EC. They could benefit from the Common Market, its free movement of goods, persons, services and capital, including agriculture and transport. In general when determining the legal form of an enterprise to be established in the EC, there is no need to give much attention to Articles 9 to 84 of Part II of the EEC Treaty concerning the foundations of the Common Market and the subjects just mentioned. These Treaty provisions protect the rights of nationals of the Member States rather than those of foreign residents. Moreover, these articles do not impede the free establishment of enterprises within the Common Market. In a way, this part of the Treaty looks inward, rather than outward, and relates to intra-Community trade for the purpose not of impeding but of stimulating the establishment of enterprises within the Common Market.

2. However, this does not to the same extent apply to some articles in Part III of the EEC Treaty (Articles 85 to 130), relating to the policy of the Community. The Community's rules on competition (Articles 85 to 94) in particular may, under certain circumstances, create barriers to the free establishment of enterprises. Here we will deal with this problem in more detail.

3. EEC competition rules are of public order, in that enterprises always have to take into account the prohibitions laid down in Articles 85 and 86. This holds true even for practices of enterprises which are located outside the EC, but affect competition and free trade within the Common Market.

4. Often the establishment of an enterprise in the EC results from independent enterprises entering into a joint venture for such purposes as research and development, production, or distribution. In some industries investments re-

11. See *Bulletin EC* 7/8 – 1980, item 2.1.19.

quire both such a broad and varied technical know-how and so much capital that it is impossible for one company, acting on its own, to make that investment pay. Hence the need for co-operation between enterprises in which each participant makes its own specific contribution.
Such co-operation will mostly exist between parties operating in the same branch of trade or industry. Assuming, for convenience's sake, the existence of a general industrial market (possibly with some submarkets), this kind of co-operation may develop between enterprises operating on both sides (supply and demand) or on the same side of the market (in which case they are competitors).
Although competition might be restricted in the event of co-operation between enterprises operating on different sides of the market, the restriction of competition is manifest where competitors co-operate. In the latter case the prohibition of Article 85(1) of the EEC Treaty will readily apply. Apparently, this will also be true for the establishment and incorporation of a joint venture within the EC, whether or not the parent companies are located within the Community.

5. Although it is likely that the prohibition in Article 85(1) applies to most cases concerning joint ventures, this does not imply that the establishment of joint ventures within the EC can hardly ever succeed. It does mean, however, that one should be aware of the applicability, in principle, of the prohibition of Article 85(1) to this increasingly popular type of co-operation and that, therefore, one will have to ask for an exemption under Article 85(3). This exemption can only be granted by the Commission of the European Communities after the parties have notified the co-operation agreement to the Commission pursuant to Article 4 of Regulation (EEC) 17/62 of the Council.

6. Until 1975 the Commission seemed to take the view that in many cases it would be possible to bring the co-operation between enterprises by way of formation of a joint venture within Article 85(1) (cf. Commission Decision (IV/26.872) SHV-Chevron, of 20th December 1974, OJ nr. L 38 12-2-75, p. 14).
It has since become evident, however, that according to the Commission the prohibition of Article 85(1) basically does apply to joint ventures (cf. Commission, Fourth Report on Competition Policy, 1975, para. 37 and seq.; Sixth Report on Competition Policy, 1977, para. 53 and seq.). The decisive question then will be to what extent the co-operation through the joint venture and the joint control over it will affect the individual conduct of the parent companies in the market. Even in the absence of particularized agreements or concerted practices between the parent companies, the Commission will assume that restrictive arrangements are more likely to be made in cases where the parties and the joint venture involved are in effect competitors, on the same side of the market. This restrictive effect which, under certain circumstances, could jeopardize the economic independence of the parties is referred to by the Commission as the 'group effect' (Commission, Fourth Report on Competition Policy, para. 39).

7. The business community does not always share the Commision's view with regard to the applicability of the prohibition of Article 85(1) to joint ventures. This policy of the Commission could easily have a considerable adverse effect on the development of trade and industry, since agreements and decisions falling within the ambit of Article 85(1) are null and void (Article 85(2)). It could be argued that under Article 85(1) the drafters of the EEC Treaty wished to prohibit the prevention, restriction or distortion of *relevant* competition in the Common Market. Therefore, not every restriction of competition, even though apparent, would be prohibited. Co-operation between independent and relatively small enterprises by way of a joint venture would indeed restrict the mutual internal competition between the participants, but the motive for such a restriction of competition is to increase the competitive force of these small enterprises in relation to the many large ones. By restricting the internal competition between the smaller enterprises, the 'external competition' between the co-operating enterprises on the one hand and the large ones on the other could lead to an increase of relevant competition in the Common Market. If the creation and establishment of a joint venture were thus to increase relevant competition in the Common Market, the general application of the prohibition of Article 85(1) to this type of co-operation between enterprises would not seem to be the appropriate way to promote a harmonious development of economic activities which is one of the main purposes of competition policy (see Article 3(f) of the EEC Treaty). Such a policy of the Community's authorities will have considerable adverse effect on the market, even if the Commission were willing to grant an exemption in many cases. Taking into account the circumstances of the market in 1981, one may wonder whether the Commission is wise in this way to give priority to competition policy over an effective industrial policy.

8. Apparently, however, the Commission remains unresponsive to the arguments of the business community (cf. Commission Decision (IV/28.796) Beecham-Parke, Davis of 17th January 1979, OJ nr. L 70, 21-3-79, p. 11, para. 32; Decision (IV/27.093) De Laval-Stork of 25th July 1977, OJ nr. L 215, 23-8-77, p. 11, para. II, 6). The Commission seems to underestimate the fact that the administrative procedure to obtain an exemption under Article 85(3) is too time-consuming and draws too much attention to new company projects to promote efficient business development, thereby hindering this development. The Commission has extended its view very far on the applicability of Article 85(1) to joint ventures. In its view, the prohibition of Article 85(1) is applicable even if no actual competition were to exist between the parent companies, but only potential competition between these partners is expected to be restricted as a result of the co-operation (cf. Commission Decision (IV/27.442) Vacuum Interrupters, of 20th January 1977, OJ nr. L 48, 19-2-77, p. 32).

9. Articles 2 and 3 of the EEC Treaty show that competition is not an objective in itself, but merely a means to achieve the objectives of the Treaty. This implies that in respect of forms of co-operation like joint ventures in the fields of research and development, of industrial production and of trade and distribution, the Commission primarily has a correcting task the performance of which may be guided by its competition policy. In this view, the application of the prohibition of Article 85(1) should be precluded if, in the end, the co-operation results in increased competition in the Common Market. However, the current policy of the Commission tends to strangle the initiatives of industry to establish joint ventures. Such initiatives are badly needed nowadays. It can only be hoped that the European Parliament is willing and able to censure this policy of the Commission.

10. In any event, when creating and establishing joint ventures within the Common Market, enterprises will have to take into account the prohibition of Article 85(1) and the need to apply for an exemption. Consequently, notification of the relevant agreements and concerted practices relating to the joint venture will almost always be necessary (cf. Article 4 of Regulation 17/62). Going ahead while the prohibition could apply and no exemption has been obtained is hazardous. In the case of a joint venture for which no exemption has been obtained one would be building on sand. The agreements and decisions involved will nearly always be prohibited and, thus, automatically be void. Bearing the risks of large investments on this basis does not seem very attractive for most enterprises where such agreements and decisions are not binding and cannot be enforced against the partner in the co-operation.

11. The aforegoing goes to show the impact of Community law on the day-to-day policy of industry and on the creation and establishment of enterprises within the EC. Although competition law covers only a small area of Community law, its consequences may reach further than many realize. Therefore it seemed appropriate in this context to give some attention to this subject.

European Company Law

I. INTRODUCTION

Paul M. Storm
Member of the Rotterdam Bar

In Europe, as elsewhere, companies have traditionally had their roots in the sovereign States. In each country company law has developed in its own way and consequently companies incorporated under different national laws often have less in common than one would be inclined to think. The differences between national company laws may hamper a company's dealings with foreign nationals and discourage them from purchasing its shares. Almost all companies are fettered by the law under which they are incorporated and this may seriously affect their international mobility; they find it virtually impossible to transfer their seat to another country or to merge with foreign companies and in some cases they even experience difficulty in being recognized abroad. Although these impediments have obviously not prevented the company from being the major vehicle for international business transactions, it cannot be denied that differences in company law from one country to another may cause problems or at least cost legal fees.

It is therefore not surprising that in the framework of the European Common Market endeavours are being made to improve the 'international climate' for companies. This is done in three different ways:

- by 'harmonizing' the various municipal company laws,
- by facilitating the cross-frontier mobility of companies, and
- by creating a supranational, European law which should serve as a basis for certain European legal entities.

It is proposed in this chapter to give a survey of what has been achieved and what is to be expected from this three-pronged approach to company law by the institutions of the European Communities. I would submit that the achievements so far justify the title of this chapter 'European Company Law'.

II. HARMONIZATION

A. General Observations

1. The harmonization of company law in the EC is based on art. 54 (3) (g) of the EEC Treaty, one of the provisions on the right of establishment. The right of establishment forms part of the free movement of persons, one of the four economic freedoms laid down in the Treaty, the other three being the free movement of goods, of services and of capital.

In the Chapter on the right of establishment the company is viewed from two different angles: as a beneficiary of the right of establishment (see art. 58 (1)), and as one of the means by which this right can be realised (see artt. 52 and 54 (3) (f)). From the first point of view, companies are assimilated to natural persons as regards their right to 'take up and pursue activities as self-employed persons'. Under the other angle, the right of establishment includes the freedom to set up agencies, branches and *subsidiaries* in other Member States (the so-called secondary right of establishment, the primary right being to establish the main business or parent company).

It is in this context that art. 54 (3) (g) provides for the co-ordination, 'to the necessary extent (of) the safeguards which, for the protection of the interests of members and others, are required by Member States of companies or firms within the meaning of the second paragraph of art. 58[1], with a view to making such safeguards equivalent throughout the Community'.

This 'co-ordination' (usually called 'harmonization') is being carried out by way of Directives[2] adopted by the Council of the EC on the basis of a General Programme for the abolition of restrictions on freedom of establishment which was adopted by the Council in 1961[3] and provided for the co-ordination to be completed by the end of 1963. This has proved somewhat optimistic, especially in view of the very wide powers the European Commission appears to be assuming under art. 54 (3) (g).

2. The Commission seems to regard this provision as little short of *carte blanche* to unify to quite some extent virtually the entire company law of the Member States, and the latter appear to acquiesce. Although so far the harmonization relates to only a few types of company, mainly the public company[4] and in two instances[5] the private company[4] and the partnership limited by shares[4], the Commission has already announced its intention to extend harmonization successively to private companies and partnerships limited by shares (to the extent previous Directives have not dealt with them) and to all other 'companies' within the meaning of art. 58. When one looks at some of the provisions of the Directives and draft Directives, one cannot help wondering what they have to do with the right of establishment. This question will only become more difficult to answer when it is proposed to harmonize the laws on, for example, partnerships.

With the growing number of Member States, each with its own legal system and traditions, one may wonder how long it will be possible to go on creating sophisticated and detailed common rules in areas of company law where harmonization is not obviously necessary.

3. In this connection it should be borne in mind that in fields covered by harmonization the legislative powers of the Member States pass to a great

1. Art. 58, para 2 defines 'companies' as companies or firms formed under civil or commercial law, including co-operative societies, and other legal persons under public or private law, except non-profit companies or firms.
2. For the concept of Directive, see the previous chapter.
3. See OJ nr. 2 of 15-1-'62.
4. See for the meaning of these terms the section on Some Terms and Abbreviations.
5. The First and the Fourth Directives.

extent to the institutions of the EC. Under art. 189 of the EEC Treaty, Directives are binding on the Member States as to the result to be achieved. Particularly in the Directives on company law, this result is often set out in great detail. The Member States are under an obligation to adapt their legislations to the Directives. It follows that, having done so, they are no longer free to amend their laws.

In my opinion, the Member States' legislative powers in fields which have been harmonized are limited by the objectives of the harmonization. As far as the harmonization of company law is concerned, these objectives can only be found in art. 54 (3) (g) viewed in the context of the right of establishment. The main objective is that the safeguards demanded from companies for the protection of shareholders and third parties be 'made equivalent'. It is within the parameters of this equivalence that the Member States retain their powers on harmonized matters. However, the further harmonization goes, the narrower these parameters will be. This poses what I would call a problem of the second generation of European Community law, a problem which is perhaps not yet felt in 1982, at a time when the Directives are so new that they have hardly been implemented by the Member States, but which is bound to materialise sooner or later. It is the *congealing effect* of Directives.

Over the last decade or so company law in many European countries has been in a state of flux. Major social and economic changes are being reflected in an increasingly rapid succession of amendments and new legislation in the field of company law. In the middle of this turmoil substantial parts of company law in Europe are now being fixed under a common denominator. It may be said that in general the Directives reflect modern thinking on company law. This is so at the time they are adopted and for some time thereafter. But for how long? There is nothing to suggest that social and economic developments in the Member States will stop at the point reached by the Directives. What will happen if in some Member States there is considerable political pressure to change a 'harmonized' law and in some other States none whatsoever? The Member States will have no power to change their own laws unilaterally. They would have to negotiate for the Directive to be changed. But in practice this requires unanimity between all 10 (possibly 12) Member States. By the time this were achieved (inevitably in a compromised form) further developments might have rendered the compromise obsolete in the view of some States.

It would seem that the further harmonization goes and the more tenuous its links with the realization of the right of establishment become, the greater the tension will be between the Community's assumption of powers and social and political reality in the Member States. The inherent risk of rebellion by the Member States should give rise to restraint on the part of the Community.

4. Apart from the very broad interpretation of art. 54 (3) (g) there are other grounds for objecting to harmonization as it is now being carried out. By its piecemeal approach to company law the Community is causing considerable hardship to government departments, Parliaments and, last but not least, the international business community. If the Commission had its way, new Directives would be adopted and implemented every year or every two years over a period of several decades (the First Directive dates from March 1968). Each time much time and effort would be required from civil servants, members of

parliament, professional lawyers and (in some cases) accountants to draft the Directives and the laws to implement them. Enterprises would have constantly to adapt themselves to new laws.
In addition, the subjects of the various Directives and draft Directives are often interrelated. Thus the Second Directive is incomplete without provisions on groups of companies (see the draft Ninth Directive) and reciprocal shareholdings, and the Fourth cannot be properly implemented without provisions on group accounts (see the draft Seventh) and on the qualifications of auditors (see the draft Eighth). Since the Second Directive does not contain any provision on, for example, the purchase of a company's own shares by its subsidiaries, the Member States (who are committed to effectively implementing the Directive) are forced to introduce their own rules on the subject, such as definitions of subsidiaries and other group companies. In this way new discrepancies are forced upon the Member States.

5. These inconveniences of the piecemeal approach could be avoided if the Council of the EC were to allow the Member States time to implement all Directives with related subjects until, say, four years after the last one had been adopted. Such a procedure would not affect the impetus of the EC's efforts in the field of harmonization, but it would greatly enhance their coherence and effectiveness. It would also do away with the present practice of providing unacceptably short periods for implementation by the Member States. A period of two years for implementing the Second Directive has clearly proved to be ludicrous. After taking twelve years to prepare this Directive, the EC forced the Member States to be in breach of Community law. What point is there in fixing a period of two years instead of three or four years? The same applies to all the other Directives, albeit that the relatively simple Third Directive allows the Member States three years.
Even in 1982 the procedure suggested above could still be adopted in respect of the Second and Fourth Directives since by early 1982 it was clear that these Directives would not be implemented by most Member States until 1982 or thereafter.

6. Another major point of criticism concerns the way in which harmonization Directives are adopted. The Commission submits its proposal to the Council and publishes it in the Official Journal and sometimes also as a Supplement to the Bulletin of the European Communities. The accompanying explanatory memorandum is usually rather sketchy. The Council passes the proposal on to the European Parliament and the ESC for their opinions. These opinions, which are often of little significance from the legal point of view, are also published in the Official Journal. In most cases the Commission then submits an amended proposal to the Council. In the case of the First and the Second Directives the amended proposals were not published. In the case of subsequent Directives and draft Directives they were. They often hardly respond even to the most cogent of the criticisms made in the EP and ESC or in legal writings.

7. It is only after the Council has received the amended proposal that it starts dealing with it through a working group of the Committee of Permanent Representatives, consisting of delegates from the relevant government Departments in Member States, representatives of the Commission and staff of the Secretariat of the Council. It is in this working group that the real negotiations take place. When only a limited number of political decisions remain the matter is referred to the Committee of Permanent Representatives (known as 'Coreper') which consists of the Ambassadors of the Member States or their deputies. If and when Coreper succeeds in solving the political problems the final text is submitted to the Council for adoption.

8. It is in particular to this latter part of the procedure, the stage within the Council, that serious objections can be made. The proceedings within the Council are totally secret. Although national delegations may consult interested parties in their countries, they are not supposed to divulge the (amended) documents which are the subject of the negotiations and one may wonder to what extent such consultations actually take place in each Member State. This secrecy would not be so objectionable if the final text of the Directive did not differ too much from the latest published draft. However, in several instances the difference has proved to be very substantial. Thus, several parts of the draft Second Directive were amended to a point almost beyond recognition during the four years of secret negotiations within the Council. A number of new provisions (e.g. art. 23) were included which were totally unknown in most Member States.

9. It is rather unfortunate that these changes could be made and new provisions introduced without the business community or professional and academic lawyers having any chance to let their opinions be heard. This contrasts sharply with the procedure for even minor changes in the company laws of most Member States. I do appreciate the difficulties with which negotiators of (now) ten different States are faced when they try to reach agreement on a complicated legal document which may have political implications. However, I feel the objections could at least be reduced to some extent if (a) the Commission in making its amended proposal paid more attention to the criticisms made in the various Member States and (b) the national delegations kept closely in touch with representatives of commerce, industry and the professions as well as with committees of their own Parliaments, particularly with respect to any major amendments or additions proposed during the negotiations within the Council.

10. Although most Directives on company law go into substantial detail, one should not expect too much of the 'equivalence' of the municipal laws after the Directives have been implemented. Many provisions in Directives contain only minimum rules. The Member States remain free to maintain or introduce more stringent rules, although in my view this freedom is limited by the requirements of a reasonable equivalence. Thus, where the Second Directive requires the Member States to provide for a minimum capital of public companies in the amount of 25,000 EUA and most Member States fix their minima at figures close to this amount, it would not be proper for a Member State to require a minimum capital of e.g. 100,000 EUA. Yet, in 1977, Italy fixed the minimum capital of the SpA at 200 million lire (at the time more than 190,000 EUA[6]).

11. Especially in the field of company law it could be undesirable to adopt rules which go beyond the minima laid down in a Directive. Indeed, company law is a system of checks and balances between the interests of various groups of persons: shareholders, third parties (including employees and debenture holders) and, possibly, the company itself. A rule for the protection of one interest could well prejudice another. The further harmonization goes, the greater the chances become that each interest is the subject of a different Directive. Going beyond the minimum laid down in one Directive could thus affect an interest protected by another Directive.

12. But it is not only differences arising from minimum rules that could affect the equivalence envisaged by a Directive. There may also be considerable differences between national laws, resulting from different interpretations of certain rules and from discrepancies in the official texts in the various (authentic) languages. It appears that there are some shocking differences in the implementation of the First Directive by the Member States (e.g. artt. 7 and 9). There are quite a number of 'mistranslations' in the various versions of the Second Directive. Such differences may perhaps be straightened out by the Court of Justice of the EC by way of preliminary rulings under art. 177 of the EEC Treaty, but this may take a very long time since the opportunity to give such rulings depends on questions being referred in private litigation.
The reader should therefore be aware of the possibility of substantial differences subsisting in 'harmonized' parts of company law. That is why, when faced with a practical problem, the businessman will always have to take advice from a local lawyer.

13. In spite of the foregoing criticism I wish to close these general observations on harmonization on a more positive note. When one considers company law in its more traditional sense, leaving aside the law relating to securities, one will find that by 1982 quite a large part of it had been covered by the existing 4 Directives and that a good deal of the remainder could be found in the draft Fifth and Seventh and the preliminary drafts for the Ninth and Tenth Directives.
Even though one cannot rely upon harmonized parts of company law being equivalent, let alone identical, in all Member States, major differences have disappeared or will soon disappear. In due course this will no doubt facilitate business relations between companies in different countries.

14. I now propose to deal in some detail with the existing Directives and in less detail with the drafts. In view of the purpose of this book, which is mainly to serve enterprises having or contemplating business activities in one of the Member States of the EC (or Switzerland), I propose to deal only briefly with the (draft) Directives on securities law, which, by the way, constitute a rapidly growing body.

6. But in January 1982 about 153,000 ECU; perhaps Italy anticipated inflation.

B. The Directives

A. THE FIRST DIRECTIVE

15. The First Directive[7], dated 9th March 1968[8], covers three areas of the law on public and private companies and on partnerships limited by shares:
- disclosure;
- validity in law of the engagements entered into by a company; and
- nullity of the company.

16. The provisions regarding *disclosure* relate to company documents (Deed of Incorporation, Statutes), and certain important information, e.g. identity of (Managing and Supervisory) Directors, annual accounts, transfer of registered office, dissolution.
As far as private companies are concerned, however, compulsory disclosure of the annual accounts was postponed until the date of implementation of the Fourth Directive (see below, sub D).
The documents and the information to be disclosed are added to a file which in every Member State forms part of either a Central Register or a Register of Commerce or a Register of Companies. In addition, they are published in the national gazette indicated for this purpose by the Member State concerned, either in full or in summary, or by means of an announcement that the document has been either added to the relevant file or entered into the Register. In principle, a company may rely on the documents and information against third parties only after they have been published in one of the ways indicated above.

17. As to *the validity in law of the engagements* entered into by a company, art. 9 of the Directive especially protects the interests of outsiders by restricting as far as possible the grounds of nullity of such engagements. The *ultra vires* doctrine which applied in most Member States has been drastically curtailed. The company is bound by acts performed by its organs, even if such acts are not within its objects, unless such acts exceeded the powers that the law confers or allows to be conferred on those organs. However, the Member States may provide[9] that the company is not bound by *ultra vires* acts if it proves that the third party knew or in the circumstances should have known that the act was outside the objects. Disclosure of the Statutes shall not of it-

7. Among the many publications on this Directive there are only a few in English, including Y. Scholten, 4 *Common Market Law Review (CMLRev.)* 1966-67, p. 377, H. Ault, 20 *Hastings Law Journal* 1968, p. 77, and F. Woolridge, *Acta Juridica* 1978, p. 327, but above all the brilliant book by Prof. Eric Stein, *Harmonization of European Company Laws*, The Bobbs-Merrill Company, Indianapolis, 1970, which deals with nearly all subjects touched on in this essay. Some outstanding articles in French are: Prof. R. Houin, *Revue trimestrielle de droit européen (RTDE)* 1965, p. 25 and *RTDE* 1966, p. 307, Prof. R. Rodière, *RTDE* 1965, p. 336, and Prof. P. Van Ommeslaghe, *Cahiers de droit européen* 1969, pp. 495-563 and 619-665.
8. Nr. 68/151/EEC, OJ nr. L65, 14-3-'68, p. 8; the draft was submitted to the Council on 21-2-'64 and not published until the ESC gave its opinion (OJ 27-11-'64, p. 3245/64).
9. In fact, all Members States except Germany have done so, but unfortunately not all in the same way.

self be sufficient proof. The company is also bound by the acts of its organs even if the limits of the powers of such organs, as set by the Statutes or by a decision of an organ of the company, have been exceeded. The only provision in the Statutes restricting the power to represent the company which may be relied upon as against third parties is a provision conferring the *general* power of representation upon one person or on several persons acting jointly.
Art. 7 provides that if, before a company in the course of formation has acquired legal personality, transactions have been carried out in its name and it does not ratify them, the persons who carried them out shall be jointly and severally liable, unless otherwise agreed. This provision has been implemented more or less literally by most Member States, but in the United Kingdom and Italy assumption by the company of the obligations entered into does not seem to relieve the person who acted of his liability.

18. Both members and third parties are protected by the provisions which limit both the grounds for *nullity of the company itself* and the retroactive operation of the declaration of nullity, and those which set a short period of time (six months) within which third parties may oppose the declaration of nullity.

19. The Directive made it incumbent upon Member States to amend their laws so as to comply with it within 18 months of the notification of the Directive (i.e. prior to 11th September 1969). Most of the original Member States implemented the Directive with a considerable delay.[10]

B. THE SECOND DIRECTIVE

20. The Commission's proposal for a Second Directive was submitted to the Council on 9th March 1970.[11] The Council did not adopt it until 13th December 1976[12] and only after having amended it very thoroughly indeed.[13] This Directive deals with the formation of public companies and the maintenance and alteration of their capital.

10. Only *Germany* was in time: Act of 15-8-'69, *Bundesgesetzblatt* 1969 I, nr. 76. *France* was a little late: *Ordonnance* nr. 69-1176 of 20-12-'69 and *décret* nr. 69-1177 of 24-12-'69. So was *Italy: Decreto* of 29-12-'69, *Gazetta Ufficiale* no. 35 of 10-2-'70; cf. also Circular letter nr. 2143/C of 20-8-'70 from the Minister of Industry, Commerce and the Professions. Very late were *The Netherlands* (Act of 29-4-'71, *Staatsblad* 1971, nr. 285, came into force on 21-6-'71), *Belgium* (Act of 6-3-'73, *Moniteur belge* of 23-6-'73 and *arrêté royal* of 7-8-'73, *Moniteur belge* of 15-8-'73) and *Luxemburg* (Act of 23-11-'72, *Mémorial*, A, nr. 72 of 13-12-'72, p. 1586). Upon or after their accession to the EC the new Member States adapted their legislation to comply with the first Directive: the *UK* in Section 9 of the European Communities Act 1972, *Ireland* in the European Communities (Companies) Regulations, 1973 (S.I. nr. 163 of 1973), and *Denmark* first by the Act of 29-11-'72 and subsequently in the context of the overall revision of its company law (the Danish Companies Act, nr. 370, and the Danish Private Companies Act, nr. 371, both of 13-6-'73). Under art. 145 of the Accession Treaty Greece should have implemented the First Directive at the time of its accession. In mid 1981 this had not yet been done.
11. OJ nr. C48, 24-4-'70, p. 8 (with explanatory memorandum); an official English version of this proposal does not seem to exist.

→

21. As far as *formation* is concerned, the Directive does not attempt to harmonize the national laws as to the way in which a public company is formed, the supervision of the formation (by a Court or by an administrative body) and the moment the company acquires legal personality. The differences proved too great for any agreement to be reached on these matters.
Consequently, the Directive only provides what information must at least appear in the Statutes, the instrument of incorporation or a separate document. This information is mainly concerned with the capital of the company, the real core of the Directive.

22. The Directive itself is not divided into parts or chapters, probably because it was considered too difficult to make a consistent division of its subjects. I feel there is some merit in distinguishing the provisions on the raising of capital (artt. 6-14 and 25-29) and those on the maintenance thereof (artt. 15-24 and 30-39). As to the *raising of capital*, a distinction can be made between the provisions concerning the raising of capital at the time of the formation of the company and those on the increase of the capital.

23. The provisions on the *raising of capital at the time of formation* include:
a. a minimum subscribed capital of 25,000 EUA (about US$ 28,000), which must be maintained at all times after incorporation;
b. provisions to ensure that shares are not issued at a price lower than their par value and that the subscribed capital consists only of assets capable of economic assessment;
c. a provision requiring a minimum of one quarter of the par value of each share issued for a consideration to be paid up upon incorporation;
d. the requirement that a report on any consideration other than in cash be drawn up by one or more independent experts, such report to state whether the value of the assets paid corresponds at least to the par value of the shares to be issued;
e. a similar requirement with respect to any asset acquired by the company from an incorporator (or, at the option of each Member State, any shareholder or other person) within not less than two years of the incorporation and for a consideration of not less than one tenth of the subscribed capital (such requirement not to apply to certain exempted acquisitions, such as those effected in the normal course of the company's business or at some exchange);
f. a provision requiring at least the same safeguards as referred to in (a) to (e) in the event of the conversion of another type of company into a public company.

12. Directive 77/91/EEC, OJ nr. L26, 31-1-'77, p. 1.
13. Some publications in English are: G. Morse, *European Law Review* 1977, pp. 126-132, C.M. Schmitthoff, 15 *CML Rev.* 1978, pp. 43-54, J. Temple Lang, *The Irish Jurist* 1976, pp. 37-58, F. Woolridge, *Acta Juridica* 1978, pp. 334-345, and the UK Department of Trade, *Implementation of the Second EEC Directive on Company Law, An Explanatory and Consultative note* (1977). Many British publications on the Companies Act 1980, which implements the Second Directive, also deal with the Directive, e.g. the long series of articles by Diane M. Hare in *The Solicitors' Journal*, July-September 1980. See also Stein, referred to in note 7, especially on the history of this Directive.

24. Any *increase in capital* is subject to certain conditions:

a. In principle such an increase must be decided upon by the General Meeting, but this body or the Statutes may authorize another company body for a maximum period of five years to increase the capital up to a maximum amount fixed by the General Meeting or the Statutes.

b. Where there are several classes of shares, the decision or the authorization to increase the capital shall be subject to a separate vote at least for each class of shareholder whose rights are affected by the transaction.
The conditions referred to sub (a) and (b) apply to the issue of securities which are convertible into shares or which carry the right to subscribe for shares.

c. The requirements referred to above in 23 (c) and (d) apply equally in the event of an increase in capital, but the Member States may dispense with the requirements of 23 (d) in the event of a merger or a public offer for the purchase or exchange of shares where the shareholders of the target company are paid with the shares issued.

d. The shareholders have a statutory pre-emption right whenever the capital is increased by consideration in cash, subject to possible exceptions for preference shares. The Directive contains certain safeguards as to information of the shareholders of their right and a minimum period of 14 days, for exercising it.
The pre-emption right may only be restricted or withdrawn by the General Meeting if certain conditions are met (including a qualified majority).
The General Meeting may delegate this power to the body referred to sub (a) above.
The pre-emption right applies also to the issue of securities which are convertible into shares or which carry the right to subscribe for shares.

25. The provisions on the *maintenance of capital* include quite a number of different subjects:

a. A prohibition of any distribution to shareholders if the net assets as set out in the company's annual accounts for the last financial year are, or following such a distribution would become, lower than the amount of the subscribed capital plus non-distributable reserves.

b. Special requirements as to the payment of interim dividends.

c. A General Meeting must be held in the case of a serious loss of the subscribed capital (in any event half of it).

d. The company may not subscribe for its own shares.

e. Acquisition by a company of its own shares is subject to strict conditions:
- authorization by the General Meeting for no longer than 18 months;
- the par value of the acquired shares, including shares previously acquired by the company and held by it, may not exceed 10% of the subscribed capital;
- the acquisitions may not have the effect of reducing the net assets below the amount of the subscribed capital plus non-distributable reserves; and
- only fully paid-up shares may be included in the transaction.

However, Member States may decide no to apply the above conditions in a number of cases, but in most of those cases the company must dis-

pose of its shares within 3 years unless the par value of all the company's own shares held by it does not exceed 10% of the subscribed capital.
Shares acquired in contravention of the above rules must be disposed of within one year or cancelled.

f. The holding by a company of its own shares is also subject to conditions (e.g. suspension of voting rights, certain statements in the annual report).

g. Subject to a few exceptions, a company may not advance funds, nor make loans, nor provide security, with a view to the acquisition of its shares by a third party.

h. The acceptance of the company's own shares as security is subject to much the same conditions as the acquisition thereof.

i. There are a number of rather complicated provisions on *reduction in the subscribed capital.* Shareholders are protected by the requirement of a decision of the General Meeting (subject to a majority of not less than two thirds of the shares represented[14]), and separate votes for different classes. Creditors have in principle the right to obtain security for their claims and the reduction shall be void or no payment may be made for the benefit of shareholders until the creditors have obtained satisfaction or a court has decided that their application should not be acceded to.
There are special provisions on reductions to offset losses incurred or to include sums of money in a reserve, on redemption of capital without reduction, on reduction by compulsory withdrawal of shares or by withdrawal of shares acquired by the company, and on the issue of redeemable shares.

j. The Member States may derogate from certain provisions of the Directive to the extent necessary for the adoption or application of provisions designed to encourage employee participation in the capital of companies.

26. The Directive allows the Member States two years to implement it, that is until 16th December 1978. Not a single Member State was able to comply with this far too ambitious time schedule. By 1st July 1981 only Germany and the UK had brought the necessary laws into force.[15] The Directive provides for transitional periods of 18 months and 3 years (for the minimum subscribed capital and the minimum paid-up capital) for companies already in existence at the date of implementation in each Member State.

C. THE THIRD DIRECTIVE

27. This Directive deals with mergers of public companies in the same Member State.[16]

14. But the Member States may provide that a simple majority is sufficient if at least half of the subscribed capital is represented.

15. *Germany* seemed to be in time with its Act of 13-12-'78 (*Bundesgesetzblatt* 1978 I, 1959), but the Act did not come into effect until 1st July 1979. The parts of the Companies Act 1980 (1-5-'80) by which the Second Directive was implemented in the *United Kingdom* came into effect on 22-12-'80. In *The Netherlands*, the Act of 15-5-'81 was brought into force on 1-9-'81. In June 1981 the Commission started Court proceedings for breach of Community law (failure to implement the Second Directive) against Belgium, Denmark, France, Ireland, Italy and Luxemburg.

16. The relatively small number of publications in English on this Directive or the draft →

The first proposal for it was submitted to the Council on 16th June 1970.[17] The Commission amended the proposal twice[18] and the Directive was finally adopted on 9th October 1978.[19]

The impact of this Directive appears limited. It deals only with some special forms of merger and not, for example, with the form of 'concentration' of enterprises which is most common in many Member States, the take-over where one company acquires the shares of another. Its main significance seems to lie in the fact that it may serve as a basis on which the EEC Convention on International Mergers[20] could be built.

28. The forms of merger covered by the Directive are basically 'merger by acquisition' and 'merger by the formation of a new company'. In the former case one or more companies are wound up without going into liquidation, and transfer to another all their assets and liabilities in exchange for the issue to their shareholders of shares in the acquiring company. In the latter case, several companies are wound up without going into liquidation, and transfer to a company they set up all their assets and liabilities in exchange for the issue to their shareholders of shares in the new company.

In both cases that part of the consideration, if any, which consists of a cash payment by the acquiring (new) company is in principle limited to 10% of the par value of the shares issued.

As a matter of law, the consequence of the merger is that the transfer of the whole of the assets and liabilities to the acquiring company becomes effective for all parties concerned, that the shareholders of the company being acquired become shareholders of the acquiring company, and that the company which is acquired ceases to exist.

An operation whereby a company sells all its assets and liabilities for cash or even for shares of the purchasing company does not therefore come within the scope of the Directive.

29. The Directive is primarily concerned with the protection of shareholders and creditors and its provisions relating thereto are largely derived from German and French law.

The management of each of the merging companies must draw up draft terms of merger and a detailed report explaining such terms and setting out the legal and economic grounds for them, in particular the share-exchange ratio. The draft terms of merger must be published in accordance with the First Directive, and examined by one or more independent experts (accountants) who must draw up a report to the shareholders in which they must in any case state

---

Directive includes the articles by J. Temple Lang, *The Irish Jurist* 1972, pp. 313-319 (on the draft) and by F. Wooldridge, *The Company Lawyer*, 1980, pp. 75-82.
See also Stein, referred to in note 7.

17. OJ nr. C89, 14-7-'70, p. 20, also, with explanatory memorandum, in Supplement to Bulletin 5-1970 of the European Communities.
18. Neither amended proposal was officially published, but the Commission documents are COM (72) 1668 final dated 4-1-'73 and COM (75) 671 final dated 22-12-'75.
19. OJ nr. L295, 20-10-'78, p. 36.
20. See IIIC *infra.*

whether in their opinion the share exchange ratio is fair and reasonable. The merger shall require the approval of the General Meeting of each of the merging companies (although this requirement may be dispensed with for the acquiring company if certain conditions are fulfilled).
The approval is subject to the same requirements as to majority and separate voting by any classes of shareholders whose rights are affected by the merger as those laid down in the Second Directive for a reduction in capital (see item 25 (i) above).

30. The adoption of the Directive has been considerably delayed by controversies relating to the *protection* of the rights *of the employees* of the merging companies. However, this problem was solved by the adoption of Directive 77/187/EEC[21] to which the Third Directive now simply refers.

31. The *protection of creditors' interests* is largely left to the discretion of the Member States. The Directive requires them to provide for an adequate system of protection which must at least provide that creditors shall be entitled to obtain adequate safeguards where the financial situation of the merging companies makes such protection necessary and where those creditors do not already have such safeguards. The same applies to debenture holders, except where the merger has been approved by them individually or by a meeting of such holders, if such a meeting is provided for under national laws.

32. The merger must be *published* in the manner prescribed by the First Directive in respect of each of the merging companies.
The Member States are required to lay down rules governing the *civil liability* towards the shareholders of the company being acquired of the members of the Managing Board of that company in respect of 'misconduct' on the part of those members in preparing and implementing the merger, as well as on the part of the experts in the performance of their duties.

33. In the event of the acquisition of one company by another which *holds all of its shares* there are important exceptions to the above-mentioned rules, and there are some exceptions in case the acquiring company already *holds 90% or more*, but not all, of the shares of the company or companies being acquired.

34. The proposals of the Commission also covered the '*division*' (in French *scission*) of a company. This is the operation whereby a company is wound up without going into liquidation, and transfers all its assets and liabilities to several companies in exchange for the issue to its shareholders of shares in the acquiring companies (which may also be newly formed). Again the cash payment may not exceed 10% of the par value of the shares issued. This subject-matter has not been included in the final text of the Directive and will now probably be dealt with by a *separate Directive* which will only have to be applied in those Member States which allow for such a division. The provi-

21. See the Chapter on European Socia

sions of this new Directive are likely to be very similar to those of the Third Directive.

35. The procedure provided for by the Third Directive is rather cumbersome. This form of merger is therefore not likely to become popular in countries where there are no special (for example tax) reasons for making use of it.

36. This Directive had to be *implemented* by mid October 1981. At that time this had not yet been done by any Member State and it looked as if most of them would still need quite some time.

D. THE FOURTH DIRECTIVE

37. The history of this Directive, too, is a long one. The First Directive already made mention of a Directive on the annual accounts of private companies which had to be adopted prior to 9th March 1970. The first official draft was not submitted to the Council until 10th November 1971.[22]
This proposal was amended in 1974.[23] The Directive was adopted on 25th July 1978.[24] It deals with the presentation and contents of *annual accounts*, the valuation methods used therein, their publication and the auditing thereof, as well as with the minimum information to be given by annual reports, in respect of public and private companies and partnerships limited by shares.[25]

38. The Directive's provisions apply equally to each of these legal forms (which are hereafter, for simplicitiy's sake, referred to as 'companies'). However, a distinction is made between *large, medium-sized and small companies*.
A company is *'small'* if on its balance sheet date it does not exceed the limits of two of the three following criteria:
- balance sheet total: 1 million EUA,
- net turnover: 2 million EUA,
- average number of employees during the financial year: 50.

Medium-sized companies are those which are not 'small' and do not exceed two of the three following criteria:
- balance sheet total: 4 million EUA,
- net turnover: 8 million EUA,
- average number of employees: 250.

22. OJ nr. C 7, 28-1-'72, p. 11 and *Supplement* 7/71 *to Bulletin EC* (with explanatory memorandum).
23. *Supplement* 6/74 *to Bulletin EC.*
24. OJ no. L 222, 14-8-'78, p. 11.
25. In view of the wealth of literature on the Fourth Directive any choice would be arbitrary. Nevertheless, some publications in English are: Ernst & Whinney, The Fourth Directive, its effects on the annual accounts of companies in the European Economic Community, *Kluwer Publishing*, London 1979; Karel van Hulle, The EEC Accounting Directives in Perspective: Problems of Harmonization, *18 CML Rev.* 1981, 121-140; C.W. Nobes, The Harmonization of Company Law Relating to the Published Accounts of Companies, *European Law Review* 1980, p. 38.

There are 'buffer periods' of two consecutive financial years prior to the balance sheet date at which the regime for small or medium-sized companies starts to apply and after the balance sheet date at which the company has ceased to exceed two of the three criteria.
All other companies are *large*.

39. It should be noted that pending subsequent harmonization the Member States need not apply the provisions of the Fourth Directive to *banks and other financial institutions* or to *insurance companies*. The Commission has meanwhile submitted a proposal for a Directive on the annual accounts of banks and other financial institutions (see item (J) *infra*).

40. The overriding principle laid down in the Fourth Directive with respect to the annual accounts is that they must give a *true and fair view* of the company's assets, liabilities, financial position and profit or loss. The Directive requires the Member States to prescribe one or both of the *layouts* (standard formats) it sets out for the balance sheet (horizontal or vertical) and one or more of the four given for the profit and loss account (also horizontal or vertical, but in addition either on the basis of the type of expenditure or revenue, or according to the type of operations). Companies must follow the formats rigidly and may not in principle change these layouts from one financial year to the next. Such formats permit greater comparability.
The Member States may prescribe special layouts for the annual accounts of *investment companies* and *'financial holding companies'*, the latter at the special request of Luxemburg.

41. Among the items to be shown in the balance sheets are 'shares in affiliated undertakings' and 'participating interests'.
'Affiliated undertakings' are not defined by the Directive, but the provisions relating thereto will not enter into force until the Seventh Directive on consolidated accounts is implemented (see item (F) *infra*). *'Participating interests'* are defined as 'rights in the capital of other undertakings, whether or not represented by certificates, which, by creating a durable link with those undertakings, are intended to contribute to the company's activities. The holding of part of the capital of another company shall be presumed to constitute a participating interest where it exceeds a percentage fixed by the Member States which may not exceed 20%'.

42. The Member States may permit 'small' companies to draw up *abridged* balance sheets and profit and loss accounts. 'Medium-sized' companies may be permitted to draw up abridged profit and loss accounts.

43. The Directive prescribes a number of *valuation rules* which include such generally accepted principles as the going concern concept, consistency of methods of valuation from one financial year to another and valuation on a prudent basis.
On the topical and controversial issue of *inflation accounting*, the Directive contains a very lengthy and complicated provision which allows Member States, subject to certain conditions (in particular disclosure in the notes on

the accounts), by way of derogation from the general principle of historical cost, to permit or require valuation on a replacement cost basis or by some other method. However, this provision is intended to be relatively short-lived since the Directive requires the Council prior to 30th July 1985 to 'examine and, where necessary, amend (it) in the light of economic and monetary trends in the Community'.

44. Pending subsequent harmonization, the Member States may permit the *valuation of holdings in affiliated undertakings* by the *equity method* provided certain conditions are fulfilled, including that the company must place in a non-distributable reserve such part of the undertakings' profits as has been included in its own profit and loss account but not yet distributed to it. This may cause problems for holding companies wishing to distribute dividends, particularly since the Second and Fourth Directives provide for further non-distributable reserves (e.g. for own shares, for formation expenses, or revaluation reserve where valuation methods other than historical cost are permitted).

45. The Directive requires the *notes on the accounts* to give certain information, including the valuation methods applied; name, registered office, proportion of capital held, etc., of undertakings in which the company holds at least a percentage of the capital which the Member States cannot fix at more than 20%; long term debts; debts covered by security; financial commitments not included in the balance sheet; and a breakdown of the net turnover by categories of activity and into geographical markets. The Member States may permit small companies to draw up *abridged* notes omitting most of this information, and medium-sized companies to omit the said breakdown.

46. The *annual report* must, *inter alia*, give an indication of any important events since the balance sheet date, the company's likely future development, and activities in the field of research and development.

47. As to *publication*, the Directive provides that *large companies* must publish (in the manner laid down in the First Directive) their annual accounts, duly approved, and their annual reports, together with the auditors' opinions.
Medium-sized companies may be permitted to publish abridged balance sheets and profit and loss accounts and slightly abridged notes. They must, however, publish their annual reports and the auditors' opinions.
Small companies may be relieved from the obligation to publish their profit and loss accounts, their annual reports and the auditors' opinions. They may be permitted to publish abridged balance sheets and notes.
The Directive lays down certain conditions which must be fulfilled whenever the annual accounts are published in full or in abridged form.

48. The Directive requires that the annual accounts of all companies be *audited*, but Member States may relieve small companies from this obligation. The audit must be carried out by one or more persons authorized by national law. The question as to what qualifications are required for such an authorization will be dealt with by the Eighth Directive (see item (G) *infra*).

49. The Directive provides for a *Contact Committee* of representatives of the Member States and the Commission to be set up under the auspices of the Commission to facilitate harmonized application of the Directive and to advise, if necessary, on additions or amendments. This new idea may to some extent help mitigate the congealing effect referred to in item 3 above.

50. The Member States had to *implement* the Directive within two years, that is prior to 30th July 1980. However, they were allowed to stipulate that their laws to implement the Directive should not apply until 18 months after the end of that period, that is 30th January 1982. Of course the Member States were unable to implement the Directive in time and even in January 1982 none of them had done so, except that in Denmark and the UK laws had been adopted by Parliament, but would not to be brought in force until 1st February 1982. Some have proposed to extend the period of two years, but this was not accepted. Instead, there seems to be agreement on an 'interpretation' of the transitional provision to the effect that the new law will only apply with respect to financial years commencing after 30th January 1982. Except in Member States where the delay is even longer, this means in effect that for companies whose financial year coincides with the calendar year the new law will not be applied until 1984.
It should be noted that the Directive permits Member States to stipulate that their implementing laws shall not apply until 30th July 1985 with respect to publication and auditing.
The transitional period of 18 months may even be extended to 8 years (30th July 1988) for shipping companies.
Pending the entry into force of the Seventh Directive and provided certain strict conditions are met, Member States need not apply most of the Fourth Directive's provisions to 'dependent companies (of any group) governed by their national laws' nor some of these provisions to such 'dominant companies'. The concepts of dependent and dominant company are not defined, but there is a fair chance that by the time there is any need to rely upon these exceptions the Seventh Directive will have been adopted.

C. The Draft Directives

51. The Council has adopted some other Directives, but these fall into the category of securities law which I propose to deal with very briefly below. In the field of company law proper there are a number of draft Directives.

E. THE DRAFT FIFTH DIRECTIVE

52. This draft, on the *structure of public companies*, is no doubt the most controversial and politically tainted, as it deals with such issues as the 'two tier system' of management and supervision and *Mitbestimmung*, the participation of labour in company bodies ('organs').[26] It was submitted to the

26. Some articles on the draft are: John Temple Lang, *The Irish Jurist* 1972, p. 319; →

Council on 9th October 1972.[27] The Council passed it on to the ESC and the EP for their opinions. The ESC gave theirs in 1974, but the EP had not yet done so in January 1982, which shows how profound the differences of view on this draft are.

53. Some of the most important points of this draft are:

- the company's structure must be such that there are three separate 'organs' (the 'two tier system'): the 'management organ' (Managing Board), the 'supervisory organ' (Supervisory Board) and the General Meeting of Shareholders;
- the members of the Managing Board are appointed and dismissed by the Supervisory Board;
- in companies which employ 500 staff or more the members of the Supervisory Board are appointed either after the example of the German law of 1952 (two thirds by the General Meeting and one third by or on proposal of the workers or their representatives) or of the Dutch model (co-optation by the Supervisory Board with a restricted power of veto for the General Meeting and the workers' representatives);
- the authorization of the Supervisory Board is required for certain important decisions of the Managing Board (e.g. closure or transfer of the enterprise or of substantial parts thereof);
- very severe provisions on civil liability of Managing and Supervisory Directors as well as auditors, not only towards the company itself, but also vis-à-vis creditors, shareholders and other third parties;
- restrictions on proxies for General Meetings;
- restrictions on voting agreements;
- rather elaborate provisions on the independence, appointment and duties of the persons responsible for auditing the accounts.

54. As to the two tier board system and *Mitbestimmung*, the draft was superseded by the Commission's 'Green Paper on employee participation and company structure in the European Community' which was issued on 12th November 1975.[28] On the basis of a comparative study of law and practice in all Member States the Green Paper gives a detailed analysis of company structure and employee participation in the EC. It seeks to demonstrate the need for Community legislation in these fields, and sets out the Commission's objectives and approaches.

As far as company structure is concerned, the Commission reaffirms its belief in the two tier system, but admits that, at least for the time being, it would not be acceptable for some Member States. The Commission therefore proposes to amend the draft Fifth Directive so as to provide for a transitional period during which companies could choose between the one board and the two tier system, as a first step to the ultimate objective, the latter system.

J.E. Hurst, *Legal Issues of European Integration* 1974/1, p. 76; and Clive M. Schmitthoff, *International and Comparative Law Quarterly* 1976, p. 611.

27. OJ C 131, 13-12-'72, p. 49 and, with explanatory memorandum, *Supplement* 10/72 *to Bulletin of the EC*.

28. *Supplement Bulletin EC* 8/75.

As to employee participation, the Commission acknowledges that certain Member States are unable to adopt, in the immediate future, the principle of employee representation on the (Supervisory) Board of a company. It now proposes that the draft Fifth Directive be amended in such a way as for a transitional period to allow companies to adopt, instead of the two tier system, a flexible system based on a body representing the employees at enterprise level. Such an institution would enable the employees' representatives to be informed about and to influence the conduct of the company's affairs, including major decisions of economic policy, without being directly involved in the Supervisory Board itself.

55. In January 1982 it looked as if the EP would agree on further changes to the draft, including a limit of 1,000 employees for the *Mitbestimmung* to apply and a maximum of 50% of employee representatives on Supervisory Boards.
I am afraid that in the heat of the debate on the political issues the Commission's very radical proposals on Directors' and auditors' liability may be overlooked. These include provisions which could be very prejudicial to the business community.
In any event, lawyers (and accountants) will have many years to combat these proposals before they have a chance of being adopted.

F. THE DRAFT SEVENTH DIRECTIVE

56. This draft, on *group accounts*, should really form part of the Fourth Directive.[29] However, it was not submitted to the Council until 4th May 1976.[30] Every effort is being made to have this Directive adopted as soon as possible, but it raises difficult problems over which there is much disagreement. On 14th December 1978 an amended proposal was submitted to the Council.[31] In January 1982 it looked as if the Seventh Directive could be adopted by the end of 1982. The reader should be aware that the final text is likely to differ considerably from the amended proposal a bold outline of which is given below.

57. In most Member States consolidation is not dealt with by statute and *consolidation practices vary widely* from one State to the other. Consequently, there are a number of *conceptual problems* in harmonizing the law on group accounts.
What enterprises should be included in a group for consolidation purposes? Only (public and private) companies limited by shares or also other enterprises, including individuals? Should minority holdings be included and, if

29. See, *inter alia*, the articles by Karel van Hulle and C.W. Nobes referred to in note 25 *supra*.
30. OJ nr. C 121, 2-6-'76, p. 2 and *Supplement Bulletin EC* 9/76 (with explanatory memorandum).
31. OJ nr. C 14, 17-1-'79, p. 2.

so, how? Should 'horizontal groups' (where there is no relationship based on dominance of one enterprise over the other, but where enterprises are nevertheless managed on a 'unified basis') be included?

58. The Commission's amended proposal contains *definitions* of 'associated', 'affiliated', 'dominant', 'dependent', and 'group' undertakings. A dominant undertaking and one or more undertakings dependent on it constitute a group if the dominant undertaking 'exercises in practice its dominant influence to the effect that all such undertakings are managed on a unified basis by the dominant undertaking'. A group can also consist of undertakings between which no relationship of dependency exists but which are managed on a unified basis.
It is interesting to note that these definitions are very wide in that they do not refer to any kind of undertaking or company. However, the draft Directive's *scope* is somewhat limited by various provisions to the effect that it shall apply to all groups where the dominant, any intermediate dominant, or any dependent undertaking is *a public or private company with its registered office within the EC*. If the dominant undertaking has its registered office outside the EC, sub-group consolidated accounts and a sub-group annual report must be drawn up for all its dependent undertakings within the EC. However, Member States may exempt dependent undertakings from this obligation if certain conditions are met.

59. The *substantive provisions* of the draft are *comparable to* those of the *Fourth Directive* and often simply refer to it. In principle, *consolidation* is to take place according to the *parent company method. Associated undertakings* (over which a significant influence is exercised, which is presumed to be the case if 20% or more of their capital is held) are treated by the *equity method*. Member States may, however, authorize the accounts of *joint venture* undertakings to be consolidated on a *pro rata basis* according to the percentage held by the group undertaking.

60. Group accounts must be *audited* and *published*, but Member States may provide for *reliefs* similar to those of the Fourth Directive (see items 47 and 48) for groups which would qualify as 'small' or 'medium-sized' companies.

G. THE DRAFT EIGHTH DIRECTIVE

61. Of course the audit requirements laid down in the Fourth and draft Seventh Directives would largely miss their aim if the persons carrying out the audit were not sufficiently qualified and if their qualifications were not at least comparable throughout the EC. This is what the draft Eighth Directive[32] seeks to secure. This essential corrollary to the Fourth and the draft Fifth and Seventh Directives was first proposed to the Council on 24th April 1978.[33] An amended proposal was submitted on 5th December 1979.[34]

32. See, *inter alia*, the article by Karel van Hulle referred to in note 25 *supra*.
33. OJ nr. C 112, 13-5-'78, p. 6 and *Supplement Bulletin EC* 4/78 (with explanatory memorandum).
34. OJ nr. C 317, 18-12-'79, p. 6.

62. The draft relates to the *approval of persons responsible for carrying out statutory audits* of the accounts of *public and private companies* as well as *partnerships limited by shares*. Such persons may be both natural persons and professional companies or associations. The draft requires such persons to be 'of good repute and independent' and to have followed a programme of professional education and training and passed an *examination of professional competence* at graduate level which is organized or recognized by the State. The examination consists of a test of theoretical knowledge covering a number of subjects set out in the draft and must follow or precede a minimum of three years' practical training with an auditor. The draft provides for *various exceptions*, in particular for persons who at the date of entry into force of the implementing provisions did not fulfil all the conditions but had the right to carry out statutory audits and had in fact engaged in such activity.

63. With a view to the fact that the qualifications set out in the draft are rather extensive and that in quite a few Member States the number of qualified auditors may well prove to be too small to carry out all the new tasks entrusted to them by the Second, Third, Fourth and draft Seventh Directives, long *transitional periods* (up to 5 years) have been provided.
The contact committee set up under the Fourth Directive will also assist in facilitating the 'harmonized application' of the Eighth (and the Seventh) Directives.

H. WORK ON THE NINTH DIRECTIVE

64. For many years officials of the Commission and experts from Member States have been working on a Directive on *groups of companies*. By the end of 1975 their efforts had resulted in two Parts of a preliminary draft[35] which were never officially published, but found their way among interested lawyers.
Since then the preliminary draft seems to have been considerably changed and slimmed down. In January 1982 it had not yet been submitted to the Council.

65. The *law on groups of companies* (rather, groups of enterprises) is rather complicated and a very difficult subject-matter for harmonization since it varies substantially from one Member State to another. Only German law deals with it in a comprehensive manner, but also with such perfectionism that the statutory provisions are hardly applied in practice. In the other Member States the law is still based on the rather unrealistic assumption that each company is an independent entity, but one finds more and more isolated provisions with exceptions to this rule. This is of course in line with the economic reality that many of the most important enterprises in the EC (and elsewhere) form part of a group. In a 'dependent undertaking' the position of 'outside' shareholders and creditors is different from their position in an independent company. This difference justifies special protection of their

35. Part I, Commission Document XI/328/74, and Part II, Commission Document XI/593/75.

interests. It could also be argued that there is a certain public interest in the transparency of the relationships between companies. This can be satisfied by various requirements for the publication of information on such relationships.

66. In 1981 it could reasonably be expected that the draft Ninth Directive would contain provisions on the *publication* of the acquisition or disposal of certain *shareholdings* in other companies and on the *protection of dependent companies* and their shareholders, creditors and employees.
The protection of the dependent company (probably only a public company) could consist in civil liability on the part of the dominant undertaking and even of the members of its Managing Board if certain conditions are met, and in the obligation to publish any transactions with, instigated by, or in the interest of the dominant undertaking and prejudicial to the dependent company.

67. An important question relating to the law on groups of companies is what conditions must be met for a group to exist from a legal point of view. The *concept of 'group'* is rooted in the concepts of dominance and dependence which are based on factual situations that cannot be simply defined. Such situations are usually said to exist where the dominant undertaking is able, directly or indirectly, to exercise a controlling influence on the dependent one. Dependence is presumed to exist if one undertaking directly or indirectly:
(*a*) has a majority holding in the subscribed capital of the other; or
(*b*) controls the majority of the votes attached to shares issued by the other; or
(*c*) can appoint more than half of the members of the other's administrative, managerial or supervisory body.[36]

The 'ability directly or indirectly to exercise a controlling influence' is too vague a notion to be permitted to trigger off the important consequences of the existence of a group. It is therefore expected that the draft Ninth Directive will, as a first step to possible further reaching measures, follow the German example of making the existence of a group, for the purpose of the application of its provisions, dependent upon a 'control contract' between dominant and dependent undertakings.

68. A *control contract* provides the legal basis of a group. By concluding it, the dependent company submits to the management of the dominant enterprise which acquires the right to manage the company and give instructions to its Managing Board.
In some Member States the law does not now recognize such a right even though it is usually exercised in practice. It is also expected that the Second Directive's prohibition of distributions in excess of profits and distributable reserves will not apply if a control contract has been concluded. But upon

36. Art. 1 of Part I of the preliminary draft referred to in note 35 *supra* and Art. 2 of the draft Seventh Directive.

expiration of the control contract the dominant undertaking would have to make good any loss in the net worth of the dependent company.
The *interests of outside shareholders* could be *safeguarded* by the obligation of the dominant undertaking to purchase their shares at a fair price, to exchange their shares for shares or debentures of the dominant company, or to make suitable annual equalization payments to them, as well as by further measures, such as a report by independent experts on the fairness of the proposals, the approval of the contract by both the Supervisory Board and the General Meeting of the company, and requirements to publish the contract and other documents.
Creditors of the dependent company could be *protected* by making the dominant enterprise liable for the debts of that company.

69. The draft is also expected to provide for the possibility of a *contract* whereby *independent undertakings* place themselves under a *unified management* (a horizontal group), although the legal consequences thereof do not yet seem to have been fully considered.

70. Part I of the preliminary draft contained provisions designed to check *reciprocal shareholdings* in excess of 10%. These provisions are *not likely* to be included in the draft.

I. WORK ON A DIRECTIVE ON DISSOLUTION AND LIQUIDATION

71. Back in the Sixties the Commission started preparatory work on a Directive on Dissolution (in the continental sense meaning a fact preceding the winding-up) and Liquidation of public companies.
A Dutch lawyer, Y. Scholten, was commissioned to draft a report which he submitted in 1971. In 1973 a revised report (Com. Doc. XI/381/73) was made, but never published. It contains a preliminary draft Directive. In 1981 this matter was still low on the Commission's list of priorities.

J. DRAFT DIRECTIVE ON ANNUAL ACCOUNTS OF BANKS AND OTHER FINANCIAL INSTITUTIONS

72. The Fourth and draft Seventh Directives allow Member States to exempt banks and other financial institutions in view of the difference in structure and content of balance sheets of credit institutions. This draft[37] should fill the gap.

73. It does not contain a definition of 'banks and other financial institutions', but refers to the definition of credit institutions in art. 1 of Directive 77/780/EEC on the taking up and pursuit of the business of credit institutions[38], a Directive adopted under art. 57 of the EEC Treaty, which deals

37. OJ nr. C130, 1-6-'81, p. 1.
38. OJ nr. L322, 17-12-'77, p. 30.

with the freedom of establishment. However, the new Directive will also apply to 'all other companies or firms whose principal activity is to receive deposits or other repayable funds, for their own account, or to grant credits (including guarantees), to acquire participating interests or make investments, in so far as they have not been made subject to the Fourth Directive.' On the other hand, the Directive will not apply to certain listed credit institutions.

74. The draft does not provide for a set of standards separate from the Fourth Directive; it rather deals with such exceptions to the rules of this Directive as are justified by the particular characteristics of credit institutions. In view of the more general scope of this book I shall not go into any details of the draft. Suffice it to say that the draft does not provide for exceptions for small and medium-sized credit institutions and that it requires the annual accounts of a credit institution having its head office in one Member State to be published in all the Member States where it is established (in the official languages of those States).

75. It will no doubt take several years for this Directive to be adopted. In addition, the draft promises 'a longer period than usual' for its implementation, without specifying such period.

K. EXTENSION OF THE PRINCIPLES OF THE SECOND AND THIRD DIRECTIVES TO PRIVATE COMPANIES

76. Officials of the Commission consider this extension as an important and urgent matter. However, it is also a very difficult matter since the differences between GmbH, sàrl, sarl, BV, pbva, ApS, EPE, and private company are much greater than between the public companies of the various Member States.
In January 1982 no preliminary draft had yet been seen.

D. (Draft) Directives on Securities Law

77. As stated above (item 14), the (draft) Directives on securities law will be dealt with only briefly. I propose just to list them:
(*a*) Directive 79/279/EEC of 5th March 1979 on the *conditions for the admission of securities to official Stock Exchange listing.*[39]
(*b*) Directive 80/390/EEC of 17th March 1980 on the drawing up, scrutiny and distribution of the listing particulars to be published for the admission of securities to official Stock Exchange listing.[40] In its draft stage this Directive used to be called the *draft Sixth Directive on Prospectuses.*
The indication 'Sixth' was subsequently dropped since this Directive does not belong to the same category as the other, numbered, Directives.

39. OJ nr. L66, 16-3-'79, p. 21.
40. OJ nr. L100, 17-4-'80, p. 1.

(*c*) Draft Directive on *information to be published on a regular basis* by companies whose transferable securities are admitted to official Stock Exchange listing, submitted to the Council on 19th January 1979.[41] An amended draft was submitted on 25th June 1980.[42]
(*d*) Draft Directive on the drawing up, scrutiny and distribution of the *prospectus* to be published when *securities are offered for subscription or sale to the public* (and are *not admitted to official listing* on a Stock Exchange in the same Member State).
This draft was submitted to the Council on 13th January 1981.[43]
(*e*) In 1974 Prof. R.R. Pennington prepared a report on *Take-over and other Bids*[44] which contains a preliminary draft Directive. In 1981 there seemed to be little enthusiasm for this draft or, indeed, for harmonization in this particular field.
(*f*) The Commission has been contemplating drafting a Directive on *Insider Trading* but in January 1982 did not seem to have prepared a draft yet.
(*g*) On 25th July 1977 the Commission adopted a *Recommendation* concerning a *European code of conduct relating to transactions in transferable securities*.[45] This Recommendation, which is not binding on the Member States, has met with considerable criticism and does not seem to have much impact on their legislations.
(*h*) Draft Directive on *collective investment undertakings for transferable securities*, submitted to the Council on 29th April 1976.[46] This draft is not based on art. 54 (3) (g) of the EEC Treaty but on art. 57, which calls for the adoption of Directives on the coordination of national laws on the taking up and pursuit of activities by self-employed persons in the context of the freedom of establishment. It therefore concerns such collective investment undertakings (CIUTS) rather than the units issued by them.

III. FACILITATING CROSS-FRONTIER MOBILITY OF COMPANIES

78. From a company law point of view, cross-frontier mobility of companies can be facilitated in essentially three ways:
- the mutual recognition of companies;
- the maintenance of legal personality in the event of transfer of seat from one Member State to another; and
- the possibility of mergers between companies that are subject to different national laws.

It is with respect to these subjects that art. 220 of the EEC Treaty charges the Member States, 'so far as is necessary', to enter into negotiations with a view

41. OJ nr. C29, 1-2-'79, p. 3.
42. OJ nr. C210, 16-8-'80, p. 5, adopted on 15-2-'82, OJ nr. L 48, 20-2-'82, p. 26.
43. OJ nr. C355, 31-12-'80, p. 39.
44. Com. Doc. XI/56/74, not published.
45. OJ nr. L212, 20-8-'77, p. 37.
46. OJ nr. C171, 26-7-'76, p. 1.

to concluding Conventions for the benefit of their nationals. Reference is made to item 22 of the Chapter 'Some Observations on the Law of the European Communities'.

A. Mutual Recognition

79. The Convention concerning the Mutual Recognition of Companies and Legal Persons was the first final text in the field of European company law. It was signed on 20th February 1968 by the original six Member States.[47] However, it never came into force since The Netherlands did not ratify it. Under the Accession Act of 1972, Denmark, Ireland and the UK agreed to accede to this Convention, but they could negotiate changes. This is what has been done since 1979. In January 1982 no agreement had yet been reached and some delegations seem to have expressed doubts as to whether the Convention still met the 'necessity' criterion of art. 220. In fact, it has been argued convincingly[48] that it is not only superfluous because companies must be recognized under artt. 52-58 of the EEC Treaty anyway, but is also to quite some extent incompatible with these Articles. It is therefore to be hoped that the negotiations, in which Greece will join as well, will continue *ad calendas Graecas*.

80. The Convention would be of little practical importance anyway because what it intends to ensure has in practice already been secured either by the national laws of the Member States or by existing bilateral Conventions. According to the Convention, the recognition of a company or any (other) legal person implies that in all Member States it has the powers which it has under its own law.
During the negotiations regarding this Convention serious difficulties arose, in particular with regard to the criteria by which the national law of a company may be determined. Recognition by another State hinges on these criteria.

81. This point is governed by either of two separate rules. On the one hand, according to the incorporation rule, mainly applied in Anglo-Saxon countries, a company may be set up in a certain State and its seat (registered office) may be situated there, even if neither its head office nor its enterprise are situated in that State. On the other hand, there is the rule of the '*siège réel*' (effective head office); according to this rule, a company is subject to the company law

47. An unofficial American translation was published in *CCH Common Market Reports* 6083 and in Stein's book referred to in note 7 *supra*. For comments and references to literature, see Stein's book, Chapter 8, § 4 and pp. 28-31. See also G.K. Morse, Mutual Recognition of Companies in England and the EEC, *The Journal of Business Law* 1972, p. 195.
48. Prof. C.W.A. Timmermans in his report *'Erkenning van vreemde vennootschappen en rechtspersonen'* for the *Netherlands Association for International Law*, Kluwer, Deventer 1980 (with summary in English).

of the State in which its effective head office is situated, even if it was not organized in this country.

The incorporation rule applies in The Netherlands[49] the United Kingdom, Ireland and, by way of an alternative in certain cases, also in Italy. The other Member States, and in general Italy also, follow the rule of the effective head office. In the latter States, the fact that the effective head office and the seat of a company are situated in two different States does not carry identical consequences: Germany may refuse to recognize a company which has established only its effective head office within its territory, whereas Belgium, France[50], Italy and Luxemburg apply the rules of their own national company law in such cases.

The Convention stipulates the latter treatment[51] in regard to companies whose seat is situated in one Member State and effective head office in another where they invoke the Convention to obtain recognition.

Since the incorporation rule applies in The Netherlands it is possible for companies having their effective head office outside the Common Market to acquire a seat within this Market. By making use of the Convention they could penetrate into the other Member States. This is what these States are apparently afraid of and it was at their request that art. 3 was included. This Article states that each Member State may declare that it will not recognize a company having its seat in one of the Member States but its effective head office outside the Common Market, if this company does not have a real connection with the economy of one of the Member States.

82. This and other more or less vague restrictions on the principle of recognition justify the fear that the effect of this Convention would be that recognition would be less safely ensured than it is now. One of the few positive things that can be said about the Convention is that the interpretation of its many ambiguous clauses would not be within the exclusive competence of national Courts. A protocol signed on 3rd June 1971[52] gives the Court of Justice of the EC competence to give preliminary rulings on the interpretation of the Convention in the same manner as art. 177 of the EEC Treaty does.

B. Transfer of Seat

83. The transfer of seat from one Member State to another raises problems that are inherent in the discrepancies between the national company laws of

49. Cf. the Act of 25-7-'59, implementing the Hague Convention of 1956 on the recognition of the legal personality of foreign companies, associations and foundations, *Staatsblad* 1959, nr. 256.
50. Cf. art. 3 *Loi sur les sociétés commerciales.* For reference to Belgian, Italian and Luxemburg law, see note 54 *infra.*
51. With the proviso, however, that the State of the effective head office may declare that it will apply only those provisions of its own law which it regards as mandatory (Art. 4 of the Convention). This declaration has, in fact, been made by all five original Member States which have ratified the Convention.
52. See item 22 of the Chapter 'Some Observations on the Law of the European Communities'.

the Member States. Transfer to another country of the seat (if it is at all possible; this is not the case in many Member States, as will be shown below), and in most cases also transfer of the effective head office, implies in principle that henceforth the company will be subject to the rules of company law of the new State of residence.

84. Such a transfer has important consequences, both for the company concerned and for the new State of residence. When, for example, a Belgian public company transfers its seat to Germany – assuming this to be legally possible – quite a number of questions with regard to its structure and mode of operation would arise. The German legal provisions which regulate the supervision at the time of formation and in the event of an increase in capital (in particular when assets in kind are brought in), the contents of the balance sheet and the profit and loss account, the publication of the annual report and other data, the rights of shareholders, etc., are so different from the Belgian provisions that Germany can hardly be expected to permit a transfer of the seat of a Belgian company to her territory unless the latter meets the German legal requirements, at least in so far as these are of a binding nature. Therefore, the 'receiving State' would generally demand[53] that the company to be received amend its Statutes so as to conform to the legal requirements of the receiving State, and that henceforth it will in all other respects be subject to the latter's internal law.[54] The examples given above show that many differences will disappear or at least be considerably reduced as a result of the implementation of the harmonization Directives. One could, therefore, wonder whether the aforesaid demand would still be justified by the time the harmonization (as adopted and drafted in 1982) had been completed.

85. On the other hand, objections also arise from the original State of residence and in practice these are much harder to overcome. In the first place, in several countries, including Germany, Belgium, the UK, Ireland, Denmark and The Netherlands, transfer of seat to another country is legally impossible. France[55] and Italy[56] do permit such transfers, although on certain conditions. In the first named countries, a transfer of seat implies liquidation and consequently taxation on the hidden reserves. Although if certain conditions are met French and Italian companies wishing to leave their State of residence may do so without winding up, they are not likely to escape the same fate as regards taxation. In addition, some States levy taxes on the transfer of real estate and on capital brought in in such cases.

53. Even in the absence, as in all Member States except Italy (art. 2505 *Codice civile*), of an express statutory provision.
54. Cf. the decision dated 13-11-'65 (*Journal du droit international* 1967, p. 141) of the Belgian *Cour de Cassation* regarding an English company which had transferred its seat to Belgium and in respect of which the Belgian statutory provision restricting the duration of the company to 30 years was applied as of the day of the transfer of the seat. Cf. also Art. 2505 of the Italian *Codice civile*, Art. 197 of the Belgian Companies Act of 30-11-'35 and the identical Art. 159 of the Luxemburg Companies Act of 10-8-'15.
55. Art. 154 *Loi sur les sociétés commerciales.*
56. Art. 2437 *Codice civile.*

86. These problems of law and taxation in the event of liquidation also arise in relation to international mergers. This is why the Commission decided to tackle these problems from the twofold angle of transfer of seat and international mergers, within the framework of art. 220. However, in view of the greater practical importance of mergers, the Commission decided to give the latter priority.

C. International Mergers

87. On 29th June 1973 the Commission, acting as secretary to a working group of experts of the Member States under the chairmanship of Professor Berthold Goldman, submitted to the Council a *draft Convention on the international merger of 'sociétés anonymes'.*[57] The working group had been discussing this matter for more than seven years and the draft is still incomplete on the vital issue of employee participation, on which no agreement could be reached.

88. From a technical legal point of view the provisions of the draft are very similar to those of the Third Directive, but there is the additional international element. This is simply dealt with by the provision in the Convention that merger of companies formed under the law of different Member States is possible. However, not every such company can benefit from this Convention. Such benefit is made subject to the company being accorded recognition under the Convention referred to above under A.
No agreement was reached as to the precise effects of denial of recognition in one of the Member States.

89. The draft provides for interpretation of the Convention by the Court of Justice of the European Communities by way of preliminary rulings in the same manner as provided in art. 177 of the EEC Treaty, with the additional possibility that an authority of a Member State may request a ruling if decisions given by courts or tribunals of this State are at variance with the interpreation given by the Court of Justice or by a decision of a court or tribunal in another Member State. Such a ruling will, however, not affect the decision in respect of which it was requested.

90. It is quite clear that this Convention would be completely pointless unless the problems of taxation connected with international mergers were resolved simultaneously. As is mentioned in the Chapter on European Tax Law, the Commission presented a draft Directive relating to these problems to the Council on 16th January 1969. Unfortunately, this draft has made very little progress towards realization.

91. In 1982 negotiations on the draft Convention were still dragging on. There seemed to be very little prospect of this Convention entering into force

57. *Supplement Bulletin EC* 13/72 with report by Prof. Goldman.

in the foreseeable future, unless political miracles happen in the fields of employee participation and taxation.

IV. PROPOSED SUPRANATIONAL LAW

A. The European Company

92. International merger is one of the instruments for achieving concentration of enterprises in the Common Market. This concentration is necessary for the adjustment of these enterprises, which in many cases are still attuned to their domestic markets, to a single market of 300 million. In addition, concentration of European enterprises is also required in view of the competition on the part of enterprises from third States, which is continually increasing and becoming more fierce.

93. But international merger as envisaged in the draft Convention does not provide a satisfactory answer to the very delicate question: what kind of company will result from the merger? Under the draft Convention this would necessarily be a company of the nationality of one of the Member States. Thus at least one of the parties to a merger would have to surrender its nationality in favour of the nationality of the other(s). This could be, and has, in fact in several instances proved to be, a serious psychological obstacle to an international merger, in particular in the case of more or less equivalent partners.
The obstacle could also be of a more substantial nature: the law governing the company resulting from the merger could be either very strict or very liberal on a subject like employee participation. Thus the absorbed company could suddenly change over from a system without any employee participation to, e.g., the German system or, conversely, escape the German system by becoming subject to a system with no employee participation at all. Neither alternative would be acceptable to all Member States. Any intermediate solution which avoided the necessity of one particular system of national law would be the first step towards a European Company.

94. It is this kind of company which could provide a satisfactory answer to the above delicate question. It is, in fact, intended as an instrument for concentration of enterprises in the Common Market. The European Company is designed as a company identical in all Member States and similar to the public company which is familiar throughout the Common Market. Enterprises will be entirely free either to organize themselves in this form or not to do so. It would therefore be a new type of company in addition to those existing in the Member States.[58]

58. Since 1959 so much has been written about the European Company that it would be impossible to give a survey in this footnote. Suffice it to mention a few publications in English: Y. Scholten, *5CMLRev.* 1967-68, pp. 9-22; P.M. Storm, *5CMLRev.* 1967-68, pp. 265-290; D. Thompson, *International and Comparative Law Quarterly (ICLQ)* 1968, pp.
→

95. According to the latest draft it could be used for three specific purposes, all resulting in concentration of enterprises across frontiers:

- for a *merger* or the formation of a *holding company* by two or more public companies from different Member States;
- for the formation of a *joint subsidiary* by any two or more companies or other legal persons from different Member States.

For companies of different nationality wishing to merge, the European Company would offer a solution to the problem of surrender of nationality: they could find each other in a 'European nationality' which is of equal value to each of them. They would not even have to choose a specific country for the seat of the European Company: it may have several seats within the Common Market.

An important advantage of the European Company could be its increased facilities for raising capital in all Member States. In none of these States would it be considered as a 'foreign' company since not only its legal form but also all its important particulars would be known in all Member States, the latter through publication in the Official Journal of the EC.

In addition, the European Company could have a unifying effect on company law in the Member States and thus promote the harmonization of company law.

But its purpose would be first and foremost to facilitate the concentration of enterprises across the frontiers of the Member States.

96. The EEC Treaty does not provide for the creation of anything like a European Company, but as early as 1959 there were lawyers in Europe who advocated it. One of the first was Prof. Pieter Sanders of Rotterdam who at the request of the Commission and with the help of a group of experts from the other five Member States made the first draft of a Statute for European Companies.[59] This Statute could best be regarded as an international Companies Act relating to one special kind of company only: the *Societas Europaea* (SE).[60]

Prof. Sanders made his draft in 1966, whereupon the Member States were to enter into negotiations on the basis of this draft. However, the negotiations which were in fact initiated got bogged down in the political controversies that at the time more or less paralysed the Council of Ministers. Meanwhile the Commission – in collaboration with Prof. Sanders – proceeded to

---

183-190; D. Thompson, *The Proposal for a European Company*, Chatham House/PEP, London 1969, 73 pp; Prof. P. Sanders, *8 CMLRev.* 1971, pp. 29-43; F.A. Mann, *ICLQ* 1970, pp. 468-482; P. M. Storm, *The Business Lawyer* 1971, pp. 1443-1453; H.-C. Ficker, *The Journal of Business Law* 1970, pp. 156-169 and *idem* 1971, pp. 167-184; J. J. Norton, *Cornell International Law Journal* 1973, pp. 111-136; and J. Micallef, *The European Company*, a comparative study with English and Maltese company law, thesis Rotterdam 1974, *Bulletin of Comparative Labour Relations* (ed. Blanpain) nr. 8/1977, Workers' Participation in the European Company.

59. Published in Dutch, French, German and Italian by the Commission in the Series '*Concurrence*', nr. 6 (Brussels, 1968). An American translation was published by Commerce Clearing House, Inc., Chicago.

60. Prof. Sanders used this term in order to give the European Company an internationally acceptable name and abbreviation in addition to the existing SA, AG, SpA, NV, etc.

amend the draft and to make some additions. This resulted in a revised draft which was submitted to the Council on 30th June 1970 in the form of a draft Regulation[61] in pursuance of art. 235 EEC Treaty.[62] The Council submitted the draft to the European Parliament and the Social and Economic Committee and their Opinions[63] prompted the Commission to revise the draft once again, not only on some politically 'hot' issues but also on many technical details.

97. This latest draft[64] dates from 30th April 1975 and contains 337 articles and four annexes, two of which are rather extensive (as against 284 articles and one small annex in the previous draft). On the one hand it is a paradigm of modern company legislation: it deals very extensively with employee participation and, somewhat less extensively but very radically, with the law on groups of companies; it recognizes the diminished role of the General Meeting of Shareholders by limiting its powers in favour of the Supervisory and Managing Boards, but protects the shareholders by giving them special rights and, above all, by providing for a considerable amount of disclosure, which also protects creditors and employees; and it contains provisions on, e.g., insider dealing, and on the reporting of shareholdings in excess of 10%.
On the other hand it is becoming tainted with political compromise and with the products of perfectionism to such an extent that even if the Regulation comes into effect one may wonder whether any enterprise would be prepared to make use of it. In this connection it is significant that the *Union des Industries de la Communauté Européenne (UNICE)*, which speaks for the whole of industry in the Common Market, considers the 1975 draft unacceptable and says it is convinced that enterprises will not give up their national legal status in favour of the SE status as it is now proposed.[65] *UNICE's* main objections concentrate on *Mitbestimmung* and the law on groups of companies, and, in particular, they have very decided views on the rigidity and unwieldiness of the proposed Statute.

98. In January 1982 an ad-hoc Working Party of the Council was still reviewing the 1975 draft, but at a rather reduced speed and leaving the political issues aside. The political and economic mood in Europe did not seem to favour any

61. Published, with a rather detailed explanatory memorandum, as *Supplement Bulletin EC* 1970, nr. 8 (also in English). For the concept of 'Regulation', see the Chapter 'Some Observations on the Law of the European Communities'.
62. As stated above, the EEC Treaty does not provide for the creation of a European Company. The Commission therefore proposes to base the Regulation on art. 235 of the Treaty, which authorizes the Council on the proposal of the Commission to take 'appropriate measures' where action by the Community proves to be necessary to realize one of the objectives of the Community and no power to do so has been granted by the Treaty. In the preamble to the draft Regulation the Commission forcefully argues that one of the objectives of the Community is the realization of the economic union and that a condition for its realization is the reorganization of enterprises on a Community level. This condition can only be fulfilled by creating European Companies.
63. Opinion of Social and Economic Committee in OJ nr. C 131, 13-12-'72, p. 32.
Opinion of European Parliament in OJ nr. C 93, 7-8-'74, p. 22.
64. *Supplement Bulletin EC* 4/75.
65. Opinion of 8th October 1975.

step forward towards the realization of the challenging idea of a *Societas Europaea*. This is why there seems to be little sense in going in this book into any detail of the 1975 draft. Suffice it to say that where originally the realization of an SE Statute was expected to act as a catalyst for the harmonization of company law in Europe, it must now be hoped that harmonization will help remove the obstacles (especially *Mitbestimmung* and the law on groups of companies) on the arduous road to the SE.

B. *The European Co-operation Grouping*

99. In 1967 France introduced the *groupement d'intérêt économique*[66] *(GIE)*, a new legal form with legal personality intermediate between the *société* and the *association*[67], intended as a means of co-operation for enterprises which wish to maintain their independence. Such enterprises could, through a GIE, join in certain activities, e.g. sales, export, import, research. From a tax point of view the GIE is transparent, which means that only its members are taxed. The GIE proved successful, and it was soon suggested that a similar legal form should be introduced for the whole Common Market. This the Commission did when, on 21st December 1973, it submitted to the Council a proposal for a Regulation on the *European Co-operation Grouping (ECG)*.[68] On 12th April 1978 the Commission submitted an amended proposal[69] which unfortunately did not take into account the justified criticism which had been raised against many (mainly technical) legal and tax aspects.

100. The ECG could best be compared with a co-operative society but its structure is looser. According to the draft, it has two or more members from at least two different Member States, who may be natural persons, firms or companies. Its purpose is to facilitate or develop the business of its members and its function must be entirely ancillary to that of its members. Its activities are therefore limited to either the supply of services exclusively to its members or to the manufacturing, processing or packaging of goods, exclusively for its members. It may not exercise management functions in respect of the business of its members and it may not have more than 500 employees.

These restrictions, which seem rather arbitrary, have been made to distinguish the ECG as much as possible from a company. If it could be used as a company, e.g. to supply services to third parties, companies could make use of it to elude certain provisions of national company law for the protection of members or third parties, and in particular rules on employee participation. Thus the Commission hopes, by introducing this emasculated

66. *Ordonnance* nr. 67-821 of 23-9-'67, *Journal officiel* of 28-9-'67.
67. These legal forms have a specific and rather restricted meaning under French law.
68. OJ nr. C 14, 15-2-'74, p. 30 and *Supplement Bulletin EC* 1/74 (with explanatory memorandum). The proposal is based on art. 235 of the EEC Treaty.
69. OJ nr. C 103, 28-4-'78, p. 4.

legal form, to avoid the political obstacles which block the road towards the European Company. Nonetheless, in its amended proposal the Commission could apparently not avoid including two provisions for the protection of the interests of employees.

101. It is proposed not to go into the details of the draft, even though it contains only 24 articles. It may suffice to say that it leaves the members a maximum of flexibility and provides, with a view to protecting third parties, for ample publicity. An ECG may not seek to make profits for itself, but if it happens to make any, they will be taxable in the hands of its members.

102. The proposal has so far been given a reasonably favourable reception, especially by those who are disenchanted with the draft SE Statute, which by its unwieldiness seems to be getting less and less attractive for small and medium-sized (and, for that matter, for large) enterprises. The ECG would seem particularly suitable for medium-sized enterprises, but there is no reason why it could not be used for co-operation between large enterprises.[70] However, as the above shows, it cannot be regarded as an alternative to the SE and it does not solve any of the problems connected with the concentration of enterprises across frontiers. In January 1982 no progress had been made on this draft and it did not look as if new life would soon be breathed into it.

70. This was underlined in the Opinion of the Social and Economic Committee, see OJ nr. C 108, 15-5-'75, p. 46.

European Tax Law

Maarten J. Ellis

The tax provisions in the Treaty of Rome are found in artt. 95 through 99 inclusive.
Art. 95 prohibits discriminatory taxation of imports.
Art. 96 prohibits export subsidies in the form of (in)direct refunds of indirect taxes exceeding the taxes levied. Art. 97, dealing with multi-stage turnover taxes, is no longer relevant since all Member States have adopted value-added tax systems.
Art. 98 prohibits exemptions and refunds of taxes other than turnover taxes, in respect of exports, and countervailing charges in respect of imports, unless approved by the Commission and the Council.
Art. 99 instructs the Commission to consider and propose measures for the harmonization of turnover taxes, excise duties and other forms of indirect taxation.
In addition to the above, art. 100 is often cited as the basis for legislative authority. It does not refer to taxation at all, but provides that the Council may issue Directives for the harmonization of laws which have a direct bearing on the establishment or the functioning of the Common Market. The legislative activities of the Commission and the Council have been concentrated in four main areas:

1. harmonization of turnover taxes and excise duties;
2. harmonization of taxes on the raising of capital and transactions in securities;
3. harmonization of direct taxes;
4. prevention of tax avoidance and evasion.

I. HARMONIZATION OF TURNOVER TAXES AND EXCISE DUTIES

A. Value Added Tax

Based on the explicit instruction of art. 99 of the Treaty of Rome, the Council in 1967 adopted the first Directive[1] setting forth the basic principles of a value-added tax system to be adopted by all Member States by 1970. (This date was subsequently extended to January 1973 by the third[2], fourth[3] and

1. First Directive, nr. 67/227 of 11-4-'67, *Official Journal*, nr. 71 of 14-4-'67, p. 1301.
2. Third Directive, nr. 69/463 of 9-12-'69, *Official Journal*, nr. L 320 of 20-12-'69, p. 34.
3. Fourth Directive, nr. 71/401 of 20-12-'71, *Official Journal*, nr. L 283 of 24-12-'71.

fifth[4] Directives). The second Directive[5], of the same date as the first, provides details of the VAT-system to be adopted. A sixth[6] Directive adopted by the Council in 1977, provides ground rules on the basis for assessment to be adopted by Member States by 1979. The eighth[7] Directive providing harmonization of refund and collection procedures with respect to intra-EC trade, was adopted in 1979. A seventh[8] Directive, still at the proposal stage, deals with works of art, used goods, collection items and antiques.
The first, second and sixth Directives have now been implemented by the nine first Member States, and the VAT-systems in effect are now harmonized to a considerable degree. The basic principle of the Value Added Tax is that each business enterprise selling goods or services collects from its customers a tax based on turnover, and gets a refund of taxes paid to its own suppliers of goods and services. As a result, the net tax collected by each business enterprise is the tax applicable to the value it has added to the product (i.e., the cost of labour and capital, and profit).
Since only business enterprises selling taxable goods or rendering taxable services are entitled to a refund of VAT paid, the non-business customer ultimately carries the full burden of the tax.
For goods and services exported to other EC-countries, the system is designed so that generally, tax is payable either in the country of production or in the country of consumption. For exports to non-EC-countries, the system is designed so that there is no turnover tax burden thereon; no turnover tax need be charged on such sales and services, while the exporter is entitled to a refund of taxes paid to his suppliers.
The Member States are, of course, free to set their own rates of VAT. Most countries have adopted a differentiated system with a low tax on basic commodities and a higher rate on luxury articles.

B. Excise Duties

As mentioned above, article 99 instructs the Commission to propose measures for the harmonization of Member States' laws in this area, and a number of Directives have been issued and proposed.
Since these Directives are only of limited interest, a detailed review of them would appear to be outside the scope of this book. Therefore, only a list of the Directives is provided.
The issued Directives concern travelers' tax exemptions (1969[9], amended sev-

4. Fifth Directive, nr. 72/250 of 4-7-'72, *Official Journal*, nr. L 162 of 18-7-'72, p. 18.
5. Second Directive, nr. 67/228 of 11-4-'67, *Offical Journal*, nr. 71 of 14-4-'67, p. 1303.
6. Sixth Directive, nr. 77/388 of 17-5-'77, *Official Journal*, nr. L. 145 of 13-6-'77, p. 1.
7. Eighth Directive, nr. 79/1072 of 6-12-'79, *Official Journal*, nr. L 331 of 27-12-'79, p. 11.
8. Proposed Seventh Directive, submitted to the Council on 11-1-'78, *Official Journal*, nr. C 26 of 1-2-'78, p. 2.
9. Directive nr. 69/169 of 21-5-'69, *Official Journal*, nr. L 133 of 4-6-'69, p. 6.

eral times[10]), small personal shipments (1974)[11] and manufactured tobacco (1972[12] and 1978).[13] Still in the proposal stage are draft Directives on an outline for excise tax harmonization on alcohol (spirits), on wines, on beer, on mixed beverages, on mineral oils, on insurance contracts, and a further directive on international travelers.

II. HARMONIZATION OF TAXES ON THE RAISING OF CAPITAL AND TRANSACTIONS IN SECURITIES

A. Taxes on the Raising of Capital

This is an area in which considerable harmonization has been achieved. A Directive was issued in 1969[14] instructing the Member States to abolish stamp duty on securities and provide for a harmonized form of capital duty. A further Directive of 1973[15] established common rates for the capital duty. It should be noted that the Directives leave the Member States free to exempt or tax respectively certain transactions.

Under the Directives, the capital duty applies to 'capital companies' which includes all forms of limited liability companies and certain other entities. The transactions that are subject to capital duty are the formation of a capital company, an increase of its capital, an increase in its assets not offset by an increase in its liabilities, the 'immigration' of a capital company from a third country into a Member State, and certain other transactions.

The taxable base is the value of assets contributed, after deduction of liabilities assumed, or (in the case of immigration) the actual value of the company's net assets.

The rate of tax was established at 1% by the 1973 Directive. A reduced rate (between 0 and 0,5%) may be provided in the case of certain mergers or reorganizations. The conditions for the reduced rate are defined rather narrowly in art. 7 of the Directive. Its application is restricted generally to assets-for-shares mergers involving EC resident companies, when a company transfers all its assets or one or more parts of its business to another in exchange ex-

10. Directives nr. 72/230 of 12-6-'72; nr. 78/1032 of 19-12-'78; nr. 78/1033 of 19-12-'78;
11. Directive nr. 74/651, of 19-12-'74, *Official Journal*, nr. L 354 of 30-12-'74, p. 57. Amended by Directive nr. 78/1034 of 19-12-'78.
12. Directive nr. 72/464 of 19-12-'72, *Official Journal*, nr. L 203 of 31-12-'72, p. 1. Amended by Directives nr. 74/318 of 25-6-'74; 75/786 of 18-12-'75; 76/911 of 21-12-'76; 77/805 of 19-12-'77; 80/369 of 26-3-'80.
13. Directive nr. 79/32 of 18-12-'78, *Official Journal*, nr. L 10 of 16-12-'79, p. 8. Amended by Directive nr. 80/369 of 26-3-'80.
14. Directive nr. 69/335 of 17-7-'69, *Official Journal*, nr. L 249 of 3-10-'69, p. 25. Amended by Directives nr. 73/79 of 9-4-'73, 73/80 of 9-4-'73 and 74/553 of 7-11-'74.
15. Directive nr. 73/80 of 9-4-'73, *Official Journal*, nr. L 103, of 18-4-'73, p. 15.

clusively for shares, and shares-for-shares mergers between companies resident in EC Member States, where the acquiring company obtains at least 75% of the other company's shares in exchange exclusively for its own shares. The Directives having been incorporated into the national laws of the first nine Member States, the provisions on capital duty have been effectively harmonized.

B. Securities Transactions

As noted above, the 1969 Directive contains a prohibition for the Member States to levy taxes on security transactions such as the creation, issue, admission to quotation on a stock exchange, loans raised by the issue of debentures or other negotiable securities.
However, the Member States are specifically permitted to charge duties on the transfer of securities, on the transfer of businesses, immovable property or business assets, and on the creation, registration or discharge of mortgages or other charges.
Considerable differences exist between the treatment of such dutiable transactions in the different Member States. The Commission, while generally favouring total abolition of such duties as the most desirable route, has in 1976 proposed a Directive[16] containing limited, and sometines optional harmonization measures. The purpose of the Directive is generally to distribute taxing powers between the Member States and providing maximum rates and mandatory exceptions, but without mandatory imposition of taxes where they are not now imposed.

III. HARMONIZATION OF DIRECT TAXES

A. General

Although only harmonization of indirect taxes is expressly provided in the Rome Treaty, some degree of harmonization of direct taxes was identified many years ago as a necessary element for the realization of a unified market. According to the 1962 Report of the Fiscal and Financial Committee, the need for harmonization exists mainly in the areas of taxes on company income or interest and dividends.
The legislative efforts of the Commission and the Council have consequently been concentrated in these areas. Six draft Directives have been submitted to the Council, and although none have been adopted so far, work is progressing and several Directives may well be issued in the not too distant future. The authority for these Directives is found in art. 100 of the Rome treaty.

16. Proposed Directive, submitted to the Council on 2-4-'76, *Official Journal*, nr. C 133 of 14-6-'76, p. 1.

B. Tax Treatment of Structural Reorganizations

This draft Directive was submitted to the Council in 1969.[17] It proposes a common system for mergers, split-ups and transfers of assets in exchange for shares. The objective is to remove tax obstacles (mainly, taxes on capital gains and distributions of reserves) to such reorganizations taking place across national boundaries.

The proposal has been thoroughly reviewed by the Council on several occasions, lastly in 1978, and is virtually ready from a technical point of view. Its adoption is blocked by two Member States that fear unfavourable political and economic consequences if trans-border mergers could be effected tax-free. The main argument is that as long as company income taxes and dividend taxes have not been harmonized to a reasonable degree, companies will attempt to migrate to the most favourable jurisdiction. The Commission has recently proposed measures to overcome these objections.[18]

C. Tax Treatment of Parent/Subsidiary Relationships

This draft Directive also dates from 1969.[19]

It proposes a common system for the taxation of profits received by parent companies from subsidiaries in other countries. The objectives are to avoid double taxation of such profits, to eliminate dividend withholding taxes, and to create the concept of taxation on a consolidated basis. The basic rule of the draft Directive is that dividends received by parent companies from subsidiaries in other Member States should be exempt from tax. Withholding tax on intercorporate dividends would be eliminated (except in special circumstances such as the split rate of tax in Germany). Furthermore, parent companies under certain conditions could elect to be taxed on a consolidated basis with their majority-controlled subsidiaries in other EC-countries. This proposal has not been under active consideration since 1973. It would appear that the discussion on the harmonization of taxes on company income and dividends (see below) has taken precedence over that on the parent-subsidiary relationship.

17. Proposed Directive, submitted to the Council on 16-1-'69, *Official Journal*, nr. C. 39 of 22-3-'69, p. 7.
18. Doc. COM (80) 203 def. of 29-4-'80.
19. Proposed Directive, submitted to the Council on 16-1-'69, *Official Journal*, nr. C. 39 of 22-3-'69, p. 7.

D. Harmonization of Taxation on Company Income and Dividends

This draft Directive[20], which was submitted in 1975, has become the centre of the harmonization efforts. It is again under active consideration by the European Parliament, which initially (1977) had reacted negatively to the proposals.

The draft Directive was preceded by extensive studies of the tax systems in force in the various Member States. The main issue in these studies is the system according to which the countries tax profits flowing through a company to a shareholder. Basically, three systems are distinguished:

(i) the 'classical' system which taxes company profits at full rates, and again taxes shareholders receiving dividends, at full rates;

(ii) the 'split-rate' system which alleviates the double tax burden on company profits by allowing for a lower tax rate on distributed profits than on undistributed profits, or by allowing a full or partial deduction for dividends paid;

(iii) the 'imputation'-system (also referred to as 'integration system' or 'tax-credit system') where the company profits are taxed at full rates but the shareholder receiving a dividend is entitled to full or partial credit for the tax paid by the company.

The draft Directive chooses in favour of the imputation system which would grant the recipient of dividends a partial credit for the tax paid by the company on its profits. The technique through which this is achieved follows the system adopted by the UK in 1975. All shareholders residents in the EC would be entitled to an equal credit.

Secondly, the draft Directive proposes harmonization of company income tax rates between 45 and 55% of profits. The tax credit to which the shareholder would be entitled would be between 45 and 55% of the company income tax imposed on the amount of the dividend plus the credit. Thirdly, the draft Directive provides for a compensatory tax payable by companies distributing dividends out of earnings that have not borne normal company income tax. The compensatory tax is equal to the tax credit to which the shareholder is entitled. Thus, the tax credit attaching to profits generated by a foreign branch or a foreign subsidiary could be transferred to the shareholder.

The fourth basic element of the draft Directive is a withholding tax of 25% on dividends. Dividends paid to an EC parent, and (optionally) dividends paid to registered resident shareholders would be exempt from such withholding tax.

All EC Member States except the Netherlands, Luxembourg and Greece have now adopted imputation systems of one kind or another. The harmonization of these systems, however, is still a mammoth task because of the very substantial differences between the systems. In addition, the 'flow-through' of tax credits through intermediary vehicles in different countries still presents

20. Proposed Directive, submitted to the Council on 1-8-'75, *Official Journal*, nr. C 253 of 5-11-'75, p. 2.

a formidable technical problem. The concept of a harmonized system of taxation of company profits and dividends is, therefore, still many years away.

E. Avoidance of Double Taxation resulting from Pricing Adjustments

One of the greatest problems in international taxation is the double taxation of company profits that results from the unilateral adjustment by the revenue of one country of transfer prices between related entities. Traditionally, countries attempt to alleviate this problem by providing in bilateral tax conventions, a procedure (the so-called mutual agreement procedure or competent authority procedure) whereby the revenue authorities of the two countries involved attempt to settle the problem by mutual agreement.

This procedure has many drawbacks, and the Commission has therefore submitted to the Council a draft Directive that proposes to settle such problems by arbitration.[21]

Several Member States, however, feel that such a matter should not be the subject of a Directive but of a multilateral convention based on art. 220 of the Rome Treaty. Others prefer the bilateral solution.

It appears that the proposal has been put on the backburner for the time being.

F. Collective Investment Institutions

This draft Directive, submitted in 1978[22], is regarded as an extension of the 1975 draft Directive on the taxation of company income and dividends. It proposes a mechanism through which in the imputation system of taxation, the shareholder's entitlement to a tax credit can flow through the intermediary of a collective investment institution. The progress of this draft Directive is linked with that of the proposed Directive on the taxation of company income and dividends.

G. Frontier and Migrant Workers

So far the only proposed Directive on individual income tax, this proposed Directive was submitted to the Council in 1979.[23] It deals with the tax posi-

21. Proposed Directive, submitted to the Council on 29-11-'76, *Official Journal*, nr. C 301 of 21-12-'76, p. 4.
22. Proposed Directive, submitted to the Council on 24-7-'78, *Official Journal*, nr. C 184 of 2-8-'78, p. 8.
23. Proposed Directive, submitted to the Council on 21-12-'79, *Official Journal*, nr. C 21 of 26-1-'80.

tion of an individual residing in one Member State who habitually works in another. The principal proposed rule is that the country where the employment is exercised may tax the employment income, while the country of residence may also tax the income but must give a credit for taxes paid in the other State.

These situations are now generally covered in bilateral tax conventions, and because of the complexities involved and the lack of harmonization this draft Directive is not expected to be issued shortly.

IV. PREVENTION OF TAX AVOIDANCE AND EVASION

A. General

In recent years, ever-increasing attention has been given politically to the problem of tax avoidance and evasion in the European Communities. Members of European Parliament regularly ask questions, and several studies have been published by the Commission on this issue. The Commission's attention is focused on three areas:

(i) *Withholding taxes on interest and dividends.* As regards dividends, a withholding tax of 25% has been proposed in the 1975 draft Directive (see 3. d. above); in respect of bond interest, the Commission generally would regard a withholding tax in the neighboorhood of 25% as an appropriate anti-evasion measure. However, the Commission is hesitant to propose concrete measures in this area, because a significant flight of capital from the Communities could result.

(ii) *Holding companies.* Consideration is being given to measures to reduce the use of tax-haven holding companies. Withholding taxes would be a prime tool in this attempt, but further measures under consideration include reversing of the burden of proof for payments to tax-haven entities (i.e., the payor would have to prove that such payments are not unjustified) and measures to avoid shifting of profits through artificial intercompany transfer pricing.

(iii) *Mutual assistance and exchange of information.* This is the only area in which concrete steps have been taken. This is dealt with in more detail below.

B. Mutual Assistance and Exchange of Information

Based on art. 100 of the Treaty of Rome, the Council on December 19, 1977 issued a Directive[24] concerning 'mutual assistance by the competent authorities of the Member States in the field of direct taxation and value-added tax'.

24. Directive nr. 77/799 of 19-12-'77, *Official Journal*, nr. L 336 of 27-12-'77, p. 15.

Initially, this Directive applied to all taxes on income, gains and capital. It was later extended (in 1979)[25] to include value-added tax.
The Directive, which in respect of direct taxes should have been (and presumably has been) incorporated in the national laws by January 1, 1979 (for value added tax, January 1, 1981), authorizes and obliges respectively the revenue authorities of the Member States to exchange information, that may be relevant in the assessment of the taxes concerned.
The authorization/obligation to provide certain information is also contained in most bilateral tax conventions. The Directive, however, contains several provisions that exceed by a wide margin, those contained in most tax conventions. The most significant thereof is the obligation contained in art. 4 of the Directive, to forward to the authority of another Member State, without prior request, information when there is a reason to suppose that taxes are being avoided by artificial transactions or otherwise. Furthermore, the Directive instructs Member States to enact legislation authorizing their revenue authorities to contact each other directly, and arrange for spontaneous and automatic exchange of information in specific cases or groups of cases.
From statements made by the Commission in reply to Parliamentary questions and on other occasions it appears that it regards this Directive as the most important and successful tool in the fight against tax avoidance and evasion. The reactions of the authorities of the Member States have been – as might be expected – quite positive, as the Directive facilitates greatly the obtaining of information that was previously difficult to obtain.
The success of the Directive is underlined by the fact that the four Scandinavian non-Members (Finland, Iceland, Norway and Sweden) have asked to be included in the mutual assistance system of the EC.

C. *Mutual Assistance in Tax Collection*

On December 6, 1979 the Council adopted Directive nr. 79/1071[26] amending Directive nr. 76/308.[27] The lastmentioned Directive deals with the mutual assistance among the Member States in the collection of certain EC-levies (agricultural levies and import duties). The 1979 Directive extends this to value-added taxes; it became effective on January 1, 1981.

25. Directive nr. 79/1070 of 6-12-'79, *Official Journal*, nr. L 331 of 28-12-'79, p. 8.
26. Directive nr. 79/1071 of 6-12-'79, *Official Journal*, nr. L 331 of 27-12-'79, p. 10.
27. Directive nr. 76/308 of 15-3-'76, *Official Journal*, nr. L 73 of 19-3-'76, p. 18.

European Social Law

*Bernard C. Dubois**
Civil-law Notary, Professor at the Law School of the University of Gent

I. GENERAL BACKGROUND AND INTRODUCTION

1. On the continent of Europe, always an area of migrating populations, both bilateral and multi-lateral international treaties governing the status and rights of migrant workers have traditionally assumed great importance.
The creation of the European Communities and thereby of a European social policy had a significant impact, not only on the status of migrant workers who are nationals of one of the Member States, but also on all other workers within the Member States. The vesting by the ECSC, EEC and Euratom Treaties in the Treaty institutions of regulatory power in certain fields opened up the possibility of putting into effect a centralised Community policy. It has resulted in far-reaching changes in the constitutional structure of the Member States since decisions taken at Community level replace the former independent power of the Member States by giving their citizens directly effective rights.

2. The fundamental basis of the Common Market is the achievement of economic aims; social measures play a limited role insofar as they are necessary to economic development.
The reluctance of the signatories of the Treaties (particularly in the case of the EEC Treaty, to which this Chapter is confined) to create extensive Community powers in the area of social policy can be briefly explained as follows: in this area, the Treaty mainly exhorts the Member States to co-operate; this inevitably restricts the implementation of an overall Community social policy; moreover, each Member State predictably guards jealously its freedom of action in the social field at the national governmental level.
As a result, Member States enjoy almost complete autonomy in social matters in comparison with other areas governed by the Treaty in which they have accepted drastic limitations of their sovereignty in favour of the supra-national European institutions.
Consequently, European social policy remains largely complementary to Community economic policy, both as a result of the wording of the Treaty and of the practice of Member States.
The draftsmen of the EEC Treaty believed that the progressive establishment of a Common Market would bring in its wake a harmonized social policy; this is the reason for the scarcity of social provisions.

* The author is indebted to Mr Herman van Hoogenbemt, member of the Gent Bar and assistant at the University of Gent, for his assistance in writing this chapter.

3. The relevant provisions of the EEC Treaty are, in summary, as follows:

a. Art. 2 sets out the *general overall aims* of the Community: by establishing a Common Market and progressively approximating the economic policies of the Member States to promote throughout the Community a harmonious development of economic activities ... *an accelerated raising of standard of living ...*

b. Artt. 48 to 51 create *specific Community powers* for the introduction and organisation of a Common Market in employment and ancillary areas (e.g. free movement of workers – harmonization of the social security systems for migratory workers and their dependants – harmonization of the right of entry and residence in the territory of the Member States).

c. Express powers in the social field are contained in Part III, Title Three of the EEC Treaty, headed 'Social Policy', which contains articles 117 to 128.

- Art. 117 gives the Community institutions *general powers* (but no power to adopt Regulations or Directives or to formulate Decisions) in social affairs by providing that Member States accept the necessity to improve living and working conditions and hence make possible their harmonization. The States also expressed their opinion that such a development will result from the functioning of the Common Market as well as from the harmonization of their legal and administrative provisions.
  Commentators disagree about the correct interpretation of article 117. For example, does it enable the Community institutions to pursue a centralised social policy, especially in a period of economic and social crisis? This suggestion is strongly rejected by some important Member States. It is, however, the duty of the Member States under the Treaty, particularly when the economic machine breaks down, to co-operate actively in the implementation of the Treaty, including its social provisions.
- Art. 118 gives the Commission the explicit task of promoting close co-operation between Member States in the social field, especially in the areas of employment, labour law and labour relations, vocational training, social security, prevention of professional sickness, labour hygiene, and the right of association.
  This article gives the Commission the power to take important initiatives either by recommendations (art. 155 EEC Treaty), or opinions, or by preparing studies which, with the co-operation of the Member States, may result in Directives under artt. 100 or 235 of the EEC Treaty.
- Art. 119 requires Member States to respect the principle of equal pay for men and women for equivalent work. In this purely social field, the Commission has, by way of Directives, set up a framework of provisions which has substantially modified national legislation in the Member States.
- Art. 123 to 128 govern the work of the European Social Fund and the establishment of a common policy in the field of vocational training. The European Fund aims, by a framework of extremely complex provisions sustained by limited proper financial resources, to contribute and assist in the retraining and resettlement of workers laid off by conversion of their industries. This aim was enlarged by special promotional measures for certain groups of workers especially endangered by unemployment: e.g. persons withdrawing from agriculture, women and young unemployed people,

migratory and disabled people. These measures are realized by numerous decisions of the Commission.
Financial support from the Fund is never granted to particular employers or workers: it reimburses, as a rule, 50 per cent of the costs which the Member States themselves or corporations of public law within them spend to achieve those aims.

4. Except for artt. 49 and 51, the above-mentioned provisions of the Treaty do not vest in the Community institutions any power to adopt Regulations or Directives or to formulate Decisions. However, there are two Treaty provisions on which the Community institutions may, and in fact have, based Regulations and Directives: artt. 100 and 235.

– *Art. 100* empowers the Council to harmonize by Directives such legal and administrative provisions of the Members States as have a direct incidence on the establishment or the functioning of the Common Market. This makes possible the harmonization of existing national laws in the social field where substantial disparities exist from Member State to Member State.
– *Art. 235* gives the Council a wide power to intervene whenever action is necessary to realise an aim of the Community where the Treaty does not provide the necessary powers. Recent history of the EEC social policy shows that the Council has in some cases intervened in the social field on the basis of this article (e.g. in relation to equal treatment for male and female workers).

5. Though the number of obligatory measures adopted in the social field under the EEC Treaty is modest, it must be emphasised that since 1974 new objectives for the European social policy have been adopted.
By its *Resolution dated 21st January 1974*[1] the Council adopted a *social action programme* through which the Community must find a 'human face' if it is to get the support of the citizens; in other words, this programme expresses the determination of the Member States to go beyond the previously limited compass of the social provisions of the Treaties in order to launch a broad and original 'social union' besides the economic and financial union. This new instrument of the Community's social policy contains a very detailed enumeration of aims and general measures which are to be taken in order to achieve these aims as well as specific measures to implement the general measures.
This new approach to European social law permitted – and permits – the Council, by way of Directives, to harmonize certain fields of the social legislation of the Member States in a European mould.
This far-reaching harmonization is exemplified by Directives on the approximation of laws concerning for example the rights of employees in the event of transfers of undertakings, collective dismissals, equal pay, and equal treatment as regards access to employment.
It remains doubtful to what extent this new impulse in the social objectives of the Community will be followed up by Member States faced with tragic na-

1. OJ nr. C 13, 12-2-'74, p. 1.

tional economic realities. For some of them the crisis which confronts them will strengthen their solidarity with the Community.

6. Mention must also be made of the considerable impact of the *European Court of Justice* in establishing and reaffirming fundamental principles of European Social Law. The judgments of the Court represent an increasingly important source of law in this field.

7. NOTE TO THE READER: TABLE OF CONTENTS
This survey on European Social Law is in the context of this book necessarily brief. The material of this survey is the result of a careful but strict selection by its author. The following is a résumé of those important areas which are briefly dealt with on the following pages:

- The *free movement of persons* – particularly *workers* – which is one of the foundations of the Common Market is dealt with in Section II.
- This is followed, in Section III, by a résumé of some of the Community *provisions on harmonization of law* in the social field:
    - Council Directive of 17th February 1975 on the approximation of the laws of Member States on *collective redundancies*;
    - Directive of 14th February 1977 on the safeguarding of employees rights in the event of *transfers of undertakings*;
    - Directive of 20th October 1980 on the protection of employees in the event of *insolvency of their employer*;
    - some other important Directives and draft Directives on the harmonization of laws in the social field.

Finally, Section IV is devoted to the *European Convention* of 19th June 1980 *on the law applicable to contractual obligations*, in particular obligations arising under *individual employment contracts*.
Although not strictly part of European social law, this important Convention which in July 1981 had been signed by all Member States but one, will be of considerable importance in the Member States when questions of conflicts of laws arise, both in general and specifically in the context of the labour law of the Member States.

II. FREE MOVEMENT OF EMPLOYEES WITHIN THE EC

8. One of the most original aspects of the EEC Treaty is the creation of on the one hand a common economic market, to which on the other hand a common labour market between the Member States was attached. The sensitive area of migration of employees, usually characterized by strong nationalism and protectionism, is within the EC the subject of a supra-national scheme in which Community interests prevail.
Artt. 48 to 51 organize the free movement of employees, whereby every form of discrimination on the ground of nationality between the employees of the

Member States is abolished, and this in the field of labour demand as well as labour supply, wages, and other working conditions.
The employees may also count on co-ordination of the application of the various schemes of social security to which they are entitled to resort by virtue of their employment in the various Member States.
The realization of this free movement was achieved in stages that culminated in the basic Regulation 1612/68 of 10th October 1968.[2] The introduction of this final scheme was accompanied by the introduction of a series of Community schemes aimed at the abolition within the Member States of all restrictions on the movement and residence of employees and their families.
This right, ensured at Community level, can only be restricted within the limits contained in the Treaty (art. 48(3)(1)) and developed in Directive 64/221 of 25th February 1964.[3]
The right was furthermore guaranteed by stand-still provisions (Regulations 15 (of 1961) and 38/64, which have been replaced in the meantime), through which the Member States were forbidden from introducing new restrictions. Since the end of the transition period (31st December 1969), the existing restrictions lost their significance. In fact, in this field the Member States have now little or no room for own initiative left; the Community schemes moreover have a direct effect, which reinforces their precedence over any national rules to the contrary.

The scope of Regulation 1612/68

9. *a. Ratione personae*: The EEC Treaty distinguishes clearly between free employee movement on the one hand (artt. 48 to 51) and the freedom of establishment (independent activities) and the free supply of services on the other (artt. 52 to 58 and 59 to 66 respectively).
Consequently, free movement of employees only relates to employees, viz. persons bound in subordination by labour, as a rule under an individual labour contract. The right only applies to those employees who are nationals of the Member States.

b. Ratione territoriae: Regulation 1612/68 stipulates that the free movement of employees applies to the entire territory of the EC, six French overseas territories, on ships and probably also (oil) platforms under the jurisdiction of one of the Member States. Generally, it applies in all relationships which can be localised within the Community, either by reason of the place where they were entered into or by reason of the place where they have their effect.[4]
Transition periods of varying lengths were provided for new Member States.[5]

c. Ratione materiae: The free movement of employees relates to all economic activities in the private sector, thereby excluding persons employed in pub-

2. OJ nr. L 257, 19-10-'68, p. 2.
3. OJ nr. 56, 4-4-'64, p. 850/64.
4. Court of Justice in case 36/74 (Walrave and Koch), ECR '74, p. 1405.
5. Thus the most important provisions of Regulation 1612/68 will only apply in the nine Member States with regard to Hellenic nationals and in Greece with regard to nationals of the Nine as from 1-1-'88.

lic administration. However, the decisions of the European Court of Justice show that the concept of public administration, being an exception to the general rule, must be given a narrow interpretation.

The basic contents of Regulation 1612/68

10. Free movement of employees is supported by a structure of Community provisions by which the employees of each Member State are granted the following rights:

a. to accept any offer of employment actually made;
b. to move freely within the Community in order to accept such an offer;
c. to stay in any Member State in which he is employed;
d. to be subject to the same conditions of employment and work as the national employees of the other Member State.

11. Regulation 1612/68 serves to abolish every national provision to the contrary that would, purely on the grounds of nationality, maintain a discrimination between employees from different Member States in the field of the supply of and the demand for work and the access to work. The Regulation specifies this principle as follows:

a. Any national of a Member State may *accept* work and any employer may *offer* work in the territory of a Member State, in accordance with the laws and regulations of such a State; this may and must not lead to discrimination in any form.
b. The employees of any Member State have therefore the *same privileges* on the labour market as the nationals of another Member State.
c. The employees have the right not only to accept a specific offer of work but also to actively *seek* work in the territory of any Member State, but this within a limited period of time (Cf. item 12 below).
d. There is *no* obligation on the part of the employee to apply for and obtain a *work permit* nor does the employer have to obtain a permit to employ such an employee.
e. The employees of other Member States receive the *same assistance* in finding employment from the national labour offices as the nationals of the relevant State.
f. An employee who is a national of a Member State may in the territory of other Member States not be treated any differently on the grounds of his nationality than the national employees as far as the conditions of employment are concerned; this is in the widest sense (right to non-discriminatory treatment). This *prohibition of discrimination* applies to wages, dismissal, rights to re-involvement in the occupation or re-employment in case of unemployment, re-schooling etc.. The equal treatment applies to all legal provisions that may influence the conditions of employment, which consequently precludes both direct and indirect discrimination of the migrating EC employee in respect of the national employee. The equal treatment applies both to individual and to collective labour legislation or social security legislation.
g. Finally, Regulation 1612/68 organizes the technical co-operation between the labour offices in the various Member States, in order to promote an efficient communication between supply and demand in the European

labour market. In this context, the Commission has developed an appropriate system (the Sedoc plan) that has now, following an experimental stage, become operational.

Entry and residence

12. The specific Community provisions in connection with entry to and residence in the territory of the Member States are in line with the above. The *right to migrate* within the Community of the nationals of the Member States has been laid down in Directive 68/360 of 15th October 1968[6], while the limitations on these migration rights have been developed in Directive 64/221 of 25th February 1964.[7] The right to permanent residence for employees in the territory of a Member State, after having been employed there, has been laid down in Regulation 1251/70 of 29th June 1970[8], while the limitations on this right have been laid down in Directive 72/194 of 18th May 1972.[9] Characteristic for these Community rules is the abolition of all national legislative and administrative provisions and practices that may set limitations on the conditions for entry and residence, while the Member States can only invoke exceptions which are supported by criteria set by the Community (Directive 64/221).

a. Directive 68/360 requires the Member States to grant eachother's nationals the right to *leave* the territory in order to accept and enter into paid employment in the territory of another Member State. To exercise this right, only a valid identity card or passport need be submitted.

b. Nationals of a Member State who are looking for work may move about freely in the territory of another Member State in order to *solicit* concrete *offers of employment*. The person involved has a minimum term of three months at his disposal for this purpose. When this term has expired and if no concrete work has been found, the stay of this person may be terminated by the Member State to which he has travelled (unpublished, unofficial Minute of the meeting of the Council in which Regulation 1612/68 and Directive 68/360 were adopted).

c. If within three months an employment contract is concluded or work is performed, the relevant employee will receive a 'residence permit for national of a Member State', without further formalities, upon submission of the following documents:
   - the official identity card or passport shown by him in order to enter the territory;
   - a statement of engagement or employment from the employer.

Close relatives are also given a residence permit. This permit is valid for five years and may automatically be extended. Only in a few cases can the permit be revoked or extension be refused: viz. in the case of a long period of voluntary unemployment, a long period of illness or an accident. The first extension may be limited to a minimum of 12 months if the employee has been involuntarily unemployed in the 'host State' for more than 12 months.

6. OJ nr. L 257, 19-10-'68, p. 13.
7. See note 2 on page 61.
8. OJ nr. L 142, 30-6-'70, p. 24.
9. OJ nr. L 121, 26-5-'72, p. 32.

The granting, extending and revocation of this residence permit are subject to very precise conditions laid down in Directive 68/360.
The Member States may only deviate from the provisions of this Directive for reasons arising from public policy, public security or public health. The exceptions have been listed in specific Community acts.

13. The Council Directive 64/221 of 25th February 1964 on the co-ordination of special measures concerning the movement and residence of foreign nationals which are justified on grounds of public policy, public security and public health.
The Directive is based on the limitation of the right to movement and residence of the EC employee (laid down in art. 48(3) of the EEC Treaty).
Directive 64/221 sets the conditions for the restrictions justified on grounds of public policy, public security and public health, but these conditions apply only to entry to and residence in the territory of a Member State so that they cannot be invoked with regard to the conditions for entry and the exercise of professional activities.
The Directive aims at co-ordinating national law with regard to these restrictions: on the one hand by a precise definition of the concepts of 'public policy' etc., on the other by ensuring possibilities to institute proceedings against the decision of a Member State to refuse entry or residence.

a. *The limitations*

(i) *Public order and security*

These concepts are neither defined by the Treaty nor by the Directive, so that the Member States have their own margin for evaluation; this is implicitly recognized by the European Court of Justice, although the Court of Justice checks every national limitation against the fundamental principles of the Treaty, *inter alia* in the context of the free movement of employees.
Moreover, the Directive limits the margin of evaluation by the following principles:

- the measures of public policy or security should exclusively be based on the personal conduct of the person involved; the reasons invoked for refusal of entry or residence must never be abused for economic purposes;
- prior convictions for criminal offences are in themselves not an adequate reason;
- removal from the territory may not merely be founded on purely administrative offences against the rules concerning the identity card or the residence permit.

(ii) *Public health*

Only such diseases as are listed in the Annex to the Directive justify refusal of entry or to issue a first residence permit. Diseases or disabilities occurring after a first residence permit has been issued shall not justify refusal to renew the residence permit or expulsion from the territory.

b. *Rules of procedure*

Any Member State that refuses entry, refuses to grant or extend a residence permit or proceeds to remove a person from its territory must observe the following principles:

(i) The person concerned must be informed of the grounds upon which the decision in his case is based.

(ii) The person concerned must be officially notified of any decision ro refuse the issue or renewal of a residence permit or to expel him from the territory. The period allowed for leaving the territory must be stated in this notification (save in cases of urgency, not less than 15 days if the person concerned has not yet been granted a residence permit and not less than one month in all other cases).

(iii) The person concerned should have the same legal remedies in respect of any such decision as are available to nationals of the relevant State in respect of acts of the administration.

(iv) Where there is no right of appeal to a court of law, or where such appeal may be only in respect of the legal validity of the decision, or where the appeal cannot have suspensory effect, the decision shall not be taken by the administrative authority, save in cases of urgency, until an opinion has been obtained from a 'competent authority' of the host country before which the person concerned enjoys such rights of defence and of assistance or representation as the national law of that country provides for.

c. *Implementation and application*

Pursuant to the obligation put on them by Directive 64/221, the Member States have adjusted their national laws.

The application of the Community principles and their implementation in national law are supervised by the European Court of Justice, mainly by means of the procedure of preliminary rulings (art. 177 of the EEC Treaty). In giving its rulings, the Court has given direct effect to quite a number of provisions of Directive 64/221.[10]

The social security of the migrating EEC employee

14. Migrating employees who, by virtue of the right of free movement within the Community, are going to work in the territory of other Member States are of course interested in the maintenance of the social security entitlements accrued to them both in the country of origin and in any other host country.

Art. 51 of the EEC Treaty therefore attaches to this free movement the need for co-ordination of the various systems of social security within the Community in order to ensure the continuity of the rights of the migrating employees. Regulations nrs 1408/71 and 574/72[11] specify this objective.

10. See items 8 and 13 of the Chapter 'Some Observations on the Law of the European Communities'.

11. Codified versions of these Regulations and all their amendments may be found in OJ nr. C 138, 9-6-'80.

General characteristics and technique of Regulations 1408/71 and 574/72

15. a. Equality of treatment:
Migrating employees from the Community are entitled to the same rights to social security as the nationals of the State in which they are employed.

b. Aggregation of the periods:
With this technique the periods of insurance, employment or residence under various national systems are all aggregated in order to determine whether there is a right to certain benefits and, if so, to what amount. In this respect, not only the periods under compulsory insurance schemes are taken into account, but also the periods assimilated with insurance periods and the periods of voluntary or optional continued insurances to the extent that they do not coincide with the compulsory periods.

c. Exporting benefits or allowances
Payment of the benefits or allowances is guaranteed to employees located in the territory of another Member State than the one under whose legislation the right to payment had accrued. The various countries of employment must each pay the migrating employee pro rata to the rights determined for him.

Scope of Regulations 1408/71 and 574/12

16. a. Ratione personae the Regulations apply to all employees or persons considered equal thereto and their families who are nationals of one of the Member States (or stateless persons or refugees residing within the Community) and who are or have been subject to the social security legislation of one or more of the Member States.
Regulation 1408/71 defines the concept of employee ('worker') or person considered equal thereto; these concepts are constantly being clarified or refined by the decisions of the European Court of Justice.

b. Ratione materiae the Regulations apply to all legislation relating to the following types of social security: sickness and maternity, invalidity, old age and death, accidents at work and occupational diseases, death grants, unemployment, family benefits and family allowances for employed and unemployed persons, and benefits for dependent children of pensioners and for orphans. The Regulations contain special provisions with respect to each of these types.
In its application, Regulation 1408/71 makes no distinction between general and special systems of social security, nor between systems supported by contributions from employer and/or employee and those supported by general taxation.
Each Member State specifies the regimes applying in its territory on a list published in the Official Journal of the European Communities.

c. Determination of the legislation applicable
The essential purpose of the Regulations is to avoid conflicts of law concerning the application of social security regimes to migrating EEC employees. Regulation 1408/71 states that the social security legislation of the country of employment is applicable. The same rule applies if the employee is posted to another Member State for an anticipated period of not more than 12 months. A worker who normally pursues his activity in two

or more Member States is subject to the legislation of the Member State in whose territory he resides or if he does not reside in any Member State, to the legislation of the Member State where the registered office or the place of business of his employer is situated. These rules are subject to various exceptions.

d. Regulations 1408/71 and 574/72 replace the bilateral social security treaties concluded between the Member States. However, the Regulations do not affect obligations arising from any conventions adopted by the International Labour Conference or the European Interim Agreements on Social Security of 11th December 1953 concluded between the Member States of the Council of Europe. Certain provisions of other conventions (for example the European Convention of 9th July 1956 concerning social security for workers in international transport) also continue to apply.

The position of employees from third countries within the EEC

17. Although in recent years the employment within the Community of employees migrating from third countries is showing a tendency to decrease, they are still significant in number.

a. *Community priority*
Regulation 1612/68 grants the nationals of one of the Member States a Community priority for employment in any of the Member States. If a Member State notifies the employment services of the other Member States of vacancies, suitable applications from nationals of other Member States have the same priority for employment over employees from third countries as the national employees of the Member State concerned. This priority remains valid for 18 days, in which period the employment of employees from third countries is blocked. During this period vacancies may be notified to third countries only if the number of available employees in the relevant occupation who are nationals of the Member States is deemed insufficient by the Member State having such vacancies.

b. *Exceptions to the above priority*
Regulation 1612/68 provides for some exceptions to the principle of priority, by virtue of which vacancies may be offered by a Member State simultaneously both to the other Member States and to workers from third countries. The above-mentioned period of 18 days does not need to be observed in such cases.
Such exceptions include *inter alia*:
- an offer made to a named worker and of a special nature in view of:
  (i) the requirement of specialist qualifications or the confidential nature of the post offered or previous occupational ties; or
  (ii) the existence of family ties between the employer and the worker asked for or between the latter and a worker who has been employed regularly for at least a year in the enterprise of the employer.
- vacancies offered expressly to workers from third countries for reasons connected with the smooth running of the enterprise, provided the employment of the Member State concerned are of the opinion that such reasons are justified.

Regulation 1612/68 does not affect the obligations of Member States arising out of

- special relations or future agreements with certain non-European countries or territories, based on institutional ties existing at the date of the entry into force of the Regulation (in the case of new Member States the date of accession), or
- agreements in existence at one of the dates referred to above with certain non-European countries or territories, based on institutional ties between them.

Workers from such countries or territories who are employed in one of the Member States may, however, not invoke the benefit of this Regulation in other Member States.

Finally, we mention that employment of non-EEC nationals in the Member States is subject to stringent rules aimed at protecting the national labour markets on the one hand and at strictly controlling access to and stay in their territories on the other. The application of these rules is discussed separately for each Member State in the national chapters.

III. HARMONIZATION OF SOCIAL LAWS

A. The Council Directive of February 17, 1975 on the approximation of the laws of the Member States relating to collective redundancies[12]

18. Although most Member States have already more or less adopted provisions concerning collective redundancies in their national law, the EC Council wished to remove the existing inevitable differences between the national laws in order to promote the approximation on the way to progress in the sense of art. 117 of the EEC Treaty. The Council proceeded on the assumption that these differences could have a direct effect on the functioning of the Common Market, for example by movement of employees to regions providing the protection of strong social legislation. The underlying argument obviously was the unfavourable position in which Member States with well-developed protective legislation in favour of the employees find themselves when compared with Member States with less favourable legislation.
The Council found a basis for issuing a Directive in art. 100 of the EEC Treaty.

19. Like all other Directives, this Directive is binding on each Member State as regards the result to be achieved, but the choice of form and means is left to the Member States. The specific implementation of the Directive in the

12. OG nr. L 48, 22-2-'75, p. 29.

legislation of every Member State may therefore be found in the national chapters of this book.
The provisions of this Directive must be implemented by the Member States by means of acts, regulations or administrative provisions, or by means of collective labour agreements. If collective labour agreements are concluded, government interference is required to give such agreement to generally binding force '*erga omnes*'.

20. Definition of collective redundancies
Two distinct sets of criteria are adopted by the Directive to define collective redundancies (art. 1).

a. subjective and qualitative criteria: collective redundancies are created through the actions of an employer who dismisses employees for one or more reasons not relating to the individual workers concerned: for example for purely economic or technical, health or hygiene, environmental protection or similar reasons. Dismissal for reasons related to the individual employee do not lead to collective redundancies. In their own legislation, the Member States can, however, limit these criteria.
b. objective, quantitative and temporary criteria: collective redundancies must concern a certain number of employees over a specific period. The Directive allows the Member States the following options:
either – over a period of *30 days*:
    1. at least 10 employees are dismissed in establishments normally employing more than 20 and less than 100 workers;
    2. at least 10% of the employees is dismissed in establishments normally employing at least 100 but less than 300 workers;
    3. at least 30 employees are dismissed in establishments normally employing 300 workers or more

    or – over a period of *90 days*:
    at least 20 employees are dismissed, whatever the number of workers normally employed in the establishment in question.

In their own internal legislation, the Member States have implemented these criteria in different ways: sometimes elements of the above definition are extended or restricted; in some cases the provisions deviate to such an extent from the principles of the Directive that it is difficult to speak of harmonization.
In practice, it is therefore necessary to examine the definition of collective redundancies as developed in the legislation of the individual Member States. It should be noted that the Directive allows the enactment by the Member States of more favourable provisions: e.g., it is possible that under the rules of a Member State certain redundancies are considered collective redundancies, while this would not be the case according to the criteria of the EEC Directive. In this respect, the approximating effect sought by the Directive should be viewed some scepticism.

21. Exceptions
Certain categories of employees are excluded from the application of the Directive:
– either because they are subject to different specific rules (crews of sea-

going vessels or employees of public administrative bodies or by establishments governed by public law);

- or because their contracts of employment were concluded for a limited period of time or for specific tasks, except where such redundancies take place prior to the date of expiry or the completion of such contracts;
- or because the activities of an establishment are terminated as a result of a judicial decision.

22. Consultation procedure (art. 2.1.)

The main purpose of the Directive is to guarantee the consultation of the workers' representatives in every case of contemplated collective redundancies. The purpose of this consultation is to find solutions to avoid the dismissals or, if at all possible, to reduce the number of employees affected. If, however, collective redundancies turn out to be inevitable, the consultations shall include a study of possible measures to mitigate the consequences of the collective redundancies for the employees: this may be effected by the development of a 'social plan'.

The Directive does not contain alternatives if the consultations do not yield positive results. Ultimately the employer alone decides on the actual execution of the collective redundancies.

23. Duty to inform (art. 2.3.)

Since consultations can only be effective if complete information is provided, the employer is bound to draw up a complete and exhaustive information file, copy of which is to be forwarded to the workers' representatives. This file contains at least the information stipulated in the Directive.

24. Procedure for collective redundancies (artt. 3 and 4)

To a certain extent, the Directive grants the competent public authority, the right of supervision on and interference in contemplated collective redundancies. During the preparatory work on the Directive the role of the authorities in this matter was a subject of serious discussion. Between the proposal of strong government interference (opposition to the collective redundancies) and neutrality of the authorities on this point, a compromise solution was agreed.

a. The competent public authority is notified of the start of the consultation procedure (see nr. 22 above).

b. The employer is bound, following the consultations, officially to inform the competent public authority of the plan for collective redundancies. The workers' representatives may also send their comments to the competent public authority.

c. The above notification has the immediate effect that:

  - the employer's decision to effect collective redundancies is temporarily suspended;
  - during this suspension the competent public authority seeks solutions for the problems raised by the projected collective redundancies;
  - the employer's decision is in principle suspended for 30 days following receipt of the notification. Extension to 60 days is possible if the initial period turns out to be too short to find a solution. The Direc-

tive leaves it to the discretion of the Member States to shorten or extend the periods in their national legislation. Extensions of the period, however, should be limited to where they are a necessity and the employer should be informed of the extension in good time.

d. Although the Directive contains no provisions on this point, of course the public authority can continuously assist the parties involved in the consultation procedure, at the request of one of the parties.

e. Although ultimately, the Directive kept the role of the public authority limited, art. 5 stipulates that the Directive does not prohibit the Member States from applying or introducing laws, regulations or administrative provisions which are more favourable to workers. Consequently, in its internal legislation any Member State may expand the role of supervision and interference of the competent public authority, provided that the objective is better protection of employees affected by collective redundancies.

25. Brief comments on the Directive

a. This Directive is far from revolutionary; most Member States already had provisions that go considerably further than the Directive. The emphasis of the Directive lies on the participation of the employees through the compulsory prior notification and the subsequent consultation procedure, and the existing relations between unions and employers in most Member States would have led to similar procedures.
The Directive does have the advantage of imposing a uniform obligation on all Member States, according to clearly defined criteria.
Due to the limited contents of the Directive, approximation of laws concerning problems other than collective redundancies cannot be expected.
For the time being, approximation in a progressive direction, i.e. in the sense of the most progressive national legislation on this matter, is unlikely. In the end the Directive has not prevented most Member States from formulating their internal law according to their own (limited or progressive) views on collective redundancies.

b. According to the Directive, the Member States had to bring into force the laws, regulations and administrative provisions needed in order to comply with the Directive within two years following its notification (February 22, 1975).
Consequently, from a practical point of view, the national legislations should by now have been adapted to the criteria of the Directive. If this should not be the case or if compliance with the Directive is unsatisfactory or only partial, the question arises to what extent and how a legal entity or individual can rely on the Directive in conflict with other persons or with the public authorities. This question is briefly discussed in items 8 and 13 of the Chapter 'some Observations on the Law of the European Communities'.

B. Directive 77/187/EEC of 14th February 1977 on the approximation of the laws of the Member States relating to the safeguarding of employees' rights in the event of transfers of undertakings, businesses or parts of businesses[13]

GENERAL COMMENTS

26. In its Resolution regarding a Social Action Programme of 21st January 1974[14], the Council stated its intention to take measures to promote the approximation of the legislation of the Member States concerning the interests of the employees in the case of mergers, concentration and restructuring of enterprises.
This led to the adoption of Directive 77/187/EEC, which, after the example of the Directive on collective redundancies, was based on art. 100 of the EEC Treaty with a reference to art. 117.

SCOPE

27. The Directive applies to the transfer of *undertakings, businesses* or parts of businesses as a result of a *legal transfer or merger* (art. 1(1)). However, the concepts of undertaking, business and part of business are not specified. This may be due to an intention on the part of the Council, as is not unknown in harmonization Directives, to introduce a certain vagueness in order to facilitate incorporation of the principles stipulated in the Directive in the national legislations. From the *case-law* of the Court of Justice concerning competition we may infer that the concept of undertaking presupposes legal and economic independence, while the set-up of the present Directive shows that a certain *'social'* autonomy is also required. The concept of business may then be deemed to refer to more or less autonomous parts of an undertaking that are not legal persons, but have a *certain 'social' independence* demonstrated by the fact that employment relationships are organized at this level.
Finally, the concept of 'part of a business' must refer to parts without any legal, economic or 'social' autonomy.
The above makes it clear that the Directive also applies to transfers of a very limited scope. It does not apply to sea-going vessels (art. 1(3)). This may be due to the fact that seamen are customarily employed for one voyage.
Transfer of an undertaking presupposes a legal change of employer. To fall within the scope of the Directive such a change should be of a *contractual* nature. Transfer through inheritance or through *unilateral government* decisions is therefore not included.

13. OJ nr. L 61, 5-3-'77, p. 26.
14. See note on page 59.

28. Notwithstanding the original intentions of the Commission, the Directive does *not* relate to operations that merely lead to one undertaking gaining *factual control* over another. This may presumably be explained by reference to the prospect of a future Regulation on economic concentration which is intended to have a wider scope. Apart from the restrictions just referred to, the scope of this Directive is very wide: it includes transfer through, *inter alia*, sale, incorporation, donation, merger, absorption, division and even lease.

SAFEGUARDING OF INDIVIDUAL RIGHTS

29. The transferor's rights and obligations arising from a contract of employment or from an employment relationship existing on the date of the transfer are, by reason of such transfer, transferred to the transferee (art. 3(1)). The transferee can therefore oblige the employees to remain in his employment. On the other hand, he has to continue to employ them on the same terms as the transferor did before him. In principle, the transfer releases the latter from any further obligations towards the employees. Nevertheless, the Member States may provide that after the date of transfer, in addition to the transferee, the transferor continues to be liable in respect of obligations arising from a contract of employment or an employment relationship (art. 3(1)(2)). As nearly all conditions and terms of employment are now no longer agreed individually but by collective bargaining, the continuation of the rights of the employees would be a dead letter, were it not for the stipulations of art. 3(2). In the said paragraph it is stipulated that the transferee shall continue to observe the terms and conditions agreed in any collective agreement on the same terms applicable to the transferor under that agreement, until the date of termination or expiry of the collective agreement or the entry into force or application of another collective agreement. Member States may limit the period for observing such terms and conditions, with the proviso that it shall not be less than one year. It should be noted that in formulating this provision the differences between the various Member States concerning the binding force of collective agreements have been taken into account.
The continuation of rights does not cover employees' rights to benefits under supplementary company or inter-company social security schemes outside the statutory social security schemes in Member States. While the French and Dutch texts leave open the possibility of continuation of rights with regard to schemes drawn up by the undertaking concerned, in the English and German texts this possibility is absolutely excluded. Consequently, the meaning of this exception is not completely clear. The Directive does provide an obligation for the Member States to adopt the measures necessary to protect the interests of employees and former employees to old-age benefits and survivors' benefits, under supplementary schemes of social security (art. 3(3)).
The sanction on failure by the transferee to respect the conditions of employment existing on the date of transfer is that if the contract of employment or the employment relationship is terminated by the employee because the transfer has led to a substantial change in working conditions to his detriment, the employer will be regarded as having been responsible for termination of the contract or relationship (art. 4(2)).

In itself, the transfer does not constitute grounds for termination by transferor or transferee. However, this provision does not prevent dismissals for economic, technical or organizational reasons entailing changes in the workforce (art. 4(1)). This weakening does of course entail that only few dismissals will be in conflict with the basic prohibition of dismissals. The provision is moreover not sanctioned. Furthermore, the Member State may provide that the prohibition of dismissals does not apply to certain specific categories of employees who are not covered by the laws or practices of the Member States in respect of protection against dismissal (art. 4(2)).

SAFEGUARDING OF COLLECTIVE RIGHTS

30. In addition to the safeguarding of individual rights, the Directive also provides for the safeguarding of collective rights in behalf of the employees. This consists, prior to or at the time of the transfer, in the obligation for transferor and transferee to inform and even, to some extent, consult their employees, through representatives, on the transfer (art. 6). In addition, there are some provisions on the status and function of the representatives or of the representation of the employees affected by the transfer.
According to art. 5, if the business preserves its autonomy, the status and function, as laid down by the laws, regulations or administrative provisions of the Member States, of the representatives or of the representation of the employees affected by the transfer, will be preserved. However, if, under the laws, regulations, administrative provisions or practice of the Member States, the conditions necessary for the re-appointment of the representatives of the employees or for the reconstitution of the representation of the employees have been fulfilled, the above provision does not apply. If the term of office of the representatives of the employees expires as a result of the transfer, the representatives shall continue to enjoy the protection provided by the laws, regulations, administrative provisions or practice of the Member States.
The principle of retaining function and position does of course not apply to members of administrative, governing or supervisory bodies of companies who represent employees on such bodies in certain Member States (e.g., the employees' representatives who are members of the *Aufsichtsräte* of the *Aktiengesellschaften* in the Federal Republic of Germany (art. 2(c)).
Transferor and transferee are required to inform the representatives of their respective employees affected by the transfer of the reasons for the transfer, the legal, economic and social implications of the transfer for the employees and the measures envisaged in relation to the employees. This information must be given in good time, viz. by the transferor before the transfer is carried out, and by the transferee before his employees are directly affected by the transfer as regards their conditions of work and employment (art. 6(1)).
Finally, if transferor or transferee envisages measures in relation to his employees, he is bound to consult the representatives of his employees in good time on such measures with a view to seeking agreement (art. 6(2)).

31. Certain deviations are possible, however. In Member States where the representatives of the employees may have recourse to an arbitration board to obtain a decision on the measures to be taken in relation to employees, the obligations to inform and consult may be limited to cases where the transfer of the business gives rise to a change likely to entail serious disadvantages for a considerable number of the employees (art. 6(3)). The obligations may moreover be limited to undertakings or businesses which, in respect of the number of employees, fulfill the conditions for the election or designation of a collegiate body representing the employees (art. 6(4)). The Member States may provide that where there are no representatives of employees in an undertaking or business, the employees concerned must be informed in advance when a transfer is about to take place. In that case there seems to be no obligation to consult.

The Directive contains no sanctions on non-compliance with the obligations to inform and consult. Any sanctions are left to the Member States.

The Member States may at all times apply or introduce laws, regulations or administrative provisions which are more favourable to employees than the present Directive (art. 7).

C. Directive 80/987/EEC of October 20, 1980 on the approximation of the laws of the Member States relating to the protection of employees in the event of insolvency of their employer[15]

GENERAL COMMENTS

32. The economic recession around 1980 more than ever before has drawn the attention of the competent authorities to the often precarious situation in which employees are placed in the event of insolvency or bankruptcy of their employer.

In such cases the employees seeking to realize claims originating in the employment relationship face the competition of other creditors. Even if the claims of the employees are given legal preference over other claims, the funds available are often inadequate to meet them. As the rights derived by employees from their employment relationship are usually their only source of income, it was considered desirable to guarantee these rights in another manner.

In most Member States the national law already provided a mechanism of guarantee of the employees' claims through institutions especially created for this purpose. The existing regulations differed, substantially from country to country, however, and moreover some Member States had no specific guarantee scheme at all. In view of the steadily-increasing social and economic links between the Member States, more uniform protection appeared necessary, especially as the existing national differences could have a direct influence on the effectiveness of the Common Market.

Directive 80/987 is aimed both at social harmonization and at the elimination

15. OG nr. L 283, 28-10-'80, p. 23.

of distorting factors from the Common Market; it is consequently based on art. 100 with a reference to art. 117 of the EEC Treaty.

SCOPE

33. The Directive applies to the employees' claims arising from contracts of employment or employment relationships (art. 1(1)). To facilitate incorporation of the principles of the Directive in the various national legal systems, the task of defining concepts such as 'employer', 'employee' etc. is left to the Member States (art. 2(2)). The Commission's proposal to extend the protection of the guarantee also to the claims arising from training relationships has not been adopted by the Council. This does not, however, prohibit the Member States from guaranteeing such claims. By way of exception the Member States may, by virtue of the special nature of the employee's contract or relationship, or of the existence of other forms of guarantee of a similar nature, exclude certain categories of employees from the scope of the Directive (art. 1(2)). The categories excluded by several Member States are summed up in the Annex to the Directive.
What is the exact meaning and scope of the concept of 'insolvency'? According to art. 2 the employer is deemed to be in a state of insolvency when a request has been made for the opening of proceedings involving the employer's assets to satisfy collectively the claims of creditors, on the condition that the claims of the employees can also be taken into account and that the competent national authority has either decided to open these proceedings or to refrain from doing so because the employer's undertaking or business has been definitively closed down and there are insufficient assets to warrant the opening of the proceedings.

GUARANTEE FUNDS

34. The Member States should ensure that guarantee institutions honour the unfulfilled claims of the employees relating to their salaries over a period that is established at the discretion of the Member States and which preceeds, either the onset of the employer's insolvency, or the notice of dismissal on account of this insolvency, or the onset of the insolvency or the termination of the employment contract or relationship as a consequence thereof (art. 3). In principle this guarantee also covers the premiums owned by virtue of the national systems of social security or by virtue of complementary systems of social provisions applying for one or more branches of industry; however, art. 6 leaves the Member States free to deviate from the rule as far as these premiums are concerned.
The payment obligation of these institutions may to some extent be curbed or limited by the Member States (art. 4). Organization, financing and working of the guarantee institutions are determined by the individual Member States. In this they must, however, observe certain principles.
In the first place, the assets of the institutions should be independent from the employers' operating capital and it should not be inaccessible to proceed-

ings for insolvency. Furthermore, the employers should contribute to the financing, unless the public authorities are fully responsible for the financing of the institutions. Finally, the institutions should be bound to honour claims, whether or not obligations to contribute to their financing have been observed (art. 5).

SOCIAL SECURITY

35. The insolvency of the employer may have negative consequences for the employees also as regards their claims to social security benefits, e.g., if the employer has failed to pay the contributions owed by him. Consequently, art. 7 obliges the Member States to take measures to ensure that non-payment of the compulsory contributions due from the employer before the onset of his insolvency does not adversely affect the employees' benefit entitlement in as much as the employees' contributions were deducted at source from the remuneration paid.
Measures should furthermore be taken to protect the accrued and accruing entitlement of employees and former employees in respect of old-age benefits and survivors' benefits by virtue of company or inter-company pension schemes outside the national statutory social security schemes (art. 8).

CONCLUSIONS

36. Of course, the Member States continue to be authorized to prevent abuse; more specifically, they may refuse or restrict the obligation to honour claims or to guarantee social security entitlements, if it appears that fulfilment of the obligations is unjustifiable because of collusion between employer and employee (art. 10). As the Directive only imposes minimum requirements, the Member States may apply or introduce regulations that are more favourable to the employees (art. 9).
Notwithstanding the approximation intended by the Directive, in the various Member States very diverse regulations continue to exist. Actually all Member States, with the exception of Ireland, already have legal provisions on the subject covered by the Directive. The Directive has been drawn up in such general terms, however, that it will probably be incapable of abolishing the differences between the laws of the various Member States. The original proposal of the Commission, which advocated further-reaching approximation, went too far for certain Member States because of the substantial financial burden it entailed. On the other hand, it was of course out of the question to force Member States with a regime which is very favourable to the employees, specifically the Federal Republic of Germany and France, to adapt to the lower standards of the other Member States.
The Council has therefore admitted that the present Directive can only be regarded as a first step towards further approximation of the national laws on this matter.

D. Some important directives and proposals for directives within the framework of the approximation of laws (Artt. 100-102 of the EEC Treaty)

A. DIRECTIVE 75/117/EEC OF FEBRUARY 10, 1975[16] ON THE APPLICATION OF THE PRINCIPLE OF EQUAL PAY FOR MEN AND WOMEN.

37. Even though art. 119 of the EEC Treaty stipulates the principle of equal pay for equal work for men and women, this stipulation was only very slowly implemented in the Member States – in spite of its direct effect. The Commission wished to end this both legally and actually unsatisfactory situation in the Member States through a Directive to affirm the principle contained in art. 119. The Directive, adopted by the Council on February 10, 1975 had as its objective the approximation of the national laws concerning the principle of equal pay.

In summary, the Directive obliges the Member States:

(i) to abolish any discrimination in the field of equal pay resulting from statutory or administrative provisions;

(ii) to declare null and void or voidable any such discriminatory provisions in collective labour agreements, wage agreements and individual labour agreements;

(iii) to offer any employee who feels prejudiced by non-observance of the principle of equal pay the opportunity to seek recourse before a court, possibly after having taken this case to another competent authority;

(iv) to protect employees against any dismissal by employers who might proceed to dismiss them because of a complaint within the enterprise or court action to enforce the principle of equal pay;

(v) to see to it that the measures to implement the Directive as well as any relevant provisions which already exist be brought to the attention of the employees by any appropriate means.

The Commission keeps a close watch on the actual implementation of the Directive. Although in most Member States the formal implementation has been carried out, in actual fact various types of discrimination still appear to exist.

B. DIRECTIVE 76/207/EEC OF FEBRUARY 9, 1976 ON THE IMPLEMENTATION OF THE PRINCIPLE OF EQUAL TREATMENT OF MALE AND FEMALE EMPLOYEES AS REGARDS ACCESS TO EMPLOYMENT, OCCUPATIONAL TRAINING, PROMOTION OPPORTUNITIES AND WORKING CONDITIONS[17]

38. The Council adopted this Directive as a logical consequence of the realization of the principles adopted in Directive 75/117. Equal pay for equal

16. OJ nr. L 45, 19-2-'75, p. 19.
17. OJ nr. L 39, 14-2-'76, p. 40.

work presupposes after all that every employee, regardless of sex, should be accorded the same treatment with regard to access to employment, occupation of training, promotion opportunities and working conditions.
The Directive regulates in detail the abolition by the Member States of all existing types of discrimination that hamper the application of the principle of equal treatment in the abovementioned fields.
The Directive consequently obliges the Member States to take measures with regard to various social and economic national regulations that are no longer justified in the context of the Directive. The required adaptation is of course a fairly complex matter, because it requires a review of situations based on historical and social traditions that are the underlying cause of a distribution of labour which puts women at a disadvantage.

C. DIRECTIVE 79/7/EEC OF DECEMBER 19, 1978 REGARDING THE GRADUAL IMPLEMENTATION OF THE PRINCIPLE OF EQUAL TREATMENT FOR MEN AND WOMEN IN THE FIELD OF SOCIAL SECURITY[18]

39. The primary objective is the achievement of equal treatment in the systems of social security of the individual Member States, but the realization of this principle will undoubtedly have a harmonizing effect on these national systems.
Every form of discrimination by reason of sex, either directly or indirectly, by reference to the marital status or family situation is outlawed, in particular with regard to access to the scheme, the payment and calculation of contributions, the calculation of the benefit and the conditions regarding duration and retention of the right to benefits. In certain fields (such as pensions) the Member States may maintain some discrimination.
The Directive does not require completely equal treatment at this stage, so that it will be necessary to draw up other, supplementary Directives. For example, by simply abolishing the term 'head of the family' and by a total individualization of benefits, equal treatment may be secured.
Ratione personae the Directive applies to the entire working population, while *ratione materiae* the sectors sickness and disability, old age, unemployment, industrial accidents and occupational diseases are covered. Survivor's benefits and child allowances are therefore excluded.
Within six years (by the end of 1984) the Member States must have implemented the Directive. The Directive introduces no major innovations: the objective is a minimum programme in which certain matters may yet be frozen for an indefinite period of time.

18. OJ nr. L 6, 10-1-'79, p. 24.

D. PROPOSAL FOR A DIRECTIVE ON PROCEDURES FOR INFORMING AND CONSULTING THE EMPLOYEES OF UNDERTAKINGS WITH COMPLEX STRUCTURES, IN PARTICULAR TRANSNATIONAL UNDERTAKINGS (SUBMITTED BY THE COMMISSION TO THE COUNCIL ON OCTOBER 24, 1980)[19]

40. With this proposal the Commission hopes to secure for employees within the community, equal treatment in respect of the right to information and consultation in matters that are of crucial importance for their enterprise. The Member States follow their own policies in granting these rights, which may distort the operation of the Common Market, so that approximation of these mutually inconsistent national regulations becomes essential.

41. First of all, the proposal aims to provide a uniform guarantee for the communication of information and the attached right of consultation to employees of transnational enterprises. The management of a dominant undertaking, whose decision-making centre is located in a Member State, would have to communicate the relevant information to employees' representatives in all subsidiaries within the EEC.
The proposal stipulates the nature and extent of this information and the time at which it should be communicated. This disclosure duty relates on the one hand to general information, based on precise criteria, that should make it possible regularly to give a picture of the activities of the dominant undertaking and all its subsidiaries, on the other to information on occasional decisions that the dominant undertaking proposes to take concerning the undertaking itself or its subsidiaries and that are liable to affect the interests of its employees. The proposed decision would have to be communicated to the managements of the subsidiaries no later than 40 days before it is due to be adopted, and these managements would then in their turn have to inform its employees' representatives.

42. The communication of this information gives the employees the right to consult with the management in order to advise on and examine the measures that are deemed necessary in the interest of the employees. The Member States are obliged to make provisions in their national legislation, so that in case of failure to observe the employees' rights to information and consultation, appropriate steps can be taken to guarantee the observance of these rights.
If the decision-making centre of the dominant enterprise is located outside the Community, at least one responsible person located within the Community should be indicated; this person will then be held responsible for the fulfilment of the obligations imposed. If no such person is indicated the management of the subsidiary that employs the largest number of employees within the Community will be responsible for the fulfilment of the obligations imposed on the management of the dominant enterprise.

19. OJ nr. C 29, 15-11-'80, p. 3 and *Supplement* 3/80 to *Bulletin EC* (with explanatory memorandum).

43. The abovementioned obligations have also been imposed on managements of enterprises whose decision-making centre is inside or outside the Community and which have one or more subsidiaries with at least 100 employees inside the Community.

44. The proposal imposes similar obligations regarding information and consultation for enterprises with a complex structure whose decision-making centre is located in the Member State in which the employees work.

45. Finally, the proposal requires secrecy from the employees' representatives involved in the disclosure of information, the consultations and advice. In communicating information the interests of the enterprise should be taken into account; secrets regarding the enterprise or its business should not be divulged.
Disputes concerning or infringements of this secrecy requirement would be brought before the national tribunal or other national bodies via a special procedure: their task would be to establish the degree of confidentiality of the information and impose appropriate penalties in case of infringement of the secrecy requirement.

46. In 1981, it is still too early to evaluate the chances of adoption of this proposal. It is a fact that certain Member States will not accept the principles on which the proposal is based without resistance. On the other hand, it is in line with other proposals of the Commission (Proposal for a Regulation on the Statute for European companies, and proposal for the Fifth Directive), in which employee participation plays a significant role.

IV. PRIVATE INTERNATIONAL LAW IN THE FIELD OF EMPLOYMENT CONTRACTS

47. An important step towards the unification of private international law within the Community was made in Rome on 19th June 1980 when the Convention on the Law Applicable to Contractual Obligations[20] was opened for signature. On that date it was signed by seven Member States and Denmark signed it later. In July 1981 the UK had not yet signed it, nor had Greece. The Convention will take effect after seven ratifications.
The Convention offers, *inter alia*, the beginning of a solution regarding the problem of the law applicable to employment contracts, but this can in no way be compared with the provisions laid down in the specific proposal of the Commission submitted to the Council on 23d March 1972.[21] As the more general Convention covers the same subject matter, albeit inadequately, the old proposal will now probably never be adopted.

20. OJ nr. L 266, 9-10-'80, p. 1, see also the Report on the Convention by Prof. M. Giuliano and prof. P. Lagarde in OJ nr. C 282, 31-10-'80, p. 1.
21. OJ nr. C 49, 18-5-'72, p. 26.

48. The objective is to achieve uniform rules concerning the law applicable to contractual obligations. Art. 3 of the Convention states that a contract shall be governed by the law chosen by the parties. This law may be that of one of the Member States or that of any third country. The Convention's approach to the choice of the law or a subsequent variation thereof is flexible. The basic principle is the autonomy of the parties, with the proviso, however, that the mandatory rules of the law of a country should be applied if all factual elements relevant to the situation at the time of the choice are connected with that country (art. 3(3)).

49. Specific rules determine the law that is applicable if no choice is made. As a rule, the contract shall be governed by the law of the country with which it is most closely connected (art. 4(1)). As this definition is not very precise, the Convention introduces certain presumptions. However, these presumptions may be disregarded if it appears from the circumstances as a whole that the contract is more closely connected with another country. This makes this Convention hardly original, as in most Member States judges involved in a case of private international law always have had to select the decisive connecting factor for determining the law applicable to a contract in each specific case among the various elements of the contract and the circumstances of the case.

50. For *individual employment contracts* the Convention gives a set of special provisions (art. 6). The principle of the free choice of law is maintained, but with one important proviso: the free choice may not have the result of depriving the employee of the protection afforded to him by the mandatory rules of the law which would be applicable in the absence of choice.
This means that if the principal elements of an employment contract are localized in a certain system of law, the mandatory rules of this law continue to protect the employee, and this according to the conflict rules specifically provided by the Convention in the case of absence of choice. The objective conflict rule is that an individual employment contract is governed by:

a. the law of the country in which the employee habitually carries out his work in performance of the contract, even if he is temporarily employed in another country, or

b. the law of the country in which the place of business through which the employee was engaged is situated, if he does not habitually carry out his work in any one country,

in both cases unless it appears from the circumstances as a whole that the contract is more closely connected with another country, in which case the contract shall be governed by the law of that country.

51. This reference '*in extremis*' to the closest connection weakens of course the precision which the Convention wished to give to the conflict rules in the case of employment contracts. On the other hand, for the larger part, conflicts concerning the law applicable to employment contracts will usually be solved by the specific reference to the law of the country where the employee is habitually employed. If this is not the case (employees working internationally) the choice of law may possibly offer a solution, save for the applicability of the mandatory rules of the law of the country where the principal elements of the employment contract are located: the evaluation of the factual situation continues to be a task for the judge to whom the dispute arising from the employment contract is submitted.

52. Art. 7 of the Convention deals with the situation where there is a conflict between the chosen law or the law that must be applied according to the Convention (for example art. 6) on the one hand and the mandatory rules of law of another country 'with which the situation has a close connection' on the other. In such a situation effect *may* be given to those mandatory rules if and in so far as, under the law of the country from which those rules emanate, those rules must be applied whatever the law applicable to the contract (*lois d'application immédiate*). As is shown by the word 'may', the courts have a discretion in deciding whether or not to give effect to those rules and in exercising this discretion they must take into account 'their nature and purpose and (...) the consequences of their application or non-application'.
This means that on the one hand the parties involved in the dispute will have to come with very well-founded arguments in order to prove or disprove the 'close connection', while on the other hand the judge will, depending on the case, have to solve the conflict of laws in fairness (to a great extent, in any case), which makes a subjective decision not impossible.
In the event of a conflict between '*lois d'application immédiate*' of various countries the Convention (art. 7(2)) provides that nothing in it shall restrict the application of such rules of the country of the court which has to decide the case.

53. Individual employment relations and especially the law on employment contracts are in most Western European countries characterized by their mandatory nature; it is therefore quite probable that, in this field, the Convention offers the judge not very much more support than he had before.

Belgium

W. Hallemeesch
M. Denys
R. Tournicourt
B. Dubois

I. INTRODUCTION

Company law in Belgium has known few sweeping developments since the main body was created in the 19th Century particularly by the law of 1873. Twentieth Century major amendments and additions were made in 1913, 1935, 1953 and lastly in 1973, pursuant to the first Directive of the European Communities. Other minor amendments have been inspired by reasons unrelated to company law proper.

The Government, aware of the obsolescence of major parts of company law and the patchwork left by the piecemeal approach of the latter years has drafted a new company bill presently pending in Parliament. However, in view of other pressing business, it is most unlikely that Parliament will enact this bill in the near future. Thus Belgium is left with a legal framework that is incomplete, patchy and behind modern thinking and developments. It does not appear, however, that this has notably hampered business in effectively managing companies.

Conversely, management has been greatly affected by the endless and unabsorbable avalanche of legislative and judicial developments in the tax and labour/social fields. Ever since in 1962, Belgian income tax law was unified in one comprehensive and logical (!) code, successive governments have incessantly tampered with it in their attempts to raise ever increasing sums of money. This has resulted in a lengthy, inextricable and often conflicting set of rules and regulations. Indeed, they have also taken the opportunity of the EC inspired introduction of VAT to increase revenue. Likewise, ever since labour law started developing rapidly in 1900 and the social security system was unified in 1944, management has had to spend more and more time, effort and money to comply with the rules.

Whole departments and large staffs have to be maintained for the purposes of applying the tax, labour and social security rules and the sums of money involved are enormous.

Some aspects important in other countries have not been developed or have not been developed at length. The Antitrust law has never had much impact in Belgium although there is a 1960 law on the books; in a small open economy such law may not be necessary.

Co-determination stricto sensu and compulsory profit sharing have not taken root. Groupements d'Intérêt Economique have found a draft form of words but are not law. Exchange control is effective through the double market system but otherwise money moves freely.

Considerable attention has been given to such portions of labour law that, quite effectively, replace co-determination and profit sharing such as the Works Council, the union delegation, the right to receive and the obligation to give information, rights to compensation on dismissal of employees on termination of their contracts and collective bargaining.

II. THE LEGAL FRAMEWORK

A. The Vehicle

1. THE WHOLLY-OWNED ENTERPRISE

1.a. THE BRANCH

(i) Setting-up – publication

A Belgian branch of a foreign company is established by the publication of the resolution by the competent organ of that company to establish the branch, together with an extract from the statutes of the foreign company (art. 198 (1) of the Coordinated Company Laws ('CCL')).[1]
Publication is made in the Annexes to the Belgian Official Gazette (Belgisch Staatsblad – Moniteur belge) after all relevant documents have been registered with the clerk of the Commercial Court having jurisdiction over the place of business of the branch (art. 10 § 1 (2) CCL).
The signatures on these documents must be declared authentic in accordance with the prescribed procedure and a sworn translation must be attached (in Dutch if the place of business is in Flanders, in French if it is in Wallonia, or in either language if it is in Brussels).
Subsequent transfers of the seat of the foreign company, amendments to its statutes and changes in the composition of its Board of Directors must also be published.
All acts, invoices, publications, letters, orders and other documents of the branch must state
- the name of the company
- the form of the company
- the seat
- the registration number in the Commercial Register
- the VAT-number.

Any action brought before Belgian Courts by a company whose statutes have not been properly published will be dismissed.
The company must also apply for registration in the Trade Register. The application is made to the Commercial Court for the area in which the branch is established. If subsequently, other branches are established in Belgium, similar applications for registration in the Trade Register must be made, if those

1. The Coordinated Company Laws are now under complete revision. A draft Law (nr. 387 (1979-1980)) was submitted to Parliament on 5-12-'79.

branches are to be situated in the area of jurisdiction of other Courts. Registration in the Trade Register must be made prior to the performance of any 'commercial act', a concept defined by art. 2 of the Commercial Code. Failing this, penal sanctions apply and legal proceedings by the branch will not be entertained by the courts.
In the application for registration, the foreign company must disclose all judicial or administrative decisions made abroad and all arrangements made under any foreign law for the protection of creditors in circumstances of payment difficulties or insolvency.

(ii) Organization

– Management
A branch represents a foreign company as an agent empowered to act on behalf of the foreign company and to bind the company in law.

– Liability
The person (either a Belgian national or an alien) entrusted with this representation is liable to third parties as if he were managing a Belgian company. Under the general law, the directors of a company are liable not only for fraud but also for faults which they commit in the carrying out of their duties. They are jointly and severally liable to the company and to third parties for all damage resulting from infringements of company law or of the statutes of the company.
Internal restrictions on the power of the agent to represent the company cannot be relied on against third parties.
The branch being a part of the foreign company, the latter remains liable for all obligations, contractual or otherwise, of its Belgian establishment.

– Accounting – auditing
Every branch of a foreign company must comply with the rules relating to accounting laid down in the Act of July 17, 1975 and its implementing Royal Decrees. For the purposes of the Act, the Belgian branch must be considered as a separate enterprise, and all its books, accounts and documents must be kept in Belgium for a period of ten years from the 1st January following the year of the closing of the books.
According to the general rule of the Act, an enterprise must keep its books in a manner appropriate to the nature and volume of its activities.
The Royal Decree of October 8, 1976 lays down detailed accounting rules. This Decree is based on the 4th Company Law Directive of the European Communities on the annual accounts of companies. Like the Directive, the Decree lays down the method of presentation of the annual accounts. The annual accounts comprise a balance sheet, a profit and loss account and an explanatory memorandum. Exceptions to the Act and the Royal Decree are made in favour of banks, insurance companies and holding companies.
Non-observance of the Act and Royal Decrees is punishable by fines and imprisonment.
Belgian law does not require the accounts of the branch as such to be audited. Foreign companies with branches in Belgium must publish annual accounts in

accordance with the rules applicable to Belgian companies. That means that the annual accounts of the foreign company must be registered with the clerk of the Commercial Court within thirty days after their approval. The clerk sends a copy of the accounts to the National Bank which is bound to provide copies to anyone requesting them.
The obligation to publish the annual accounts lies with the directors of the foreign company. Directors who fraudulently fail to publish the annual accounts are punishable under the criminal law (art. 204 CCL).

1.b. THE SUBSIDIARY

Two forms of business association are commonly used to establish a subsidiary in Belgium:

I. the private limited company (personenvennootschap met beperkte aansprakelijkheid PVBA – société de personnes à responsabilité limitée SPRL);
II. the public limited company (naamloze vennootschap NV – société anonyme SA).

Such companies constitute legal entities.

I. THE PRIVATE LIMITED COMPANY (PERSONENVENNOOTSCHAP MET BEPERKTE AANSPRAKELIJKHEID PVBA – SOCIÉTÉ DE PERSONNES À RESPONSABILITÉ LIMITÉE SPRL)

I(i) Setting-up – publication

The company must be incorporated before a notary public. The number of members must be at least two. Spouses may together establish a private limited company. The maximum number of members is fifty. Only natural – not legal persons may be partners.
The objects of a private limited company must not include the business of insurance, finance or a savings bank, or extending mortgage loans, or exchange brokerage.
The statutes must be deposited with the Registry of the Commercial Court having jurisdiction over the private limited company within fifteen days of its establishment. Thereafter, they must be published by way of extract in the Annexes to the Belgian Official Gazette within a further fifteen days.
Any action brought before Belgian Courts by a company whose statutes have not been published in this way will be dismissed. The company must also apply for registration in the Trade Register. The application is made to the Commercial Court for the area in which the private company is established.
Registration in the Trade Register must be made prior to the performance of any commercial act. Failing this, penal sanctions apply and legal proceedings by the company will not be entertained by the Courts.
All acts, invoices, publications, letters, orders and other documents of the private company must state:

– the name of the company;
– the form of the company;
– the seat;

- the registration number in the Commercial Register;
- the VAT-number.

I(ii) Organization

I(ii)(a) Capital Shares and Transfer of Shares

- Capital

The minimum capital is 250,000 BF. The capital must be fully subscribed and at least one fifth must be fully paid up with a minimum of 250,000 BF.
Contributions in kind must be fully paid up before they can be incorporated in the capital.

- Shares

The capital is divided into shares (deelbewijzen – parts sociales). The shares must have a par value of not less than 1,000 BF. The law provides that each share confers equal rights in the allocation of profits and to the balance upon winding-up.
It is impossible to create preferred stock. No non-capital shares are permitted. The shares are indivisible.
All shares must be recorded in the register of members. This register is kept at the seat of the company. Any interested party may inspect it.
It should contain a detailed description of each member, his respective shareholdings and all transfers of shares.

- Transfer of shares

The law stipulates certain minimum restrictions on the transfer of shares. The statutes may provide further restrictions. The transfer of shares is subject to the agreement of at least half the number of members representing three quarters of the capital not being transferred.
However, this agreement is not required (unless the statutes provide otherwise) in case of transfers to members, spouses, ascendants or descendants or to persons accepted in the statutes.
The transfer must not raise the number of partners above 50. As against the company and third parties a transfer is effective from the date of entry of the transfer in the register of members.

I(ii)(b) Management – Representation

The company is administered by one or more managers (zaakvoerders – gérants) who need not be members or Belgian nationals.
Frequently they are named in the statutes of the company; they also may be appointed by the General Meeting of Members. The appointment can be for a limited or unlimited period of time.
Managers appointed in the statutes are normally appointed for the duration of the company's activities and may be removed only for serious reasons.
Every manager has the power to perform any act necessary or useful for the attainment of the objects of the company. This power covers all acts that are not expressly reserved by law for the general meeting. The statutes may restrict the powers of the manager, such restrictions are no defence against third parties, even if they have been published.

I(ii)(c) General Meeting of Members

Irrespective of the number of members, a private limited company must hold

a General Meeting of Members every year. The rules applicable to the general meetings of public limited companies also apply to general meetings of private limited companies (art. 136 and 137 CCL).
Members are authorized, unless the statutes provide otherwise, to be represented by a proxy or to vote in writing.
Decisions are taken by a simple majority of votes, unless the statutes impose special majorities for certain resolutions.
Each share confers one vote.
The general meeting has no other powers than those reserved to it by law; these are

- the appointment and removal of the managers;
- approval of transfers of shares;
- approval of the annual accounts;
- allocation of profits;
- amendment of the articles;
- to increase or decrease the capital;
- to wind up the company.

I(ii)(d) Liability of the Managers

As regards their liability to the company and to third parties the managers are in the same legal position as the directors of a public limited company. Art. 132 CCL provides that the liability of managers must be considered according to the rules applicable to the liability of directors. These rules are dealt with in the chapter on public limited companies, below.

I(ii)(e) Accounts and Auditing

- Accounts

Private limited companies must comply with the accounting rules laid down in the Act of July 17, 1975 and its implementing Royal Decrees. These accounting rules apply to branches and to subsidiary companies (private as well as public limited companies), and are dealt with in the chapter on branches, above.

- Auditing

The appointment of one or more auditors is only compulsory in the case of a private limited company with more than five members (either at the time of incorporation or thereafter). The auditor may be appointed in the statutes or by a General Meeting of Members.
The auditors have the same powers and responsibilities as the auditors of public limited companies, but they may be appointed for more than six years and are not required to deposit shares by way of guarantee.

I(ii)(f) Publication of Accounts

A private limited company must file its accounts with the Registry of the Commercial Court within thirty days after their approval by the General Meeting. The clerk of the Court must send a copy of these accounts to the National Bank which must provide copies to anyone requesting them.
The obligation to file the annual accounts lies with the manager. Managers who fraudulently fail to register the annual accounts are punishable under the criminal law (art. 204 CCL).

II. THE PUBLIC LIMITED COMPANY (NAAMLOZE VENNOOTSCHAP NV – SOCIÉTÉ ANONYME SA)

II(i) Setting-up – publication

II(i)(a) Substantive conditions

By art. 29 of the CCL the incorporation of a public limited company is subject to the following three conditions:

- There must be at least seven shareholders who may be natural as well as legal persons, nationals or foreigners.
- The capital must be fully subscribed. The minimum capital is 1,250,000 BF.
- One fifth of each share must be fully paid up in cash or in kind (non-monetary assets). In case of capital contribution in kind, the president of the Commercial Court having jurisdiction over the place where the Deed of Incorporation is executed, will appoint a public accountant, member of the Institute of Public Accountants (bedrijfsrevisor – reviseur d'entreprise) who will report on the value to be attributed to these contributions.

In case of capital contributions in cash, the funds must be deposited, before incorporation, in a bank account opened in the name of the company and at its sole disposal. The bank must issue a certificate stating the amount of the deposit; this certificate is attached to the notarial Deed.

II(i)(b) Conditions of form

Belgian law recognizes two methods of incorporation: direct incorporation and Incorporation by the public subscription.

- Direct incorporation

The public limited company must be incorporated by a notary public. The Deed of incorporation must certify that the three substantive conditions have been fulfilled.

The statutes must state (art. 30 CCL):

- the precise objects of the company;
- the contributions in kind and their equivalent in shares;
- the bank where the funds in cash have been deposited;
- an abstract of title relating to immovable property contributed to the company;
- any mortgages or charges on the immovable property contributed;
- privileges granted to the founders;
- costs incurred in incorporation.

The statutes must be deposited within fifteen days of incorporation at the Registry of the Commercial Court having jurisdiction over the place where the seat to the company is situated.

An extract of the statutes will then be published by the Registry in the Annexes to the Belgian Official Gazette. The company exists vis-à-vis third parties as soon as the statutes have been published.

Any action brought before Belgian Courts by a company whose statutes have not been published as aforesaid will be dismissed.

- Incorporation by public subscription

Incorporation by public subscription is seldom used for new companies.

If any of the conditions of art. 29 CCL are not fulfilled the incorporation is not void.

The founders, however, are personally and jointly and severally liable for all obligations contracted by the company until it has seven shareholders and for any part of the capital which has not been subscribed and for the full payment of the subscription up to one fifth of the capital (art. 35 CCL).
Under art. 13 bis CCL they are also jointly and severally liable for all transactions entered into on behalf of the company before its establishment, unless such transactions are ratified by the company within two months of incorporation, or if the company is not formed within two years.
A new article (29ter) further obliges the founders to prepare a financial plan containing a statement of the capital of the company to be established. This document is not published, but in the event of a dispute concerning the founders' liability for undercapitalisation, it must be placed at the disposal of the Commercial Court.
The founders can be held liable for the obligations of the company in the event of insolvency of the company within 3 years of its incorporation if the capital was obviously insufficient for the normal course of its business over a period of at least two years.
The company must apply for registration in the Trade Register, as described above for branches and private limited companies.
All acts, invoices, publications, letters, orders and other documents of a public limited company must include the same statements as are required in the case of branches and private limited companies.

(ii) Organization

II(ii)(a) Capital, Shares and Transfers of Shares

- Capital

The share capital (the total of the contributions of the shareholders) is divided into shares.

- Shares

– Shares may have a par value or no par value.
– The company may issue shares which do not represent the assets or funds contributed to the company (winstaandelen – parts bénéficiaires).
– Belgian law also recognizes preference shares (bevoorrechte aandelen – actions de priorité or actions privilégiées) which sometimes entitle their owners to a greater dividend and some preferential treatment in case of winding-up.

Shares are registered shares or bearer shares. The names of the holders of registered shares are entered in a special register kept at the seat of the company.
Shareholders can always request the conversion of bearer shares into registered shares. Shares which have not been fully paid up must remain registered, i.e. may not be in bearer form.
Shares entitle their owners
– to vote at a general meeting of shareholders
– to a dividend, if any
– to participate in the distribution of the company's assets upon winding-up of the company.

- Transfers of shares

In principle the shares are freely transferable unless the law (art. 46 CCL – partly paid up shares), the statutes (only for registered shares), or an agreement between shareholders restricts their transferability. However, restrictions that, in practice, result in the shares not being transferable are void.
Bearer shares are transferred by delivery and registered shares by agreement between the shareholders.
Transfers of registered shares must be duly executed by the parties concerned and entered into the share register.

II(ii)(b) Management and Representation

- Board of Directors

The public limited company is administered by a Board of Directors, consisting of not less than three members (no maximum), who need not be shareholders or Belgian nationals.
They are appointed by a general meeting of shareholders for a period not exceeding six years. Members of the Board of Directors are eligible for re-election. The directors are subject to removal by the shareholders at a general meeting at any time.
Legal persons may also be appointed directors. The law disqualifies certain persons from acting as directors: persons who have been declared bankrupt or have been convicted of certain crimes (such as counterfeiting share certificates, forgery and theft), members of the Judiciary and of the Council of State, notaries, civil servants, military personnel, and members of the Institute of Public Accountants.
Directors may be remunerated if the statutes so provide. Except for managing directors, the directors are not employees of the company for social security purposes and must make their own social security provision.
Each director must deposit a certain number of shares (specified in the statutes) as a guarantee for the fulfilment of his functions. These must be registered shares.
According to art. 54 CCL the Board of Directors has the widest powers to perform all acts which are necessary or useful for the attainment of the company's objects. All powers not expressly assigned to a general meeting of shareholders by company law or by the statutes are exercisable by the Board of Directors.
The Board represents the company vis-à-vis third parties.

- Representation

The company may be bound in dealings with third parties in one of the following three ways:

1. an act of one of its 'organs';
2. an act of one of its 'special proxies';
3. an act of an 'apparent proxy'.

1. Act by organs

Within the limits laid down in the CCL, which may not be altered by the statutes, the organs are deemed to be the company. The competence of one organ in no way affects the competence of any other organ. The CCL list these organs, which are four in number.

a. A General Meeting of shareholders, with respect to those matters which are within its competence, as laid down by CCL art. 54, (1).

b. The Board of Directors, with respect to all other matters. The Board's competence may not be limited vis-à-vis third parties (art. 54, (3)).

c. One or more members of the Board of Directors, acting singly or jointly, when all of the following three conditions are met:

- the delegation of powers is provided for in the statutes;
- the whole of the Board's powers to represent the company to third parties is delegated;
- the document containing the delegation of powers is published in the Annexes to the Belgian Official Gazette.

When only limited powers to represent the company are delegated, the delegation is automatically extended to include all such powers (art. 54, (4)).

d. One or more persons entrusted, singly or jointly, with the day-to-day management of the company, when the following three conditions are met:

- the delegation of powers is published in the Annexes to the Belgian Official Gazette;
- the delegation covers only the day-to-day management of the company;
- the delegation covers all matters of day-to-day management (art. 63). (See also 2 below).

There is an automatic extension to cover all matters of day-to-day management. The statutory limitation to day-to-day management can be relied upon against third parties.

2. *Act by special proxies*

Powers based on a special proxy are valid in the case of a director, and hence even more so in the case of employees.

A distinction has to be made between published and unpublished special proxies. In no circumstances, however, can a proxy cover the management or the conduct of the day-to-day business generally. It must therefore always relate to a specific act or series of acts. If a proxy does not comply with this rule, the company will be validly bound on the ground of 'apparent power', but third parties will not be bound (Civil Code art. 1998 (2)).

Where the statutes do not provide for delegation of the powers of representation, there is no real danger that the publication of a special proxy to one director will result in that director having full power to bind the company as an organ in the sense of art. 54, (4). Nor is there any such danger where the statutes allow only a delegation to two directors jointly, and a special proxy to one director only is published.

On the other hand, if the statutes state that the day-to-day management may be delegated to one or more persons, a director to whom delegated powers in respect of such day-to-day management are given will have full power to so represent the company, since he was given such powers on the basis of a provision in the statutes.

Furthermore, when the articles state that one director may be entrusted with the power to represent the company, a special proxy cannot be given to a director without giving him all powers.

The reason for this is that as third parties do not have to take account of any limitations mentioned in the publication of a delegation of powers, there is also no reason why they should take account of a statement that the delegation is made on the basis of a special proxy rather than on the company's statutes.

Special proxies relating to day-to-day management are not valid even if published, since, by contrast with the situation discussed above, a distinction cannot be made according to whether such delegation is based on the statutes. Any proxy so published would be automatically extended to the entire day-to-day management.

On the other hand, in those cases where publication of a special proxy to a director is possible as such (i.e. in the absence of a relevant clause in the statutes, or where there is a joint signature condition), it will naturally also be possible to entrust the day-to-day management to a director and to publish such delegation without further consequences.

Publication of a delegation of powers relating to part only of the day-to-day management will automatically be extended to cover the entire day-to-day management.

But such a director will be an organ of the company on the basis of art. 63 CCL, since, in the absence of a specific clause in the statutes as provided for in art. 54 (4), he cannot become an organ in the sense of art. 54, and for this reason the statutory limitation of art. 63 remains applicable.

Finally, it is always possible to grant an unpublished proxy to any person on condition that it does not relate to the management or the day-to-day conduct of business generally.

3. Acts by apparent proxies

The company is liable under the general law for the 'apparent proxy' of employees acting within their known sphere of competence or of a director where the company publishes a general proxy applying to one director in the sense of art. 54, and there is no appropriate clause in the statutes, or a clause requiring a proxy to two directors. In such cases the company will be bound, but third parties will not be. Finally it should be noted that the rule that irregularities in the appointment of an 'organ' cannot be relied upon against third parties (art. 13) applies only to such organs, and not, for example, to unpublished special proxies (if they are published and if they relate to the day-to-day management, the person granted the powers becomes an organ), or general proxies given to non-organs. Except where the company is responsible for a misrepresentation in this respect, a third party must in these cases himself verify the validity of the proxy.

II(ii)(c) General Meeting of Shareholders

A General Meeting regularly constituted represents the entire body of shareholders. It consists of all shareholders who have complied with the statutes.

A General Meeting must be held at least once a year. It must take place on the date and at the place specified in the statutes. This constitutes the Ordinary General Meeting of shareholders; any other general meeting is an Extraordinary General Meeting. The powers of both meetings are the same.

Each shareholder has the right to vote proportionally to his participation in the share capital.

Unless company law or the statutes provide otherwise the resolutions of a General Meeting shall be carried by a majority of votes, irrespective of the number of shares represented.

The voting power of a single shareholder may not exceed one fifth of the total number of shares or two fifths of the voting shares represented at a General Meeting.

The procedure to be followed during a General Meeting is laid down in the statutes of each public limited company; the range of provisions that can be made is extremely wide: for example the statutes may provide for a General Meeting to be held abroad.
The powers of a General Meeting are those given to it by company law and the statutes and include:

- appointment and removal of directors and auditors;
- approval of the annual accounts;
- declaration of dividends;
- special resolutions:
  - amendments to the statutes;
  - extension of the life of the company;
  - winding-up of the company and appointment of liquidators;
  - increase or decrease of the share capital;
  - merger;
  - transformation.

II(ii)(d) Liability of Directors

The directors, as the mandated agents of the company, are not personally liable for commitments entered into by the company.

- Liability to the company

In accordance with the principles of the law of agency, directors are responsible for carrying out their mandate and are liable for failure to do so.
This liability for errors and failures in the fulfilment of their mandate is a personal one. An action for damages may only be brought by the company, and not by third parties or shareholders.

- Liability for breaches of company law and/or the statutes

By art. 62 (2) CCL the directors are also liable for all damage resulting from a breach of company law or of the statutes. They may only be exonerated from this liability if they had no part in the breach, if no fault is imputable to them and if they reported the breach to the next General Meeting after it was known to them.
Directors are jointly and severally liable and an action for damages may be brought by third parties or by the company.

- Finally, by a recent Law passed in 1978, any director, former director, or manager of a company can be held jointly and severally liable for the whole or a part of the debts of the company if it is established (i) that the liabilities exceed the assets and (ii) that his evident and serious fault contributed to the insolvency.

II(ii)(e) Accounts and Auditing

- Accounts

Public limited companies must comply with the rules concerning accounting laid down in the Act of July 17, 1975 and its implementing Royal Decrees. These accounting rules have been dealt with in the chapter on branches.

- Auditing

The business of a public limited company must be supervised by one or more auditors, who need not be shareholders or Belgian nationals.

They are appointed by a General Meeting of shareholders for a term not exceeding six years. The General Meeting determines their number and remuneration and may remove them at any time.

Auditors are eligible for re-election. Should the number of auditors be reduced, through death or otherwise, by more than half, the Board of Directors must call a General Meeting forthwith to fill the vacancies (art. 64 CCL).

The law further provides that companies which have or have had recourse to the public capital market must appoint at least one auditor who is a member of the Institute of Public Accountants (art. 64bis § 2 CCL). He is appointed for a period of between three and six years, but may be removed by a General Meeting at any time.

The auditors (except members of the Institute of Public Accountants) must deposit a number of shares of the company as a guarantee for the fulfilment of their duties.

The auditors have an unlimited right of supervision and inspection of all the company's business. They may examine documents, books, correspondence and minutes, without removing them.

At an Ordinary General Meeting the auditors must report on their investigations and may make any remarks and recommendations they think appropriate. The auditor who is a member of the Institute of Public Accountants makes a separate report.

II(ii)(f) Publication of Accounts

The public limited company must file its accounts with the registry of the Commercial Court in accordance with the same rules as apply to private limited companies.

III. GROUPS OF COMPANIES

– *General*

Unlike other legal systems, Belgian statute law does not contain any provisions relating to groups of companies or to mergers as such.

However, case law has developed rules especially regarding mergers.

– *Mergers*

A distinction is made between two forms of merger: merger by absorption of one or more existing companies and merger by setting up a new company.

- Elements

A merger supposes:

– at least two existing companies.
  The merger requires at least the combination of two existing companies which, prior to the merger, were legally independent of each other.
– at least one of these companies ceases to exist.
  At least one company must disappear entirely and contribute the entirety of its assets and liabilities or of net assets to the other or new company.
– the shareholders in the absorbed company become shareholders in the absorbing company.
  The contribution of the capital of one company to the other is compensated by the issue of shares in the absorbing company which are divided among the shareholders in the absorbed company.

• Conditions

The right to decide to merge rests with a General Meeting and is made by special resolution. This General Meeting must take place before a notary public.

The power of a General Meeting is, however, restricted. The General Meeting may not change the 'essential elements' of the company, such as its object, its corporate form or nationality. Changes in these elements will require the application of special procedures.

(iii) Checklist for incorporation

1. The company:
   - name of the company
   - objects of the company
   - amount of subscribed capital
   - nature and number of the shares
   - identity of the founders.
2. Establishment before a notary public and appointment of the directors and auditor(s).
3. Registration with the registry of the Commercial Court and publication in the Annexes to the Belgian Official Gazette.
4. Inclusion in the Trade Register (Registration number).
5. Registration with Ministry of Finance (VAT).
6. Costs: Taxes for registration (registratierechten – droits d'enregistrement): 1% on the subscribed capital.

1.c. OTHER FORMS

Besides the two forms described hereabove Belgian company law recognizes other forms of commercial companies. All are legal entities.

(i) General partnership (vennootschap onder gemeenschappelijke naam – société en nom collectif)

A general partnership is created between two or more persons for the purpose of carrying on a business under a trading name (art. 15 CCL). It can be established by private contract. The Deed of establishment of a general partnership has to be published by way of extract in the Annexes to the Belgian Official Gazette.

All partners are jointly and severally liable without limitation for all obligations entered into by the partnership (art. 17 CCL).

(ii) Limited partnership (vennootschap bij wijze van eenvoudige geldschieting – société en commandite simple)

A limited partnership is created between one or more partners with unlimited liability (gecommanditeerden – commandités) and one or more partners with limited liability (stille vennoten – commanditaires) and whose liability is

limited to the amount of the funds contributed to the partnership (art. 21 CCL).
A partner with limited liability is not allowed to manage the partnership in any way, not even under a proxy.
The rules relating to establishment and publication are the same as those for unlimited partnerships.

(iii) Partnership limited by shares (vennootschap bij wijze van geldschieting op aandelen – société en commandite par actions)

This form of company has almost completely disappeared in Belgium. It consists of one or more partners with unlimited liability and shareholders with limited liability (vennoten – actionnaires): their liability is limited to the amount of capital contributed (art. 105 CCL). It is a combination of the limited partnership and a public limited company.
The provisions concerning public limited companies are applicable to partnerships limited by shares (art. 107 CCL).

(iv) Co-operative partnership (samenwerkende vennootschap – société coopérative)

This partnership consists of associates whose number and contribution are variable (art. 141 CCL). The liability of the associates is limited. The assignment of shares to non-associates is restricted.

2. THE JOINT VENTURE

2.a. The jointly owned company

At the present time, no statutory rules exist in Belgium concerning the concepts of joint venture, shared participation, reciprocal participations or parent and subsidiary companies.

(i) Shareholder agreements

Unlike in many other legal systems, agreements between shareholders relating to the exercise of voting rights are considered invalid in Belgium.
The prevailing opinion is that shareholders attending the General Meeting must be free to form their views from the discussions and information they receive at the meeting. Certain agreements however are valid, e.g. the agreement to consult each other before the General Meeting in order to reach a collective opinion.

(ii) Minority rights

The protection granted to corporate minorities is rather limited in Belgium. This follows from the structure of the Belgian economy, in which industrial stocks are generally held by members of the same family and where, even in the case of many companies whose stock is traded on the Brussels Stock Exchange, the controlling power is held by a few persons who are related to each other. Nevertheless, a minority of more than 25% of the votes can veto any amendment to the articles (art. 70 CCL).

If the proposed amendment refers to the object and to the transformation of the company, a minority of more than 20% can block the proposal (artt. 70bis and 168, § 1, CCL).

As noted above, no single shareholder can have a voting power above one-fifth of the remaining shares or two-fifths of the shares actually represented at the meeting (art. 76). But this protection is illusory, as there is no statutory provision prohibiting pooling.

Art. 73 contains a strict requirement that board members must call a shareholders' meeting if requested by shareholders representing at least 20% of the shares. But, again, a meeting does not necessarily mean a favourable decision. More important is art. 191, which, although it has been practically unused, does provide for an investigation on behalf of a minority representing 20% of the capital. Such a minority can request the competent Commercial Court to appoint special auditors to verify the corporate books and documents. The Court will grant the application only if the applicants can show that there has been a serious lack of care in accounting procedures. However, if the special auditors discover irregularities, a majority vote of the board can still exonerate the persons responsible.

Art. 103 entitles a 25% minority to wind up the company if three-quarters of the capital is lost. The right is considered as a means of protecting the company against the risk of bankruptcy.

The idea behind these provisions is not to punish directors for incompetence, but to protect minority shareholders from their intentional fraud.

2.b. Consortia

Besides the forms dealt with in chapter 1 Belgian law recognizes two forms of commercial partnership without legal personality:

- tijdelijke vereniging – association momentanée
- vereniging in deelneming – association en participation.

The 'association momentanée' is frequently found in practice.

Association momentanée

According to art. 175 CCL the 'association momentanée' is a partnership having as its object the acomplishment of one or more business transactions. The 'association momentanée' has no name.

– Characteristics

The 'association momentanée' has a transient character and cannot be established for an indefinite period of time. If this were attempted, it would be considered as an unlimited partnership (vennootschap onder gemeenschappelijke naam – société en nom collectif).

The 'association momentanée' is established by private contract. It is not governed by the provisions of the CCL.

The partners are jointly liable for all obligations to third parties with whom the 'association momentanée' does business.

– Organization
The partners are entirely free to organize the 'association momentanée' as they think fit.

– Object
Practice shows that 'associations momentanées' are used for a wide variety of purposes:
- construction;
- delivery of machines and equipment;
- sale of goods;
- turn-key projects.

Normally the contract sets out the precise obligations of each partner.

– Management
The partners usually constitute one or more organs to manage the 'association momentanée' such as:
- a managing committee: comprising a representative of each partner and having the power to take all decisions useful for the achievement of the common purpose; it may be compared with the board of directors of a public limited company;
- a committee entrusted with the day-to-day carrying out of the instructions given by the managing committee.

Association en participation

According to art. 176, CCL the 'Association en Participation' is a partnership in which one or more persons participate in commercial acts performed by other persons in the latters' own names. It is established by private contract. It is not governed by the provisions of the CCL.

2.c. Other forms

The Belgian Government has presented to Parliament a draft Law for the creation of a 'Groupement d'intérêt économique – groepering van bedrijfseconomische samenwerking' (GIE) (Second Chamber, nr. 848 of April 18, 1976). This draft has been inspired by the French Law of September 23, 1967 and the draft Directive of the EEC-Commission on the same subject.
Some characteristics
The GIE is an instrument of cooperation between enterprises, aimed at the development and rationalisation of their businesses by bringing together certain activities in order to reduce production or sales costs of goods or services.
It is created by a written contract and has a legal personality. Vis-à-vis third parties it takes effect as from publication in the Annexes to the Belgian Official Gazette.

It need not be listed in the Commercial Register, but must be entered in a special Register kept at the Registry of the Commercial Court.
It exists for a period defined in the contract. All partners of the GIE are jointly liable to third parties for all the obligations of the GIE.
The management of the GIE lies with one or more natural or legal persons. The managers are not necessarily partners of the GIE. The managers are jointly liable to the GIE and to third parties. The assembly of the partners has full power to take any decision or perform any act necessary or useful for the attainment of the objects of the GIE.
The contract may, however, restrict these powers or entrust them to other bodies of the GIE.

B. External Controls

1. EXCHANGE CONTROLS

In the Belgian exchange system there are two separate markets: an official market for commercial transactions and a free market for financial transactions.
Financing of foreign investment in Belgium should, in principle, pass through the free market. In this case investment is free and funds may be repatriated freely if they pass back through the same market. Investment and repatriation can also be made through the official market. In this case the authorization of the Belgo-Luxemburg Institute of Exchange (Belgisch-Luxemburgs Instituut voor de Wissel – Institut Belgo-Luxembourgeois du Change) has to be obtained.
The principles of exchange control are laid down in artt. 7 and 8 (as amended) of a Decree of October 6, 1944. The Institute is empowered to issue Regulations relating to Exchange Control.

2. TAKE-OVER CONTROLS

Bank Commission
Public take-over bids are controlled by the provisions of the Royal Decree nr. 185 of July 9, 1935 (artt. 26-34) and the Acts of June 10, 1964 (art. 22) and July 10, 1969 (art. 1). All forms of public take-over bids, including bids not leading to the taking over of control of a company as well as bids relating to bonds, especially convertible bonds, are covered by these Laws.
Every take-over bid must be reported to the Bank Commission fifteen days before it is made. If the Bank Commission is of the opinion that the take-over may disrupt the capital market or that subscribers are being misled, and if the bidders do not take account of this opinion, the Bank Commission has the right to forbid the take-over for three months and to publish its opinion.
Although the Bank Commission is only empowered to postpone the take-over for a limited period and to publish its opinion, in practice this power is sufficient to wreck any take-over bid of which it disapproves. Moreover, the

Minister of Finance can, at the request of the Bank Commission, forbid the registration in the Stock-Exchange List (prijscourant – prix courant) of any shares and bonds acquired contrary to the advice of the Bank Commission.

Government

Further, all take-over bids have to be notified in advance to the Ministries of Economic Affairs and Finance if they apply to one third or more of the capital of enterprises situated in the country (Act of December 30, 1970, art. 36, as amended). Finally a public take-over bid of public quoted stock requires the authorization of the Minister of Finance if the take-over bid is made by or on behalf of non-EC nationals or non-EC enterprises. (art. 108 Commercial Code).

3. ANTI-TRUST

Belgian anti-trust law is embodied in the Act of May 27, 1960 on Protection against Abuse of Economic Power.

Economic power is defined as the power possessed by a natural or legal person acting alone or by a group of such persons acting in concert to exert, within the territory of the Kingdom, through industrial, commercial, agricultural or financial activities, a dominating influence on supplies of goods, on the capital market or on the price or quality of specific goods or services.

Under this Law, a company or group of companies is entitled to occupy a dominant position in a particular market but is prevented from abusing its economic power. The test of abuse of economic power is non-compliance with the general interest.

An abuse is committed when one or more persons having economic power do harm to the public interest by means of practices which distort or restrict the normal effect of competition or which interfere with the economic freedom of producers, distributors or consumers or with the development of production or trade.

The administrative procedure for enforcing this Act is very complicated: it requires arbitration by the Council for Economic Disputes and can result in a 'cease and desist' order issued in the form of a Royal Decree.

Up to now, administrative enforcement of the Act has only once resulted in a Royal Decree (November 7, 1973).[2]

4. ENVIRONMENTAL CONTROLS

It is possible under the general law to bring proceedings against an offender for damage resulting from noise, water or air pollution: Civil Code artt. 1382 et seq. (action for misdemeanour causing damage), or Civil Code art. 544 (nuisance from neighbours sensu stricto, theory of equilibrium). Monetary

2. A draft Law relating to competition and inspired by the EEC-rules was presented by the Government a few years ago, but has met with many objections and has, consequently, not been enacted.

compensation or measures ending the nuisance may be ordered.
Apart from the above, there is specific legislation relating to:

- dangerous, unhealthy and disruptive businesses (principally the Decree of the Regent of February 11, 1946): system of licensing based on 'de commodo et incommodo' examination;
- town and country planning and urbanisation (Act of March 29, 1962): construction plans, building licences;
- water pollution (principally the Act of March 26, 1971 relating to the protection of surface waters against pollution, and the relevant orders): licence for discharging waste waters;
- air pollution (principally the Act of December 28, 1964 and the relevant orders): technical requirements, prohibitive regulations;
- nuisance by noise (principally the Act of July 18, 1973 and the relevant orders): noise standards.

5. STATE MONOPOLIES

- *Real Estate sector*:
  - The National Housing Company (Nationale Maatschappij voor Huisvesting – Société Nationale du Logement) has a de facto monopoly for the construction of subsidized homes.
  - Inter-commune companies exist for the preparation of building land for industrial and commercial purposes.
- *Water supply*: National Water Supply Company (Nationale Maatschappij der Waterleidingen – Société Nationale des Distributions d'eau): inter-commune companies, communal 'régies'.
- *Electricity and gas supply*: de facto monopoly of the communes.
- *Telegraph and telephone*: RTT monopoly.
- *Transport*:
  - air transport: heavily state controlled via Sabena
  - railways: NMBS and NMVB monopoly
  - trams: monopoly of inter-commune companies in the five largest cities
  - road passenger and freight transport: NMBS and NMVB competing with private sector
  - transport by water: state exploitation of some waterways, the Ostend-Dover ferries, and the harbour installations.
- *Post Office*: state monopoly.
- *Social Security*: state monopoly in the fields of pensions, family allowance, unemployment benefit, illness and disability pensions, holiday pay and industrial illness. Control, but no monopoly in the sector of industrial accident insurance.
- *Financial sector*: state dominated by the National Bank, the savings institutions Algemene Spaar- en Lijfrente Kas – Caisse Générale d'Epargne et de Retraite, the investment company Nationale Investeringsmaatschappij – Société Nationale d'Investissement and the credit institution Nationale Maatschappij voor Krediet aan de Nijverheid – Société Nationale de Crédit à l'Industrie.

6. PRICE CONTROLS

The law relating to the control of prices (Act of January 22, 1945 as amended and, lastly, by the Act of July 30, 1971) applies to the prices of all products sold and of most services rendered in Belgium.

- The Minister of Economic Affairs has the power to impose maximum prices and price limits per sector or per product.
- He also may recommend normal prices which are published in the newspapers.
- Any price increase must be reported to the Ministry of Economic Affairs. Within a set period (which can be up to three months) after notification, prices may be increased within the limits of the notification unless the Minister decrees otherwise.

III. TAXATION

A. Corporation Tax

1. ENTITIES SUBJECT TO TAX

Corporation tax is charged on the whole of the income of a corporation, whether distributed or not and of whatever type. The law provides that any company, association or organisation is subject to corporation tax if it meets the following conditions:

- it is incorporated under Belgian or foreign private or public law;
- it has its seat or principal establishment or administrative or management headquarters in Belgium; the seat is nearly always also the principal establishment, which means the place from which the corporation is governed, managed and controlled. 'Administrative or management headquarters' refers to corporate bodies which do not have a seat;
- it is engaged in industrial, commercial or agricultural operations or in other transactions of a profit-making nature. Consequently, a company in liquidation is not subject to corporation tax, provided its activities are confined to its winding-up. A real estate company is, however, assessable for corporation tax on any property transactions during liquidation.

The tax therefore applies to the following types of corporation:

- any Belgian corporate body having the form of a commercial company, i.e.:
  - *a.* a body with corporate capital, either a public limited company or a partnership limited by shares;
  - *b.* a private limited company, a co-operative partnership, a general partnership and a limited partnership.

In certain circumstances, the companies, mentioned under b above, may opt for the assessment of their profit as a personal tax liability of their partners.

- Belgian corporate bodies other than commercial companies, i.e.:
  a. public bodies or public utility enterprises which are engaged in operations of a profit-making nature;
  b. non-profit-making associations (VZW – ASBL) which, despite their non-profit-making status are engaged in operations of a profit-making nature.
- companies formed abroad but whose seat or principal establishment is in Belgium and which are engaged in transactions of a profit-making nature. It is, in fact, rare for a foreign company to meet these conditions; foreign companies are normally subject to taxation as non-residents.

Corporation tax is not levied on

- unincorporated associations, that is to say 'tijdelijke verenigingen – associations momentanées', 'verenigingen in deelneming – associations en participation' and 'feitelijke vennootschappen – sociétés de fait'. The profits of such bodies have to be declared in the personal income tax return of the members themselves.
- non-profit-making bodies or bodies not normally engaged in profit-making activities.

2. COMPUTATION OF PROFITS

Corporation tax is charged on the total company income of whatever type and from whatever source. All such income is taxed as 'trading income'.
The taxable income of companies by shares is divided into:

- reserved profits
- non-allowable expenses
- remuneration of directors
- dividends.

The taxable income of a partnership is divided into:

- reserved profits
- non-allowable expenses
- income from capital invested.

2.a. Reserved profits

a. The reserved profit is the difference between the total taxable income at the end of a financial year and the total taxable reserves at the end of the previous financial year. Taxable reserves consist of:

1. *Book reserves*: the reserves entered in the annual accounts of the company, such as the balance sheet and the profit and loss account carried forward, the legal reserve and other reserves such as the extraordinary reserve, special reserve, etc.
2. *Hidden reserves*: the reserves resulting from a fiscal adjustment of the books to take into account assets of the company which are not showing in the annual breakdown. These include:
   - under evaluation of assets such as stock, shares, claims, etc. entered at

a lower value than is laid down by the regulation on tax assessment;
- over evaluation of liabilities, such as a creditor account, which does not correspond to the real debt;
- excessive depreciation, that is the difference between amounts written off and the amounts permitted in the regulations.

2.b. Non-allowable expenses

In principle, a company may deduct from its taxable profits any expenses incurred in connection with its trading activities for the purpose of earning or retaining taxable income. The expenses must have been incurred in the financial year, i.e. actually incurred or entered as such in the books. The expenses must be evidenced in the manner laid down by law.
The following are typical trading expenses which are generally recognized as deductible:
- rent of buildings and materials as well as all the related costs of maintenance and repair;
- the interest payable on loan capital, which however may not exceed by more than three points the official rates quoted by the Belgian National Bank. If the interest rate of the National Bank is less than 6%, interest may be deducted up to 9%.

This limitation on deductible interest does not apply when the interest is paid to a bank or other recognized financial institution;
- wages and all related Belgian social security payments;
- depreciation: the straight-line method is adopted as a rule. The declining balance formula may be adopted at the request of the company;
- commissions as well as fees and retainers, the beneficiary of which are disclosed with a statement of names and addresses.

All expenses, which are deducted from the income by the company but are not considered as operating expenses for tax purposes, are grouped under the heading 'non-allowable expenses' and added to the taxable income.

Examples
- Secret commissions i.e. professional fees and retainers the beneficiary of which is not disclosed, or which cannot be substantiated by relevant evidentiary documents.

In addition, such commissions and fees are assessed separately as well as being subject to Corporation Tax: hence the total tax payable on such fees can amount to 202.5%. Secret commissions and fees may, however, subject to strict conditions, be allowed as operating expenses for the purpose of Belgian Corporation Tax.
- Interest, royalties, indemnifications, paid to a person, enterprise or holding company established in a foreign country, where it benefits from a tax regime substantially more favourable than the Belgian, except when it can be proved that the payments involve a normal operation.
- Expenses in connection with hunting, fishing, yachts and vacation houses, as well as clearly unreasonable expenses.
- Direct taxes.

Whenever a Belgian enterprise, which has direct or indirect ties with a foreign company, provides by virtue of such ties abnormal or benevolent advantages to the foreign company or to other persons from enterprises having common interests with the Belgian company, all such advantages are likewise added to the profits of the Belgian company.
The same rule applies to all abnormal advantages granted to companies and persons established in a foreign country when they benefit from a substantially more favourable tax regime.

2.c. Directors' remuneration

Fees and bonuses paid to directors and auditors are in principle part of the taxable profit. However, remuneration paid to directors exercising real and permanent functions within the company may be considered by the company as operating expenses to the extent that the amount paid to them exceeds the bonuses paid to honorary directors without real functions.
An active director may indicate two companies in which he has real and permanent functions and which may deduct his remuneration as an operating cost.

2.d. Dividends

Corporation tax is assessed on the amount which the General Meeting resolves to distribute by way of a dividend.
In the case of a partnership, a profit element is represented by income from invested capital, that is to say:
- interest paid or deemed to be paid on the capital invested by the partners. The portion of income from invested capital attributed to the active partners is established at the same percentage as the income attributed to non-active partners, in case the statutes are silent on this subject. When there are no non-active partners the percentage of the income from invested capital is fixed at 6%.
- interest on money advanced to the company by the partners, their spouses and children if the partners have the legal right to the income of their children.

2.e. Operating losses

A net operating loss for any given taxable period may be carried forward and offset against taxable income during the following five years.
This time limitation does not apply to losses arising from events beyond the control of the company (force majeure) occurred after January 1st, 1960.
Companies formed after the 1st of January, 1972 may also carry forward indefinitely their start-up losses sustained during the first five years following their incorporation. The five year limitation does not apply to losses occurred since the financial year following the 31st of December 1976 to the extent that such losses either do not exceed depreciation accepted according to taxation standards or could have been set off within the five year period if there had not been depreciation.

The last hypothesis applies equally to losses sustained before the 31st of December 1976, which could have been set off within the five year period if there had not been depreciation accepted after the 31st of December 1976.

2.f. Capital gains

In principle, realized capital gains are part of taxable profits. However, capital gains on real estate, machinery and participations are exempted up to the amount of the revalued cost price, provided that these assets belonged to the company for more than five years before the realization of the gain.
The amount then exceeding the revalued cost price is taxed separately at a lower rate, at present 24%.
There is also an exemption for compulsory gains i.e. capital gains which arise from compensation for a compulsory sale, disasters, etc., provided the amount received is entered on a special debit account but also provided the amount is reinvested in the company within a period of three years.

2.g. Income from dividends

When a Belgian company receives a dividend from another company (Belgian or foreign) this income is excluded from the taxable income, provided that the shares have been held by the company during the entire taxable period.
The exemption amounts to 95% or 90% of the dividend received, depending on whether the source is a trading company or a holding company, the latter being a company, whose assets consist of shareholding of a value exceeding 50% of its capital.
The dividend received is increased either by the real withholding tax (20% of gross amount for Belgian dividends) or by a fictitious withholding tax (5% of the amount received). This withholding tax is deductible from the final tax to be paid.

2.h. Income from liquidation

A Belgian company may also receive income from a liquidated company in which it held shares. That income is treated almost the same way as the income from dividends outlined above.
Its share in the net result of the liquidation is exempted, amounting to 95 or 90% of the income, upon which a fictitious withholding tax of 25% is calculated.

2.i. Difference between tax and accounting legislation

A Royal Decree of October 8, 1976 implemented the Law of July 17, 1975, concerning the accounting regulations.
Although the tax authorities made an assurance that the application of the accounting principles would not affect the application of the tax rules, there were some areas where it was necessary to clarify the taxation principles:
- provisions: although a company can be forced to make provisions for possible future risks which may occur, these provisions are only acceptable

for tax purposes when the circumstances from which the risks appear, become apparent during the year the provision is formed;

- depreciation: the tax authorities maintain their position that depreciation has to be calculated on the historic cost price. If another basis is taken, the difference should appear on a special debit account 'capital gain of revaluation' in order to avoid taxation;
- evaluation of stock: the accounting legislation allows several methods for the evaluation of stock, provided the same method is applied during the entire year and changes appear in the annexes to the annual accounts. The tax authorities maintain that all gains on stock shown in the accounts, become immediately subject to taxation.

3. RATES OF TAX

3.a. Normal rates

- where profits do not exceed 1,000,000 BF: 33%;
- where profits are between 1,000,000 BF. and 1,700,000 BF: 33% on the first 1,000,000 BF. and 50% on the remainder;
- where profits are between 1,700,000 BF. and 3,000,000 BF: 40%;
- where profits are between 3,000,000 BF. and 15,000,000 BF: 40% on the first 3,000,000 BF. and 50% on the remainder;
- where profits exceed 15,000,000 BF: 48%.

The flat rate of 48% applies to all the profits of:

- holding companies, i.e. companies whose holdings of shares represent 50% or more of their capital and reserves; this is because the bulk of their income consists of dividends which are deductible from taxable profits;
- affiliated companies, i.e. companies which have at least 50% of their capital held by another company or companies; this is to prevent profits being split up between companies in order to obtain assessment at lower rates.

The rates of assessment are reduced by 3/4 in respect of taxable foreign income subject to tax abroad and not exempt under double taxation treaties.
Application of the foregoing rates is conditional upon payments in advance of all tax liabilities on the dates fixed for this purpose. Four quarterly dates (April 10th, July 10th, October 10th and December 20th) are provided for prepayment of taxes. The penalty for failure to prepay is calculated under a complex system which results in an average increase of about 20% per annum.

3.b. Capital gains

Capital gains from real estate, machinery and shareholdings which are not exempt are taxable at a rate of 24% provided the company owned the asset for more than 5 years.

3.c. Purchase-back of shares

When a company purchases back its own shares from the shareholders in the course of a reduction of capital, a special levy at a rate of 48% applies to that portion of the amount paid which is in excess of the amount of capital which was brought in for that share. This special levy is in addition to the normal corporation tax.

3.d. Liquidation of the company

Tax liability on the income of the company ceases upon its dissolution, except for gains in its liquidation.
Reimbursement of the capital brought in by the shareholders, possibly revalued, is exempt from tax.
All amounts paid out to the shareholders in excess of the stated share capital of the company i.e. previously formed reserves and newly appearing increases in value, are taxed with a special levy fixed at a rate of 48% for the existing reserves and 24% for the other amounts.
No tax is payable by the shareholders receiving the distribution except for companies where the liquidation bonus is treated as received dividend.

3.e. Consolidation – Splitting – Merger – Transformation

Dissolution of the company following merger, consolidation, or split-up is normally taxed in accordance with the rules set out in the foregoing paragraph with regard to capital gains on realization.
However, the Belgian income tax code provides rules for neutral reorganizations, subject to the following conditions:
– that the companies resulting from a consolidation or split-up have their registered office or main establishment in Belgium;
– that the contribution of the assets of the company to the merged or consolidated companies is made in consideration for shares only;
– that where the dissolution of the company has not been decided on for the express purpose of consolidation or splitting-up, the liquidators have not previously distributed part of the capital and surplusses thereby taking advantage of the corresponding exemption from taxation.

The transformation of the legal form of the company does not necessitate dissolution of the company where such change is made under the terms of art. 165 to 174 CCL, provided the assets and liabilities, capital and reserves included, are not altered as a result of such a change in the legal form.

4. TAX CREDITS, ADVANCE LEVIES

In order to calculate the final tax liability of a company, one has to take into account the advance levies already paid by the company as well as the tax credits.

a. Advance levy on real estate (onroerende voorheffing – précompte immobilier). The property is taxed on the basis of its fictitious rental income (kadastraal inkomen -- revenu cadastral). This tax can be deducted from the tax finally due with a maximum amount of 12.5% of the 'revenu cadastral'.

b. The advance levies on dividends and interests received in Belgium at a normal rate of 20% is entirely deductible from the corporation tax, and will even be reimbursed.
Dividends received by the company, and generated by non permanent shareholdings, are not deductible to establish the taxable basis, but give raise to a tax credit at a rate of 57.5% of the amount received.

c. Income from a capital dividend from foreign sources, taxed abroad and not qualifying for the deduction as a permanent shareholding, is entitled to a tax credit in Belgium of 15% of the amount received.
This does not apply to income from capital invested in a foreign branch.

5. WITHHOLDING TAX ON DIVIDENDS, INTEREST AND ROYALTIES

Income paid by a company to its shareholders in the form of dividend, interest paid to its creditors, as well as royalties, are all subject to withholding tax.
This withholding tax is levied on the debtor established in Belgium. The normal rate is 20%.
There are numerous exceptions to this principle exempting the income or reducing the rate of the withholding tax.
In addition double taxation treaties provide for relief or reduction of the withholding tax:

- dividends: 15% (sometimes down to 5% in case the beneficiary company owns a minimum amount of shares);
- interest: 10% (sometimes total exemption for interest paid to a foreign enterprise);
- royalties: zero.

However, the rate fixed in the treaty for dividends, may be applied to that portion of a royalty which is in excess of a normal amount, agreed upon in at arms' length dealing.

B. Registration and Stamp Duties

1. A duty of 1% is charged on the value of assets brought into the business in return for shares when a company is formed or its capital is increased, if, either the company's principal place of business is in Belgium or the seat is in Belgium and the principal place of business is outside the EC. The minimum basis for assessment is the resale value of the assets.
If the assets consisting of real estate are not paid for with shares, they will be considered to have been sold to the company and taxed at the rate of 12.5%.
In order to prevent double taxation of assets brought into a business which are also subject to VAT, the VAT Code provides that such assets are exempt from VAT, provided the company taking over the assets, is subject to VAT.

2. A lower duty of 0.5% is charged on assets brought into a business as a result of merger, absorption or splitting of companies, provided that the company bringing in the assets had its actual or registered place of business in an EC-country, and at least 90% of the value of the assets are paid for by shares or compensated by previously existing debts of the contributing company.

3. In order to prevent the avoidance of registration duties on transfers of real property by the device of transfers through a company formed for that purpose, a duty of 12.5% applies to:
- transfers of real property located in Belgium from a public limited company or co-operative partnership to one or more of its partners;
- any transfer of such property, other than by way of contribution of assets to a company, from a partnership, to one or more of its partners, except:
  a. by way of re-transfer of assets previously brought into the company to the partner who brought them in;
  b. in the case of real property previously bought by the company on which the duty on sales has been paid, provided the intended transferee was already a partner at the time of the earlier purchase.

4. A fixed fee of 225 BF. is due for registration of the incorporation, an extension of the life of a company for decrease of capital, for dissolution and for amendment of the statutes of companies.

C. Individual Taxation

Individuals living in Belgium are subject to personal income tax, as residents, as well as non-residents.
Residents however are subject to tax on their world wide income, i.e.
- income from real estate;
- income from shares, bonds and other capital;
- income from earnings;
- some other categories as e.g. speculative income, alimony payments, etc.

Capital gains are taxable when part of the assets are invested in a business.
Gains realized on private property are taxable under certain conditions:
- unbuilt real estate when sold within 16 years after acquisition when it is situated in a building zone.
  The rate is 33% when sold within 10 years and 16.5% when sold within 16 years;
- shareholdings of at least 25% in a company when sold to another company. The rate is 16.5%;
- real estate purchased and sold within a short period of time can be regarded as speculative and taxed at 33%.

The tax rates are progressive:
- up to 750,000 BF.: average %: 33%
- 750,000 – 1 m. BF.: 47.5%
- 1 m. – 1.5 m. BF.: 52.5%

- 1,5 m. – 2 m. BF.: 57.5%
- 2 m. – 3 m. BF.: 63%
- 3 m. – 4 m. BF.: 69%
- above 4 m. BF.: 72%

The average basic rate may not exceed 67.5%.
The tax has also to be paid in advance by business people and free professions; otherwise it undergoes a substantial increase of circa 20%.
Expatriates benefit from a substantial reduction of their taxable income.
It concerns management employees or highly qualified personnel, working in Belgium for subsidiaries of foreign enterprises.
The reduction is normally 30% of the gross remuneration.
Employees travelling more than 50% of the time abroad are only taxable on the salary earned for the time spent in Belgium.
The 30% rule is however limited to 450,000 BF. (calculated on 1,500,000 BF.) and 1,200,000 BF. (calculated on 4,000,000 BF.) for staff personnel working in coordination centres.

D. Indirect Taxation

Sales of goods, including imported goods, and the provision of services are subject to VAT, charged at three different rates:
25% on luxuries, 6% on goods and services 'of prime necessity' and 16% on other goods and services.
A VAT return must be made each month setting out the turnover of the preceding month.
Foreign enterprises with a fixed establishment in Belgium are treated in the same way as Belgian tax payers with respect to the transactions of the establishment.
Foreign enterprises with no fixed establishment must appoint a representative to carry out VAT formalities with respect to goods delivered and services performed in Belgium.
Special provisions apply to small businesses and agricultural enterprises, which provide for a lump sum basis of assessment and, in the case of small retailers, for equalisation tax.

E. Government Incentives

1. GOVERNMENT INCENTIVES FOR GRANTING CREDIT AND EQUITY-CAPITAL FINANCEMENT

1.a. Act of 1959 on General Expansion

Under this Law, interest relief, state guarantees or capital premiums can be granted for long-terms loans in order to establish, enlarge, modernize, rationalize or reorganize an undertaking, or to preserve or increase employment.

1.b. Act of 1970 on Regional Expansion

Investments are encouraged in some 25 'development areas', i.e. areas where there is structural unemployment, a substantial decline in employment, a generally low standard of living or a recession of economic activity.
The incentives can consist of interest relief grants, capital premiums, state guarantees, repayable interest-free loans or employment premiums.

1.c. Act of 1978 on Economic Reorientation

Special support, such as interest relief grants or the Guarantee Fund security, can be given to young self-employed people in business for the first time, to companies with a majority of shareholders younger than 35, and to the newly self-employed of any age in skilled manual trades, such as plumbers. Only small or medium-sized enterprises are eligible, i.e. those which employ less than 40, 50 or 70 workers.

1.d. Incentives for Research

The Institute for the Promotion of Research into Industry and Agriculture subsidizes research projects by undertakings individually or jointly, or by research centres.
The Ministry of Economic Affairs grants interest-free loans for research into prototypes, new products or manufacturing processes. Such loans are only repayable if the research results in a remunerative industrial and commercial application.

2. EMPLOYMENT GRANTS

Numerous schemes operate to mitigate the effects of unemployment.
The Government requires and subsidizes the recruitment of young and encourages the early retirement of older workers, gives employment premiums to small and medium-sized enterprises, or repays their social security contributions, or temporarily reduces these contributions if the number of employees is increased.
The Unemployment Office contributes to the salary of 'hard case' unemployed, such as older, disabled or handicapped workers, and assists the establishment, enlargement or reorganization of enterprises by assuming part of the workers' training cost.

3. TAX INCENTIVES

In order to promote economic expansion and employment, various permanent or temporary tax reliefs are allowed to enterprises, such as:

a. exemptions from real estate tax;

b. doubling of the normal annual linear depreciation allowance for investment in material and equipment and the improvements of land;

c. exemption from registration duty for capital brought into companies;
d. exemption from capital gains tax, conditional on reinvestment;
e. temporary exemption from corporation tax for certain dividends paid on newly contributed capital;
f. special temporary relief on taxable income re-invested;
g. 'Ad libitum' depreciation percentages (up to 110%);
h. additional reduction of taxes on value added for additional or employment-generating capital assets.

4. INCENTIVES TO EXPORT

The Government subsidizes export financing by allowing interest relief grants, it also insures exchange-rate risks and the export of industrial equipment, and gives social and tax privileges to Belgians employed abroad.
The Belgian Foreign Trade Service informs the business world on foreign markets, helps enterprises in prospecting these markets, and generally promotes Belgian products abroad, with the assistance of Belgian diplomats all over the world.
The Belgian Foreign Trade Fund subsidizes or grants interest-free loans for various schemes promoting Belgian exports.

F. Double Tax Treaties

Belgium has treaties with the following countries:

Australia	October 13, 1977
Austria	December 29, 1971
Brazil	June 23, 1972
Canada	May 29, 1975
Czechoslovakia	June 19, 1975
Denmark	October 16, 1969
Finland	May 18, 1976
France	March 19, 1964 and February 15, 1971
Germany	April 11, 1967
Greece	May 24, 1968
India	February 7, 1974
Indonesia	November 13, 1973
Ireland	June 24, 1970
Israel	July 13, 1972
Italy	October 19, 1970
Ivory Coast	November 25, 1977
Japan	March 28, 1968
Luxemburg	September 17, 1970
Malaysia	October 24, 1973
Malta	June 28, 1974

Marocco	May 4, 1972
The Netherlands	October 19, 1970
Norway	June 30, 1967
Philippines	October 2, 1976
Poland	September 14, 1976
Portugal	July 16, 1969
Rumania	October 14, 1976
Singapore	February 8, 1972
South Korea	August 29, 1971
Spain	July 2, 1965 and March 7, 1967
Sweden	July 2, 1965
Switzerland	August 28, 1978
Thailand	October 16, 1978
Tunisia	February 22, 1975
United Kingdom	August 29, 1967
United States	July 9, 1970.

IV. LABOUR ASPECTS

A. Principles of Law on Employment

1. GENERAL

The Act of July 3, 1978 regulates the labour contract law of manual workers and non-manual workers, salesmen and servants.
The Act regulates conditions of employment so comprehensively that there is little room for individual agreements between employees and employers. Most of the provisions of the Law are binding to the extent that the parties can only deviate from the Law through clauses that are in favour of the employee; agreements in conflict with the Law are voidable, i.e. the nullity can only be invoked by the parties to the agreement. Some provisions, however, are mandatory, such as those relating to the language to be used, the minimum period of notice and regulations based on Collective Labour Agreements. Terms of agreement in breach of these provisions are absolutely void, i.e. for a period of 30 years the nullity can be invoked by any party, and a judge must do so ex officio.

2. CATEGORIES OF EMPLOYEES

Labour law makes an initial distinction between manual workers and non-manual workers. The Law of 1978 lays down general principles applying to both categories of employees and specific regulations for each category. The result is that different systems govern manual workers and non-manual workers. The non-manual worker does mainly office work.
It is the real nature of the work done which in law determines the status of the employee and not the label put on it by the parties in the contract of

employment. The judge's ruling is decisive in case of dispute. The distinction is very important in relation to periods of notice: those applicable to non-manual workers are longer than those applicable to manual workers.

The distinction is also relevant in relation to Collective Labour Agreements; trade unions incorporate the distinction in their structures; CLA's deal with the two categories separately, and the same is true in joint committees.

Supervisory and managerial personnel, even at the highest level, can legally be classified as non-manual workers: under the law on contracts of employment they have the same rights and obligations as non-manual workers. Their special position is only taken into account in certain provisions of collective labour law.

The Act of 1978 also governs the status of salesmen. These are persons employed under a contract by which they agree in return for payment to search for and visit customers with a view to negotiating and concluding business under the authority, for the account, and on behalf of one or more principals. As a rule, they have the status of non-manual workers; however, certain specific additional provisions entitle them to specific compensation when they cease to be employed.

Temporary employees are governed by the provisional Act of June 28, 1976, which is in force for 4 years with a possible extension of 1 year; hence their conditions of employment have yet to be definitively established by legislation.

The provisional Law governs strictly:

1. the use of temporary staff (only permitted in a few specific cases);
2. the method of recruitment, either by sub-contract or through temporary employment agencies;
3. the conditions of employment of these workers on their wages, security of employment, and social security. As a rule their conditions of employment are the same as those of permanent workers. Their employment is closely supervised by the authorities and there exist substantial penalties for breaches of the law.

3. FORM AND DURATION OF CONTRACTS OF EMPLOYMENT

In principle, a contract of employment need not be in writing except in cases specifically provided for by law, i.e. contracts of employment for a limited period or for a specific kind of work. Normally, contracts of employment are entered into for an indefinite period. A succession of contracts of limited duration gives rise to a contract of employment for an unlimited period unless the employer is able to justify using a succession of such contracts.

As a result of the language laws, the contract of employment must be in the language of the region where the enterprise is established, otherwise it is absolutely void: for the Flemish region, the Decree of July 19, 1973; for the Walloon region, the Decree of July 12, 1978. In Brussels, the language normally used by the worker is applicable.

Translations into other languages are acceptable under certain conditions.

Incidentally these language obligations go beyond the contract of employment and cover all dealings with employees.

Probationary periods are permitted, but must be laid down in writing, the periods being fixed for each category of workers:

- for manual workers a minimum of 7 days and a maximum of 14 days;
- for non-manual workers a minimum of 1 month and a maximum of 3 to 6 months according to whether the annual pay is lower or higher than 300,000 BF.

Prior to the expiration of the probationary period, the employer must clearly indicate whether he wants to continue the employment or not. If he fails to give any indication, the contract will become one for an unlimited period.

4. CONTENTS OF CONTRACTS OF EMPLOYMENT

The comprehensive legal regulation of contracts of employment is evident in the provisions governing the contents of the contract: several laws on employment, together with generally applicable Collective Labour Agreements, closely circumscribe the contractual freedom of the parties.

These are, inter alia:

- the Act on Employment of March 16, 1971 concerning working-time and Sunday rest, which applies nothwithstanding the specific rules for each branch of industry provided for by Collective Agreements and given effect by Royal Decree;
- the Royal Decree of June 28, 1971 on holidays, supplemented by specific CLA's; the Law of January 4, 1974 on paid public holidays;
- the Act of April 12, 1965 on the protection of wages, which principally regulates the time and methods of payment. Wages themselves are freely negotiated between the parties, but account must be taken of the minimum pay fixed for each branch of industry and for each category of employee in the various CLA's made by joint committees and by the National Labour Council. The principle of equal pay for equal work is guaranteed by the national Inter-Industry Labour Agreement nr. 25 of October 25, 1975;
- the Act of April 8, 1965 on the introduction of conditions of work, which regulates conditions of work inside the enterprise;
- the range of social security regulations which impose obligations both on the employer and on the employee.

The Law on contracts of employment expressly forbids certain provisions:

1. A provision whereby the employer reserves to himself the right to change the conditions of the agreement unilaterally is void. This prohibition is to be strictly applied. If the agreement does not expressly or implicitly provide for certain conditions of employment, the employer may make amendments in the interest of the company, but no change may be made to the essential conditions (e.g. job description, pay, etc.).
   In case of dispute, the Labour Court is empowered to interpret the contract, though this power is limited.
2. Provisions stipulating that marriage, maternity, or reaching the legal or

contractual retirement age automatically terminate the agreement are void.

3. Disputes arising from the contract of employment may not be settled by arbitration except where there is an express agreement to this effect with non-manual workers whose annual pay is higher than 500,000 BF. and who carry out functions at the highest level of the company.

5. SUSPENSION OF THE CONTRACT OF EMPLOYMENT

Certain events outside the control of the employer may suspend the contract of employment. The employee may or may not retain his right to pay, according to the circumstances. As soon as the suspension ends, the employee must be re-employed. The following cases *a.* to *e.* apply to all categories of employees, *f.* applies to manual and non-manual workers, and *g.* to *i.* to manual workers only.

a. Working hours lost by employees willing to work but unable to do so for various reasons (e.g. technical problems or delays in transport – exceptions are strikes and force majeure): they are entitled to their normal pay for the lost hours.

b. Obligations arising from military service laws for the period concerned.

c. Inability to work owing to illness or accident.
The employee must comply with certain formalities (notice, medical certificate, medical examination). During the suspension, a manual worker has the right to his normal weekly pay, and a non-manual worker to his normal monthly salary. After this period, he comes under the social security system.
Pregnant women have the right to their normal pay; moreover, they have the right to 14 weeks maternity leave, of which at least 8 weeks must be taken after childbirth; the other 6 weeks may be taken entirely or partly before the birth.

d. Notice must be given in advance for absence from work owing to personal or family circumstances (e.g. birth, marriage or bereavement) or for the purpose of complying with civil obligations, with the right to pay.

e. Time off for political duties for employees holding political posts: the right to wages or salary is protected within certain limits.

f. During the annual closure and the employee's holiday the employee has the right to the payments laid down by the law on holidays.

g. Interruption of work owing to bad weather: the contract is suspended without pay provided notice is given beforehand.

h. Interruption of work owing to breakdown of equipment: the employee must continue to receive his normal pay for up to 7 days, but the employer may put him onto similar substitute work.

i. Interruption owing to a shortage of work because of economic conditions: the employer may either suspend work for a maximum period of 4 weeks or introduce a system of short-time working provided he gives notice to the employee. After four weeks, the employee is treated as unemployed.

6. TERMINATION OF THE CONTRACT OF EMPLOYMENT

Apart from the normal ways in which obligations are terminated under art. 1184 of the Civil Code (for example voidness of the contract, mutual agreement, etc.) a contract of employment is terminated in the following cases:

a. end of the agreed period or completion of the work contemplated by the contract;

b. special circumstances, such as force majeure or the death of the employee (as a rule, however, not the death of the employer);

c. termination without notice when one of the parties has committed gross negligence;

d. termination by notice by one of the parties if the contract was concluded for an indefinite period;

c. and *d.* require further discussion.

a. Immediate termination for just cause

Either party may invoke a just cause to terminate the contract immediately (i.e. without notice). A 'just cause' is a fault so serious that further cooperation is rendered impossible. The burden of proof is on the party invoking it, and, in case of dispute, the judge alone will rule whether the reason invoked in fact constitutes a just cause.
Not surprisingly there is extensive and very detailed case-law on this question. Interesting problems are raised in cases where a unilateral modification of essential working conditions by the employer is invoked as a just cause for immediate termination of the contract by the employee.
The law strictly regulates termination for cause i.e. (i) it is void if the reason invoked has been known for more than 3 working days to the party who wishes to invoke it; and (ii) the reason must be notified by registered mail within 3 working days of the termination (and within 3 working days of the time the reason becomes known).

b. Termination through the service of notice

Either party can terminate a labour contract of unlimited duration by serving notice on the other party. Unless the law exceptionally and specifically so rules, it is not necessary to give reasons for the termination. But strict formalities and minimum periods of notice apply.

Formalities

The other party must be served with a letter stating the beginning and duration of the period of notice; notification by way of a writ served by a process server or a registered letter is also possible.
For manual workers the period of notice starts on the Monday following notice; for non-manual workers on the first day of the month following notice.

The period of notice

For manual workers this period is 28 days if the employer serves the notice and 14 days if the worker does so. These periods are doubled for workers who have been with the same enterprise, (considered as an economic unit) for more than 20 years.
For some categories of manual workers special periods have been fixed by Royal Decree.

– For non-manual workers with a maximum annual salary of 250,000 BF.

The minimum period of notice to be observed by the employer is 3 months for a worker with less than 5 years' service in the enterprise. This period is increased by 3 months for each additional period of 5 years' service.

> Example: a non-manual worker with 21 years' service and an annual salary of less than 250,000 BF. must have a minimum period of notice of 12 months.

If the employee gives notice then the period is reduced to half the time applicable to the employer, buth with a maximum of 3 months.

– For non-manual workers with a minimum annual salary of 250,000 BF.

The period can be agreed by both parties after the termination notice but not before. In the absence of an amicable settlement the employer must fix the period of notice, but at the risk of having it disputed by the employee. In such circumstances he will refer the case to the Labour Court which will then establish a reasonable period of notice.
The law imposes two limitations on the contractual freedom of the parties:
a. the legally fixed periods of notice for non-manual workers with an annual pay of maximum 250,000 BF. are minimum requirements;
b. if a non-manual worker serves the notice, the period of notice may not exceed $4\frac{1}{2}$ months if the annual pay is less than 500,000 BF. and 6 months if the annual salary is higher.
These regulations regularly lead to disputes, mainly because parties with such contradictory interests cannot easily reach an amicable settlement, but also because the law provides no specific rules for determining a reasonable period of notice for this category of non-manual workers.
In case of dispute, the Court will base its ruling on a combination of several criteria in order to determine a reasonable period. Such criteria are: job security (very important), salary and other benefits, seniority, the nature and level of responsibility, and the difficulty of finding a similar job on the labour market. The period of notice is often an expression of the manner and faithfulness with which a non-manual worker has served the enterprise.
Middle and senior managers generally receive substantial periods of notice (up to $3\frac{1}{2}$ years) from the Court.
An exception concerns non-manual workers reaching the normal retirement age (65 years for men, 60 years for women). Notice can be legally served on such people with a period of 3 months if their seniority in the enterprise is less than 5 years and 6 months if their seniority is higher. If the workers serve notice, these periods are halved.
Non-manual workers on whom notice has been served may terminate the contract on short notice during the period of notice by means of a *counter-notice* and on the condition that they have found another job.

The short period of notice lasts between 1 and 6 months, depending on the annual pay of the dismissed employee who serves the counter-notice.

General

It occurs that high level non-manual workers regularly disagree with the period of notice unilaterally fixed by their employer. If no agreement can be reached, the employer, as already mentioned, is forced to state what he considers it a reasonable period. If the employee rejects the employer's offer, the case will be referred to the court.
Senior managers are particularly tempted to take such disputes to court.
If the judge supports the employee he will determine a reasonable period and compensation equal to the current salary for that period that exceeds the period served by the employer. The right to such compensation is normal since the agreement is automatically terminated as soon as the notice has been served by the employer and the employee is released from any further work. The remaining part of the period of notice fixed by the judge must be compensated in money.
As a rule the periods of notice for high level employees in Belgium exceed those applicable in other EC countries. This partly compensates for the right to terminate employment contracts without motivation.

c. Special compensation

In some specific cases, employment contract law provides for special compensation, apart from the normal period of notice or compensation.

Special compensation for salesmen
Unless the employer proves that the termination of the contract is not to the detriment of the salesman, a dismissed salesman has a right to special compensation, i.e. the indemnity of eviction if he can prove that he has introduced new customers. Compensation is only due after 1 year of employment. It must be equal to 3 months pay for a salesman with 1 to 5 years seniority, and be increased by one month's pay for each additional five year period.

Special compensation for employees who are unfairly dismissed
If a manual worker is dismissed for reasons that do not relate to his capability or behaviour, or to economic or company interests, he can demand from the employer compensation for unfair dismissal calculated at at least 6 months' salary, unless a CLA provides another kind of compensation.

Special laws
Some special laws and Collective Labour Agreements provide for additional compensation e.g. to members of the Works Council, the safety committee, and trade union delegates and in the case of the closure of the enterprise or party thereof or of collective dismissals.

Closure of enterprises (Acts of June 28, 1966 and July 20, 1968)
Workers in a company with at least 20 workers are upon its closure, enti-

tled to normal and supplementary compensation, the latter being 2,494 BF. per year of employment with that enterprise up to a maximum of 49,880 BF. as well as 2,494 BF. for each year that the worker is older than 45 years, also to a maximum of 49,880 BF.
This compensation is paid by the employer, or if he does not do so, by a special fund which afterwards reclaims the amount from him. This fund may also pay the normal notice compensation, with right to subrogation, if the employer fails to pay it.
The fund is also authorized to decide which cases are equated with the closure of an enterprise.

d. Collective dismissals

This material is regulated by a series of interprofessional agreements concluded by the National Labour Council.
When an enterprise with at least 20 workers dismisses at least 10% of its personnel (with a minimum of 6), for economic or technical reasons, within a period of 60 days the dismissed workers are entitled to special compensation. Over a period of 4 months the employer must pay compensation equal to half the difference between their (maximum) salary and the employment compensation or the wage they would receive from a new employer.
However, if they receive a normal term of notice or compensation of more than 3 months' salary then the period of 4 months is reduced to the part of the term of notice (over 3 months). If the collective dismissal coincides with a closure of the enterprise, then the first compensation is cancelled.
Before a collective dismissal or closure of an enterprise, the employer must inform and seek advice from the head of the Works Council, the union delegation or the representative of the workers. Certain government authorities must also be informed.
Breach of an employment contract of unlimited duration without notice by the employer will entitle the employee to compensation based on the wage corresponding to the normal period of notice. Breach of an employment contract of limited duration or for specific work before expiration or completion of the work requires compensation equal to the wage due until the expiration or completion, but must not be in excess of twice the amount payable if the contract had been for unlimited duration.

e. Rights and obligations of the parties during the period of notice

During this period the contract remains in effect, thus the dismissed employee continues to work to the last day of the period and the employer must strictly observe the terms at the risk of breaching the contract.
For management personnel it often happens that, for psychological reasons, and by mutual agreement the employer pays the dismissed employee an amount equal to the salary he would have received during the normal period of notice. The contract is then terminated forthwith and each party is released from its obligations.
During the period of notice the dismissed employee may, on the conditions provided by law, leave his workplace to look for a new job while retaining his wage.

If an employee signs a receipt for the balance of his account when the period of notice ends or the agreement is broken it does not mean that he waives his rights; he is still able to claim, in court, additional compensation calculated for the normal period of notice.

f. Provisions of the employment contract that remain in effect after its termination

The principal provision which remains in effect is the covenant of non-competition. Such covenants which undoubtedly limit the freedom of employees are strictly regulated by law.
These covenants must always be laid down in writing and are:
1. considered inapplicable to employees with an annual salary of less than 250,000 BF.;
2. applicable to employees with an annual salary between 250,000 BF. and 500,000 BF., but only for jobs covered by a CLA or an agreement between the employer and the representative trade unions;
3. applicable to all employees with an annual pay higher than 500,000 BF., unless they are explicitly excluded by CLA or another agreement.

Moreover, the covenant is only valid under the following strict conditions. It must:
a. relate to similar activities;
b. be limited geographically to locations where competition is possible (effective only within Belgium);
c. be effective for no longer than 12 months.

The employer must be able to prove that the former employee can damage the enterprise by using the commercial or industrial knowledge that he has acquired for himself or for a competitor.
A covenant of non-competition should require the employer to pay a single lump sum as compensation, unless he renounces the application of the covenant within 15 days of the termination of the contract.
For manual workers this compensation is fixed by the Law of 1978; for non-manual workers it is fixed by the CLA nr. 1 bis.
The Law of 1978 further specifies that the covenant of non-competition is not effective if the contract is terminated:
- during the probation period; or
- by the employer without just cause; or
- in the case of resignation of the employee for just cause.

However, the law allows certain exceptions if they are provided by a National Labour Council CLA and when the enterprise concerned meets one of the following conditions:
a. it has an international field of activity or important economic, technical or financial interests in the international market;
b. it operates a research department.

Such exceptions only apply to non-manual workers who, through their position, have acquired knowledge that would be harmful if used outside the enterprise.
The exceptions are fixed by National Labour Council CLA nr. 1 of February 12, 1970 as amended by CLA nr. 1 bis of December 21, 1978 and provide

1. that for the aforesaid category of non-manual workers all exceptions to the covenants of non-competition are determined by an industry-wide CLA or in the absence thereof, either the level of the enterprise or by individual agreement. The Law of 1978 allows exceptions relating to the territory and term of the covenant;
2. that in contrast to the law, the covenant will take effect if the employer dismisses the worker. If the dismissal is given during the probation period, the covenant of non-competition will only be effective for a period equal to the time during which the employee has been in the enterprise;
3. that the compensation which the employer must pay under the terms of the covenant must be fixed by mutual agreement. This compensation will depend on the following elements: the nature of activities, term and territory in which the covenant is applicable and the salary. However, the minimum compensation is half the gross salary payable during the term of the covenant;
4. that a Commission of Good Services will be established, which, at the request of the employer and employee involved, may give advice as to whether the exceptions to the covenant are within the Law and the aforesaid CLA. This commission can only advise, thus the normal powers of the Labour Courts remain unaffected in case of dispute. So far this commission has rarely been called upon to intervene.

7. THE RIGHTS OF EMPLOYEES IN CASE OF A CHANGE OF OWNERSHIP OF THE UNDERTAKING

On February 14, 1977 the Council of Ministers of the EC issued a directive urging the member states to adapt their national legislation to preserve workers' rights in case of changes of ownership of enterprises.
In Belgium this has been regulated by the National Labour Council CLA nr. 32 of February 28, 1978.
The following regulations are currently in effect:

1. The rights of the employees are guaranteed in all cases of change of ownership (e.g. change of legal status, transfer, merger, takeover; but not in the case of concentration or restructuring which does not lead to a change of employer).
2. The rights and obligations effective at the moment of transfer are passed on to the new owner. The employee keeps aal rights resulting from employment contracts, except rights to complementary systems of social security unless these were fixed by CLA or law.
3. The change of ownership does not constitute a reason for dismissal for either the former or the new employer.
4. The workers changing employer may, however, be dismissed for urgent reasons or for economic, technical or organizational reasons leading to changes in employment conditions.
5. If the employment contract is terminated because the change in ownership is to the disadvantage of the employee, then the contract is considered to be terminated by the employer. This entitles the employee to compensation. This provision is particularly applicable to senior and topmanagers whose situation often becomes unfavourable because of reorganization at the time of a change in ownership.

8. DISPUTES ARISING FROM EMPLOYMENT CONTRACTS

Disputes arising from individual employment contracts can only be submitted to the Labour Courts and appealed in the Labour Court of Appeal. These Labour Courts consist of a professional judge, and laymen designated in equal numbers by the representative professional organizations of employers and employees. These Courts are considered to be able to make a pronouncement in labour disputes in a better and more expert way than conventional courts. Adapted rules govern the proceedings.

B. Organizational Aspects

1. TRADE UNIONS

The rise of the Belgian trade unions has been very rapid. From small, ineffective unions they have turned into powerful pressure groups, especially since World War II. They have succeeded in improving their position in Belgian economic, social and political life. A characteristic feature of these unions is their adherence to certain religious or ideological principles. They also give their sympathy and support to the political parties that hold similar views.

The trade unions are not organized on an occupational or craft basis, but rather by type of industry.

The main trade unions are also split up into separate organizations for manual and non-manual workers, irrespective of the company that they work for.

Manual workers are usually organized into local groups by branches of industry. The non-manual workers are grouped, irrespective of the branch of industry, in trade unions with proper structures. Both the local groups and the trade unions for non-manual workers are coordinated on a national level. It is the national trade unions which, as a rule, are involved in overall economic and social policy-making. These policies come about either through direct discussion and decision-making, or through national committees on which they have permanent representatives. Although the creation of trade unions is entirely free, the government recognizes only a few of them as being representative on the basis of their influence and authority. The law provides no clear criteria for being recognized as representative. The representative trade unions possess a virtual monopoly on social consultation in its widest sense. About 70% of all Belgian workers are unionized and most of them belong to one of the following representative trade unions:

1. ACV-CSC (Confederation of Christian Trade Unions) with approximately 1,300,000 members (1979). This trade union is based on Christian principles and is closely related to the Christian Democratic Parties.
2. ABVV-FGTB (Belgian General Federation of Labour) with a slightly lower number of members than ACV-CSC is based on a pronounced socialist ideology and in principle supports the policies of the Belgian Socialist Parties.
3. ACLVB-CGSLB (Federation of Liberal Unions of Belgium) has approximately 200,000 members and is closely related to the Belgian Liberal Parties.

In Belgium, leading personnel including senior and middle managers are considered to be non-manual workers. Unions for these employees are of the classic type and link non-manual workers from all industries.
It must be said that unionization among management personnel is not very high. However, a growing number of them are becoming members of a trade union specifically for management personnel. So far this union has not been accepted as representative, which in practice severely limits its impact on collective labour relations.
Employers also have an organization, in this case the VBO-FEB (Federation of Belgian Industries). It is composed of a number of smaller organizations that group employers by industry e.g. Fabrimetal, the organization of the metal-working industry.
This federation is recognized as the representative organization of employers. Strongly centralized and structured, the VBO-FEB practically has a monopoly on all Belgian industry.
Small and medium-sized enterprises and agricultural enterprises also have their own organizations which have influence in proportion to their relative importance.

2. BUSINESS ORGANIZATION

Through their representative organizations, employers and employees influence a number of institutional boards and committees. Here they defend, on an equal basis, their social and economic interests. Such committees can be found at national, industry, and company levels. The agreements concluded there may be interprofessional (national level) or purely professional (other levels). If the situation requires, the government may bring together the representative organizations to support certain policies or even to develop solutions. This cooperation may lead to a social programme in the mid-term or to far-reaching economic decisions, for example the restructuring of certain branches of business, implementation of an active employment policy or government initiatives. As a rule, all social policy is the result of such consultations.
Cooperation between these representative organizations and the government is necessary because it is impossible for one party to act without the consent of the others. It is evident that this consultation machinery must be very intricate and subtle. It is often based on a shaky equilibrium which is easily unbalanced in times of crisis.
The chart below shows the responsibilities entrusted by law to the councils and committees.

	Economic matters	*Social matters*
Nationally	Central Economic Council	National Economic Council
By branch of industry	Industrial Councils	Joint Committees
By company	Works Council	Works Council

3. THE SYSTEM OF COLLECTIVE BARGAINING

1. Collective Labour Agreements (CLA's) can only relate to matters that are not legally regulated or which can be further developed only when the law sets minimum norms.
Here we should note that there are extensive laws governing individual and collective labour and social security problems in Belgium. The strong presence of trade-union-oriented members of parliament is not unrelated to this. Also the cabinet has a substantial number of trade-union-supported members. Certain matters such as wages and working conditions are, in principle, left to the social partners.
2. There are no fixed rules of procedure for collective bargaining. As a rule, proposals are advanced by trade union delegations at the industry level. These proposals are then forwarded to the national trade union. After amendment (if any), the proposals are sent to the joint committees i.e. industry-wide bodies composed on a parity basis. Proposals developed there are usually submitted to the members for ratification.
3. Although the CLA's are made formally in the National Labour Council and particularly in the joint committees, there is a growing trend towards single company agreements. In flourishing companies which are strongly unionized the CLA concluded on an industry-wide level is used as a basic agreement and is developed further in the company itself.
4. As a rule the CLA's are supported by at least the two most important representative national trade unions. Although strongly competitive, these two trade unions usually try to stand together.
5. There are different CLA's for manual and non-manual workers. The structures of the negotiating bodies also reflect this distinction. Supervisory and senior management personnel are usually not involved in the collective bargaining process; the low level of unionization in this group partly explains this practice.
6. The legal status of the CLA's and the joint committees entrusted with the negotiation and conclusion of such agreements are regulated by the Act of December 5, 1968. Apart from formal provisions regulating the conclusion of CLA's, the Act also confirms the monopoly of the representative unions, defines the composition and power of the joint committees, and determines the scope of the CLA's.
The contents of the CLA's are legally subdivided into two parts: the normative regulations, which determine the content of the individual and collective agreements between employees and employers and the obligatory regulations which impose obligations on the contracting parties (trade unions and employers or their associations). There is an important legal regulation that, by Royal Decree, agreements concluded in a joint committee can be rendered generally binding if one of the organizations represented on it so demands. This makes the CLA binding for all employees within its scope and who are under the jurisdiction of the joint committee. Violations of the provisions of the CLA's will be penalized. This is extremely important since a CLA that has not been rendered generally binding will only apply to those employers who either personally signed the CLA or who are members of the organizations which committed themselves to it.

Hence, in the hierarchy of labour relation agreements, generally binding CLA's follow next after the law itself; next come the not generally binding CLA's, whereby the employer is involved because of his membership of the organization that signed the agreement, and finally the individually written labour agreement. This order is sustained by law and clearly emphasizes the importance of the CLA in Belgian labour law.

7. A party to a CLA can only be forced to pay a penalty for violating it if this is explicitly stated in the CLA. In practice, such terms do not exist.

8. If a company is partly or fully taken over, the new employer must respect the agreement binding the former employer until it expires.

9. In general all collective disputes, including those arising from the provisions of a CLA or the negotiations for concluding or reviewing it do not fall under the jurisdiction of the Labour Court. Conciliation and mediation are organized either by the joint committees, the government, or lower ranking government bodies. A department of the Ministry of Employment and Labour can place a team of specialized social mediators at the disposal of the parties involved in the dispute.

Violations of the normative regulations of a CLA can be brought before the Labour Court by the employees or their trade unions.

C. The Works Council

1. GENERAL

During the difficult years of the reconstruction of the Belgian economy after World War II, the idea arose to set up a cooperative body at enterprise level to confront employer and employee interests in a peaceful way. In 1948 the Act on Economic Organization created the Works Council. It has undoubtedly substantially influenced Belgian social history although its workings and achievements have often been questioned.

However, one must admit that the results, good or bad, obtained through Works Councils strongly depend on the general social and economic climate in the enterprise, the spirit of cooperation between management and trade unions, and the honesty with which they respect the rules of the game.

On the other hand, it has been found that in the course of the years, since the basic Act of 1948, the status and powers of the Council have undergone basic changes under the impact of the legislator, the government or the social partners concluding national Collective Labour Agreements. This evolution is still continuing be it in a rather radical direction.

2. CREATION

In principle, the Act of 1948 provides for the creation of Works Councils in enterprises employing 50 or more people as the Executive may direct. In practice the Executive had to moderate this principle.

1. Compared with the original 200 (later 150), today Works Councils are

compulsory in enterprises employing 100 people or in enterprises with at least 50 workers if after the preceding elections a Council was set up or re-elected (R.D.October 11, 1978).
2. The term 'enterprise' does not refer to the legal entity, but to the technical entity of exploitation. This entity is specified on the basis of economic and social criteria, the latter prevailing. Hence, the existence of social autonomy will suffice for determining a technical entity of exploitation, even though there is no economic or technical autonomy (ruling of the Supreme Court October 22, 1979).

Enterprises which, as legal entities, employ at least 100 employees, irrespective of the number of workers employed in the different plants, are subject to the same regulations.

The Act also provides for presumptions that different legal entities are considered as one technical unit unless there is evidence to the contrary. Hence, a technical unit may comprise several legal entities (the reverse also is possible).

This greater rigidity in the practical application of the principle as carried through since 1978 aims at neutralizing various schemes to circumvent the obligation to set up a Works Council. It is also supported by the Courts.

The Act also regulates the continuity of Works Councils set up in enterprises that were subject to transfer, split-up, merger or takeover.

3. COMPOSITION

The Works Council is composed on a parity basis of, on the one hand, the employer and his representatives, and on the other hand, representatives of the employees who are elected for four-year terms. The election procedure is regulated in great detail.

The initiative for setting up a Works Council must emanate from the head of the enterprise. The actual elaboration is the responsibility of the trade unions which are free to organize elections.

In case of a positive decision, the unions start looking for candidates. Lists reflecting the quantitative proportion between manual and non-manual workers as reliably as possible are prepared by the representative unions.

Managerial personnel cannot vote or be elected. This category includes people entrusted with the daily management of the enterprise as well as their subordinates having supervisory functions. The nature of the job is decisive (responsibility, delegation of power, cooperation with senior management, etc.).

The management designates its representatives unilaterally. At each social election this designation leads to serious disputes, i.e. the trade unions consider this an attack on employee solidarity. However, the Courts still make a clear distinction between dream and reality.

4. POWERS

As stated above, according to the Act of 1948 Works Councils should form a bridge between the opposed interests of labour and capital; cooperation must

prevail over conflict. Therefore, the Council needed specific powers which, on the basis of equality between employer and employees, must make such co-operation possible. In principle, senior management stays in charge of decision and policy making. However, there has been a tendency to expand the powers of the Works Council both qualitatively and quantitatively.
The strongest emphasis has been placed on the informative and advisory roles and the areas where there is a certain right of joint decision remain fairly small. The Council only has decisive power in purely social matters (social services, etc.).

a. Information

Although in 1948 the informative powers of the Works Council were strongly emphasized by law, management was reluctant to pass them on entirely to the Council. As a result of the social conflicts of the 60s and 70s the government and the social partners redefined the said powers and organized the information flow more efficiently.
1. A CLA concluded at the NLC (March 9, 1972, nr. 9) granted the Council access to comprehensive information on employment issues relating to the enterprise (prospects, recruitment, lay-off policy, etc.).
2. Various Royal Decrees realized the right to information on economic and financial issues relating to the enterprise:
- R.D. of September 25, 1972 whereby state-subsidized enterprises are forced to inform the Council of the modalities and employment of the subsidies;
- R.D. of November 27, 1973 on economic and financial information.

This very comprehensive regulation intends to bring about a horizontal and vertical examination of the enterprise and possibly also of the economic or legal entity to which it belongs.
The information to be supplied is split up into four sections:

(i) Basic information:

All fundamental data on the legal, economic and financial structure of the enterprise. Whenever a new Council is elected this basic document is transferred to the members and clarified and discussed wherever necessary. Regular adjustments must be made.
This information must be formalized according to the criteria clearly specified by law:
- status of the enterprise and, if relevant, of the legal, economic, or financial entity of which it is a component;
- competitive market position of the enterprise or of the legal entity;
- production and productivity;
- financial structure, budgeting method, and cost price calculation either by product or by component;
- personnel costs (global by category);
- programme and general prospects;
- government subsidies (nature, amount, and destination);
- organization chart of the legal, economic and financial entity of which it is a component.

(ii) Annual information

This information is supplied to the Council in writing and covers the situation and evolution of the enterprise during the past year and states the objectives for the next year. It comprises at least one copy of the balance sheet, the profit and loss account, the annual survey, and the report from the company's auditor(s). The management is expected to clarify this report according to legal criteria.

(iii) Periodic information

This information is to be supplied quarterly. It should draw an accurate picture of the evolution of the enterprise, turnover, order-book, cost price calculation, etc.

(iv) Occasional information

This kind of information is to be supplied whenever events occur which may profoundly affect company life or whenever internal decisions of substantial impact are contemplated (transfer, merger, concentration, closure, etc.).

- The law explicitly provides for the possibility of exceptions to the obligation to supply information on certain issues if this would be harmful to the interests of the enterprise.
  The matter must be settled by an official of the Ministry of Economic Affairs. Both the request and the decision must be motivated.
- The information supplied may be the subject of extensive discussions and criticism in the Council. The management must answer any questions or rebut any criticism raised.
- The Council members may involve external experts in certain activities of the Council, either to receive additional technical information or advice or to have additional examinations conducted. Rejections are possible, but only in limited cases. If there is a continuing dispute about the expert, the matter can be submitted to the official of the Ministry of Economic Affairs.
- Violations of the aforementioned regulations must be referred to the Courts.

b. Right of Co-decision

There is a limited right of joint decision in the following matters:

- setting and changing internal working rules;
- defining the general criteria for rehiring or dismissing workers; however, the employer keeps the right to decide on individual dismissals or hirings;
- fixing the dates of the collective holiday periods;
- managing social works in the enterprise unless this is the exclusive right of the employees;
- moving legal holidays.

c. Advisory Task

The Works Council has the right to offer preliminary advice on a whole series of important decisions falling under the exclusive authority of management. The decision contemplated will therefore be communicated to the Council, after which it may or may not offer advice which the management may or may not take.

Legally, the advice cannot prevent the management from making a decision. This right of advice relates to training problems, personnel policy, labour organization (technical organization included), changes to the legal or economic structures of the company (closure, merger, concentration, takeover, etc.). The Council can also offer advice on the general criteria for recruiting employees. This does not mean on each specific case of hiring an employee which is the exclusive right of the employer, but on the general criteria of recruitment (professional skill, age bracket, categories, etc.).

d. Control Task

The Council supervises the implementation of any measure affecting company interests, both on the social level and on that of the criteria for determining professional qualification levels, and also on the application of labour law. In case of violation, it can inform the competent labour inspection authorities.

5. PROCEDURE OF THE COUNCIL

The Council is convened every month by the management to meet on its agenda during working hours. However, a request by 50% of the employee representatives can also convene the Council. The proceedings are formal (minutes, etc.). Reports of the meetings are distributed among the personnel.

Voting in the Council must be unanimous. The members must observe professional secrecy about the proceedings.

6. SPECIAL PROTECTION OF WORKER REPRESENTATIVES

In conformity with the rules fixed by the ILO, worker representatives on Works Councils enjoy special protection against dismissal, change of work station or working conditions, or any form of discrimination. This protection covers candidates for membership and elected members.

Basically, the protection covers dismissal unless such dismissal is based on economic or technical reasons preliminarily recognized by the competent joint committee.

The protection period for elected Council members or first-time candidates extends from 30 days before the publication of the elections to the day on which they are succeeded by the newly elected members who take office (as a rule 4 years). The protection period for non re-elected candidates or for second-time candidates extends from the same starting day as above until two years after the result of the elections.

An unlawful dismissal gives the person concerned the right to be re-integrated in the enterprise. If the employer refuses, he must pay, apart from the normal dismissal compensation, an amount equal to the current salary corresponding to a period of 2 years if the employee has less than 10 years' service, 3 years for between 10 and 20 years, and 4 years for more than 20 years' service.
Dismissing worker representatives often creates unrest in the enterprise. Such conflicts are usually hard to settle.

7. TRENDS

Both intrinsically and as far as actual results are concerned the Works Council remains an important issue.
Moreover, certain unions oppose the legal parity structure in the light of the factual, psychological and professional inequality between worker representatives and management.
Ideologically, there also is doubt about the cooperation principle because of the fundamental conflict of interest between labour and capital. In this respect, cooperation with the neo-capitalist system is looked on as an abnegation of the socialist view of society.
This opinion prevails mainly in socialist trade-unions. These unions consistently shift the emphasis from co-determination to growing powers of information and control with eventually a possible veto on the employer's decision.
The Christian Trade Unions advocate the replacement of the present parity Works Council by an autonomous worker council.
Apart from greater decision-making powers in some matters, a more extensive informative and advisory task would greatly influence management. Much attention is also paid to work consultation (influencing labour organization). These very schematic reform proposals will undoubtedly play a role in the future evolution of the Belgian Works Councils.

8. UNION DELEGATION

Following a national CLA concluded in 1971, the employers recognize that employees affiliated to a trade union are represented by a union delegation. Its members are appointed or elected among the employees. Among others, the powers of the union delegation relate to:

1. labour relations;
2. CLA negotiations or company-level agreements which do not affect CLA's on other levels (industry or nation-wide);
3. the application of labour legislation, CLA's, working regulations, and individual employment contracts in the enterprise;
4. safeguarding the general principles for establishing these delegations: respect for the legitimate company authorities, promotion of parity relations, reconciliation, appointment of skilled and competent members.

This basic agreement was further elaborated for each specific industry by means of special CLA's. Dozens of detailed CLA's were concluded whereby the powers of the union delegation, its creation and composition, and the

conditions of fulfilling mandates, were expounded in great detail.
Considering the high degree of unionization among Belgian employees, the importance of this institution need not be stressed.
Union delegates are specially protected against discriminatory treatment by the employer (i.e. against arbitrary dismissal). Any decisions for dismissal must be discussed in advance with the union delegation and the trade union to which the delegate belongs.
If this procedure is not observed or if the Court considers the dismissal illegal, the employee will be entitled to a lump sum compensation of one year's gross salary in addition to the normal dismissal compensation.
The discharge of a union delegate very often is the cause of intense social conflicts in the enterprise.
In spite of the principles governing the working of the union delegations set out in the basic agreement of 1971, this body has grown to a great extent into a combative and strongly critical body. In some critical situations, it has taken an independent course, without the approval or cooperation of its union. This obviously brought the unions into difficult situations.
The union delegation undoubtedly fulfils an active and militant role in social difficulties. Strongly associated with the employees, it concentrates most efficiently the opposition to the employer's authority. The real division of power between employer and trade union is more than ever checked by the union delegation. Therefore, it should be no surprise that certain progressive groups in the trade unions want to turn the delegation into a spearhead in the attack on the capitalistic structure of the enterprise.
To some militants the delegation represents the strongest trade union weapon in the enterprise, particularly from the point of view of ideology.
The current, clearly critical evolution in the attitude of the union delegations towards labour relations on company level will undoubtedly affect the social climate in Belgium.

D. Co-determination

The Belgian concept of co-determination requires some clarification.
a. First it must be emphasized that the participation of *worker* and *employer associations* on national level and also industry-wide is very intense. Nationally, these organizations participate in general economic and social policy-making through institutional parity bodies where they have a consultative and advisory voice. We can refer to the Central Economic Council and the National Labour Council. Moreover, in Belgium there is a system of tripartite consultations involving Government and these organizations, e.g. through the National Committee for Economic Expansion. Occasionally, national conferences are held between the same bodies whenever economic or social situations so require. On the industry level, policy-making is also determined by employer and worker organizations through specific committees e.g. audit committees in the public utility sectors, the steel industry and the oil industry. Finally, informal 'ad hoc' tripartite meetings often precede important economic or social government decisions.

b. The participation of the employer and worker associations is most clearly visible at industrial level through joint committees on which collective bargaining prevails.
c. On company level, the same organizations have acquired specific powers in the Works Council. The trade unions have done so more specifically through the union delegation. As a rule, these bodies possess strong advisory, consultative, and informative powers, but formally, they stay *outside* company management.
If we consider participation as direct participation of the workers in the management of the enterprise, then we must admit that today Belgium has no regulations which make such participation possible.
Therefore in companies:
1. the employees do not sit on the managing bodies and, unless so elected by the shareholders, do not have access to the Board of Directors which is charged with decision-making and daily management. Nor are they, as a rule, members of the General Meeting of shareholders;
2. the Works Council and union delegation do not *formally* possess decision-making powers in corporate policy. But the law does grant them a far-reaching controlling function so that the employees can informally and by way of pressure influence corporate policy, if not determine it. But, they have no responsibility at all in decision-making which is the exclusive right of the Board of Directors and the General Meeting;
3. collective bargaining, in all its forms, remains the most adequate means for employees to ensure their objectives individually and collectively. However CLA's do not lead to participation in the direct management of the enterprise. This remains the prerogative of management.

Evolution
As in many European countries, Belgium is currently faced with the problem of worker participation in company management. Opinions among trade unions are strongly divided, whereas the employees adopt reticent attitudes. The government initiatives are not convincing because of the lack of consensus among the social partners. The evolution can be summarized as follows:
1. A trend to strengthen the strict application of the regulations for economic and financial information.
2. The Christian Trade Union wants to turn the Works Council from a parity body into an exclusive worker committee (worker council) with the right to joint decision in certain economic and financial issues that so far have been the exclusive territory of management.
3. Worker participation in the managing structures of the company remains an open point of discussion among the unions. On the one hand, the Socialist Trade Unions reject any form of co-management or cooperation by workers on the German Mitbestimmung model. For ideological reasons these unions stick to the strategy of worker control whereby they do not assume management responsibility. But, on the other hand, on the basis of good information they try to influence on decision-making in order to safeguard their direct interests. Any form of joint responsibility in corporate management is radically rejected.
   The Christian Trade Union as of 1980 is not against the reform of com-

pany law to split the present unitary Board of Directors into a managing board and a supervisory board. The latter would be tripartite: $\frac{1}{3}$ shareholders, $\frac{1}{3}$ elected by employees and $\frac{1}{3}$ coopted by the first two groups (representation of 'general interest'). According to this trade union, the group of employees would never be in a minority position to the suppliers of capital. The supervisory board would:
(1) give preliminary approval to all important decisions;
(2) exert general control on the management;
(3) appoint and discharge the management.
Hence, this trend is in principle in favour of legally organized participation in the formal supervisory body.

4. The Government adopts a wait and see attitude.
If the EC Council of Ministers approve the fifth directive which proposes worker representation on corporate management level, this would necessarily lead to concrete initiatives by parliament and government. However, the approval of this EC directive is deadlocked.

E. *Residence and Work Permits for Aliens*

Two sets of rules govern this matter: first the public law rules governing access to and residence and establishment in Belgian territory by aliens, and, secondly, the labour law rules regulating applications for work, employment, the supply of services, trading and industrial activities.
These two sets of rules are separate. Public law rules are mainly based on public policy, whereas employment law is chiefly based on socio-economic factors, such as the internal situation of the labour market, the economic situation, the views of trade unions, etc.
Employment law is characterized by flexibility; the government will tighten or relax its provisions according to socio-economic conditions in the country. This area is mainly governed by the commitments undertaken by Belgium in international agreements. Hence, a distinction must be made between EC nationals and nationals of other countries.

1. EC NATIONALS

– The EC Treaty (artt. 48 to 51) and the regulations and directives under it provide for the free circulation within the EC of nationals of Member States wishing to take up employment.
Therefore, any EC national has the personal right to enter and reside in the territory of any Member State in order to apply for and to perform work as an employee.
Only very specific exceptions (public order and security, public health) restrict this right. The case-law of the European Court of Justice gives wide scope to its exercise. There is no discrimination whatsoever between the nationals of the country of employment and those of other Member States.
– The Treaty (artt. 52 to 66) also guarantees to self-employed persons the

right of residence and the right to supply services under the same conditions as those applying to nationals.
The implementation of this principle is proceeding more gradually than has been the case for employees.
It is for the EC authorities to lay down the necessary rules for each economic activity or independent profession.
The supply of services in trade and industry has now been regulated for substantially the whole territory of the Community.
As a rule, the right may be freely exercised subject to the restrictions imposed on the nationals of the Member State in question.
Regulations governing the practice of the free professions, however, apply to the whole territory of the Community. EC regulations are already in force for certain professions (e.g. doctors), and are being prepared for others.

2. OTHERS

– *Employees*: their employment is governed by the Act on Foreign Labour of July 20, 1967. This is a strict Act which eases or restricts the right of entry depending upon the situation on the Belgian labour market (e.g. the unemployment rate).
The Act is based on a system of preliminary licences which must be applied for by the employer (work permits) and by the employee (employment card) from the Ministry of Employment and Labour.
Depending on their duration and the nature of the work, three types of employment cards are issued:
Type B: work with a named employer or in a named branch of industry; maximum duration: 1 year.
Type C: applies to skilled trades in which services are not normally used by one employer only; maximum duration: 1 year.
Type A: applies to all paid labour and is of unlimited duration. This card can be obtained by foreign workers who have worked in Belgium on a regular basis and have resided in Belgium without interruption for between 3 and 5 years. Close relatives of Card A holders are also eligible for Card A.
These cards are only issued to nationals of countries with which Belgium has concluded international labour agreements or treaties. Since 1974 there has been a halt on immigration into Belgium.
However, the relevant Minister has power to accede to requests for permission to work for the following categories of foreigners:
- persons exercising management functions in a subsidiary of a foreign company;
- specialists in professions which require special skills not possessed by nationals;
- highly skilled personnel.

Irrespective of the situation on the Belgian labour market, such people will almost certainly receive an employment card, even if they are nationals of a country with which Belgium has concluded no international labour agreement or treaty.

– *The exercise by non-EEC nationals of self-employed work in Belgium.* This requires a personal professional card issued by the Ministry for the Middle Classes. The card contains a precise description of the trade or profession which may be practised and specifies the duration of the permit (maximum 5 years with the possibility of renewal, R.D. November 25, 1965).
International treaties may provide for exemption from the requirement of a professional card. For independent professional activities in certain small and medium-sized enterprises, the Act on Establishment (Act of December 15, 1970) provides for strict ability requirements to be met by Belgian and foreign applicants.

V. BIBLIOGRAPHY

Blanpain R., Belgium (Labour Law) International Encyclopaedia for Labour Law and Industrial Relations, 1979, vol. 2. Kluwer-Deventer.

Claeys Bouuaert, Ignace, Principes de l'imposition des sociétés en Belgiques (Larcier, Brussels, 1970).

Colens, a.o., Le contrat d'emploi, 1980. Larcier, Brussels.

European Taxation, Belgium, Kluwer-Deventer.

François L., Introduction au droit social, 1974, Liège.

Frédéricq L., Traité de droit commercial belge (Fecheyr, Gent, 1950).

Gregoire A., Manuel des Sociétés Anonymes, 2nd edition (Bruylant, Brussels, 1973).

Kirkpatrick John, L'imposition des revenus des sociétés belges par actions, et de leurs actionnaires, obligateires, et organes (Larcier, Brussels, 1968).

Lenaerts H., Dubois B., Leboucq E., Inleiding tot het Sociaal Recht, Story-Scientia, 1973, Gent.

Linard de Guertechin, Ch., L'impôt des personnes physiques, Larcier, Brussels, 1968.

Megret J., Louis J.-V., Vignes D., Waelbroeck M., Le droit de la CEE, t. VII Politique sociale, 1973, Brussels.

Megret J., a.o., Le droit de la CEE t. III, libre circulation des travailleurs. Etablissements et services. Capitaux et Transports, 1974, Brussels.

Raucq A., Sociétés Anonymes, 1972.

Ribas J.J., Jonczy M.J., Séché J.C.,, Traite de droit social Européen, 1978, PUF Paris.

Schnorr G., European Communities (Labour Law), International Encyclopaedia for Labour Law and Industrial Relations, 1980, vol I, Kluwer-Deventer.

Schreuder E., Les impôts sur les revenus (Bruylant, Brussels, 1957).

Tel Pierre, Le régime fiscal des filiales et succursales des sociétés étrangères – Droit belge et perspectives communautaires européennes (Bruylant, Brussels, 1973).

Tiberghien A., Manuel de droit fiscal, Brussels, (annual edition).

't Kint J., Ghyselinck R., Les Sociétés Anonymes, Guide Pratique, Brussels, 1975.

Tschoffen A., Lamalle A., Les sociétés de Personnes à Responsabilité Limitée, Brussels, 1980.
Van Houtte J., Traité des sociétés de personnes à responsabilité limitée, 3rd edition (Scientia, Ghent, 1962-1963), compl. 1967 (2 volumes).
Van Ryn J., Principes de droit commercial (Bruylant, Brussels, 1966).
Verstraete B., La réforme du code des impôts sur les revenus. Commentaire de la loi du 25 juin 1973 suivi de la coordination officieuse du code des impôts sur les revenus (Presses Universitaires de Namur – Larcier, 1975).
Zondervan R., Les impôts sur les revenus de l'extranéité (Pauwels, Brussels, 1967).

Denmark

Hans Lindegaard
Eskil Trolle

I. THE WHOLLY-OWNED ENTERPRISE

Foreign companies can conduct business in Denmark, by establishing or participating in different legal forms of undertakings which are similar to the undertakings in other European countries such as a Public Company, General Partnership, Private Company limited by shares, Limited Partnership, Joint Venture, etc. By far, the majority of foreign companies conducting business in Denmark have chosen to establish a public or a private limited company or a branch office. In this context we shall principally deal with companies and branches.

Danish legislation similar to the law of the other EEC countries, recognizes two types of companies, viz. Public Companies (aktieselskab, abbreviated A/S) and Private Limited Companies (anpartsselskab, abbreviated ApS).

With regard to company tax liability in Denmark there is generally no difference whether business is conducted through a branch or by establishment of a company, and the tax liability is equal for public and private limited companies. The choice whether the business form should be that of a branch or a company will therefore primarily depend on whether direct ownership and responsibility through a branch is more desirable than the more indirect ownership through a company, or whether possible capital investments are expected from another source. The decisive factor with regard to the choice between a branch and a company will often be the tax legislation in the country of the investor.

A. Branch

A Foreign company wishing to conduct business in Denmark through a branch office must be one legally existing in its own country of incorporation and must be a public company or a private company both according to the law of the country of incorporation and according to Danish law.

The activity to be performed by the branch must be included within the objects clause of the parent company. Any branch which is set up has to be registered with the Danish Register of Companies situated in Copenhagen. The branch has to be managed by one or more branch managers, who must reside in Denmark, unless the Minister of Industry grants dispensation from this rule. The registration with the Register of Companies has to be signed by the branch manager. The following documents should be attached to the registration form:

1. official evidence to the effect that the parent company is legally existing

in its country of incorporation e.g. a certified copy of the company's domestic registration documents;

2. a statement from the 'parent' company, signed by those entitled to bind the company, that the parent company undertakes to subject itself to Danish law and consent to jurisdiction of- and execution by Danish courts in all matters of law arising from the company's activities in Denmark;
3. original powers of attorney for the branch manager or duly certified copies of the same;
4. a copy of the company's statutes;
5. evidence that managers comply with the Company Act.

The Danish Registrar of Companies decides whether this documentation must be submitted in an authorized translation.

Registration of a branch involves the parent company in a duty to publish its own annual accounts. Not later than one month after approval, a certified copy of the annual accounts of the parent company has to be submitted to the Danish Register of Companies, endorsed by the company's auditor, or with his report. Further a separate report regarding the branch, and separate accounts of the branch, have to be filed with the Registrar of Companies. The public has access to this information in the Register of Companies.

Essential changes in the particulars registered for the parent company must also in principle be reported to the Danish Register of Companies.

The branch has to include the parent company's name in its own name with the addition of the designation 'branch office' and with a clear indication of the company's nationality. Letters and order forms have to state the company's name, its domicile and the registration number under which it is entered in the Register of Companies.

B. Subsidiary

A subsidiary can be established as a public company (aktieselskab, abbreviated A/S) which is comparable to the German 'Aktiengesellschaft' AG, and the French 'Société Anonyme' S.A., or a private company (anpartsselskab, abbreviated ApS) similar to the German 'Gesellschaft mit beschränkter Haftung' GmbH, and the French 'Société a responsabilité Limitée' SARL.

Since the rules governing the two types of companies are to a large extent identical, the term 'company' will be used to cover both. If the rules differ, this will be specifically stated.

1. FORMATION OF THE COMPANY

Upon the establishment of the company, the founders must draw up and sign a memorandum of association containing a draft of the statutes. The statutes must comply strictly with the provisions of The Companies Act. The number of founders must be at least three, for establishing an A/S (public company) whereas an ApS (private company) can be established by one founder.

A decision about the establishment of a public company is made at a statutory meeting. The establishment of a private company does not require any statutory meeting.

2. CAPITAL OF THE COMPANY

In Danish companies all the shares can be owned by one person. The share capital shall be at least D.kr. 100,000 for public companies and D.kr. 30,000 for private companies. At least 50% and at minimum D.kr. 100,000 or D.kr. 30,000 respectively, has to be paid up before registration, and the balance not later than one year after. The capital can be represented in cash or values other than cash.

If the company is being established by taking over an existing business, the profit and loss account and balance sheet of the business in question have to be presented when the deed of incorporation is signed. The accounts should relate to the two previous accounting years, or any shorter period during which business may have been carried on, as well as the profit and loss account and balance sheet for such of the current accounting year as may have elapsed prior to the take-over. Furthermore, an opening balance sheet for the company is required as well as a declaration stating that the financial circumstances of the business have not deteriorated in the period between the take-over and the establishment of the new business. This declaration is generally a statement from the new business's auditors, who will be elected at the new business' shareholders' meeting.

The Register of Companies does not make any actual assessment of the assets invested in the company, but the assets have to be of such a character that they are appropriate to form the basis for the company's activities with the objects it has registered.

Goodwill can be included in the assets to be taken over by the new company, but usually not in an amount larger than $1\frac{1}{2}$ times the average of the previous three years' net earnings. Knowhow, patent rights and sole agencies can further be part of the new company's capital.

3. SHARES AND VOTING RIGHTS

The main rule is that all shares have equal rights in the company. However, the statutes may lay down that there shall be different classes of shares with different rights. Each share in a public company has to carry a vote: if there are different classes of shares their voting powers can be increased, but not by more than ten times the voting power of any other share of the same denomination. In private companies there can be shares carrying no votes.

Share certificates may be registered in the name of the holder or issued to bearer. With regard to registered shares the statutes can limit the transferability of the shares. In private companies the company is not required to issue certificates as proof of the shares.

The company must keep a special register of shareholders who own 10% or more of the voting rights or 10% or more of the share capital in excess of D. kr. 100,000.–.

The register of shares must be accessible to public authorities, shareholders, board members, and a representative of the employees, if the latter is not represented on the board.
The company in general meeting can pass a resolution about the raising of loans against an issue of bonds or instruments of debt, which may later be converted into shares. The resolution passed by the company at the general meeting has to specify the loan terms and the rules for the conversion of the bonds.
The company can at a shareholder's meeting resolve to issue convertible bonds, or issue variable-rate interest-bearing notes, the amount of interest being dependent on the dividend with the company's shares yield or the year's profits.

4. BOARD OF DIRECTORS

The Danish company law is based on the two-tier-system. Public companies (A/S) must have a board of directors with a minimum of three members. If the share capital is less than D.kr. 400,000 the board can consist of one member only, but in that case a deputy director has to be elected. The board is elected by this company at a general meeting of shareholders.
In companies with an average staff of at least 50 during the last three years, the employees have a right (in addition to the board members elected by the company at the general meeting) to elect a number of board members corresponding to at least one half of the number elected by the shareholders and not less than 2 members. In case of an unequal number of board members, the number of board members to be elected by the employees is increased. With regard to groups of companies the board members to be elected by the employees of the parent company are to be elected by the employees from all employees in the group by indirect election.
Companies with a share capital of D.kr. 400,000 or more must have a board of management of at least three members. Private companies (ApS) with a capital of less than D.kr. 400,000 can dispense with a board, unless the employees have a claim to be represented on the board.
All general managers and one-half of the members of the board must have their permanent residence in Denmark, unless the Minister of Industry makes a special exception from this regulation, i.e. for EEC citizens.
Members of the board and the management have authority to sign for the company. The statutes may, however, lay down that the company can only be found by the signature of two or more such persons jointly. Further internal restrictions on authority cannot be binding against third parties.
Generally the fees of the board members are fixed by the company at a shareholders meeting, while the remuneration of general managers is usually fixed by the board of directors. Fees of board members may from time to time be limited by price laws on the profit margin.
The company's annual accounts, and in the case of parent companies consolidated accounts also, have to be signed by the board of directors and the management.
Under Danish law, as compared to the law of other European countries, board

members are less likely to be held liable for mismanagement of a company. It may be added that a company which is not registered cannot, as such, acquire any rights or contract obligations. As regards an obligation entered into on behalf of the company before registration, the persons who have undertaken the obligation are liable jointly and severally. On registration the company assumes responsibility in accordance with the company's contract after the statutory meeting.

5. GENERAL MEETING OF SHAREHOLDERS

The shareholders' direct influence is exercised at the shareholders general meeting of the company. Not later than six months after the end of each accounting year the company must meet in an ordinary general meeting of shareholders. Annual accounts and the auditor's report have to be submitted to the company at the general meeting. The annual accounts consist of a balance sheet, profit and loss account and annual report. A parent company must in addition submit the consolidated accounts. The company at an ordinary general meeting then resolves whether or not to adopt the profit and loss account and balance sheet and how to use the profit or cover the loss. Apart from that the company may make other resolutions which, subject to the statutes have to be decided by the company at a general meeting. Extraordinary general meetings are held when the board of directors, the auditors or shareholders owning one-tenth of the share capital so desire. Resolutions passed by the company at a general meeting are by simple majority, unless the law or the statutes stipulate a qualified majority. Amendments to the statutes have to be adopted by a minimum of two-thirds of the votes cast as well as of the share capital entitled to vote which is represented at the general meeting.

6. MINORITY PROTECTION

There is no general protection for minority shareholders against actions by the majority which might damage the company's financial position. If a parent company owns more than 90% of the shares in a subsidiary company and the parent company has more than 90% of the voting rights, the parent company is entitled to purchase the remaining shares of the subsidiary company. In the absence of an agreement the shares are valued by outside experts.
General meetings may be dispensed with by private companies, if all quotaholders agree to making the decisions without holding any general meeting or without observing the rules of procedure relating to general meetings.

7. AUDITING

The company at a general meeting elects one or more auditors. They are elected for a period fixed by the statutes, normally one or more accounting years at a time. In public companies a minimum of one auditor has to be a chartered or registered accountant, whereas a similar requirement does not apply to private companies. Shareholders owning one-tenth of the share capital can demand that the Chief Registrar of the Register of Companies appoint one further auditor to participate in the examination of the accounts for the period up to and including the next ordinary general meeting. A minimum of one of the auditors must have his permanent residence in Denmark or be an EEC citizen.

If the company's shares are quoted on the Stock Exchange, two auditors have to be elected, one of whom must be a chartered accountant. In other companies, shareholders holding one-tenth of the share capital can demand the election of a chartered accountant.

The audit balance sheet, the profit and loss account and the financial information in the annual report of the board of directors are available to the public. Since the auditor's task is generally of a continuing nature, it is usual for him to examine the accounts several times in the course of the year. Apart from this, the auditor must submit a report at the general meeting, containing a statement to the effect that the annual accounts are drawn up in accordance with the requirements of the law and the company's statutes. Furthermore, he is responsible for the accuracy of the final audit.

In 1974 the concept of 'scrutiny' was introduced. Scrutinizing can refer to certain accounts or the administration of the company and be used to clarify the reasons why the company's financial circumstances have improved or deteriorated. A resolution for 'scrutinizing' is passed by simple majority at a general meeting. If the proposal is not carried, but is, however, supported by shareholders representing 25% of the share capital, a shareholder can request the local court to appoint 'scrutinizing officers'. If the court finds the request sufficiently justified, the request must be complied with.

8. PUBLICATION

Anyone can obtain information about the registered facts concerning the company from the Company Registry. The board of directors, the management and the auditors must be registered and moreover the statutes are registered. The annual accounts i.e. balance sheet, profit and loss account and annual report, are accessible to the public in the Company Registry. For private companies the rule is that companies whose assets do not exceed D.kr. 2 million need not prepare an annual report but only submit a copy of the balance sheet including comments to the Register of Companies.

9. STATUTORY RESERVE FUND

Public companies (A/S) have to transfer a minimum of 10% of the profits each year to the statutory reserve fund, until this represents 10% of the share capital, thereafter 5% of the annual profits have to be transferred until the reserve fund represents 25% of the share capital. The statutory reserve fund can be used to cover deficits that are not covered by free net capital and for distributions of bonus shares. If the statutory reserve fund does not represent one-tenth of the share capital, the dividend has to be restricted to a maximum of 6% of the share capital. There are no requirements for a statutory reserve fund in the case of ApS companies.

II. OTHER COMPANY FORMS

A. Limited Partnerships

Under Danish law it is possible to establish companies with any type of structure independent of company law. If none of the participants or owners of the company are personally liable for the obligations of the company, and profit of the company is shared between the owners according to their capital deposit, the company will be taxable according to the Company Tax Law.
Other companies such as limited-partnerships ('Kommanditselskaber') are not considered taxable subjects under Danish Tax Law. The participants are taxed separately and individually according to their tax status. Establishment of such companies by foreign investors requires permission from the Danish foreign exchange authorities if the investment in the company exceeds D.kr. 1 mill. per calendar year.
Associations, societies, unions, leagues, foundations and institutions are not taxable subjects. However if they are engaged in business operations they are taxed on the profit of the business activities according to the Company Tax Law. As such legal entities are not suitable for foreign investors they will not be further dealt with here.

B. Cooperative Societies

Cooperative Societies are not taxed according to their income or profit, but the tax is assessed with a basis in the value of assets of the company.
The taxable income of cooperative societies is assessed at a percentage of 4-6% of the net assets invested in the society. The tax amounts to 15% of the income. The income tax to be paid by cooperative societies can, therefore, be characterized as symbolic, as it is not based on the profits.
These companies are therefore quite favourable from a tax point of view. To be taxed as a cooperative society the business should be carried out solely with the members or owners of the cooperative society. For this reason such a company has no interest for foreign investors.

C. Partnerships

Partnerships are not considered taxable subjects in Denmark and are not liable at all to taxation. This means that the partnership is disregarded for tax purposes and the individual partners will be assessed for tax according to their individual interest in the partnership. Income of the partnership is therefore allocated for tax purposes to the partners in proportion to their individual interest. It is to be noted that it is up to each partner to decide whether and to what extent he will depreciate and write off the assets of the partnership. Depreciations made in the accounts of, the partnership are disregarded in respect of the assessment of the partner for tax purposes, and the partner may depreciate at his choice on a pro rata basis in proportion to his individual interest in the depreciable assets, independent of the partnership and the other partners.

Any change in the percentage of a partner's undivided interest will for taxation purposes be equated with the sale or purchase. For tax purposes a retiring partner will be regarded as a seller.

A partnership may have foreign partners. It is to be noted that a foreign partner of a Danish partnership will be liable to limited taxation in Denmark in case the partnership is considered to have a permanent establishment in Denmark. Then the rules on 'Permanent Establishments' in relation to the double taxation conventions will apply, and the foreign partner will be taxable in Denmark according to his share of profit in the partnership.

D. Foundations

At present Denmark has no legislation on *foundations*, and foundations can be established for any purpose. Foundations are only taxed on income derived by business enterprise, and are not taxed on income deriving from dividends or interest. The foundation has to be independent of the founder and the investment in the foundation must under no circumstances return to the founder. Independent persons have to be represented on the board of the foundation. Legislation is currently being considered which would tax foundations, especially those not having charitable purposes. Because Foreign investors do not usually establish foundations as vehicles for investment in Denmark, these rules will not be described further.

E. Joint Ventures

If a foreign enterprise is doing business in Denmark in a *Joint Venture* with a Danish enterprise, the Joint Venture is likely to be a partnership, and as such not liable to Danish taxation. However, according to the tax law, a foreigner is liable to limited Danish taxation in case he participates in business with a permanent establishment in Denmark, or is entitled to a part of the profit of such an enterprise.

The foreign partner in a Danish Joint Venture will therefore often be liable to limited taxation, and if a double taxation convention is entered into between Denmark and the state of a foreign partner, double taxation will be avoided according to the provisions of the double taxation convention.

F. Royalty and Interest

In this respect distinction has to be made between a participation in profit sharing and a right to receive *royalty or interest* in the investment of a Danish enterprise. The right to receive royalty or interest on investments does not make the foreigner taxable in Denmark, and it is to be noted, that there is no withholding tax in Denmark on royalties or interests.

III. FOREIGN EXCHANGE

Direct investments in Denmark may be made by non-residents without permission from the Ministry of Industry if the investment does not exceed D.kr. 1 mill. per calendar year. Investments in excess of D.kr. 1,000,000 per calendar year will in general be permitted.
Direct investments will always require permission from the Ministry of Industry if the investment is made in a business enterprise carrying out exclusively or to any considerable extent, capital investments abroad; or financing of non-residents; or if the investment is made by a foreign business enterprise in which a resident directly or indirectly possesses assets representing a direct investment.
Transfer of money to the business enterprise in Denmark should be made through an authorized foreign exchange dealer. All the major Danish banks are authorized foreign exchange dealers. Declaration should be made to Danmarks Nationalbank (Central Bank) about the investment and the purpose of the investment.
Foreign Exchange control does not prevent the free transfer of profits and dividends from Danish enterprises to owners abroad, and capital proceeds originating from the liquidation of a company may freely be transferred to a foreign owner. Prepayments in conjunction with trade in goods and services may without permission from Danmarks Nationalbank only be made or received from abroad when the prepayment is in conformity with normal commercial practice for the particular line of business. Prepayments for import may be granted for up to one year prior to the expected date of import, but up to five years for capital goods, purchased for an amount of 1,000,000 kroner or more.
Danish enterprises can finance their imports and exports by raising loans in foreign currencies. In case a Danish enterprise is financed by credit on purchase of goods from the parent company abroad, the credit must not exceed the normal commercial practice for that particular line of business. Loans from a parent company to a Danish enterprise to finance the business must not be unrealistic when compared to the equity – financing of up to four times the equity which is at present generally acceptable to Danish authorities. For further details it is advisable to contact a Danish bank.
In general it can be said that foreign exchange control does not cause any severe problems in procedure for foreign investors in Denmark, under the current law.

IV. MONOPOLY MATTERS

A. Merger- and Take-over Control

There is no merger control, nor any take-over control in Denmark.

B. Monopoly and Antitrust

If a business enterprise has essential influence on the Danish market or essential influence within limited markets within Denmark, the Registry of Restrictive Trade Practices can claim that the enterprise is registered in the Monopoly Register. After registration the enterprise must file any changes in its practicies.

C. Profit Freeze and Price Stop

The Danish Parliament passes from time to time Profit Freeze Laws or price stop laws to reduce inflation, usually in connection with collective agreements between the employers and the trade unions.

V. TAX

1. Company Tax Rate

Companies registered in Denmark are taxed on their world-wide net-income at a rate of 40%, covering both national and municipal tax. The rules for calculation of the net-income are the same as for individuals with a few essential exceptions.
Danish companies doing business abroad are only taxed by 1/2 of the tax amount which proportionally corresponds to the income derived from abroad. If the activities abroad are carried out through an independent subsidiary with a registered office abroad the deduction is granted only if the Danish company and its subsidiary are taxed jointly and report income on a consolidated return.
Danish Companies do not pay tax on net wealth.

2. *General Danish Tax Principles*

In assessing the taxable income, the working expenses (known as 'expense account') that were necessary in order to obtain the income are deducted. A loan granted to a subsidiary is not deductable, but the interest is. There is no withholding tax on interest payments even to a foreign lender. Depreciation for plant and machinery is computed on the basis of the book value at the beginning of the financial year with a deduction for sales of plant and machinery in the course of the year, plus the total puchase price of plant and machinery in the first 6 months of the financial year, and 50% of plant and machinery bought in the second half of the year.
The maximum annual depreciation for ordinary plant and machinery is 30% of the book value. Plant and machinery whose life does not exceed 3 years and the purchase price of which does not exceed D.kr. 1,800 may, however, be written off in full in the year of procurement. Furthermore, advance depreciation of assets is possible if their value amounts to more than D.kr. 700,000.
Factory buldings, buildings for plant and machinery and ancillary storage facilities are depreciated linearly subject to certain rules, with percentage rates of 4-6% based on the original purchase price.
Section 12 of the Corporation Tax provides that the taxation authorities are entitled to assess the company's income based on an estimate, if the company is under the control of a foreign business and in its commercial or financial relations with the said foreign business is subjected to conditions other than those which should apply to an independent enterprise (dealing at arm's length). However, the Danish taxation authorities have made use of this provision only in a few cases, recently in the oil business; but the tax court has recently rescinded the decision by the tax authorities, who thereafter have been forced to accept the accounts prepared by the Danish oil companies being subsidiaries of the seven sisters.
If the enterprise owns real estate, property tax has to be paid. The amount of tax depends on where the property is situated.
If a dividend is paid, an interim tax of 30% is retained, unless this rate is alterable by virtue of double taxation agreements.
Tax on value Added (VAT) amounts to 22%.
Danish income taxes are not deductable. Income taxes paid to foreign countries from sources in that country are deductable. Ordinary indirect taxes are deductable.

3. *Special Tax Incentives – Valuation of Inventory*

The rules on valuation of inventory shall be noted as by these rules tax payment can be postponed to some extent.
According to Act. nr. 255 of 10th May 1973 on inventory valuation, taxable subjects, – persons and corporations etc., – can choose between the following ways of valuation of inventory:

1. The market value at the end of the accounting year.
2. The cost-price (purchase price) with addition of freight, custom duties, etc., or
3. The production costs, if the inventory is produced by the taxable subject itself. Production prices will include materials and direct labour costs, but not normally overheads. In determining the production price, the first-in-first-out method is normally used and accepted.

The taxpayer can choose between the above valuation principles for each group of goods in his stock, but once the principle of valuation is chosen, the taxpayer cannot change principle without previous consent from the tax authorities.

When the inventory has been valued according to the above principles, the taxpayer can reduce the value at a percentage between 1 and 30.

This reduction reduces his taxable income. However, the inventory valuation used at the end of the year shall next year be used at the beginning of the new accounting year. This means that the reduction of profit in principle is taxable next year, but at the end of the next year, the taxpayer can again make a reduction up to 30% of his stock. The size of the stock of inventory will accordingly influence the taxable income if the law is used.

If the taxpayer has reduced his inventory valuation by 30% he can only get further postponement of tax payment to the extent to which the size of the inventory at the end of the second year is increased. If the taxpayer has no inventory at the end of the following year, the reduction made at the end of the preceding year will automatically be taxable.

If, on the other hand, the taxpayer's enterprise is expanding, he can push forward taxable profit in an amount equaling 30% of the value of his inventory at the end of his accounting years.

If the enterprise shows a net loss for a given tax year, the taxpayer can apply a smaller percentage in reducing inventory valuation ('cash his inventory reserve') and thereby offset the current year's loss with profit from previous years.

4. Withholding Taxes on Dividends, Interests, Royalties, Licenses

Dividends from Danish companies are subject to withholding tax. The withholding tax rate is 30%, and for non-residents of Denmark the withholding tax is final. Double-taxation agreements between Denmark and other countries normally restrict the right of Danish tax authorities to collect withholding taxes, so reducing the withholding tax from 5-15%, depending on the content of the double-taxation agreement in question.

There is no withholding tax on royalties, interests or licenses, not even to foreign residents/companies.

By an Act of 1976 Denmark introduced an item which approached the French 'Avoir Fiscal Principle': a reduction of the Danish shareholder's liability to pay income tax on dividends received, but with a tax-credit rate of only

15% of the gross dividend. The tax credit is not available for non-resident shareholders.

5. *Registration and Stamp Duties*

When a Danish company is formed a certain stamp duty called Capital Supply Revenue must be paid. The rate is 1% of the capital invested or, if taking over a company, the value of the assets contributed to the company reduced by the amount of liabilities assumed. If the company has to be registered a registration fee has to be paid to the Register of Companies at a rate of D.kr. 1,100 + 4‰ of the capital for public companies and D.kr. 600 + 4‰ for private companies. The total costs including lawyers fees will normally amount to 4-5% of the equity of the company.

6. *Taxation of Individuals*

Danish residents are liable to pay National Income Tax, municipal income tax, county income tax, pension contribution, church tax, capital gain tax and net worth tax. The taxes are calculated upon the net taxable income.
The income tax rates are progressive with a maximum of around 75%.
Special rules apply to foreigners who become liable to pay tax in Denmark by establishing residence in Denmark. They are allowed a deduction for increased living costs connected with their stay in Denmark. The deduction requires special consent from the Tax Authorities.
'Danish residents who temporarily perform work abroad are permitted a Tax Credit Note but due to the progressive rate structure, the tax due will be greater than if the foreign-source income had been exempted, and tax computed only on the domestic-source income according to the following formula:

$$\begin{matrix}\text{Tentative Tax} \\ \text{On Total Income}\end{matrix} \times \frac{\text{Foreign income}}{\text{Total income}} = \begin{matrix}\text{Amount of} \\ \text{Tax credit}\end{matrix}$$

Generally speaking, if a double taxation agreement applies, each calendar year is analysed separately, and the taxpayer will be eligible for the credit only if at least 183 days of the calendar year were spent working abroad. In case of work abroad lasting at least two months' (but not 183 days) a deduction of 10% for calculated extra expenses incurred is allowed if the work is performed in Western Europe, 25% if the work is performed outside Western Europe. This deduction is based on salary received for work performed abroad.

7. *Indirect Taxation – VAT*

In Denmark there is no sales tax but a tax on value added, VAT. The original Act has been amended several times, and the tax rate is at present 22%.
The characteristics of the VAT-system are:
1. that the tax is levied on all stages of the turnover and,
2. that on account of specific rules of deduction, the result will be that for the individual turnover stages a tax will only have to be paid on the increased value which is added to the product in the individual stage of the turnover.

The taxpayer is liable to pay tax on all products which are sold commercially (also articles of food) and all services unless expressly exempted.
The tax liability is not incurred on the purchase and sale of real estate and letting of houses or apartments.
All firms and companies which carry on a commercial business with goods or the services stipulated in the Act must register with the Customs Authorities. When selling the goods and services subject to taxation, the registered firm or company must collect the tax of 22% stated in the act. The tax shall be charged regardless of whether the firm sells the goods or the services to the consumer, or to another firm or company.
When purchasing raw materials and other products or purchasing services, the firm and the company which charges the tax has itself paid a tax of 22% of the price of such goods and services. The tax paid to the registered firms and companies must be calculated by the end of each quarter as a principle (but there are of course certain modifications), and the tax which is payable to the Danish state by the individual firm or company comprises the difference between the taxes charged on the one side and taxes paid to the other firms and companies for the purchase of goods and services. If, at the end of a quarter, the taxes paid by a firm or a company exceed the taxes charged by the firm or the company during the same period, the difference will be reimbursed by the Customs Authorities.
In order to make the tax system neutral with respect to exports, no tax is due on goods exported out of EEC countries. This means that Danish firms and companies which export the greater part of their products at the end of each quarter have paid more taxes than they have charged during the same period. Such firms and companies will therefore ordinarily have a claim against the Customs Authorities for reimbursement of taxes paid at the end of each quarter.
When importing goods a tax shall be paid to the Customs Authorities amounting to 22%.
The Minister of Finance may promulgate rules under which any person who buys taxable services abroad shall pay 22% tax on the consideration paid for such services.
The Minister of Finance may bring in regulations regarding the refund of tax paid by foreign enterprises in connection with purchase, processing, etc., storage or transportation of exported goods.
Foreign enterprises which carry on independent commercial turnover of goods and taxable services in Denmark must submit to registration. If the enterprise

has not a branch, etc. in Denmark, it must be registered by a person living in Denmark or by an enterprise which has a business office in Denmark.

8. *Capital Gains Tax (Special Income Tax)*

A. IN GENERAL

Certain types of gains or profits are taxable under a special income tax law, the Capital Gains Act (nr. 454 of 19th July 1977). The provisions of this act are applicable to both corporations and individuals. However, different rates of tax apply. Individuals are taxed at 50%, and they can deduct D.kr. 6.000 each year, which means that profit below D.kr. 6.000 is tax free. The taxable income of joint-stock companies and other companies subject to the Company Taxation Act includes normal taxable income, and income calculated according to the Capital Gains Act. This means that capital gains earned in companies are taxed at 40% without deduction of D.kr. 6.000. Special rules in relation to the calculation of the size of capital gains regarding real estate and goodwill shall be noted, see below.

A. Gains subject to Capital Gains Tax

The following items are subject to capital gains tax:

1. Profit or loss arising from sale or disposition of machinery, equipment, ships and vehicles used entirely for business purposes, when sale or disposition is connected with sale or disposition of the business enterprise in question.
2. Profit from the sale of buildings and installations having been depreciated for tax purposes ('regained depreciations'). Gain which exceeds the total amount of yearly depreciation is also taxable, but the size of the gain is subject to special computation.
3. Profit from the sale of immovable property.
4. Profit or loss arising from the sale of goodwill, patents, copyrights, design patents, trademarks, and lease contracts, etc.
5. Profit or loss arising from the sale of shares or of other parts of limited companies, or profit and loss in connection with the sale of rights to subscribe for shares in a company.
6. Profit or loss arising from liquidation of companies and corporations. Dividends from companies or corporations in the year when the company or the corporation is woundup.
7. Compensation received when resigning from employment.
8. Gifts and gratuities received by employees at retirement or at the employers' anniversary.
9. Profits derived by an employer from the cancellation of a pension liability which has previously been deducted.
10. Compensation in connection with an undertaking of agreement of non-competition.
11. Gifts or grants received from public funds, legacies, cultural foundations when the gift or grant is given entirely in recognition of services of the recipient.

However, in some instances *profit is not considered taxable under the Capital Gains Act*, if the assets have been acquired as part of the taxpayers' business as a *dealer in such assets* or if the taxpayer has acquired such assets with the intent of *speculation.* In such cases, profit is *regarded as general taxable income.*
Capital gains tax is not applicable in the following special instances:

1. when shares have been sold within 2 years after the date of acquisition, or if dealing in shares is the taxpayer's trade,
2. when rights of limited duration, such as patents, copyrights, design patents and trademarks have been created by the seller,
3. when shares are sold to the issuing cooperative or company,
4. when compensation for loss of employment replaces regular salary,
5. when ships are sold within 5 years after the date of acquisition.

B. COMPUTATION OF GAIN OR LOSS

Capital Gain is computed for each item individually, and the gain or loss is normally the difference between the selling price, and the purchase costs reduced by tax depreciation. Special rules apply to the sale of immovable property, goodwill and shares. Loss in capital gain can be off-set against general taxable income.

C. IMMOVABLE PROPERTY AND REAL ESTATE

Profit earned by the sale of houses for one or two families is tax free if the owner or his family has lived in the house for at least 2 years. There are, however, some exceptions in this respect which are too extensive to describe here.
For other gains in respect of sale of real estate, special and quite favourable rules apply as to the calculation of the taxable profit. The starting point for computation of the gain or loss is the adjusted acquisition costs, which is based on the actual purchase price. If the property was acquired before January 1, 1966, the taxpayer can choose to substitute the value at which the property was assessed by the public authorities on 1st August 1965.
The purchase price – or the valuation – is increased by 30% plus 8% per year for the first two years after the date of acquisition, 9% for the next three years and 10% for the years following. These additions allow to a great extent tax-free profit, to some extent corresponding to the inflation.
If the selling price still exceeds the adjusted acquisition costs, a further reduction of the taxable gain of D.kr. 40.000 or 60.000 may be made.
If the selling price still exceeds the adjusted acquisition costs, the profit is increased by 30% for an individual taxpayer, and by 80% in case of a company. The resulting figure is taxable capital gain.
If the selling price is less than the adjusted acquisition cost, the loss is not deductable from either general income or other capital gains.

D. GOODWILL

Individuals selling goodwill can deduct the profit at a rate from 10%, if he has owned the business enterprise for 5 years, or up to 35% if he has owned the enterprise for 10 years or more. The total deduction must not exceed a maximum amount of D.kr. 75,000.

E. SHARES

The basis for the acquisition costs is the average acquisition costs during the period of ownership. If the seller has owned the shares on January 1, 1962, he may substitute the average acquisition costs, if the value of the shares was higher on that date.
The law does not allow reduction in the profit according to the inflation.

9. *Double Taxation Agreements*

Double Taxation Agreements have been concluded with the following countries:

Republic of Arab
Argentina
Austria
Belgium
Brazil
Bulgaria
Canada
China
Ceylon
Czechoslovakia
Faroe Islands
Fiji
Finland
France
Germany
Great Britain
Greece
Iceland
India
Ireland
Israel
Italy
Japan
Jordan
Kenya
Korea
Kuwait
Lebanon
Malta
Malaysia
The Netherlands
New Zealand
Norway
Pakistan
Philippines
Poland
Portugal
Rumania
Singapore
South Africa
Spain
Sweden
Switzerland
Tanzania
Thailand
Tobago
Trinidad
U.S.A.
U.S.S.R.
Yugoslavia
Zambia

VI. LABOUR ASPECTS

1. Collective Agreements

Labour relations in Denmark are based on voluntary collective agreements between the Trade Unions and the Employers Organization. The agreements are usually renegotiated every second year. The collective agreements deal with minimum wages, termination periods, holidays, etc.

2. Employees

Employment contracts are in principle free, but the Employment Act stipulates rules of the termination period, which is 3 months after 6 months' employment. After 3 years' employment the termination period is increased to 4 months. After 6 years' employment the termination period in 5 months, and after 9 years employment the termination period is at maximum 6 months. In addition the employee is entitled to compensation similar to one, two or three months' salary after employment in 12, 15 or 18 years.

The Employment Act further contains provisions to the effect that the employees are entitled to organize themselves, and the employer is obliged to negotiate with the organization of the employees.

Employees are entitled to 5 weeks holiday per year. The employee is paid his normal salary or $12\frac{1}{2}\%$ of his normal salary. In the latter case 1% of last years salary is paid out when the holidays begin.

3. Social Security Premiums

Social Security Premiums consist of holiday allowance, $12\frac{1}{2}\%$, day money fund and casual insurance premium. The Social Security Premiums do not exceed 15% of the total salary expense.

4. Compulsory Profit Sharing and Pension Schemes

At present, no compulsory profit sharing and pension schemes apply in Denmark.

France

Maurice Letulle
Claude Lucas de Leyssac *Jean Possoz*
Denis de Ricci *Jacques Tuot*

I. INTRODUCTION

The very important political change occurred in France with the election of a socialist President and a large left wing majority in the Parliament will certainly result in substantial modifications in the actual legislation as hereinafter described.
The legal framework is not likely to change, at least in the near future, except for a very probable reinforcement of anti trust legislation.
Exchange control rules, which had just been largely liberalized, both for french investments abroad and foreign investments in France might incurr changes if the monetary situation does not improve.
However company law and the legislation related to the Groupements d'Intérêt Economique (GIE) as well as to real estate companies (sociétés civiles) are likely to remain largely as they are actually.
For many years now every new government coming into office has announced a basic reform of the french tax system: it is quite obvious that such will now certainly be the case but it is far too early even to give an idea of the general trend of such a reform except that high personal incomes will support a much heavier taxation and that an annual tax on capital will be created.
Labour law will also be modified but, there again, it is extremely difficult to estimate to what extent.
Codetermination, which does not exist in the actual french legislation will certainly be introduced but major changes might not occur for a certain time and, as will be indicated in the third chapter, the complicated structures through which employees exercise a right of control will probably remain because France has already reached a high degree of socialisation in this sector.

II. THE LEGAL FRAMEWORK

A. The Vehicle

1. THE WHOLLY OWNED ENTERPRISE

1.a. THE BRANCH

1.a.(i) Setting-up

A company which opens a branch in France must comply with registration requirements contained in the décret nr. 67-237 of March 1967.

If a branch is opened within the jurisdiction of the Commercial Court (Tribunal de Commerce) where the parent company has its registered office, all that is necessary is to record this fact in the Companies Register. If the branch is opened in another area, then it must be registered in the Companies Register for that area, after which it will be allotted a number of its own. The Companies Register in which the parent company is registered will be altered to show the existence of the branch. In either case the formalities must be completed within two months of the commencement of business.

The requirements for branches in France of foreign companies are the same, although in addition there are further provisions which apply when first opening a branch in France. Any further branches opened will be treated in the same way as those of a French company.

Copies of the memorandum and articles of association and all modifications thereto must be lodged with the Commercial Court for the area concerned upon opening a branch. In each two copies translated into French are required, copies being freely obtainable from the Clerk of the Court.

1.a.(ii) Organization

There are no compulsory legal requirements for the organisation of a branch. The legal representatives are those of the parent company and have to be registered as such in the Companies Register. The manager of the branch may also be registered but as an employee with no specific legal powers others than those which have been delegated by the representatives of the parent company.

Since a branch is regarded as being part of the parent company, the latter is legally bound by any contract or obligation entered into by the branch, although in practice the position is somewhat confused.

In theory the creditor of a French branch can sue the parent company of that branch through the French courts, the parent being regarded as liable for the debts of that establishment. However the projection of this principle is that a French judge could thus declare a foreign company bankrupt. Conversely the powers of the liquidator of a foreign company could extent to cover the branch in France.

However, these extreme consequences are largely tempered by the general rule according to which a foreign judgment cannot be enforced in another country without a local preliminary procedure (exequatur in France) and although, at present, judgments obtained in one of the members of the Common Market can be executed relatively easily in the other CEE countries the Convention on the jurisdiction of courts and the enforcement of decisions in civil and commercial matters signed in Brussels on 28th September 1968 excludes judgments concerning bankruptcy so that the examples just mentioned are unlikely to be encountered in practice.

There is no theoretical obligation for a branch to have a separate accounting system. However in practice for a branch of a foreign company this is an absolute necessity for tax reasons as the profits made by the branch are submitted to french corporation tax.

Although a branch has no separate legal existence for taxation purposes, its profits are considered separately from those of the parent company. If profits

are earned in France, corporate income tax is payable even though the parent company may have made an overall loss for the year in question.
Thus if a branch in France did not have separate books of accounts the computation of the profit earned by that unit could be almost impossible. In practice, the tax authorities are empowered to base their assessment of the profits earned in France on an average of the gross profits earned by similar undertakings in the same field, or even the result obtained by the parent company in its operations in another country. Due to the risk of a high assessment being made under these circumstances, it is clearly desirable that proper books are kept by a branch.

1.b. THE SUBSIDIARY

French law recognizes all the traditional types of business organisations and the following kinds are commonly used in France:
a. Société en nom collectif (ordinary partnership)
b. Société en commandite simple (limited partnership)
c. Société en participation (business on joint account)
d. Société en commandite par actions (partnership limited by shares)
e. Société anonyme (SA) (public limited company)
f. Société à responsabilité limitée (SARL) (private limited company)
All these types of business organisations are regarded as commercial companies regardless of their purpose.
From a tax point of view, partnerships (en nom collectif and en commandite) have regained their importance as a result to the tax reform passed on 26th December 1959, which eliminates certain of the double taxation provisions. Members of partnerships of this type are now only liable to the normal Income Tax (IR), which is a graduated tax, with a maximum rate of 60%. We shall however limit our detailed comments to the SAS and the SARLS which remain, by a very great margin, the most commonly used types.

1.b.(i) Setting-up

For both SAS and SARLS filing of articles of association with the Clerk of the Commercial Court of the area in which the company has its place of business, one or more advertisements in specialized journals, and registration in the official Register at the Commercial Court, are formalities which have to be complied with, and, regardless of its type, a company only becomes a separate legal entity upon registration in the Register of companies: (Registre du Commerce et des Sociétés – RCS).
No government permit of any kind is needed whichever type of company is chosen but, in certain cases, permission must be obtained from the Direction du Trésor of the Ministère de l'Economie et des Finances before a foreign investment is made in France (see hereunder).
Whereas SARLS are usually constituted by an instrument under hand[1], signed

1. The subscribed capital of an SARL must be totally paid before incorporation. The paid-up capital is blocked in a bank account until final registration of the company: this rule applies to all types of companies.

on the day of incorporation, the setting up of an SA entails a notarial attestation of subscription and payment of capital with the result that most SAS are established by notaries.
The setting up of an SA when shares can be purchased by the public entails various supplementary formalities including filing the draft articles of association with the Clerk of Court and signing subscriptions forms.

1.b.(ii) Organization

1.b.(ii)a Capital – shares – transfer
In order to be properly constituted, every French SA must have at least seven members, and failure to observe this requirement will not only render the company ineffective but make it liable to penalties. The company must have a minimum capital of F. 100.000 and each of the shares must have a minimum par value of F. 100. Twenty-five per cent of the nominal amount of the shares must be paid up.
By contrast, an SARL only requires two members but its status must be changed to that of an SA when the number of members exceeds fifty.
The minimum capital required is F. 20.000 divided into shares having a minimum par value of F. 100. (A law of 31st December 1981 has introduced certain changes in french company law in particular to take into account the Second Directive of the European Commission. The minimum capital for an SA has been increased to F. 250.000 for an ordinary company and to F. 1.500.000 for savings institutions.) All the shares must be fully subscribed and paid up on formation. If the number of members required by law falls below the minimum for a period exceeding one year, the company may be declared dormant, which implies its winding-up.
In order to become a member of an SA, it is necessary to acquire shares, but French law also recognizes debentures which can be convertible into ordinary shares.
Subject to any provisions to the contrary contained in the articles of association of the company, the shares are freely transferable.
Pre-emption clauses are strictly controlled. They may be applied neither in the case of a lineal succession or between a married couple or in the case of transfers among shareholders, this last provision being often troublesome.[2]
Moreover such a restriction can never prohibit the right of a shareholder to transfer of his shares: short of acceptance of the clause by the proposed transferee (s), the other shareholders must repurchase or have the shares bought from the seller.
Shares carrying more than one vote can only be issued on certain well defined conditions and may never carry more than two votes. All companies formed after the law of 24th July 1966 came into force are prohibited from issuing founders' shares. The shares may be registered shares, or bearer shares, or they may be preference shares, but the benefits attaching to the latter are mainly economic. The finance laws for 1982 prohibits, for the future, the creation of bearer shares. Moreover all existing bearer shares in all french companies must

2. A proposal before Parliament for a law to consider the acceptance and pre-emptive rights valid toward third parties even in case of transfer among shareholders is still under consideration.

be transformed into registered shares at the latest on 1st October 1982.
The issue of transferable debentures to the public is now subject to exacting conditions imposed by relatively new legislation. The principal requirement of such legislation is that in cases where the issue of debentures exceeds F. 15 million, a declaration must be made to the Ministry of Finance before the issue is made.
The debenture holders form a special group whose representatives can exercise some control over the company.
Membership of an SARL is by means of shares (parts) which are not freely transferable. There are strict rules governing the transfer of these securities which are designed to maintain the private character of this type of company. Unless otherwise stipulated in the articles of association, a transfer between members, or by reason only, requires written notification to be given to the company. However, if shares are to be transferred outside the company, the law requires that such transfers are approved by a majority of members representing at least 75% of the share capital. If this approval is not obtained, the members themselves must purchase the shares proposed to be transfered from the transferor at a price which will be fixed by experts.
Preference shares may be issued giving the holder the preferential right to dividend but such shares must not carry more than one vote.
Finally, an SARL may never invite the public to subscribe for its shares and may therefore never issue debentures.

1.b.(ii)b Management – representation
An SA is managed by a board of directors (Conseil dAdministration) elected by the shareholders in general meeting.
The board of directors elects a chairman who assumes full responsibility for the overall management of the company and also has full executive power. The chairman can be assisted by one or several General Directors (directeurs généraux) nominated by the board. The powers of the director general are fixed by the board but towards third parties, they have the same powers as the chairman.
An alien can only be the chairman of the board of directors or director general of a French SA if he holds a foreign trader's card (carte de commerçant étranger). Commom Market country residents are not required to hold this card for most commercial and a number of industrial activities, and exemption from the requirement may be granted subject to certain conditions.
The decisions of the board are valid only if at least half of the directors are physically present. They need a simple majority vote unless otherwise specified in the articles of association, which can stipulate a higher (but not a lower) majority.
Voting by proxy is permissible unless specifically prohibited by the articles of association. Directors must hold shares and must deposit theses shares as collateral security. An alien may be a director of a French SA except in unusual circumstances, even though he is not domiciled in France.
Recent legislation relating to companies now allows the setting up of an SA in the same manner as in Germany; the board of directors not exceeding five in number (directoire), plus a supervisory board (Conseil de Surveillance). There are significant differences between the legal status of members of a

board of directors of the classical type of an SA (Conseil d'Administration) and members of a 'directoire'.

An SARL is managed by one or more managers (gérants) elected by the shareholders in general meeting. Managers need not be members, they can be dismissed by a resolution of the members who represent more than 50% of the share capital, but they are entitled to claim damages in the event of dismissal without proper cause. On the other hand, should a manager be guilty of misconduct, any interested party can apply to the court for his dismissal. A manager has extremely wide authority on behalf of the company and if there is more than one manager, each has the same powers. Third parties dealing with the company cannot be affected by any contractual limitation on the manager's authority, and an alien may be manager of an SARL provided that he holds the foreign trader's card (unless exempted by membership of the Common Market).

1.b.(ii)c Shareholders meetings

In both an SA and an SARL the shareholders in general meeting have very wide powers. The company may hold ordinary or extraordinary meetings, the former taking place at least once a year to conduct such business as approval of the accounts, appointments whenever necessary.

At the present time, voting by letter is not permitted at a general meeting of an SA and shareholders may only be represented by their husband or wife or by another shareholder. This prohibition on voting by letter has led to a loss of interest on the part of small investors, who have adopted the habit of sending blank proxies (pouvoirs en blanc) thus making it possible in some cases for a minority to control a meeting through the use of blank proxies. A majority is constituted by percentage of share capital represented by the votes cast and not by the numbers of shareholders present. The law of 30th December 1981 stipulates that in shareholders' meeting the majority will be calculated in future with respect to the number of shareholders present or represented, which means that the shareholders who abstain from voting will be considered as voting against the proposed resolutions.

Resolutions are passed at an ordinary general meeting by a simple majority, whereas at extraordinary general meetings resolutions can only be passed by a two-thirds majority of the share capital represented by the votes cast at the meeting.

Moreover, there are legal provisions relating to quorums which are unalterable by the articles of association.[3]

Members of an SARL are only required to have an annual general meeting to approve the accounts since they can otherwise vote by letter. By contrast with the case of an SA, the members of an SARL may be represented at meetings by non members if expressly stipulated in the articles of association.

Any amendment to the articles of association of an SARL can only be effected by a majority decision of members together holding shares representing at least 75% of the company's capital.

3. The quorum requirements are as follows in the SA: at the first annual general meeting 25%. No quorum is required for subsequent meetings, but for extraordinary general meetings the quorum is 50% for the first one held and 25% for any subsequent meeting.

For transfer of shares to a non partner, as mentioned above, a double majority is required (majority of existing members plus 75% of the share capital).

1.b.(ii)d Liability

In principle the parent company has no liability whatsoever towards a subsidiary. The only exception is in case of bankruptcy: exceptionally if the accounts of the parent and the subsidiary and the business of both companies are so indetermingled that the Court considers that it is in fact one sole enterprise, it can be decided by a judgment to include both companies in the same bankruptcy proceedings notwithstanding the fact that only one of the companies is technically bankrupt.

The liability of directors is, of course, much stricter.

Both the chairman and general director of an SA and the manager of an SARL are regarded as traders (commerçants) so that, should the company become bankrupt, they can suffer the same loss of rights as any other bankrupt trader.[4]

In case of bankruptcy, if the assets are not sufficient to cover the debts, the Court can decide that a proportion of the debts, which the Court determines, will be personally paid by the chairman, the director general and, eventually, the members of the board of an SA if the latter do not prove, to the satisfaction of the Court, that they have managed correctly the business of the company.

The same rule applies to managers of SARL and to any person who, whatever the form of the company, has, in fact, managed the business of a company without the legal status of director or manager.

1.b.(ii)e Accounts and auditing requirements

The accounts of an SA must be audited by auditors (commissaires aux comptes) appointed in general meeting. The law contains provisions intended to ensure their independence as regards the companies which they serve, and, in addition, at least one of the auditors or the sole auditor of an SA which invites the public to subscribe the capital, must be elected from a list of auditors which is prepared within the jurisdiction of each Court of Appeal.

The auditors' task has become greater since the introduction of new legislation, in particular relating to the balance sheet which must be declared by them to give a true and fair view.

The new legislation also makes arrangements for the protection of minorities and deals with the information which must be given to shareholders. It is also provided that a minority group may convene a shareholders' meeting or require a matter to be put on the agenda; however it is too early to assess the efficacy of this reform.

An SARL is obliged to have one or more auditors (commissaires aux comptes) if it has a share capital of F. 300.000 or more, although those companies

4. Any individual trading under his own name can be declared bankrupt. He can then be deprived for a certain time of a number of rights such as, in the last resort (but only in case of fraudulent bankruptcy), the right to manage or to be a director of a company. In the case of bankruptcy of a company, the chairman of the board or manager (SARL) can suffer the same consequences.

having a smaller capital are free to choose whether or not they appoint an auditor.

1.b.(ii)f Publication of accounts

Only the accounts of an SA have to be deposited every year with the companies Register who will deliver copies to any interested third party.
This rule applies to no other form of commercial company.
However companies quoted in a stock exchange, whatever their form are subject to disclosure of their yearly accounts.

GROUPS OF COMPANIES

There are no regulations in France with respect to groups of companies.
However companies whose shares are listed on the stock exchange must publish the accounts of their subsidiaries whereas all public companies (SA) must list these subsidiaries.
Moreover the idea of groups of companies may be used from the fiscal point of view (worldwide or consolidated profits).
Finally, jurisprudence may call on this idea in regards to social regulations (e.g. worker's committees, participation in profits) and most often in matters of bankruptcy as mentioned above.

1.b.(iii) Checklist for establishing a subsidiary

I. The formation of an SARL or an SA starts with the signing of the statutes which may be preceded by an interim agreement (a protocol) in which the founders enumerate the characteristics of the company to be created.
The statutes may be notarized or be a private agreement. However a notarized version is obligatory every time there is any kind of real-estate advertisement such as in the case of the bringing in of real-estate. These statutes must include the provisions stated in art. 2 of the law of July 24th 1966 and in art. 55 of the decree of March 23rd 1967.
If non cash holdings are brought in, reports of the commissaire aux apports must be annexed along with a signed document listing the steps taken for the account of the company being formed.
A copy of the statutes must be given to each associate (art. 20, paragraph 2 of the decree of March 23rd 1967).

II. After the signature of the statutes, the following procedure must be undertaken:

a. Registration:
The statutes, and other documents as the case may be (notarized declarations of subscription and of payment in the case of an SA, the minutes of the constitutive Assembly if there was a public offer of shares) must be formally registered for fiscal reasons.

b. Legal newspaper notice:
The official notice must include the provisions of art. 285 of the decree of March 23rd. 1967 and must be signed by one of the first partners who must have a special power of attorney. No lapse of time is required for this formality.

c. Filing with the Clerk of the Commercial Court:

- 2 copies of the statutes executed and authenticated by a notary or 2 originals if by private agreement,
- 2 copies of the acts nominating the first members of the management, the administration, the audit and the control of the company,
- 2 copies of the certified statements containing on one hand, the list of all the transactions previous to and in view of the forming of the company and on the other hand, the solemn affirmation that this formation was carried out in conformity with the law and regulations (art. 6, paragraph 1 of the law of July 24th. 1966).

In case of omission or irregularity, this declaration establishes the responsibility of those concerned.

- 2 copies of the report from the 'commissaire aux apports' if non-cash holdings are brought in,
- 2 copies of the notarized declaration of underwriting and of payment for the SA.

d. Registration in the official Trade Register with the Clerk of the Court of the main office. The request is made in 3 copies signed by the manager or the chairman of the board of directors. To back this request it is necessary to produce the following:

1. documents relative to the constitution of the company,
   - the receipt of the filing at the registror's office,
   - a copy of the legal newspaper containing the formation notice of the company,
2. documents concerning the member of the board,
   - a birth certificate, less than three months old,
   - for foreigners, other than those from a country belonging to the Common Market, who will occupy a management position, a foreign traders card (carte de commerçant étranger) must be produced,
   - for a corporate legal entity administrator, an extract from the Trade Register. Regarding a foreign company, an extract of its registration in its country or else a copy of its statutes,
   - the deed justifying the possession of the premises where the main office is established.

e. A declaration of existence with the Administration.

III. Cost of the formalities:

1. Registration fee: 1% for the ordinary contributions (art. 810-1 and 2 of the Code Général des Impôts) and 11, 40% for the contributions for valuable consideration and for those intended for a person subject to company tax from a person who is not subject to it.
2. Cost at Clerk of Commercial Court from a THOUSAND to FIFTEEN HUNDRED FRANCS.
3. Cost of the publicity from TWO THOUSAND FIVE to THREE THOUSAND FRANCS.
4. Fees –
   These vary as to whether a lawyer, a legal consultant or a notary is called upon.

The notaries are bound by tariff regulations; the drawing up of the statutes entitles the notary to a fee of a THOUSAND FIVE HUNDRED AND SEVENTY FIVE FRANCS to which is added an additional fee rated on a degressive scale of the brute value of the contributions.

Example : up to 200.000 F. 0,75%, over 60.000.000 F. 0.005% plus 16.000 F.

For the lawyer and the legal consultant, the fees are freely discussed with the client and depend of course of the importance of the consultations and of the time and assistance given. For foreign investors for instance, the eventual necessity of obtaining an authorisation from the Treasury must be taken into account.

In general terms, for a straight forward formation of a company without any complications or extra factor, fees range from TWO THOUSAND FIVE to FIVE THOUSAND FRANCS for a private limited company (SARL) and FIVE THOUSAND to SEVEN THOUSAND for a public limited company (SA).

5. Length of time for the formation of an SA or of an SARL:
   This will amount to between 50 and 90 days until the delivery of the extract from the Trade Register registering the company.
   The company does not acquire its legal corporate personality until its registration on the Trade Register.

1.c. OTHER FORMS

Sociétés Civiles Immobilières

Mainly for tax reasons, the normal types of commercial companies are rarely used for the activities related to building promotion.

But although the economic crisis has not spared the construction sector, building promotion is still one of the largest branches of activity which reflects a deep French affection 'for bricks and mortar'.

Under art. 632 of the Commercial Code the buying of properties with a view to later resale (whether as a whole or by units) after having built, is not considered as a commercial act.

The basic law on building problems is law 71-579 of July 10th. 1971.

Three types of companies may be considered: The Sociétés d'attribution, the Sociétés coopératives, the Sociétés constituées en vue de la vente.

It is under this last form (companies formed with a view of sale) that most of the building promotion in France is done, allowing the promotor to associate financiers to his transactions and leading him to form a particular type of company in order to commercialize each program.

Next to promotion and construction, we find in France the Sociétés Civiles considered to be real-estate companies because of their purpose which is to buy and manage property. These companies offer nothing special as compared to the typical Sociétés Civiles which are ruled by the art. 1832 and following of the Civil Code.

It is necessary though to mention the Sociétés Civiles de placement collectif which can be created in order to mobilise savings in large building transactions consisting of buying real-estate for commercial use and offices to rent.

Due to the ever growing importance of the Sociétés Civiles, the legislator has

taken special provisions with the law 70.1300 of December 31st. 1970 and with the decree nr. 71.524 of July 1st 1971.
The Sociétés Civiles formed with a view of selling real-estate are governed by Title I of the law of July 16th. 1971 and by the artt. 1382 and following of the Civil Code.

1.c.(i) Setting-up

The statutes must be set down in writing and must take into account the provisions of art. 6 of the decree 72-1935 of December 29th. 1972, especially those concerning the answering to the calling of funds.
The purpose of the company is the construction and the selling of real-estate, this being for both commercial and housing use.
The formation of the Company calls for the following formalities:
- The insertion of a legal notice in a newspaper qualified to receive such a notice and this in the department of the main office,
- Filing with the Clerk of two originals of the statutes and two copies of the nomination acts of the managers,
- Registration of the Company on the Trade Register.

The company has a separate legal entity from the day of this registration.

1.c.(ii) Organisation

The construction-selling Company may be managed by one or more persons associated or not. Firms may be associates.
Each manager is individually responsible to the Company and to third parties whether it be in regards to violation of laws, breaching of statutes or mistakes made in the management itself.
The associates are liable indefinitly for social debts but only to the extent of their respective contributions of capital; they are thus not jointly liable.
Art. 1856 of the Civil Code states that the manager (s) must once a year give an account of his (their) management.
The accounts must include a written report on the Company's activities especially concerning the profits and losses.
The nomination of an external auditor (a commissaire aux comptes) is not compulsory but always permissible.

2. THE JOINT VENTURE

2.a. THE JOINTLY OWNED COMPANY

Two or more companies can form a company for a joint venture, which is usually owned in equal shares. The implementation of such a structure is frequent but it should be noted that legal opinion makes reservations about the validity of this structure if the companies associated in the joint venture are not legally and economically distinct. In practice though, such reservations do not usually hinder the formation of a jointly owned company among companies belonging to a single group.

The subsidiary is managed by the rules of the social form adopted; and, in absence of group company rights, these rules may conflict with the interests of the associates expressed in different annex agreements. This conflict is particularly acute in the case of an SA. In effect, it is frequent that the protocol organizes for example the alternation of directors or the distribution of administrative posts, or even the different mechanisms in view of violating certain fundamental principles of law of the SA such as the revocation ad nutum of the managing board or the freedom of deliberation and vote.
In the case of such a conflict, it is obvious that the traditional rules forbidding shareholders agreements as contrary to the principle of the freedom of vote or to that of securing the protection of minority rights, should override the whims of the parties expressed in such agreements. However it appears that the courts do consider practical imperatives and in absence of group company rights, they apply less strictly the principles of company rights when they differ with the organisation of the common branch. Such was the case SCHNEIDER-MARINE FIRMINY: the Commercial Court of Paris refused to declare void clauses violating the freedom of vote of shareholders (Trib. Comm. Paris August 1st. 1974, Rev. Soc. 1974-685, note J.J. BURST).
The jurisdictional tendency having been underlined, there remains the fact that the common law rules concerning vote agreements or minority rights are generally applied to the jointly-owned company which creates numerous uncertainties.
Since it is not certain that the voices in favor of an elaboration of group rights will be heard, these uncertainties might continue to weigh down upon the jointly owned company's activities.

2.b. OTHER TYPES OF LEGAL ORGANISATIONS FOR JOINT VENTURES

A specifically French type of organisation for a joint venture is the GROUPEMENT D'INTERET ECONOMIQUE (GIE) but, for temporary joint ventures the SOCIETE EN PARTICIPATION will also appear useful.

Groupement d'intétêt économique
The GROUPEMENT D'INTERET ECONOMIQUE is considered as an organisation of support, of assistance or of transition; as a pooling of resources.[5]
The essentially distinctive feature of a GIE, as compared to other companies, is hard to pinpoint.
One of the obstacles to the creation of a GIE lies in the impossibility of transforming it into a company of a normal type without losing its separate legal personality, this entailing the liquidation of the grouping with all its fiscal implications. Where growth and development will be an important consideration, the creation of a company is thus to be preferred, more especially as juridictional uncertainties have arisen about the ability of a GIE successfully to maintain in all circumstances its separate legal personality. This has resulted in disagreable consequences such as the refusal of the right to commercial property.[6]

5. LE FOLL – Possibilities and limits of the GIE in Bilan, objectif et stratégie du GIE, p. 44, Paris 1970.
6. December 18th 1975 D. 75, p. 366.

The participation of a foreign company in a GIE is possible. Its fiscal system was stated precisely in a ministerial order (BOCD nr. 24 of June 19th 1968). It is used particularly for export promotion but may reveal itself to be insufficient if one wants permanent commercial structures.

2.b.(i) Establishment

Besides certain special regulations concerning either the purpose or the quality of its members, the GIE has the advantage of a flexible regulation.
The GIE is formed by a written contract which freely fixes the organisation in agreement with the provisions of an executive decree of September 23rd. 1967.
The contract must contain certain obligatory indications stated by the art. 6 of the heresaid executive decree. The deed of incorporation is in general accompanied by an interior regulation.
Two originals of the deed of incorporation and two certified copies of the nomination acts of the administrators must be filed with the Clerk of the Commercial Court of the area concerned.
Every GIE must be registered on the Trade Register whatever its object.
The deed of incorporation must be registered in the month of its signing. The contributions, once executed, give rise to a payment of 1% registration tax. The contributions acquired for valuable consideration are taxed as are sales (CGI art. 809-1).
The formation of a GIE without capital and without contributions entails the payment of a fixed fee (CGI art. 822).
A letter of existence must be addressed to the fiscal Administration.

2.b.(ii) Organisation

The executive decree of September 23rd. 1967 states that the GIE has an Assembly (art. 8) and that it is administered by one or several persons. Subject to abiding by this provision and to the rule that the limits of power are not valid as against third parties, the organisation is freely determined by the terms of the contract.
The members of the GIE are indefinitely and jointly liable for its debts and this on their own patrimony. A GIE, whether its purpose is civil or commercial, may be put into liquidation (Law 57-563 of July 13th 1967, art. 1).
The GIE are subject to the same accounting obligations as the civil or commercial companies according to their object. When a GIE issues debentures, the control of the accounts must be performed by one or several external auditors (commissaires aux comptes).
The fiscal system of the GIE is that of fiscal 'transparency'. The members, who are individual persons, are personally liable for income tax for the share of the profits that correspond to their interests in the company. Any corporate members who are subject to company tax, are also subject to this same tax for their share of profits in the GIE.

La société en participation
Due to its simplicity, the SOCIETE EN PARTICIPATION may be used for

different reasons and is found in all the branches of commercial activities. One can particularly call upon it for prompt transactions whose importance and risks bring individuals and firms to agree for example upon fulfilment of a supply contract or for a special undertaking.

There is nothing to prevent foreign individuals and firms from taking part in a Société en Participation subject to French law.

1. The Société en Participation is a company in which the associates have agreed that it will not be registered, which implies the following consequences:
   - an absence of the separate legal personality,
   - an absence of publicity, giving it an occult character, in principle at least.
2. The associates freely agree on the object, the operation, the liquidation and the conditions of the Société en Participation.

   The freedom of the parties is confined only to respecting the fundamental principles of corporate law such as results from the Civil Code through its artt. 1832 and following.
3. Each associate remains the owner of his contributions.

   The Company may be administered by one or several managers. However the associates, due to the occult character of its structure, are personally responsable when dealing in their own name with third parties, unless they reveal the existence of the Company. Each participant is indefinitely and jointly liable for the debts of the Company.

   The title of the associates can not be represented by shares: each associate must make his own arrangement for proof of his participation. Proof may be given by any means (July 2nd 1969, Revue des Sociétés 1970, p. 274).

   Although the Société en Participation does not have a separate legal personality and the associates remain owners of their contributions, the deeds of incorporation are subject to the general system of company contributions.

   The associates are personally subject either to income tax for individual persons, or to corporate tax according to their nature.

   However, the registered Sociétés en Participation can opt to be subject to corporate tax.

B. External Controls

1. EXCHANGE CONTROLS

Until very recently all investments by residents in France (whatever their nationality) in another country and all investments in France by non residents were subject to prior consent by the Direction du Trésor of the Ministère de l'Economie et des Finances.

Theoretically this permission could not be refused for investments originating from Common Market countries.

However, the Direction du Trésor on certain occasions, requested further time to consider the application, in which case the proposed formation could be delayed for an indefinite period of time.

These rules have been fundamentally modified by a decree nr. 80-617 published on August 4th 1980.
All investments from French residents in a Common Market country or from residents in a EEC country in France are free provided:

a. they originate from a physical person resident in a EEC country or from a moral person (corporation) or establishment controled directly or indirectly by EEC residents.
b. they concern:
   - the creation or the extension of branches or subsidiaries wholly owned by the investor, or the complete take over of existing enterprises;
   - the participation in newly created or existing enterprises in view to create or maintain permanent economical relations;
   - the granting of loans for more than 5 years provided their purpose is to maintain permanent economical relations.

However, except for certain types of operations which may be dispensed of this formality[7], a prior notification for all such investments must be sent to the Direction du Trésor. If, within a delay of two months from the receipt of this notification, the Direction du Trésor has not indicated that the proposed investment is not conform to the above mentioned conditions, the investor can proceed.
Prior consent remains necessary for all investments which could have an influence on public order, public health or public security. Such is the case for manufacture or trading concerning weapons and ammunition.

2. TAKE-OVER CONTROLS

The external control of take-over controls is organized by the regulation of:
1. the offre publique d'achat (OPA) ou d'échange (OPE) (take-over bids or exchange of shares);
2. the disposal of a controlling block of shares.

These two procedures aim particularly to secure a certain protection of minorities in the take-over transactions; but they are only applied to companies listed on a stock exchange, in such a way that for companies which are not listed on a stock exchange, freedom of action remains the rule subject only to the fundamental principles of corporate law. This situation is not entirely satisfactory as has often been remarked.
The COB (Commission for stock exchange transactions, similar to the Securities and Exchange Commission in the US) tries sometimes to use its moral authority in order to influence promoters of take-over transactions of non-quoted companies. In a bold decision, it has even extended the rule so as to apply to a disposal of a controlling block of shares in a case which appeared not to be within the scope of regulation (decision of February 27th 1973).

a. The OPA and the OPE

Inspired by the anglo-saxon regulation of the take-over bids, the OPA or OPE procedure is contained in art. 178 (and following) of the general regulation of

7. The principle of these possible exceptions is indicated in the decree nr. 80-618 dated August 4th 1980.

the French stockbrokers association to which must be added a decision of the COB of January 13th 1970 modified by another decision of July 24th 1974.
The project of an OPA or OPE is presented before the Stock Exchange Committee (Chambre Syndicale des agents de change) by one or several banks. In order to be accepted, the project must conform to certain imperative rules. It is published in a special official bulletin referred to as the 'Cote' along with other information. The possibility of a counter-OPA is catered for. The result is published by the Committee.
A more simplified procedure is followed when the initiator of the offer holds at least 90% of the capital or when the transaction concerns a limited number of shares or a limited amount.

b. The disposal of controlling blocks of shares

Art. 201 and following of the general regulation of the Stockbrockers association (Compagnie des agents de change) try to assure a certain equality among shareholders on the occasion for a disposal of controlling blocks of shares.
The Committee determines whether the conditions for a disposal have been met. If so, a notice is published on the day when the transaction takes place and the buyer must then maintain his offer at the same price for fifteen stock exchange sessions in order to give the minorities the possibility of releasing their shares at the same price as that of the seller of the control shares.
For the buyer, this procedure is more dangerous than an OPA or an OPE for he becomes obliged to buy all the shares offered; it can though be simpler and less expensive.

3. ANTI-TRUST

French internal law established a regulation of understandings (ententes) under art. 419 of the Penal Code, and then with art. 59bis, ter and quater of the executive decree of June 30th 1945 which became art. 50 to 59 as modified by the law of July 19th 1977. This is a penal regulation.
Alongside this general control of understandings and of dominant market positions exercized by the Commission de la Concurrence (competition comittee), the law of July 19th 1977 established a more specific control of concentrations of establishments. This regulation is inspired by european projects but with an important difference in as much as it does not contain an authorisation procedure or a previous notification measure. The companies may alert the ministry of their project in order to provoke a control but they can also wait and let the control be brought about.
A concentration is forbidden when it endangers competition, giving a company more than 40% of the domestic market of similar products or services or 25% in the case of a vertical concentration.[8]

8. The law is applicable: In the case of a horizontal concentration (similar products and services) when the turnover realized by all the firms included in the concentration, on the domestic market only, represents more than 40% of national consumption; In the case of a vertical concentration (products or services of different nature), when the turnover on the domestic market of two at least of the firms or groups included in the concentration represents more than 25% of the national consumption for each of these two firms or groups.

The law applies to various types of concentration: 'Any legal act or transaction of any form, conveying property transfer or the total or the partial use of goods, rights and duties of a company or aiming at permitting an enterprise directly or indirectly to exercise on one or several other companies an influence that might govern or even guide the management or the operating of the latter'. (art. 4 – L. 1977)
After consulting the Commission de la Concurrence, the minister has the power to order companies either not to follow through with their project or if the project has been completed, to take steps in order to restore competition.
Non-compliance with such an injunction entails fines but no further penalties (unless the concentration also constitutes an understanding or an abuse of a dominant market position both of which are subject to penal sanctions).

III. THE FISCAL SYSTEM

A. *Corporate Income Tax*

1. The entities that are liable to corporate Income tax are: the SA, SARL, limited partnerships and partnerships limited by shares, for the share of the silent partner's profits;
   The entities that may opt for it are: limited and ordinary partnerships for the manager's share; civil companies; undertakings on joint accounts and sociétés de fait.
2. The profits that are taxable are based on the increase of the net assets between the opening and the closing of each financial year which does not have to correspond to the calendar year; there must nonetheless be at least a profit and loss account during the calendar year. The profits must take into account the new contributions or the withdrawal of money by associates. Profits include not only the ordinary profits and losses of the company but also the capital gains and losses.
   The difference in net assets is explained by the accounting which must be kept according to the General Accounting Plan, as modified eventually by particular accounting plans adapted to certain specific trading activities. Furthermore, these accounts must be declared on the obligatory accounting forms of the administration.
   Tax exemptions are limited and defined by regulations and include in particular 92,5% of the dividends received from subsidiaries as well as, within certain limits and time limits, the amount of dividends distributed in cash for subscribed shares.
   Fiscal losses of the five preceding years may be deducted from the profit of the year.
   Corporate income tax, and generally the dividends distributed, do not form an allowable expense. The finance law for 1982 contains completely new rules concerning payments made by french companies or french residents to persons of firms residents in countries considered as tax havens. These rules concern particularly the non deductibility of expenses unless strictly justified or dividends and profits paid to residents in tax haven countries.

3. The normal rate of corporate tax is 50%. Rebates or reductions are rarely based on the net taxable profits (which however are reduced for certain small, new companies), but apply to the rate which is reduced to 15% or 25% on capital gains on long term investments, that is for those held for over two years.
4. Quarterly instalments are paid in February, May, August and September, on the basis of 10% or 12,5% of the profits of the preceding financial year. The payment of the balance is required within three months and a half of the end of the bookyear: for example, before April 15th when the bookyear ends on December 31st.
5. Annual accounts are received and checked by local centres reporting to the Direction Generale des Impôts, whose inspectors can rectify the accounts of the four preceding years: in 1981, these inspectors may thus examine and reassess the profits of the financial years ending in 1977, 1978, 1979 and 1980.
   Disagreements regarding the assessment of the Inspector are brought before the head of the Centre or before the local tax service. Against their acceptance or refusal, appeal may be filed with the Administrative Court. The judgment of this court may finally be brought before the Conseil d'Etat whose decision cannot be appealed.

B. *Withholding Taxes*

Profits distributed by French companies to their non-resident shareholders are normally liable to tax at the rate of 25%, which is deductable at source, and which is only refundable if the shareholder in question is liable to tax in France on other income.
Dividends which are paid to shareholders resident in France are included in the computation of their Income Tax (impôt sur le revenu, IR), which is a graduated tax varying between nought and 60%. Dividends received by shareholders on which the usual 50% Corporation Tax has been paid are not liable to deduction of tax at source, and entitle the holder to a 'tax credit' against his liability for Income Tax.[9]

Example:

A company earns a profit of	F. 200
It has to pay 50% Corporation Tax	F. 100
To be distributed to the shareholders	F. 100
If the distributed dividend amounts to	F. 80
– F. 40 is due to shareholders domiciled or permanently resident in France	
– F. 40 is due to non-resident shareholders	
the respective tax liabilities are:	
– shareholders in France, regardless of their nationality receive	F. 40
plus a tax credit of	F. 20
They must declare a taxable income of	F. 60
and their tax liability is	F. 20

9. This tax credit is the so-called 'avoir fiscal'.

- non-resident shareholders receive after deduction at source (40 – 10) F. 30

plus a 'tax credit' of F. 10 which can only be used if the shareholder has other taxable income arising in France, such as an income from a business activity. If the shareholder is resident in a country with which France has a double taxation agreement, tax is not always deducted at source but becomes payable at a reduced rate, in which case the amount paid can be set against the recipient's liability to tax in his own country.

Moreover certain countries have obtained, for the residents, the advantage of the tax credit which can be refunded under certain conditions and modalities.

As regards profits obtained by French branches of foreign companies, these profits, whether or not transfered, are submitted to art. 7.1 of the law passed on 12th July 1965 which is now art. 115quinquies of the General Tax Code. Broadly the effect is as follows:

1. If in any year there is no trading profit in France, or if there is a loss in France but the foreign parent company nevertheless pays a dividend in the same year, then the 25% deduction at source does not apply;
2. If in any year a trading profit is made in France and the parent company does not pay a dividend in that year, the amount which will be deducted at source is provisionally computed by reference to the taxable profits arising in France, subject to certain corrections which are not within the scope of this paper. For the purposes of calculating the profits the amount of Corporation Tax paid may be deducted.

The provisional assessment referred to in 2. above may be revised if the company shows that the actual dividend was smaller or has been distributed to persons having their residence or place of business in France.

It should be noted that these principles have been modified or overridden by the provisions of a number of tax agreements, among which the following should be mentioned:

- For French branches of German companies there is no deduction at source.
- For French branches of British and US companies, the basis of assessment is limited to two-thirds of the net profit of the French branch, and the rate is 15%,
- For French branches of Belgian and Italian companies the basis of assessment can be limited (option) to 25% of the taxable income at the normal rate of 25%,
- For French branches of Swiss companies the basis of assessment is the normal one, but the rate is reduced to 5%.

Interest paid to non residents in principle is subject to the deduction of tax at the rate of 38%. This deduction can be waived or reduced to 10% or 15% when the creditors are domiciled in a country with which France has an international fiscal agreement.

Rents, fees and other remunerations (except salaries which are subject to a special deduction) paid to non-residents are subject to a deduction at a general rate of 33,33% which is usually reduced by international conventions.

The reduced rates on dividends and rents are as follows for the principal countries having a fiscal convention with France:

	% of withholding	
	Dividends	*Rents*
Belgium	15 *c.* 10 *d.*	0
Canada	15	10 (except 3, 4 art. 12 Convention)
Denmark	0	0
West-Germany	0 *a.* 15 *b.*	0
United-Kingdom	15 5 *f.*	exemption
Greece	15	5
Italy	15	0
Japan	15	10
Luxembourg	15 5 *e.*	0
Netherlands	15 5 *e.*	0
Spain	15 10 *e.*	
Sweden	15 *c.* 5 *e.*	0
Switzerland	0 15 *q.*	
USA	15 *c.* 5 *f.*	5

a. If right to avoir fiscal or if the shareholder is a parent company owning 25% or more of the capital,
b. profits other than those comprised in a) above,
c. countries whose residents benefit from avoir fiscal,
d. if the shareholder is a parent company owning at least 10% of the capital,
e. if the shareholder is a parent company owning at least 25% of the capital,
f. if the shareholder is a parent company owning at least 10% of the capital and with special conditions,
g. if the shareholder is a parent company owning at least 20% of the capital with special conditions.

C. Registration and Stamp Fees

Company's statutes and certain documents, more particulary those destined to be registered such as notarial deeds, powers of attorney, must be executed on stamped paper whose basic cost is F. 10 for a sheet of 21 x 29,7 centimeters.

The registration of the company's deed of incorporation costs 1% of the paid-up capital if this is paid in cash. The rate is the same for payments in kind obtained from another company but it is increased to 12% for those obtained from individuals.

An increase of capital by capitalisation of profits or reserves is taxed at a rate of 12%, but the rate is provisionally reduced to 6%, and even 3% in some cases.[10]

Mergers are registered at a fixed fee of F. 600 or 1,20% of any excess of the value of the contributions of the acquired companies over the amount of their nominal capital which is absorbed in the merger.

Transformation of companies within the same category, for instance from an SA into a SARL, only requires a fixed fee of F. 200. Nevertheless, when a partnership goes public and vice versa, and in certain other cases, the existence of reserves may entail a distribution tax.

Dissolution are registered at a fixed fee of F. 600.

The transfer of participants' rights such as SARL shares, ordinary and limited partnership's shares is subject to a registration fee of 4,80% on the value of transfer. The same applies to the transfer of shares of an SA or of a partnership limited by shares whenever they are recorded in a bilateral agreement (including a simple exchange of letters). The transfer price may be adjusted by the administration if it considers that the true value of the shares is not involved. Simple transfers or conveyances of shares are always free from registration fees as long as there is no written bilateral agreement.

An important aspect of French tax case law should be underlined here.

If nearly all the shares of a commercial or industrial company were sold simultaneously or within a short period of time to one or several buyers, the tax authorities could claim that the operation corresponded in fact to the sale of the goodwill.[11]

The consequences were disastrous: seller and buyer were jointly liable for the payment of 16,8% registration tax (plus penalties) on the value of the goodwill. Moreover the company whose shares had been sold could be considered as liquidated which involved payment of the corporate tax on capital gains and the distribution tax on the surplus left by the liquidation.

10. This provisional reduction is valid actually until December 31st. 1981 but has already been extended a certain number of times.

11. Goodwill is the nearest translation to the French notion of 'fonds de commerce' which normally includes the right to use the name of the company, the clientele, lease rights, etc... In certain cases, even with a 16,8% registration tax, buying the 'fonds de commerce' is a better proposition than buying the shares in as much as the buyer of the 'fonds de commerce' acquires all the assets of the company without the liabilities.

However a recent official interpretation dated March 3rd. 1981 has commented on the answer which had been given by the Minister to a member of Parliament.[12]

The French tax authorities now consider – and this is a very substantial change from the former case law – that the simultaneous sale or transfer of all the shares, or of a majority of the shares of a commercial company (2/3 for an SA and 3/4 for a SARL) can only be considered as a disguised sale or transfer of the companies assets, or, still worse, as a liquidation of the company whose shares have been sold or transfered followed by the floating of a new company, if a certain number of important changes occur within a certain delay i.e. normally within 3 to 5 years after the sale or transfer of the shares.

These important changes may be the dissolution or a merger, or the sale of most of the assets or of essential assets or important amendments concerning the object for which the company has been established.

The list of these important changes is certainly not limited but it now appears that the simultaneous sale of even 100% of the shares of a French commercial company is possible if, as underlined, no major changes are considered within a reasonable period of time as regards the existence, the assets and the activities of the company.

D. Individual Taxes

1. All French or foreign individuals who are resident in France for tax purposes are liable to income tax.

Residents are those who have their family home or their main residence or the center of their financial interests or those who pursue a profession in France. In principle, income from all sources is subject to tax except foreign income which by virtue of international conventions is taxed in another country.

2. Taxable income can be divided into the following categories:

a. Income from personal effort, salaries receiving a standard deduction of 10% and then 20%; pensions and life annuities after the same deductions subject to a maximum amount; net income from real estate; net profits from farming; net profits from industrial and commercial activities; net profits from non-commercial activities, which includes all the other types of income.

Income from bonds and shares includes interest from loans which may be released outright from tax entirely by the payment of 25% of the interest of non-indexed bonds or of 38% for that of loans and accounts.

Dividends are taxable to the extent of the net amount paid by the distributing company, together with a tax credit (avoir fiscal) of 50%, which will later be deducted from the tax to be paid.

12. Members of Parliament have the right to submit any practical or theoretical problem to the competent minister in the form of a 'written question' (question écrite). The Minister's answer is published in the official gazette (Journal Officiel). It has no legal value and Courts are in no way obliged to accept the interpretation contained in this answer (réponse à une question écrite) which however is normally respected by the administration itself.

b. Taxable capital gains include capital gains on real estate which are determined by retaining an indexed value for real-estate; they are generally taxed at a fixed rate of 15%. This rate also applies to capital gains on shares and stocks transferred by associates owning more than a fourth of the capital. Moreover, certain capital gains regularly obtained on the stock exchange are taxed at 30% or may even be combined with the other income and be subjected to income tax if they form most of the taxpayer's revenue.

c. Exemptions include income taxed abroad, for instance interest and certain capital gains which have been subject to a withholding tax. They also include income from abroad for which international conventions allocate taxation to the country of origin. But in this case, these tax-exempt revenues are nevertheless taken in account in determining the tax rate applicable to other income ('exemption with progression').
General deductions include certain financial and other expenses for the main residence and certain pensions paid for example to aged parents without resources.
Further deductions include, within certain limits, certain stock market investments, life-insurance premiums and gifts to charitable institutions.

3. Income tax is applied at progressive rates up to 60% with 13 brackets; marriage and family dependents determine a family quotient by person, dividing the income and reducing the progression. Taxable income is divided by the appropriate quotient; tax is computed on the result and then multiplied by the quotient to arrive at the tax liabilities. The finance law for 1982 has created an exceptional increase of 10% for all those who pay more than F 25,000 income tax. Also the effect of the family quotient has been limited.

4. Gift and inheritance duties are fixed at rates varying from 0 to 20% for free transfers of ownership in a direct line of succession (ascendants, descendants) or between husband and wife. This rate is raised; 35% and 40% between brothers and sisters, to 55% and even 60% between distant relatives or between different families.
Some life-insurance benefits are exempt from tax; this also applies under certain conditions to woods, forests and rural real-estates rented on a long term basis, for 3/4 of their value.
Housing real estate built between 1948 and September 1973 is tax exempt for a first transfer (inheritance or gift).
Inheritance duties are payable within six months of the death in cash, or by public loans or works of art if they are accepted by the State. Heirs of property without usufruct may delay the payment of the duties until the death of the tenant but only under certain conditions and guarantees. Heirs in a direct line of an estate mostly comprising real estate or assets not quoted on the stock exchange may request that payment be spread out over five to ten years, with interest.
The finance law for 1982 has created a yearly tax on capital. This new 'Impots sur les Grandes Fortunes' applies to all natural persons whose fortune amounts to more than 3 million francs. It applies, under certain conditions, to non residents for their estate in France. The rate is 0,5% for the bracket

between 3 and 5 million, 1% between 5 and 10 million and 1,5% over 10 million francs.

E. Indirect Taxes

These include mainly the value added tax (VAT), reorganized after 1979 to conform to the EC sixth directive. The VAT concerns all deliveries, imports or sales in France and almost all of the services rendered to individuals resident in an EC country. The general rate is 17,60% on the price or the value without tax; it is reduced to 7% for certain services and basic food products. The rate is increased to 33,33% on gems and precious materials, jewerly, photographic equipment, recordplayers; this higher rate also applies to private cars and large motorcycles.
All salaries and certain fees (doctors, lawyers, notaries, insurance experts), insurance and bank transactions as well as exports are tax exempt.
The tax is paid monthly by the supplier who bills his customer for it; the latter recuperates the tax if he himself is subject to it and this with a delay of one month and under certain conditions; other delays apply in respect of fixed assets (constructions equipment).
Various ad valorem taxes are collected under different systems and rates other than that of the VAT on various consumer products added on to the VAT. Professional banking and financial activities are exempt from VAT and are subject to a tax on loans consented in french francs.
High excise taxes apply to the production, import and sale of alcohol. Wine, cider and various drinks are subject to a transportation fee as well as to different para-fiscal taxes. A wheel-axle tax applies to certain road vehicles (for a weight of 16 tons or more).

F. Fiscal Incentives

Fiscal incentives consist of exemptions from or reductions of the basic corporate tax or income tax for new enterprises or others set up in regions with high unemployment.
A fiscal incentive for investment in new equipment reduces the tax by 10% of the excess of investments over those of the previous year; this incentive concerns new equipment for industry and commerce and allows also accelerated depreciation.

G. Social Security

Compulsory insurance premiums for various risks (sickness, accidents at work, unemployment, family allowances, additional old age and retirement pensions) of wage-earners reach 50% up to a maximum salary, 40% of which is paid by the employer, and 10% is withheld from the employee's wage. Above this salary ceiling (F. 79.080 in 1982) the premiums of the general system are discontinued or reduced to 10% for sickness; but on the part of the salaries surpassing the ceiling there are generally special dues for the retirement of higher level employees ranging from 8% to 16% of these amounts.

H. Various Local Taxes

In order to furnish funds to townships, departments or regions, local taxes are imposed on real estate owners and occupants who pay either a private housing tax or a professional tax (the former 'patente'[13] for industrial or commercial use).

The taxable base includes the rental value of the premises and the equipment used, as well as salaries paid or turnover. Its amount may vary substantially depending on the financial needs of the local authorities where the factory or offices are set up. Partial exemptions are foreseen for drawing new industries to regions suffering unemployment.

I. International Conventions to Avoid Double Taxation

France has concluded numerous international conventions to avoid double taxation; among those are:

Algeria	October 2, 1968	Italy	October 29, 1968
Australia	April 13, 1976	Japan	November 27, 1964
Austria	Ocotber 8, 1959	Lebanon	July 24, 1962
Belgium	March 10, 1964	Luxembourg	April 1, 1958
Brazil	September 10, 1971	Monaco	May 16, 1963
Canada	March 16, 1971	Morocco	May 28, 1970
Czechoslovakia	June 1, 1973	Netherlands	March 16, 1973
Denmark	February 8, 1967	Norway	September 23, 1953
Finland	September 11, 1970	Pakistan	July 22, 1966
West-Germany	July 21, 1959	Spain	June 27, 1973
Greece	May 22, 1968	Sweden	December 24, 1936
India	March 26, 1969	Switzerland	September 9, 1966
Iran	June 27, 1973	Tunisia	May 28, 1973
Ireland	March 21, 1968	United-Kingdom	May 22, 1968
Israël	August 20, 1963	USA	July 28, 1967

J. Withholding Taxes

Withholding taxes on dividends interest and rents have been mentioned in chapter B. 1 but tax is also withheld from the following:

13. The 'patente' has been recently replaced by the 'taxe professionnelle' which is now a serious political issue and will probably be modified in the near future.

- salaries of non-residents for their activity in France: 15% from 25.800 to 76.100 of annual salaries and 25% beyond 76.100;
- fees and other remunerations for independent work in France by non-residents; a withholding tax at the rate of 33,33% applies, which is usually waived in international conventions which provide taxation in the country of residence.

K. Companies with Special Status

Industrial and commercial enterprises, almost always SA or SARL, may form a *société en participation* (see above page 173) without fiscal or legal individuality; for instance for a specific work (building of a dam or a building, producing a motion picture) in which they would share the work to be done and in which they would split the results, profits or losses.
For a longer cooperation, enterprises may group various technical and commercial means in *'groupements d'intérêt économique'* (GIE) (see above page 172) which has a moral personality but is fiscally 'transparent' so that the partners must include their share of the results in their taxable profits.
Civil companies are often formed to acquire and to build real-estate and to manage it; they may be fiscally transparent: each associate, firm or individual, must then declare his share of the results. In certain cases, however the partners can elect that the company be treated as a taxable entity.

IV. LABOUR ASPECTS

A. Principles of Labour Rights

The very recent political changes in France will almost certainly result in important modifications in labour rights.
It is probable that the lay-off of employees will be rendered more difficult. At the present time it is not expected that the complicated structure of employees delegates, works committees and union delegates will be fundamentally modified but their powers will almost certainly be increased and whereas, for the time being there is no real system of co-determination in France it is probable that this situation will be modified in the near future.

1. GENERALITIES: SUBORDINATION, THE CRITERIA OF A WORK CONTRACT

At the top of the pyramid are the shareholders representatives who receive their directive and administrative powers from their mandators, the associates or shareholders.[14]

14. The French legal terminology for shareholder representatives is 'mandataires sociaux'.

The essential feature common to employees, workers and executives is that all are subject to a higher authority, or, in other words, they are all subordinates. This situation of subordination is the criterium allowing one to qualify contract relations as pertaining to labour rights.
It is thus clear that the shareholders representative – gérant, Président – directeur général or Président du Directoire[15] – at the top of the pyramid, escapes all subordination: he does not receive orders, he gives them. On the other hand, he must, as any other representative account for the execution of his mandate to the associates or shareholders, to the Board of Directors or to the Supervisory Board.
It is true nonetheless that the same person may, under certain conditions which we will examine, hold both the offices of shareholders representatives and employee.

2. EMPLOYMENT

a. Length of time

The employee and the employer may conclude a contract for a limited period of time or for an indefinite period.
The choice is important for the system of an employment contract; its nature depends on its duration.
If the contract is concluded for a limited period of time, it may be renewed once or not renewed at all; the length of time may be fixed from one date to another, for a season, for a task or for a works site. If the employment continues after the time limit of the contract, it automatically becomes a contract for an indefinite period.

b. Form

The contract for a limited period of time, must necessarily be a written document. An ordonance of 5th February 1982 has strictly limited the cases in which an employment contract may be concluded for a limited period of time and has also modified the rules applying to this type of contract. The decree due to complete this ordinance has not yet been published. All information hereafter on this type of contract is based on the situation existing before this ordinance and future decree.
The indefinite contract way be oral or in writing. However collective agreements invariably prescribe that the contract be the object of a letter containing all necessary details concerning for example, the office to be held, qualifications and remuneration.

c. Trial period

Before the employee is definitively employed, it is always possible for the parties to agree on a period during which they have a chance to evaluate each

15. The 'gérant' is the manager of an SARL. The Président Directeur Général or Président du Directoire is the head exécutive of an SA.

other. During this period, each party, the employer as well as the employee, has the possibility of termination without having to justify himself. The termination is thus discretionary resulting in a certain insecurity for both parties. In order to remedy this, customs and collective agreements usually limit the trial period and, if such is the case, the parties may not extend or renew the period unless a collective agreement has provided for such an extension or renewal. For employees with an indefinite contract, the trial period is about one month whereas for executives it is generally three months. For a contract limited time wise, it depends on the length of time for which it was concluded.

3. MODIFICATION DURING AN EMPLOYMENT

In French law, the manager of a company has the possibility, deriving from his power of organization, of modifying the employment contract of his employees but of course under the condition that he does not use this power in an arbitrary or abusive way. Against this necessary power, the employee has an identical one which is to be able to refuse modifications that change the substance of the contract initially concluded. The employee must have time to evaluate and to appreciate the modification. If he refuses and if the employer maintains his decision, the contract will inevitably be ended but the financial consequences caused by the termination will be assumed by the employer who took the initiative to modify the initial agreement.

4. END OF EMPLOYMENT CONTRACT

During the employment contract, the employer may come across several types of difficulties:

a. The employee may be incompetent or undisciplined or make mistakes.
b. The economic situation may force the company to lay off employees.
c. The employee may be ill, and therefore absent and this absence severely upsets the functioning of the company.
d. The employee retires.
e. By mutual agreement the employer and the employee may decide to terminate the contract.
f. The employee may resign unilaterally.

These points are considered successively below.

a. The employee is incompetent

The manager of a company, after having reprimanded the employee, notices that he does not improve.

The Law of 1973 provides for a procedure, rather complicated, concerning companies with more than eleven employees, designed especially for indefinite contracts when the length of service of the employee in the company has exceeded a year. Before making the decision to dismiss the employee, the latter must be summoned and informed that his dismissal may eventual-

ly be considered and that he may be assisted during the meeting by anyone of his choice among the company's personnel. After this meeting and as a precautionary measure, the employer must consider his decision for forty-eight hours before sending the employee a letter of dismissal, without any obligation to state the reason. The employee thus dismissed has a short time to ask the employer to reveal, in a written document, both the real and serious reasons for his dismissal. The employer must reveal these reasons within a period of ten days after having received the employee's request.
The procedure is laid down in the law and is easy to follow, just as in a guide-book.
On the other hand, it is quite important to draw the attention to the fact that in case of litigation, the employer has to prove that the reasons which motivated the dismissal were real and serious, such as the fact that the company's functioning was hindered. If he is not able to prove the existence of real and serious reasons, the company may be sued for damages with a minimum of six months salary.
If the reason of the dismissal is faulty behaviour, a first difficulty arises when evaluating this faulty behaviour.
A second difficulty lies in the nature of the offence which may be qualified as a serious or as a grievous offence[16] which, if proved, can justify an immediate suspension of the employment contract. Before considering the specific consequences of a serious or a grievous offence, the consequences generally of termination of the contract are considered.
In the termination of an indefinite contract the employee is entitled first of all to a previous notice period which may range from two to six months depending on his position in the hierarchy, a period during which he will continue to work but will have the chance to look for a new employment; secondly, the employee will receive a dismissal indemnity which amount varies according to years of service in the company, age and conditions laid down by collective bargaining.
In the case of a contract limited time-wise, the employee has the right to work and therefore to be paid until the date agreed upon in the contract. A serious offence is necessary in order to interrupt the contract. If such an offence is not established and proved, the employer risks paying both the amount of salary that the employee would have received had he continued working until the end of his contract and damages, if any.
In any case, if the offence is serious, the employee loses his rights to previous notice and dismissal indemnity. If the offence is grievous he is not only deprived of the previous notice and the indemnity but he also loses the right to holiday allowance for the period preceding the grievous offence.

b. The economic situation puts the company in a critical position whether temporarily or definitely

Although the behaviour of the employee is not in any way a factor it is nevertheless his future that is involved.

16. French law makes a difference between a serious offence (faute grave) and a grievous offence (faute lourde).

A law passed in 1975 provides protection for the employee.
Prior to the decision to lay off employees for economic reasons and after having followed a special procedure in the company, the manager of the company must ask the permission from the Labour Inspection (Inspection du Travail) which is part of the Ministry of Labour.
Labour Inspection is entitled to initiate a thorough investigation and may be called upon to give the reasons for its refusal or authorization.
Any company that decides to lay off some of its personnel, even if it concerns only one employee, without having previously asked the authorization from the appropriate labour inspector risks prosecution and the payment of damages.
The legal system for economic lay offs guarantees a substantial financial protection for the employee for at least one year; it also prohibits the manager of a company that has used this procedure to engage new employees or to lay off whoever it may be without the previous authorization from the Labour Inspection.

c. Illness

The employment contract may also be broken if circumstances outside one's control arise; such is the case of a continued illness upsetting the correct functioning of the company to such an extent that it becomes necessary to replace the sick employee.
According to certain collective agreements, the employee may, in case of illness, claim a dismissal indemnity even though the employer does not wish either in fact or in law to end the contract.

d. Retirement

The arrival of the retirement age, as defined by a collective bargaining, provides a natural end to the employment relationships. The person concerned is often entitled to a departure indemnity, similar to the dismissal indemnity.

e. Termination by a mutual agreement

The two parties are completely aware of the impossibility to continue their cooperation and decide on the circumstances in which they will terminate it. On the condition of the implementation of the first steps of the termination procedure and the drawing up of a settlement, the termination will be considered as a lay off giving the employee right to unemployment benefits paid by social security funds.

f. Resignation

It is not uncommon that an employee resigns to seek better fortune in another company. Doing so he cannot count on a dismissal indemnity and must continue to work for the time of notice necessary for the employer to find a substitute. Precautions should be taken so that the resignation does not appear to have been given under pressure.

5. SHAREHOLDER APPOINTEES AND EMPLOYMENT CONTRACT

In French law, the Presidents of the Board of Directors and of the Directoire, Directeurs Généraux and managers are removable at any moment, and without reason, from their appointed position.
These shareholders appointees may nevertheless, under certain conditions, be simultaneously shareholder representatives and employees but this plurality of offices is often used in an attempt to shelter these appointees from the risk of immediate removal by the shareholders or associates.
The Courts have declared invalid employment contracts concluded in such conditions if they are not related to the real activity of the employee and if the employee was not actually subordinated and especially paid for the work provided.
It should however be underlined that the unpaid appointee benefits from social protection created especially for employees, social security and pension for instance.

6. CONTROL AND LITIGATION

Labour inspectors and controllers form a body of specialized civil servants with extensive powers.
Their task is to ensure that all the rules concerning employment, work conditions, hygiene and security are followed.
Special Courts, the Conseils de Prud'hommes, which exist since the 19th century – the second one created in France is at Rouen and was decided by Napoleon at Tilsitt – are the only courts having jurisdiction in matters concerning employment contracts. There is still doubt as to whether or not executives may appeal to ordinary Courts; decisions rendered in this matter have been contradictory.

B. Wage Negotiations

One must distinguish between negotiations in which the manager of the company participates personally, and those in which he does not participate but whose consequences will apply to him as member of a certain branch of trade or industry.

COLLECTIVE BARGAINING

Within each branch of economic activity, professional organisations have been created, employer's associations on one side and labour unions on the other. After long negotiations these organisations sign collective agreements which regulate, in each branch, all relations between employers and employees.
These agreements are always concluded for a short period of time renewable by tacit agreement. In principle, if a company is not a member of the organisations who have signed the agreement, it is not obliged to abide by its rules.

Nevertheless, if the Ministry of Labour extends, by decree, the application of the agreement to all companies operating in the particular branch, the company is obliged to comply with the clauses of the agreement from the day of the extension decree.
If the employer is asked to install one of the representatives mentioned above, he cannot refuse to implement the procedure specific for each type of delegate.
To refuse would be to risk penalties for having impeded the normal practice of employee's representation; such prosecutions are becoming more and more frequent and are automatically followed by penalties.
It should be noted as a striking difference between labour law and general law that it is not necessary for the prosecuting party to prove malicious intent in order to obtain a conviction.

C. Employee Representation

Since 1945 in particular, French law has developed several forms of employee representation whose duty it is to reveal the employees' wishes and demands. It is expected that the function, the powers and prerogatives of the whole system of employee's representation will be affected by major changes during 1982, but details are as yet uncertain. The following should be mentioned:
1. Employee delegates (délégués du personnel).
2. Representatives in the works committee (représentants au comité d'entreprise).
3. Union delegates (délégués syndicaux).
4. Union representatives at the works committee (délégué syndical au comité d'entreprise).

Before reviewing in more detail each of these types of 'social partners' it should be noted that they are installed with the help of the manager of the company but not on his initiative.

1. EMPLOYEES DELEGATES

Designation

As soon as the company has normally more than eleven employees, they may demand that an election for employee delegates be held.
The number of delegates varies with the number of employees: it ranges from one delegate plus one deputy if the number of employees is between 11 and 25, to nine delegates with nine deputies if the number of employees is between 501 and 1000. For larger companies, there is one additional delegate and one deputy for each extra bracket of 500 employees.
The election system is rather complicated and lawsuits concerning the elections are referred to the Tribunal d'Instance (the Magistrate's court).
Delegates are elected for one year and are eligible for re-election.

Function, powers and prerogatives

Their function is fixed by the law but its extent can be modified and extended by collective agreements.
Employee delegates must first of all report to the manager of the company all individual or collective claims concerning the application of salary rates, professional classifications, laws and regulations concerning protection, hygiene, security, social funds and paid holidays.
They are free to go to the Labour inspector with all complaints and observations concerning the application of legal regulations whose control is expressly given to this authority.
If a company does not have a works committee, the powers of the employee delegates are much increased: they are then empowered to discuss with the employer all suggestions regarding:

- social works,
- internal regulations,
- work hours: division on daily and weekly basis,
- compensating rest,
- number of work hours,
- lay-offs for economic reasons,
- handicapped persons,
- worker training,
- seminars for executives and for youth counselors.

On the other hand, if a works committee has been established the employee delegates form, with the members of the committee, a special body which chooses the members of the hygiene and security committee.
It is obvious that the delegates' function is to assert themselves at the heart of the company and during work hours.
Therefore, they have the right to devote part of their working hours not to the work that they have been assigned to do and which they must accomplish under their employer contract, but to making various contacts with their mandators.
They are thus entitled to fifteen hours per month paid as working hours by the company.
Other facilities are given to the delegates such as the possibility to move about freely in the workrooms, offices, and even outside company premises if the mandate requires it; or the possibility of using an advertising billboard which must be put at their disposal by the company to enable them to publish notes which they wish to communicate to the personnel.
The company is moreover obliged to put at their disposal a meeting room in which they may only discuss official matters.
The law also obliges the manager of the firm to meet with the employee delegates collectively at least once a month and at their request, in case of emergency.
Beside these periodical meetings the manager must also meet with delegates at their request either individually or by category (employee, executive, worker), or by workroom, department or professional specialty, depending on the issues at stake.
At their request, the employee delegates may receive external assistance in

the person of a representative of the union of their profession when they are to meet with the employer.

Dismissal of employee delegates

Employee's delegates function as the echo of all the demands inside the company. This may cause the management to feel a strong desire to sever relations with these persons who may be, by definition, a particular nuisance.
The law therefore contains a protective system that makes the dismissal of an employee delegate most difficult.
If a works committee exists, it must be consulted. The manager can address a dismissal letter as provided by law only if the committee gives its approval.
If the works committee refuses to approve the dismissal of the employee delegate, or if no such committee has been set up, the company must, before any definite decision, request the authorization of the competent Labour Inspector.
The Labour Inspector's decision is reached after a complete investigation carried out inside the company.
In case of a refusal, the company may appeal either to the administration or to the court.
The employer may not disregard these preliminaries to the dismissal of an employee.
Failing to comply with them, he is exposed to certain sanctions which are very severe; first a penal sanction (fine), then the reinstatement of the employee ordered by a summary procedure, and finally damages which may be granted to the employee representative as well as to the union to which the representative belongs.

2. REPRESENTATIVES IN THE WORKS COMMITTEE

Designation

If a company employs at least 50 employees, a works committee must be set up.
The number of personnel representatives in the works committee varies with the number of employees.
It ranges from 3 representatives and 3 deputies if there are 50 to 75 employees, up to 11 representatives and 11 deputies if there are over 10.000 employees.
Representatives in the works committee are elected by employees who have been working in the company for more than 6 months.
Here again, the law thoroughly regulates the eligibility requirements as well as the electoral process.
In case of litigation, the Tribunal d'Instance has jurisdiction.
The employer may have several establishments in places more or less distant from each other: when an establishment reaches the necessary number for the setting up of a works committee, elections must be held for an establishment committee.

The rules are identical to those governing the works committees.
If a company has several establishment committees, a central committee must be formed, composed of a number of delegates elected from the different establishment committees and an equal number of normal representatives. Nevertheless, the central committee may not include more than 15 delegates and 15 deputies.

Powers of the works committee

In professional, economic and financial fields, the powers of the committee are strictly advisory: it receives information and gives its opinion.
On the other hand, in the social field, it has management powers.

The works committee as a consultative body

Advance consultation of the committee, which in no way binds the manager of the company is necessary for any important decision that might affect the general functioning of the company, its employment level and work conditions.
The management is obliged to make at least one annual report add, sometimes quarterly reports are required.
Moreover, in public limited companies (SA) two members of the works committee must participate in all the sessions of the Board of Directors or of the Supervisory Board but only in an advisory capacity.
The absence of these delegates at one of the sessions results in the invalidity of the resolutions.
Moreover, still only for the SA, the works committee is entitled to receive, before its presentation to the General Meeting of Shareholders, the profit and loss account, the annual balance sheet of the company, the auditor's report and generally speaking all the other documents to be submitted to the General Meeting of Shareholders.
To examine all the information that it receives, the works committee may request the assistance of a chartered accountant whose fees are paid by the company.
As regards the work situation, there cannot be a decrease of employment or collective lay offs for economic reasons, if the matter has not been referred in advance to the works committee allowing it to give its opinion on the operations contemplated by the company.
Also, no individual dismissal of the supervisory staff may occur without previous notification of the works committee.
The works committee must be consulted in connection with improvements of work conditions that are desired or that are contemplated by the company; as well as on everything having to do with the employment situation for the youth, women and handicapped persons and with discipline rules which must be followed by all employees of the company.
In respect of work hours, a certain number of very specific points must be referred to the works committee such as individual hours, paid holidays, compensating rest etc.
Just as in matters pertaining to professional training, the works committee

must be consulted on general problems relating to professional improvement and training of employees.
The works committee is also directly concerned with the participation of the employees in the profits of the company and in its economic growth: these points are reviewed in more detail below.
Generally speaking, since 1977 the company is obliged, under certain conditions related to the number of employees, to establish a social balance sheet and to submit it to the works committee every year.

The works committee as a management body

The works committee manages social services by means of a budget financed by payments made by the company proportionate to the total of salaries. Its role in this field may be of considerable importance.
These social services include: pension funds; the improvement of welfare conditions (for instance, canteens, co-ops, housing, family gardens, public day-nurseries, children holiday camps); sport and leisure activities; professional or educational institutions connected to the company (such as apprenticeship and professional training centres, libraries, study circles, domestic science and general culture courses); the welfare of the worker in the factory; the medical service of the company and social projects.

Functioning of the works committee

The works committee meets at least once a month at the request of the manager of the company. If the majority of the members of the committee express the desire, further mensual meetings must be held.
The chairman of the meeting is ex officio the manager of the company.[17]
The agenda of the meetings is set by the manager of the company and the secretary of the committee. Beside the President, only the members are entitled to vote. The deputy members and union representatives are consulted.
The variety of tasks attributed to the committee is such that it may be desirable to create specialized commissions for the preparation and study of specific problems such as hygiene, security, professional training and employment, etc.
To ensure that the members have the time and independence needed to assume these responsibilities, they are entitled to a number of working hours which are paid even though they devote this time to their works committee tasks. Except in exceptional circumstances, the maximum is 20 hours per month. They must of course devote these hours to the tasks described. In addition, the time used for committee and commission sessions is paid by the employer.

Dismissal of members of the works committee

The activity of the members of the works committee may involve conflicts with the management.

17. Gérant of a SARL, Président du Conseil d'administration or Président du Directoire of an SA.

In order to avoid arbitrary dismissals, the elected members enjoy special protection which is in force for the duration of their mandate and a period of six months following its expiration.
The procedure is the following: the manager must announce his intention to dismiss the employee representative and summon the works committee to examine the request and its reasons.
If the committee approves the proposal, the dismissal may be carried out. If the committee refuses, the manager must apply to the Labour Inspector who gives his opinion. The party who is not satisfied with the opinion given by the Labour Inspector may ask the Ministry of Labour to overrule the decision. Furthermore the disagreement can be brought before the Tribunal Administratif (Administrative Court).
It is essential to underline that unless the employer has received the necessary authorization, he is paralysed. He cannot dismiss an employee representative without risking serious problems such as penalties and damages. At the same time, by a summary procedure, the employee may obtain his reinstatement in the company against the company's will.

3. UNION DELEGATES

So far, only representatives elected by the other employees have been discussed.
We must now review a quite different situation, one in which external discussion partners are imposed upon the manager of the company, whose presence it is difficult to challenge. This concerns union delegates and union representatives in the works committee, both of whom are employed by the company but are entrusted with a mandate by external bodies viz. departemental federations of labour unions.
The union delegate may only function in companies employing usually more than 50 employees; his role is to ensure the protection of employees' professional interests inside the company. He is therefore prohibited from acting in favour of a political party whichever it may be. The union's activities are set out explicitly by law which provides as their only object 'the study and the protection of economic, industrial, commercial and agricultural interests'. Political activities therefore cannot be the purpose of a union.
Unions may create, inside the companies themselves, union branches.
However, the concept of a union branch was not defined by the legislation of 1968.
It is now recognized that the designation of a union delegate suffices to prove the existence inside a company of a union branch. The manager of the company need not have been previously notified.
At this point, it is useful to consider briefly a very important feature in French law, i.e. union representation.
There are unions that are representative on a national scale: they participate in all social negotiations where employer representatives are present. They have the following charateristics: large number of members, independence, volume of contributions paid by members and a patriotic attitude during the

german occupation. The following unions are considered as legally representative: the CGT, FO, CFTC, CFDT and the CGC.[18]
It is unusual that the employees of a company form a 'house' union. They must prove, contrary to those unions mentioned above, that the union actually represents employees inside the company.
There cannot be more union delegates than the number fixed by law, that is one delegate for companies or establishments employing from 50 to 1000 employees and a maximum of four delegates for companies or establishments with more than 6000 employees.
To become a union delegate one must meet a certain number of conditions based on age and years of service inside the company. The mandate is not fixed for a certain period; it only ends with the repeal.
The range of the mandate is quite wide; it contains:

1. Informing members of the union branch on the union's activities as well as on all questions with which the union is concerned;
2. Information on union problems occurring inside the company or the establishment;
3. Discussion and signing of agreements, if any concerning employee profit-sharing schemes;
4. Assistance to employee delegates upon their requests;
5. Discussion and signing of agreements concerning professional elections (employee delegates, works committee);
6. Discussion and signing of establishment agreements.

In order to accomplish these duties, the delegate has a workroom at his disposal as well as an advertising billboard, a number of working hours (10 or 15 depending on the number of employees in the company) and protection similar to the one described for the other representatives except that the Labour Inspector is the only person competent to give authorization for dismissal.

4. UNION REPRESENTATIVE AT THE WORKS COMMITTEE

The most representative unions in the company may designate, beside the union delegate, a second person who must be one of the company's employees and satisfy the conditions for eligibility to the works committee. This person's only role is to make the union's opinion known and therefore, he must attend the sessions of the works committee in an advisory capacity.

D. Co-determination

At present, there is no system of co-determination in France. The nearest system to it is the regulation already mentioned concerning the obligation for

18. Confédération Générale du Travail, Force Ouvrière, Confédération Française des Travailleurs Chrétiens, Confédération Française des Travailleurs; Confédération Générale des Cadres.

SA's to admit personnel delegates to participate in sessions of the Board of Directors or of the Supervisory Board.
Nevertheless, since this participation is limited to two delegates, irrespective of the number of Board members (minimum 3, maximum 12); and since both these delegates have only an advisory capacity, it is not possible to regard this as even the beginning of a co-determination system.
As is the case in other EC countries, several plans exist aiming at modifying the actual situation: the recent changes occurred in the political situation in France might well lead to a very substantial modification of the actual situation.

E. Compulsory Retirement Plans and Profit Participation

1. PENSION SCHEMES

An important part of the contributions required to finance the obligatory retirement plans is provided by companies. Next to the general systems, there are special ones for certain branches of trade and industry, such as the building trade, chemical industries, etc.
It is not possible to review all of the systems actually in force. Therefore, we shall only deal with the obligatory system concerning all employees. It is enough to know that many collective agreements for specific industries contain graduated pension schemes. The normal retirement age is 65.
One of the major changes instituted by the socialist government is that the normal retirement age should, step by step, become 60 instead of 65. This will certainly involve important changes in all retirement plans.

Old age pension of the social security

There is first of all the old age pension which is part of the general system of the social security.
In 1982, this system, under certain conditions, provided an annual pension of at least F. 24.000 with a maximum of F. 39.540.
The contributions, with a maximum amount fixed by decree are born by the company for 8,20% and the employee for 4,70%.
A complementary system created in 1957, the system of the Union Nationale des Institutions de Retraites des Salariés – UNIRS – at first optional, was made compulsory by successive agreements and now benefits workers and executives who must participate.
The contributions that finance this system must be paid until the age of 65. Their rate is 4% of the salary paid within the maximum fixed for social security contributions.[19] The burden is shared: 60% is paid by the employer and 40% by the employee. The amount of the benefits entitlement is calculated

19. The so-called 'plafond de la Sécurité Sociale' is modified from year to year.

by multiplying the number of retirement points of the employee by the value per point.

Retirement and provident scheme for executives

The agreement that created this system goes back to 1947. Designed for five years, it was first renewed by tacit agreement. Its application was initially reserved for the groups that signed the agreement. It was given general application by an Act of Parliament in 1972, followed by two decrees in 1973.
This system now covers all executives, except those in banks or in companies whose retirement scheme is fixed by legislation or regulations (such as the SNCF, EGF, Air France) or in the bodies subjected to Mutual Insurance (agriculture).[20]
This system includes:
- a compulsory contribution of 8% which is paid partly by the employer (6%) and partly by the employee (2%),
- a further compulsory contribution by the employer alone, used to cover benefits in case of death, (1,50%).

The rate of the 8% contribution can be increased at the company's option to a maximum of 16%.
Contributions by executives and employers are calculated on the gross salary as it appears in the pay and salary declaration given every year by the employer to the tax administration.
The amount of the benefits entitlement is calculated by multiplying the number of acquired points by the entitlement per point.

Retirement and provident scheme for VRP's (agents)

This concerns a specific system applying to non-executive commercial representatives, with very special rules.

2. PROFIT SHARING

Profit sharing

This optional system enables the employees to share in productivity increases or company profits.
A freely negotiated profit sharing system must be drawn up in a contract, for a length of three years; it may be concluded within a branch of trade or industry by a collective agreement or simply within one particular company. The way in which the personnel will be kept informed of the profits must be specified as must be the way of controlling the execution of the system.
The contract must be deposited with the Clerk of the Tribunal d'instance and confirmed by the administrative authority. Any form of pay effectively enabling employees to share in the development of the company may be considered. Nevertheless, the most common forms are:

20. SNCF: French Railways, EGF: Electricity and Gas Supply Board.

– a participation in profits,
– a participation in capital or in equity financing,
– a participation in an increase of productivity.

The company will benefit from tax and social security exemptions for the participation paid to its employees.

The amount of participation paid in cash is deductible for the employer, and not taxable to the employees.

When profit sharing is carried out by creating or distributing shares, the exemption also covers the taxes and duties attached to the transaction.

Moreover, the sums paid to employees are not part of the salary, and are therefore exempt from all social insurance contributions.

Participation in the company's growth

This system is compulsory for companies normally employing more than 100 employees; others may submit themselves to it.

A share of the company's enrichment, measured by the non-distributable profits, is distributed among employees, with a counterpart of fiscal advantages.

The employee's rights are calculated at the close of each financial year on the basis of the fiscal profits made by the company in France and they must be transferred to a special account.[21]

Every employee has rights proportional to the salary that he received during the financial year on the basis of which the participation reserve is calculated.

Employees who either have less than 6 months of service with the company or have been present less than three months are excluded from the distribution.

The personnel is informed of the development of the special reserve by notices posted in public places and in an annual report addressed to the works committee or, as the case may be, to each employee within 6 months following the close of the financial year.

Participation agreements concluded between the company and the employees determine the nature of the employees' rights and the way in which they will be managed.

Except for additional agreements recognized by the Centre d'Etudes de Revenus et des Coûts (Centre of Cost and Revenue Studies) and ratified by a joint decree of the ministers of finance and social issues, participation can only occur in one of three forms:

(i) attributing company shares to employees;

21. The rights are calculated according to the following formula:

$$\frac{I}{2}\left(B - \frac{5}{100}C\right) \times \frac{S}{VA}$$

- B: net profit
- C: capital and reserves
- S: total amount of salaries paid
- VA: added value is obtained as follows: staff salaries and social charges + financial expenses + amount of depreciation + amounts appropriated to reserves + trading profits + taxes and contributions (with the exception of VAT and corporation income tax).

(ii) recognition of a company debt: sums set apart in a fund that the company must devote to investments. The employees are then owed an amount that may take the form of bonds or of frozen accounts;

(iii) use on the financial market:

- registration of the name of each employee for shares in investment companies (Sicav) or mutual funds, or
- allotment of the participation to an open account under the name of each employee in connection with a company savings plan forming a collective portfolio of stocks and shares.

The rights credited to employees by virtue of the participation are not negotiable (if it concerns stocks and shares) or due (if it concerns debts) until the expiration of 5 years from their being granted. They cannot be sold or transferred before the expiration of this period except in some cases restrictively laid down.[22]

The amounts brought to the participation reserve during a financial year are deductible, to the extent attributed to each employee, from the overall corporate tax. They are not liable to income tax once in the employee's hands.

3. EMPLOYEE SHAREHOLDING

Stock options

The system, purely optional, enables companies to grant all or part of its personnel options to acquire company shares.

The decision is made by the Board of Directors, after previous authorization of the Extraordinary General Meeting of Shareholders. The conditions of the options are fixed by the Board of Directors: according the rules laid down by the Extraordinary General Meeting of Shareholders, the Board may set conditions such as prohibiting the resale of the shares within five years, and impose the registration of the shares.

However, the employees' rights in respect of the option are the subject of various legal restrictions.

Employees owning more shares than the maximum fixed by the General Meeting of Shareholders (more than 5%) may not benefit from further options.

The maximum option rights that may be granted is determined according to the size of the company from 5% to the part of the share capital not exceeding 10 million francs, to 3% of the part between 10 million and 50 million francs, and 1% of the part of capital above this figure.

The maximum period during which the option may be exercised is five years from the day it is granted; no minimum time is required.

The value of options granted to a single employee cannot, taking in account the options already owned by the employee, exceed either twice the annual salary, or ten times the maximum fixed for social security contributions (the so called 'plafond de la Sécurité Sociale').

22. They are: marriage of the concerned party, dismissal, retirement, invalidity or death of the beneficiary or spouse, building or purchase of main residence.

Subscription or buying of company shares by employees

This applies to company shares quoted on the stock exchange.
These companies may raise their capital with the increase being reserved for their employees either on an individual basis or through the intermediary of an investment fund created inside the company in the context of the participation described above.
If the shares need not be paid up in full immediately, equal and regular deductions may be made from the subscribers' salaries.
The shares subscribed are registered and non-transferable for 5 years.
The raising of capital carried out in this particular context is exempt from the 1% registration tax.

Distribution of shares in favour of the employees
(Law nr. 80-834 of October 24, 1980. Official Gazette of October 25, 1980).

The law permits joint-stock companies, that have distributed dividends at least twice during the last five financial years, to proceed with an exceptional distribution of free shares to employees.
The decision whether or not to proceed with this distribution belongs to the Extraordinary General Meeting of Shareholders.
The shares to be distributed must be the result of a capital increase which must be equal to 3% of the capital without exceeding an average of 5,000 F. per benefiting employee.
Companies that use this possibility will receive a credit from the State, payable in ten years, and equal to 65% of the negotiable value of the distributed shares.
To be eligible employees must have at least two years' service with the company or with subsidiaries on the condition that they do not already benefit from a share distribution from another company directly or indirectly holding more than half of the share capital of the company employing them.
Finally, the value of the distributed shares is not subject to income tax in the hands of the employees, nor to any taxes or duties on salaries paid by the company. Furthermore they are not taken into consideration for the application of labour legislation or Social Security.

F. Residence and Work Permits for Foreigners

Foreign workers must be distinguished in those from other EC countries, and others.

1. THE FOREIGN WORKER FROM A NON EC COUNTRY

French law in this field, like that of many nations, is the desire to control the hiring of foreign labour. Numerous bilateral agreements have been signed with

other countries.[23] defining the status of nationals of each country in the reciprocal territories. We will not discuss these special agreements which may provide rules differing from those mentioned below.
Although the number of foreign workers admitted in France is not fixed, its proportion in regard to the total volume of employees is limited. In companies carrying out public works or supply contracts for the State and for public communities, the percentage of foreigners may not exceed 5%.
For all other companies, the minister of Labour is entitled to fix in each department, by decree, the maximum number of foreign workers allowed to be hired in industrial and commercial establishments.
Hundreds of thousands of companies are subject to these strict rules. In order to verify that they are respected, every employer is obliged to keep a register of foreigners which he must show at the request of Labour Inspectors whose duty it is to control the application of labour legislation.
To be registered as a foreign worker in France, the employee will have to follow a special procedure of which we will indicate the main stages and which the employer must enforce under risk of penalties.

Residence permit

Any foreigner residing in France for more than 3 months must request a residence permit at the Prefecture.
This temporary residence permit may be replaced by an ordinary one whose validity lasts for 3 years and which authorizes foreigners to have a residence in France.
Finally there is the privileged residence permit which is valid for ten years and renewable automatically; it is granted by the departmental prefect after investigation. No appeal is allowed against the prefect's decision.

Work permit

All foreigners pursuing in France a paid professional activity either part or full-time, must be in possession of a valid work permit.
The applicable procedure is similar to the one concerning the residence permit:

- The temporary authorization to work for a specific employer, valid for a maximum of six months, is given to foreign employees whose activity is limited in time either by its nature or by circumstances;
- A seasonal permit may be given to seasonal workers, valid for a maximum of 3 months;
- The temporary work permit is valid for one year for a specific professional activity;
- The ordinary work permit specifies the professional activity that the foreign worker may exercise: it is valid for 3 years;
- The work permit for all paid professions is valid for 10 years. It may be given with or without certain conditions.

23. *Inter alia*, Algeria, most french-speaking African countries, former Indochina.

These work permits, except for the seasonal work contract, are of course renewable after certain formalities.
Foreign workers may change profession or department as long as they have been authorized to do so by labour and prefectoral authorities.
To obtain these various types of work and residence permits, one must comply with certain procedures. They differ as to whether the employer initiates the introduction of foreign labour (introduction procedure) or whether the foreigner requests the regularization of his personal status, which is employee rather than tourist (regularization procedure) or whether the foreigner, having resided in France for several years, wants to take on, for the first time or not, a paid activity (admission procedure).
Once he has obtained the right to work in France, the foreigner has the same rights as a french employee, including access to unemployment benefits and to the office of union delegate, employee's delegate, and representative in the works committee.
Apart from these foreigners wishing to 'establish' themselves as employees in France, there is a large number who come on an assignment and who are already employees of a foreign company. For example, technicians working for a foreign firm in France for some time to assemble material sent to a French customer. A temporary work authorization, valid for 6 months, non-renewable, is automatically given after presentation to the labour authorities of a certificate drawn up by the French customer and of a letter of assignment from the parent company.
Some French companies may also wish to use for a short time the services of, for example, a technical assistant or a financial inspector, normally employed by a foreign company having no establishment in France. There again, a very simple procedure will procure the delivery of temporary work authorization valid for 6 months and renewable once or (exceptionally) twice.

2. EC NATIONALS

The Treaty of Rome set down the rule of free movement of workers inside the Community.
French regulations have complied with Community requirements.
EC nationals may pursue a professional activity without a work permit.
Their only restraint is that they must hold a residence permit. Within 3 months of their arrival in France, they must request a temporary residence permit which will be changed into a permit valid for 5 years for the whole country.
This permit will be renewed for 10 years.
In case of temporary or seasonal work, and for border workers, the formalities are again simplified.
Nationals of EC countries are submitted to France's general system of Social Security.

V. REFERENCE MATERIAL

1. List of Abbreviations

CGI	Code Général des Impôts – General tax code
GIE	Groupement d'intérêt économique
OPA	Offre publique d'achat – Take over bid
OPE	Offre publique d'échange – Take over bid by exchange of shares.
SA	Société anonyme – public limited company
SARL	Société à responsabilité limitée – private limited company.
TVA	taxe à la valeur ajoutée – VAT

2. List of Names/Translations of most Important Statutes Referred to

- Articles of association: statuts.
- Auditors: commissaires aux comptes.
- Board of Directors: Conseil d'Administration or directoire which, in both cases, concerns an SA.
- Business on joint account: société en participation.
- Chairman of the board of directors: président du Conseil d'Administration.
- Collective bargaining: convention collective.
- Companies Register: Registre du Commerce et des sociétés (RCS).

Corporation tax: Impôt sur les sociétés – IS.
Direction du Trésor: Treasury Département of the Ministry of Finance.
Director General: directeur général.
Extraordinary meeting of shareholders: assemblée generale extraordinaire.
Employment contract for a limited period of time: contrat à durée déterminée.
Employment contract for an unlimited period of time: contrat à durée indéterminée.
Foreign traders card: carte de commerçant étranger.
Income tax: Impôt sur le revenu des personnes physiques IR.
Limited partnership: société en commandite simple.
Lay off for economic reasons: licenciement économique.
Manager of a SARL: gérant.
Notarized declaration of underwriting and of payment: déclaration notariée de souscription et de versement.
Ordinary partnership: société en nom collectif.
Ordinary meeting of shareholders: assemblée générale ordinaire.
Partnership limited by shares: société en commandite par actions.
Private limited company: société à responsabilité limitée SARL.
Public limited company: société anonyme.

Registration fee: droit d'enregistrement.
Shareholders representatives or appointees: mandataires sociaux.
Social Security: Sécurité Sociale.
Supervisory board: Conseil de Surveillance.
Tax credit on distributed dividends: avoir fiscal.
Works committee: comité d'entreprise.

3. *Bibliography*

There is, of course, a vast amount of publications in the fields covered by the preceding studies and we have consequently limited the list to those which are currently used by practitioners.
A first list includes publications in French.
A second list concerns publications in English.

FRENCH

On company law
Memento pratique des sociétés commerciales: Editions Francis Lefebvre.
Digest with the same characteristics as the Memento pratique du contribuable.
LAMY sociétés: published by société des Services Lamy, 155 bis Rue Legendre, PARIS. Also a digest but more detailed than the former.
Dictionnaire Joly: 21 Avenue Georges V, 75008 PARIS. This is a loose-leaf publication with one series of 6 volumes for the sociétés anonymes, limited partnerships and partnerships limited by shares, and another series of 3 volumes for the private limited companies.

On tax problems
Memento Pratique du Contribuable: published every year by Editions Francis Levebvre, 15 Rue Viete, 75017 PARIS, A very remarkable digest which gives accurately all the essential information on all classical tax problems.
Feuillets de Documentation Pratique: also published by Editions Francis Lefebvre, this is a loose-leaf publication with 5 volumes for direct taxes, 2 volumes for indirect taxes, 2 volumes for turnover taxes and 1 volume for registration taxes.

On labour law problems
LAMY social – published by société des Services Lamy 155 bis Rue Legendre Paris, A quite comprehensive and useful digest.
LEGI – Social – 54 Rue de Chabrol – 75010 PARIS. A monthly publication giving accurate informations on all new laws and case law.
MEMENTO PRATIQUE – Social – Securité Sociale – Droit du Travail.
Editions Francis LEFEBVRE – Similar digest to the ones published by the same editor and concerning company law and taxes.

ENGLISH

On company law
'French Company Law'
Editions BUTTERWORTHS – 1980 – LONDON
'Doing Business in FRANCE'
Editions PRICE and WATERHOUSE June 1979
European Commercial law library – General editor – Robert R. Pennington
– French Company law.

On tax problems
'Taxes in FRANCE'
Editions BUTTERWORTH – 1980 – LONDON
'French Measures for the Prevention of International Tax Evasion'
(by Jean Michel TRON)
International Trade law and Prentice
April 1978
Editions MASSON – PARIS – 102 Bd Saint Germain
75280 PARIS CEDEX 06.
European Commercial law library – General Editor – Robert R. Pennington
French business taxation.
A Butterworths Taxbook – Halpern
– an English adaptation of Francis Lefebvre's 'les impôts en France'.

Federal Republic of Germany (including West Berlin)

Wolfgang Rosener

I. INTRODUCTION

1. When a foreign undertaking considers starting a business in the Federal Republic of Germany (including Berlin West) on its own, rather than by merely appointing an agent or a representative, or by setting up a sales office or similar place of business with restricted competence, it may either establish a branch or a subsidiary.
Whereas the concepts of branch and subsidiary are separately treated in the part of this chapter dealing with the legal framework, a distinction in the taxation and labour sections will not generally be made.
Thus the statements concerning taxation and labour aspects apply to both subsidiaries and branches, unless the contrary is specifically mentioned.

2. The most common types of incorporated companies in Germany are the *Gesellschaft mit beschränkter Haftung* (GmbH) which is broadly comparable to the private company limited by shares or the close corporation and the *Aktiengesellschaft* (AG) which is equivalent to the public limited company or stock corporation. Although hereafter for convenience the English expressions will sometimes be used, it must always be kept in mind that the forms are not identical and that there are many differences of detail. The use of the English terms is therefore a simplification justified only by practical requirement.
In practice, the GmbH is by far, the more widespread type of company. This had been foreseen by the German legislators when they 'invented' the GmbH in 1892 as the simpler alternative to the AG for multiple purposes of normally only a few shareholders. Whereas there are about 2,000 AGs, mainly chosen by enterprises of large-scale industries, the number of GmbHs has meanwhile, surpassed 200,000.
Therefore it is appropriate to split the part of this chapter dealing with the subsidiary into one general part and two special parts, one covering the GmbH, the other one the AG.
This will then be followed by a short survey of other forms of subsidiaries and by a special section necessary in the German chapter, dealing with groups of companies for which German law contains quite detailed provisions.

3. There have been several changes in German commercial legislation recently concerning business law, among them two of major importance which are reflected in this chapter.
One is the Amendment Act of July 4, 1980 to the GmbH Act, which came into force on January 1, 1981. The legislation has been in preparation on this

subject for a number of years and as early as 1970 a Bill for a completely new GmbH Act was tabled.
However, the Bill was withdrawn after intensive public discussions, criticising (among other aspects) the obvious perfectionism of the Bill, which was said to modify the GmbH so as to become a 'small AG', thus disqualifying this legal vehicle from serving the multiple purposes hitherto served by it.
In reaction to this criticism the Federal Ministry of Justice drafted a Bill merely proposing reforms of certain areas of the Act. However, even this Bill finally has been considerably tightened by the competent parliamentary committees; as a result, in place of lengthy paragraphs dealing with a great many subjects, only those amendments which were necessary or advisable have been enacted in a language also comprehensible to non-lawyers, equivalent to the original text of the law. The flexibility of the GmbH, after all, has been retained.
The second important change was the introduction of a new corporation tax system abolishing the internal double taxation of company profits by means of a tax credit.

II. THE LEGAL FRAMEWORK

A. *The Vehicle*

1. THE WHOLLY-OWNED ENTERPRISE

1.a. THE BRANCH

Although the German Commercial Code (*Handelsgesetzbuch*, HGB) does not contain a general definition of a branch (*Zweigniederlassung*), but instead only gives general rules pertaining to its organization, there is practically no difference of opinion as to the characteristics of a branch:

- Branches are never independent legal entities; they are part of the commercial enterprise operated by the head office. This is one of the main distinctions from subsidiaries.
- A branch enjoys a certain independence; it must have at least some business relationships of its own so that, if necessary, it may by itself become the head office in case the original head office is closed down.
- In particular, a branch must have a manager with authority to act independently in matters of more than minor importance.
- Internally, a branch is considered as a component part of the parent company. Externally it is registered as such with the Trade Register so that third parties may know they are dealing with a branch rather than with an independent company.
- The branch may not be registered at the same address as the head office. The business of the branch may be carried on in the same general locality but not in the same building.

- Business establishments are only regarded as branches if they are set up for a substantial period of time.
- Separate accounts must be kept of the branch's assets and the business it transacts.

If a place of business does not have the features set out above, as in the case of a warehouse, a sales office or the like, it will probably still be a permanent establishment within the meaning of the tax law, but not a *Zweigniederlassung* as envisaged in the Commercial Code.

1.a.(i) Setting-up

The legal provisions concerning the formation of branches of foreign companies are laid down in the Commercial Code, the Stock Corporation Act (*Aktiengesetz*, AktG) and the Act concerning companies with Limited Liability (*GmbH-Gesetz*, GmbHG).

The name of the undertaking must be one that is permitted in Germany. The branch must have the same name as the head office but an addition to the name of the head office is permitted. One very important point is that the name must be such that there is no danger of confusion with the name of another already existing undertaking. Art. 18, para. 2 HGB provides that no addition may be made to the name of the undertaking which might lead to mistaking the nature or importance of the business or the position of the enterprise's owner.

By art. 13 b HGB, the local court (*Amtsgericht*) of the district where a branch is set up is the sole competent authority for the filing of notifications and the registration of branches of foreign companies in the Trade Register. For purposes of registration, branches of existing foreign companies, and newly formed German undertakings are basically subject to identical rules. This implies that all the managing partners in the case of a partnership (*Personengesellschaft*), all the members of the managing board or board of directors (*Vorstand*) in the case of a public company or stock corporation, and all the managing directors (*Geschäftsführer*) in the case of a private company or close corporation must give notice of the formation of the branch. Their signatures must be certified by a notary. If the head office is a foreign company, the notification has to be signed by officers of the head office equivalent to those mentioned above. Certification should be effected by the German Consulate in the country concerned, which is equivalent to notarial certification. All documents prescribed by law which serve to prove that the conditions required for registration have been fulfilled, must be filed at the time of notification.

The Commercial Code, the AktG and the GmbHG contain detailed provisions concerning the documents which must be filed upon notification.

The main conditions are as follows:

- the foreign head office must be in existence at the time of notification;
- the parent undertaking must be of a type which may be registered in the Trade Register in Germany;
- if the object of the enterprise or the business to be transacted in Germany requires a special licence, such licence must be obtained.

There are special provisions regarding branches of foreign parent companies in certain fields of activity: branches of foreign credit institutions must obtain

a licence from the Banking Supervisory Board (art. 53, para. 2 of the Banking Act (*Kreditwesengesetz*), KWG). This licence may be refused if it appears unjustified in view of general economic conditions.
By art. 105 of the Insurance Companies Supervisory Act (*Versicherungsaufsichtsgesetz*. VAG), a licence is required for branches of foreign insurance companies. The Federal Minister of Economic Affairs is the competent authority to issue such licences (art. 106 VAG) which he must do in accordance with certain legal provisions.
Certain commercial activities are only allowed with a licence issued by the trade supervision departments (*Gewerbeaufsichtsamt*); details may be found in the Trade Regulations (*Gewerbeordnung*, GewO), the Restaurant Licensing Act (*Gaststättengesetz*) and in other regulations.
The Trade Regulations generally stipulate (art. 12, para. 1 GewO) that foreign legal persons must have a permit from the authority competent for economic affairs of the relevant German State (normally the Ministry of Commerce) to transact business within the territory of the Federal Republic. No such permit is required, however, for legal persons who are established according to the laws of a member state of the EC and have their registered office or head office within the EC.
As with every new business, whether German or foreign, branches must register with the local trade office (*Gewerbeamt*) and with the tax office (*Finanzamt*) having jurisdiction over the district, town, or city where the branch is situated.
The setting up of the branch is published in the Official Gazette, together with all particulars of the foreign company itself which German law requires to be registered and published. Consequently, subsequent changes in the particulars relating not only to the branch but also to the foreign company itself must be registered and published.

1.a.(ii) Organization

– *Management and representation*
Branches are generally considered to be managed by the managing board or board of directors of the head office; a branch cannot have a board of its own, since its manager is the proxy of the true board of directors. A special manager authorised to represent the enterprise is, however, required, as already pointed out. In the case where a branch office has a name which differs from that of the head office by the addition of one or more words to the company name, the representative's authority with legal effect against all third parties may be restricted to the business of the branch.
There are no special provisions regarding the domicile and nationality of persons authorised to represent branches. Special regulations, however, apply to branches of foreign credit institutions and insurance companies: a permit to set up a branch is only granted if the foreign enterprise undertakes to nominate as heads of its branch at least two proxies domiciled in Germany (art. 53, para. 2 KWG; art. 106 VAG).

– *Liability*
Both foreign and domestic companies are fully liable for all acts and obliga-

tions of their branches as these have no separate legal status. For taxation purposes it follows that any loss suffered by a branch is treated as a loss of the parent company, subject to recognition by the tax authorities.

– *Accounts and publication*

Whether a branch must in general possess assets of its own (and consequently its own capital) is still open to question. However, with the exception of the branches of foreign credit institutions, there are no special regulations applying to branches of foreign enterprises.

A branch of a foreign enterprise must keep within the Federal Republic of Germany complete accounting records complying with the requirements of the Commercial Code and the tax law. Publication of financial statements is, however, not required.

1.b. THE SUBSIDIARY IN GENERAL

There is no legal definition of the term 'subsidiary company' (*Tochtergesellschaft*) but it is generally regarded as a separate legal entity in which the parent company holds the majority of shares or at least has the majority of votes, or which is otherwise controlled by the parent company. Consequently the term comprises wholly owned subsidiaries as well as companies in which a minority interest is held by another enterprise or several other persons.

The term 'subsidiary' used in a broader sense, however, covers also affiliates organized in the form of a partnership, which under German law is not a legal entity but shows most of the characteristics of one.

In theory, a German subsidiary may be organized either as a partnership, which does not constitute a separate legal entity, or as a public or private company, which does. A partnership may be organized as an *Offene Handelsgesellschaft* (OHG, general partnership – see also page 233) or a *Kommanditgesellschaft* (KG, limited partnership), but in practice a subsidiary company is almost always set up as a *Gesellschaft mit beschränkter Haftung* (GmbH) or an *Aktiengesellschaft* (AG) (or acquired by taking over an existing enterprise of either of these types). Though the AG is broadly comparable to a public limited company or stock corporation and the GmbH to a private limited company, it must be borne in mind that they differ in detail substantially.

The following information will therefore in principle be limited to the two types of companies prevalent in practice, although some details on partnerships will also be given.

At first, general aspects affecting both types of companies will be treated, while the details of each follow in the later paragraphs.

The AG and the GmbH present the same basic characteristics:

1. The company constitutes a separate legal entity.
2. The shareholders are not liable for the debts of the company.
3. The shareholders subscribe to the shares into which the capital is divided.
4. The company is a commercial company which aims to make a profit.

There are, however, differences in the structure of these companies. The AG is conceived as a company which may invite the public to subscribe for the necessary capital. The GmbH, on the other hand, is usually limited to a very small number of shareholders. Thus the legal rules regulating AGs are generally mandatory: in view of the great number of shareholders, the individual cannot exercise his rights unless they are clearly defined. Since a GmbH has only a small number of shareholders, the law allows a large measure of freedom regarding the contents of its statutes.

In principle, no prior governmental or administrative licence or certificate is required the formation and operation of a subsidiary company regardless of its nature, unless the purpose of the company lies within the compass of those activities which are regulated; a licence is required for such companies even when they are entirely controlled by German capital.

As in the case of branches, notification of starting up a business must be given to the local trade office (*Gewerbeamt*) and the competent tax office (*Finanzamt*) and subsidiaries must be entered in the local trade register. It should be stressed, however, that the court official is bound to register a GmbH (as well as an AG) if he finds that all formation requirements have been fulfilled.

In some particular cases, formation requires a special licence before registration. The following provisions are of special importance:

1. Companies wishing to engage in financing (credit institutions) require a licence (the same rule applies to mortgage banks).
2. Insurance companies require a licence from the supervising authorities concerned; the same rule applies to building societies.
3. Accounting firms require a licence.
4. Certain activities are only permitted when duly authorized by the trade supervision departments (*Gewerbeaufsichtsamt*); details may be found in the *Gewerbeordnung,* the *Gaststättengesetz* and other regulations.

In addition, commercial law contains special supervisory provisions pertaining to other branches of commerce where a licence is required before business can be commenced.

AGs and GmbHs that have been formed in accordance with German law and registered in Germany, are subject to German law irrespective of the nationality of their shareholders since these are German companies. There are no provisions limiting the investment of foreign capital of the voting rights of aliens. In practice, companies partially or wholly owned by aliens and those entirely owned by German nationals receive the same treatment.

The members of the managing boards of AGs or the managing directors of GmbHs, as the case may be, may be chosen freely irrespective of their nationality. Neither the members of the managing board nor the managing directors need be domiciled in Germany. Insurance companies are an exception; a decision of the supervising authorities stipulates that the managing board of an insurance company must have a majority of German nationals domiciled in Germany. It is desirable, however, that also in other companies at least one of the members of the managing board or managing directors be a German national. In any case, the managing board or the supervisory board of a German company may be entirely composed of foreign nationals, subject of course to the application of the regulations concerning aliens residing in Germany. If, however, all the executive personnel of a German company reside outside the country, this fact may influence the tax position of the German subsidiary company. Thus the Anglo-German double taxation treaty, for example, stipulates that German companies controlled by British nationals are regarded as residing in Great Britain, if their directors also reside in Great Britain rather than in Germany (cf. also III. below, page 230).

The name of the subsidiary must contain the abbreviation AG or GmbH, as the case may be. It should be noted that certain courts competent to register companies still require the complete term *Gesellschaft mit beschränkter Haftung* to be used in full.

Unless the subsidiary continues to use the name of an enterprise which it has acquired, the name of a GmbH must furthermore comprise the name of at least one of the shareholders or must indicate the business of the company; in case of an AG, while the name will normally indicate the nature of the business, the court may, however, permit another type of name. For both types of companies the combination of a personal name and an indication of the business (so-called mixed firm) is admissible. As in the case of a branch, the name must be one that is permitted under German law and there must be no danger of confusion with the name of another already existing company.

Prior to registration of the company the local chamber of commerce must be consulted on the question of admissibility of the name.

1.c. THE GMBH

1.c.(i) Setting-up

The incorporators may be natural persons or companies. The formation of a GmbH by proxy is permitted. Until 1980 a GmbH had to be incorporated by at least two persons, although subsequently all shares could be transferred to one shareholder.

However, this has been simplified. One of the important innovations of the GmbH Amendment Act is the recognition of incorporation of a 'one-man GmbH', making the formation of a wholly-owned subsidiary is easier than before.

The founder or founders must establish the company's statutes (*Gesellschaftsvertrag* or *Satzung*) which must be recorded by a notary. This single document, the deed of incorporation, contains essentially the same items as covered in the two basic documents used in the United Kingdom (memorandum of association and articles of association) and the United States (certificate of incorporation and by-laws or articles of association).

The minimum capital requirement beginning on January 1, 1981 is DM 50,000, the capital being the total sum subscribed to by the shareholders. The minimum single share is DM 500 and each shareholder may subscribe for one share only. The shares may, however, have different nominal values, but the amounts must be in multiples of 100. Contributions in cash must be paid up at the time of incorporation only to the extent of 25% of the value of each share, but an aggregate amount of at least DM 25,000 must be paid up initially. In the case of incorporation by one person only, a security for the payment of the full capital requirement must be established unless the founder pays the whole amount at the very beginning. Contributions in kind must be made in full. No certificate is issued with respect to a shareholding in a GmbH but naturally the shares may be inherited and transferred.

Such transfer, however, requires a notarial deed, so that the negotiability of

GmbH shares may be restricted. It is quite common to provide in the statutes that no transfer of shares may be validly effected without consent of the other shareholders and to give them a right of first refusal or a pre-emptive right over such a restricted share.
Legally, the company comes into existence only upon registration of the particulars required by law in the Trade Register, namely:

- the name
- the domicile
- the object of the company
- the amount of the share capital
- the amount of the contribution of each shareholder
- the name(s) of the managing director(s)

which, together with the indication of the fiscal year, represent the minimum contents of the statute. Names of the members of the supervisory board, if any, must be added.
Those particulars are published by the Trade Register in the Official Gazette. Subsequent changes in these items, except changes in the composition of the shareholders, must be entered into the Trade Register and published. As to the shareholders, the managing directors are obliged to file an updated list with the Trade Register annually, in the month of January.

1.c.(ii) Organization

– *Management, representation*

The GmbH usually has only two organs:

- the executive(s), namely one or more managing director(s) (*Geschäftsführer*)
- the shareholders' meeting.

Normally, the appointment of the managing director(s) is decided at a shareholders' meeting. The managing directors represent the company vis-à-vis third parties, and their powers may not be limited. The shareholders may, however, limit internally the managing director's right of representation and management by imposing the requirement of their prior approval for certain transactions. Sometimes, particularly when the company employs more than 500 persons or is subject to co-determination under the Co-Determination Act, 1976 (cf. IV. D. below, page 251), a GbmH must have a supervisory board, in which case its employees have the right to be represented on it. In addition, and irrespective of the aforementioned conditions, the shareholders may exercise the legal option to voluntarily install a supervisory board by providing for the establishment of such a board and by defining its over-all functions in the company's statutes.

– *Shareholders' meeting*

The shareholders of a GmbH may pass resolutions orally, in writing or at meetings. A meeting is required for the passing of resolutions concerning the capital measures, such as an increase of capital, and for other amendments to the statutes, since in these cases, resolutions, to become effective, must be recorded by a notary and filed with the Trade Register.
For such resolutions and for voluntary winding-up, a majority of 75% of the

votes is required, called the 'qualified majority'. A minority of more than 25% of the votes entails a veto on such resolutions and consequently is called the 'blocking minority' (*Sperrminorität*). All other matters require only a simple majority. The statutes may increase the qualified majority, thus reducing the blocking minority, but not decrease it.
The GmbH's shareholders, as opposed to those of an AG, are entitled to give instructions to the managing directors, even if there is a supervisory board.
The protection of the minority in a GmbH was very limited until 1980, being restricted to the following: shareholders holding 10% of the shares could request the calling of a shareholders' meeting, or a court order dissolving the company and appointing a liquidator, or bring an action to have the company declared invalid. The GmbH Amendment Act, however, has introduced in addition the right of each shareholder irrespective of the amount of his shareholding, to demand information from the managing directors and to inspect the books of the company.

– *Liability*
The personal liability of the shareholders for the obligations of a GmbH is in principle strictly limited to the amount of their investment. This also applies to wholly owned subsidiaries, except for very rare cases where such limitation of liability on the part of the sole shareholder would appear to be an abuse of rights.
(For specific liability provisions of the Stock Corporation Act concerning controlling or dominating AGs which also apply if the subsidiary is a GmbH cf. below under d) (liability, page 222)). Consequently, losses of a GmbH have in principle no influence on the tax position of the controlling foreign enterprise.
The managing directors must fulfil their duties with the diligence of a prudent businessman; if the fail in their so defined duties they are jointly and severally liable for the loss caused. The liability exists only vis-à-vis the company, whereas the managing directors in principle are not directly liable to the shareholders.

– *Accounts and auditing requirements; publication of accounts*
There are few legal requirements for the accounting and financial statements of a GmbH, but the German Implementing Act complying with the Fourth EC Harmonization Directive (see European chapter) will change this state of affairs. In practice, today the provisions of accounting in tax law (cf. III. A. 2. below, page 232) are therefore, as a rule, more important for a GmbH than those in commercial law.
At present, the balance sheet of a GmbH needs not to be audited, nor filed with the trade register, nor published, except for GmbHs in the banking business. In practice, the balance sheets of many GmbHs are audited when the shareholders so decide.
Substantial GmbHs often publish their balance sheet voluntarily.
Already, however, some large GmbHs which fulfill certain criteria, must publish their financial statements by virtue of the Disclosure Act (*Publizitätsgesetz*). The provisions of this Law apply to all large undertakings, irrespective of their legal form, if two of the following conditions are present:
– balance sheet total exceeding DM 125 million

– annual sales exceeding DM 250 million
– average number of persons employed during the year more than 5000

(banks: balance sheet total of DM 300 million; insurance companies: proceeds from premiums exceeding DM 100 million).

1.c.(iii) Checklist for incorporating a GmbH

(Normal procedure, if business requires special permits etc., further steps are necessary)

1. Advisable first step: checking with local Chamber of Commerce whether intended company's name is admissible and still available.
2. Establishing the statutes before a notary public, this is done by one or more incorporator(s).[2]
   Minimum statutory regulations
   – Name and seat of company
   – object of enterprise
   – amount of share capital
   – amount of share capital subscribed to by each shareholder.
3. Appointing the first managing director(s), normally by shareholders at the same time as 2.
4. Opening an account in the name of the company to be incorporated or of managing director(s); before registration: pay 25% share capital, at least DM 25,000 (in the event of only one incorporator: pay up full or give security for the balance). Contribution in kind to be effected in full.
5. Signing (before notary public, normally at the same time as (2)) of application to Trade Register for registration of company by (all) managing director(s) with affidavit that minimum amount is paid up and is at the disposal of managing director(s) and his (their) specimen signature(s).
6. Payment of capital investment tax (1% of amount paid up; since January 1, 1981 this is no longer a precondition of registration).
7. Filing with the court (Trade Register) on application for registration (normally through notary public acting as per (2) and (5)), accompanied by:
   – statutes
   – list of name, address, occupation and amount of share capital subscribed by each shareholder
   – not required but advisable to shorten registration procedure: approval of Chamber of Commerce as per (1).
8. Together with (7): payment of registration fees.
9. Entry of company into Trade Register; publication in Official Gazette effected by the Court; Court transmits notice of entry to incorporators with certified extract from Trade Register upon request and for a small extra fee.

2. Proxies of incorporators must present notarised power of attorney (in the case of proxies for companies: with notarial certificate that the executives giving the power of attorney are entitled to represent the company in this respect); acting executives of companies may present certified extracts from the commercial register showing their power to represent the company. Non-domestic powers of attorney and extracts from trade register must be legalised, e.g. by the German consulate in the respective country, and translated by a sworn translator.

10. From the moment of registration managing director(s) may act exclusively on behalf of the company (for acts prior to registration acting persons are personally liable).
11. Notification to Trade Office.
12. Notification to Tax Office.
13. Letters and certain other printed matter must show at least the particulars required under the first EEC Directive:
    - legal form (GmbH)
    - seat of company
    - Trade Register with which the company is registered
    - registration number
    - surname and at least one christian name in full of each managing director (and chairman of supervisory board, if any).

Time required:
Incorporation – comprising steps (1) to (9) – usually takes about four weeks, but can be substantially shortened by help of a notary public according to local circumstances.
Note: provision of legalised powers of attorney or extract from trade register as per footnote on page 218 may take considerable time.

Cost (approximately):
For incorporating a GmbH with capital of DM 50,000 (DM 25,000 paid up)

– notarial fee for incorporation deed	DM 420
– notarial fee for certifying of application for registration	DM 80
– capital investment tax (1% on 25,000 DM)	DM 250
– court fee for registration in Trade Register	DM 300
Total	DM 1050
For GmbH with capital of DM 200,000 (fully paid up)	DM 3,850

1.d. THE AG

The AG is in certain basic respects similar to the GmbH. This is not surprising since both are corporate entities and the AG, as pointed out, was to some extent the model for the simpler GmbH. However, since it is designed as a company with a wide shareholding, the legal provisions governing the AG are far more complex and, as a rule, are mandatory, so that the legal protection for this large number of anonymous shareholders and creditors of the AG is maintained (the *Aktiengesetz* has more than 400 paragraphs as opposed to the *GmbH-Gesetz* which ends with paragraph 85).

1.d.(i) Setting-up

An AG also comes into existence when the Court enters its particulars in the Trade Register. The conditions to be fulfilled and the procedures leading to registration are much more complicated than in the case of a GmbH.

The major items are as follows:
At least five persons, natural or corporate, are required as founders, and they must sign the statutes (*Satzung*) and subscribe to the shares; this requires a notarial deed. In the case of an AG, a wholly owned subsidiary can be created only by subsequently transferring all shares to one shareholder.
The minimum statutory provisions required are similar to those of a GmbH, though somewhat more comprehensive.
The minimum share capital is DM 100,000, which must be divided into shares of a minimum face value of DM 50. At least 25% must be paid up at the time of incorporation. Any premium or contributions in kind must be fully paid up.
By contrast with the GmbH, share certificates are issued. Normally shares are issued in the form of bearer shares, but registered shares are permitted, and they are required as long as the shares have not been fully paid in.
AG shares are freely transferable, and there are no notarial requirements to be fulfilled. The statute may, however, provide that the transfer of registered shares requires the consent of the company (*vinkulierte Namensaktien*).
The statute may furthermore provide for ordinary and preferred stock, but cumulative voting rights are prohibited unless sanctioned by the Minister of Economics of the respective federal state.
The incorporators must appoint the first supervisory board (*Aufsichtsrat*).
The supervisory board appoints the managing board (*Vorstand*). The incorporators must make a written report of the incorporation. Both boards must review the steps of the incorporation and in certain cases auditors must carry out an examination.
The application for entry into the Trade Register must contain a statement to the effect that the amount of cash demanded for each share has been properly paid and is definitely at the free disposal of the managing board.
The following documents must, inter alia, be filed with the application:
- proof that the amount paid up is at the free disposal of the managing board;
- statutes and notarised documents by which the incorporators established the statutes and subscribed the shares;
- documents stating
  - remunerations or expenses paid to promotors and other advantages obtained by them,
  - particulars of contribution in kind;
- documents regarding the appointment of the managing board and supervisory board;
- formation report on incorporation and reports of the investigations of the members of the managing board and of the supervisory board, and of the auditors, if any;
- the certificate of Government approval, if the object of the company or other provisions of the statutes render such approval necessary.

As in the case of the GmbH, the particulars of the AG mentioned above are published in the Official Gazette at the time of registration, as also changes which may occur.

1.d.(ii) Organisation

– *Management and representation*
The AG has three organs.
Besides the general or shareholders' meeting, there are the two further bodies already mentioned

– managing board (*Vorstand*)
– supervisory board (*Aufsichtsrat*).

Though legally one managing director would be sufficient, the AG usually has a managing board. Its members are appointed by the supervisory board. The managing board has responsibility for managing the company and does not receive any instructions from the other organs.
The supervisory board has the function of control only. The managing board represents the company vis-à-vis third parties.
The powers of the managing board can be restricted internally but such restrictions have no external effect. The acts of its members are therefore binding on the company even if they contravene such internal restrictions. If there is a contravention, it will, however, lead to internal consequences.
The supervisory board must consist of at least three members. The number of members must always be divisible by three. In principle, the supervisory board is chosen by the shareholders meeting, but one-third of its members are nominated by the employees. (For large companies with more than 2,000 employees etc., cf. IV. D. below, page 251.)
It supervises the managing board and may stipulate that certain transactions require its approval, although not to such extent that the activities of the managing board are paralysed.

– *Shareholders' meeting*
The general or shareholders meeting of the AG must always be minuted by a notary. Resolutions can therefore only be passed at meetings. A qualified majority of 75% is required for the same transactions as in the case of a GmbH and for further special decisions such as the issuing of convertible bonds. The Stock Corporation Act, however, differs from the GmbH Act by permitting in certain cases a lower requirement of a simple majority.
Again differing from the case of a GmbH, the annual balance sheet and profit and loss statement are not as a rule approved by the general meeting. Instead, joint approval is given by the managing board and supervisory board after an audit by chartered public accountants. The shareholders meeting then decides on the distribution of profits.
The law provides for certain group minority rights; there is, however, no right of proportionate representation of the minority on the supervisory board under the Act, but the company statutes may so provide.
There are several rights which may be exercised by a minority of shareholders of an AG holding at least one-tenth of the share capital, or, in some cases, the nominal amount of DM 2 million; e.g. to request for a separate vote on the discharge of board members; to make claims for damages on behalf of the AG against board members and others or to request special auditors (to be exercised by a court order only). One-twentieth of the share capital suffices for calling a shareholders meeting, if necessary by court order. Each shareholder is

entitled to demand information from the management at the shareholders' meeting; the Act contains detailed regulations which specify when and under what circumstances management may refuse to give such information. In case of doubtful refusal the shareholder is entitled to appeal to the court.

– *Liability*

Basically what has been said in this respect with regard to the GmbH applies also to the AG. In addition thereto, the Stock Corporation Act expressly lays down that the provisions concerning the standard of diligence applicable to the managing board as well as the extent of liability shall apply accordingly to the members of the supervisory board.

Furthermore, if a parent company holds a controlling majority in a subsidiary company, the parent company will be liable to the subsidiary and under certain circumstances to its minority shareholders (if any) for any disadvantage caused to the subsidiary by the controlling influence. In addition, the members of the managing and supervisory boards of the controlling company will be personally liable in such cases, if they have neglected their duties.

If the companies have entered into a control and profit transfer agreement (cf. also below under f, page 224) – law on groups of companies), the dominating company must cover losses of the dominated company, if any, during the lifetime of the agreement, and after the termination of the agreement, must, upon request, give security to creditors of the formerly dominated company.

– *Accounts and auditing requirements; publication of accounts*

The Stock Corporation Act contains very detailed regulations regarding the annual accounting and reporting of AGs. These provisions will be amended by the implementation of the provisions of the Fourth EEC Harmonization Directive (see European chapter). However, as compared with the GmbH the modifications will be limited, because the present German provisions for the AG have been to a certain degree the model for the Directive.

The law provides in general that the annual financial statements shall conform to proper accounting principles (*Grundsätze ordnungsgemäßer Buchführung*). These principles come partly from usage or common practice, but are, however, to a large extent now fixed by law. There are provisions against excessive reserves, in particular, hidden reserves, and over- and undervaluation etc.

The managing board is responsible for drawing up the balance sheet with profit and loss statements, and the business report, which is then examined and confirmed by the auditors elected at the shareholders meeting. Thereafter they are submitted by the managing board to the supervisory board for further examination and approval.

Only when both boards disagree the financial statements are put before the shareholders meeting for approval. In practice this rarely happens.

The balance sheet, the profit and loss account and the business report of an AG, together with the audit certificate, must be filed with the Trade Register and published at least in the Federal Gazette (*Bundesgesetzblatt*).

1.d.(iii) No separate checklist for AG

A checklist for incorporating an AG will not be given here. In outline, reference can be made to the GmbH checklist, but in detail, the list for an AG would be substantially longer. In view of the rarity of incorporating a subsidiary in the form of an AG and the necessity to consult specialists in such an event, the lengthy checklist is not appropriate here.

1.e. OTHER FORMS

In addition to the private and public limited companies (GmbH and AG) which constitute separate legal entities, German law also regulates partnerships that are not legal entities. It must be stressed, however, that despite of their lack of legal personality, partnerships may acquire rights, enter into obligations, acquire real estate, may sue and be sued in their own name.
There are two types of partnerships:
– general commercial partnership (*Offene Handelsgesellschaft*)
– limited partnership (*Kommanditgesellschaft*).
An *Offene Handelsgesellschaft* (OHG) is an association between two or more persons for carrying on business in common with a view to profit. The partners are jointly and severally responsible for the liabilities of the firm and the liability of each partner is unlimited.
Each partner may participate in the running of the partnership, but this may be restricted to certain partners by a partnership agreement. Each partner is therefore entitled to represent the firm in so far as he has not been excluded from such representation by the agreement.
Any association between two or more persons for carrying on business in common with a view to making profit in which the liability of one or more of the partners is limited to the partnership capital brought in by him or them (non-active partners, limited partners, *Kommanditisten*), and when the liability of the other partners is unlimited (active partners, *persönlich haftende Gesellschafter* or *Komplementäre*), is a limited partnership (*Kommanditgesellschaft*, KG). The rules which apply to active partners are identical to those which apply to the partners in a general partnership. Non-active partners are excluded from the running of the partnership and cannot represent it.
A particular feature of the law is that legal persons as well as individuals can become partners in both general partnerships and limited partnerships. It is not even necessary for any of the partners to be natural persons. A company which is an active partner is liable up to the full amount of its assets for the obligations of the partnership; but the shareholders of the company are not personally liable beyond the shares they hold. Based on this legal situation, the GmbH & Co. KG has become a very popular type of company in Germany. As the KG according to the German legal concept for partnerships is not a separate legal entity, no corporation tax is levied; but the liability of all partners is still limited as in the case of a company.
Partnerships are established by the simple conclusion of a partnership agreement, but must be registered in the Trade Register. The names, first names, professions and domiciles of all partners, the purpose of the partnership and the place of business of the new firm must be notified as well as the date of its commencement. It is important to note that in principle a partnership is not established by the act of registration, since registration here is only in the nature of a declaration.
The limitation of the liability of the non-active partners, however, becomes effective upon registration only.

As in the case of incorporated public and private limited companies, partnerships intending to act as credit institutions, insurance firms and building societies require a licence from the supervising authorities. In addition, various other activities require a licence from the trade supervision department. Partnerships engaging in these activities are subject to the same governmental supervision as incorporated companies.

Partnerships registered in Germany are subject to German law regardless of the nationality of the partners; such a partnership is considered German even if all or some of the partners are aliens.

It may be mentioned that there is still another type of partnership: the silent partnership (*Stille Gesellschaft*). It is based on an agreement under which the silent partner contributes to the business of another party and participates in the profits of this business. He is not known to third parties, not liable for the debts of the business and no entry is made in the Trade Register.

1.f. LAW ON GROUPS OF COMPANIES (*KONZERNRECHT*)

So far no special law governing subsidiaries (dependent companies) has been enacted in Germany.

However, the new Stock Corporation Act (Aktiengesetz, AktG), which came into force on January 1, 1966, contains for the first time 'special rules of law governing connected enterprises' (art. 291 ff., AktG).

Among legally independent companies, the following are regarded as connected enterprises (art. 15 ff., AktG):

1. undertakings linked by a majority participation;
2. undertakings either directly or indirectly controlling another undertaking (dependent and controlling enterprise);
3. undertakings mutually holding participations in each other;
4. undertakings under the same central management (members of a group of companies);
5. undertakings which are partners to an enterprise agreement.

In addition to these definitions the term 'participation' should be mentioned, as it is of importance in drawing up the balance sheet. In case of doubt, ownership of 25% or more of the share capital of another limited company constitutes a participation (art. 152, para. 2 AktG).

Thus defined, these terms are only applicable for the purposes of the Stock Corporation Act; but in legal parlance they are also used for other types of companies.

More often than not, connected companies fulfil more than one of the requirements indicated in items 1 to 5 above: a company may hold more than 50% of the share capital of another company and may thus simultaneously control the dependent company and have in addition entered into an enterprise agreement with the dependent company.

The legal consequences of the linking of enterprises are nowadays more fully regulated than ever before. Up till now, the regulations have only been intended to guarantee financial soundness, to prevent deviation from the purposes of the company and to provide additional information for the public, but now they also serve to protect minority shareholders against detrimental actions on the part of the majority. In this connection very briefly some provisions may be mentioned which have been introduced by the new Stock Corporation Act:

1. If an enterprise either directly or indirectly controls a stock corporation, usually through a majority interest, an annual report of dependence has to be made by the managing board of the dependent corporation. The report must state any detrimental effects caused to the dependent company by the dependence relationship and the latter may claim damages.
2. If a stock corporation and another company mutually own more than 25% of each other's share capital, they are only entitled to exercise rights out of their shareholdings up to 25% of the total shares of each of the companies.
3. Enterprise agreements such as control agreements, agreements to transfer profits, profit pools, shop leasing agreements, business transfer agreements and management agreements, require the approval of a 75% majority of the shareholders. Where both parties to an enterprise agreement are stock corporations, approval from a 75% majority of shareholders from both companies concluded at their respective shareholders' meeting is required. The other contracting party must therefore, for this, as well as for tax reasons, hold the majority of the voting stock of either the dependent stock corporation or of the corporation undertaking to transfer profits. The former is liable for the liabilities of the latter. In the case of a control agreement and an agreement to transfer profits, the other contracting party must guarantee a fixed dividend for the thirdparty shareholders of the dependent company and propose an indemnification in the event of such shareholders wishing to dispose of their shares.

A new method of organization has been introduced by law in the form of an integration (*Eingliederung*) of a stock corporation into another stock corporation registered in the Federal Republic. The integration decision is made by a 75% majority vote of the shareholders at the shareholders' meeting of both companies. To effect integration, the principal company must hold at least 95% of the share capital of the other company. Shares which have not up till then been acquired by the principal company thereupon become its property. Those shareholders who are consequently eliminated are generally compensated by shares in the principal company. This procedure preserves the legal independence of the integrated company; but in all other respects it is treated as a place of business of the principal company.

Groups of companies (*Konzerne*) must prepare and publish consolidated financial statements comprising a business report. If more than 50% of a company's share capital belongs to a parent company in a group of companies, it must be included in the consolidated balance sheet of the dominant company, unless it is of no importance in determining the financial position and results of trading of the group. All companies which are members of a group and are registered in the Federal Republic must be included in the group business report. This report must also indicate which companies have been included in the balance sheet of the group and which companies are registered outside the Federal Republic. The balance sheets of the consolidated companies of the group must be attached to the business report, which must also comment upon any important differences shown by the balance sheet in comparison with the preceding balance sheet. The business report must also contain particulars concerning:

1. the reasons for, and the nature of, any difference between the amounts of the participations in the consolidated enterprises and the amounts of equity of those enterprises corresponding to the participation, which must be shown in the consolidated balance sheet;
2. the legal and business relations with companies which are registered in the Federal Republic and which are not a part of the group, but connected with a company belonging to the group.

2. THE JOINT VENTURE

Joint ventures in Germany occur, as in other countries, in two forms: either as a jointly-owned company, established for a longer or indefinite period, or in the more loosely composed form of a business consortium for a specific project, which legally as a rule is a civil-law partnership (*BGB-Gesellschaft*). In both events one must have regard to the provisions of the anti-trust law: the former may in particular be subject to merger control, the latter may conflict with the regulations against the restraints of competition (cf. also B. 3. below, page 229).

2.a. The jointly-owned company

Also for this type of joint venture the corporate forms, in particular the GmbH, are considered the most suitable legal framework. Therefore in general reference can be made to the relevant passages above.
A special feature which is often, though by no means exclusively, found in cases of jointly-owned companies is the shareholders' agreement. Such agreements may be entered into by two or more shareholders. The subject of such agreements is normally the obligation to vote in the general meeting in a certain way or to abstain from voting. Furthermore they usually contain obligations concerning the transfer of shares underlying the agreement.
The voting agreement may either cover all resolutions to be passed by the general meeting or govern only important subjects such as (which is mostly the case) the election of members of the managing and supervisory board or managing directors respectively, or other subjects such as amendments and changes of the statutes, increases in capital, distribution of dividends, merger and liquidation decisions and transfer of shares.
The latter concerns prior consent to transfer of shares as provided by the statutes, making the consent a condition of the validity of the transfer, whereas often in place of, or in addition to, statutory regulations on this subject the shareholders' agreement itself contains such provisions. They may provide that the shares of the partners to the agreement may not be sold without the prior consent of these partners, and that they may only be sold to certain persons, or that the other partners have a pro-rata right of first refusal.
Case law and legal writings state that shareholders' agreements are permitted and are valid under German law, in particular because the Stock Corporation Act declares such agreements invalid in one specific case only, thus, impliedly permitting shareholders' agreements in all other events. The specific prescription concerns agreements whereby shareholders undertake to vote according

to instructions of the stock corporation itself, or the management, or the supervisory board.
Furthermore, the sale or purchase of votes, i.e. an agreement to vote in a certain way or to abstain from voting in consideration for any advantage, is invalid.
Shareholders' agreements need not be disclosed to the company or published by it in order to become valid and binding.
They may be entered into for a fixed period of several years or for an indefinite period of time. In the latter event it is advisable and therefore customary to fix the details concerning the notice of termination since otherwise according to civil law, the agreement, which legally is deemed to be a civil-law partnership, may be terminated at any time.
In the past, a controversial question existed as to whether or not a claim for specific performance of the voting agreement could be made or a simple claim for damages or contractual penalty (if provided for) only. The Federal Court has now held in the case of a GmbH, that specific performance can be claimed. According to the Civil Procedural Code, final judgement in such event is deemed as a casting of the vote. It may be added that with respect to those parts of the shareholders' agreement concerning transfer of shares, damages for breach of contract can be claimed only if a party to the agreement has in violation thereof sold his shares to a third party. This is so because the shareholders' agreement has no effect vis-à-vis third parties so that a transfer in breach of the agreement becomes nevertheless effective.
Shareholders' agreements basically are a suitable means of pooling the interests of shareholders in such way as to produce a blocking minority or a majority. They are therefore sometimes called pool agreements.

2.b. Consortia

Apart from the specific types of banking and insurance consortia, which will not be dealt with here, business consortia have been customary in Germany for a long time in the field of contracting and civil engineering. For large building projects, the resources of one undertaking alone were often insufficient, and bidding for public contracts, in particular, seemed more promising for an *Arbeitsgemeinschaft* (working combine, consortium).
This type of co-operation has meanwhile been adopted for all sorts of national and international large-scale projects for industrial development, erection and installation of plants and equipment, etc. As long as different types of enterprises co-operate in such a way for one given project, e.g. a civil engineering company, manufacturer of machinery, and an electrical installation firm, usually no anti-trust problems arise. The position is different if several undertakings in the same branch of industry co-operate over one or more projects because this carries with it the danger of restraining competition.
There are several forms of consortium agreement: the bidding consortium as opposed to the collaborative consortium, the external consortium (where the client deals with the consortium), and the internal consortium (where only one member of the consortium deals with the client), etc.
In law, a consortium will nearly always be a civil law partnership. Under civil law, among other things, all partners are jointly and severally liable and must pass a resolution unanimously. This may require to be modified by internal

agreement; in particular, management, representation and liability questions of the consortium and many other details require a careful and thorough drafting of the consortium agreement. As the relevant civil law is to a large extent not mandatory, the parties are free to frame an agreement closely adapted to the business requirements of each case.

B. External Controls

1. EXCHANGE CONTROLS

Foreign trade has to a large extent been liberalised and as a matter of principle there are no exchange control restrictions, so that in both respects branches or subsidiaries of foreign companies may carry on business without the requirement of obtaining licenses.

The Foreign Trade Act (*Außenwirtschaftsgesetz*, AWG), however, sets out certain conditions under which the government is authorised to impose restrictions on the import and export of goods as well as on capital transactions. The government may, for example, require a cash deposit (*Bardepot*) for capital imports if this appears to be necessary in order to prevent an influx of foreign capital which could endanger the German economy.

Funds permanently invested in a branch office and adequate equity contributions to a subsidiary by a foreign parent company would be exempt from this regulation. At present no such cash deposits are required.

It may be mentioned that certain transactions under the Foreign Trade Act require a notice to the Federal Reserve Bank. Violation of these obligations is punishable by a fine, but does not affect the validity of any investment measures.

2. TAKE-OVER CONTROLS

Under German law there are no specific judicial or administrative procedures available as protection against unwanted take-over bids, such as exist in some other countries.

If a take-over results in or reinforces a dominant market position and fulfils certain other criteria of German anti-trust law, it may, however, be prohibited by the Federal Cartel Office (see below, 3, page 229).

Furthermore, there are a few sectors where the law requires a German majority, as in the case of aviation companies.

In all other events defensive measures against unwanted take-overs can only be provided for in the statutes of the respective companies. As discussed above, the statutes may provide that share transfers are valid only if the prior consent of the general meeting is obtained.

Instead, the validity of a transfer may be made subject to the prior approval of the board, which may be more suitable in companies with many shareholders. Finally, the statutes may limit the voting rights of shareholders, so that no shareholder, irrespective of the amount of shares held by him, may exercise for example more than 10% of all existing voting rights.

The provisions mentioned can be included in the statutes of both private and public companies but, in practice, few of the latter have availed themselves of this opportunity. Share transfer restrictions are very common, however, for private companies (GmbHs).

3. ANTI-TRUST (MERGER CONTROL)

In 1973 the Cartel Act, or Act against the Restraint of Competition (*Gesetz gegen Wettbewerbsbeschränkungen*, GWB) was amended in several respects. The most important amendment was the introduction of comprehensive merger control provisions. After some years of experience the Fourth Amendment Act, which came into force on January 1, 1981, has further tightened merger control. As the field of anti-trust law, particularly merger control is far too complex for an adequate treatment here, only some aspects of merger control are discussed. (With regard to the EC aspects, reference is made to the European Chapter.)

Under certain conditions the Federal Cartel Authority must be notified of mergers, e.g. if the undertakings concerned attain a market share of 25% or more by means of the merger or if one of these enterprises already holds such a market share prior to the merger.

The term merger is defined widely: e.g. acquisition of a participation of 25% or more in another company is regarded as a merger as well as incorporation of a joint subsidiary.

The notification must be accompanied by a report of certain features of the merging companies and all connected enterprises (cf. A. 1. f) above, page 224), e.g. market shares, sales figures, balance sheet totals, numbers of employees, etc.

If two of the merging companies have annual sales volumes exceeding DM 1 billion each, or one of them has annual sales exceeding DM 2 billion, the merging companies must give notice in advance and the merger must not, in principle, come into effect for a period of four months after notification. The Federal Cartel Authority has to decide within this period whether the merger is to be prohibited, but it may shorten the period by giving earlier notice that it will not prohibit the merger.

The Federal Cartel Authority must forbid a merger if a position of market domination would thereby be created or strengthened, unless the merger at the same time improves competition and this improvement outweighs the disadvantages of the market domination.

Merger control under German law applies in the same way where foreign companies are involved, since it is sufficient that the transaction concerned has an effect on the German market.

The detailed provisions are very complicated and far-reaching. It is therefore essential to take them into consideration early in the planning stage of an envisaged acquisition or co-operation which may be considered a merger within the meaning of the act.

4. ENVIRONMENTAL CONTROLS

Based on art. 74 of the German Constitution the legislature as late as 1974 passed the comprehensive Federal Immission Protection Act (*Bundesimmissions-Schutzgesetz*, BImSchG). Together with the complementary Intromission Protection Acts of the federal states and official regulations, these laws cover the whole scope protection of men, animals, plants and other matters against intromissions caused by emissions of industrial plant and equipment and other installations. Prior to the BImSchG, of course, there were already similar provisions in other acts, such as the Trade Regulations (*Gewerbeordnung*). Now the BImSchG and the complementary legislations completely cover the subject and provide for the necessary procedures.
The most important regulation concerning industrial investment is the necessity of an official permit for certain installations exhaustively listed in the BImSchG. They are only allowed if their emissions are within the limits of the BImSchG and the complementary regulations.
Industrial and other refuse has to be disposed of in refuse pits in accordance with the Refuse Disposal Act (*Abfallbeseitigungsgesetz*).
Further restrictions or investment may be imposed in the interest of preserving nature (Federal Nature Preservation Act; *Bundesnaturschutzgesetz*). The production of food and medicine is supervised. Food may only contain pesticides and other noxious substances within certain limits. Medicine must be tested, to ensure that it is not harmful to human beings.

5. STATE MONOPOLIES

The two major institutions run by the state which are in principle closed to private enterprise competition are the Federal Railways and the Federal Postal Administration. In addition, there are a few state monopolies. One may mention the distilled spirits monopoly and the monopoly on matches.

6. OTHER CONTROLS

Some branches, in particular credit institutions, insurance companies and building societies are subject to Government supervision after incorporation. Such companies must submit regular reports to the supervising authorities concerned and these authorities may audit the companies' records and books, intervene under some circumstances in personnel matters, and also prescribe or proscribe certain material measures.

III. TAXATION

A. Corporation Tax

Preliminary remarks:
In 1977 there was a major change in the German corporation tax system. As

part of the German Corporation Tax Reform Act the Corporation Tax Act (*Körperschaftsteuergesetz*, KStG 1977) came into force. It was applicable for the first time for the assessment period beginning on January 1, 1977. This law introduced the tax credit system, thus abolishing, in principle, the internal double taxation of corporate income which had long been criticized. Previously corporate income was subject to a 51% corporation tax if not distributed, and 15% (effective rate: 23,44%) if distributed. The dividend received by the shareholder was then again subject to income tax in the case of an individual or, in general, to a corporation tax if it was a corporation.

At present the full amount of corporation tax attributable to the distributed dividend is credited against the individual income or corporation tax debt of the shareholders.

Although this basic principle is very simple, the German legislator, in order to create a just system providing fair solutions for all possible eventualities, has elaborated a law which is highly complicated in detail. Therefore, only its main features are set out here.

This will include, however, also certain provisions of the German Income Tax Act (*Einkommensteuergesetz*):

As the corporation tax is only a specific form of income tax, the general provisions of the Income Tax Act are applicable to a large extent for the purposes of the corporation tax also.

Finally a preliminary remark concerning the impact of the new tax credit system on international business relations:

As the benefit of the tax credit system is only available to persons or corporations receiving domestic income subject to German taxation, the tax credit is not available to foreign shareholders not receiving such direct internal income apart from dividends.

Other arrangements have been attempted by foreign shareholders in order to circumvent this discriminating effect of the German tax credit system for non-resident shareholders, but the German authorities are expected to block such arrangements. On the other hand, however, there are efforts to mitigate the disadvantages for foreign shareholders by certain revisions of double taxation treaties.

1. ENTITIES SUBJECT TO TAX

There are two categories of corporation tax liability, namely unrestricted and restricted liability.

a. Corporation tax liability is unrestricted for all companies (among others AG and GmbH) where the management or domicile is situated in the Federal Republic of Germany (resident companies). In principle their world-wide income is subject to corporation tax; but such taxation is limited by the many double taxation treaties (cf. I. below, page 245).

b. For companies without management or domicile in Germany (non-resident companies; foreign companies) the corporation tax liability is restricted to their 'domestic income' earned within Germany. If the non-resident company has a permanent establishment in Germany (e.g. a branch) all income derived from German sources through the permanent establishment in Germany is subject to tax. If the company has no permanent establishment, only the income falling into certain classes of income defined as domestic income of non-resident companies is taxed. The main classes are

- income from domestic farming and forestry (domestic in the present context always means within the Federal Republic of Germany);
- business income not obtained through domestic permanent establishments but
  - through permanent representatives or through owned or chartered sea ships or aircraft operating between domestic points or between domestic and foreign ports or
  - by selling a participation in a German corporation;
- income from capital investments, in particular dividends and certain types of interest, e.g. dividends of subsidiaries;
- rental or royalty income flowing from domestic real estate or industrial property rights;
- income from the sale of domestic real estate or other goods, if sold within two years (real estate) or six months (all other goods) after purchase.

For the purposes of corporation tax, all these different types of income are treated as business income of the foreign corporation.

Again, the incidence of corporation tax in the event of receiving such income may be excluded or reduced by applicable double taxation treaties (cf. I. below, page 245).

Partnerships are not subject to corporation tax, the income obtained through partnerships is taxable in the hands of the partners. The income of partners being individuals is subject to income tax, while that of partners being corporations falls under the corporation tax.

2. COMPUTATION OF PROFITS

2.a. Income

The range of income subject to corporation tax has been indicated under 1. above.

The taxable income of a corporation is defined as the difference between the net assets of the company at the end of the fiscal year and the net assets at the end of the preceding fiscal year plus capital withdrawn and less capital paid in.

The net assets of corporations must be established as per the end of each fiscal year by means of a balance sheet which basically must be drawn up in accordance with proper bookkeeping principles under commercial law. The balance sheet for tax purposes (or tax balance sheet) therefore in principle is based on the commercial balance sheet, required by the tax law.

In practice, however, except for AGs and certain other large companies, most companies and in particular GmbHs draw up only one balance sheet incorporating the adjustments necessary under the tax law without first preparing a commercial balance sheet.

Some principles of tax law are mentioned below which modify the normal commercial accounting principles and restrict valuation alternatives granted by the commercial law etc.

aa. Property, plant and equipment must be written off over the expected useful lifetime of each individual asset. Depreciations omitted in one fiscal year may not, therefore, as a rule be made up for later on. Depreciation of land is not allowed.
The Federal Minister of Finance publishes lists of uniform depreciation rates for the different sectors of business. Although they are not mandatory the taxpayer has the burden of proving the justification of any departure from these rates.
Straight line depreciation is allowed for all assets, although the declining balance method for movable property investments is allowed in the alternative. In the latter case, however, the annual depreciation rate may not exceed the corresponding rate given by the straight-line method by more than two and a half times and may not be higher than 25%.
In certain cases more favourable depreciation rates apply as an incentive (cf. F) below, page 241).
Items of property with minor value (for the time being up to DM 800 may be written off completely in the year of acquisition.

bb. The taxable income may not be reduced by a hidden distribution of profit (*verdeckte Gewinnausschüttung*). Such distribution can be effected by manipulated transactions between a corporation, its shareholder, and other affiliated companies. Transactions like the purchase or sale of merchandise at unusual prices or special discounts or rebates, leases at unusual terms and conditions, loans at unreasonably high or low rates of interest, licence agreements with unreasonable royalties, employment contracts with unduly high salaries or other tax compensation are examples.
If, and insofar, as the considerations paid in such transactions prove to be unreasonable, such consideration is deemed to be a hidden distribution of profit and will for tax purposes be allocated to the income of the company, subject to tax. The question of whether the consideration is unreasonable, may for example be answered by applying the 'arm's length' test, according to which expenditures are only allowed by the tax authorities, if they equal those agreed upon with independent parties.

cc. Under certain circumstances a subsidiary is not amenable to tax on its income, which is instead taxed as income of its parent company. This is so in the case of an *Organschaft* (integrated intercompany relationship). In such a case the controlled subsidiary (then called an *Organgesellschaft*) must from the beginning of its respective fiscal year be wholly integrated (i.e. financially, economically and organisationally) into another German corporation or into the German branch of a non-resident corporation (*Organträger*). A partnership or a person may become an *Organträger*.
A profit and loss pooling agreement (*Ergebnisabführungsvertrag*) must be concluded for a period of at least five years.
In such a case, the profit of the controlled subsidiary is not distributed as a

dividend, but accrues directly to the controlling company, which is taxed on it. The same applies to losses of the controlled company which have to be absorbed directly at the level of the *Organträger*.

2.b. Capital gains/losses

aa. Whereas, for individuals, capital gains on assets not connected with a business are generally free of tax if held longer than six months (real estate: two years), capital gains for corporations generally constitute ordinary taxable business income, and are taxed at the normal rates.
However, under certain circumstances the gains flowing from the sale of certain fixed assets may, at the election of the taxpayer, be set off against the cost of certain other fixed assets acquired in the same fiscal year or, alternatively, set aside as a tax-free reserve for future acquisition of such fixed assets. Such assets comprise land, buildings, assets having an expected lifetime of at least twenty-five years, ships, and shares in domestic or foreign corporations. The gain from selling some of these types of fixed assets is not available for reinvestment in each and every type of fixed assets mentioned above. If a tax-free reserve has been set aside, it must be used within a period of two (in certain cases four) years, thus permitting a tax-free exchange of assets. If not made use of during the said period, the reserve must be dissolved and becomes ordinary taxable income.
Furthermore, gains flowing from recapitalisations and reorganisations such as a reduction with a simultaneous increase of a corporation's capital, including also cancellation by all creditors of all or part of the corporation's debts, are deemed as rehabilitation gains (*Sanierungsgewinne*) and do not form part of the taxable income. Such gains need not be set off against the corporation's losses carried forward.

bb. Losses of a corporation can be carried back for 1 year and up to DM 5 million. Beyond that they can be carried forward for five years, however, there must be not only legal, but also economic identity between the enterprise incurring the loss and the one applying it against its profits. If a corporation has totally changed its object and character, it is no longer considered identical. The acquisition of corporate shells (*Mantelkauf*) therefore is of no purpose, if the only intention is to obtain a tax-deductible loss carried forward.

2.c. Exemptions, deductions, rebates

aa. The Income Tax Act contains a long list of income exempted from tax and there is a catalogue of institutions exempted from corporation tax. From the first category it may suffice to mention interest on certain government and other bonds, specifically exempted from tax. Within the second group for example certain pensions funds for employees are exempted.

bb. Whereas business expenses can in principle be deducted, certain expenses are not deductible from taxable income. The most important categories are

- payments of or provisions for corporation tax (including capital yields tax, being merely a form of levying) and income corporation tax net worth tax and value added tax on inhouse consumption,
- half of the payments to members of a supervisory board, administrative board or other persons charged with supervision of the management,
- expenses directly related to non-taxable income (see above under *aa*),
- expenses for gifts to non-employees, except for gifts clearly marked for use as advertising and being of minor value,
- expenses for entertainment of non-employees (e.g. clients, businessfriends) unless recorded individually on printed forms officially prescribed by the tax authorities and indicating names, event, amount etc. (often to be found on the back of restaurant bills). However, even correctly recorded expenses of this nature are not deductible if they are unreasonable.

3. RATES OF TAX

The tax rates for German corporations with unrestricted tax liability are in principle as follows:
- profits not distributed to shareholders 56%,
- profits distributed to shareholders 36%.

These rates are reduced by 22,5% in the case of profits made in West-Berlin (see below F., Incentives, page 214).
The rate of tax on non-resident companies is the same, if they have a permanent establishment in Germany. If they have not, all classes of income are subject to the same tax rates except dividend and interest income. On this income, a withholding tax is levied (see below B. 1, page 236). It should be noted already here that in order to calculate the complete tax burden of a company in particular the trade tax must be taken into consideration (cf. H. 1. below, page 243).

4. TAX CREDITS

Tax credits, as pointed out above, are granted to the shareholders of a company covering the 36% corporation tax paid on the gross profit out of which the dividend is distributed to them. The tax credit thus amounts to 9/16 of the dividend paid (out of 100, 36 are paid as tax, 64 are distributed as dividends; 36/64 equals 9/16).
On the other hand, tax credits for withholding taxes levied by the tax authorities in other countries on dividends distributed are available for the German corporation under the existing double taxation treaties (cf. I. below, page 245).

5. TIMING OF PAYMENT

The tax year is identical with the calendar year. For companies with a different business year, assessment is based on the business year ending in the respective calendar year.

Returns should normally be filed after the completion of the calendar year by a date fixed by the tax authorities from time to time. This usually in the middle of the following calendar year unless professional tax advisors are employed, in which event the term is upon application usually extended to September 30.
This corresponds with the fact that, for example, GmbHs must draw up their annual accounts within 3 months or, if the statutes so allow, 6 months after the end of their fiscal year.
On the basis of the return, the tax office issues a notice of assessment. Tax amounts exceeding the prepayments (see below) must usually be paid within one month; overpayments are refunded or set off against other tax liabilities. Corporation tax is prepaid in quarterly instalments, usually based on the last preceding tax assessment. Prepayments may be adjusted if the current income is considered to differ substantially from the total amount of prepayments fixed for the respective calendar year.

6. REVIEW AND APPEAL

The assessments based on the returns are not final, they are subject to the results of tax audits (*Betriebsprüfung*). Taking into consideration the normal period of limitation for tax liabilities, namely five years, the law provides that such audits shall be made at least once every three years, but in practice the intervals are often longer.
Where the assessments of the fiscal office (*Finanzamt*) are considered incorrect an appeal may be made to the tax court (*Finanzgericht*). The basic rules applied by these bodies in addition to the specific provisions governing corporation tax (or other taxes) are set out in the Fiscal Code (*Abgabenordnung*, AO). For a final decision further appeal is possible to the Federal Tax Court (*Bundesfinanzhof*) in Munich. Upon application by the taxpayer payment of tax amounts under appeal may be deferred until after the final decision.

B. Withholding Taxes on Dividends, Interest, Royalties

(see also below: J. Schedule of withholding taxes, page 246).

1. INCOME CATEGORIES SUBJECT TO WITHHOLDING TAX

Income from German sources received by non-resident companies is in principle subject to corporation tax. Non-resident companies for the purposes of the tax laws are defined as those having neither their domicile nor their management in the Federal Republic of Germany.
As mentioned above, only dividends and interest are subject to a special withholding tax, the so-called *Kapitalertragsteuer* (capital yield tax) if the non-

resident company has no domestic permanent establishment. In all other cases (for example, royalty payments or income received through a German permanent establishment) the normal corporation tax is levied instead of the *Kapitalertragsteuer.*

If the foreign undertaking is not a corporate body but an individual or a partnership, corporation tax is not levied, but such individuals or partners are subject to a regular income tax deduction (see below D. Individual Taxation). If there is no German permanent establishment, dividends, interest and royalties are subject to a withholding tax with special rates.

2. COMPUTATION OF INCOME

For computation of income, the principles set forth above under A. 2., page 232 apply.

3. RATES

The rate of capital yields tax levied on dividends is 25%. The same rate applies to interest, e.g. interest on profit-sharing and convertible bonds, other bonds etc., whereas interest from loans (excluding bond loans) secured by immovables situated in Germany is subject to corporation tax at the normal rate, i.e. 56%. Royalties received by a non-resident company are also subject to the normal corporation tax rate of 56%.

For non-resident recipients the withholding tax levied at the above rates (or other rates fixed by double taxation treaties, see below under 4.) is the final tax. This does not apply, however, if the dividend, interest or royalty income is obtained by the non-resident company through a permanent establishment in Germany, in which case it becomes taxable at the full rate of corporation tax. It therefore makes a substantial difference in this respect also whether a foreign company runs its German business through a subsidiary or a branch, because branches are permanent establishments under tax law.

In case of a foreign natural person, the rate of withholding tax on dividends, interest and royalties is 25%. If they are earned through a permanent establishment in Germany, the rate varies from 22% to 56% (see below D. Individual Taxation, page 239).

List of tax rates

Recipient / *type of income*	*Incorporated Company*		*Natural person, personal partnership*	
	with German permanent establishment	*without German permanent establishment*	*with German permanent establishment*	*without German permanent establishment*
dividends	56%	25%	22%-56%	25%
interest	56%	25%	22%-56%	25%
royalties	56%	56%	22%-56%	25%

4. EFFECT OF DOUBLE TAXATION TREATIES

a. As far as capital yield tax on dividends is concerned, most double taxation treaties between EC countries provide a refund of 10% upon application, unless the recipient non-resident company owns directly or indirectly 25% or more of the voting shares of the German company, making the effective rates 15% and 25%, respectively.

b. The 25% withholding tax on interest in the case of convertible and profit sharing bonds is often reduced by a refund of 10% upon application, bringing the effective rate down to 20%, 15% or 10%; tax on interest on other bonds is often fully refunded upon application, whereas the treatment of interest from loans secured by immovables situated in Germany differs. Under the treaties between EC countries (and certain other treaties) interest from all other sources remains free from German withholding or other taxes.

c. With regard to royalties the same applies for withholding taxes (except for Luxemburg), whereas a value added tax is levied in Germany.

C. Registration and Stamp Duties

1. REGISTRATION DUTIES

A capital investment tax (*Gesellschaftsteuer*) as one of the two categories of capital transaction tax, is levied on capital invested in a German branch at the time of investment at the rate of 1%, provided the head office is a public or private limited company. If this is not the case, no tax is due.
All companies are subject to this tax, computed on the basis of the paid up capital; the tax is also payable in the event of an increase in capital. Long term loans and credits which are directly or indirectly put at the disposal of the subsidiary company by one or more of its members are also subject to this tax, if the tax authorities are of the opinion that these loans and credits are intended to avoid an increase in capital. As the tax is in principle due at the time of registration of a new company or of a capital increase, the tax may be classified as a registration duty.
This tax is already harmonized within the EC (see European chapter).
There are no other registration duties.

2. STAMP DUTY

The only stamp duty existing in Germany is the bills of exchange tax. This 0.15% tax is levied on all bills of exchange and negotiable promissory notes issued in Germany or issued abroad and acquired in Germany. The tax rate is reduced by one-half if the bill is drawn in Germany on a foreign drawee and payable abroad or drawn abroad on a domestic drawee and payable in Germany.

D. Individual Taxation

1. PERSONS SUBJECT TO TAX

All persons resident in Germany are subject to income tax, in principle, on the whole of their income from all domestic and foreign sources. Generally a person is regarded as resident in Germany after a stay of six months.
Non-residents are subject to income tax on their domestic income from certain defined sources (cf. insofar the respective passage concerning corporation tax, A. 1. above, page 231).

2. COMPUTATION OF INCOME

a. Of the several sources of income, the income from employment is of main interest in the context of this book, because this is the sort of income a foreign manager will receive in Germany.
Such income includes all benefits in cash or in kind received by the person, except certain pension benefits which the employer is obligated to grant.
Only tax on the employment income of residents is withheld at the source by the employer who must pay it to the tax authorities as payroll tax (*Lohnsteuer*). However, any person whose employment income exceeds DM 24,000 p.a. must file an annual income tax return; in which all withholding taxes are set off against the full tax debt. Domestic income of non-residents is always subject to a withholding tax.

b. Capital gains of individuals obtained from sales of privately owned land or other assets, including shares, are free of tax if such assets were held prior to the sale for a period exceeding two years in the case of real estate or six months in all other cases.

c. The major allowances and deductions of employees to be set off against the taxable income are
- employees allowance (DM 480 p.a.)
- christmas allowance (DM 400 p.a.)
- expenses incurred in earning income (*Werbungskosten*) (lump sum deduction DM 564 p.a., unless higher expenses proved)
- special expenses (*Sonderausgaben*), in particular contributions for sickness, accident, liability and life insurances up to certain ceiling amounts.

Certain of these amounts are higher for married employees and those with children.

3. RATES OF TAX

Taxation of the income of individuals begins at a very low level of annual income. The tax rates can be taken from official tax tables. The tax rate in the so-called proportional zone is 22%. The progressive tax rates start with an an-

nual income of DM 16,000 up to a maximum rate of about 56% in the highest bracket (which is reached at DM 130,000). Married persons may choose to be assessed jointly or separately.
Residents of West Berlin and persons working there for a period exceeding three months with regard to income obtained in West Berlin enjoy a reduction of 30% of the amount due in accordance with the tax tables.
Non-residents, as pointed out, are only taxable on their German sources of income, subject to exemptions under double taxation treaties. Normally they cannot choose to be taxed jointly with their spouse and generally they are not entitled to the allowances mentioned above, except certain allowances if they receive income from employment. A tax is always withheld at the source. The non-resident tax rate is 25% and the rate for members of the supervisory board is 30%. On employment income, only the payroll tax is levied, the rate of which is the same as that of the income tax, i.e. from 22% to 56%.

4. SUCCESSION DUTIES

Whereas the real estate transfer tax applying to the sale of land is dealt with below under H. 3. (page 244), inheritance tax (*Erbschaftsteuer*) should be mentioned here. All transfers due to donations or inheritance are subject to this tax. Various tax-free allowances are provided for transfers between spouses and relatives. They are rather high, e.g. for spouses up to DM 540,000.
The rates are progressive in proportion to the amount and vary for different classes of persons fixed by the Inheritance Tax Act.
Rates vary from 3% to 35% in class I (spouses, children) up to 20% to 70% in class IV (non-relatives). The highest rate is reached only when there is a transfer of more than DM 100 million.

E. Indirect Taxation

1. TURNOVER TAX

In accordance with the concept of harmonization of the indirect tax systems of the EEC countries, on January 1, 1968 the former cumulative allstage turnover tax was replaced by the VAT (Value Added Tax, *Mehrwertsteuer*). The national law introducing further harmonization in compliance with the Sixth EC Directive on turnover tax came into force on January 1, 1980.
This tax is levied on the price received for goods delivered or services rendered within Germany. The normal tax rate is 13% but a reduced rate of 6.5% applies, inter alia, to foodstuffs, printed matter, dentists' services, and transport. It is not now relevant whether the goods are sold for industrial purposes or to the final consumer. The sales price and the tax are invoiced to the buyer separately. The undertaking deducts from the turnover tax payable to the tax authorities, the amount of turnover tax charged by its suppliers (this is called the pre-tax deduction (*Vorsteuerabzug*)). The result of this preliminary deduc-

tion is that an undertaking only pays a turnover tax on the value added. Export rebates have been discontinued. The law provides for compensation for the pre-tax within the framework of the turnover tax by allowing exporters to deduct the pre-tax on exported goods from the turnover tax which they have to pay.

Since the tax applies directly to the value added, it no longer enters as an element in the calculations, but is merely a transferable item. Consequently like income tax and net worth tax, and in contrast with other taxes, the turnover tax is no longer an allowable deduction when the taxable profit is determined. For further details reference is made to the European chapter.

2. OTHERS

Other indirect taxes, namely stock exchange turnover tax and real estate acquisition tax, are treated below under H. 3. (page 244).

F. Incentives

A broad variety of tax benefits and government incentives are available to branches and subsidiaries doing business in Germany, in particular West Berlin and other assisted areas.

Special advice on these questions should therefore be sought before setting up new business operations in Germany and in particular before deciding where a branch or subsidiary should be situated. Only a survey of the major tax benefits and incentives can be given.

1. MAIN TYPES OF INCENTIVES

There are, besides a range of other measures, three types of incentives which are the most important, all or some of which are applied in most promoted areas, namely:

- accelerated depreciation by application of elevated depreciation rates;
- tax-exempt investment premiums;
- loans on favourable terms and guarantees.

2. AREAS FOR ELEVATED DEPRECIATION RATES

Elevated depreciation rates and other incentives have already been provided for, in a general way, under the regulations of the Income Tax Act for:

- residential construction;
- assets applied for environmental protection;
- fixed assets of private hospitals.

Other main areas of promotion by elevated depreciation subject to special legislation are among others:

- property, plant and equipment used exclusively or primarily for research and development purposes,
- foreign investments, in particular in developing countries,
- promotion of certain German regions, e.g. along the border with the German Democratic Republic (zonal border development area, *Zonenrandgebiet*).

3. INVESTMENT PREMIUMS

The Investment Premiums Law (*Investitionszulagengesetz*, InvZulG) provides premiums for new investments in regions which are officially declared to need promotion, if the investment is in accordance with the aims of national economy and the regional development plans (*Raumordnung, Landesplanung*). All regions along the border with the German Democratic Republic (*Zonenrandgebiete*) are promoted regions. The rate of the premium is 10% of the value of the investment in the *Zonenrandgebiet*, but 8.75% in all other regions.
Furthermore, the InvZulG provides a premium of 20% for investments on research and development, and a premium of 7.5% for investments which help to save energy.

4. LOANS

Loans on favourable terms and government guarantees may be obtained from the Federal Government, the states, the regions and from the districts.
Furthermore, the *Kreditanstalt für Wiederaufbau* lends the capital funds of the European Recovery Program (ERP, *Marshall-Plan*). Guarantees for foreign trade and foreign investment may be obtained from the *HERMES-Kreditversicherungs AG*. These incentives are given out for regional promotions as well as for the promotion of rationalization, research and development, energy saving, environmental protection, job security, and the industries of housebuilding, coal and steel, petrol, navigation, docks, fishing and for the press.

5. BERLIN PROMOTION

A specific area of emphasis is the promotion of West-Berlin.
Main incentives for the investment phase are tax-exempt investment premiums amounting to between 10 and 40% of the cost of certain fixed or movable assets used in businesses in West-Berlin, accelerated depreciation of up to 75% in the first year or over any of the five years, and low interest rate loans from Marshall Plan (ERP) funds and other sources, as well as government guarantees.
Valuable incentives during the operation phase are reductions of value added taxes for West-Berlin businesses, amounting to between 4.5% and 10% for companies operating in West-Berlin, and an amount equal to 4.2% for West German firms purchasing goods and services from West-Berlin.
As already mentioned, corporation taxes in West-Berlin are cut by 22.5%, and the tax rates on personal income earned in West-Berlin by 30%.

G. Social Security Premiums

Social insurance in Germany entitles employees to old age pension, the sickness benefits, accident insurance (industrial injury compensation), unemployment insurance and furthermore provides for special benefits for example in the event of maternity.
Whereas, employer and employee each contribute 50% of the premiums for pension, sickness and unemployment insurance, premiums for industrial injury compensation insurance are payable by the employer alone.
The full premiums amount to the following percentage of the income:

– old age pension		18%[3]
– sickness	average	12 – 13%[4]
– unemployment	max.	2%[5]
– workmen's compensation (accident)	average	1.5%[6]

The income limits to which contributions must be paid vary; in 1982 this limit is DM 4,700 per month, for sickness insurance 75% thereof, i.e. DM 3,525. Persons earning more than DM 3,525 per month are therefore exempted from compulsory sickness insurance.

H. Other

1. TRADE TAX

This tax levied by the municipalities (*Gewerbesteuer*) is composed of two parts. In addition to corporation tax, undertakings in Germany pay trade tax on profits (*Gewerbeertragsteuer*) at a rate of about 13%. This tax is computed on the basis of the actual profit plus interest paid on long term loans or credits and various other costs. However, for the purposes of the *Gewerbesteuer*, certain items including the tax itself, which are not allowable deductions for the purposes of corporation tax, may be deducted. Thus the assessable basis differs from the basis of corporation tax. An annual tax of 0,5% is also levied on the operating capital plųs longterm loans and credits (*Gewerbekapitalsteuer*).

2. NET WORTH TAX

In Germany all enterprises of any type must pay an annual tax of 1% on their net assets as determined according to a special law (*Vermögensteuer*). This net worth tax, which in other states is often unknown, has been levied in Germany for many years. For the evaluation of the assets a financial statement as at January 1 must be drawn up in accordance with the Valuation Act (*Bewertungs-*

3. In the mining branch 23.5%, 8.5% to be borne by the employee.
4. Fixed by the insurer.
5. Fixed by the Federal government.
6. Fixed by the insurer, average 1.5%, mining branch 7.6%.

gesetz) which, inter alia, provides that real property is assessed at a special value determined for tax purposes (*Einheitswert*). Foreigners operating directly, e.g. through branches, in Germany are subject to this tax on certain of their German assets only, as set out in the Valuation Act; among these are:

- real estate property,
- business assets,
- patent rights registered in Germany,
- assets leased or licensed to a German undertaking.

3. OTHER TAXES

Among several other taxes which are of minor importance, the following may be mentioned:

Stock exchange turnover tax (*Börsenumsatzsteuer*), levied on contracts for the acquisition of shares or other securities for a consideration; the tax rate varies between 0.1% and 0.25% of the consideration paid; but these rates are reduced by onehalf if one party to the agreement is a foreigner and the agreement is concluded abroad.

Real estate acquisition tax (*Grunderwerbsteuer*) applies to all transfers of real estate and also in the event of acquisition by one person of all the shares in a company owning real estate. The tax rate generally amounts to 7% of the consideration given for the transfer or, in the case of share acquisition, 7% of the taxable value of the real estate. Vendor and purchaser are jointly and severally liable for tax.

4. GERMAN TAX EVASION ACT

Within the broader framework of the International Transactions Tax Reform Act (*Außensteuerreformgesetz*) of September 8, 1972, a tax evasion law was passed called *Außensteuergesetz*. It provides, inter alia, that the income of foreign tax-haven companies not transacting active business operations will be attributed to their German shareholders.

On the other hand, it also introduces, as a unilateral tax relief, the concept of the 'indirect tax credit' for foreign income tax paid by controlled foreign subsidiaries, and under certain conditions, sub-subsidiaries on their distributions of profits.

Of particular interest in the context of this chapter is the power now given to the tax authorities to adjust income and deductions if the income of a German taxpayer, in particular a German company, was reduced because of non-adherence to the arm's-length principle in dealing with a related foreign party.

5. TAX REORGANIZATION ACT

Finally, it should be mentioned that under the provisions of the Tax Reorganization Act (*Umwandlungsteuergesetz*) certain tax disadvantages which would otherwise bar or at least burden mergers, transformations of corporate forms or other types of reorganization of companies, have been removed.

I. Double Taxation Treaties

The Federal German Government has concluded many treaties for the avoidance of double taxation, notably with all of the EEC countries. The treaties, though differing in detail, contain the following basic principles regarding the right to tax income earned in more than one state:

1. TAXATIONS OF BRANCHES

Profits of branches which are regarded as 'permanent establishments' of the foreign company are taxed in the country where the branch is situated at the rate normally applicable in that country. This system solves all problems as regards this income, provided a tax credit (or tax relief) system applies in the country of registration of the parent company, in which case the gross income, which has already been taxed in the state of residence of the branch, is again liable for tax; but the tax paid abroad is an allowable deduction for purposes of taxation, and a tax credit is granted.
Sometimes, however, income earned abroad, although not taxable in the home country, must be taken into account when computing the income tax liability.

2. TAXATION OF SUBSIDIARIES

The profits of a German subsidiary of a foreign parent company are subject to taxation in the same way as the profits of any other German company; thus, the problem of double taxation mainly arises with regard to dividends. Subsidiaries must withhold at source 25% (some treaties provide for a reduction) of all profits distributed to its shareholders, including amounts not paid in the form of dividends; this is paid to the German tax authorities to the account of the shareholders. As a rule, the recipient pays tax on the gross dividend in his own country while the 25% (or the reduced rate) withheld at the source constitute a tax credit against his liability. This does not apply, however, if the dividend income is derived through a permanent establishment in Germany, in which case it becomes taxable at the full rate. Such an arrangement should therefore be avoided.
In accordance with the directives of the OECD, the more recent treaties regard participations in public and private limited companies as assets. For taxation purposes, the criterion of the country of residence applies to income from these assets, while the source country has the right of withholding at source.
A short list will now be given of the existing double taxation treaties. Under J. a schedule of withholding taxes follows, showing the effect of the double taxa-

tion treaties on the most important types of income derived by foreign companies from German sources, namely dividends, interest and royalties. The schedules include, in addition to the EEC countries and Switzerland, USA, Canada and Japan.
For cross references see the European chapter.

List of Double Taxation Treaties (all ratified)

Country	*Signing Date*	*Revisions under negotiation etc.*
1. Belgium	11.04.67	
2. Denmark	30.01.62	
3. France	31.07.59/9.6.69	Revision-Treaty under negotiation
4. Greece	18.04.66	
5. Ireland	17.10.62	
6. Italy	31.10.25	Revision-Treaty under negotiation
7. Luxemburg	23.08.58/15.6.73	
8. Netherlands	16.06.59	Revision-Treaty initialled on 04.04, 1979
9. United Kingdom	26.11.64/23.3.70	Revision-Protocol initialled on 31.01, 1975
10. Switzerland	11.08.71	Revision-Protocol signed 30.11.1978, ratified by German Parliament 13.6.1980
11. United States of America	22.07.54/17.9.65	Revision-Treaty under negotiation
(new version)	17.08.66	
12. Canada	04.06.56	Revision-Treaty under negotiation
13. Japan	22.04.66/17.04.79	

J. Schedule of Withholding Taxes

German withholding taxes on *paid to non-resident recipient company in*	*Dividends*[7, 8] *paid to a company which owns at least 25% of the German company*	*in other cases*	*Interest*[8, 9]	*Royalties*[10]
	All figures mean tax rates, taking into consideration double taxation treaties			
1. Belgium	25	15	0	0(13)
2. Denmark	25	15	0	0(13)
3. France	25	15	0	0(13)
4. Greece	25	25	10	0(13)

7. Capital yields tax (*Kapitalertragsteuer*).
8. Original deduction irrespective of possible refunds upon application.
9. Interest from other sources than: a). convertible and profit sharing bonds; b). other bonds; c). loans secured by immovables situated in Germany, which are normally subject to withholding tax of 25% (a), (b) or corporation tax (c), but often fully or partially refunded upon application.
10. In brackets: Value added Tax (*Mehrwertsteuer*) paid by the German company.

German withholding taxes on paid to non-resident recipient company in	Dividends[7,8] paid to a company which owns at least 25% of the German company	in other cases	Interest[8,9]	Royalties[10]
	All figures mean tax rates, taking into consideration double taxation treaties			
5. Ireland	20	15	0	0(13)
6. Italy	25	25	0	0(13)
7. Luxemburg[11]	10	15	0	5(13)
8. Netherlands	25	15	0	0(13)
9. United Kingdom	20	15	0	0(13)
10. Switzerland	15	15	0	0(13)
11. United States of America	25[12]	15	0	0(13)
12. Canada	15	25[13]	15	0(13)
13. Japan	25	15	10	10(13)

K. Special Types of Companies

The mixed enterprise type of company mentioned above on page 223, namely the GmbH & Co. KG, is often preferred also because of certain tax advantages (in particular in so-called depreciation companies (*Abschreibungsgesellschaften*).
This is only mentioned here without further details in order to complete the survey in this area since these tax advantages are not available to foreign investors.

IV. LABOUR ASPECTS

A. Principles of Law on Employment

1. EMPLOYMENT

Employment contracts are in principle based on the law of service contracts and the general rules for contracts as contained in the Civil Code. In addition, there are protective laws concerning maximum working hours, certain work-

11. Indicated rates for non-holding companies.
12. In cases where a U.S. company owns at least 10% of the German company and the dividend is re-invested in the German company.
13. Basic German withholding tax; no provision in the treaty. The draft of the new treaty limits the tax to 15%.

ing conditions, legal holidays, unjustified dismissal, status of apprentices, special protection for pregnant women and disabled persons. As yet, there are no legal provisions concerning minimum salaries or wages.
Wages and other working conditions are as a rule more commonly fixed by collective bargaining agreements (*Tarifverträge*), resulting from collective bargaining (see below under B., page 249).
The government can declare collective labour agreements generally binding, which has the effect of introducing compulsory minimum wages. This is only common in the case of employees in the construction industry and the restaurant business. The German constitution guarantees occupational liberty and forbids closed or union shops.

2. TERMINATION OF EMPLOYMENT

Termination of employment is subject to several protective laws, which as a rule contain mandatory provisions. They do not apply to company executives (GmbH: *Geschäftsführer*; AG: *Vorstand*) and only partly to so-called executive employees (*leitende Angestellte*). In all other cases, a distinction must be made between wage earners and salaried employees, for whom different basic periods of notice are fixed. Further protection is granted according to age and seniority, in the event of pregnancy or incapacity, to members of the works council and supervisory board, etc.
Wage earners must normally receive two weeks' notice. This is extended to
  one month after five years of service;
  two months after ten years of service; and
  three months after twenty years of service.
In the first two cases notice must expire at the end of a month and, in the third case, at the end of a calendar quarter.
The notice for salaried employees must be given six weeks before the end of a calendar quarter. It may be shortened by agreement of the parties, however, to one month and notice is to be given one month before the end of a calendar month.
The period of notice is extended to
- three months after five years of employment;
- four months after eight years of employment;
- five months after ten years of employment; and
- six months after twelve years of employment,

before expiring at the end of a calendar quarter. Time spent working before reaching the age of twentysix is not counted. The said periods may not be reduced in advance.
Termination without notice period is admitted only in the event of what is called 'serious cause'.
The works council must always be heard beforehand, otherwise the dismissal is void except for dismissal of company executives and executive employees.
In addition, generally the provisions of the Dismissal Protection Act (*Kündigungsschutzgesetz*) apply. According to this Act any salaried employee or wage owner over age 18 and having been employed by the undertaking for more than six months cannot be dismissed, if this would be 'socially unjusti-

fied', provided the undertaking regularly employs more than five persons. A social justification exists in the event that the dismissal is caused by reasons related to the person or the conduct of the employee or if urgent business requirements prevent the further employment of the person concerned. In the latter event, however, the dismissal would be socially unjustified if the employer had disregarded the opportunity to employ the person at a suitable place elsewhere in the undertaking or has not sufficiently considered social aspects when choosing the person to be dismissed.

If the employee is of the opinion that the dismissal is socially unjustified, he must bring the matter before the Labour Court within three weeks after receipt of the notice of dismissal. The Court may either uphold the dismissal or rule that the employment contract is not terminated and either order the employment to be continued or award damages to the employee of up to eighteen months' salary. Employment for a trial period or for a predetermined period of time is, however, admitted within certain limits, in which event the Dismissal Protection Act does not apply.

Special provisions apply to collective dismissals. In the case of undertakings employing more than 20 persons a prior written notice to the competent state labour office is a precondition of such dismissals becoming effective. Such notification must be accompanied by an opinion of the works council. Statutory periods apply for this notification, differing according to the number of dismissals in relation to the size of the undertaking. For one month following the notification, dismissal cannot take effect without specific approval from the labour office.

If collective dismissal is the result of total or partial closure of the undertaking, a so-called social plan must be negotiated with the works council, providing redundancy payments for the dismissed employees.

B. Labour Procedures

The collective bargaining system in Germany is well developed and of great practical importance. The employers' association concerned on one side and the corresponding trade union on the other side regularly negotiate and conclude collective bargaining contracts (*Tarifverträge*) in accordance with the provisions of the Collective Bargaining Contracts Act (*Tarifvertragsgesetz*). For each undertaking only one employers' association and one union are involved. The contracts, normally on a regional basis, usually govern wage and salary rates, working hours, length of vacation, etc., for the particular industrial branch, thus supplementing the provisions of the labour law.

Strikes and lock-outs as the ultimate applicable sanction are legal if certain rules are complied with. The unions have recently mounted political campaign against the admissibility of lock-outs, but the Federal Labour Court has ruled that, in principle, lock-outs complying with the rules of the Act are constitutional.

Upon application the competent state authority may make a declaration of universal validity for a specific collective bargaining contract. However, even without this declaration the conditions agreed to are normally granted to all employees of an undertaking which is party to this contract, irrespective of whether or not they are union members. As mentioned, there are no closed or union shops in Germany.

In practice, the agreed rates are minimum rates; often higher wages are paid. In addition to the law and collective bargaining contracts, so-called 'shop agreements' may be concluded and these three sets of rules supplement individual employment contracts. Such agreements are negotiated between the individual employer and the works council as representative of the employees of the undertaking in question. The shop agreement, which must be in writing, may only provide for matters which are not covered by the applicable collective bargaining contract.

C. *Works Council*

1. ORGANISATION

The Labour Management Relations Act 1952 (*Betriebsverfassungsgesetz*), which was completely revised in 1972, requires each undertaking or plant with five or more employees to have a works council. The management, however, is not obliged to initiate the formation of a works council. It has to consist of between 1 and 31 members depending on the number of the employees. In undertakings with more than 9,000 employees the works council is further increased by two members for each additional 3,000 employees.

The members of the works council are elected every three years between March 1, and May 31. Wage-earning and salaried employees shall be represented in proportion to their respective numbers. The works council elects a chairman and a deputy chairman. In the event that the works council has nine or more members a committee must be formed consisting of the chairman, the deputy, and between three and nine additional members depending on the total number of members of the works council. Furthermore, a special economic comittee must be established in all undertakings with more than 100 employees.

The members of the works council do not receive any remuneration for their activities, but they are released from their work without a reduction of their wages or salaries to the extent necessary to fulfill their duties. Undertakings with more than 300 employees must release certain numbers of employees completely from their ordinary work.

In undertakings with several works councils for different plants, a general works council must be established consisting of one or two members of each works council.

Within a group of companies (*Konzern*) the general works council may resolve to establish a group works council.

2. COMPETENCE

As far as management decisions are concerned the works council participates in social matters, general and individual personnel decisions and in economic matters on the basis of the following rights:

Right of information regarding the
  contemplated employment or changes therein as far as employees are concerned.

Right of information and consultation concerning
  the economic and financial situation, production and sales, investment planning, working methods or procedures, personnel planning, training of personnel, vacation regulations.

Right of consultation with the possibility of making objections regarding
  dismissals, which are invalid without consultation of the works council.

Right to claim for
  suitable measures to prevent, mitigate or compensate particular burdens placed upon employees by changes or working procedures or working places etc.

Right of veto in matters defined by the law regarding
  individual personnel matters (for example employment, classification, transfer).

Right of veto in general matters regarding
  personnel questionnaires, selection guidelines.

Right to negotiate
  a compromise and a social plan in order to neutralise or mitigate disadvantages to employees resulting from operational changes (restriction, closing or relocation of works or parts thereof, merger with other undertakings etc.).

In order to cooperate in social, personnel and economic matters, the employer and the works council must meet at least once a month for consultation. They then discuss disputed matters with sincere intentions of reaching an agreement. If necessary, differences are settled by a board of conciliation consisting of an equal number of members appointed by the employer and by the works council, and an independent chairman agreed upon by both parties or (if no agreement can be reached) appointed by the Labour Court.

D. Co-determination

There are three types of co-determination structures under different legal provisions:

1. COAL AND STEEL CO-DETERMINATION ACT 1951 AND SUPPLEMENTARY ACT 1956

These acts (*Montan-Mitbestimmungsgesetz*), supplemented in 1956 by the Supplementary Act to the Coal and Steel Co-Determination Act (*Mitbestimmungsergänzungsgesetz*) apply to corporate bodies active in the fields of coal, steel and mining corporations with more than 1,000 employees.

The supervisory board (*Aufsichtsrat*) of such companies must consist of an equal number of shareholder and labour representatives. The supervisory

board must elect a further 'neutral member', the so-called 'labour relations director' (*Arbeitsdirektor*).
Labour unions are in a position here to control the appointment of the labour representatives of the supervisory board. They have not only the right to nominate a part of the members of the labour section, but also the right to object to nominations made by the works council concerning the other part of the members of the labour section.

2. LABOUR MANAGEMENT RELATIONS ACT

This act (*Betriebsverfassungsgesetz*) applies to stock corporations (AGs) and to partnerships limited by shares (except family controlled enterprises with less than 500 employees), which have not more than 2,000 employees, as well as limited liability companies with between 500 and 2,000 employees.
These companies must have a supervisory board, the size of which may be determined by their statute, but must be a number divisible by three. One third of the members of the supervisory board must be labour representatives elected by the employees. If the supervisory board consists of at least six members, one of the labour representatives must be a wage-earner and one a salaried employee.
If the supervisory board consists of nine or more members, two of the labour representatives must be employees of the company, while the other labour representatives must be outsiders (for example trade union officials).

3. CO-DETERMINATION ACT 1976

a. This act (*Mitbestimmungsgesetz*) is the result of a long lasting political struggle and has had a major impact on the large industries in Germany. As opposed to the Coal and Mining Co-Determination Act, it does not only cover a specific industrial branch, and when it is applied, it supersedes co-determination under the Labour Management Relations Act.
The act is applicable to companies, which
- are stock corporations, partnerships limited by shares, companies with limited liability, mining corporations, business or trade cooperatives, and
- employ as a rule more than 2,000 employees.

Thus co-determination under the Act is practised in about 650 companies. It must be mentioned that the Act does not apply to branches of foreign companies.

b. All companies concerned must have a supervisory board with an equal number of members representing the shareholders and the employees. The number of the board members depends on the number of employees:

	Number of Employees		
	2,001 to 10,000	10,001 to 20,000	more than 20,001
Board members elected by			
– Shareholders	6	8	10
– Employees (or their delegates) from candidates proposed by			
– employees themselves	4	6	7
– trade unions	2	2	3
	12	16	20

There are three groups of employees to which the principle of proportionate representation within the number of board members appointed by the employees applies: wage earners, salaried employees and executive employees; provided always that each group has at least one representative among the board members.
While the shareholders' representatives have to be appointed according to the relevant company law (e.g. by the shareholders' meeting) the labour representatives will be elected either directly by the groups of employees (in companies with less than 8,000 employees) or indirectly by delegates elected by the employees (in companies with more than 8,000 employees).
In the latter case the wage earners and the salaried employees in separate ballots elect the delegates of their groups, which must be represented among the delegates in proportion to their respective numbers. The delegates of these groups elect the board members representing the wage earners and the salaried employees respectively, but all delegates jointly elect the representatives of the labour unions, who may but need not be employees of the company.
The members of the supervisory board elect the chairman and the deputy chairman with a two-thirds majority. If such a majority cannot be obtained the chairman will be elected by the shareholders section and the deputy chairman by the labour section. This procedure is of special importance, insofar as only the chairman and not the deputy chairman is allowed to cast the tie-breaking vote in case of deadlock.

c. The supervisory board does not exercise management functions but appoints and controls the management.

aa. According to ordinary company law the supervisory board appoints the board of management (AG: *Vorstand*; GmbH: *Geschäftsführung*) by simple majority. This procedure is substantially modified for the co-determined companies. In principle the appointment of the board of management now requires two thirds of the votes. If this majority is not reached at the first voting, a mediation committee is created which consists of the chairman, the vice-chairman, and one representative each for the shareholders and the employees.

This committee must then propose a list of candidates for the managing board one month after the first unsuccessful voting. The supervisory board then appoints the managing board by simple majority. If this majority is also not obtained, there must immediately be a second ballot in which the chairman has an additional, casting vote. This vote is not available for exercise by the vice-chairman, who is an employees representative. It is thus ensured that in the event of a controversial election, a managing board will be appointed only after approval by the shareholders' representatives or the supervisory board.

bb). Although the managing board is responsible for all business activities, its permanent control enables the supervisory board to affect business policy, too. Management is more or less not in a position to realize an important economic or financial plan which is not in accordance with policies set forth by the supervisory board. For this reason the trade unions have through co-determination attained a position of considerable influence in the business policy of large undertakings. It must be stated in this connection that this influence sometimes creates conflicts of interest. Since the deadline for introducing this system of the Co-Determination Act 1976 was as recently as July 1, 1978, experience during time must still be gathered to evaluate this new system.

E. Compulsory Profit Sharing and Pension Schemes

Under German Law there exists no compulsory profit sharing system, and as far as pension schemes are concerned only the respective contributions to social insurance as stated under III. G., page 243, above are mandatory.
However, several undertakings have introduced, on a voluntary basis, profit-based additional payment to employees; and voluntary pension schemes which supplement the social insurance are often found. Therefore, a short survey on this subject seems appropriate.

1. PROFIT SHARING

a. Management's share of profit

Employment contracts with company executives and executive employees often provide for some profit sharing as an incentive. The contract in such event provides for a profit- or dividend-linked bonus which sometimes increases in proportion to the duration of the employment. Such payment is called a *Tantieme*. For stock corporations, the act contains a model provision to this effect for the managing board and the supervisory board; this regulation, however, is not mandatory.

b. Bonus

For all other employees a voluntary extra payment called a *Gratifikation* is often provided, though not, or at least not directly linked to the annual profit or dividend. Usually it is paid as a so-called thirteenth monthly salary partly before the holiday period and partly before Christmas. If not provided expressly in the employment contract, a claim to such payment may nevertheless arise if the payment has become customary, i.e. has been effected for years without any express reservation concerning its voluntary character and its revocability.

c. Voluntary profit sharing systems

There are, furthermore, certain systems, some still in the experimental stage which border on the line between profit-sharing and employee participation in the enterprise.
Some undertakings distribute profit-based additional payments and at the same time offer to their employees shares in the company or obligations at advantageous conditions. If the business is a partnership, such participation, however, is effected in the form of silent partnerships or loans, purely to prevent the employees being deemed to be partners for tax purposes with their income subject to trade tax as a consequence.
The legislature had in the early seventies intended to introduce a mandatory participation system aiming at what was called employees' creation of wealth (*Vermögensbildung*), but owing to the intensified and finally successful endeavours for introducing co-determination, these plans were shelved.

2. PENSION SCHEMES

In small businesses, pensions, if provided for at all, are usually available only to executive personnel, whereas, larger companies very often offer pension schemes to all employees which supplement social insurance.

a. Systems

Various systems are applied. Often staff pension funds (*Pensionskassen*) or relief funds (*Unterstützungskassen*) are created, either within the company or as separate legal entities such as a GmbH. The allocation of funds to such a GmbH are deductible expenses; if no separate entity has been created, reserves for future pensions may be set aside reducing the taxable income, insofar as firm obligations to pay the respective pensions have been entered into by the company.
Alternatively, the employer may conclude insurance contracts in favour of employees with insurance companies; both single and group contracts occur. The employer may also choose to pay additional premiums to the social insurance in order to create an increased social pension entitlement for the employee.
It is advisable to take the advice from an expert before deciding which of the above or other existing systems should be adopted.

b. Retirement Pension Security Act

The benefits paid under such voluntary pension schemes are often not very high since such benefits are purely supplementary to the social insurance.

However, they are secured in several ways. According to the Retirement Pension Security Act (*Betriebsrentengesetz*. BetrAVG) each employee after ten years of employment with the enterprise and on reaching the age of thirty six acquires an expectancy (which does not lapse) to receive the benefits available under the pension scheme upon retirement.

This means that payment is effected by the undertaking upon the retirement of the employee even if he leaves the enterprise (after fulfilling the aforesaid conditions) but before reaching his retirement age. Naturally, in such an event only a pro-rata amount becomes due according to the duration of his employment.

Furthermore, the payment is also guaranteed in the event of bankruptcy of the employer. A mutual pension insurance association has been established into which all employers with voluntary pension schemes must pay the premiums; this association assumes the obligation to pay the pension in the event of bankruptcy.

Finally, in principle, the amount of the benefits must be adapted to the cost of living; under the provisions of the Retirement Pension Security Act a review by the employer takes place every three years.

F. Residence and Work Permits for Aliens

In principle, German labour law applies also to foreign nationals employed in Germany. Its application may be excluded, however, if the employer is also a foreigner and the relations between both parties are as a whole is materially subject to foreign law.

Foreigners intending to stay longer than 3 months in the Federal Republic of Germany must obtain a residence permit (*Aufenthaltserlaubnis*), generally before they leave for Germany. The application should be made to the German Embassy or Consulate competent for the domicile of the applicant. Initially the permit will be granted for a period of up to 12 months. Applications to extend the period of residence should be made to the aliens department of the local police authority. While this still applies to subjects of the EC member countries as well as to others, EC subjects are no longer required to obtain a work permit (*Arbeitsgenehmigung*), which is otherwise necessary if a foreigner intends to take up employment in Germany. In the latter event, it must be applied for jointly by the employer and the employee, usually at the local labour office through the local police authority. Work permits, however, are not required for executive personnel.

V. REFERENCE MATERIAL

1. Names, Abbreviations and Translations of the Most Important Acts Mentioned

COMMERCIAL LAW

Aktiengesetz	AktG	Stock Corporation Act (Public Company Act)
GmbH-Gesetz	GmbHG	Law concerning companies with limited liability (Private Company Act)
Gewerbeordnung	GewO	Trade Regulations
Handelsgesetzbuch	HGB	Commercial Code
Kreditwesengesetz	KWG	Banking Act
Publizitätsgesetz	PublG	Disclosure Act
Versicherungsaufsichtsgesetz	VAG	Insurance Companies' Supervision Act

TAX LAW

Aussensteuergesetz	AStG	Tax Evasion Act
Bewertungsgesetz	BewG	Valuation Act
Einkommensteuergesetz	EStG	Income Tax Act
Erbschaftsteuergesetz	ErbStG	Inheritance Tax Act
Kapitalverkehrsteuergesetz	KVStG	Capital Investment Tax Act
Körperschaftsteuergesetz	KStG	Corporation Tax Act
Umsatzsteuergesetz (*Mehrwertsteuergesetz*)	UStG	Turnover Tax Act (Value Added Tax Act)
Vermögensteuergesetz	VStG	Net Worth Tax Act

LABOUR LAW

Betriebsrentengesetz	BetrAVG	Retirement Pension Security Act
Betriebsverfassungsgesetz	BetrVerfG	Labour Management Relations Act
Kündigungsschutzgesetz	KSchG	Dismissal Protection Act
Mitbestimmungsgesetz	MitbestG	Co-Determination Act
Tarifvertragsgesetz	TVG	Collective Bargaining Contracts Act

VARIOUS LAWS

Aussenwirtschaftsgesetz	AWG	Foreign Trade Act
Bundesimmissionsschutzgesetz	BImSchG	Federal Immission Protection Act
Gesetz gegen Wettbewerbsbeschränkungen	GWB	Cartel Act or Act against Restraints of Competition

2. *Bibliography*

a. TRANSLATIONS INTO ENGLISH AND BILINGUAL TEXT EDITIONS GERMAN-ENGLISH

1. Goren and Forrester, *The German Commercial Code* (translation and introduction), (Deventer, London, Boston and Frankfurt, 1979), 250 pages.
2. Peltzer, Jung, Allen, German Commercial Code, Synoptical Translation with introduction (Köln, 1980), 260 pages.
3. Mueller and Galbraith, *The German Stock Corporation Law*, bilingual edition with introduction (Frankfurt am Main, 1976), 550 pages.
4. Juenger and Schmidt, *German Stock Corporation Act*, translation (with introduction and German text) (New York, 1967), 299 pages.
5. Peltzer, *GmbH – German Law Concerning the Companies with Limited Liability*, translation (with German text) and introduction (Köln, 1981), 60 pages.
6. Mueller and Schneider, *The German Law on Restraints of Competition* (Gesetz gegen Wettbewerbsbeschränkungen), bilingual edition with introduction (Frankfurt am Main, 1973), 207 pages.
7. Peltzer, *Labour Management Relations Act* (Betriebsverfassungsgesetz), bilingual edition (with commentary) (Frankfurt am Main, 1977), 370 pages.
8. Peltzer, Codetermination Act 1976, German-English Text with Introduction (Köln, 1976).
9. Hoffman, *The German Co-Determination Act 1976* translation with introduction (Deventer, London, Boston and Frankfurt am Main, 1976), 96 pages.
10. Peltzer, *German Insolvency Laws* (Konkurs- und Vergleichsrecht), bilingual edition with introduction (Köln, 1975), 218 pages.
11. Siebel, *German Restrictions on Capital Transactions with Foreigners* (Geld-Kapitalverkehr im deutschen Aussenwirtschaftsrecht), bilingual edition (Frankurt am Main, 1973), 175 pages.
12. Schmidt, Döser, Bellstedt, *Das Mehrwertsteuergesetz* (Value Added Tax Law), English-German text with short introduction (Köln, 1968), 363 pages.
13. Ault and Rädler, *The German Corporation Tax Reform Law 1977* (translation and commentary), (Deventer, London, Boston and Frankfurt am Main 2nd. ed. 1980), 118 pages.

14. Bellstedt, *Aussensteuerreformgesetz* (International Transactions Tax Reform Act), English-German text with introduction (Köln, 1972), 88 pages.
15. Broenner, *Berlin Promotion Law* (Berlin-Förderungsgesetz), English translation (without German text), including a brief commentary (Freiburg, 1972), 128 pages.

b. GERMAN TEXTS AND COMMENTARIES (SELECTION)

1. Schönfelder, *Deutsche Gesetze*, an unofficial loose-leaf collection of Federal Law, with references and an index, regularly up-dated by supplements (München and Berlin).
2. *Steuergesetze*, an unofficial loose-leaf collection of all Federal Tax Laws and regulatory ordinances, with references and an index, regularly updated by supplements (München and Berlin).
3. Korn and Dietz, *Doppelbesteuerung* (Double Taxation), looseleaf commentary, (München and Berlin), 3 volumes.
4. Baumbach and Hueck, *Aktiengesetz*, Commentary on the Stock Corporation Law (München and Berlin), 14th edition under preparation.
5. Baumbach and Hueck, *GmbH-Gesetz*, Commentary on the Law concerning Limited Liability Companies, 13th edition (München and Berlin, 1970), 555 pages.
6. Baumbach and Duden, *Handelsgesetzbuch*, Commentary on the Commercial Code (including the law of branches, general, limited and silent partnerships), 24th edition (München and Berlin, 1980), 1312 pages.
7. Mueller, Henneberg, Schwartz, *Gesetz gegen Wettbewerbsbeschränkungen und Europäisches Kartellrecht*, Commentary on the German Law on Restraints of Competition and the European Cartel Law, 3rd edition (Köln, 1972-79).
8. Bühler and Paulick, *Einkommensteuer-Körperschaftsteuer*, Commentary on the Income Tax Law and the Corporation Income Law, loose-leaf, updated by supplements (München and Berlin, 3rd edition 1979.

c. LEGAL DICTIONARIES

1. Romain, *Wörterbuch der Rechts- und Wirtschaftssprache*, Part I: English-German, 2nd edition 1979, 760 pages, Part II: German-English, 1980, 848 pages (Berlin and München).
2. Doucet and Fleck, *Wörterbuch der Rechts- und Wirtschaftssprache*, 3rd edition, Part I: French-German, 1979, 432 pages, Part II: German-French, 1979, 509 pages (Berlin and München).
3. Conte, *Wörterbuch der Rechts- und Wirtschaftssprache*, 3rd edition, Part I: Italian-German, 1980, 355 pages, Part II: German-Italian, 1980, 458 pages (Berlin and München).
4. Herbst, *Dictionary of Commercial, Financial and Legal Terms*, 3 volumes:
   I: English-German-French, 1979, 1138 pages
   II: Deutsch-English-Französisch, 1979, 1100 pages.
   III: Français-Anglais-Allemand, 1980, 979 pages (Zug, Switzerland).

5. Dietl, Moss and Lorenz, *Wörterbuch für Recht, Wirtschaft und Politik*, 2 volumes:
I: English-German (München and Berlin, 1979).
II: Deutsch-English under preparation.

Greece

Dimitri C. Lambadarios
George N. Stathopoulos
Criton Anastassopoulos

I. INTRODUCTION

The Greek Chapter follows closely the general outline as set down by the Working Group.

In the case of Section II, 'The legal framework', however, due to the nature of the Greek Company Law, a certain deviation from the outline was necessary particularly with the subheadings. In addition, a more detailed analysis was given to Section III F, referred to as 'Incentives' as this is significant information for foreign investors, particularly so with the new incentives law nr. 1116/1981 (January 14, 1981) entitled 'Providing Incentives for Regional and Economic Development' which is bringing the Greek tax, credit and other incentives in line with EEC principles.

It should be pointed out that due to Greece's entry on 1st January, 1981 in the EEC there will be substantial harmonizational and structural changes taking place in terms of company Law, exchange-controls, labour legislation, taxation etc.

These changes will be reflected in future updatings and alterations of the book as they evolve.

In fact harmonizational changes have already started with the new Incentives Law 1116/1981 encompassing cash grants and other incentives dealt with further on in the Incentives Section and which are in line with EEC policies. In indirect taxes, Greece has already agreed to adopt the EEC VAT system at the latest by January 1st, 1984.

Exchange controls have also already started easing up, and, through a gradual process, by the end of 1985 they will be in line with the EEC rules.

In the Labour Law area, it should be pointed out that the concepts of Works Council, Co-determination and Compulsory profit sharing and pension schemes are not dealt with extensively in the Greek Chapter, inasmuch as no Legislative measures exist at present. However, changes in the EEC direction are expected in this area in the next five years.

Finally, a word is said about the special purpose companies. The first, refers to the Law 89/67 Offshore branches established in Greece. These offshore branches have been very successful in Greece using Athens and Piraeus as their headquarters primarily for Middle East activities. The 'holding' type legislation has not had much success in Greece as this vehicle, due to strict conditions imposed, has not met with anticipated popularity.

II. THE LEGAL FRAMEWORK

A. *The Vehicle*

1. THE WHOLLY–OWNED ENTERPRISE

1.a. THE BRANCH

Foreign partnerships or limited partnerships as well as foreign companies may operate in Greece without forming a new Greek partnership or company, the basic rule being that an undertaking having no matter what form of business organization which is lawfully established and operating in the home country, can exercise all its rights in Greece and have access to the Courts both as plaintiff and defendant in the same manner as a similar Greek entity, under the condition of reciprocity. The same principle has been included also in many Conventions and Treaties to which Greece is a party.

In the case, however, of companies taking the form of a société anonyme or a limited liability company some simple formalities of administrative nature have been established by specific laws and these are necessary for such legal entities so that they may fully carry out their activities in Greece with all the attached benefits.

In the case, however, of a somewhat permanent establishment taking the form of a branch or agency, the law 2190 on companies (S.A.) (art. 50) has made mandatory that before its establishment the foreign company must submit the following to the Ministry of Commerce:

a. a copy of their representative's or agent's power of attorney, duly certified by the appropriate Greek Consular authority including the essential appointment of a special attorney for the acceptance of a service of documents;

b. a declaration of the year of their establishment and the name of the persons representing them at their registered office. Any alteration of the above mentioned items subsequent to the above notification must be immediately reported to the Ministry of Commerce.

In practice the Ministry of Commerce usually requests an up-to-date copy of the Statutes.

The law further requests that the balance-sheets be submitted anually together with a report on the company's operations.

The above prerequisites are necessary to inform the public and eventually check the legality of the operation of the company and should not be construed as 'an operating license'. However, the Ministry of Commerce does check carefully the importance and the objects of the company that intends to establish the 'branch' or the 'agency' and in some cases has refused such an establishment either because of too little capital or the objectives pursued e.g. dealings in foreign securities.

Although the law does not state so the Greek authorities require that a foreign parent company (S.A.) establishing a branch in Greece must have at least the

minimum share capital required by law for Greek S.A. companies, i.e. the equivalent of Drs. 5.000.000 wholly paid-up.
Where no permanent establishment is sought (e.g. in the case of contractors performing a certain task for a relatively short time) it is then not necessary for the foreign enterprise to be established under art. 50 above.
Similar provisions are applicable for the establishment of branch offices of foreign limited liability companies.
Here also the foreign limited liability company wishing to register a branch in Greece must have a capital of at least the equivalent of 200.000 drachmae which is the minimum capital requirement for a Greek limited liability company.
The approval to establish a branch office or agency is published in the Official Gazette and all foreign corporations and limited liability companies must register with the Chamber of Commerce and Industry, including in their records the relevant copy of the Official Gazette in which the appointment of the manager of the branch or the agent is published and copy of the relevant power of attorney. If the representative is a foreigner then his residence and work permit must also be enclosed.

Parents Liability
Since the branch is not a separate legal entity the foreign company remains liable for all the activities of the branch.

Special Branch of Law 89/1967
Law 89/1967 has created the possibility for foreign enterprises to establish offices in Greece enjoying special privilege provided such offices are dealing exclusively in commercial transactions whose objects lie outside Greece.
This law has been extensively used in the past and particularly in relation to the Lebanon crisis which has necessitated the removal of the regional offices of many enterprises from Beirut. For the registration under this law, the following documents are necessary:

a. A certified true copy of the Company's Statutes.
b. A certificate from the appropriate authority in the home country stating that the applicant is a company legally operating in that country.
c. Balance sheets of the two last accounting periods of the company.
d. Resolution of the Board of directors of the company for the establishment of the office in Greece.
e. A declaration from the applicant company to the effect that they are prepared to deposit a Bank letter of guarantee issued by a recognized local or foreign Bank, which shall be forfeited in favour of the State in case of breach on the part of the company's personnel, of the provisions under E.L. 89/67.
f. A signed Declaration that the applicant foreign company will deal exclusively with commercial activities having their objects outside of Greece and that the office to be established in Greece, will perform no commercial activities whatsoever in Greece.

For foreign shipping companies the application is submitted to the Ministry of Mercantile (Merchant) Marine. To the above documents a statement should be added as to the ships that the enterprise owns or manages and in case the branch office in Greece represents ships belonging to other enterprises, a statement of the owner to the effect that it has entrusted the office to be established in Greece with the representation of its interests.

When completing the application the applicant must also state:

a. The legal form in which it operates.

b. The current object of the company's business in every possible detail.

c. The object (in detail) of the company's office to be established in Greece, as well as the names of the countries towards which the activities of the office are to be oriented.

d. Name and surname of the manager of the office (provided it is known in advance).

e. The yearly amount of foreign exchange to be imported for any kind of operational and payroll expenses. This calculation is based on the number of persons which the company intends to employ, at the current rate of 50,000 US $ for four employees. This minimum amount is increased to 100.000 US $ for 8 employees and by 12.000 US $ for each additional employee thereon.

f. The number of foreign and local personnel to be employed.

Approval by the Ministry of Coordination is necessary in order for a company to acquire an official establishment, and the establishment becomes official from the moment the letter of guarantee provided for in art. 1 paragraph 2 of Law 89, is filed. The amount of this letter of guarantee is currently established at US $ 5.000. Such a guarantee is forfeited if the company or its employees violate the provisions of Law 89. To our present knowledge there has as yet, no such forfeiture been necessary.

The advantages of such an establishment can be summarized as follows:

1. Licence to conduct overseas business from Greece.
2. Foreign Currency accounts for the enterprise and its employees.
3. Granting of work and residence permits to foreign personnel and residence permits to their families.
4. Freedom of foreign staff to depart from and re-enter Greece at will.
5. Freedom to import office and business equipment free of tax and duties.
6. Freedom from local taxes and duties etc.
7. Freedom from keeping records in Greek.
8. 'Diplomatic' posting privileges.
9. Free importation and exportation of advertising material and samples of 'no commercial value'.
10. All personnel can be employed overtime subject to proper payments being made.
11. Freedom to import and re-export household belongings of foreign employees without tax or duties.
12. Ownership of duty-free car with free plates.
13. Freedom to exit from Greece without impounding of car or other personal property.

A company established under Law 89 does not have to keep the official accounting books normally required under the tax laws in Greece. Such companies must, however, keep a book of receipts and expenditures for the purpose of checking payments which involve tax liabilities of individuals.

The original text of Law 89/1967, provided for an exemption from Greek

income taxes for the salaries of foreign personnel working in the Greek branches of foreign companies established in Greece by virtue of law 89/67. The above exemption was abolished by para 1(d) of art. 29 of law 27/75, passed in April 1976 for the salaries of foreign employees earned in Greece. Due to the latter, foreigners working in branches where law 89/67 applies are subject to the provisions of Greek income tax legislation.
Further the law 89 branches must keep payroll records in order to calculate the salary withholding for their employees. Such records are also used to evidence that the foreign exchange amounts required under the Governmental Approval (by which the branch 89 has been established) is in fact imported. The foreign currency imported is controlled after the first year of operation of the branch. All payments are effected through an established bank in Greece upon issue of a relevant pink slip which is the actual proof of importation of foreign currency.

1.b. THE SUBSIDIARY

Foreigners may also form, either with other foreigners or Greek nationals, corporations and limited liability companies. These forms of business organization are more interesting for foreign investors.

SOCIÉTÉ ANONYME (A.E.)

1.b.(i) Setting-up

The basic corporation law concerning the A.E. is law 2190 enacted in 1920 as codified by Legislative Decree 174/1963.
For the formation of a Société Anonyme (A.E.) the following steps must be taken.

a. Ensuring that the Statutes are executed by a notarial deed and duly signed by at least two incorporators either individuals or companies.
b. A decision of the Minister of Commerce approving the legality of such Statutes.
c. Publication of the Ministerial decision and the Statutes in the Official Gazette.
   The Statutes must include provisions relating to:
   - The name and object of the company
   - The seat of the company
   - Its duration (which is usually 50 years)
   - The amount and manner of payment of the share capital
   - The number and issue of the shares
   - The convening composition, operation, and competence of the Board of Directors
   - The convening composition, operation, and competence of general meetings of shareholders
   - The auditors
   - The shareholders' rights

- The balance sheet and distribution of profits
- The dissolution of the company and liquidation of its assets.

1.b.(ii) Organization

Capital

The minimum share capital required for the incorporation of an A.E. company is 5.000.000 drachmae which must be wholly subscribed at the date of incorporation of the company. The above the minimum capital amount can be paid up in instalments at the latest within 10 years from the date of incorporation but provisions for such payment must always be made in the Statutes.[1] If however, the capital is offered for public subscription, then the minimum capital required is Drs. 10.000.000.–. For the formation of an insurance company the minimum capital is Drs. 30.000.000.–, and for Banks Drs. 300.000.000.–.

Within two months following the establishment of the Company or any increase of the capital thereof, the Board of Directors shall hold a special meeting to ascertain whether such capital has been paid or not. Within the same period of time the Chairman of the Board of Directors shall submit to the Ministry of Commerce a copy of the minutes of this special meeting.

In case the capital is offered for public subscription the prior approval of the Greek Capital Committee is required.

The Statutes may provide that during the first five years following the incorporation the Board of Directors has the right to increase, by a resolution passed by a majority vote by 2/3 of the Members of the Board, the share capital in whole or in part, by issuing new shares up to twice the amount of the paid up share capital. If such provision is not made in the Statutes, any increases in the capital of the Company are considered by law as an amendment of the Statutes and can only be effected by a decision of the General Meeting of Shareholders.

Corporate name of an A.E.

The corporate name of an A.E. company must respond to the object of the company. It may, however, contain additionally the name of some founder of the company or of a person or the name of another company. It may be expressed in a foreign language but in any case it must strictly respond to the truth. The words 'Anonymos Etaira' or the abbreviation 'A.E.' must also be part of the name.

The corporate name is mentioned in the Statutes and submitted to the Chamber of Commerce in complete form as described above, but in practice it may be used in a shorter form for reasons of convenience in the business practice. Change of the corporate name occurs upon decision of the General Meeting of Shareholders which is competent to decide on the alteration of the Statutes and must be approved by the Minister of Commerce and submitted to the Bulletin of A.E. and Limited Company.

1. After Greece's entry into the Common Market the provisions of the Second Council directive on Company Law providing for a minimum capital of 25.000.–, US and a five year payment by instalments for the above the minimum capital, may be applicable.

Shares
Art. 34 of the Commercial Code requires that the capital of the A.E. be divided equally into shares.
Shares can be issued either to the bearer or registered, the par value being a minimum of 100 drachmae and a maximum of 30.000 drachmae. In some corporations, however, due to their object, shares must be registered (i.e. banking, insurance, aviation, etc.). The shares are freely transferable provided, in case of registered shares, that the transfer is effected in the special register of the Company and signed by both parties, or their legal representatives. With regard to registered shares the Statutes can limit the transferability of the shares.

Preferred shares
The statutes can also provide for the issue of preferred shares which may enjoy the following privileges:
a. A priority right in the payment of the compulsory 6% first dividend. The statutes can provide that preferred shares are entitled to payment of dividends in spite the fact that in one or more years no dividends are distributed.
b. A priority right in the repayment of capital which has been invested by the shareholder in case of liquidation and the right to share the remaining amounts equally with the common shares after their repayment.

Founder's shares
Such shares having no par value may not represent more than 1/10 of the total number of issued shares. They may confer to their owners the right to enjoy no more than one fourth of the profits left after deduction of the compulsory dividend and the necessary amounts to create the ordinary reserve. Such shares do not confer to their owners the right to participate in the administration of the company or to share in the company's assets on liquidation. Such shares are subject to redemption by the company ten years after their issue at a price provided in the Statutes such price not exceeding an amount equal to the capitalisation at 15% of the average dividend paid during the previous three years to the founder's shares.

Administration of the A.E.
The S.A. company is represented generally by a Board of Directors acting collectively. The directors may be removed at any time by their appointers and replaced by others. Their term of office may not exceed six years, but they can be re-elected.
There are no restrictions in Greece as to the nationality of the members of the Board except in some specific cases, where a certain percentage of the directors must be Greek nationals, e.g. for insurance companies where 2/3 of the members of the Board must be Greek nationals.
The Board of Directors meets at the place where the Company's seat is situated at least once in every calendar month. Exceptionally and after approval of the Minister of Commerce the meeting may take place abroad provided such place is referred in the Statutes. The Board may validly transact the company's business if a quorum of half the directors plus one are present or

represented at any meeting, provided no less than three directors are present. The directors elect the General Manager of the Company who may also be a member of the Board. The directors have authority to decide on every matter relating to the management of the Company, the administration of its property, and the pursuance of its objects. They are responsible to the corporation for any fault committed by them in the management of the corporation affairs, and they are particularly responsible for any omissions or false entries in the balance sheet concealing the actual position of the Company. Each director's liability is waived if he proves that he has managed the company's affairs with the diligence of a 'wise head of a family' whereas the Managing Director is only relieved from such liability if he has exercised utmost diligence. Each member of the Board of Directors must maintain absolute secrecy with respect to confidential matters of the corporation which have been made known to him in his capacity as a director.

General Meeting of Shareholders

The General Meeting of Shareholders is the highest authority of the company and must be held at the seat of the company at least once every year and within 6 months from the end of the business year, and extraordinarily whenever the Board of Directors shall deem it necessary, or whenever such a meeting is requested by the Company's auditors or by shareholders representing at least 1/20 of the paid-up capital.

The General Meeting of Shareholders is the only body competent to decide on:

- any amendment to the Statutes
- the election of the members of the Board of Directors and the election of the Auditors
- the approval or amendment of the Balance Sheet of the Company submitted by the Board of Directors
- the distribution of the annual profits and on the issue of a loan through bonds
- the extension of the duration or merger or dissolution of the Company and the appointment of liquidators
- the approval of election by the Board of Directors of provisional members of the Board.

Every shareholder has the right to vote and may participate in the General Meeting of Shareholders either in person or by proxy, who need not be a shareholder, provided he has deposited his shares with the treasurer of the Company or with the Consignment Deposits and Loans Fund or with any Bank established in Greece at least five (5) days before the General Meeting. The General Meeting of Shareholders is in quorum if at least 1/5 of the paid-up capital is represented. If no such quorum is present, the meeting shall be held again within twenty (20) days from the day of the cancelled meeting. A new meeting shall form a quorum and may validly transact the business contained in the Agenda of the original meeting, irrespective of the amount of paid-up share capital represented. If only one person is present at the meeting, the meeting shall be attended by a representative of the Ministry of Commerce or a Notary who countersigns the minutes. Exceptionally, decisions which correspond to an amendment of the Statutes of the company and concern the changing of the object of the company, its nationality, the increase of shareholders obligations, the increase of the share capital, an issue of a debenture loan, a change in the manner of distribution of profits, a merger of amalgamation of the company, an extension of the duration or the dissolution of the company must be taken by a General Meeting of Shareholders where at least 2/3 of the paid-up capital is represented.

Protection of minority shareholders

The law specifies various minority rights the most important being the following:

Minority shareholders representing at least 1/20 of the paid-up share capital have the right:

a. To request the President of the appropriate Court at the seat of the company to examine the books of the company, or to order an audit in a case where it has been assessed that the company's affairs have not been correctly administrated. This provision is not applicable where the requesting minority is represented in the company's Board of Directors.

b. To request an extraordinary General Meeting of Shareholders.

c. To request once, at any general meeting, the postponement of a decision on a given item on the agenda.

d. To request that the Board of Directors may provide at the next regular meeting of shareholders information on any sum paid to members of the Board, the managers, or other employees of the company.

Shareholders representing one tenth of the paid-up capital may request that any decision of the general meeting be taken on the basis of a roll call vote.

The auditors

The auditors (at least two) are appointed by the General Meeting of Shareholders and have as their task to examine the Balance Sheet before submission by the Board of Directors to the General Meeting of Shareholders of the company and generally to supervise the management of the company. Such auditors must be graduates of the High Commercial or business schools. More specifically they have the right of access to any book, account, or document, including the minutes of the General Meeting and the Board of Directors. They make all necessary suggestions to the Board of Directors and report to the supervising Minister of Commerce any instance of violation of the provisions of the law or the Statutes.

At the end of the accounting period they examine the Balance Sheet and the Profit and Loss Account and submit to the Ordinary General Meeting of Shareholders a report of the result of their audit.

The report must show clearly, through an examination of the company's books for accuracy and legality of the entries, whether the Balance Sheet represents the financial position of the company on the day of termination of the audited accounting period and the Profit and Loss Account shows the actual results of that period.

It is permitted that Greek A.E. companies may appoint chartered accountants to act as auditors. In such cases, these companies may appoint one chartered accountant to carry out the ordinary audit, instead of the two (2) auditors as mentioned above.

Distribution of Profits

The law on the matter of distribution of profits provides that the company must appropriate each year at least 5% of the net profits in order to create an ordinary reserve. These payments of the ordinary reserve cease to be obligatory once the ordinary reserve reaches 1/3 of the Share Capital. After this appropriation the company is required to distribute out of net profits a first dividend equal to 6% of the paid-up Share Capital or 35% of net profits whichever is higher. In case the 35% of net profits exceeds the 6% of the paid-up Share Capital, the General Meeting of Shareholders representing at least 80% of the paid-up Share Capital can vote not to distribute the above the 6% of the paid-up capital amounts. In this case, the non distributable dividends (at least up to the amount of the 35% of the net profits) is capitalized through the issurance of new shares offered to the shareholders in relation to their stock. This last capitalization requirement can be also waived by the General Meeting of Shareholders representing at least 95% of the paid-up Share Capital. The rest of the profits are distributed as provided in the Statutes.

Distribution of interim dividends or percentages is also permitted if at least twenty (20) days before the day of such distribution, an accounting report of the company's property is published as soon as it is drawn up, in one of the Athens daily newspapers which in the Director's opinion has the widest circulation, and in the Bulletin of A.E. Companies and Companies of Limited Liability of the Government Gazette and is submitted to the Ministry of Commerce.

Dividends or other items so distributed may not exceed one half of the net profits shown in the accounting report.

Dissolution and Liquidation of the A.E.

The company is dissolved if (a) the period for which it has been incorporated expires, (b) by decision of the General Meeting of Shareholders taken with a 2/3 increased majority, and (c) in case the company is declared bankrupt. In addition, the Board of Directors is obliged to convene the General Meeting in order to decide whether to dissolve the company, in a case where the value of the company's assets at the time the Balance Sheet is drawn, after deduction of the liabilities, is less than 1/2 of its paid-up capital. The fact that the total number of shares is owned by one shareholder does not consititute a reason for the dissolution of the company.

In case of (a) and (b) above, dissolution is followed by the liquidation of the company's assets. In case of (a) above, unless the Statutes provide otherwise, the Board of Directors is responsible for carrying out this function whereas in case of (b) above, the liquidations are appointed by virtue of the same decision of the General Meeting of Shareholders which voted for the dissolution of the company. The appointed liquidators must effect an inventory of the assets of the company and publish in the daily Press and the Bulletin of A.E. and Limited Liability Companies Official Gazette the Balance Sheet showing the exact financial situation of the company. A copy of the Balance Sheet is also submitted to the Ministry of Commerce. During the process of liquidation the General Meeting of Shareholders retains all its rights and all liquidation accounts are subject to its approval.

LIMITED LIABILITY COMPANY (EPE)

A limited liability company is a company whose capital is divided in parts and where shareholders are liable for any debts in relation to the parts they own. The basic law which regulates the EPE company is Law 3190/1955.
For the establishment of a limited liability company the following procedure must be followed:

a. The execution of a notarial deed between at least two partners.
b. Forwarding of the above deed to the Court of first Instance.
c. Publication within a month in the official gazette of a summary giving the name of the company, the name of the partners, the capital of the company, the name of the administrators, the seat, the duration of the company, the number of the contract and the name of the notary and the number of the act of entry in the Court of First Instance.

Capital
The minimum capital required for the formation of an EPE is 200.000 drs fully paid-up at the moment that deed is executed by a notary and divided in parts of at least 10.000 drs each or its multiple. Half of the minimum amount i.e. 100.000 drs must be in cash.
Transferability of the part is free provided no provision for the contrary is stipulated in the Statutes. Such transfer must be executed by a notary deed which must include the name, profession, place of residence, nationality of the person acquiring the part and becomes effective for the company from the date of registration in the company's books. It is not permitted for the company to acquire its own parts.

Corporate name of the limited liability company (EPE)
The corporate name of the EPE consists of either the name of one or more shareholders or it must reflect the object of the company's business.
The name of a non-shareholder cannot be used in the corporate name. In addition it is obligatory that the corporate name of such company contains the words 'Company of limited liability' fully written.

Administration
For the administration of the Company no Board of Directors is required, the Company being administered by one or more administrators freely appointed and recalled by the General Meeting of the Shareholders except when appointed by Statutes and for an unlimited period of time. In such a case a court decision is necessary for serious reason and after decision by the General Meeting of Shareholders. Such administrators have full authority to represent the Company, except for certain items (amendments of Statutes, approval of balance sheet) for which a decision can only be taken by the General Meeting of Shareholders.

General Meeting of Shareholders
The General Meeting of the Shareholders acting collectively, is the highest authority of the company and must be held at least once a year. Every shareholder has votes equal to the parts he owns. The ordinary decisions are

taken with a double majority of the number of shareholders and the capital and the extraordinary decisions (any change in the Statutes, dissolution before the term referred in the Statutes) by a three fourths double majority. Unanimity is required for the change of the nationality of the company, the increase of the shareholders liabilities, diminishing their rights or authorising the administrators to act in competition with the company.
The EPE is not subject to the supervisory authority of the Ministry of Commerce, its publicity being secured by forwarding any changes of the Articles of Incorporation, administrators etc. to the Secretary of the Athens Court of First Instance. The EPE must publish its annual balance sheet as well as any corporate changes, in the Government Gazette.

Dissolution and liquidation of an EPE
The dissolution of an EPE may occur a) for any reason provided by the law or by the Statutes of the Company, b) by a decision of the General Meeting of Shareholders taken by a 3/4 double majority i.e. of the number of Shareholders and the capital in case the Statutes do not provide for a different majority, c) by a court decision upon request of any shareholder representing at least 1/10 of the capital for serious reason, d) in case of bankruptcy and e) by a court decision upon request of any person having legal interest in case all the parts are owned by one person.
Bankruptcy or death of any shareholder brings the company into dissolution only if specifically provided in the Statutes.
Further, in a case where half of the capital of the company is lost the administrators are obliged to convoke a general meeting of the shareholders in order to decide upon either the dissolution of the Company or the decrease of the capital which in no way may become less than the 200.000 drs minimum amount provided by Law.
Liquidation of the Company is carried out by the administrators unless either the Statutes or the General Meeting of Shareholders provide otherwise. In case the liquidators are appointed by the Statutes they can only be revoked for a serious reason, whereas if they are appointed by the General Meeting of Shareholders they can be revoked at any time. Their duty as soon as appointed is to effect an inventory of the company's assets and draw a balance sheet reflecting the company's financial position. Such a balance sheet is published in the bulletin of the S.A. and Limited Liability Companies of the Official Gazette.

1.b.(iii) Checklist for establishing a subsidiary

A. FOR AN A.E. COMPANY

1. Procedural and documentary requirements:
   a) Execution of the Statutes by a Notarial Deed between at least two founders.
   b) A decision of the Minister of Commerce approving such Statutes.
   c) Publication of the above Ministerial decision and the Statutes in the Official Gazette.
2. Time required for the establishment of an A.E. Company is about forty-five (45) days:
3. Various costs amount to approximately Drs. 25.000.–.

B. FOR AN E.P.E. COMPANY

1. Procedural and documentary requirements:
   a) Execution of Notarial Deed between at least two partners.
   b) Forwarding of the above deed to the Primary Court.
   c) Publication within one (1) month in the Official Gazette of a summary of the Statutes.
2. Time required for the establishment of an EPE Company is about twenty five (25) days.
3. Various costs are:
   - Stamp duties and various other contributions amount to 5% on the equity capital.
   - Notary fees approximately Drs. 3.000.–.
   - Various other costs Drs. 2.000.–.

1.c. OTHER FORMS

General partnership – limited partnership

There is no prohibition for foreigners to form general partnerships or limited partnerships and no administrative formalities special to foreigners exist for their establishment except again for the necessity of obtaining work permits to register with the Chamber of Commerce.
Under the Commercial Code a partnership exists when two or more persons associate themselves under a common name for the purpose of engaging in commercial activities. Each partner is jointly and severally liable without limitation for the obligations undertaken in the name of the partnership. The administration of the business may be carried out by all the partners, provided the partnership contract does not stipulate otherwise.
The limited partnership consists of one or more general partners with unlimited liability and one or more special partners whose liability is limited to the amount each has contributed to the capital of the partnership. The special partner must not interfere with the administration of the business and if this restriction is violated, the special partner assumes the liabilities of a general partner. Moreover, a special partner is not ipso facto a 'merchant'.
Both forms of partnership must be created either by a notarial deed or a private contract executed in as many originals as there are partners. In some cases (such as where immovable property is contributed to the partnership) a notarial deed is obligatory.
A summary of the partnership agreement must be registered in accordance with art. 42 of the Commercial Code, with the Primary Court. In case such formalities have not been observed, third parties may assert the nullity of the partnership ab initio. Moreover, any partner may demand the annulment of the partnership; he may not, however, assert such lack of compliance with formalities, against third parties.

Silent partnership

A 'silent partnership' is a form of business organization whose main characteristic is that third parties ignore the existence of an association and one of the partners carries on the business in his own name for the benefit of all partners while the silent partners who may not act in the name of the association, only take part of the profits or share the losses.

2. THE JOINT VENTURE

A Joint Venture can take the form of either a jointly owned company or of a cooperation of companies for a specific purpose. More specifically:

2.a. The jointly owned company

A Joint Company which can take any of the legal forms described under II.A.1.b. above, and has, apart from the general conditions already covered, certain special considerations, the most common of which are control of management, increased minority rights, increased quorum and majority requirements in basic Shareholders and Board of Directors decisions, participation on the Board of Directors, limitations in the transfer of shares etc. ...
Such limitations can be secured either through special provisions in the Statutes of the Company provided the law governing the specific form of Company allows such provisions or through a Shareholders Agreement. It is generally advisable to include as many as possible of the increased minority rights or other special agreements in the Statutes since the provisions of its signatories, may not be enforceable against the Company itself. In such a case, the shareholder violating his contractual obligations is liable for damages in favour of the injured party.
It should be noted that in the case of an Anonymos Etaira the law does not permit the establishment in the Statutes of an increased majority for all decisions in the Shareholders Meetings. On the other hand qualified majorities on items specifically enumerated in the Statutes are legal and fully enforceable. A practical problem may arise in case of a 50/50 division of the shareholding between two shareholders, since unanimity will be necessary in order to take a decision on those issues which are the exclusive competence of the General Meeting of Shareholders. In such a case, a decision on those issues cannot be reached and consequently the Company cannot be administered.
Of course, in such cases the law permits a shareholder to request from the Court the appointment of a temporary Board of Directors with limited responsibilities. Eventually, such shareholders may try to obtain the dissolution of the Company, if it becomes obvious that the Company cannot operate any more.

2.b. Consortia

A Joint Venture can also take the form of a cooperation agreement between individual persons and legal entities without the formation of a separate company (e.g. consortia). In such cases, the member entities retain their individual status but are jointly represented in the Venture according to the provisions of the Joint Venture Agreement, signed between the parties. Such agreements are not governed by any specific legislation and the parties are free to decide their relations. The basic provisions of such agreements normally cover the representation and decision making process of the Venture which could be either unanimous or by majority; the participation in the profits or losses of the Venture; liability of each member towards his partners and third parties etc. ... It should be noted, that in certain cases and especially for consortia of construction companies undertaking State of Public Companies contracts, the liability of the members towards the owner of the works is joint and it is up to the parties and the Consortium Agreement to secure guarantees in case one (1) member fails to perform.

B. *External Controls*

1. EXCHANGE CONTROLS[2]

Among the most important impediments to foreign investment is the imposition of exchange controls which limit the use of foreign exchange and which have severely hindered the transfer abroad of income from foreign investments.
Generally speaking anyone wishing to export any funds from Greece must either secure implementation of the Greek investment laws, in particular L.D. 2687/53, or have an ad hoc decision of the Greek currency Committee, which is granted on a case by case basis.
As far as the capital invested and the profits deriving from such investment are concerned repatriation provisions contained in the various investment laws are summarized as follows:

The repatriation provisions and the possibility of re-investment of profits

The repatriation of the investment is regulated by artt. 5 and 14 of L.D. 2687 in connection with several other provisions included in different laws, that give additional benefits under certain conditions. The terms under which the imported capital can be repatriated and earnings can be remitted are as follows:

a. Repatriation of equity capital and loans

The equity capital or loans can be repatriated in annual instalments not exceeding 10% of the total capital imported, but no payment can be made before the end of one year from the date the enterprise begins to operate and in any case not before the end of one year from the date of its importation (art. 5 para 1).

2. Under the Accession Treaty of Greece's entry into the EC such foreign exchange restrictions will be substantially relaxed. In particular the repatriation of capital invested and profits deriving from such investments effected after June 12, 1975 will be free as from January 1, 1981. Investments effected prior to June 12, 1975 will be subject to transitional period up to December 31, 1983.

Deviation from these provisions may be permitted if the enterprise is considered of special importance to the Greek economy, as decided by the Council of Ministers. However, the Government is extremely reluctant to give additional remittance percentages in the case of equity capital, if there is no special reason for it. Additional amounts for repatriation of loans are more easily granted, probably because immediate repayment of a loan will mean a lesser burden on the foreign exchange balance because of smaller interest payments.

b. Remittance of foreign exchange for payment of dividends and interest on loans

Profits for payment of dividends may be remitted at an annual rate not exceeding 12% of the amount of equity capital imported.
Despite the fact that the law clearly provides for the calculation of the 12% on the amount of 'equity capital imported' in practice this percentage is calculated on the amount of such capital not yet repatriated.
However, for enterprises under Law 4171/1961 (productive investment exceeding 150.000.000 drachmae or expansion exceeding 50.000.000 drachmae, a percentage of the profits not exceeding 6% annually on the repatriated part of the capital is allowed to be remitted abroad on condition that this percentage is not more than 8% of the foreign exchange receipts obtained by the enterprise from sales of its products abroad.
The exportation of foreign exchange under such circumstances shall be made in the currencies acquired from the exports of the enterprise and in proportion to each currency so acquired, unless the Bank of Greece, on the request of the party concerned, authorizes exportation in other currencies (L. 4171/1961 art. 2 para 13, L.D. 916/1971 art. 1 para 1 and 5, L. 159/1975 art. 5 para 1 and 2).
Art. 5 permits cumulative remittance of dividends in case the full quota is not used in any one year. This privilege is defined in the law and thus the Government cannot refuse to grant it. As a result, the annual amount allowable is increased since, normally, an enterprise will have small profits if indeed it has any, during the first years of its operation. Thus the investor will be able to take advantage of his unused quota in future years, when his profits will be high enough to permit remittance of more than 12%.
Remittance for payment of interest on loan capital is permitted at an annual rate not exceeding 10% of such capital not yet repatriated. In practice, the average remittance permitted by the licenses does not exceed 8%. The current licenses however, taking into account inflation in the international market, have permitted interest rates of 10%.
A practical problem has arisen, in connection with the time in which payment of loans can commence. As has already been noted, the remittance of capital cannot begin before one year after the production of the enterprise has started. The Government does maintain the view that this provision is also applicable in the case of repayment of loans.

c. Obligation of the Bank of Greece to allocate foreign exchange

Art. 6 of L.D. 2687 provides that the Bank of Greece shall be required to allocate the foreign exchange necessary for any remittance provided in the license.

The meaning of this provision is that, after the certification by the Ministry of Coordination, the Bank is obliged to allocate the currency, and that the investor has a direct cause of complaint against the Bank in case of undue delay or refusal.

Blocked Funds

If implementation of any Greek Investment Law or an ad hoc decision of the Greek Currency Committee have not been secured by the investor no funds can be exported from Greece but instead they must be deposited in a blocked account in Greece.[3]

2. TAKE-OVER CONTROLS

No specific legislation exists in Greece dealing with take-over controls.

3. ANTI-TRUST

Until recently Greece had no antitrust legislation, the provisions of unfair competition being the only weapon in the hands of the authorities in dealing with unfair practices.

Since late 1977 however Greece has enacted Law 703/1977 on Monopolies oligopolies and protection of free competition. This law came into force in June 1978. Law 703 follows very closely the language of artt. 85 and 86 of the Treaty of Rome and their implementing regulation 17. Thus, agreements decisions and concerted practices which have as their object or effect the prevention, restriction or distortion of competition, are prohibited (art. 1 of the Law). Further it is unlawful for one or more undertaking to exploit their dominant position on the market (art. 2).

The drafters of the new legislation have also taken under consideration jurisprudence of the Court of Justice particular as far as unjustified refusals to sell are concerned which are specifically included in both artt. 1 and 2 of the Law.

Up to date enforcement of the new legislation has been very mild and only two official decisions of the Competition Protection Board are published. We believe however that enforcement from now on will be more serious and expect a number of decisions in the near future.

3. Under the Accession Treaty of Greece's entrance into the EEC such funds blocked in Greece belonging to persons resident in the present Member States will be progressively released by equal annual instalments from Accession until December 31, 1985, in six (6) stages, the first of which will begin on January 1st, 1981.

Environmental controls

To date there is no specific legislation dealing with the matter of protection of the environment. What is only existing at the moment are various health regulations which must be observed by the Industries and which entail various penal sanctions in case of non observance.
Recently the Ministry of Industry which grants the necessary operation license for new industries, requires, before granting such licenses, that various measures for the protection of the environment are observed. It is evident that in the near future legislation similar to that in the EC on the protection of the environment will have to be enacted.

State monopolies

Greece although following the principle of free enterprise has certain sectors of the economy excluded to private investors. These sectors include matches, playing cards, salt, saccharin and although not in the strict sense, state monopolies and all public utility enterprises.

III. TAXATION

A. Corporation Tax

1. ENTITIES SUBJECT TO TAX

Taxability

A domestic corporation is liable to be taxed on the entire amount of income derived from Greek or foreign sources.
Foreign corporations, limited liability companies, and general and limited partnerships are subject to tax on income derived from Greek sources and on profits earned through a permanent establishment in Greece.

2. COMPUTATION OF PROFITS

2.a. Income

Corporations are taxed not only on profits derived directly from their activities but also on income derived from dividends, interest, royalties, and real estate, as well as on capital gains. Income derived from illegal operations is also taxable.

2.b. Capital gains/losses

Capital gains

Income from commercial enterprises is considered to include the gain derived from: (a) the transfer of any kind of right or privilege (lease, patent, mineral rights, etc.); (b) the transfer of goodwill; and (c) the sale of business assets, with the exception of real estate and ships. Such capital gains are taxed separately from the ordinary business profit at a flat rate of 30% in the year of their realization or appreciation in the books.
However, gains derived from the sale of plant and machinery used in the enterprise are not taxable if they are reinvested in fixed assets of the enterprise within two years.

Losses

Commercial company losses may be carried forward for three years while industrial companies may carry forward losses up to five years. There are no provisions allowing carrying back of losses.

2.c. Exemptions, deductions, rebates

(i) Tax exemption of interest and dividends

Income derived from interest and dividends for which a tax exemption is provided in favour of individuals is also exempted from tax when such income is acquired by a corporation.

(ii) Refund of income tax paid by corporations-intercompany dividends

When a corporation distributes accumulated profits in subsequent years in the form of dividends or fees to directors, etc., then the amount already paid for nondistributed profits is deducted from the withholding tax levied on such distributions. If the amount of tax paid in previous years is higher, the difference is refunded.

3. RATES OF TAX

The basic tax rate for undistributed profits for domestic corporations as well as for foreign corporations, limited liability companies and partnerships is 40%. This rate is subject to a surcharge of 15% for the Farmer's Insurance Fund (OGA) (total 46%). Since this OGA surcharge is a deductible expense, the effective rate is decreased to 43.4%. In the case of domestic mining and industrial corporations listed on the Stock Exchange this effective rate of 43.4% for net undistributed profits is reduced to an effective rate of 38.25%. Gross income (real or presumptive) derived by the above entities from real estate situated in the area of Athens is taxed in addition with 3% for the Water Supply Works.

4. TAX CREDITS

The main characteristic of the Greek tax system is that domestic corporations are subject to tax only for that part of their profits which is not distributed, while the distributed part is taxed in the hands of shareholders as income from dividends.
In several countries the tax is imposed on both distributed profits and non-distributed profits (the latter at full or split rates), but no other EC country provides a complete exemption from tax on distributed profits, as is done in Greece.
The Greek tax system on corporate profits, owing to its structure, is also considered as extremely favourable in the case of affiliated or holding corporations, since the transfer of dividends from company to company (inter-company dividends) does not raise any questions of double taxation.

5. TIMING OF PAYMENTS

The tax due on the basis of the tax return, after a deduction of any withholding tax at the source and the prepaid tax (mentioned below), is payable in 10 equal monthly installments from March to December in the respective fiscal year. If the entire amount is paid at the time the first installment is due, the taxpayer corporation is given a 10% discount.

6. REVIEW AND APPEAL

When no agreement is reached on the disputed assessment, with the Tax Authorities, the taxpayer may file an appeal with the Tax Court of First Instance. At the same time, the taxpayer normally pays an amount equal to 20% of the disputed tax, which is later refunded to him if he wins in the Tax Court or deducted from the tax to be eventually determined by the Court, as the case may be.
However, Law 820/1978 has made this rule more flexible so that the 20% prepayment of disputed taxes and penalties need not be paid in certain cases specified by the law (e.g. where the taxpayer can show that he has good prospects with the litigation or that he is unable to pay).
If either the Taxpayer or the Tax Authorities are dissatisfied with the decision of the Tax Court of First Instance (which is often the case), either may appeal to the higher court, the Tax Court of Appeals.
The final word, however, on tax disputes is given by the Council of State which adjudicates only points of law and not of fact.

B. Withholding Taxes on Dividends, Interest, Royalties

1. INCOME CATEGORIES SUBJECT TO WITHHOLDING TAX

Corporations, limited liability companies, partnerships and sole proprietor undertakings, are required to withhold the tax on dividends, directors' fees, interest, royalties, salaries, wages and pensions, remuneration paid to lawyers, doctors, engineers, and other professionals as well as to auditors, experts, etc., as the case may be.

2. RATES

The rate of withholding tax is as follows:
1. – Dividends
a. from shares registered in the Stock exchange
  (i) registered shares at 38%
  (ii) bearer shares at 41%
b. from shares not registered with the Stock Exchange
  (i) registered shares at 43%
  (ii) bearer shares at 47%
2. – Directors' fees and remunerations: at the progressive income tax rates for individuals
3. – Interest
a. to individuals: at the progressive rates.
b. to corporations, etc.: if resident, 25%: if non resident, 40% plus 15% of the tax which is deductible i.e. 43,4% effective rate.
4. – For royalties:
15% plus 15% OGA surcharge i.e. effective rate 17.25%;
but for royalties subject to approval under L. 4171/1961: 10% which is credited to the final rate due.
5. – Salaries, wages and pensions: at the progressive rates.
6. – Remuneration and fees paid to professionals: 8%.
7. – Payments made to contractors: at 1,50%.
All withholding taxes are refunded or credited by the Government within the time limits fixed by the law on the basis of a tax return filed with the competent Tax Director.

3. EFFECT OF TAX TREATIES

This is a summary of relief from Greek tax at source on dividends, interest, and royalties, in accordance with double taxation agreement between Greece and the following countries:

Country of recipient's fiscal residence	*Dividends* %	*Interest* %	*Royalties* %
U.S.A.	Normal rate	Normal rate	Exempted
U.K.	Normal rate	Exempted	Exempted
Sweden	Normal rate	10	5
France	Normal rate	10	5
W. Germany	25%	10	Exempted
Italy	25	10	Exempted
Cyprus	25	10	Exempted

Country of recipient's fiscal residence	*Dividends %*	*Interest %*	*Royalties %*
Belgium	25	15	5
Austria	Normal rate	Exempted	Exempted[4]
India	Normal rate	Normal rate	Normal rate
Finland	Normal rate	10.	0 (for intellectual property) 10 (for intellectual property)
Holland[5]	35	8 banking and other credit institutes 10	5 (for intellectual property) 7 (for industrial property)

C. Registration and Stamp Duties

1. STAMP TAX

Stamp taxes are essentially taxes upon documents rather than upon transactions. However, in the following cases the stamp tax is payable even when no documents are issued in respect of:

a. Salaries, wages, fees, remunerations, commissions, and brokerage;
b. Wholesale sales of goods, etc., to other enterprises;
c. Rents derived from the lease of buildings and real estate in general; and
d. Dividends paid by corporations.

In addition, the stamp tax is payable when the transaction is proven by the books of an enterprise even though no document is issued, such as in the case of loans granted to corporations, limited liability companies, and partnerships by their shareholders, members, or partners, and vice versa, and in respect of partners' withdrawals against the company, etc.

In principle, stamp duties are paid on written instruments concerning transactions concluded in Greece between persons individuals or legal entities) regardless of their nationality, residence, or domicile. However, certain transactions and documents, although issued abroad, are subject to stamp tax in Greece, e.g. invoices for sales to buyers in Greece and bills of lading for transport of goods to Greece.

Most documents and transactions are liable to stamp duty. The rates vary between 0.50% for bank overdrafts to 3.6% for the transfer of limited liability Co. (EPE) shares. Stamp duties are also imposed on sales and commercial transactions, payments of royalties, interest, etc.

Some examples of stamp duties in effect today are as follows:

	Percent
– Sales invoices for goods and services:	2.40
– Import invoices:	2.40 to 6.00

4. 10% if Australian company owns 50% or more of the Greek company.
5. The Greek-Holland tax treaty has been signed, but not yet ratified.

– Professional fees (from consultations with members of medical, legal professions etc.):	1.20
– Commissions:	2.40
– Director's fees:	1.20
– Loans between businesses or between individuals and A.E.s or E.P.E.s (and interest on such loans):	2.40
– Bank overdrafts:	0,50
– Capital of partnerships and E.P.E.s:	1.80
– Profits of partnerships and E.P.E.s:	1.20
– Transfer of E.P.E. shares:	2.40 or 3.60

D. Individual Taxation

1. PERSONS SUBJECT TO TAX

This is a general tax levied on the total annual income of individuals after a deduction of personal and family allowances. Tax rates are highly progressive (from 0% to 60%). However, due to the surcharge of OGA (Agricultural Insurance Fund), the effective maximum rate is increased to 69%. Earned income is treated more favourably than certain passive incomes such as income from real property, profits of a limited liability company, interest, directors fees, etc., which is charged with an additional 3% tax. However, income from dividends is exempt from this 3% tax.

2. COMPUTATION OF INCOME

2.a. Income

The term 'Income' is not defined in the tax law. Instead, income chargeable to tax is calculated under seven categories (schedules), according to the nature of the source from which it is derived. Net income of each separate category is first computed separately, according to rules which vary from category to category. Income from all such categories is then combined and the total is the statutory income. From the aggregate the losses from one or more categories may be deducted.

The seven schedules mentioned above cover income from the following sources: (a) Buildings; (b) The lease of land; (c) Movable capital; (d) Business; (e) Farming in general; (f) In respect of dependent personal services, including pensions; and (g) In respect of independent personal services and in general income not falling under any of the foregoing cases and not accumulating from capital.

2.b. Capital gains

As a general rule, capital gains realized from the alienation of real property or movable capital outside the ordinary course of business are not subject to income tax. Thus, a benefit accrued to an individual from the sale of shares or securities or real property, in which he has invested his capital, is not liable to tax.

2.c. Exemptions, deductions, rebates

The individual income tax is levied on the total annual income of individuals after a deduction of personal and family allowances and certain other expenses.
The basic exemptions and deductions for each source of income mentioned above are as follows:

1. *Income from buildings*

DEDUCTIONS
- 25% of gross annual income from rental of apartments.
- 10% in the case of offices, warehouses, stores etc.

2. *Income from land*

DEDUCTIONS
The chief deductions are any direct taxes (except income tax), dues, and fees levied on the property, the interest on debts owed on the property and secured by mortgage, 5% of the gross income for depreciation and for the upkeep of the land, and any expense for flood control works and for draining marshes.

3. *Income from movable capital*

EXEMPTIONS
- Interest derived from all kinds of deposits with Greek and foreign banks operating in Greece;
- Dividends of shares of domestic corporations whose profits are subject to the special tax;
- Dividends received by policy holders of life insurance companies up to the amount of Drs. 15.000 per year (from one or more such companies);
- Dividends derived from shares of domestic corporations registered in the Stock Exchange, up to the amount of Drs. 25,000 per annum per corporation with a maximum exemption of Drs. 100,000 overall per year.

4. *Income from business*

All ordinary and necessary business expenses as defined in the Tax Laws related to and justified by the business qualify as deductions.

5. *Income from agricultural enterprises*

THE FOLLOWING IS EXEMPT FROM TAXATION
An amount of the gross income equal to Drs. 200,000 per year, increased to Drs. 500,000 provided that the taxpayer or members of his family are themselves working on the farm, even if they employ other workers.

6. *Income from dependent personal services (schedule F)*

DEDUCTIONS
- A special allowance up to 40% of this income, with a maximum limit of Drs. 90.000 per annum.

7. *Income from independent personal services (schedule G)*

DEDUCTIONS
- A special deduction of 25% on the gross income, with a maximum limit of Drs. 20,000 per annum.

Note: The total deductions of a taxpayer who has income both from schedule F (income from dependent personal services) and schedule G (income from liberal professions) cannot exceed the sum of Drs. 90.000).

Add: Personal and family allowances
In computing the net taxable income in a given year, the taxpayer is entitled to the following deductions:
Drs. 20,000 as a living allowance for himself, Drs. 20,000 for his wife, Drs. 15,000 for the first child, Drs. 15,000 for the second, Drs. 25,000 for the third, Drs. 35,000 for each child above the third one and Drs. 15,000 for every other dependent. Dependents are: children up to the age of 18 (25 for students), the parents of both spouses, disabled children, and unmarried daughters, regardless of age. All these are deemed to be dependents as long as they do not have a separate income in excess of Drs. 25,000 per annum.

3. RATES OF TAX

The rates of tax are 0% for a net annual income of Drs. 80.000 which progress to as much as 60% for a net total income of Drs. 3.000.000. However, as explained previously, the maximum effective rate is increased to 69% due to the OGA surcharge.

4. SUCCESSION DUTIES (ESTATE TAXES/GIFT TAXES)

Under the Greek Tax System, as established by basic Law 1641 of 1919 (and amendments), gift, inheritance, and dowry taxes are imposed on certain transfers of movable and immovable property. The amount of tax which burdens such transfers depends upon the value of the particular property transferred and upon the degree of relationship between the testator (or donor) and the recipient. The actual rates of both the inheritance and gift tax are based on graduated rate schedules and are the same in both cases differing only as per category. The rate of dowry tax, however, is equal to only one half of the inheritance and gift tax.
After deducting the debts and charges against the estate, the net remaining amount of inheritance is subject to tax calculated according to each recipient's tax rate category corresponding to the relationship between the reci-

pient and the testator. There exist four general categories (A, B, C and D) of recipients, each with a different schedule of rates. The closer the relationship between the testator and the recipient, the lower is the tax rate.
According to the recent Law 1041/1980, the above mentioned four categories of recipients, receive tax free, the following amounts per category:
1. Category A, Drs. 500,000.–
2. Category B, Drs. 250,000.–
3. Category C, Drs. 200,000.–
4. Category D, Drs. 100,000.–.

E. Indirect Taxation

PRINCIPAL INDIRECT TAXES

Turnover taxes

1. Characteristics

This tax is an ad valorem tax levied on industrial and handicraft enterprises; banks; insurance companies; transportation enterprises; electric, gas and telecommunication enterprises; advertising companies; repair and maintenance of automobiles; beauty parlours; and hotel enterprises.
Imported goods are also liable to turnover tax at the same rate as domestic products.
The Greek turnover tax resembles the French added value tax (*impot sur la valeur ajoutee*). However, in Greece, this tax is currently imposed only at the time the products are sold by the manufacturer to other processing enterprises or to a wholesale dealer, retailer, or, even directly, to the ultimate consumer.
According to the Greek-EEC Accession Treaty, Greece has agreed to adopt the EEC VAT system by January 1, 1984. Already, there is substantial work done in this direction.

2. Tax rates

The normal rate is 8%, but reduced rates are provided for certain products: namely 2% for certain products in common use (rice, fats, fish, etc.) and 4% for certain types of trucks and buses, spare parts, soap, cattle foods, and some other foodstuffs.
Also under the incentives programme the normal 8% may be reduced to 6% or 4% depending on the geographical location of the enterprise.

A. EXPORTS
No turnover tax is imposed on manufactured goods which are exported.

B. BANKING ENTERPRISES
A 4% tax rate is levied on gross receipts from interest, commissions, discount, etc., earned in Greece.

C. INSURANCE ENTERPRISES

The tax is levied on insurance premiums and related dues of all branches.
The tax rates indicatively are as follows: life insurance premiums 3%, other insurance premiums 8%.

D. ELECTRIC AND GAS ENTERPRISES

The tax rate is 8% levied on gross receipts. Electric current for agricultural and industrial purposes is exempt from tax.

E. TRANSPORTATION ENTERPRISES

The tax rate is 7% levied on gross receipts from passenger fares within Greece.

F. ORGANIZATION FOR TELECOMMUNICATIONS

The tax rate is 8% levied on gross receipts.

3. Tax returns–payment of tax

This tax is paid on the basis of tax returns filed with the competent Tax Office each month. As an exception, insurance companies may file their tax returns quarterly.

F. Incentives

In this section of 'Incentives', (due to the new Incentives Law 1116/1981 mentioned in the Introduction) we must distinguish between investments made up to December 31st, 1980 and those made as of January 1st, 1981.
For those investments made up to December 31st, 1980 the 'Old Regime' applies (i.e. incentives granted for regional development by all prior Laws to Law 1116/1981), while for investments made as of January 1st, 1981 the new incentives of Law 1116/1981 are applicable.
It is in this light that the presentation of this section follows.

I. OLD REGIME INCENTIVES (INVESTMENTS UP TO DECEMBER 31ST, 1980)

General

In order to promote regional development and to promote provincial industries certain special tax incentives for the development of less developed regions in Greece were introduced. To this end, Greece was geographically divided into five areas (A, B, C, D, and E) and certain investment allowances and working capital allowances were made available as deductions from net profits. These areas geographically are indicated as follows:

Area A: Attica area except municipality of Lavrion

Area B: Lavrion, districts of Thessaloniki, Boetia, Corinth and province of Halkis

Area C: All other areas of Greece

Area D: Industrial zones determined within Region C in certain specified areas in the districts e.g. of Kilkis, Xanthi, Lesbos, Serrai etc.

Area E: Frontier areas (i.e. 20 kilometers from the Greek boundaries) of such regions as Ioannina, Kastoria, Florina and other specified regions.

Law Decrees 1078/1971, 1313/1972 as amended by L.D. 1377/1973, Law Decree 289/1976 and Law 849/1978 divided Greece into these five regions and granted the various tax and credit incentives enumerated below.

To take an example, as regards deductions from net profits and working capital deductions from investments realized in a particular Area, enterprises of Area E, for instance (except hotel enterprises on Rhodes) will be entitled to deduct from their net profits an amount equal to 150% of the value of the expenses involved with new investment if such profits are realized within five years from the filing of the application to become qualified. Also, the abovementioned enterprises may, for the purpose of building up working capital, deduct from their net profits an amount equal to 25% of the value of such investments.

Other incentives

1. Incentives for scientific research

Greek industries, handicraft industries and mining concerns purchasing new machinery or equipment between January 1, 1973, and December 31, 1977, used exclusively for scientific research, or for the improvement of industrial or mining production, were allowed to deduct the value of such. The deduction was not allowed to be higher than 10% of the annual net profits for the fiscal year in which such purchase took place and the following years up to December 31, 1982.

2. Turnover tax reductions

The turnover tax is reduced from the normal rates for industries or handicraft enterprises located in certain areas outside Athens-Piraeus (Area A) as follows:

a. By 25% if located in Lavrion, Boetia, Corinth, Thessalonika, and the isles of Attica and Chalcis.
b. By 50%, if not located in (a) above nor in the remaining parts of Attica.
c. By 75% if a qualifying enterprise in Area E.

3. IKA (social security contributions) reductions

The employer-employee contributions to IKA as well as other insurance funds or remunerations from January 1, 1973, to December 31, 1982, are reduced by:

a. 20%, if the industries or handicraft enterprises are located in Area C and the isles of Attica.
b. 40%, for industries and handicraft enterprises located in area D (as determined by Art. 5 of L.D. 1377/73).
c. 50%, for qualifying enterprises in Area E.

Credit incentives

Apart from the above tax incentives, certain financial and credit incentives are granted. For example, the State will cover part of industrial construction costs under certain conditions (Area D is granted 25% coverage in the form of a cash payment of the expenses of construction of building installations).
New credit incentives in the form of Government loans for the reduction of pollution, electricity consumption, and for installing laboratories for research were established by Law 849/1978.

1. Relocation loans

Industrial and handicraft enterprises from Regions A or B relocated or transferred to Regions C, D, E or to the industrial area of the Hellenic-Industrial Development Bank (ETBA) in the District of Thessalonika between January 1, 1978 and December 31, 1982, may receive a certain percentage between 25% to 50% of the relocation costs as a Government loan.

2. Moving expenses

In order to encourage decentralization of industry away from the Athens-Piraeus area, relocation, rental and other similar allowances are granted (Law 849/1978) to persons moving to take on jobs in other than area A.

3. Special Incentives

A. REDUCTION OF POLLUTION
A loan in the amount of 50% of the investment is approved for investments made between January 1, 1978 to December 31, 1985, in order to reduce air, soil, water, and subsoil pollution so long as the loan amount does not exceed:
(i) 10% of the book value of the fixed assets before depreciation, and
(ii) Drs. 20 million per investment.

B. ENERGY CONSERVATION
A loan of up to 35% of any investment made from January 1, 1978, to December 31, 1985 is offered when such investment results in the reduction of the use of electric or other energy derived from solid, liquid, or gas fuels so long as the loan amount does not exceed:
(i) 15% of the book value of the fixed assets before depreciation, and
(ii) Drs. 30 million for each investment.

C. RESEARCH FACILITIES
A loan of up to 50% of the total investment may be granted in order to expand existing laboratories in industry, for mining research and mining pilot plants, provided the loan amount does not exceed Drs. 30 million.

Government subsidies

1. Interest subsidies

The following maximum interest subsidies in percentage points are allowed per region for investments made between January 1, 1978, and December 31, 1982:

a. *Region B* (within the ETBA industrial Zone)
   (i) Bank Loans 1.5%
   (ii) Bond Loans 2.0%
b. *Region C*
   (i) Bank Loans 3%
   (ii) Bond Loans 4%
c. *Region D*[6]
   (i) Bank Loans 4%
   (ii) Bond Loans 5%
   The above subsidies are granted provided that 40% (Region B), 30% (Region C), and 25% (Region D) of the investment is covered by the company from its own funds.
d. *Region E*[6]
   (i) Bank Loans 7%
   (ii) Bond Loans 7%
   (These interest subsidies of 7 percentage points in Region E are granted by Law 289/1976. For Region E, Law 849/78 also provides interest subsidies and one must chose either of the two laws).

2. Construction subsidies

Domestic industrial or handicraft enterprises making new investments in Region D between January 1, 1973, and December 31, 1982, receive a subsidy equal to 25% of the cost of construction of manufacturing facilities or other related buildings. This subsidy may not, in any case, exceed the amount of Drs. 150 per cubic meter. Provided the enterprise covers 25% of the total investment cost from its own funds, this subsidy is in addition to the subsidy granted in Region D.

II. NEW TAX INCENTIVES OF LAW 1116/1981 (FOR INVESTMENTS MADE AS OF JANUARY, 1981)

Preliminary comments

Law 1116/1981 (Published in the Government Gazette on January 14, 1981) entitled 'Providing Incentives for Regional and Economic Development' became law very timely, just a few days after Greece's entry in the EEC. It was promulgated in order to offer incentives to Greek and foreign investors in

6. The above interest subsidies in percentage points referred to in Regions D and E, are increased by *30% (Region D) and 50% (Region E)*, by article 9 par. 7 of Law 1116/1981.

harmony with other EEC country incentives and in line with EEC rules of competition.

To this end, the above Law 1116/1981 divides Greece into three Geographical areas (A, B and C), in lieu of the five Areas as foreseen in the 'Old' Incentives Regime.

The three geographical areas for industry and craft enterprises according to Law 116/1981 are:

Area A: District of Attica (except for the province of Kithira), part of the district of Corinth bordering Attica and up to the Corinth Canal, the province of Salonica of the district of Salonica (except for the section west of the river Axios and except for the industrial area of (ETBA) Hellenic Industrial Development Bank).

Area B: Districts of Corinth (except for the section bordering the district of Attica and up to the Corinth Canal and except for the areas of the previous municipalities Pheneos, Stymfalias, Pellinis and Nemea), Achaia (except for the province of Kalavryta), Boetia, Euboia (except for the island of Skyros), Magnesia (except for the province of Skopelos), Larissa (except for the province of Elassonos) the district of Pierria, the Province Imathia of the district of Imathia, the province of Yianitsa of the district of Pella, the district of Kilkis (except for a 20 kilometer zone distance from the borders), the province of Lagatha, the section west of the river Axios and the industrial area of ETBA of the district of Salonica, the district of Halkithiki, the district of Fthiotidos (except for the province of Domokos and the area within the town plan of Iraklion, Crete).

Area C: Rest of Greece and the industrial areas of ETBA which are situated in Area B (except for the Industrial area of ETBA of the district of Salonica which falls into Area B).

The most important incentives provided for by Law 1116/1981 are noted below as follows:

A. Direct cash grants

The Government direct cash grants (on a free basis) include the following percentages from total investment amounts made in the geographical areas as follows:

Area A: No cash grants are given.

Area B: the Government cash grants are 20%, 25% and 30% of investment made, depending correspondingly on the type of activity involved (low, medium or high support category).

Area C: the Government cash grants are increased to 40%, 45% and 50% respectively again depending on whether it concerns a low, medium or high support category investment in that order.

Note that these cash grants may be increased by another 10%, if the investment is located within an 'industrial zone' area, or in areas in which special programmes for regional development exist.

Also cash grants are granted for relocation of firms as follows:

– From Area A to Area C 50% of the relocation expenses and from Areas A to B and B to C (under certain conditions) 30% of the relocation expenses.

B. Government interest subsidy

The Government, in addition to the direct cash grants provides for interest subsidies for investments in the various Areas as follows:
Up to 30% and 50% of the amount of interest on the loan agreed to and necessary for the financing of a particular investment in Areas B and C respectively.
Certain conditions are however attached in order for the Government to give the direct cash grants or the interest subsidies. The most important of which are:

- The firm must provide from its own capital part of the investment involved as follows: Area A 30%, Area B 25%, Area C 20%.
- In addition, if a new investment is involved it must be at least 5 million Drs. and if it involves an extension of an existing investment at least 3 million Drs.
- It should be noted that in the case of Government 'cash grants' referred to above, for each investment concerned at least 10 new permanent jobs must be created as a result.

C. Tax free allowances

In conjunction with the direct cash grants, *but as an alternative* (i.e. both systems are not given cummulatively to the investor), the following percentage amounts may be deducted from net company retained profits for productive investments made up to the end of 1985.

1. In Area A, up to 20% of the investments made.
2. In Area B, up to 50% of the investment made.
3. In Area C, up to 80% of the investment made.

It should be noted that the amounts deducted from net profits annually may not exceed the following sums: Area A 30%, Area B 60%, Area C 90%.

D. Increased depreciation allowances

The New Law also provides for *increased* depreciation allowances for assets acquired as of January 1, 1981 and thereafter from *the normal rates*, depending on the Geographical Area and number of shifts of the industry in question as follows:
Area A: 1 shift 0%; 2 shifts 25%; 3 shifts 50%
Area B: 1 shift 25%; 2 shifts 50%; 3 shifts 75%
Area C: 1 shift 50%; 2 shifts 100%; 3 shifts 150%
In order for the second and third shifts to be granted the above increased depreciation rates, a certain specified percentage of the number of workers of the first shift must be employed in the second and third shifts.

Incentives for mergers

1. Mergers proper

According to LD 1297/1972, as amended by Law 849/1978, certain acts are exempted from all taxes, stamp duties or other duties in favour of the state or

other parties. These acts include the contribution and transfer of assets of the merging companies, every relevant act or agreement concerned with the contribution or the transfer of assets or liabilities or other rights or obligations, the publication in the Official Gazette, and the recording of relevant acts. As a condition to the tax exemption the merger must involve a minimum capital of Drs. 10.000.000.
If the company resulting from the merger is dissolved within five years from the time of the merger all taxes or stamp duties in favour of the state must then be paid.

IV. LABOUR ASPECTS

A. *Principles of Law on Employment*

1. LABOUR LEGISLATION

The Greek labour legislation is extremely extensive. Sources of labour law are found in the Constitution, in legislative enactments (laws and legislative decrees), acts of the Council of Ministers, decisions of the Minister of Labour, and in accepted local custom and tradition. Greece has ratified the Conventions of the International Labour Organization (ILO). Their provisions have the force of internal law. Labour law covers issues of hiring, working hours, employment of women and children, industrial safety and health, days of rest and public holidays, compensation for dismissal, social security, trade unions, collective labour agreements, arbitration courts for the settlement of disputes arising from collective labour agreements, protection of veterans, sickness, annual leave, compulsory bonuses etc.
The Minister of Labour and various offices, such as the Labour Inspectors, have wide responsibility in supervising the enforcement of labour law.

2. EMPLOYMENT CONTRACTS

Employment contracts may be either in writing or verbal and may be concluded for either a specified or an indefinite period of time.

3. EMPLOYEES AND WORKERS

Greek law distinguishes between *workers*, whose work is primarily manual, and *employees*, whose work is primarily non-manual. Workers are usually paid on a daily or weekly basis. Employees are paid on a monthly basis. Interim payments are deemed advances. Workers are usually employed on a temporary basis. Employees are employed on a continuous basis. The importance of this distinction is significant in: severance payments, working hours, holidays, remuneration etc.

4. HIRING

The employer is obliged to report to the local office of the Ministry of Labour giving the name of any employee or worker hired and to obtain a work permit within eight (8) days from commencement of employment.

5. EQUALITY BETWEEN MEN AND WOMEN

Since 1978, women's wages must be equal to those of men for the same type of work.

6. HIRING OF MINORS

Employment of persons under 14 years of age is prohibited. Other prohibitions include: employment of women in underground work, of male persons under 16 and female under 18 in jobs deemed dangerous and/or unhealthy, and of male persons under 18 and of women for night work.

7. CERTIFICATES OF PROFESSION OR TRADE

Only qualified technicians may perform certain jobs, therefore official certificates of profession or trade or diplomas must be presented before hiring.

8. WORKING HOURS

In a week of six (6) working days, normal working hours may not exceed eight (8) hours a day and forty eight (48) hours a week. In a week of five (5) working days, normal working hours may not exceed nine (9) hours a day and forty five (45) hours a week. From October 1, 1980 to September 30, 1981 the normal weekly payment covers only 43 hours. After October 1, 1981 it shall cover only 42 hours.
Additional payment is due for the extra hours up to the 48th hour inclusive. The maximum hours per work day for most corporate employees is reduced to seven (7) hours and the work week to forty two (42) hours. Banks, as a rule, are closed on Saturdays (and, of course, on Sundays).
Employers must provide at least one day of rest a week (Sunday as a rule). Sunday is an obligatory holiday.

9. OVERTIME

The law distinguishes between legal and illegal overtime. Illegal overtime is subject to an overtime premium of 100% from the very first hour. Legal overtime is subject to the prior approval of the Ministry of Labour. Each industrial branch and each geographical district (Prefecture) is permitted a

number of overtime hours per worker per calendar semester based on unemployment and other economic conditions.
The overtime premium for legal overtime is computed on a yearly basis and is paid as follows:
i. 25% of the hourly rate for hours 1 to 60
ii. 50% of the hourly rate for hours 61 to 120
iii. 75% of the hourly rate for each hour after the first 120 hours per year.
Under the provisions of Law 4171/1961, art. 9 para. 3, of Law 89/1967, art. 2, para. 1 and of Law 378/1968 foreign technical, commercial, industrial and shipping companies qualifying under these Laws are allowed overtime work by their office personnel without any restrictions as long as such work is absolutely necessary and the overtime premium is paid to their personnel.

10. WORK ON SUNDAYS OR AT NIGHT

Work on Sundays (and legal holidays) is paid at an hourly rate increased by 75%. Work at nights is paid at an hourly rate increased by 25%. Night work on Sundays is paid at an hourly rate increased by 100%. In case such work is also overtime the overtime premium is computed on the basis of the increased hourly rate.

11. LEGAL HOLIDAYS

In addition to Sundays, the following six (6) days of the year are recognised as legal holidays:
a. March 25th (Independence Day)
b. Easter Monday
c. May 1st (Labour Day)
d. August 15th (Ascension of the Virgin Mary)
e. October 28th (National Day)
f. December 25th (Christmas Day).

12. CUSTOMARY HOLIDAYS

Depending on the category of employees or workers, and the type of undertaking, business sector, district etc. certain other holidays are also customarily recognized nationwide or in certain districts. The following are the most important:
a. January 1st (New Year's Day)
b. January 6th (Epiphany)
c. First Monday in Lent
d. Good Friday
e. Whit Monday
f. September 14th (Holy Cross Day) and
g. December 26th (Day after Christmas).

13. WAGES

Wages may not be agreed below the minimum wage rates determined by collective bargaining agreements or by compulsory arbitration. In addition to the nationwide minimum wage rates for unskilled workers, minimum wage rates are determined by various collective agreements or by compulsory arbitrations for various categories of skilled workers in the various branches of industry, trade and the services. Various factors such as age, length of service, skill etc. account for a variation in the escalation of minimum wages.

14. COMPULSORY BONUSES

Employers are required to pay their employees and workers, in addition to their salaries and wages, the following compulsory bonuses:

a. A Christmas bonus equal to one month's salary or 25 days wages.

b. An Easter bonus equal to 1/2 of a month's salary or up to 15 days wages.

c. An annual leave (vacation) bonus amounting up to 1/2 of a month's salary or up to 13 days wages. An annual leave bonus is granted to those who are entitled to an annual leave i.e. after one year's employment with the same employer and it is equal to the number of working days in their leave subject to the above maximum limit of 13 days or 1/2 of a month's salary.

15. ANNUAL LEAVE

After one year's employment with the same employer a person is entitled to a paid annual leave of at least twelve (12) working days. With each additional six months of service the initial length of the leave is increased by one (1) working day up to a maximum of 26 working days. For purposes of calculation of the annual leave Saturdays are considered 'working days'.
In case the employer does not provide for an employee or worker to take his annual leave in whole or in part, the employer is obliged to pay him his normal remuneration increased by 100% for the unused days of leave as well as the annual leave bonus.

16. OTHER LEAVES

Pregnant women are entitled to a paid leave lasting 42 calendar days before the expected day of birth and they are entitled to 42 more calendar days of paid leave after the actual day of birth.
Students of Universities or Technical Colleges are entitled to a paid annual leave of absence of at least 18 days.
In order to participate in examinations they are entitled to a special unpaid leave of absence of up to six days every year.

17. SICKNESS

Sickness does not terminate an employment contract. Persons insured with the Social Insurance Organization (IKA) receive an allowance during their sickness. The employer is obliged to pay the difference between the IKA allowance and the person's normal remuneration for a period of up to one month. After the lapse of one month the employer has no obligation to make any further payments.

18. FRINGE BENEFITS

Under collective labour agreements certain fringe benefits have become compulsory. As a rule, all fringe benefits, including those voluntarily given by the employer, are added to the employee's taxable income as long as they are provided as additional remuneration in consideration for services rendered.

19. DISMISSAL OR DISCHARGE

Employment contracts of a definite duration may not be terminated before the expiry of a specified term except for 'a serious cause'. Thus, dismissal prior to the expiration of the specified terms entails payment to the employee of compensation for the remaining period of the contract.
Employment contracts of an indefinite duration may be terminated by the employer at any time provided: 1) The discharged person is given an advance notice of termination a copy of which should also be forwarded to the Labour Inspection Office and the Unemployment Office and 2) the discharged person is paid a severance indemnity. The notice and the amount of payment vary with the length of service with the present employer. In case the above conditions are not observed the termination is not valid and the person may be deemed to continue being in the service (and on the payroll) of his employer.
In the case of termination with immediate effect (instant discharge) of an employee (without observing the period of advance notice which is prescribed by the law) the employer must pay a severance indemnity from 1 to 24 month's earnings (depending on the length of service) which is exactly equal to the required respective period of advance notice of termination.
Under the same circumstances a worker should be paid a severance indemnity varying from 5 to 52 daily earnings. For the purpose of calculating severance indemnity all earnings under the person's full employment status are included in the calculation both in money and in kind (such as salary or wages, family allowances, bonuses, free meals, free housing, premiums for increased production, regular commissions etc.). All such earnings must have been received by the person in an ordinary and regular fashion during the last period of his employment and their granting should be provided for under the law, collective agreements or the employment contract.
Employers are limited to the number of employees and/or workers they may dismiss within a brief period of time. In case of collective dismissals a prior approval of the Ministry of Labour is required.

20. PROTECTION OF RESERVISTS

Employees and workers alike are protected from dismissal from the date of issue of the order by the Ministry of Defence calling them to military service until one year following their discharge from military service. Within a month from their discharge they must inform their employer of their desire to be reemployed and they must assume work then within 15 days. Should the employer wish to dismiss them before the lapse of one full year after their discharge he should pay them both their usual severance indemnity plus a special indemnity equal to six month's earnings. An employer may be relieved of the payment of the special indemnity by applying to the Special Judicial Committee at the Court of First Instance and requesting approval for dismissal of the reservist for an 'obviously justifiable cause' such as incompetence, indifference, injurious behaviour etc. A precondition requires that the employee or worker was employed for at least six months before called up for military service.

21. PROTECTION OF TRADE UNIONISTS

The President, Vice-President, Gen. Secretary, Deputy Gen. Secretary and the Treasurer of a duly established Union of employees or workers having at least 100 members are protected from dismissal. The same protection is accorded to the President and Gen. Secretary of a Union having at least 80 members which are all engaged by the same employer. The said persons may not be dismissed from the date of their election until one year following their last day in one of the above offices unless the employer obtains an approval from a Special Judicial Committee for dismissal on certain specified serious grounds, such as:

a. submission of fraudulent certificates in order to be given greater pay.
b. betrayal of trade secrets, accepting commissions from third parties against employer's interests.
c. grave insults or serious threats against the employer and/or his family.
d. refusal of service, insubordination where reasonable orders are given, habitual drunkness, endangering persons or property persons by his negligence.
e. incompetence to perform the stipulated work, failure to perform essential duties, or non-essential ones despite repeated warnings.
f. absence from work for more than 15 days (if he is an employee) or more than 10 days (if he is a worker).

22. RETIREMENT

Male employees and workers in private undertakings generally reach the retirement age at 65, while female reach it at 60. An employment contract may deviate from this rule. The granting of private pensions by employers in Greece is very seldom practiced at present.

23. SOCIAL SECURITY

Greece has an unusually large number of social security funds. These are grouped in 'main' and 'auxiliary' funds. The most important of the 'main' funds is the Social Insurance Fund (IKA). The greatest number of persons employed by private enterprises is insured with IKA. The other 'main' funds cover persons under employment contracts or self-employed. The benefits provided by 'main' and 'auxiliary' funds are: – old age or disability pensions, medical services and hospitalization, family allowances, maternity allowances, unemployment allowances etc. Efforts to consolidate the smaller funds have not yet been successful. Their total administrative costs are quite high in proportion to their revenues. Contributions to the funds vary. Contributions to IKA are calculated in percentages of salaries earned up to a monthly salary of 63.000 drachmas approximately. They vary according to the risks covered, the industry concerned, the employee's occupation etc. They are lower in the case of provincial enterprises and where the employees are also insured with certain auxiliary funds. As an approximate average, the employer's contribution is 20% and the employee's contribution is 10% of the latter's earnings. Foreign nationals for Greek employers in Greece are obliged to contribute to the social security funds. In case their employment in Greece is intended to be temporary they may apply to the respective social security funds to be granted an exemption. Employment of less than one year is considered temporary. In exceptional cases social security funds have granted exemptions of up to three years.

24. APPLICATION OF EEC SOCIAL SECURITY LAW PROVISIONS

As from January 1, 1981, when Greece became a full Member State of the European Communities, the Community's legislation concerning Social Security schemes on the application of Social Security to employed persons and their families moving within the Community is also applicable in Greece.
Such legislation is contained in the basic Regulation (EEC nr. 1408/71 re-application of Social Security schemes to employed persons and their families moving within the Community as well as Regulation (EEC) nr. 574/72 fixing the procedure for implementing Regulation (EEC) nr. 1408/71.
Competent authority in Greece for the implementation of the above is the Ministry of Social Affairs and the Social Insurance Fund (IKA).

B. Labour Procedures

TRADE UNIONS

Specific legislation covers the formation of trade unions. Various requirements must be met for a trade union to qualify as such under the law. A trade union's object is to maintain and advance the common professional interests of its members.

A trade union may enter into collective bargaining agreements and may participate in the arbitration for the settlement of collective labour disputes. Greek citizens are free to form trade unions subject to the stipulations of the law. Any attempt to obstruct the formation of a trade union or to coerce anyone in joining a trade union is punishable. The deed of incorporation of a trade union must specify what sort of work one must do or the name of the employer by whom one must be employed in order to qualify for membership. The deed of Incorporation must be approved by a judicial decision of the local Court of the First Instance for conformity with the law and filed with the Clerk of the same Court. Subsequent amendments to the deed of Incorporation, a list of the names of the officers of the trade union together with a copy of the resolution of the trade union's general assembly regarding the election of every officer to his respective office are also filed with the Clerk of the Court of the First Instance.
Trade unions may establish federations of trade unions.

STRIKE

Employees and workers have the right to strike provided a) such a strike has been declared by the trade union or federation to which they are members b) such a trade union or federation has been lawfully established and operates lawfully c) the strike aims at maintaining and advancing the economic, working or social security interests in general of those employed in one undertaking or of their specialty or professional branch which are represented by the trade union or federation going on strike. 'Abusive' strikes are prohibited. A trade union may not go on strike without giving the employer(s) or the employers organization prior notice with the purpose of giving them an opportunity to hold negotiations immediately with the aim of settling the disputes.
If a strike has been decided and put into effect contrary to the stipulations of the law all protection accorded by law to the trade union or federation officers who voted in favour of the unlawful decision is withdrawn. Participation in a strike which has not been declared by a lawfully established and operating trade union or federation brings about an automatic severance of the contractual relationship between the strikers and their employer at no cost to the employer.

COLLECTIVE BARGAINING

Competent trade Unions and federations may solve labour disputes with competent representatives of the employers by means of direct negotiations and by the signing of collective agreements. Such agreements are filed with the Ministry of Labour and subsequently published in the Government Gazette.

COMPULSORY ARBITRATION

In case direct negotiations fail to produce an agreement any interested party may request the intervention of the Ministry of Labour for the purpose of reaching a collective agreement.
The competent Ministry official invites all parties to the negotiations and participates in them as a mediator. In case these negotiations fail, the disputes are submitted to the Administrative Arbitration Court of the First Instance. An appeal against a decision of the said Court may be made before the Appellate Administrative Arbitration Court.
Both Courts are presided by a Judge whose vote prevails in case of a tie. The other members are: – one official of the Ministry of Labour; one representative of the labour organizations; and one representative of the employers organizations. An irrevocable decision of an Administrative Arbitration Court is binding upon all parties concerned upon its publication in the Government Gazette together with a decision of the Minister of Labour declaring the said Court decision 'enforceable'.
From the time a labour dispute has been referred to compulsory arbitration a strike or a slow down strike or a lock-out is not permitted for 45 days (in case of appeal: for 60 days). Strike actions in this case are deemed illegal and constitute grounds for termination of the employment contracts at the expense of the party which has infringed the law (Double severance payment if the employer is responsible, no severance payment whatsoever if the employed is responsible).

C. Works Council

Up to the present there is no legislation regarding the introduction of works councils in management. In fact, there is no evident activity in this direction.

D. Co-determination

There is no movement in this respect up to the present.

E. Compulsory Profit Sharing and Pension Schemes

Until present there is no legislation establishing any requirements for profit sharing. Private pension plans are not required under Greek law. Only a very small number of Greek companies (mostly subsidiaries of foreign multi-nationals) provide private pensions for their employees.

F. Residence and Work Permits for Aliens

As a general rule, foreigners are not freely permitted to assume employment in Greece. Residence and work permits are required for foreign nationals who are planning to work in Greece.
Residence permits are granted by the Ministry of the Interior. Work permits are issued by the Ministry of Labour.
The Greek employer must apply to the Ministry giving the specific reasons for employing a foreigner. In order to protect local employment work permits are granted in small numbers and only for specialists possessing skills which are in shortage or not available in Greece.
An exception to this practice applies to employees of foreign commercial, industrial and shipping undertakings establishing offices, branches or agencies in Greece under Law 89 of 1967 (as amended) as well as for employees of undertakings which have been granted special privileges pursuant to laws regarding the protection of imported foreign capital and laws granting incentives for establishing major productive investments. Work permits are usually valid for one year and they may be extended. The foreign personnel of an undertaking having established offices under Law 89 of 1967 may be granted work and residence permits valid up to two years. These permits may be extended.

V. BIBLIOGRAPHY

i) Taxation in Greece by Nicholas M. Mosholios.
ii) Investing in the Eastern Mediterranean, J.F. Chown and George Stathopoulos.
iii) The Taxation of Companies in Europe: Chapter on Greece: International Bureau of Fiscal Documentation.
iv) Greece Investment Guide: Hellenic Industrial Development Bank (ETBA).
v) Doing Business in Greece: Price Waterhouse.
vi) Tax and Trade Guide: Arthur Andersen and Company.
vii) Greece – Business Crossroads of Three Continents (Briefing Paper – Business International Roundtable).
viii) Investment Bank, Athens, Greece (3rd ed.) May 1981, Tax and Other Incentives Available in Greece to Foreign Investors.
ix) Tax Management Washington DC, Foreign Income Portfolios, Business Operations in Greece by G.N. Stathopoulos, Tax and Investment Consultant, Athens.

Ireland

John N. Ross
Richard Rice

I. INTRODUCTION

The term 'Ireland' is used throughout this chapter to refer to the twenty-six counties of the Republic of Ireland and does not in any way refer to Northern Ireland, which is part of the United Kingdom (UK) and for which see the chapter on that country. The name of the state is 'Ireland' in the English language, and 'Eire' in the Irish language.

Irish law is firmly based on English law and this is particularly true of company law.

The corner-stone of Irish company law is the Companies Act 1963 (the 1963 Act). Readers familiar with the British Companies Act 1948 will find many identical sections in the 1963 Act, but the two Acts are not identical: for example, in the powers to acquire compulsorily the shares of dissenting shareholders in a successful take-over bid.

In practice, English post-1922 case law is frequently quoted in the Irish Courts and, although not binding on them, is usually followed in Irish judgments. Here too there are important exceptions, but the similarities are far more numerous than the differences and anyone conversant with UK company law and practice will find himself on very familiar ground.

As in the UK, an incorporated company has its own legal personality distinct from its shareholders, but a branch of that company has no legal personality separate from the company itself. However for exchange control purposes the Central Bank of Ireland will treat an Irish branch of a non-resident company as being a quite separate entity and required to conform to the exchange control regulations in the same way as any other Irish resident (see Exchange Control page 312 below).

Although there is at present no effective exchange control in the UK, Ireland still has her own controls and since February 1979 the Irish pound (or punt) no longer maintains parity with the pound sterling. Irish exchange control legislation is very similar to that operating in the UK prior to its abolition.

It will be seen from the part of this chapter dealing with Taxation that most companies established before 1st January 1981 have complete tax exemption until 1990 on profits from the sale of exported goods manufactured in Ireland as well as from certain warehousing, service and office activities in the Shannon Free Airport Development Area. Manufacturing companies established after 1st January 1981 have the benefit of an incentive tax rate of 10% until the year 2000, and generous tax allowances are available in respect of expenditure on industrial buildings, plant and machinery.

Independent of these statutory tax concessions, there are substantial government incentives to industrialists who wish to set up manufacturing plants in

Ireland. These, for the most part, cover non-repayable cash grants towards the cost of fixed assets such as sites, site development, buildings, new machinery and equipment (other than office equipment) as well as for training workers to fit them for the new industries.

The Industrial Development Authority (the IDA) was established by the Irish government to promote industrial development in Ireland, and is the main organization dealing with such grants.

A non-resident contemplating a commercial operation in Ireland by way of branch or subsidiary company, will be influenced by a number of factors: the political factor, exchange control, and in the case of a manufacturing company the attitude of the IDA, but in many instances, and particularly in the case of a manufacturing company whose profits are taxable at the low 10% rate, the primary factor is likely to be taxation, and the ability to make the best use of the profits generated in Ireland.

II. THE LEGAL FRAMEWORK

A. The Vehicle

1. THE WHOLLY OWNED ENTERPRISE

1.a. The branch

1.a.(i) Establishment

No government licence or consent (other than Exchange Control see page 00 below) is required to establish an Irish branch of a non-resident company provided that it is not going to engage in banking, money-lending or insurance. Particular statutory restrictions apply to these activities, some of which are discriminatory against non-Irish persons, but EEC directives have to some extent relaxed these in favour of EEC nationals.

No government consent is required for the use of the non-resident company's name but, as in the UK, care must be taken that this does not resemble the name of an existing company trading in Ireland in the same goods, since such resemblance could result in an action by the existing company for 'passing off'. This is rare in practice because usually the company which establishes its branch in Ireland has already been trading in the Irish market, and will thereby have protected its trading name.

Under Part XI of the 1963 Act, a company incorporated outside Ireland which establishes a branch in Ireland must, within one month of the establishment, lodge with the Registrar of Companies:

1. a certified copy of its Charter, Statutes or Memorandum and Articles, and also a certified translation if the original is not in the English or Irish language;
2. a list of its directors and secretary;
3. the names and addresses of one or more persons resident in Ireland authorized to accept service of proceedings or notices served on the com-

pany, and the address of its principal place of business in Ireland.

Details of all changes must be lodged and, unless it is equivalent to an Irish private company (but see publication of accounts page 306 below), the company must also once in every calendar year lodge a balance sheet and profit and loss account.

Under Part X of the 1963 Act, a foreign company may in certain circumstances be wound up even though it has already been dissolved or ceases to exist under the laws of the country where it was incorporated. The winding up will be limited to the assets within the jurisdiction of the Irish courts, but foreign creditors are entitled to prove debts in such a winding up.

The Central Bank regard the branch of a non-resident company as quite separate from its head office and as resident in Ireland for exchange control purposes. The branch, therefore, will be treated as any other wholly Irish resident entity. All are subject to the same controls relating to the raising and investment of capital within Ireland and the transfer of funds from Ireland to any other monetary area including the UK (but see Exchange Control page 312 below).

1.a.(ii) Organization

Management and representation

There is no legal requirement for a branch to have any managerial structure, but as has been seen above it must appoint a representative resident in Ireland authorised to accept service of proceedings. In the case of small branches this is frequently a partner in the offices of its law firm, in larger branches it is more likely to be the branch manager.

Once a branch has commenced trading a branch manager is likely to be appointed. In the light of Irish Tax considerations and the establishment of his own authority locally the powers and authorities vested in him should be carefully defined. This should be done either by board resolutions of the 'parent' company on specific issues such as limitations on capital expenditure, opening and operating bank accounts, entering into tenancy or other agreements on behalf of the company, or on more general matters by the company entering into a Power of Attorney under seal (if it has one) in his favour.

Liability of 'parent'

A branch of a foreign company has no separate legal identity from its 'parent' and the company itself is therefore liable for all the contractual obligations of its branch and for its tortious and criminal acts.

As has been seen already a foreign company with a branch or place of business in Ireland must register under the 1963 Act and service of proceedings can be effected in Ireland on the foreign company by service on its authorised appointee. A judgment in Ireland against a foreign company can be enforced against the assets of the Irish branch.

Even if a foreign company fails to register, proceedings may still be served on it at its Irish place of business and ultimately it may be wound up under the terms of the 1963 Act liquidation procedure which will apply to the Irish assets.

Liability of management

There is a presumption in Irish law that a branch manager has powers to contract on behalf of the company to the extent that someone dealing with him might normally expect. These implied powers will vary in accordance with the size and type of business carried on by the branch. A branch manager would certainly be expected to have powers to hire and fire most staff, to purchase usual office equipment and furniture and deal with matters of day to day expenditure.

It may be that the company has restricted the branch manager more severely but provided that he acts within his *implied* authority the company will be estopped from denying that authority to contract with a third party in good faith.

If the branch manager oversteps the authority given to him by the company in such circumstances the remedy of the company lies against him, not against the third party, unless the third party knew of the limitation.

Accounts and auditing requirements

Unless the company is equivalent to an Irish private company it must produce a balance sheet and profit and loss account once in every calendar year. There is no present requirement in company law to produce branch accounts but they will be necessary for tax purposes.

There are no statutory auditing requirements for the branch as such but in practice it is clearly advisable for the company to employ Irish based auditors for its branch accounts so that the latter can work closely with their foreign counterparts to make as much use as possible of Irish tax concessions and double tax treaty provisions.

Publication of accounts

If the company is not the equivalent of an Irish private company it must lodge accounts annually with the Registrar of Companies. It is anticipated that the Fourth EEC Directive on Company Law will come into force in 1982. This will mean that the current privilege exempting private companies from lodging annual accounts will come to an end.

1.b. The Subsidiary

1.b.(i) Establishment

The meaning of 'subsidiary' is defined in Section 155 of the 1963 Act whereby one company is deemed to be the subsidiary of another, if that other company is

1. a member of it, and controls the composition of its board of directors; or
2. holds more than half in nominal value of its equity share capital; or
3. holds more than half in nominal value of its shares carrying voting rights (save in special circumstances).

There are detailed sub-sections setting out the meaning of such terms as 'control' and 'equity share capital', and rules as to nominees' shares held in a fiduciary capacity.

The Irish law and procedures for the establishment of a subsidiary are so similar to those in the UK that it would be merely repetitive to set them out in detail here. But when referring to the relevant sections of the UK Chapter (see page 557) ons should keep in mind that there are a number of differences in both law and practice: the following are the most important:

Although exchange controls are no longer operating in the UK Ireland still has significant controls (see page 312 below).

The functions and powers of the Department of Trade in the UK are in Ireland vested in the Minister for Industry Commerce and Tourism.

References in the UK Chapter to the European Communities Act 1973 should be disregarded. In Ireland under the European Communities (Companies) Regulations, 1973, which implemented the provisions of the First EEC Directive on Company Law with effect from the 1st July 1973, the obligation to publish notice of the issue of its certificate of incorporation in the Official Gazette (Iris Oifigiuil) rests with the company itself and not the Registrar of Companies, but in practice the Registrar, without accepting any responsibility, publishes the notice.

The modification of the ultra vires doctrine by the European Communities (Companies) Regulations, 1973, in favour of a person dealing with a company in good faith had been preceded by a similar, but not identical, modification contained in Section 8 (1) of the 1963 Act, which provides that 'any act or thing done by a company ... shall ... be effective in favour of any person relying on such act or thing who is not shown to have been actually aware, at the time when he so relied thereon, that such act or thing was not within the powers of the company ...'

The more stringent provisions of the British Companies Acts of 1976 and 1980 have not yet been followed in Ireland.

There is a short Irish Companies (Amendment) Act of 1977 and a bill of 1981 but both deal entirely with administrative matters.

Before incorporation consent to the use of the proposed name of the company should be sought from the Registrar of Companies. It is common practice to choose the name of the foreign parent company with the addition of 'Limited' or frequently '(Ireland) Limited'. It is not now the practice of the Registrar to allow the use of the word 'Eire' unless 'Teoranta' is substituted for 'Limited', and any other words descriptive of the company's activities are also in the Irish language. The Registrar will not approve a name considered to be too like that of an existing company without that company's consent, but there are no present restrictions on the use of such words as 'Irish', 'national', 'international', or 'trust'. Words describing banking or insurance activities may not be used unless the company complies with the appropriate provisions of the Central Bank or Insurance Acts.

The companies' file kept by the Registrar contains a copy of each company's Deed of Incorporation, its Memorandum and Articles of Association and the address of the registered office. Each company must file a register of mortgages, debentures and other charges, a list of directors, secretary and shareholders with an annual return bringing this up-to-date. A public company must also file a copy of its latest balance sheet, profit and loss account and auditors' and directors' reports. Anyone can inspect any file on payment of a small fee.

A company intending to carry on business under a trading name other than

its own name must register the trading name in a special Register of Business Names which is also kept by the Registrar of Companies.
The Registrar will register any name put before him by a company or any other person having a place of business in Ireland without enquiry as to whether the name is already registered. Registration of itself gives the person effecting the registration no proprietary rights in the name, but registration and use of a trading name already used by another person in a similar field of activity may well result in a passing off action being taken by the existing user of the name.

(ii) Organization

Again excluding the British 1976 and 1980 Companies Acts the similarities of Irish and British law are so great that it is sufficient to refer to the relevant sections in the UK Chapter with the following differences:
A private company, unlike a public company, is not at present required to file with its annual return copies of its accounts and directors' and auditors' reports. The directors' report need not contain particulars of turnover, the number of employees, the total of their remuneration, political or charitable gifts or exports.
The obligation to publish in the Official Gazette notice of the delivery to or issue by the Registrar of Companies of the documents and particulars specified in the European Communities (Companies) Regulations, 1973, rests with the company, but again in practice the Registrar publishes the notices.
The Minister for Industry Commerce and Tourism may appoint an inspector or inspectors to investigate the affairs of a company and report on them on the application of not less than 100 shareholders or of shareholders holding not less than one-tenth of the issued share capital. Otherwise, the circumstances in which the Minister may or must appoint inspectors are as in the UK.
Where the rights of one of a number of classes of shares are varied, the holders of not less than 10% of the issued shares of that class may apply to the court to have the variations cancelled.
Under Section 205 of the 1963 Act the statutory protection afforded to oppressed minority shareholders differs from that in the UK in that a shareholder may apply to the court for an order on the grounds that the affairs of the company are being conducted or that the powers of the directors are being exercised in a manner oppressive to him or any of the shareholders or in disregard of his or any of the shareholders' interests as shareholders.

1.c. Other forms

In practice foreign investment in Ireland takes no other form. Partnership is impracticable not only because of its unlimited liability but also because the valuable tax reliefs for manufacturing are only available to companies.

(iii) Checklist for Establishing a Subsidiary

Procedure or Documentary Requirement	Time Required	Cost involved in IR £
1. Apply to Registrar of Companies to use desired name: have alternative(s) in case first choice not available.	Two to three weeks from application.	
2. Apply to Central Bank of Ireland (Exchange Control) for consent to invest foreign funds by way of share capital or loans and for future repatriation of capital and profits.	One to four weeks from application depending on complexity of financial structure.	
3. Apply to Department of Labour for permit to employ non-EEC nationals.	One to three weeks from application (procedures 1, 2 and 3 should be followed as soon as a decision has been taken to establish the subsidiary and as early as possible in the planning stages).	
4. Lodge with Registrar for approval draft Memorandum and Articles of Association signed by two subscribers for a private company or seven for a public company together with: (i) Statutory Declaration of Solicitor forming the company. (ii) Statement of authorised share capital.	Six to eight weeks from lodgment (to be followed as soon as practicable after procedures 1, 2 and 3 have been cleared).	Registration fee on lodging documents £ 80.50 including £ 1 capital duty on two subscribers shares, £ 4 on filing forms and 50 pence for counterpart.

Procedure or Documentary Requirement	Time Required	Cost involved in IR £
5. Hold first meeting of Board of Directors.	The meeting should be held as soon as possible after receiving certificate of incorporation from the Register.	
	Returns should be filed with the Registrar:	Registration fee on £ 1 per return.
(i) Note appointment and file Return of Directors and Secretary with Registrar.	(i) Appointment of Directors and Secretary within 14 days of appointment.	Failure to lodge a return within the requisite time makes the company and every officer of the company in default liable to a fine not exceeding £ 100.
(ii) Establish registered office and file Return of its situation with Registrar.	(ii) Notice of Situation of Registered Office within 14 days of the incorporation of the company.	
(iii) Approve transfers of subscribers' shares and issue of share capital. File Return of Allotments and Capital Duty Statement with Registrar.	(iii) Return of Allotments and Capital Duty. Statement within one month of allotment.	Capital Duty is payable ad valorem at 1% of the issued share capital. Failure to lodge a Capital Duty Statement within the month will incur interest on the duty at the rate of £ 1.25 per cent per month.
(iv) Adopt the Company's Seal.		
(v) Appoint auditors.		
(vi) Appoint bankers.		
6. Apply to register the company with:		
(i) Customs & Excise for V.A.T.	(i) As soon as it can be seen that taxable turnover is likely to be reached.	
(ii) Revenue Commissioners for P.A.Y.E. in respect of employees salaries.	(ii) On or before the engagement of first employees.	

2. THE JOINT VENTURE

2.a The jointly owned company

Quite often foreign investors want to involve an Irish partner in their new enterprise or to take a substantial interest in an existing Irish company. Less frequently, two or more foreign investors may co-operate in the formation of an Irish company.

In all cases unless the operation is contrary to the Mergers and Takeovers and Monopolies (Control) Act 1978 (see page 313) such a company will be established in the same way as the subsidiary described above, but normally with the following shareholders' checks and balances:

(i) Shareholders' agreements

It would be most unusual for the investors in a joint company not to set out their respective interests and liabilities in a comprehensive agreement. This will cover in particular such points as: the extent and limitations of the proposed activity, its location, the capital and working capital needed, the investment, (initial and progressive) committed by each shareholder and the manner and proportions in which it is to be made, the composition of the Board and who shall be Chairman, the representation required for board and shareholders meetings, the pre-emptive rights of shareholders and the manner of calculating the value of shares which may pass from one joint owner to another, and finally the circumstances in and terms on which the joint venture may be terminated.

In practice many of these points will be covered in the company's Articles of Association particularly the appointment and number of directors, quorums, and the sale and value of shares.

By these means a minority shareholder may obtain very substantial negative controls over the operation of the joint company.

(ii) Minority rights

Quite apart from such rights as he may negotiate under a shareholders' agreement, the minority shareholder has the statutory rights of Section 205 of the 1963 Act referred to at page 308 under Subsidiary (ii) Organisation.

2.b Consortia

The same basic principles apply to the setting up of a consortium as to a joint venture: the shareholders' agreement and the Articles of Association will be more complicated, but otherwise there will be very little difference. It is highly advisable for all the parties however minor to be separately represented in the negotiations.

2.c. **Other**

None.

B. External Controls

1. EXCHANGE CONTROLS

The Exchange Control authority is the Central Bank of Ireland, and application must be made to it to permit any investment from outside Ireland whether by way of shares in or loans to a subsidiary company, or by direct investment in the assets of a branch to be established in Ireland. The general policy of the Central Bank is to expect branches or subsidiaries of companies resident out the EEC to obtain their fixed asset financing by way of equity or loan capital raised from outside Ireland in foreign currencies. Consent is freely given to raise working capital in Irish pounds.

Branches or subsidiaries of EEC controlled companies will however be allowed to raise their entire financial requirements in Ireland provided they are not for the purpose of portfolio investment.

Exchange Control consent should be sought prior to the making of the investment in Ireland, and is freely given for the following:

a. the making of investment by way of shares and loans from non-Irish sources;

b. the payment of dividends on shares and interest on loans at reasonable commercial rates in currencies other than Irish pounds;

c. the repatriation of proceeds of sale of such shares, including all profit, and the repayment of the principal of the loans;

d. the payment of a reasonable amount in respect of royalties, management fees and technical services, including marketing services.

The Central Bank does not at present require that provision must be made for tax or other liabilities before consents for such payments on repatriation are granted.

Exchange Control consent is also necessary where a subsidiary company wishes to invest its accumulated profits outside Ireland. This consent is freely given where it can be shown to the Central Bank that such an investment will be made in another EEC country or in a non-EEC country on production of an auditor's certificate that the investment is being made out of undistributed profits.

Initial applications are usually made on behalf of the company by its professional advisers, but current payments for items such as the purchase of raw materials or for services are normally dealt with by the company's bankers to whom the Central Bank delegates authority.

As already indicated, the policy of the Central Bank for Exchange Control purposes is to treat an Irish branch of a non-resident company as if it were a separate entity from its foreign base, and earnings from the Irish branch activities must be lodged to an account of the branch in Ireland. Remission of profits outside Ireland by a branch or subsidiary requires Central Bank consent. In both cases this is easily got on production of an auditor's certificate that such profits are available.

In practice, there may be greater foreign currency flexibility for a branch than for a subsidiary. The former merely has to remit certified profits to its external head office; the latter must declare and pay a dividend or remit in some other approved way, which may take longer.

Under the Exchange Control regulations remittances to Ireland in currencies other than Irish pounds must generally be converted into Irish pounds on receipt in Ireland. It frequently happens that a company making raw material purchases abroad and receiving remittances on sales from abroad finds itself at a disadvantage if it has to convert receipts to Irish pounds and then buy back the same foreign currency to pay for raw materials. Only the bank benefits from the commission on two exchanges, while its customer may run a devaluation risk. In such circumstances the Central Bank will normally give consent for trading or 'hold' accounts to be opened and maintained in specified foreign currencies.

Balances on such accounts must normally be cleared and converted into Irish pounds at the end of each month except for payments known to be due in the following month. In exceptional cases the Central Bank may agree to an extended holding period, but it is important to negotiate this at the time of establishing the account.

2. TAKE-OVER CONTROLS

The Mergers, Take-overs and Monopolies (Control) Act 1978 applies to a proposed merger or takeover if in the most recent financial year the value of the gross assets of each of the two or more enterprises involved is not less than IR £ 1.25 million or the turnover of each is not less than IR £ 2.5 million. As soon as an offer capable of acceptance is made each of the enterprises involved in a proposed merger or takeover must notify the Minister for Industry Commerce and Tourism. The Minister can then decide either not to make an order or to refer the proposal for investigation to the Examiner for Restrictive Practices. If the case is referred to the Examiner the latter will report back to the Minister with recommendations. The Minister, whose criterion is 'the exigencies of the common good', will after consultation with any other minister concerned, then make an order either prohibiting the proposal or allowing the merger or takeover on the conditions specified in the order. Orders must be confirmed by the Oireachtas (Parliament) within twenty-one days.

The Act also defines a monopoly as existing when an enterprise or enterprises under common control supply or provide not less than half of the goods or services of a particular kind in a particular year, but specifically excludes enterprises which export 90% of their output. The Act does not apply to a monopoly if in its most recent financial year the sales or purchases of the relevant goods or services did not exceed IR £ 1.5 million. The Minister also has power to have an apparent monopoly enquired into by a Commission and after getting its report may in the interests of the common good prohibit the monopoly save on conditions or require it to be divided. The affected company has a right of appeal to the High Court.

It will be seen therefore that it is most important for a foreign enterprise wanting to establish itself by way of takeover or merger to first clear the position with the Department of Industry Commerce and Tourism. This department has a special section for this purpose and will normally be able to process swiftly matters referred to it for clearance.
There is one other restriction on a take-over of an Irish public company. The Irish Stock Exchange is part of the British Stock Exchange so that in practice an intending purchaser of an Irish public company must also comply with the British City Code on Take-over and Mergers (see page 574).

3. ANTI TRUST

A Restrictive Practices Commission was established in 1972 to prepare and publish rules covering fair practice conditions for the supply and distribution of goods and services. This Commission is empowered to examine a number of specified unfair practices. These practices include any measures, rules or agreements put into effect (or intended) by a person alone or through merger, trust, control, monopoly or other means which in any way 'operate against the common good or are not in accordance with the principles of social practice'.
Schedule III to the Restrictive Practices Act 1972 sets out a long list of the offending actions. These include the unreasonable limitation of free and fair competition, the unreasonable restraint of trade, the unjust enhancement of prices, the unjust prohibition or restriction of supplies of goods or services, the imposition of unjust or unreasonable conditions for such supplies and the exclusion without good reason of new entrants to a trade or business.
The Commission has powers to enquire into all such matters and to summon and examine witnesses on oath: it reports to the Minister of Industry Commerce and Tourism recommending whether he should make an order prohibiting specified restrictive practices. The Minister may then by order prohibit the relevant practice or such part of it as he thinks fit.

4. ENVIRONMENTAL CONTROLS

There is comprehensive legislation in the Local Government (Planning and Development) Acts of 1963 and 1976 and the Regulations of 1977 which provides for control of town and country development. Development is effectively defined in the first Act as 'the carrying out of any works on, in, or under land or the making of any material change in the use of any structures or other land'.
Any such development requires the prior approval of the local planning authority. This will be the County or Town Council of the place where the proposed development is intended.
There are two categories of planning permission: full permission which is complete in itself, and outline permission which is consent in principle to the development subject to compliance with specific conditions laid down by the local planning authority. The formal approval of the planning authority is not lightly given, and applications should be prepared carefully and fully.

Every planning authority has divided its local area into zones allocated to different purposes: residential, agricultural, commercial, light and heavy industrial etc. and all authorities are concerned with environmental control with particular emphasis on such matters as the preservation of amenities, scenic beauty, and the purity of rivers. Proper treatment of effluent and the curbing of noise and vibration in public places are therefore matters to which great attention must be paid.

Subject to this however there are many areas in which prospective industrialists will find all their needs well catered for, and in any case the local authorities will give every reasonable help and encouragement to employment prospects in their area.

Once Planning Approval has been given it is open to any aggrieved person to appeal: the applicant company may do so if the conditions attached are too stringent, or local residents or bodies if they consider the approval has been given without due consideration. An applicant has one month from the decision being communicated to him in which to appeal, but a third party must appeal within 21 days from the date of the decision. The appeal is made to an independent planning board (An Bord Pleanala) whose decision is final.

A planning permission must be acted upon within five years of being granted or it will lapse automatically.

5. STATE MONOPOLIES

There are a number of State and semi-state bodies which have a monopoly of certain public services. Public Transport is very largely monopolised by the State, Aer Lingus controlling the Irish end of international air routes and Coras Iompair Eireann (C.I.E.) the rail and bus systems. The B & I, a government owned shipping line without legal monopoly status, competes for passenger and freight traffic to the UK. Postal services, telephones, wireless and television are all controlled by independent semi state boards. Electricity is produced and sold by the Electricity Supply Board (E.S.B.), a semi-state company, but gas is still supplied by independent gas companies in various cities and towns. There is no state monopoly of other forms of fuel such as petrol, oil or coal, although peat is produced and marketed by Bord na Mona (the Turf Board) in such substantial quantities as to have effective control of that particular market.

III. TAXATION

A. Corporation Tax

1. ENTITIES SUBJECT TO TAX

Bodies corporate, private and public, limited and unlimited, are liable to corporation tax. Throughout the remainder of this chapter the word 'company' will be used to describe entities so liable. The principal statute is the Corporation Tax Act, 1976.

Subject to special exemptions, all the profits and gains of a company which is resident in Ireland are chargeable to corporation tax. A company is regarded as resident for Irish tax purposes in the country in which its affairs are controlled, and this normally will be the place where meetings of directors are habitually held and policy (as opposed to day-to-day management) decisions are taken. Non-resident companies trading in Ireland through a branch or agency are liable to corporation tax on all the income of that branch or agency unless they benefit from one of the exemptions discussed below. Non-resident companies are also liable to corporation tax in respect of capital gains arising on the disposal of assets used for the purposes of a trade carried on through a branch or agency in Ireland. Non-resident companies are chargeable to Irish income tax at a rate of 35% on income arising in Ireland which is not chargeable to corporation tax.

The position as above stated with regard to non-resident companies may be affected by the provisions of the Double Taxation Agreements which Ireland has negotiated with other countries. These Agreements are referred to in I below.

2. COMPUTATION OF PROFITS

2.a. Income

In general, the income of a company for the purposes of corporation tax is calculated in the same way as that of an individual under income tax law.

Corporation tax is charged by reference to tax accounting periods, the first of which begins when the company comes within the charge to corporation tax. The tax accounting period corresponds (with a few exceptions) to the company's financial period of account. However, a tax accounting period cannot exceed twelve months in duration, and if the company's period of account exceeds twelve months an apportionment must be made.

Income of different types is charged to tax under separate statutory heads called Schedules and Cases. A company's total chargeable profits are established by aggregating the amounts computed under the different Schedules and Cases and the amount of the capital gains (reduced as explained in (b) below). This total is reduced by losses (see below), charges on income (for example royalties or annuities), management expenses (in the case of an investment holding company) and group relief (under which one member of a group may 'surrender' trading losses to another).

Trading losses of a company may be relieved against the company's income of any description of either the accounting period in which the losses are incurred or the twelve months preceding that accounting period. Trading losses may also be carried forward indefinitely against profits of succeeding accounting periods of the trade in which they are incurred. Allowable capital losses may be relieved but only against chargeable capital profits of the same or a succeeding accounting period.

Any relief for trading losses available to a company may be 'surrendered' to another company where both are Irish resident and both are members of the same group (i.e. one is a 75% subsidiary of the other or both are 75% subsidiaries of a third company). Trading losses may also be surrendered by an Irish resident 90% subsidiary of a consortium to the Irish resident consortium members in proportion to their interests. In determining whether one company is a subsidiary of another for group or consortium relief purposes, regard is had to the beneficial ownership, direct or indirect, of the ordinary share capital.

Trading income is calculated for corporation tax purposes largely by reference to accepted accountancy principles. Profits shown in the accounts of a company are adjusted to exclude deductions not allowed for tax purposes and to reflect special tax reliefs. Deductions from trading income are permitted for revenue expenses wholly and exclusively expended for the purposes of the trade. Dividends and other distributions of a company's profits are not deductible.

Amounts provided by way of depreciation of fixed assets are added back but extensive tax depreciation, called 'capital allowances', is given. Capital allowances are part of the Irish industrial incentives scheme, and they are described more fully in F.1(a) below.

While interest on money borrowed wholly and exclusively for the purposes of the trade is deductible, other interest in excess of £ 2,400 will generally not be deductible. However, it should be noted that loan interest paid by an Irish resident subsidiary to a foreign parent company owning 75% or more of the shares in the Irish subsidiary will be treated as a distribution and therefore will not be deductible.

Up to 1980, there was no significant anti-avoidance provision in Irish taxation law governing pricing in transactions between associates. The Finance Act, 1980, which introduced a new system (discussed below) whereby certain manufacturing companies enjoy a 10% rate of corporation tax, contains a number of comprehensive provisions to prevent abuse of the new system by the use of artificial prices. Under the Act, tax liabilities must be computed on the basis of substituting arm's length prices where prices are not at arm's length.

2.b. Capital gains/losses

The Capital Gains Tax Act, 1975, introduced capital gains tax on disposals occurring on or after 6 April, 1974. Companies were chargeable to capital gains until 5 April, 1976. In respect of disposals on or after 6 April, 1976, companies are liable to corporation tax on capital gains calculated in accordance with the rules contained in the Capital Gains Tax Act 1975. 66.67% of the gains so calculated is included in arriving at a company's total income so that the gains are charged at an effective rate of 30%. The treatment of allowable losses has been described above.

3. RATES OF TAX

The full rate of corporation tax is 45% and this rate is chargeable unless a company qualifies for a specific exception provided for in tax legislation.

Where the profits of a company do not exceed IR £ 25,000, the rate of corporation tax is 35%. Where the profits exceed IR £ 25,000 but do not exceed IR £ 35,000, the rate will vary between 35% and 45%.
Public utility companies and certain special companies are subject to a rate of corporation tax of 30%.
From 1 January, 1980, certain qualifying manufacturing companies enjoy a rate of corporation tax of 10%. (See F.1.(d) below).
Capital gains liable to corporation tax are charged at an effective rate of 30%.

4. TAX CREDITS

Irish resident companies no longer deduct income tax from dividends. In the case of a dividend or other distribution made on or after 6th April, 1976, part of the corporation tax on the profits underlying the dividend or distribution is imputed to the shareholder by way of a tax credit of an amount specified in the legislation in force from time to time. The present amount is 30/70 of the dividend or distribution. The tax credit in respect of dividends or distributions made out of profits of qualifying manufacturing companies chargeable at the 10% rate is equal to 1/18 of the dividend or distribution.
An Irish resident company receiving a dividend or distribution from another Irish resident company will not be chargeable to corporation tax on that dividend or distribution.
A person who is not resident in Ireland will not be entitled to repayment of the tax credit unless this is provided for by a Double Taxation Agreement (and at the time of writing the only Agreement to contain such a provision is Ireland's Agreement with the United Kingdom); such a person will be chargeable to income tax on the actual amount of the distribution, but his liability will be reduced by an amount equal to income tax at the standard rate (which for this purpose is 30%) on the amount of the distribution.

5. TIMING OF PAYMENTS

Corporation tax is payable in two equal instalments. Usually, the first instalment is payable nine months after the end of the accounting period in respect of which the tax is payable, and the second instalment is paid twelve months after the end of accounting period. Penalty interest is charged for late payment and such interest is not deductible for tax purposes.

6. REVIEW AND APPEAL

Returns of income must be made when required by an Inspector of Taxes or authorised officer. Every company commencing to trade in Ireland must notify the Inspector to that effect within 30 days. A company which has not filed a return in respect of an accounting period within a year of the end of that accounting period must so notify the Inspector.
Assessments to corporation tax are made by an Inspector of Taxes. Non-resi-

dent companies may be assessed in the name of any agent, manager or representative. In the absence of satisfactory information, estimated assessments may be made.

Any company aggrieved by an assessment may appeal within 30 days, specifying the grounds for appeal. Unless a settlement is reached with the Inspector, the appeal is heard by the Appeal Commissioners. Decisions of the Appeal Commissioners may be appealed by the taxpayer to the Circuit Court where a complete rehearing of the questions of fact and law will take place. Decisions of the Circuit Court Judge as to questions of fact are conclusive, but decisions on questions of law by the Appeal Commissioners or the Circuit Court may be appealed to the High Court by either the taxpayer or the Inspector. Decisions of the High Court may be appealed to the Supreme Court.

B. Withholding Taxes on Dividends, Interest, Royalties

1. INCOME CATEGORIES SUBJECT TO WITHHOLDING TAX

Dividends paid by a company resident in Ireland are not generally subject to any withholding tax, even where the recipient of the dividends is resident abroad.

In the case of annual interest payable by a company, the company must deduct income tax except where the interest is payable in Ireland by a bank carrying on a banking business in Ireland or is payable by such a bank in the ordinary course of its business or in certain other circumstances, for example, where the company has been authorised to pay the interest without deduction of tax.

Where annual interest is payable by any person (whether a company or an individual) to a person who is resident outside Ireland, income tax must be deducted.

Short interest (as distinct from annual interest) may always be paid without deduction of tax.

Tax must be withheld from payment of patent royalties, mineral royalties, annuities and certain other 'annual payments'. Copyright royalties and licence fees for the use of trademarks, designs and 'know-how' may be paid without deduction of tax.

Where rent in respect of premises within Ireland is payable to a person resident abroad, income tax must be deducted.

The principal example of tax withholding is the Pay As You Earn (PAYE) System under which employers deduct tax from the income payable to their employees.

2. COMPUTATION OF INCOME

In the case of most categories of income (excluding income from an Irish employment) payable subject to withholding tax, the payer computes the amount of tax by reference to the gross amount of the sum payable, withholds that amount of tax and pays the net sum to the person entitled. In the case of income from an Irish employment, the tax to be withheld is computed by reference to the net amount of the income after deduction of the appropriate allowances and reliefs.

3. RATES

The standard rate of income tax, at present 35%, is the rate at which tax must generally be withheld, although this is not so in the case of employment income (in which case the appropriate different rates of tax are applied) or where a Double Taxation Agreement has modified the usual rule.

4. EFFECT OF DOUBLE TAXATION AGREEMENTS

With certain exceptions (for which see J. below), the Double Taxation Agreements concluded by Ireland provide that interest and royalties (other than mineral royalties) payable by an Irish resident to a resident of the relevant other country are exempt from Irish tax. In such cases, the Irish resident should obtain the approval of the Revenue Commissioners before paying the interest or royalty without deduction of tax.

In accordance with usual principles, the Double Taxation Agreements do not relieve foreign residents from liability to Irish tax on Irish rents and mineral royalties, so that the obligation to deduct tax from such payments when made to non-residents is not affected.

C. Registration and Stamp Duties

The registration fees payable in connection with the incorporation of a company limited by shares amount to IR £ 80.50 and there is a stamp duty (known as capital duty) charged at the rate of 1% on the net value of the assets subscribed for shares in the company. Capital duty is also payable on the same basis whenever the issued share capital of a limited company is increased.

As mentioned in A.1. of Part II, a company incorporated outside Ireland which establishes a branch in Ireland is obliged to file certain documents with the Registrar of Companies. The registration fees charged in this case amount to IR £ 3.00.

A variety of legal documents are chargeable with stamp duties. Some duties, such as the 3p duty payable on cheques, are of fixed amount. The amount of other duties is related to the value of the transaction, e.g. transfer of Irish registered stocks and shares (except Government securities which are exempt) are chargeable at 1% of their value, and transfers of other dutiable property (such as land and buildings, goodwill and book debts) are chargeable at progressive rates according to their value, the highest rate being 6% in the case of property with a value in excess of IR £ 50,000. In the case of leases of land or buildings, any premium payable will be chargeable with stamp duty on the same basis as on the transfer of land or buildings, and a duty will also be payable by reference to the amount of the annual rent, the rate of duty varying from 1% where the term of the lease does not exceed 35 years to 12% where the term exceeds 100 years.

D. Individual Taxation

1. PERSONS SUBJECT TO TAX

1.a. Income

An individual resident and domiciled in Ireland is generally chargeable to income tax on his worldwide income.

Where an individual is resident in Ireland but not domiciled there (or is a citizen of Ireland but not ordinarily resident there), he will be chargeable to income tax on all his Irish and United Kingdom income but only on so much of his other foreign income as he remits to Ireland. This rule, known as the 'remittance basis', may be of considerable value to a foreign national taking up employment in Ireland without intending to live there permanently; further, the remittance basis will apply not only to his unearned foreign income, such as dividends and interest, but also to earned foreign income which could include income paid to him outside Ireland in respect of services provided under an employment contract entered into outside Ireland with a foreign employer, even if the services are to be performed in Ireland. Such a person may reduce his Irish income tax liability by limiting the amount of his foreign income which he remits to Ireland, and, if he has capital moneys available to him abroad (which would not upon remittance be chargeable to income tax but might in certain circumstances be chargeable to capital gains tax), it may be advantageous for him to remit to Ireland capital rather than income.

An individual who is not resident in Ireland is chargeable to income tax only on his income arising in Ireland.

The above general statements are subject to the provisions of any applicable Double Taxation Agreement.

Briefly an individual will be treated as resident in Ireland for Irish tax purposes in any tax year if he spends an aggregate of 183 days in Ireland in that year, if he has been habitually (e.g. in each of four consecutive years) visiting Ireland for substantial periods (e.g. three months), if he or his wife has a place of abode in Ireland available for his use and visits Ireland at any time in the tax year, or if he enters Ireland during the tax year with the intention of establishing residence there. There are special rules in the case of a United Kingdom resident.

b. Capital gains

An individual who is resident or ordinarily resident in Ireland is in general chargeable to capital gains tax on all gains accruing to him on the disposal of assets, wherever the assets are situated.

However, if such an individual is not domiciled in Ireland, only so much of the gains accruing on the disposal of assets situated outside of Ireland and the United Kingdom as he remits to Ireland will be chargeable.
A person who is neither resident nor ordinarily resident in Ireland is in general chargeable only on gains arising on the disposal of interests in Irish land, buildings or minerals, hydrocarbon exploration or exploitation rights in the Irish Continental Shelf, or assets in Ireland used by him for the purposes of a trade carried on by him in Ireland through a branch or agency.
A gift constitutes a disposal by the donor, but in case of an inheritance there is no disposal by the deceased and the beneficiary is deemed to have acquired the inheritance at its market value at the date of death of the deceased.

2. COMPUTATION OF INCOME

a. Income

For the purpose of calculating the total taxable income of an individual, the amount of each category of his income is computed according to the rules applicable to that category, and from the aggregate of those amounts there are deducted the personal allowances and reliefs to which the individual is entitled, the balance being his total taxable income. His tax liability will be the amount (less any tax credits) resulting from the application of the appropriate tax rates to his total taxable income.
Different rules apply to the computation of the different categories of income. In the case of trading or professional income, the income of the accounting period ended in the preceding tax year will generally be the basis of the computation for the current tax year, and the rules of computation as to allowable deductions and other such matters will be similar to those applicable to the computation of the trading income of a company for the purposes of corporation tax.
Income from an Irish employment is generally computed on the basis of the actual income for the current tax year. Benefits-in-kind, such as the provision by the employer without charge of accommodation or a motor car, are taxable. Expenses incurred by the employee are allowed as deductions only in limited circumstances.
Interest, rent and royalties (wherever arising) and foreign income are, if not subject to deduction of Irish income tax, normally taxed on the basis of the income of the preceding year.
Interest, rent, royalties and foreign income (where these are payable subject to deduction of Irish income tax) are usually taxed on the basis of the current year's income. Irish dividends are also taxed on a current year basis.
In the case of computation for tax purposes of the amount of passive or non-trading income, the general rule is that expenses are not deductible, although in the case of income from letting premises such items as head rents, repairs and insurance will be allowed.

2.b. Capital gains

The basic method of computing the taxable capital gain on any disposal is to subtract from the amount of the sale price of the asset the aggregate of its

original acquisition cost, the cost of permanent improvements carried out and the expenses of purchase and sale.
However, only the gains accruing from 6th April, 1974, are taxable, and accordingly when the asset was acquired before that date the original acquisition cost is taken to be the market value of the asset on 6th April, 1974.
For the purpose of avoiding the taxation of gains which merely reflect inflation, the acquisition and improvement costs are increased by reference to the increase in the Consumer Price Index between the time they were incurred and the time of disposal.
Capital losses in any year may be set off against the capital gains in that year, and any excess of losses may be set off against gains of future years.

3. RATES OF TAX

3.a. Income Tax

The rates of income tax are as follows: –

Part of taxable income	*Rate of tax*
First IR £ 1,000	25%
Next IR £ 4,500	35%
Next IR £ 2,000	45%
Next IR £ 2,000	55%
Remainder	60%

A married couple are entitled to be jointly taxed in which case each of the amounts of income in the above Table will be doubled.

3.b. Capital gains tax

The normal rate of capital gains tax is 30%. However, an individual (but not a company) resident or ordinarily resident in Ireland is taxable at progressively lower rates depending on the length of the period for which he has held the asset. The rates vary from 25.5% where he has owned the asset for 3 years to nil where the period of ownership is more than 21 years. These reduced rates will not be available if the asset disposed of is Irish development land or minerals, hydrocarbon exploration or exploitation rights in the Irish Continental Shelf, or shares in an unquoted company the greater part of the assets of which is constituted by such assets.

4. EXEMPTIONS, DEDUCTIONS AND REBATES

4.a. Income Tax

The principal personal allowance or deductions are: Single person or each spouse IR £ 1,115, married couple IR £ 2,230, dependent child IR £ 195 and PAYE employee an additional IR £ 600. There are also reliefs in respect of (inter alia) life insurance and medical insurance premiums, certain health expenses and contributions towards certain retirement annuities.

The general rule is that an individual resident outside of Ireland will not be entitled to any of the foregoing allowances or reliefs, unless he is an Irish citizen or a British subject.
While there is no limit on the allowability of interest incurred for trade or business (including property rental) purposes, only the first IR £ 2,400 (IR £ 4,800 for a married couple) of interest incurred for other purposes is allowed, unless the money borrowed is used for special purposes such as acquiring in certain circumstances shares in a trading or business company of which the individual is a member of the management or a share in a partnership in which he is actively involved.

4.b. Capital gains tax

The first IR £ 500 (IR £ 1,000 in the case of a married couple) of net gains in any year is exempt from tax. Any gain on the disposal of an individual's principal private residence (including up to one acre of land) is exempt, as are gains on the disposal of specified government securities, chattels sold for no more than IR £ 2,000, and wasting assets (tangible moveable assets with an expected life of less than 50 years). Gains on transfers between spouses are not chargeable, but the spouse acquiring the asset is deemed to acquire it at the original cost.
A gain on the disposal by an individual on retirement to his child of a business, farm or shares in a family company will in certain circumstances not be chargeable if the consideration or value does not exceed IR £ 150,000, nor will a gain by such an individual on the disposal outside his immediate family of such assets if the consideration does not exceed IR £ 50,000. The tax on any gain arising on the transfer by an individual of his business to a company may be deferred until a disposal by the company takes place.

5. INHERITANCE AND GIFT TAX

Capital acquisitions tax is a tax on gifts and inheritances, and the recipient is accountable for the tax. If the donor or deceased is domiciled in Ireland or the proper law of the disposition is Irish, the entire property comprised in the gift or inheritance is taxable; otherwise only the property situated in Ireland is taxable.
The tax is charged at progressive rates applied on a successive slice system to the cumulative total of the gifts and inheritances between the parties, with four different scales of rates, the applicable rate being determined by the relationship between the parties. For example, inheritances between a husband and wife or from parent to child aggregating no more than IR £ 150,000 will not give rise to any tax, but above that level the rate of tax on successive slices rises from 25% to 50% in respect of any excess over IR £ 400,000. In the case of an inheritance between persons not having a close family connection, the rates of tax on successive slices above IR £ 10,000 rise from 20% to 60% in respect of any excess over IR £ 98,000. The rates of tax applicable to a gift are three-quarters of the rates applicable to an inheritance of the same amount.
A special relief is given in the case of agricultural property, whereby if the

donor or deceased is a farmer the value of the property is for tax purposes reduced by IR £ 150,000 unless the property is sold within six years and not replaced by other agricultural property.

E. Indirect Taxation

Value added tax is chargeable, with certain exceptions, on the supply of all goods and services within Ireland in the source of a business and on goods imported into Ireland.

There are three rates of tax: zero %, which applies to (inter alia) goods exported, services supplied outside Ireland, clothing and most foodstuffs; 15%, which applies to (inter alia) building materials, road vehicles, television sets, most secondhand goods (including imported antiques), books and newspapers, and most services; and 25%, which applies to all goods and services not exempt or taxable at any other rate.

Exempted activities include banking, insurance, medical, legal and accountancy services, and the services of employees. Building work and sales in the course of business of land developed since 31st October, 1972, are taxable at an effective rate of 3%.

Every two months every person accountable for the tax must make a return to the Revenue Commissioners of the tax charged by him on the goods and services supplied by him and the tax paid by him on the goods and services supplied to him, and must remit the amount of any excess of the former over the latter (the amount of any excess of the latter over the former will be refunded to him). The difference between a zero-rated activity and an exempt activity is that in the case of a zero-rated activity, but not in an exempt activity, credit is granted for any tax paid on inputs.

The excise duties mentioned in H below are the only other form of indirect tax in Ireland.

F. Incentives

1. TAX INCENTIVES

1.a. Investment in buildings, machinery and equipment

The original purpose of the scheme of tax allowances called 'capital allowances' was to recognise for tax purposes the depreciation of buildings, machinery and equipment due to wear and tear from use in a trade. In due course, as industrial development emerged as a national priority, capital allowances became an important part of the general scheme of incentives. Capital allowances are available for both companies and individuals. The system is described here with reference to companies but substantially the same rules apply to individuals.

Buildings

Industrial buildings, hotels, holiday camps, holiday cottages, agricultural and market garden buildings all qualify for initial and annual allowances for taxation purposes. An 'industrial building' is defined as a building or structure in use for the purposes of a trade carried on in a mill, factory or other similar premises.

Industrial buildings allowances are available to persons (individuals or companies) who incur expenditure in providing or improving industrial buildings rather than the persons who actually carry on trades in them. In respect of capital expenditure on industrial buildings incurred in the period to 15th January, 1975, the initial allowance was 20% and the balance of expenditure was written off by way of an annual allowance of 2% on a straight line basis. Expenditure incurred on or after 16th January, 1975, is eligible for an initial allowance of 50% and an annual allowance of 4% for the balance on a straight line basis. Since 1 February, 1978, a first year write-off of 100% is available to those who incur qualifying expenditure and who occupy the buildings for the purposes of a trade. Where a new building changes hands before it is used, the allowance is granted to the person who invests in it with the intention of putting it to industrial use, and where the eligible person is a second or subsequent owner the allowance is based on the lesser of the amount which he paid for the building and the amount invested by the first owner.

Market garden buildings and certain agricultural buildings qualify for an initial allowance of 20% and an annual allowance of 10% on a straight line basis. Hotels, holiday camps and holiday cottages constructed after February 1978 qualify for a first year allowance of 100% in the case of claimants occupying them for trade purposes. Otherwise they qualify for a writing down allowance on a straight line basis at the annual rate of 10%.

State grants towards the cost of qualifying buildings are deducted in arriving at the amount on which allowances are granted.

The consequences for tax purposes of disposing of or ceasing to use qualifying buildings are similar to those in relation to machinery and equipment discussed below.

In 1981, special incentive capital allowances were introduced in respect of construction expenditure incurred in the provision of moderate-cost rented residential accommodation, multi-storey car parks for use by the general public, and certain toll roads, bridges etc.

Machinery and equipment

The cost of new machinery and equipment (with the exception of road vehicles) may be written off in full against the profits of the tax accounting period in which the expenditure is incurred or the machinery and equipment is put into use for the purpose of a trade. A 100% write-off is given in the case of machinery and equipment which when purchased is new, unused and not secondhand, and which is purchased for use in a trade or profession, or for leasing to others.

Machinery and equipment is widely interpreted and includes heating and electrical fittings, boilers, special acoustical or suspended ceilings and other

items normally regarded as parts of buildings.
There are two methods of obtaining the 100% write off:

(i) If the 'wear and tear' or annual allowance is claimed, the claimant may specify the amount of expenditure claimed up to 100% subject to having to take a minimum annual allowance in respect of each asset of between 10% and 25% depending on the estimated useful life of the asset. Notwithstanding the compulsory minimum, this allowance is commonly referred to as 'free depreciation'.

(ii) An 'initial allowance' of 100% is available in the year in which expenditure is incurred even if the asset is not put into use in that year.

In the case of road vehicles (for which the annual allowance is 20%), second-hand or used assets and new assets in respect of which a 100% allowance is not claimed, the annual allowances (varying from 10% to 25% depending on estimated useful life) are given annually on a reducing balance basis.
The allowance claimed in respect of an asset cannot exceed the cost of that asset. When an industrial building, machinery or equipment is sold or ceases to be used, any deficiency or excess in the capital allowances already granted, after account is taken of the proceeds of sale, insurance etc., is adjusted by means of a balancing allowance or balancing charge. However, no balancing charge or balancing allowance will apply after twenty five years in the case of an industrial building nor after ten years in the case of a hotel, holiday camp or holiday cottage.
State grants to assist in the purchase of machinery and equipment are not deducted in arriving at the amount on which the tax allowances are calculated.

1.b. Export sales relief

Ireland's best known tax incentive, no longer available to new applicants, has been the special relief available to a company in respect of profits derived from the export by it of goods manufactured in Ireland by it or its 90% parent, 90% subsidiary or 90% sister company, or manufactured by another company and exported by the claimant as wholesaler. The relief is available only to companies or partnerships involving companies, but a company does not need to be incorporated or resident in Ireland in order to qualify. A foreign company trading in Ireland through a branch qualifies.
Export sales relief is no longer available to new claimants after 31 December, 1980. However, companies already entitled to the relief at that date may complete their periods of relief.

The relief provides a 100% reduction of the corporation tax attributable to the qualifying export activity for a period of 15 years and a withdrawal period of five years during which the tax charge gradually increases to the full rate. However, no relief is available after 5th April, 1990.
Relief from Irish income tax is extended to the shareholders of companies which qualify for export sales relief. Dividends paid out of wholly relieved profits are free of Irish income tax in the hands of shareholders, while dividends paid out of partially relieved profits (where there is a mixture of export and other income or where a company is in the withdrawal period) are relieved of Irish income tax to the same extent as the profits from which the dividends

are paid are relieved from corporation tax. An Irish resident company which receives a dividend from another Irish resident company which has benefited from export sales relief is not chargeable to corporation tax in respect of that dividend whether it is paid from a fund which has suffered corporation tax in full measure or a fund which has not been charged to corporation tax because of export sales relief.

From 1 January, 1981, a new scheme of corporation tax at a rate of 10% operates for manufacturing companies whether exporting or not. A company claiming export sales relief may elect to change to the new scheme if it is thought beneficial to do so. This election once made cannot be reversed.

1.c. Shannon exemption

A company, whether incorporated in Ireland or not, carrying on within the customs-free area of Shannon Airport trading operations which were certified by the Minister for Finance before 1 January, 1981, to be 'exempted trading operations' is entitled to complete exemption from corporation tax on its income from those operations up to 5th April, 1990.

Exempted operations consist of: –

(i) the sale for export by a company carrying on all or part of its business within Shannon Airport of goods which it either produces or processes within the Airport or packages or handles within the Airport after they have been imported into Ireland;

(ii) other trading operations deemed by the Minister for Finance to contribute to the use or development of the Airport, and trading operations which are ancilliary to the trading operations designated above; and

(iii) the repair or maintenance of aircraft within the Airport or outside of Ireland or the rendering within the Airport or outside of Ireland of services involving the use of air transportation.

The exemption from Irish taxation with respect to a company's profits from exempted trading operations extends also to dividends paid by it out of such profits.

The new manufacturing relief applies to manufacturing operations in Shannon Airport but, as mentioned in (d) below, it may also apply to certain non-manufacturing operations carried on there.

1.d. Manufacturing relief

As a result of pressure from Ireland's partners in the EEC, the Irish government introduced provisions in the Finance Act, 1980, to terminate the system of export sales relief and the Shannon exemption described above. The same Act contains the main Irish tax incentive or 'relief' for the period 1981 to 2000 in the form of a reduced burden of corporation tax at an effective rate of 10% for certain manufacturing companies. The relief is in the form of a reduction of corporation tax chargeable in respect of income from the sale of goods manufactured in Ireland. There is no requirement that the goods should be exported.

The relief is available to companies only, but a claimant company need not be incorporated in Ireland or resident in Ireland for tax purposes. Accordingly, a non-resident company trading in Ireland through a branch may qualify for the relief.

The basic requirement for qualification is that the claimant company derives income from the sale of goods manufactured by it in Ireland. The relief is also extended to a company which sells goods manufactured by a company with which it has a 90% relationship. A 90% relationship exists where either the seller or the manufacturer beneficially owns 90% of the ordinary share capital of the other or where a third company beneficially owns 90% of the ordinary share capital of both the seller and the manufacturer.

A company which carries on a trade consisting of or including the rendering to another person of services by way of subjecting commodities or materials belonging to that person to any process of manufacturing will also qualify for the relief.

The production of fish on an Irish fish farm, the cultivation of mushrooms in Ireland, the repair of ships in Ireland, and the rendering in Ireland of design and planning services in connection with chemical, civil, electrical or mechanical works executed outside the EEC are deemed to be the manufacture in Ireland of goods.

The relief applies to the manufacture of goods within Shannon Airport, but it is extended to the repair or maintenance of aircraft within the Airport, operations within the Airport which contribute to the use or development of the Airport (service industries may qualify under this category) and operations within the Airport which are ancilliary to any of the foregoing.

For the purpose of avoiding abuse of the relief, the legislation provides that where a company benefitting from the relief buys from or sells to a company which is under common control with it and the prices charged are not arm's length prices, the income and losses of buyer and seller must be computed by reference to prices which would have been charged had the parties been dealing at arm's length.

Goods which qualify for the relief are referred to in the legislation as 'goods' and goods which do not so qualify are referred to as 'merchandise'. Where a company's sales include both 'goods' and 'merchandise', the income from the sale of 'goods' is deemed to be that amount which bears to the income from the sale of both goods and merchandise the same proportion as that which the sales turnover in respect of 'goods' bears to the sales turnover in respect of both goods and merchandise. This method of calculating the relief may sometimes make it advantageous to have separate companies for selling 'goods' and 'merchandise' where the overall profit contribution of 'merchandise' is lower than that of 'goods'.

Profits which have been taxed at the special 10% rate and which have not been distributed by way of dividend or otherwise constitute a special fund for tax purposes which is referred to in the legislation as the 'primary fund'. Dividends or other distributions from this fund carry a tax credit of 1/18 of such dividend or distribution (contrasting with the tax credit of 30/70 attaching to dividends and other distributions out of profits which have suffered corporation tax at the full rate). Where a company has profits which have been taxed at the special 10% rate (i.e. a primary fund) and also profits which have been taxed or relieved from tax on any other basis, dividends or other distributions

paid or made by the company will be deemed to be paid first out of the primary fund.
The normal rule whereby an Irish resident company is not chargeable to corporation tax in respect of dividends or other distributions received by it from another Irish resident company applies to distributions out of profits taxed at the special 10% rate, but such distributions will constitute or form part of a primary fund of the recipient company.

1.e. Taxed-based financing

Interest received by lending institutions in the normal way is taxable at the standard 45% rate of corporation tax. However, Irish resident corporate lenders are not subject to corporation tax in respect of distributions received from Irish resident companies. For several years it has been an attractive method of financing companies which are exempt or virtually exempt from tax to structure their loans in such a manner that the interest is treated as a dividend or distribution.
Since the lending institutions are not taxed on distributions, they are in a position to offer such financing at comparatively low cost. The fact that the 'distributions' made to the lending institutions are not deductible for tax purposes will not concern the borrowing companies in view of the Irish tax-exempt status.
The leasing of machinery and equipment by lending and other institutions has become an important feature of financing in Ireland. The scheme of capital allowances described in F.1.(a) above is of little or no value to a company which has a low or nil burden of taxation. However, if a lending or other institution subject to tax at the normal rate purchases machinery and equipment and leases it to such a company, it will be entitled to the capital allowances and thereby reduce its tax liability for the year of purchase by 45% of the cost. The lessor may also obtain government grants (see F.2.(a) below) in respect of the machinery and equipment and the availability of such grants will not diminish the amount of the capital allowances. In view of the tax and grant advantages, the lessor will be in a position to lease the machinery and equipment to the lessee at a favourable rent.

1.f. Scientific research

Expenditure of a capital or non-capital nature incurred by a company or an individual on scientific research may be written off in one year against the profits of a trade carried on by that company or individual whether or not the scientific research relates to the trade.

1.g. Exemption on patent royalties

A person, including a company, resident in Ireland and not also resident elsewhere, is entitled to exemption from Irish tax on any royalty or other sum paid for the user of an invention to which a 'qualifying patent' relates. A 'qualifying patent' is, in general, a patent of an invention developed in Ireland.

2. FINANCIAL INCENTIVES

2.a. Capital grants

The Industrial Development Authority which is the statutory organisation responsible for promoting industrial investment in Ireland, offers a wide range of financial incentives to the promoters of manufacturing and service industries in Ireland.

The principal incentive in this category is cash grants towards the cost of fixed assets, including sites and site development, buildings and new machinery and equipment. In the case of medium-sized and small projects, the maximum level of the grant available in the undeveloped areas (generally speaking, the western half of the country) is 60% of the cost of the fixed assets and 45% in the rest of the country. In the case of larger capital intensive projects, the grants are related to the location and the number of employees. A grant will become repayable only in the event of serious breach of the terms of the grant, ceasing to trade or liquidation within ten years after payment of the grant.

Reference has already been made in F.1.(e) above to the fact that, for tax reasons, it may be more economic for a company to lease rather than to purchase its machinery and equipment. The lessor may obtain a grant from the IDA in respect of the machinery and equipment, and since the IDA requires the benefit of the grant to be passed on to the lessee, the rental terms will become even more attractive.

Udaras na Gaeltachta (the Gaeltacht Authority), a statutory body charged with the promotion of development in the Irish-speaking areas, offers attractive incentives, including generous capital grants, to industries establishing in those areas.

The IDA has recently introduced a major new scheme designed to encourage service industry project. Under the scheme, employment grants of up to IR £ 5,000 per job created, training grants (see below) and capital grants of up to 50% of costs of fixed assets are available to promoters of suitable projects.

2.b. Training grants

The IDA also provides training grants of up to 100% of the cost of training programmes for workers in new industries. The grants extend to the cost of sending workers abroad for training, the remuneration and expenses of training personnel, management training expenses and the cost of hiring training consultants. AnCo (the Industrial Training Authority) operates training centres in a number of locations throughout the country.

2.c. Industrial estates and advance factories

The IDA owns many serviced industrial sites throughout Ireland which are available for sale to new industries approved by the IDA. It builds advance factories on these industrial estates for new industry so that accommodation for new industry is readily available. This standard factory space may be purchased or rented, with the benefit of subsidy by the IDA.

2.d. Other IDA incentives

The IDA has a special programme to encourage the development of small industrial projects (i.e. employing less than 50 persons and with assets of less than IR £ 400,000). Re-equipment grants to encourage the modernisation and expansion of existing industries are provided up to a maximum of 35% of fixed assets in the undeveloped areas and 25% elsewhere. The IDA also subsidises the cost of in-house research and development.
Other assistance available from the IDA includes the guarantee of loans, subsidisation of interest payable on loans and the provision of finance by means of participation by the IDA in the share capital of the company being promoted.

2.e. Shannon industrial estate

The purpose of Shannon Free Airport Development Company Limited ('SFADCO') is to encourage the development of manufacturing and service industries in the Shannon Industrial Estate (near Shannon Airport in the south-west of Ireland) and adjoining areas. SFADCO offers incentives similar to those of the IDA.
The exemption from taxation available to companies established in the Shannon Airport area has been referred to above.
Since this area is customs-free, goods of all kinds can be imported into and exported from the area without payment of any customs duties.

2.f. Other financial incentives

There are many other forms of incentive available. For example, Coras Tractala (the Irish Export Board) makes grants towards the cost of export marketing, market research, consultancy and export advertising campaigns.
Under an employment incentive scheme, employers in a wide range of industries may become entitled to tax-free premiums if they increase the numbers of their employees above certain levels.
Grants and loans are available from the European Agricultural Guidance and Guarantee Fund (FEOGA) and the European Investment Bank respectively.

G. Social Security Premiums

With few exceptions, all employees must be insured under the Pay-Related Social Insurance scheme administered by the State. Contributions towards the scheme are calculated as a percentage of the employee's earnings (not in excess of IR £ 7,000), and are shared between the employer and employee. The total contributions, as a percentage of earnings, vary from 14.3% to 1%, and the employer's share is generally greater than that of the employee, whose share is collected in the same way as his PAYE tax. The benefits provided under the scheme include Unemployment Benefit, Disability Benefit, Contributory Old Age Pension and Contributory Widow's Pension.

H. *Other Taxes*

1. LOCAL TAXES

Local taxes (known as 'rates') are imposed by local authorities on owners or occupiers of land and buildings other than residential property. Rates are generally not burdensome and are deductible for tax purposes in the case of trading profits and rental income.

2. CUSTOMS AND EXCISE DUTIES

As a member of the EEC, Ireland has progressively reduced its import/export duties on its trade with other EEC members in manufactured goods, so that there is now, with few exceptions, free trade between Ireland and the other member countries in such goods. Ireland is also a party to the General Agreement on Tariffs and Trade.

Excise duties are levied on certain goods produced or manufactured in Ireland. The rates of the duties vary as between different commodities, which include spirits, beer, oils, tobacco and motor cars.

I. *Double Taxation Agreements*

Ireland has entered into Double Taxation Agreements (all of which have been ratified) with the following countries:

Austria	(24 May 1966)	Luxembourg	(14 Jan. 1972)
Belgium	(24 June 1970)	Netherlands	(11 Feb. 1969)
Canada	(23 Nov. 1966)	Norway	(21 Oct. 1969)
Cyprus	(24 Sept. 1968)	Pakistan	(13 Apl. 1973)
Denmark	(4 Feb. 1964)	Sweden	(6 Nov. 1959)
Finland	(21 Apl. 1969)	Switzerland	(8 Nov. 1966)
France	(21 Mar. 1968)	United Kingdom	(2 June 1976)
Germany (FR)	(17 Oct. 1962)	United States	(13 Sept. 1949)
Italy	(11 June 1971)	Zambia	(29 Mar. 1971)
Japan	(18 Jan. 1974)		

Note: dates of signature are shown in parentheses.

All of the above Agreements relate to Irish income tax and Irish corporation tax on income. The Agreement with the United Kingdom also relates to taxation of capital gains, and is the only Agreement that recognises the extension for tax purposes of Irish territory so as to include the Irish Continental Shelf and its natural resources. A later agreement with the United Kingdom deals with gift and inheritance taxes. An agreement relating to taxation of profits from air and sea transport has been concluded with South Africa.

1. GENERAL

All of the Agreements are in accord with the general principles of the OECD draft model taxation convention.

2. IRISH BUSINESS PROFITS

The general rule in Ireland's Double Taxation Agreement is that profits of a trade or business carried on in Ireland by a resident of another country are taxable only in that country unless the trade or business is carried on through a permanent establishment in Ireland. If the trade or business is carried on through a permanent establishment in Ireland, only the profits attributable to the permanent establishment may be taxed in Ireland. A permanent establishment usually means a branch, factory, office, place of management or other fixed place of business.

In all of the Agreements the country of residence either exempts the profits arising to the permanent establishment in Ireland or grants a credit for the Irish tax payable. If the Irish tax on the profits of a permanent establishment is reduced by incentive tax reliefs, the effect of the Agreement and/or the domestic law of the country of residence is, with certain exceptions (the principal of which are Austria, Canada, Italy, the United Kingdom and the United States), to provide exemption in that country or alternatively credit ('matching credit') for the Irish tax that would have been payable had the incentive relief not been available. Where it is proposed to establish an Irish branch to which the manufacturing relief will apply, any such exemption or matching credit provisions should be checked so as to ascertain whether they operate in the case of the manufacturing relief.

3. DIVIDENDS FROM IRISH RESIDENT SUBSIDIARIES

Save in exceptional circumstances, dividends paid by an Irish resident company are not subject to any Irish withholding tax, and a foreign resident corporate shareholder is in practice exempt from further Irish tax on those dividends. However, a foreign shareholder (other than a United Kingdom portfolio investor) is not entitled to recover the tax credits attaching to the dividends. Since all of the Irish Double Taxation Agreements except that with the United Kingdom were entered into prior to the introduction in Ireland of the imputation system of corporation tax, the question of recovery by the foreign shareholder of Irish tax credits did not then arise.

In the case of dividends paid by an Irish resident subsidiary to a parent company resident in a country with which Ireland has a Double Taxation Agreement, the tax treatment in that country of the dividends will depend on whether and to what extent the domestic law and/or the relevant Agreement provide for exemption of the dividends or credit for the underlying Irish corporation tax. Where the dividends have been paid out of profits wholly or partially relieved under any of the Irish tax incentives, it will be important, where credit rather than exemption is the method of relief applied in the

parent company's country of residence, to ascertain whether the relevant Double Taxation Agreement grants credit for the underlying Irish corporation tax that would, but for the tax incentive, have been payable on the subsidiary's profits.
Where the parent company of the Irish subsidiary is resident in one of the countries with which Ireland has a Double Taxation Agreement, full or partial relief in respect of the Irish corporation tax underlying the dividends paid by the subsidiary to its parent will be available in each country by way of exemption or credit under the relevant Agreement and/or the domestic law.
In cases where the Irish subsidiary is relieved from Irish tax by virtue of the export sales relief or the Shannon exemption, dividends paid by the subsidiary to a parent company resident in all of the countries with which Ireland has an Agreement, except the United Kingdom and the United States, are wholly or partially relieved from tax in the hands of the parent company by virtue of exemption or matching credit granted by the relevant Agreement and/or the domestic law.
If it is proposed to establish an Irish subsidiary which will be entitled to the manufacturing relief, the exemption or matching credit provisions of the relevant Agreement and the domestic law of the country of residence of the parent company should be examined so as to ascertain whether they will apply to dividends paid by the subsidiary.

4. IRISH DIVIDENDS, INTEREST AND ROYALTIES

a. Dividends

A dividend paid by an Irish resident company to a foreign resident individual shareholder is not subject to any withholding tax. However, in the absence of a provision to the contrary in a Double Taxation Agreement, that shareholder is, strictly speaking, chargeable to Irish income tax in respect of the dividend; since he is entitled to a notional tax credit equal in normal circumstances (i.e. where tax incentive relief is not enjoyed by the Irish company) to 30% of the dividend, little or no income tax at the standard rate of 35% may be payable, but if the amount of the dividend or his other Irish income is substantial, income tax at the higher rates may strictly speaking be payable; however, such income tax is in practice not collected nor sought to be collected.
A foreign individual shareholder will not be entitled to recover the Irish tax credit attaching to the dividend, unless this is authorised by any relevant Double Taxation Agreement, nor will he be granted in his country of residence a credit for the Irish tax underlying the dividend unless this is sanctioned by the relevant Agreement and/or the domestic law. Only the United Kingdom Agreement provides for recovery of any of the Irish tax credit which under present law amounts in normal circumstances to 30/70ths of the dividend;
in this case, the Irish Revenue Commissioners retain 15% of the aggregate amount of the dividend and tax credit, and the balance (usually equal to approximately half of the tax credit) is payable to the shareholder who will receive credit for the 15% retained against his United Kingdom tax liability.

In the case of certain other countries, the effect of the relevant Double Taxation Agreement and/or domestic law, while not permitting recovery of the tax credit, is to grant full or partial credit for the Irish tax underlying the dividend against the individual shareholder's tax liability in his country of residence. In the remaining cases revision of the relevant Agreements is required in order that the consequences for foreign shareholders of the adoption by Ireland of the imputation system of corporate taxation be taken into account.

Where the dividend is paid out of profits relieved from Irish tax under the export sales relief or the Shannon exemption, full or partial matching credit (by virtue of the relevant Double Taxation Agreement and/or domestic law) for the underlying Irish tax spared is available where the shareholder is resident in such countries as Denmark, France and Switzerland. If such matching credit is available, it should not be assumed without prior enquiry that it will also be available in cases where the 10% manufacturing relief is applicable to the profits of the Irish company.

b. Interest and royalties

In the absence of a Double Taxation Agreement, interest, patent and copyright royalties and payments made for the use of trademarks, designs and 'know-how' are subject to Irish tax if they arise in Ireland, and, if they are payable to persons resident outside of Ireland, income tax at the standard rate of 30% must be withheld.

Where the recipient is resident in a country with which Ireland has a Double Taxation Agreement, the general rule is that the payment will be exempt from Irish tax. The Table in J below sets out the rates of Irish withholding tax in the case of payments of dividends, interest and patent royalties to residents of certain other countries.

Rents from Irish premises and Irish mineral royalties payable to foreign residents remain subject to Irish tax even where there is a Double Taxation Agreement, and income tax at the rate of 35% must be withheld.

Where there is a withholding tax in the case of any of the payments mentioned above, credit for that tax in the recipient's country of residence is granted under all the Double Taxation Agreements.

J. Schedule of Withholding Taxes

The following Table sets out the rates of Irish withholding tax in respect of dividends, interest and patent royalties payable to residents of the countries listed.

Recipient resident in:	*Dividends*[1]	*Interest*[2]	*Patent Royalties*[2]
Belgium	Nil	15%	Nil
Canada	Nil	35%	35%
Denmark	Nil	Nil	Nil
France	Nil	Nil	Nil
Germany (F.R.)	Nil	Nil	Nil
Greece	Nil	35%	35%
Italy	Nil	10%	Nil
Japan	Nil	10%	10%
Luxembourg	Nil	Nil	Nil
Netherlands	Nil	Nil	Nil
Switzerland	Nil	Nil	Nil
United Kingdom	Nil	Nil	Nil
United States	Nil	Nil[3]	Nil[3]

Note 1. While there is no withholding of tax from dividends except in special circumstances, the tax credit is not recoverable by the recipient unless he is resident in the United Kingdom in which case partial recovery is permitted.

Note 2*a*. If the recipient has a permanent establishment in Ireland with which the source of the payment is connected, or if a special relationship exists between the Irish payer and the recipient, the nil or reduced rate of withholding may not be permitted.

b. Even where the payment is, by virtue of a Double Taxation Agreement, exempt from or subject to a reduced rate of Irish tax, the payer should obtain the approval of the Revenue Commissioners before paying without deduction at the standard rate.

Note 3. If the recipient is not subject to U.S. tax or is engaged in business in Ireland (or, in the case of interest, if the recipient owns more than 50% of the voting power of the payer) the normal rate of withholding will apply.

IV. LABOUR ASPECTS

A. *Principles of law on employment*

The mid 1970's saw the enactment of a number of statutes which together form the basis of Irish employment law. Apart from the statutes outlined below there were such other Acts as the Holidays (Employees) Act 1973, the Anti-Discrimination (Pay) Act 1974 and the Protection of Young Persons (Employment) Act 1977. Their titles alone give an indication of the rapid evolution of employment law.

Under the Minimum Notice and Terms of Employment Act 1973 an employee (which excludes civil servants, members of the defence forces and the police) is entitled to have the terms of his employment set out in writing and to be given a period of notice of termination varying from one to eight weeks depending on length of service.

The Unfair Dismissals Act 1977 extended the employee's security: provided he has had not less than one year's continuous service with the employer any dismissal, whether with or without notice, is considered unfair unless the employer can show substantial grounds to justify it and the employee may be reinstated or compensated with up to two years' pay. No distinction is made between executives and other employees. There are certain exceptions: for example a period of probation or training, or a contract for a specified purpose or for a fixed term without renewal and expiring by effluxion of time.

If the employee is dismissed because of pregnancy or trade union activities or membership, the one year's qualifying period will not apply and the rights under the 1977 Act will accrue from the commencement of employment.

An employee is also entitled on being given notice to know the reasons for his dismissal and the dismissal procedures operating within the undertaking.

The Protection of Employment Act 1977 provides for consultation in the case of threatened group redundancies.

B. Labour Procedures

There are a number of workers' organisations and, although there are a few medium to large-sized employers who do not have unionised staff, by far the greater number of employers do negotiate with their employees through the latter's unions.

Collective bargaining will therefore start as a voluntary discussion between management and union representatives. If agreement is not reached the parties may appear before a Rights Commissioner who may make recommendations. If these are not acceptable appeal may be made to the Labour Court.

Neither the recommendations of the Commissioner nor of the Labour Court are legally enforceable yet the arrangement is frequently effective and a very high percentage of the Court's decisions is accepted and implemented by both sides.

Very often procedures in the Labour Court start by one of its officers acting as a conciliator and it is estimated that 60% of the cases brought before the Court are settled in this way.

Since 1970 employers and trade unions have negotiated (seven) National Wage Agreements, but 1979 saw a new initiative called 'the National Understanding for Economic and Social Development'.

Here for the first time the government took a hand as a third party in the negotiations. As its name suggests its scope is very wide and includes taxation, employment, education, health services, social welfare benefits as well as wages. It allowed for greater pro rata increases for the lower paid, but also gave broad guide-lines for all employees.

It seems to have worked which supports the view that in spite of inflation the end of the seventies saw a substantial diminution of the wide industrial unrest of the sixties. Certainly there was a significant reduction in the number of man days lost, but inflation made it necessary to re-negotiate the wages provision. At the end of 1980 the National Understanding was renewed but any increase in the rate of inflation may make it unrealistic to keep to the provisions relating to wages.

C. Works Councils

Ireland lags behind Western Europe in the development of 'industrial democracy'. There is no legislation referring to Works Councils; where they exist they are very few and are practically unknown in the private sector.
In the public sector there is worker representation in a number of semi-state companies. The Workers Participation (State Enterprises) Act 1977 provides for the settling aside of one-third of the seats on the boards of seven such companies. Nominations for election may only be made by bodies recognised for collective bargaining in the undertaking.
Most of the companies concerned have already held their elections, but it is too early yet to see how the experiment will work or whether it will be followed in the private sector.

D. Compulsory profit sharing and Pension Schemes

Compulsory profit sharing is unknown in Ireland: nor is there any active encouragement by way of tax concessions for voluntary profit sharing schemes which are rare.
With very few exceptions and regardless of earnings every employee over the age of 16 must be covered by a pay related social insurance scheme operated by the State. The cost of contributions to the scheme are shared between employer and employee. Among the benefits provided by the scheme are retirement pensions at age 65.
Apart from the State pensions most commercial or industrial firms have their own private pension schemes. Until comparatively recently these were restricted to executive and white collar personnel, but now such schemes frequently extend to workers on the shop floor. These are both contributory and non contributory but modern practice is moving towards non contributory schemes. The schemes have considerable tax benefits for both employer and employee who get tax rebates on their contributions.
Any new enterprise of any size establishing itself in Ireland should include a private pension scheme in its employment package.

E. Residence/Work Permits for Non-nationals

Nationals of EEC member states may take up residence and work in Ireland without either a residence or work permit.
Residence permits: Nationals of British Commonwealth and former Commonwealth countries do not require a residence permit.
After three months' residence, all other nationals (except those from other EEC member states) must apply for a permit from the Department of Justice, in Dublin application is made through the Aliens Office in Dublin Castle, and in the rest of the country through the local Superintendent of Police. Permits

are issued for one year or the duration of their work permit.

Work permits: Application from non EEC nationals must also be made for work permits from the Department of Labour, preferably before the employment is to be taken up. Nationals of Commonwealth and former Commonwealth countries do not require work permits but do need employment certificates which are issued by the Department of Justice. Permits are not usually given for employment for which an Irish national is available, but no problem normally arises in connection with management personnel or other key workers from abroad with special skills or knowledge.

V. BIBLIOGRAPHY

Guides to European Taxation, Vols I and II, International Bureau of Fiscal Documentation.

Irish Income Tax and Corporation Tax, Kelly and Carmichael, 11th Edition (1980) HFL (Publishers) Limited.

The Taxation of Capital Gains, Appleby and Roche (1980), The Institute of Taxation in Ireland.

Income Tax, McAteer and Reddin (1981), The Institute of Taxation in Ireland.

Principles of Corporation Tax in the Republic of Ireland, A. Graham Williams (1981), The Incorporated Law Society of Ireland.

Italy

Giovanni M. Ughi
Michael C. Kirkham
Giovanni P. Sacchetti

I. INTRODUCTION

Italian law does not in general make any distinction between nationals and foreigners in the field of private law. Thus, if a foreign company incorporated in accordance with its national law is considered in its own country as being a legal entity, distinct from its shareholders, it is also recognized as such in Italy and its shareholders are therefore not responsible for its liabilities in excess of its subscribed capital. Foreign companies can also transact business in Italy, provided they comply with the same legal requirements as laid down for Italian companies.

However, if a foreign company, having its registered office located in a foreign country, has its principal establishment in Italy or if its main business is carried on in Italy, then it must also meet certain requirements of Italian law in order for it to be recognized in this country as a validly existing entity, just as if it had been originally incorporated in Italy. It must be entered in the Registry of Companies and its deed of incorporation and statutes must also be filed with the Registry. Furthermore, it should be mentioned that all companies organized abroad in forms unknown to Italian law are regarded as companies limited by shares (*società per azioni*) as far as the registration requirements in the Registry of Companies and the liability of their directors are concerned.

Quite often, however, companies wish to operate in a foreign country through a local organization of their own, rather than from abroad. In this connection they have first to decide whether they want to operate through a local wholly-owned enterprise or through some form of joint venture. They must then decide the legal vehicle for their operations whether it be a branch of the foreign company or a company with liability limited to its subscribed capital or a partnership with unlimited liability, or a consortium. Such a decision is also affected by legal and tax considerations. Thus a foreign company intending to establish an organization in Italy must consider certain aspects of the business law of this country.

The company law of Italy is almost exclusively contained in the Civil Code of 1942 as amended by legislation in 1974 and 1977. An extensive reform of company law has been studied and debated over the past two decades. In fact the Italian Government produced in 1965 a draft bill, prepared by a group of legal experts, providing for a pervasive reform of limited companies (SPAs and SRLs), which then, as a result of an opinion given by the National Council for Economy and Labour, was submitted to Parliament in 1967 in an amended form. This bill lapsed because of the dissolution of that Parliament. Only in 1972 another bill was submitted to Parliament which was substantially different and less extensive in scope. This bill also lapsed as a consequence of the dissolution of Parliament. In 1973 a new bill was submitted based on the 1967 bill, although with changes of some relevance and a more limited scope. Finally, in 1974 the Government issued an urgent executive order, subject to approval by act of Parliament within a short deadline, with the principal aim of establishing the Companies and Stock Exchange National Commission (CONSOB) and also providing for the regulation of dealings in securities. The resulting Act of 1974 constitutes a limited reform of the law governing companies, principally SPAs, including many of the provisions of the 1973 bill and largely aimed at those SPAs having shares quoted on the stock exchange. However, certain provisions, such as those laying down the required elements of the profit and loss statements, are directed to all limited companies.

The 1977 Act, mostly dealing with taxation matters, simply provided for updated minimum capital requirements.

One problem which the reform did not solve is that of the plurality of Registries of Companies. Although the advantages of establishing one single Registry of Business Enterprises for the whole country have often been stressed, no such provision has ever been enacted and to-day there is one Registry of Companies attached to each district court (*tribunale*). Companies and partnerships must therefore register with the court having territorial jurisdiction. The existence of so many registries often causes complications.

As far as tax law is concerned, a thorough reform has been adopted by fairly recent legislation. By the Tax Reform Act of 1971 the Italian Parliament gave authority to the Government to enact by delegated orders (*decreti delegati*) a thoroughly reformed tax system along broad lines which were specifically set out in the Act; this constituted a drastic change in respect of the system previously in force.

By virtue of such delegation, in 1972 Registration Tax was partially reformed. In the same year Value Added Tax was introduced by a separate act to replace the *Imposta Generale sull' Entrata* (IGE), the turnover tax previously in existence, and a new tax on Increases in Value of Real Property (INVIM) was enacted. These taxes all came into effect on 1st January 1973.

It was however with regard to income taxes that the most thorough and complete reform was introduced. A set of nine separate orders containing a quite complete and systematic new regulation of income taxes was enacted on 29th September 1973 and came into effect on 1st January 1974.

The most important of these orders regulate separately the taxation of the income of individuals and legal entities (respectively IRPEF and IRPEG), the so-called local income tax (ILOR), assessment and collection of taxes in general, and tax exemptions. Since then many small amendments have been enacted. The new resulting tax system will be outlined in this Chapter on Italy based on the very few decisions made since it became effective.

Essential details on the development of labour legislation are given in the appropriate section.

II. THE LEGAL FRAMEWORK

A. The Vehicle

1. THE WHOLLY-OWNED ENTERPRISE

As stated above, foreigners are in general treated by Italian law in the same way as Italian nationals. Thus, generally speaking, no prior governmental permit, license or approval is required for the incorporation of a company in Italy by foreigners, whether it be a subsidiary or not. Such incorporation, in fact, is treated exactly the same as that of a company which is to have only Italian shareholders. The same applies to the setting up of a branch of a foreign company. Governmental approval is however required if the foreign company's organization in Italy is to engage in certain activities specifically regulated by law such as transport, aviation and navigation, insurance, banking, hydro-carbon research or exploration, activities in the nuclear field and certain other activities to which special regulations apply because they are in the public interest. It should be noted that, normally speaking, similar restrictions also apply to Italian enterprises which operate in the same fields.

1.a. THE BRANCH

1.a.(i) Setting-up

The legal requirements which a foreign company must comply with to establish a branch in Italy (defined by the Civil Code as a *sede secondaria con rappresentanza stabile*, which in effect means a place of business having power to bind the foreign company in carrying on trade on a permanent basis) are simpler, in principle, than those for the incorporation of a subsidiary company, whether it be a *Società per Azioni* (SPA) or a *Società a Responsabilità Limitata* (SRL). They only consist in the filing of certain deeds and data with the appropriate registries. The establishment of a branch and its operation, however, are not dependent on compliance with any requirement of substantive law.
A branch exists, de facto, when a foreign company regularly transacts business in Italy through a local organization of its own. However, the establishment of a branch without complying with the requirements relating to notice by publication referred to below means that, in accordance with art. 2508 of the Civil Code, all persons acting on behalf of the foreign company are jointly and severally liable, without limitation, for the obligations undertaken through them by such a company in Italy.
To formally establish a local branch of a foreign company and to avoid the liability described above, the documents set out below must be filed within thirty days of the foreign company's resolution establishing the branch with the Registry of Companies of the court (*tribunale*) of the district where the branch is to be set up:

1. The deed of incorporation and the statutes of the foreign company together with the resolution establishing the branch and a certificate of existence and good-standing of the company in question; these documents having been notarized and legalized by the Italian Consulate or in accordance with The Hague Convention of 1961 and translated into Italian.
2. Specimen signatures of the persons having authority to permanently represent the branch in Italy.

Such documents have also to be filed within fifteen days with the local Chamber of Commerce. In the event of non-observance of the latter requirement a modest fine may be imposed.
Following the filing of these documents, the Registry of Companies and the Chamber of Commerce issue appropriate certificates evidencing of the establishment of the branch. It should be noted, however, that the Registry of Companies does not subject the documents filed to any evaluation of their substance and registration cannot be refused on the grounds that the foreign company does not comply with the provisions of Italian law relating to companies.

1.a.(ii) Organization

– *Management and representation*
The filing of the names of persons having authority to permanently represent the foreign company in Italy for the purposes of the branch completes the process of the establishment of the branch as a fixed place of business of the foreign company with power to bind the same in trading matters. The resolution which appoints the manager or managers must also specify the powers that they are granted which may be wide or limited depending upon the needs of the case. Any replacement of the manager or managers or alteration in their powers must be effected by an appropriate resolution of the parent company which again must be filed with the Registry of Companies and the Chamber of Commerce. The same applies to other changes such as that of the address of the branch.

– *Liabilities*
A foreign company is fully liable for all debts and other obligations undertaken by its branch, and its directors, together with the local management of the branch, are responsible for the latter's non-compliance with the various requirements of Italian law. The rationale of this is that, save for the specific purposes mentioned below, the foreign company and its local branch are one single legal entity. Thus, from an economic and legal standpoint, the losses and profits of a branch (office, factory or other facility, as the case may be) are treated as losses and profits of the foreign company and as such are included in the latter's balance sheet. However, for exchange control purposes the branch is considered as a legal entity distinct from the company to which it belongs and the same is the case in respect of tax.

– *Accounts and auditing requirements and publication thereof*
In the light of the fact that for tax purposes branches of foreign companies are considered as being distinct from their parent companies, they are re-

quired to keep separate books and to prepare annual accounts which constitute the basis for local taxation. Such accounts must be filed not only with the tax authorities but also with the Registry of Companies. There are not, however, any requirements as to the auditing or certification of these accounts and no further publication is needed. In addition, the annual accounts of the foreign company must, at least in theory, be filed with the Registry of Companies. It is apparent that the latter accounts must comply, in respect of auditing and the like, with the requirements imposed upon the foreign company by the law of its country of origin.

1.b. THE SUBSIDIARY

The Italian Civil Code provides for two types of business company having legal personalities separate and distinct from those of their shareholders or quotaholders as the case may be. They are the *Società per Azioni* (SPA), which more or less corresponds to the French Société Anonyme, the German Aktiengesellschaft (AG) and the English Public Limited Company, and the *Società a Responsabilità Limitata* (SRL), which substantially corresponds to the French Société à Responsabilité Limitée, the German Gesellschaft mit beschränkter Haftung (GmbH) and the English Private Limited Company. The differences between these two types of company, which until recently were essentially theoretical, have been accentuated by a law passed in 1977 which increased the capital requirements for both, thus introducing a significant difference between them.

The SPA has partially returned to being the appropriate type of business organization for enterprises of a larger size especially where the capital is to be contributed by a large number of investors, who are not connected with each other by ties of family, friendship or close business interests. An SPA must comply with stricter requirements and with more cumbersome formalities for the protection of shareholders. The SRL, on the other hand, in theory and to some extent in practice, is reserved for smaller groups of persons who wish to carry on a commercial, industrial or other activity and yet have their liability limited to the capital they have contributed.

Apart from the capital requirements, the rules governing SPAs and SRLs differ, for practical purposes, only to a limited extent and in many cases the SRL can be considered as the most suitable vehicle for subsidiary companies, either of Italian or of foreign parent companies, as their equity capital is usually held by only two members, the main part by the parent company and the remainder by a second shareholder.

It should also be noted that true 'public' companies, which are the SPAs the shares of which are quoted on a stock exchange, are subject to somewhat more extensive controls and publication requirements than those needed for other SPAs. In view of the fact that quoted companies will not be of great interest to readers of this book, only a brief mention of these additional requirements will be made at the end of this section, which will thus concentrate on the unquoted SPAs and will indicate, as appropriate, the differences between SPAs and SRLs.

1.b.(i) Setting-up

The requirements for the incorporation of a subsidiary company in principle involve compliance with a greater number of provisions of substantive law than those for the establishment of a branch. However, in practice the procedure is not much lengthier. In the first instance, the deed of incorporation, including the statutes, of both an SPA and an SRL must be executed by the incorporators (or persons holding powers of attorney for them) before a notary who is personally liable, jointly with the incorporators, for the payment of the registration tax and other fees on incorporation. The notary also ensures that the deed is entered in the Registry of Companies of the court in the jurisdiction of which the registered office of the company is situated. At this point application must also be made for registration of the company with the local Chamber of Commerce and income tax office, and a value added tax number must be applied for. The deed of incorporation and the statutes, which are annexed thereto, are required to comply with Italian substantive law. Thus, for example, a court will not approve the statutes of a company which has an object clause in too general terms. In all cases of non-compliance, the court refuses to approve the deed and statutes until they have been properly amended. Since the company can only be entered in the Registry of Companies after this approval has been obtained and since its incorporation as a legal entity distinct from the shareholders becomes effective only as a result of such an entry, the court's refusal extends the period during which persons transacting business on behalf of the company are liable to third parties, jointly and severally with the company and without any limitation, for acts performed in the name of the company.

At the time of incorporation, the capital of SPA's or SRL's must fulfill the minimum requirements provided by law which are specified in the section dealing with capital and, prior to incorporation, an amount corresponding to 30% of the subscribed capital must be deposited with the Bank of Italy for later release to the company. On incorporation both SPA's and SRL's require a minimum of two shareholders (or quotaholders in the latter case). All shares or quotas may thereafter be transferred to one person but this means that, although the company remains a separate legal entity, limited liability is lost as is described below, if the company becomes insolvent.

1.b.(ii) Organization

– *Capital, shares, transfer*

As has been referred to in the introduction, company law was amended in 1977 and the minimum capital requirement for an SPA was increased to two hundred million lire and for an SRL to twenty million lire. Companies with capital below these minima had time to the end of 1980 to increase their capital or to be converted into companies of a different kind with lower capital requirements or to be liquidated.

Contributions to an SPA's or an SRL's capital may be made in kind on the basis of a valuation made by an expert appointed by the court, which must, if made at the time of incorporation, be annexed to the deed of incorporation or, if subsequently, to the resolution authorizing the increase in the company's capital. The directors and *sindaci* (a type of auditor appointed by law, to whom reference is made below) have six months in which to verify the valuation contained in the report of the expert and, if good reason exists, are bound to revise it. Until such examination has been made, the shares which represent the contribution in kind are non-transferable and are kept by the company. If it is shown that the value of the contribution in kind was lower than the certified value by more than one fifth, then the company is required to reduce its capital proportionately.

At this point it should also be noted that the incorporation of a company with a capital in excess of two thousand million lire requires an authorization from the Treasury. This also applies to increases in capital other than those made for no consideration and to issues of debentures. It is not allowed to circumvent the above rule by a series of resolutions having the effect of increasing the capital or issuing debentures in excess of the limit during one year. However, on good authority it can be said that contributions in kind to the capital of a company are not subject to the observance of the above rules.

All increases or reductions in the capital of a company must be effected by a resolution adopted at an extraordinary shareholders' meeting, which also amends the statutes of the company. Such an alteration consists of a change in the number of shares, or in the nominal value of the existing shares. Increases in capital occur because of new contributions or because of the capitalization of reserves. A preferential right for the subscription to new shares is enjoyed by existing shareholders at the time of the increase, but such right can in certain cases be waived by a resolution of the extraordinary shareholders' meeting with a special majority. Reductions in capital are resolved upon either to make partial repayments to members or to cover losses incurred by the company. Whenever the capital of a company is diminished by more than a third as a result of losses, the directors must without delay call a shareholders' meeting to take appropriate action. A report on the financial situation of the company must be presented at such a meeting. If, within the following year, the loss has not decreased to less than a third of the capital, the shareholders' meeting which approves the annual accounts must resolve to reduce the capital in proportion to the losses. If it does not, the directors and the *sindaci* must request the court to take action.

Where, however, because of the loss of more than a third, the capital of the company falls below the minimum provided by law, the directors must immediately call an extraordinary shareholders' meeting to resolve upon the appropriate reduction of capital and its contemporaneous increase to a figure not less than the minimum or, alternatively, upon the conversion of the company into an SRL, in the case of an SPA, or a partnership (since partnerships have no minimum capital requirements).

An important difference as regards capital between SPA's and SRL's concerns the nature of shares and quotas respectively. Shares of an SPA, unlike quotas, are indivisible units, equal in par value and embodying certain rights such as the right to vote at shareholders meetings and to receive dividends and a proportionate share of the assets on winding up. Certificates representing the shares are regarded as genuine negotiable instruments which can be freely transferred unless the statutes limit this. An SPA may even, provided that certain conditions are satisfied, purchase its own shares without being obliged to reduce its capital accordingly. However, the shares so purchased do not carry voting rights so long as they are owned by the company.

Normally speaking, a share in an SPA is transferred by endorsement. The vendor makes the appropriate endorsement on the certificate and his signature is authenticated by a notary or stock exchange agent. If the share is not fully paid-up the purchaser must also sign the endorsement. The SPA must then be notified of the transfer and after the appropriate amendment to the shareholders register has been made the new shareholder can exercise his rights.

A holding in the capital of an SRL, on the other hand, takes the form of a quota which simply represents the specific proportion of capital contributed to the SRL and entitles the person holding the quota to exercise his voting rights and to receive dividends (and assets or proceeds from the sale thereof, upon winding up) in the same proportion. The par value of a quota in an SRL must be one thousand lire or a multiple thereof and the quotaholder is entitled to one vote for each thousand lire. Documents certifying the ownership of quotas may be issued but, as distinct from share certificates, they do not constitute negotiable instruments of any kind.

Quotas may be transferred either by a written instrument signed by the transferor and the transferee, and in this case the register of quotaholders is amended on production of such an instrument, or by means of an entry in the register of quotaholders signed by the transferor and the transferee and witnessed by a director.

A practical consequence of the difference in nature between shares and quotas is that the share certificates of an SPA may be sent abroad and may be negotiated there. It is true that documents certifying the ownership of quotas may also be sent abroad but, as they are not negotiable instruments, this is of little significance.

Currently only registered shares can be issued by SPAs in spite of the fact that the Civil Code also provides for bearer shares. This provision of the Civil Code has been indefinitely suspended but it is possible that it may be relaxed some time to bring the matter into line with the practice in other countries of the EC.

The statutes may include provisions restricting the transfer of the SPAs' shares or of the SRLs' quotas. In the case of the SPA the restrictive provisions may make the transfer of shares conditional on compliance with certain requirements but may not amount to an absolute prohibition. For this reason, clauses stipulating that the transfer of shares is not effective unless approved by resolution of the board of directors or of the shareholders, have been declared void by the courts as not being based on objective reasons. The transfer of the SRL's quotas, on the contrary, can even be forbidden completely by the statutes.

SPA's may issue preference shares but they may only carry advantages in respect of the normal distribution of profits during the existence of the company or of its assets in the event of winding up. In no event may shares carry multiple votes but the statutes may contain a provision excluding preference shares from having a vote at an ordinary shareholders' meeting.

An SPA may issue different classes of ordinary shares, each class carrying different rights, provided all ordinary shares have equal voting rights. At first sight, this rule would seem to exclude a possible sub-division of the ordinary shares into two or three classes so as to grant to their respective holders a right to vote for the appointment of a number of directors. Nevertheless, statutes of companies which contain provisions to this effect have in recent years been approved by various courts of law at the time of registration of the company involved. It is, however, perfectly possible that the courts may come to the opposite conclusion if this matter were submitted to them in connection with legal proceedings, rather than on the occasion of the registration, especially if the purpose of such a sub-division were to permit some shareholders to appoint more directors than warranted by the proportion of the capital held by them. There is, in fact, a tendency to waive the rule that directors must be elected by an absolute majority, if this is to enable various groups of shareholders to be proportionally represented on the boards of companies.

SPAs, but not SRLs, may issue debentures which give to the holders a right to interest and to repayment at a fixed date. The issue of debentures must be resolved upon by an extraordinary shareholders' meeting and their total amount may not exceed a sum equal to the amount of the paid-up and existing capital, i.e. not reduced by reason of losses. Provision is made for debenture holders to hold meetings and to appoint a representative to safeguard their interests, who may also attend shareholders' meeting.

Debentures are easily transferable and those of the more important companies are quoted on the Stock Exchange. Debentures which have their values indexed to the cost of living at the time of issue are becoming more usual as are convertible debentures, which may be converted into shares of the company which issued tham at dates set in advance. On the conversion of the debentures, the company must make an appropriate increase in capital and in view of this, convertible debentures must first be offered to existing shareholders as in the case of an increase in capital.

The promoters of both an SPA and of an SRL may allot a portion of future net profits of the company for themselves provided that the total amount of such benefit does not exceed 10% of the net profits and is limited to a maximum period of five years. No further benefits are allowed concerning profits, voting rights, preferential option rights and such like.

It should finally be noted, under this section, that, from the net profits of an SPA and an SRL, a sum equivalent to 5% must be deducted each year and placed in a special reserve. This requirement ceases to exist when such a reserve reaches one fifth of the company's capital.

– *Management and representation*

Both SPAs and SRLs are managed by one or more directors, the number of whom is not restricted by law. The first directors are appointed in the deed of incorporation for a period which for SPAs cannot exceed three years. Thereafter, they are normally elected by an absolute majority at an ordinary shareholders' meeting again, in the case of an SPA, for a maximum of three years, save in case of interim vacancies when the board itself, provided that the majority remains in office, may nominate director who holds office until the next shareholders' meeting. Whereas in the case of an SRL, unless the statutes provide otherwise, the directors must be quotaholders, it is not required by law that the director of an SPA be a shareholder. As a security against liability incurred by them, the directors of an SPA must deposit with the company, shares of the capital of the same or government bonds equal to at least one fiftieth part of the company's capital. However, the statutes may provide, as they practically always do, that the amount of this security *is not to* exceed two hundred thousand lire (an amount which had significance in 1942). Often shares are lent to the directors explicitly for this purpose.

Meetings of the board of directors are called by giving appropriate notice as specified in the statutes. They are validly constituted when a majority of the directors in office attend, although the statutes may provide for a larger quorum. Board meetings are also valid, even if no notice has been given, if all directors, and *sindaci* if appointed, attend. Resolutions passed at board meetings are only valid if approved by the majority of directors present although the statutes may provide for a higher majority. Voting by proxy or by letter is not allowed and, in this connection, it will be appreciated that, although there is no legal requirement that any directors should be Italian or Italian residents, it can often be advantageous to have some persons resident in Italy on the board.

Directors are subject to dismissal at any time by a resolution of the ordinary shareholders' meeting. However, where such a dismissal is without 'just cause', the director concerned is entitled to claim damages for loss of office. A director may also resign at any time but, if because of his resignation a majority of the board does not remain in office, the resignation is not effective until the majority has been reconstituted.

Any limitations of the powers of those who have general authority to represent the company, whether the sole director in a company without a board or the chairman, or the managing director, when there is a board, have no validity in respect of third parties even if notice of them has been given to the public in general, unless evidence is given that such thrid parties acted in bad faith.

The day to day management of the company is entrusted to a sole director by the shareholders where the statutes so provide. Where a board of directors exists some of its powers are delegated to the chairman of the board and more often to one or more managing directors or, sometimes, in the case of larger companies, to an executive committee. However, normally, the chairman does not perform executive functions and his primary duties are those of convening and presiding over board and shareholders' meetings and issuing and accepting proceedings. It can be often advantageous, so as to overcome the cumbersome formalities required for calling a board meeting, to grant a managing director full powers for certain matters specified in advance. The exercise of the more important of such powers can be made subject to receiving approval by letter from a majority of the other directors.

There is no requirement that the managing director of a company should be an Italian or reside in Italy and, although such residence may be an advantage, a managing director can carry out his functions from abroad making only occasional visits to Italy. If necessary, residence permits can easily be obtained for managing directors.

– *Shareholders' meetings*

Ultimate authority in respect of the management of an Italian company, whether it be an SPA or an SRL, is vested in the shareholders at their meetings, whether they be ordinary or extraordinary depending upon the business of the meeting.

Such meetings must be regularly convened and the means of calling them differs for the two kinds of companies. Meetings of SPAs are called by publishing notice thereof in the Official Gazette at least fifteen days before the date set for the meeting, and statutes often provide that notice be also given to the shareholders, directors and *sindaci*. The notice should contain the time and place of the meeting and its agenda. In the case of an SRL notice calling the meeting must be given by a registered letter to the quotaholders, directors, and *sindaci* if appointed, at least eight days before the date set for the meeting. Meetings are however valid, even if proper notice has not been given, provided that all the directors and *sindaci* attend and the whole share capital is represented either in person or by proxy.

Ordinary shareholders' meetings may be held abroad provided, in the view of certain courts, that the countries involved are specified in the statutes. However, in view of the fact that, at least some of the directors and above all the *sindaci* should be present, this can be inconvenient. Furthermore, as shareholders can be represented by proxy provided that the proxy holders are not directors, *sindaci* or employees of the company, necessity that shareholders meet abroad does not really exist. It should, however, be noted that proxies are only valid for a single specified meeting and may not be issued carte blanche. Both SPAs and SRLs must hold at least one ordinary shareholders' meeting within four months of the end of each financial year to approve, in the light of the *sindaci's* report, the balance sheet and the directors' report. The statutes may provide that this term can be extended to a maximum of six months when circumstances require. At such meetings directors and *sindaci* whose terms of office have expired in accordance with the law and the statutes are also replaced or re-elected and matters relating to the general management of the company discussed. Extraordinary meetings, which are held before a notary, are called to deal with particular kinds of business such as alterations in the statutes, increases or reductions in the share capital, issue of bonds, the winding up of the company and any other matters specified as being extraordinary business in the statutes.

At least half of the share capital of an SPA must be present or represented at an ordinary meeting held on first call and, to be effective, resolutions require the approval of the majority of the shares present or represented. At extraordinary meetings, on the other hand, resolutions to be valid must be approved by a majority of the subscribed capital unless the statutes require a larger majority.

If no quorum is present at the meeting on first call, a second meeting must be convened to be held within thirty days. On second call no quorum is required for ordinary meetings and, for extraordinary meetings, resolutions must be approved by a majority representing more than one third of the issued capital unless the statutes require a larger majority. Furthermore, in respect of certain major matters, such as the change of the company's object or the transfer abroad of the registered office, also at extraordinary meetings on second call the approval of more than half of the issued capital is required.

Resolutions of ordinary meetings of an SRL, whether on first or second call, require the approval of the majority of the subscribed capital and a majority of two thirds of such capital is required to approve resolutions at extraordinary meetings. However, this rule is subject to variation by the statutes and, in

effect, requirements in relation to an SRL's extraordinary shareholders' meeting may be less exacting than those of an SPA.
Voting at meetings of both kinds of companies is subject to an important restriction which is relevant where there are shareholders with different interests. A shareholder having an interest in conflict with the company should, in fact, abstain from voting. If such a shareholder does not abstain, the resolution may be declared invalid if it could damage the company and if it would not have been passed without that shareholder's vote. This restriction is particularly important in matters relating to directors liability, in respect of which shareholders who are also directors cannot vote.

– *Liability*
A director is required to carry out his duties with the diligence which is normal in the management of a company. His prime duties consist in giving effect to the resolutions of the shareholders' and the board of directors' meetings, complying with the statutes of the company and ensuring that its business is properly conducted. These duties are, of course, more relevant for a managing director.
Failure to carry out the above duties because of lack of normal diligence or fraud can involve the directors in two kinds of responsibility. In the first instance, they will be jointly and severally liable to the company for losses resulting to it from their failure. Secondly, as a director's duties include that of guarding the interests of creditors, he can be considered responsible for the failure to preserve the company assets. The director may however be released from liability if he dissents from a decision of the directors, records his dissent in the minute book of the board and immediately gives written notice thereof to the chairman of the board of *sindaci*.
A director has a duty not to compete with his company and to abstain from voting on matters where a conflict of interest exists, after having disclosed the conflict to the other directors and *sindaci*. Failure to observe these provisions can expose directors to an action for damages and criminal sanctions and the resolution can be declared invalid as in the case of a shareholders' resolution.
There are also various other more specific provisions which apply to directors and which expose them criminally if they violate them. These violations includes for example, the issue of new shares if the capital of a company is not entirely paid-up, the failure to call shareholders' meetings within the time-limits provided by law, the disclosure of confidential information, and the taking of loans from the company or from a company which it controls or is controlled by. It should also be borne in mind that directors of a company may, jointly with the company, incur criminal liability for breaches of taxation, exchange control and other specific provisions of law. A general manager, even if he is not a director, may incur similar liabilities and is civilly liable to the company for losses resulting from his failure to act with proper diligence in the same way as a director as described above.
Finally, it should be noted that a director incurs liability to a third party or a shareholder when his negligence or fraudulent acts have directly damaged such a third party or shareholder, independently from the provisions described earlier.
As has been mentioned above, SPAs and SRLs are legal entities separate from

their shareholders who are thus in no way responsible for their debts. This, however, is subject to one limitation to which reference has already been made, namely, that where a company has only one shareholder, he will in case of insolvency be responsible without limitation for the company's obligations which arose during the period of sole ownership. It is normally considered that, to avoid this risk, it is sufficient that one share is in the hands of a shareholder other than the principal shareholder. A cautious interpretation of the above requirement, however, suggests that such shareholder should be wholly independent of the principal shareholder and that his holding should consist of a meaningful part of the capital, such as 3 to 5%. If the principal shareholder is unwilling to have another independent shareholder, then it is normal practice (a) that the other shares be held by a foreign fiduciary company, which is not bound to disclose on behalf of whom the shares are held, or (b) (although this is much less advisable) by an individual employee of the principal shareholder. It should be appreciated that the above provision is of a particular importance in the case of the subsidiary of a foreign parent and, if such parent is adamant in requiring the second shareholder to be a wholly-owned subsidiary, it should be made clear that some risk exists that the limitation of liability which is sought may not hold.

– *Accounts and publication thereof and auditing requirements*

Both SPAs and SRLs are required to draw up annual accounts, including a balance sheet and profit and loss statement, which on the recommendation of the board of directors and the *sindaci* must be approved by an ordinary shareholders' meeting of the company within four months from the end of its financial year, which, as has been mentioned, may be extended to six months, if necessary.

Details regarding the contents of the accounts are contained in the Civil Code as are specific rules for the compilation of the profit and loss account. The most relevant of the rules contained in the Civil Code relating to the compilation of the balance sheet provide that the company's fixed assets should be carried at a value not exceeding their cost price reduced as appropriate to take account of depreciation. Raw materials and other goods must be valued at the lower rate of cost price and fair market value as determined at the end of the financial year. Intangible assets may be carried at purchase price but are depreciated in accordance with their economic lives. The directors have a discretion in relation to the valuation of shares and other securities but should take into account market conditions for shares quoted on the Stock Exchange and these valuations are subject to a specific check by the *sindaci*. Receivables have to be valued in accordance with their presumed value on realization. It is possible for the directors to adopt valuation rules different from those set out in the Civil Code but, if they do, the directors and the *sindaci* must specifically state this and justify it in their reports.

If a company has subsidiary or associated companies, its shareholdings in such companies together with their appropriate values must be stated on a list attached to its balance sheet, and the balance sheets of the subsidiary companies and a summary of those of associated companies must also be attached. Finally, it should be noted that for taxation purposes different valuation rules are adopted for certain items.

Save for quoted companies the accounts of SPAs and SRLs are not required to be audited in the generally accepted sense of this word. However, all companies, save for the SRLs with a share capital not exceeding one hundred million lire, must appoint a committee of three to five *sindaci* and two substitutes. Such *sindaci* are appointed in the deed of incorporation and thereafter by the ordinary shareholders' meeting for terms of three years which may be renewed. The *sindaci* must check the accounting books of the company and ensure that the legal requirements and the provisions of the statutes have been complied with. In effect, their potential liabilities are akin to those of directors and they have a general responsibility to check the company's affairs and the activities of the board of directors.

Detailed regulations exist to ensure the independence and professional qualification of the *sindaci*. At least one of the *sindaci* and of the substitutes must, in fact, be chosen from the lists of members of the accounting professions which only include Italian nationals. If the share capital of the company amounts to five hundred million lire or more, one of the three or two of the five *sindaci* and one of the substitutes must be chosen from the national register of certified accountants. *Sindaci* are required to attend all meetings of directors and shareholders unless they have good reasons for not being present.

It should be noted that, although wide in principle, the role of *sindaci* especially in small companies has, until very recently, remained somewhat theoretical in nature and it has been unusual for them to act as a real check on the activities of companies. However, in recent years, the judicial authorities have tended to hold the *sindaci* responsible for the companies' breaches of the law and thus the extent of their powers and the need to exercise them have been highlighted.

– *Quoted companies and groups of companies*

At this point it is appropriate to mention the special rules which apply to the SPAs which have their shares quoted on the Stock Exchange. These rules were essentially introduced by the Act of 1974 which reformed company law and which introduced the CONSOB (the Companies and Stock Exchange National Commission), as stated in the Introduction.

The provisions of the 1974 Act are generally intended to provide better protection for minority shareholders and small investors. They require SPAs to disclose more detailed information about their financial statements and about the state of their businesses, under the supervision of CONSOB if the shares are quoted on the Stock Exchange. They also expressly regulate the issue of debentures convertible into shares.

The 1974 Act also makes provision for quoted companies to issue 'savings' shares (*azioni di risparmio*). These shares must receive on the distribution of profits a sum equivalent to 5% of their nominal value prior to distributions to other shareholders and if there are sufficient profits for distribution to other shareholders, the dividend to be paid to the holders of 'savings' shares must be at least 2% higher than the dividend paid to other shareholders.

The same Act makes provision in relation to the disclosure of the remuneration of directors and *sindaci* of quoted companies and of shareholdings held by them in an attempt to avoid insider trading. Further, it also requires quoted companies to submit certain information to CONSOB at periodic intervals and gives CONSOB power to secure further information from such companies.

Most important is that following the reform of 1974 a decree law was issued in 1975 which made it mandatory for quoted companies to have their accounts certified. Such certification may only be effected by accounting firms registered with CONSOB and which have to satisfy certain rigorous requirements. The obligation for quoted companies to have their accounts certified is being introduced gradually.

The 1974 Act also amended the law in relation to controlled and associated companies (groups of companies). A controlled company exists where: (1) another company controls a sufficient number of votes to obtain a majority on resolutions in ordinary shareholders' meetings; or (2) the company by the latter is effectively under the control of another company because of the number of the shares held or because of particular contractual links with the same; or (3) it is controlled by an other company through the shareholding of the latter in a third company which in its turn controls the controlled company.

A company is considered an associated company where another company holds at least 10% of its share capital.

A controlled company is not allowed to subscribe to or purchase shares in its controlling company save where the same are purchased from its reserves other than its legal reserve. Furthermore all shares which are purchased in a controlling company must be fully paid and a controlled company is prohibited from voting at meetings of its controlling company. In the case of violation of the above rules, there are provisions which require the controlled company to dispose of the shares in question.

1.b.(iii) Checklist for Establishing a Subsidiary Company

Action	*Time*	*Cost*
1. In the case of foreign investment each prospective shareholder transfers 30 per cent of the capital to be subscribed to an Italian bank with appropriate instructions to the bank, which should contain a specific reference to Law No. 43 of 7th February 1956, to notify the Italian Exchange Control Authorities and credit the sums received with the notary public who will draw up the Deed of Incorporation.	Allow 1 week	
2. The notary public, acting on behalf of the prospective shareholders, deposits with the local branch of the Bank of Italy the 30 per cent of the capital subscribed to.	Allow 2 days	

1.b.(iii) Checklist for Establishing a Subsidiary Company

Action	Time	Cost
3. Tax code numbers are obtained for the foreign shareholders unless they already have them.		
4. If the shareholders are not present in person at the time of the formal drawing up of the Deed of Incorporation, powers of attorney should be obtained in good time from them for others to act on their behalf.		
5. The Deed of Incorporation and Statutes are formally drawn up before the notary public.		1% Registration Tax must be paid on the capital subscribed in cash or other movable property (higher rates apply if real property is contributed) and 67,550 Lire of Government Concession Duties.
6. The notary public submits the Deed of Incorporation and Statutes to the local Court for approval and subsequent entry in the Registry of Companies.	Allow 5 weeks from date of the deed	
7. The notary public submits application for registration to the local Chamber of Commerce.	Allow 5 weeks from date of the deed	6,500 Lire charge
8. The notary public submits application for IVA registration number and registers the Company with the income tax office.	Immediately after the deed	
9. Tax code numbers are obtained for directors of the company unless they already have them.	Immediately after the deed	
10. Acceptances of appointment from the directors and *sindaci* are obtained for filing at Court within 15 days from the date of the deed and, for the directors, for filing at the Chamber of Commerce.		

1.b.(iii) Checklist for Establishing a Subsidiary Company

Action	Time	Cost
(They may be obtained immediately after the drawing up of the Deed of Incorporation).		
11. A Board of Directors meeting is held to grant powers to directors including those to withdraw the sum deposited with the Bank of Italy following approval by the Court of the company's incorporation and to open bank accounts.		

1.c. Other forms

In theory, foreign investors can use other collective forms of business organization rather than the SPA and the SRL. There are two forms of partnership available for commercial activities. Both must be formed by a public deed drawn up by a public notary or by a private contract authenticated by him.

In the general partnership (*Società in Nome Collettivo*) all partners are responsible without limit for the liabilities of the firm, although creditors must first take legal action against partnership property.

In the limited partnership (*Società in Accomandita Semplice*) there are two classes of partners, namely general partners and limited partners. The former are responsible without limit for the liabilities of the partnership although a creditor, as described above, must first take proceedings against the partnership itself. Management of the partnership may only be carried out by general partners. Limited partners are only liable for the firm's debts to the extent of their participation in the firm's capital. They are not permitted to participate in the management of the partnership and if they do so, even in the most limited way, they become responsible without limit for its liabilities as with general partners.

Finally, there is another type of business organization which is a hybrid form between a limited partnership and a company limited by shares. It is known as the *Società in Accomandita per Azioni*. It takes the form of a company with a share capital and many of the rules which apply to the SPAs and SRLs apply equally to it. However, the shareholders are divided into two classes just as in the case of partners of a limited partnership. The first class is responsible without limit for the liabilities of the company, whether or not they act as directors. The second class of shareholders is only responsible to the extent of their participation in the capital and may not act as directors of the company.

In view of the nature of the organizations described above, and especially of the fact that they do not have the advantage of limited liability for all members, it must be said in general that the SPA, the SRL and the branch are the only forms of wholly-owned enterprise which can really be recommended to the foreign investor.

However, reference should also be made to the so-called Liaison Office (*Ufficio di Collegamento*). This form is available particularly to foreign companies which wish to engage in non-income producing activities such as advertising and market-research for themselves or their local distributors. The concept of a liaison office is not expressly provided for in Italian law and has developed over the years mostly for tax reasons. To set up a liaison office, a resolution of the board of the foreign company is required which should also grant the powers to the manager of the office. This resolution, together with the deed of incorporation and the statutes of the foreign company and a certificate of existence must be filed, duly translated, with the local Chamber of Commerce but no documents need to be filed with the Registry of Companies.
Foreign companies may also open Buying Offices (*Uffici Acquisti*) for the sole purpose of purchasing goods in Italy for export to the foreign company. These take essentially the same form as branches but are often excluded from taxation by virtue of the relevant double taxation treaty.

2. THE JOINT VENTURE

A joint venture may take the form either of an agreement between two separate companies which gives rise to no separate structure, or by the formation of a company jointly owned by the parties to the agreement or by using the special structure provided in Italian law for consortia. Since the first approach does not imply any special vehicle, only the other two approaches will be examined.

2.a. The jointly owned company

Italian law makes no distinction between companies which are actually wholly-owned by one shareholder, those which have a plurality of shareholders and those which, in effect, are jointly owned by two shareholders (although only in the latter two cases the provisions of company law protecting minority rights are relevant). When a company is effectively owned by two independent shareholders it is normal to find that the two shareholders attempt to regulate their relationship by means of a private agreement. In addition the statutes of the jointly-owned company, be it an SPA or an SRL, may contain special provisions which are appropriate to a joint venture such as special quorums for the validity of resolutions of the Board of directors and of the shareholders' meetings on certain items.

(i) Shareholders' agreements

The concept of shareholders' agreements is not specifically dealt with in Italian law either in the Civil Code or in other legislation. However, as a result of academic writing and court decisions, it can be said that the prevalent view is that shareholders' agreements will be held to be valid provided that they do not deprive the functions of the shareholders' meeting of any real significance on a permanent basis, they do not bind the parties to vote in a way conflicting with the interests of the company or in favour of persons

being in conflict with such interests, they do not aim at binding the votes of directors, and they do not limit the freedom of vote in order to create a fictitious majority at shareholders' meetings.
In connection with the last point, it is normally accepted that an agreement whereby shareholders undertake to pool their votes and cast them in the way the totality may decide, is valid, and that, conversely, an agreement whereby shareholders undertake to vote jointly as the majority of them may decide, is open to question depending on the circumstances. It will be appreciated that this can significantly reduce the efficacy of such agreements. Provisions in such agreements which require shareholders to limit the powers conferred on directors, but not their votes are normally considered valid. Finally, it should be noted that an order of specific performance cannot be obtained from the court for the enforcement of the provisions of a shareholders' agreement.

(ii) Minority rights

The protection given to minority interest in Italian companies is somewhat limited although in certain cases quite effective. The principal means of enforcing the rights of a minority are set out below.
A minority representing at least 20% of the capital of an SPA or an SRL may request the directors to convene a shareholders' meeting without delay and if they fail to do so, the *sindaci* are obliged to. If the *sindaci* in their turn, fail to call the meeting, the President of the Court having jurisdiction must convene it and appoint its chairman.
In both the SPAs and SRLs, any shareholder or quotaholder has the right to submit to the *sindaci* any question which he considers should be discussed at any shareholders' meeting and the latter are obliged to take note of these questions in their annual report. Furthermore, if such a complaint is made by shareholders or quotaholders representing a minimum of 5% of the capital, the *sindaci* must examine the facts immediately and submit their conclusions and proposals to the next shareholders' or quotaholders' meeting and, if urgent action is required, convene it forthwith.
If there is ground for suspicion of serious irregularities on the part of directors and *sindaci*, legal proceedings of a particular nature can be instituted by shareholders representing a minimum of 10% of the share capital. The court is bound to hear the directors and *sindaci* and, if circumstances warrant it, the court can dismiss the directors and *sindaci* from office and appoint a judicial administrator for a period of time and with powers to be specified by the Court, including the authority to institute normal proceedings for liability against the directors and *sindaci*.

2.b. Consortia

The law in relation to consortia was amended in 1976 and, whereas previously such undertakings were only regulated when entered into companies engaged in the same field this is no longer the case. A consortium is now defined as a common organization between enterprises to carry out specific parts of their business, such as manufacturing, distribution and the like. General control by the government on the activities of consortia is still provided for.

The contract establishing a consortium must be in writing and has a duration of ten years unless otherwise agreed. It may simply regulate the internal relationships between the enterprises which are parties to the consortium or provide also for the establishment of facilities to carry on its activities vis-a-vis third parties. In the latter case, a common fund is established which is used to meet the debts of the consortium and which may not be distributed to the members of the consortium whilst the consortium remains in existence. The liability of the consortium is limited to the amount of its common fund.
The managers of the consortium are responsible to the members of it to act with reasonable diligence and certain of the criminal sanctions which apply to company directors also apply to them. If the consortium's management undertakes properly an operation on behalf of an individual member, such a member is jointly and severally liable for it together with the consortium although the latter is only liable up to the amount of the common fund.
Consortia are required to draw up and file annual accounts, in accordance with the rules applying to SPAs. Consortia may also be established in corporate form.

B. External Controls

1. EXCHANGE CONTROLS

Italian exchange control regulations affect all cross-border transactions, such as sales of goods, provision of services, licensing industrial property, financing and the like. They are aimed at restraining the transfer of wealth abroad, especially by Italian residents, unless such transfer is justified by a purpose which the law regulations or, in specific cases, the exchange authorities recognize as being beneficial to the Italian economy. Within this general system of restriction there are provisions to attract foreign investment and loans. Here attention will be given mostly to the latter provisions, although all other exchange control regulations obviously affect also branches and subsidiaries of foreign companies. The rules governing foreign investment in Italy are principally contained in an Act of 1956. Foreign investment must comply with certain requirements in relation to the importation of foreign currency and its conversion into lire and the Act divides such investment in two classes. The first class relates to 'productive investment', which is that made for the creation of a new productive enterprise or the enlargement of an existing one. Such enterprises are those for the production of goods and services and reference is made, under this definition, in particular, to the installation of factories and other construction works. Profits from such investment and the proceeds of disinvestment in respect thereof may be transferred abroad without limitation, independently from any administrative restriction.
The second class of investment relates to all other kinds of investment. In this connection the 1956 Act provides that the transfer abroad in foreign currencies of the profits may not exceed 8% per annum of the sum invested and that the transfer of capital may not exceed the amount of the foreign currency originally imported and may not take place until two years after the

investment has been made.
The above act is important as an investment which is made in accordance with it, is given guarantees against the restrictions which may be imposed by the government in the future. At present the Italian banks are authorized to transfer any sum in excess of the limits set forth for non-productive investment. Whilst it is true that such regulations can be withdrawn, it can be said that they have been in force for a considerable number of years. It should, however, be noted that before repatriating the proceeds of a disinvestment, in the case of a sale of shares to an Italian resident, the bank effecting the transfer needs to be satisfied that the price for the shares is fair. Evidence of this is normally provided by a certificate issued by the local Stock Exchange Committee. The same situation, in fact, applies when a resident sells shares to a non-resident.
To effect a non-productive investment is very simple and requires few formalities, whereas to have an investment recognized as productive, notice must be given to the Treasury in order that the actual status of the investment be ascertained.
The provision of loans to an Italian subsidiary by its foreign parent is also governed by the exchange control regulations. The general rule is that any loan by a non-resident to a resident requires a specific authorization from the authorities. However, particularly in respect of loans given to subsidiaries, there are important exceptions to this rule, which only require notification to the authorities. Thus, loans made for a period in excess of five years designed to establish long-lasting economic links such as those by foreign shareholders to their Italian subsidiary, fall within the ambit of these exceptions when they originate from OECD countries. Loans up to five years given by residents in EC countries, provided that the Italian recipient of the loan has not received loans totalling in excess of two hundred and fifty million Lire under the same head, also fall within the exceptions, irrespective of whether they are granted to subsidiaries or not.
Further, if foreign investors wholly own an Italian enterprise and their investment has been classified as productive, medium and long-term loans, including debentures, from local sources may not exceed 50% of such investment. Otherwise its productive status is lost and the investment is treated as non-productive. If they own less than 100% but more than 30%, loans from local sources can be obtained in excess of the above limit provided that for the amount in excess there is a foreign loan on the same terms in an amount proportional to the foreign investment. If the investment is below 30%, no limit applies to borrowing from local sources.
In general, Italian banks have a duty to satisfy themselves of the fairness of any consideration in dealings between residents and non-residents, all of which must pass through the banks, and this not only in respect of foreign investment but also in general trade. Doubtful cases are submitted to the authorities. The consideration must be fair and if it is not, the suspicion arises that an illegal export of currency is being made. The existence of such illegality can involve serious penalties, including criminal proceedings against the persons directly responsible. This particularly relates to trading transactions which must respect the criterium of being at a 'normal' price. Payments of service fees, royalties and the like must also be at a normal open market price and it

is particularly important that written contracts supporting them exist and proper documentation of the reasons for the payments is preserved. Payments of amounts related only percentagewise to the turn-over of an Italian subsidiary are not as a rule allowed.

2. TAKE-OVER CONTROLS

As stated in the introduction, the regulation of the securities market was reformed in Italy in 1974 and the CONSOB set up. The CONSOB has various regulatory powers in the securities field. It must however be said that as yet it has not had a great effect on the market.

Anyone who wishes to buy or sell shares by offers to the general public must notify CONSOB, which, establishes within 20 days, the formalities for such offers. The omission to make such a notification is subject to a fine of from 2 to 20 million Lire.

There is no other kind of supervision of the acquisition of shares. There are however rules whereby companies which come to own more than 2% of a quoted company and Italian quoted companies which come to own more than 10% of an unquoted company must give notice in writing to the other company involved and to CONSOB within 30 days of acquiring such interest. If this notification is not made, voting and option rights in respect of the shares involved may not be exercised. Penalties are imposed if the above is not complied with.

The same rules apply to foreign companies as regards the purchase by them of shares of Italian quoted companies.

3. ANTI-TRUST

Apart from the Economic Community Regulations on this subject, there are no Italian laws dealing with anti-trust matters.

4. ENVIRONMENTAL CONTROLS

Environmental controls in Italy are in general relatively lax and difficulty has been encountered in putting into effect the laws which exist. By virtue of a recent law a prior license from the local authorities must be obtained for the discharge of waste water, sewage and the like. This law sets out in detail various maximum pollution standards to which new industries must adhere and which existing industry must meet over a period of time, but implementation of the more strict standards has been delayed.

There are other laws of minor importance in relation to the protection of environment.

5. STATE MONOPOLIES

As in most European countries, the production of electric energy is reserved to a state concern and so are many activities in the field of public transport and telecommunications. In addition, and more unusually, the sale of tobacco products, but not of the tobacco leaf, is a monopoly of the state as is also the sale of salt.

III. TAXATION

A. Corporate Income Tax

1. ENTITIES SUBJECT TO TAX

Corporation Tax (*Imposta sul Reddito delle Persone Giuridiche*, known as IRPEG) is payable by corporate bodies, in particular companies (wherever they are incorporated), which have their registered offices or 'managerial headquarters' in Italy or carry on the 'principal object of their business' there and are therefore considered resident in the country. Subject as stated below, IRPEG is also paid by other corporate bodies and unincorporated associations and partnerships which neither have their registered offices or managerial headquarters in Italy, nor carry on the principal object of their business in the country, and are therefore not considered to be resident. For the purposes of IRPEG, only resident companies and non-resident companies and partnerships are dealt with.

Resident companies are subject to IRPEG on their worldwide income. Non-resident companies and partnerships are subject to such tax only in respect of the income they derive from trade carried on in Italy through permanent establishments situated there. It may be worthwhile noting here that, while resident partnerships are not subject to IRPEG, their members being instead subject to the income tax applying to individuals (*Imposta sul Reddito delle Persone Fisiche*, known as IRPEF) as described later in this section, non-resident ones are subject to IRPEG in respect of their Italian income.

As mentioned above, according to Italian tax law companies are considered resident in Italy when their registered offices or their managerial headquarters are located there, or the principal object of their business is carried on there. The concept of location in Italy of the company's managerial headquarters largely corresponds to the residence criterion of the 'place of management' adopted in several countries and in the OECD Double Taxation Model Convention. Hence, the elements which under the legislation of such countries are considered to determine that there is a place of management (such as the place where the board of directors usually meets) are also supposed to be relevant for Italian law. On the other hand, the circumstance of having the 'principal object of the business' in the country is a rather unusual criterion for determining tax residence and one potentially difficult to identify in practice. The notion of company residence adopted in Italian tax law is therefore more extensive than that embodied in the rules accepted in other countries. Where strictly interpreted, it would raise dual residence problems, although such cases have been rare in practice.

The existence of a permanent establishment in Italy determines whether non-resident entities, both companies and partnerships, are subject to IRPEG. The concept of permanent establishment is not defined by Italian tax law and in the past, the interpretation of the notion of permanent establishment by the Italian tax authorities was in certain respects open to question, especially in respect of commission agents. The Italian Ministry of Finance has however recently ruled that the provisions of Article 5 of the OECD Model Convention will be followed in dealing with the concept of permanent establishment for domestic income tax purposes. The detailed provisions of the commentary accompanying the OECD Model Convention are therefore also expected to be relevant as guidelines.

It is, further, worth mentioning that such a concept does not exactly correspond to that of a branch of a foreign company which is provided for by the Civil Code as explained earlier. In fact, the Civil Code is principally concerned with subjecting the foreign company, in respect of its Italian branch, to the publication requirements and other provisions of Italian law regulating the exercise of business activities. Tax law, on the other hand, aims at establishing a sufficient link between the carrying on of a business activity in Italy by a foreign company and the payment of a contribution to Italian public expenditure, when the benefits of such expenditure are also shared by the foreign company concerned. Thus, the appointment of a permanent representative with authority to act in the name of, and bind the foreign company, although provided for by the Civil Code, is not essential in order that the foreign company be deemed to have a permanent establishment in Italy for tax purposes, and for the profits it makes through such permanent establishment to be subject to IRPEG. It is, in fact, sufficient that business operations be carried on in Italy by a foreign company through Italian-based salesmen or independent commission agents who hold stocks of goods in Italy or have authority to bind the foreign company.

On the other hand, where a mere 'liaison office' is established in Italy by a foreign company to perform activities clearly not yielding any direct profit (such as the coordination of the advertising operations of the foreign company or of its local subsidiaries, or the coordination of relations with existing customers supplied and serviced from a foreign country) there should be no assumption that the foreign company derives any taxable income from such an office. In practice, such a liaison office must be registered with the appropriate local Chamber of Commerce only (thus being able to hire employees and obtain public services), and not with the Registry of Companies, and the local representative (usually a single employee) is granted extremely limited authority to represent the company. This is described in more detail in the section dealing with the legal structure. Under the above conditions, if the liaison office is only used for performing the activities mentioned here, no taxable income is deemed to have been produced by such a foreign company in Italy as a result of the operation of the liaison office.

2. COMPUTATION OF PROFITS

IRPEG is paid on the total net profits of a company. Such total net profits consist of the net trading income plus capital gains. They are determined on the basis of book income, as shown on the profit and loss statement drawn up in accordance with company law, but adjusted in accordance with the criteria which are set down by the tax law. Notwithstanding the importance thus in fact given to accounting principles, there is no well settled body of normal accounting principles in Italian practice. Although certain rules are embodied in the Civil Code, for tax purposes computation of profits has also to be made in accordance with rules which are laid down in tax statutes. The principal instances in which the tax rules depart from normal principles of accounting will be emphasized in the following description of computation of taxable profits.

2.a. Trading income

The principal item included in the gross trading income is the gross receipts derived from transactions constituting the object of the company's business. Tax law also qualifies as gross receipts those which are produced by the sale of raw materials, work in progress and goods originally intended to be used in production. Gross receipts must be increased by an amount equal to the fair market value of goods distributed to shareholders or used for purposes not included in the company's business. Where derived from a non arm's-length transaction with a non-resident controlling company, the proceeds from such a transaction must also be increased by an amount equal to the difference between such receipts and the fair market value of the goods sold or services rendered. Any other kind of receipts not mentioned above (such as dividends, interest and royalties) must also be included in gross income.

The law specifically provides that, in addition, the so called 'windfalls' go to make up gross income. They consist of: (i) sums received in respect of items charged as costs and expenses or accounted for as liabilities in previous financial years, or derived, indirectly, from the cancellation of such costs, expenses or liabilities, (ii) gifts or cash grants, the latter, however, being allowed to enjoy potentially endless deferral from tax, and (iii) dividends in shares and increases in the nominal value of shares without payment. The latter amounts are not, however, included in gross income when issued in connection with increases in the paid-up capital effected through the transfer to capital of special reserves formed by the revaluation of fixed assets, or by premiums paid by subscribers at the time of the issue of new shares.

2.b. Capital gains and losses

Capital gains, which are defined as gains made on the sale or exchange of a company's assets, save where such sale or exchange is the principal object of the company, are taxed on their full amount as income at the standard rate. Capital gains are also taxed, even if no transfer in fact takes place, when the value of the assets concerned is increased on the balance sheet as, for example, on the revaluation of assets, save that recent legislation exempted this from

income tax and similar provisions may well be enacted again shortly.
The taxation of capital gains can be deferred if they are placed in a special reserve and reinvested in depreciable assets within two years. The law provides that the reserve is transferred to the depreciation fund in respect of the new assets and that future depreciation can only be calculated on that amount of the value of the new assets which exceeds such an initial fund so that, in effect, the gains are taxed over the conventional life of such assets. If they are not so reinvested, the gains are taxed at the end of the two-year period.
Amendments to income tax law adopted by a delegated order of 30th December 1980 provide for the taxation of foreign residents on capital gains realized by the transfer of shares of SPAs not quoted on the Stock Exchange (or of quoted SPAs, if the vendor could exercise a 'dominating influence' on the company the shares of which are sold) and by the transfer of quotas of SRLs. Such transfers of shares or quotas are subject to taxation regardless of where they actually take place, of the nationality or residence of the transferees and of the absence of links between the transferor and Italy.
The extent to, and the manner through which such new provisions will actually be implemented are still being debated. In many instances, however, double taxation conventions derogate from this new regulation, as they prevent Italy from taxing such capital gains.
Capital losses incurred upon the transfer, whether by sale, exchange or distribution to shareholders, of any assets are fully deductible. However, unlike capital gains, capital losses arising other than as a result of transfer, can only be deducted when they refer to the decrease in value of inventory or portfolio securities valued in accordance with the criteria set out below.

2.c. Deductions

Italian tax law normally allows costs and expenses to be fully deducted from gross income provided that they are related to the production of such income and are certain and determinable. Further, they must be supported by sufficient documentary evidence. Deduction of costs and expenses incurred other than in the purchase of goods and services required for the production of the company's income is governed by detailed rules which often differ from normal accounting practice. The rules applicable to the more important of these items are now outlined.
Formation expenses may be fully deducted over the first five financial years but not in an amount exceeding 50% in any year. Thus, such deductions need not be made in equal annual instalments.
Depreciation in Italy is calculated on the basis of the actual cost of the assets by the straight line method. The Ministry of Finance fixes the maximum rates for determined categories of assets according to their presumed useful lives. Further, accelerated depreciation is normally allowed up to a maximum of a further 15% per annum but for a period not exceeding three financial years. Intangible assets are depreciated using the same rules as for other assets, but they must be depreciated in equal instalments over their useful lives, whether determined by law or by contract.
Research and development expenses incurred by a company may be deducted entirely in the financial year in which they were borne, or in five equal an-

nual instalments including the first year.
It may also be of interest to note that deductions for bad debts may not exceed 0.5% of outstanding receivables, but where the reserve amounts to 2% of such receivables the rate is reduced to 0.2%. In any event, when the total bad debts reserve equals 5% of outstanding receivables, no further deduction is allowed.
Finally, interest may be deducted for its total amount, except that the part of the interest apportionable to tax exempt income may not be deducted. Interest on loans for the purchase or construction of capital assets must be capitalized together with the relevant assets.
Special rules also apply to directors' fees, donations, employees' leaving indemnities, repair and maintenance expenses and advertising expenses. Further, operating losses may be carried forward and set against profits for five years.

2.d. Exemptions

There are no particular exemptions which apply to companies as such, other than those provided by law in relation to specific kinds of income or of enterprises. Cash grants (from private or government bodies) received by companies can enjoy potentially endless deferral from tax where they are set aside in special reserves to cover operating losses but, if the reserves are used for different purposes, they are included in the company's gross income.

3. RATES OF TAX

IRPEG is levied at a flat rate of 25%. Taking into account ILOR, the so-called Local Income Tax, which is described below, levied at a rate of 15% but which is deductible in the determination of net income for IRPEG purposes, the net combined tax rate on companies is 36.25%. This may be temporarily increased to about 39% for 1982.

4. TAX CREDITS

a. Italy adopted the so-called 'integrated system' for the taxation of dividend income in 1977. The law allows the shareholder for the purpose of calculating the amount of tax to gross up the dividends received by one third (which corresponds to the amount of IRPEG tax paid by the company making the distribution) and to deduct this amount from the tax subsequently due. Thus, at the standard IRPEG rate of 25%, the law represents a full imputation system, when the shareholder having the benefit of the credit is a company, with the consequence that the recipient company pays no further IRPEG tax on such dividends. The credit is not, however, granted on dividends paid to non-resident shareholders unless they have a permanent establishment in Italy and the dividends are included in the latter's gross income. Dividends paid to resident companies from foreign affiliates are only taxable in Italy on 40% of their total amount.
b. Italian law also provides, of course, for a different type of tax credit,

namely, a foreign tax credit for taxes paid by resident companies to foreign governments on income derived from foreign sources. This operates as a unilateral relief against double taxation in the absence of an appropriate treaty dealing with the subject.

c. No other credits against IRPEG, such as investment credits and the like, are allowed by Italian law.

5. TIMING OF PAYMENTS

Italian companies must file their tax returns within a month following the approval of their balance sheets by their annual general meetings. Tax must be paid at the time the return is filed. However, since 1978, companies have had to pay in advance a certain amount of tax, now equal to 90% of the IRPEG tax paid in the previous financial year, at the end of November of the current financial year.

6. REVIEW AND APPEAL

Local income tax offices can review a company's return and assess its income by serving a notice of assessment within five years from the year in which the return was filed. The authorities can request the company to provide supplementary information and to show its accounting and other statutory records. They can also obtain information from certain public bodies and request copies of documents deposited with public notaries and other public officers. The tax authorities may also search the taxpayer's business premises (and, with a warrant, business premises other than those of the taxpayer) in order to find evidence of tax evasion.

In the above connection, the rules concerning banking secrecy are important. The authorities are permitted to obtain full details of a company's bank accounts and transactions when it has not filed a return and they have evidence that it has earned income amounting to more than one hundred million lire, or, where a return has been filed, there is evidence that income has been earned amounting to more than four times the amount declared and the difference is greater than one hundred million lire, or, finally, where the company has not kept the prescribed books and records for three consecutive financial years.

Companies can appeal against assessments made by Local Income Tax Offices to tax commissions which determine disputes concerning income taxes and the other principal taxes. The time limit for appealing to the Tax Commission of First Degree is sixty days from the service of the notice of assessment. An appeal may be made against the decisions of this commission to a Tax Commission of Second Degree and thereafter a final appeal to a Central Tax Commission on questions concerning the application of procedural and substantive law or factual issues other than the mere determination of the amount of taxable income. Appeal from the Central Tax Commission to the Supreme Court may be made on questions of law only.

Notwithstanding any appeal, one third of any tax disputed must be paid

following service of the assessment by the Local Income Tax Offices, and 50% of any amount determined by the Tax Commission of First Degree must be paid forthwith following such a finding. The full amount of any tax held to be due by the Commission of Second Degree must be paid notwithstanding any further appeal.
A social administrative procedure is available for recovery of disputed tax which has been already withheld or which is paid at the time the return was filed.

B. Withholding Taxes

The Italian tax system, as most other modern tax systems, provides for two types of withholding tax. The first type consists of advance payments made on account of taxes, the amount of which is determined at a later date, and the second consists of taxes in their own right which are levied on the gross amounts of certain items usually when they are remitted to a non-resident beneficiary. Only withholding taxes of the latter type, which are relevant for foreign investors and which relate to interest, royalties and dividends, are dealt with here.
Any kind of interest paid to a foreign resident is, as a rule, subject to a withholding tax of 15%. However, interest paid by an Italian bank to a foreign bank on current or deposit accounts is not subject to any withholding tax.
As regards royalties, IRPEG is withheld at a rate of 30% on seven tenths of their gross amount paid to foreign residents. The effective rate is therefore 21% of the gross amount.
The taxation of royalties paid to foreign licensors, including the rate set out above, was affected by the amendments to the income tax law made by the delegated order of 30th December 1980 mentioned above. The new provisions replaced preexisting provisions on this subject which were challenged by foreign licensors, who maintained that no withholding or other tax was to be assessed on royalty income whenever the foreign-based beneficiary had no permanent establishment in Italy. The result was that royalty income was often qualified by tax commissions as trading income, if earned in carrying out a business, and thus held to be non-taxable in respect of foreign licensors without a permanent establishment in Italy.
Today, as a result of the above amendments, a specific source rule has been adopted for the taxation of royalties remitted to foreign-based beneficiaries. This withholding tax has now been clearly qualified as a tax in its own right, according to the distinction set forth at the beginning of this paragraph.
Another very important effect of such amendments is that royalties paid to foreign licensors are no longer subject to ILOR. The application of such tax was disputed under the preexisting provisions, but the matter has now become clear-cut as ILOR excludes from tax, income already subject to withholding tax.
Royalties paid to foreign associated companies can only be deducted where they represent consideration that would be received in an arm's-length transaction.

As regards dividends, taxes are withheld at a rate of 30% on the gross amount of dividends paid to foreign residents. However, if such non-residents can prove to have paid an equal or higher amount of taxes in their country of residence on the same dividend income, they are entitled to a refund of up to two-thirds of the amount of tax withheld in Italy.
If a foreign company has a permanent establishment in Italy, dividend income received by such a permanent establishment enjoys the benefit of the imputation system described under tax credits above and forms part of the permanent establishment's gross income.
It should also be noted that when the profits of a branch are remitted to the foreign company, they are subject to no withholding at all.
In the light of the above, it will be seen that, if a foreign company has a permanent establishment in Italy and also holds shares of an Italian company, the tax burden on dividend income in Italy can be lightened. This is because, if the dividend income is paid to the permanent establishment, it does not, in effect, pay IRPEG by virtue of the operation of the imputation system described earlier in respect of tax-credits and, when subsequently remitted to the foreign company as part of the permanent establishment's profits, it is not subject to any withholding tax.
Most tax treaties to which Italy is a party reduce the withholding rates described above. The treaty rates are generally fixed at 10% for interest, 0 to 10% for royalties, 15% for port folio dividends and from 0 to 5% on direct investment dividends.

C. *Registration Tax and Stamp Duties*

A large number of written and oral transactions are subject to Registration Tax (*Imposta di Registro*) which is charged at varying rates depending upon the nature of the transaction. This tax is not paid on transactions which are subject to Value Added Tax. Furthermore, certain transactions, such as agreements executed abroad are only subject to Registration Tax when embodied in an administrative deed. The tax must be paid within twenty days of the making or carrying out of the agreement involved, whichever is earlier.
Deeds for the formation of limited companies and those which incorporate resolutions increasing the capital of a company, are always subject to Registration Tax at a rate of 1% on the capital involved. If, however, factories are contributed, the rate is 4% and the rate for other real property is 8% save for agricultural land for which it is 15%. In addition, the same deeds have to pay a so-called Government Concession Duty (*Imposta di Concessione Governativa*) of 22,500 Lire. Registration Tax has also to be paid on the assets attributed to a branch of a foreign company in Italy.
A large number of documents and records are also subject to the payment of stamp duties. Again, documents on which Value Added Tax is paid are exempt and certain other documents are only subject to these duties when produced before a court or embodied in an administrative deed. There are also certain other similar taxes on mortgages and the like.

D. Individual Taxation

1. PERSONS SUBJECT TO TAX

Individuals are subject to Personal Income Tax (*Imposta sul Reddito delle Persone Fisiche*, known as IRPEF) on, in the case of residents in Italy, their world-wide income subject to a foreign tax credit as relief against double taxation. Individuals are also subject to a so-called Local Income Tax (*Imposta Locale sui Redditi*, known as ILOR) on certain kinds of income produced within Italy.

A person is considered resident in Italy for tax purposes, not only if he is registered as a resident but also if he lives there for more than six months in a calendar year or has the centre of his business and interests there or is an Italian national living abroad in the service of the State. Resident foreigners are taxed in the same way as Italians resident in Italy.

Non-residents are only taxed on income accruing from sources within Italy. Strictly speaking, they are bound to present an annual tax return. The appropriate withholding of tax should be made in the case of income from employment, as in the case of residents. Income from professional services and the like remitted to foreign residents or fees paid to foreign resident directors of Italian companies for services performed within Italy are subject to a withholding of 20%. These provisions are often modified by virtue of the treaties against double taxation between the non-resident's country and Italy. Thus, for example, in the case of Switzerland, income from professional services rendered by a Swiss resident is alone taxed in Switzerland unless the Swiss resident has a fixed base available in Italy, in which case appropriate attribution of such income is made to that fixed base. Salaries and other similar remuneration of a Swiss resident are only taxed in Switzerland except in respect of employment carried out in Italy in which case any remuneration derived therefrom will be taxed there. Notwithstanding this, such remuneration is only taxed in Switzerland if the recipient is present in Italy for a period or periods not exceeding in aggregate one hundred and eighty-three days in the year and if the remuneration is paid by a non-resident employer without a permanent establishment or fixed base in Italy. The same treaty, however, provides that directors' fees and the like paid to a Swiss resident by an Italian company may be taxed in Italy.

The taxable income of partnerships is determined in accordance with all the provisions of IRPEF but they are not taxable entities as such. In fact, partnership profits are deemed to be distributed to the partners in proportion to their participation in the partnership and each partner is taxed on his share of the partnership profits as part of his own income at progressive rates.

A non-resident partner's share of the income of an Italian partnership is expressly classified as income from sources within Italy and taxed as such. As mentioned above, foreign partnerships having permanent establishment in Italy are subject to IRPEG on their Italian income.

2. COMPUTATION OF INCOME

2.a. Gross income

Individuals are taxed on their income whether in money or in kind received from any source. The IRPEF law sets out the basic rules for the determination of gross income including profits and the applicable principles have been explained in dealing with IRPEG.
Italian law adopts the method of collection of tax on income from employment by withholding at source on the 'pay as you earn' basis and this has been extended to several other fields of activity. Thus, it now applies at different rates to salaries, directors' and statutory auditors' fees and remuneration received for professional services.
Income from real property in Italy is taxed on the so called 'cadastral' income unless such property constitutes an asset used in a business. The 'cadastral' income is a notional income attributed to and registered against real property. It applies to income from land, agriculture and urban property. It may be of interest to note that it also includes the homes of private individuals. IRPEF is levied on the cadastral income even if no actual income is in fact produced.

2.b. Capital gains

Capital gains, other than those made on the transfer of assets used in a business, are only taxed when they arise from a transaction made with the intent to resell at a gain, known as a 'speculative intent'. Such intent is a question of fact to be ascertained on a case by case basis although in certain instances there is an irrefutable presumption that it exists as, for example, on the purchase and resale of shares in property companies when they are not listed on the stock exchange and the sale is made within five years. In other cases, the interval between purchase and resale is an important element in determining the existence of a speculative intent.
Gains are taxable when the property disposed of is located in Italy or the income producing activities are carried on there, and consist of the difference between the consideration received on transfer and the purchase price plus any incremental expenses. Gains are included in the individual's income and usually taxed on their full amount.
Capital gains deriving from the liquidation of an individual's business, which in any event are taxable, are taxed separately from other income at an average rate in accordance with the rules set out below.

2.c. Deductions

Two broad groups of deductions are made from an individual's gross income to determine his net taxable income. The first group consists of costs and expenses incurred for the production of such income and the detailed rules applying here are substantially similar in the case of a business to those for IRPEG. As a general rule, deductions are not allowed on income from capital (interest and dividends) and only minor deductions may be made in respect of salaries and fees paid to directors and statutory auditors.

The second group of deductions refer to the personal circumstances of the taxpayer. Thus, medical expenses, mortgage interest, life insurance and the like may be deducted subject to certain limits and maintenance payments may also be deducted. There are also certain personal allowances whereby a taxpayer may deduct 36,000 lire from the amount of tax in respect of himself, and certain amounts in respect of his wife and dependants. A further personal allowance is also available to pensioners. Finally the amount of ILOR paid may be deducted from the gross income for IRPEF purposes. Certain of these items and, in particular, those relating to ILOR and those relating to pensions may also be deducted by non-resident taxpayers.
Refundable tax credits are provided when dividends are included in gross income as described above. They are also provided in order to take account of differences in timing between the taxation of income abroad and the allowance of double taxation relief.

3. RATES OF TAX

IRPEF is a progressive tax and rates vary from 10% on the first bracket (up to three million lire) to 72% on the last one (in excess of five hundred and fifty million lire). Thus, for example, an income of ten million lire is taxed at an actual rate of 17.55%, one of twenty million lire at 20.95% and one of one hundred million lire at 36.65%. The personal deductions described earlier are designed to favour persons with low incomes.
The law provides that certain kinds of income which are received in one year but have matured over a period of several years, should be excluded from the tax base and subject to separate taxation. This applies for example, not only to the liquidation of a business mentioned above but also to employees' leaving indemnities. The rate applying to income separately taxed is the average of the rates paid by the taxpayer in the two preceding years.

4. SUCCESSION TAX

4.a. Taxation on inheritance

In 1972 the succession tax system in Italy was reformed, when the two succession taxes then existing, which applied to the total net value of the estate and to each individual inheritance were abolished, and a single tax introduced. The burden of the new tax is however applied at rates which depend upon the status of the beneficiaries. The deceased's spouse and direct descendants or ancestors are subject to lower rates while other legatees and heirs are taxed at higher rates which increase according to the distance of their relationship from the deceased.
Tax is levied on the net value of the estate whether it is located in Italy or abroad but partial or total credits are allowed in respect of succession tax paid on assets abroad. Where the deceased was not resident in Italy at the time of death, tax is only paid on the value of the property located there.
All the property of the deceased is included in his estate for the purposes of

Succession Tax and there is a presumption that money, valuables and other personal property exist for a value equal to 10% of the estate's net value even if they are not declared.

Property is valued for the purposes of Succession Tax at its actual value and the law provides specific rules for the valuation of such items as real property, ships and aircraft, shares and other securites, annuities and debts due to the deceased. The debts of the deceased, medical and funeral expenses are the principal items which may be deducted from the gross value of the estate. Debts must meet very strict requirements in relation to their validity and date to qualify as deductions and there must be documentary evidence thereof.

Property bequeathed to the State, other public bodies, charities and private bodies with educational and similar purposes is exempted from tax. Further, certain items such as art collections, state bonds and debts, the legal validity of which is uncertain, may be excluded from tax.

4.b. Taxation of gifts

Gifts are taxed in the same way as transfers of property on death. The burden of tax again depends on the status of the donee and most of the basic rules relating to the tax base and valuation are the same as described above for succession tax.

E. Indirect Taxation

Italy has adopted Valued Added Tax (*Imposta sul Valore Aggiunto*, known as IVA) as a general tax on turnover in line with other EC countries. IVA is charged on the majority of supplies of goods and services in Italy made in the exercise of a business or profession. The tax is normally collected through the companies or persons making taxable supplies and the input-output system is used. Taxpayers collect IVA on supplies of goods or services made by them which constitute their outputs, deduct IVA paid on goods or services received by them which constitute their inputs and pay the balance to the State. Returns are filed and payments made monthly or, in special cases, at longer intervals. Thus, the supplier of goods and services transfers the amount of the IVA he has paid to the next link in the taxable chain together with an additional amount of IVA on the value he has himself added. Agreements not to charge the full amount of the tax to the recipients of goods and services are null and void.

The basic rate of IVA is 15% but this is increased to 18 or 35% for certain goods and reduced to lower rates (2 and 8%) for essential goods and services. Certain categories of supplies such as rents, salaries, wages, insurance, shipbuilding, education and certain public services are exempt from IVA.

As is mentioned above, IVA is charged on supplies made in Italy. Goods are considered to have been supplied in Italy if, in general, they relate to goods situated there. Services are supplied in Italy when supplied by persons domiciled or resident in the country although this rule is subject to exceptions in particular in relation to services supplied to other EC countries. Furthermore, exports and international services, for example, freight forwarding, but not professional services connected with them, are zero rated.

F. *Incentives*

Incentives, especially those related to tax, were in the past extremely complex in Italy. Prior to the reform of the tax system, there were a large number of taxes and levies coupled to an equal number of exemptions, the purpose of which was to make the tax burden lighter. The aim of this system was to encourage the economic development of the poorer parts of the country and tax benefits were provided by the tax law itself and by special legislation. The two most common forms consisted of absolute exemption from taxation and the so-called 'substitute regimes' whereby special forms of payment were adopted for certain taxes, thereby reducing the overall burden.

The tax reform of 1973 has greatly simplified this system and abolished most of the substitute regimes. Further, a special law has codified the surviving benefits. Those which are of interest to companies consist of incentives to new or further industrial investment. They are available equally to foreign and Italian investors. The restrictive size of this book makes a detailed description of the incentive system out of place and thus only a general outline of the principal items is set out below.

1. TAX INCENTIVES

1.a. Regional incentives

Most of the incentives have been introduced to encourage the industrial development of Southern Italy. Companies establishing their registered offices in the development areas to engage in manufacturing or tourist development there, are entitled to a reduction of 50% of the rate of IRPEF for ten years from the date of formation and to total exemption from ILOR from the year in which they start making taxable income. The exemption from ILOR is also granted to investments for the reconstruction, modernization, expansion or reactivation of existing manufacturing facilities in the development areas, in respect of profits attributable to such investments.

Any Italian company, regardless of the location of its registered office, is entitled to an exemption from ILOR of up to a maximum of 70% of that part of its taxable income which is to be invested in manufacturing facilities in the development areas, or in other companies having their own manufacturing facilities in such areas for use in such facilities.

Tax incentives are also granted to investments in undeveloped areas in Central and Northern Italy. These are limited to small and medium size manufacturing enterprises, as large size industries are already concentrated in these areas. A company qualifies for such incentives when the total value of all its fixed assets does not exceed two billion lire. The incentives consist of a ten year exemption from ILOR from the incorporation of the new company or from the investment in manufacturing industry by an existing company.

1.b. Non-regional incentives

Only a few of such incentives are of general interest to all companies. Some of them consist of deferred taxation of capital gains which, as stated above, are taxed as income. In addition to the case already mentioned in respect of IRPEG, taxation of capital gains realized on mergers or conversions of companies from one type to another is, on certain conditions, deferred to the year in which the gains are distributed to shareholders or converted into share capital. Full exemption from all income taxes is granted to interest from bonds issued by the State, regions, provinces, municipalities or other public bodies. Finally, full exemptions from ILOR tax is granted to profits invested for the exploration for hydrocarbons on the Italian continental shelf.

1.c. Non-tax incentives

These incentives primarily consist of government cash grants and low interest finance, provided to foster the industrial development of the South. Projects eligible for such aid must be in the development areas referred to above and involve the construction or development of manufacturing or tourist facilities. In general, it may be said that cash grants are made to defray the higher costs of operating in areas with poor infrastructure. Low interest finance is also provided by banks to cover development costs and is subsidized by the State. Repayment of loans for the construction of manufacturing facilities is spread over fifteen years and those for other purposes over ten years. The amount of the said cash grants and low interest finance depends upon the nature of the investment and may cover more than half the actual outlay. Some incentives in the form of low interest finance are also provided for the development of tourist facilities in other areas in Italy outside the South.

G. Social Security Contributions

Social security contributions are not considered as taxes in Italy although there are certain common fundamental features in the collection of tax and the social security contributions. The social security system is based upon a number of obligatory contributions and, although organized under the general supervision of the State, is administered by various State agencies which are in no way connected with the taxation authorities. This distinction means, for example, that pay-roll taxes paid to foreign governments for social security expenditure would not probably qualify for a tax credit in Italy as they are not considered to represent 'taxes on income' as this expression is understood in this country.

The Italian social security system is comprehensive as it provides not only free assistance in the event of illness and pensions but also death, accident and disability, maternity and unemployment benefits and makes provision for the payment of family allowances. It is financed mostly by mandatory contributions in percentage terms on wages and salaries, of which some 80% are paid by employers and 20% by the employees themselves. The latter are deducted at source by the employers who then pass the total contributions to the administering agencies at monthly intervals.

Contributions are calculated on gross remuneration which not only includes monthly salaries and wages, whether in money or in kind, but also bonuses of a continuous nature and certain allowances such as those to cover cost of living increases. Family allowances, leaving indemnities, and the reimbursement of expenses are excluded from the calculation. It is difficult to give an idea of the general cost of such contributions as they vary considerably according to the status of the employee and the type of insurance. It can, however, be said that they are approximately 30 to 45% of gross salaries and wages with an average of some 40% for employees insured against accident and disability and engaged in dangerous work. This burden is, however, gradually being reduced as legislation has been progressively enacted whereby the State assumes the burden. In fact, in southern Italy, very reduced contributions are now generally applicable.

The general rule is that social security contributions must be paid in respect of all Italian based employees regardless of the nationality and residence of the employer. This rule however is subject to numerous exceptions as a result of international and bi-national arrangements. Thus, a national of an EC country who is posted to Italy by his normal employer is subject to the social security legislation of his state of origin for the first twelve months of his stay in the case of a temporary transfer, and in certain circumstances this may be extended for a further period not exceeding twelve months. Further, the treaty relating to social security contributions between Italy and the USA provides that a US national, who works in Italy for a US employer and is covered by US social security, has his social security contributions in respect of pensions and similar items (but not health and accident insurance) paid in the USA and is not subject to the same in Italy.

H. Other Taxes

In addition to the taxes and levies dealt with above, there are two taxes of particular importance to the businessman. These are ILOR and the Municipal Tax on the Increase in Value of Real Property.

1. LOCAL INCOME TAX

Local Income Tax (*Imposta Locale sui Redditi*, known as ILOR) is a proportional tax payable on certain classes of income which was introduced in addition to IRPEG and IRPEF for two reasons. The first one was to provide finance to local administrative bodies, which were to assist in determining the rate of tax and receive all the proceeds. The law provides that rates can vary between 9.4% and 14%. However, ILOR is, in fact, now assessed and collected by the Central Government at a standard rate of 15%. The Government then pays to the local bodies amounts which are actually larger than the proceeds of the tax.

The second reason for the existence of ILOR was to favour income from employment, as salaries and wages were in fact excluded from the tax. However, recently the Italian Constitutional Court has held that the discrimination between income earned through wages and salaries and that from self-employment is against the principles of the Italian constitution and so excluded all earned income from the ambit of the tax. ILOR now only applies to business income, income from real property and also income from intangible property.

Companies and partnerships are both subject to ILOR. Taxable income is, in principle, computed in the same way as income for IRPEG and IRPEF purposes. However, dividend income is not subject to ILOR. Partnerships are considered as separate entities from their individual partners for ILOR purposes and taxed as such. Thus, individual partners do not pay ILOR on their shares of partnership profits. Furthermore, where partnership income is produced by the personal services of the partners, the amount of income subject to ILOR is reduced.

ILOR is paid by both residents and non-residents on their income from sources within Italy but not on their world-wide income as in the cases of IRPEG and IRPEF. Business income is considered to derive from Italian sources unless it is the income of a permanent establishment abroad with separate management and accounting.

Finally, as has been mentioned above, ILOR is deductible from the computation of taxable income for the purposes of both IRPEG and IRPEF.

2. MUNICIPAL TAX ON THE INCREASE IN VALUE OF REAL PROPERTY

This tax (*Imposta Comunale sull'Incremento di Valore degli Immobili*, known as INVIM) is a tax on the gains from appreciation in the value of real property. It is charged on gains made on the transfer of real property located in Italy whether by reason of sale, gift or death and paid by the vendors, donees, heirs and legatees as the case may be. It is also charged on unrealized increases in the value of property held by companies, other than that used in their business, at ten year intervals. In this case, INVIM is a periodical levy to avoid such property escaping the tax net.

The tax is collected by the Central Government but its proceeds are allotted to the municipalities where the property is situated. The municipalities also establish the rates of tax at periodic intervals within the general limits provided by law.

The calculation of the appreciation in the value of real property is the crucial point of the tax which is levied on the difference between the initial value and the final value of the property concerned as ascertained for Registration Tax purposes (or for IVA purposes where the transfer is subject to such tax) except that to the initial value are added all expenses connected with the original purchase or transfer. These include legal expenses and Registration Tax and also those expenses incurred in the improvement of the property

provided that they are properly documented.
In the years following the enactment of the law, it became apparent that a large part of the increase in value so calculated was accounted for by inflation and did not represent real appreciation. Originally a deduction of 4% of the initial value per year of ownership which was later increased to 10% was made to compensate against the effects of inflation. However, the Constitutional Court held that INVIM's failure to properly take account of the number of years of ownership was against the Constitution. As a result of this decision, the Italian Parliament has now repealed it and amended the way in which the taxable gain is determined by taking into account the length of ownership. This has, however, failed to resolve the problem as the tax has become more burdensome on long-term gains, irrespective of the fact that they may be due to inflation.
INVIM is levied at progressive rates which depend upon the ratio between the taxable gain and the initial value and the number of years of ownership. Rates vary from 3 to 30%.

I. Double Taxation Treaties

Italy has entered into treaties against double taxation and for the prevention of tax evasion and also certain agreements limited to the avoidance of double taxation on transport income with the following countries:

Austria	:	German treaty of 31st October, 1925 Extension of 26th August, 1950
Belgium	:	Treaty of 19th October, 1970
Brazil	:	Treaty of 3rd October, 1978
Canada	:	Treaty of 17th November, 1977
Czechoslovakia	:	Agreement of 28th August, 1973 (shipping and air transport profits)
China (People's Republic of)	:	Agreement of 8th September, 1972 (shipping profits)
Cyprus	:	Agreement of 24th November, 1972 (air transport profits)
Denmark	:	Treaty of 10th March, 1966
Dominican Republic	:	Agreement of 31st December, 1971
Egypt	:	Treaty of 26th March, 1966 Agreement of 18th April, 1977 (air transport profits)
Ethiopia	:	Agreement of 21st November, 1971 (air transport profits)
Finland	:	Treaty of 21st May, 1971
France	:	Treaty of 29th October, 1958 Amending agreement of 6th December, 1965
Gabon	:	Agreement of 9th March, 1972 (air transport profits)

German Federal Republic	:	Treaty of 31st October, 1925
Ghana	:	Agreement of 23rd August, 1968 (air transport profits)
Greece	:	Treaty of 19th March, 1965
Hungary	:	Treaty of 16th May, 1977
India	:	Agreement of 3rd February, 1970 (air transport profits)
Iran	:	Agreement of 29th September-7th October, 1969 (air transport profits)
Irish Republic	:	Treaty of 11th June, 1971
Israel	:	Treaty of 22nd April, 1968
Ivory Coast	:	Agreement of 19th February, 1968 (air transport profits)
Japan	:	Treaty of 20th March, 1969
Jordan	:	Agreement of 9th February, 1970
Lebanon	:	Agreement of 9th June, 1966 (air transport profits)
Libya	:	Agreement of 28th May, 1977 (air transport profits)
Mauritius	:	Agreement of 7th July, 1975 (air transport profits)
The Netherlands	:	Treaty of 24th January, 1957
Nigeria	:	Agreement of 22nd February, 1977 (air transport profits)
Norway	:	Treaty of 16th March, 1968
Philippines	:	Agreement of 25th January, 1969 (air transport profits)
Poland	:	Agreement of 9th November, 1973 (shipping and air transport profits)
Rumania	:	Treaty of 14th January, 1977
Senegal	:	Agreement of 20th April, 1972 (air transport profits)
Sierra Leone	:	Agreement of 6th May, 1970 (air transport profits)
Singapore	:	Treaty of 29th February, 1977
South Africa	:	Agreement of 26th June, 1953 (shipping and air transport profits)
Spain	:	Treaty of 8th September, 1977
Sudan	:	Agreement of 19th October, 1968 (shipping and air transport profits)
Sweden	:	Treaty of 20th December, 1956
Switzerland	:	Treaty of 9th March, 1976 Agreement of 3rd October, 1974 (commuting employees)
Syria	:	Agreement of 20th December, 1973 (shipping and air transport profits)
Thailand	:	Treaty of 22nd December, 1977
Trinidad and Tobago	:	Treaty of 26th March, 1971

Tunisia	: Agreement of 20th November, 1969 (shipping and air transport profits) Agreement of 7th December, 1973 (air transport profits)
Union of Soviet Socialist Republics	: Agreement of 16th September, 1971 (air transport profits) Agreement of 26th October, 1972 (shipping profits)
United Kingdom	: Treaty of 4th July, 1960 Exchange of notes of 4th July, 1960 Amending Protocol of 28th April, 1969
United States of America	: Treaty of 30th March, 1955
Venezuela	: Agreement of 3rd March, 1978 (air transport profits)
Yugoslavia	: Agreement of 24th May, 1967 (air transport profits)
Zaire	: Agreement of 9th May, 1973 (shipping and air transport profits)

The impact of these treaties must be determined on a case by case and country by country basis but there are certain underlying common principles which can be deduced from them.

Most of the treaties adopt the 'place of management' principle and consider that a company is resident in the country where it is actually managed although a different criterion is used in the treaty with the USA. This principle is a limitation on the concept of company residence embodied in Italian law, which also refers to the 'principal object of the business' as a criterion for the determination of residence.

Domestic law coincides in the main with the provisions of the various treaties in respect of the determination of trading income as Italy has adopted the OECD Double Taxation Model Convention's definition of permanent establishment for income tax purposes, although certain treaties differ slightly from this definition. The treaties also contain the principle that a permanent establishment's income should be taxed as that of an independent enterprise even so far as the company (of which it is a branch) is concerned. This should allow the deduction of interest and royalties paid to such a company from the permanent establishment's gross income, as is stressed in the OECD Model, but Italy is normally very strict in applying this rule.

All the treaties to which Italy is a party affect withholding tax on dividends, interest and royalties as is set out below. The rate of withholding tax applicable to dividends is further reduced in many treaties when they are paid to foreign companies owning the majority of the shares of the company paying the dividends. Some treaties (such as those with Denmark, Finland, France, Ireland, Switzerland, and the United Kingdom) appear to accept the principle of the 'force of attraction' of the permanent establishment in respect of such receipts. Thus, royalties paid to licensors resident in the above countries which have permanent establishments in Italy should be included in such permanent establishments' gross income even though the royalties are in no way connected with the permanent establishments. Dividends, however, should, in any case, benefit from the tax credit provided by the imputation system.

The treaties also include various general principles relevant to the taxation of individuals. The great majority of them define a taxpayers' country of residence as that where he has the 'centre of his interests'. This derogates from the automatic attribution of such a status after six months residence in a year provided for in Italian domestic law. Many of the treaties also modify the source rules found in Italian law, as for example, in the case of employment income where the OECD model clause is commonly adopted. Further, private pensions and annuities are normally attributed to the country of residence of the recipient, except in the case of France, and income from professional services is only taxable in Italy when performed through a 'fixed base' there, save in the case of remuneration to artists and sportsmen.

In relation to the methods of avoiding double taxation, it should be noted that certain treaties, namely those with Belgium, France, Norway and Sweden, adopt the principle of 'exemption with progressivity' whereby exempt income is included in the calculation for determining the tax rate applicable to non-exempt income. All the other treaties adopt the tax credit method, but many provide that several items of income should only be taxed in one of the contracting states.

All the treaties provide for procedures for settling disputes arising out of them and most have a clause dealing with the exchange of information. Certain of the treaties, namely those with Belgium, France and the United States, provide some rules in relation to assistance in the collection of taxes.

J. Schedule of Withholding Taxes

	Interest	*Royalties*	*Dividends*
Belgium	15 per cent	Nil	15 per cent
Canada	15 per cent	10 per cent	15 per cent
Denmark	Nil	Nil	15 per cent
France	15 per cent (1)	Nil (2)	15 per cent
German Federal Republic	30 per cent	15 per cent	Nil
Greece	10 per cent	Nil	25 per cent
Japan	10 per cent	10 per cent	10 per cent 15 per cent (4)
Irish Republic	10 per cent (1)	Nil (2)	15 per cent (5)
The Netherlands	Nil	Nil	30 per cent Nil (6)
Switzerland	12.5 per cent (1)	5 per cent (2)	15 per cent (5)
United Kingdom	15 per cent (1)	Nil (2) (3)	15 per cent 5 per cent (5) (7)
United States of America	No provision	Nil	15 per cent 5 per cent (8)

(1) Where the beneficiary of the interest maintains a permanent establishment in the other contracting state, no withholding is applied and interest is taxable in the latter as income of the permanent establishment even if it is actually not 'effectively connected' with such a permanent establishment.

(2) Where the beneficiary of the royalties maintains a permanent establishment in the other contracting state, royalties are taxable in the latter country as income of the permanent establishment, even if they are actually not 'effectively connected' with such a permanent establishment.
(3) Film royalties are treated as ordinary trading income.
(4) Tax is withheld at the rate of 10% where the non-resident recipient is a company which owns at least 25% of the voting shares of the payer for a period of six months immediately preceding the end of the relevant financial year. The rate of 15% is applied in any other case.
(5) Where the recipient of the dividends maintains a permanent establishment in the other contracting state, no withholding is applied and dividends are taxable in the latter state according to its domestic law as income of the permanent establishment, even if they are not 'effectively connected' with such a permanent establishment.
(6) Italy levies no withholding tax where the non-resident recipient is a company owning at least 75% of the payer's paid-up capital.
(7) Tax is withheld at the rate of 5% where the non-resident recipient is a company owning or controlling at least 51% of the voting shares save in exceptional cases.
(8) Tax is withheld at the rate of 5% where the non-resident recipient is a company owning, directly or indirectly, at least 95% of the payer's voting shares and not more than 25% of the recipient's gross income is represented by dividends received from its own subsidiaries.

K. Special Types of Companies

The Italian legal system does not include provision for any special type of company with the purpose of attracting certain categories of business or investors neither are there particular features in Italian tax or commercial law, other than those examined above which make, per se, the formation of any particular type of company more advantageous than another.

As has already been explained, owing to the mechanism of the Italian imputation system resident holding companies do not, in effect pay IRPEG on the dividends received from other resident companies, whilst dividends received from foreign affiliates are only taxed on 40% of their amount. There do not, however, appear to be good reasons for incorporating holding companies in Italy given the tax and legal treatment they are granted in certain other countries.

IV. LABOUR ASPECTS

A. Principles of Law on Employment

The freedom of contract in employment matters in Italy is limited by legal restraints aimed at protecting the employee. Such restraints are present, in particular, both at the time of the engaging of an employee and in the event of his eventual dismissal.

The sources of labour law are legislative and contractual. As will be explained in further detail, the latter mainly consist of collective agreements made by the employers association and trade unions in particular fields of activity.

1. ENGAGEMENT

The law provides that employees may only be engaged through employment exchanges which are run by the State and operate at provincial level. In practice, anyone wishing to work must have his name entered on the appropriate list for his trade, and employers may only take on employees through the employment exchanges. The prospective employer may not make a selection from such a list but only request the employment exchange to send him a certain number of employees from the appropriate list. The only exception to the above regulations relate to the employment of members of the employer's family and to limited categories of highly-skilled employees.
It should be noted that the system of recruitment through employment exchanges described above is now heavily criticized by both employees and employers.
A further requirement applies to employers with more than thirty-five employees. They are bound to recruit 15% of their total personnel from persons in specific categories such as military and civilian disabled, widows and orphans, refugees and the like. The law also sets out detailed regulations concerning these persons and the reasons for which their employment may be terminated.

2. INDIVIDUAL CONTRACTS OF EMPLOYMENT

Although this is not required by law, a written contract is envisaged in most of the collective agreements for management personnel and staff. It is required to set out the place of employment, the date of commencement, status and salary, the duration of any trial period and other special conditions of employment, if any. Written agreements are now very common.

3. DURATION AND TERMINATION OF EMPLOYMENT

A contract of employment is presumed to be of unlimited duration and may be for a definite term only when certain specific circumstances occur, such as that the job is of a seasonal nature, in substitution for workers absent for illness, maternity and the like, or for the performance of special services for a pre-determined period of time. Contracts with executives may always be for an initial definite term.
The applicable collective agreement establishes the duration of the trial period which is usually different for executives, staff and other workers. The extension or renewal of the trial period is not allowed. During such a period the employment may be terminated by either party at any time without notice or any right to compensation other than the employee's accrued salary.
The dismissal of an employee is strictly regulated by detailed legislation which applies to all commercial and industrial concerns having more than fifteen employees.
Whilst there is no condition whatever which limits the right of the employee to resign at any time, provided that he gives the appropriate period of notice, a number of limitations are imposed by law or by the collective agreements in

the case of the dismissal of an employee. The grounds for dismissal are dealt with by two basic laws, namely Law nr. 604 of 15th July 1966 which established the fundamental principle that an employee may not be dismissed without 'just cause' or 'justified motive' and Law nr. 300 of 20th May 1970 (known as the 'Charter of Employees' Rights') which further specified and made the principles established by the previous law stricter.

'Just cause' exists where the employee has committed a breach of duty of a seriousness that does not permit the continuance, even on a temporary basis, of his employment.

'Justified motive' exists where the breach of duty by the employee, though substantial, is not sufficient to justify dismissal without notice or where an individual redundancy situation exists.

Whilst the employee is not entitled to receive advance notice in case of dismissal for 'just cause', advance notice must be given by both the employer and the employee in any other case of termination. The length of notice is provided for by the collective agreements according to the status of the employee and his length of service with the employer. Failure to give such notice gives the other party and thus also the employer, if so be the case, a right to compensation in lieu of notice equivalent to the remuneration for the notice period.

In all cases of dismissal, including those for 'just cause', the employee has the right to receive a leaving indemnity (for which annual allocation is made during his employment). The amount of this indemnity depends on the length of service and is calculated on the basis of his final remuneration.

The employer must always give notice of dismissal in writing stating the grounds. The employee may dispute such grounds and, where the dismissal is found to be unjustified or illegal, the court disallows it and orders the reinstatement of the employee who is also entitled to receive his salary for the period from the court decision to his actual reinstatement plus a penalty equal to not less than five months salary and appropriate damages.

The legislation referred to above does not apply to small units with fifteen employees or less where dismissal is at the discretion of the employer provided the appropriate notice is given. It does not equally apply to executives (*dirigenti*) where, because of the nature of the executive's position, dismissal by the employer is permitted at any time. However, an executive who considers that he has been wrongfully dissmissed without 'just cause' or 'justified motive' may go to arbitration under the applicable collective agreement and, if the arbitrators uphold his position, he is awarded a supplementary indemnity but not reinstatement.

4. COLLECTIVE REDUNDANCY

There is no legal definition of collective redundancy. It can be said, however, that a redundancy situation exists when an employer discontinues or intends to discontinue (in whole or in part) his business or where the employer's requirement for employees of certain categories changes as a consequence of the technical or financial reorganization of his business.

There is a clear distinction, at least in law, between collective dismissals and individual dismissals and the former are more liberal from the employer's point of view than the latter. Attempts to combine the two disciplines have not been successful and a recent decision of the Italian Supreme Court has affirmed the net distinction between them and confirmed the principles which are now set out.

Collective redundancy is disciplined by a law passed in 1960 giving general effect to a collective agreement which permits collective dismissals where 'management finds it necessary to reduce the number of the employees of a business because of a reduction in size or a transformation of the business or the work process'. It will thus be noted that the law permits collective dismissals where, in the judgement of management, a need exists to reorganize a business in whole or in part or even close the business or part of it.

The procedure established by the law may be summarized as follows. Notice of dismissal setting out the reasons therefor must be given to the employees concerned. If this is contested, the employer must show that the reasons actually exist but the duty of the court does not go beyond the ascertainment of the existence of the relevant factors and does not cover the evaluation of them which is a question of judgement for management.

It is of great practical importance to mention the collective agreement signed on 5th May 1965 between the trade unions and the employers' associations although it does not have the force of law as explained below. It provides for a conciliation procedure in which the trade unions and the employers' associations participate. Whilst conciliation is in progress, the employer may not put into effect the dismissal. If the conciliation is not successful, the employer may proceed with it. If the dismissal does not concern all the employees or those of an individual unit, then the employer must act in accordance with certain criteria such as length of service and the like. Those dismissed have the right to be taken on by the same employer if he wishes to engage other similar employees within one year.

The observance of the above procedure does not concern the validity of the reasons for the collective redundancy but is a pre-requisite for putting it into effect. If the employees concerned contend that the conditions for collective redundancy do not exist, or question the observance of the procedural rules they can resort to legal proceedings and submit the matter to the courts.

Employees dismissed in the above way are entitled to unemployment benefits and have the right, as mentioned above, to be re-employed if the firm involved takes on new labour within one year. In addition in many cases they enjoy preferential treatment when industries of the same kind take on new labour.

B. Labour Procedures

Italian labour relations are characterized by the formal juxtaposition of the employers' organizations and the trade unions.

There are three principal trade union organizations and membership is mainly divided not according to the crafts of their members but rather their political allegiance. The three organizations are: the CGIL (Italian General Labour Confederation), communist and socialist inclined, the CISL (Italian Trades

Union Confederation), predominantly Christian Democrat, and the UIL (Italian Labour Union) the membership of which includes socialists, social democrats and republicans.

On the employers' side there is principally the General Confederation of Italian Industry, an organization which represents the vast majority of private industrial firms, whilst Intersind represents companies controlled by the state or by state agencies.

One of the main if not the principal function of the employers' organization and the trade unions is to negotiate collective agreements for various sectors of industry and commerce. These collective agreements govern the general aspects of labour relations and cover in detail all matters regarding employment.

The Italian Constitution foresaw that such collective agreements would have a general effect within the ambit of the industry or business concerned. However, detailed legislative provisions giving effect to this article of the Constitution have not, as yet, been made so that the agreements are only binding upon members of the employers' organizations and the trade unions which are parties to it. It is of interest to note, however, that the courts, in giving effect to another article of the Constitution which guarantees the employee a proper standard of living have taken the view that any contract granting an employee less benefits than those provided by the appropriate collective agreements is invalid and in this way have given general efficacy to the essential provisions of such collective agreements.

The procedure applying to labour disputes should also be mentioned. A law passed in 1973 significantly amended the procedure for resolving labour disputes and those in relation to social security matters. A new procedure was adopted based upon the hearing of oral evidence and speed, and competence in such matters was given to a local judge (*Pretore*). His decision is given at the end of the hearing and becomes immediately effective although it is subject to appeal.

C. Works Councils

Prior to 1970 employees within individual companies were protected through so-called Internal Commissions (*Commissioni Interne*). These were composed of persons elected directly by the employees and were not formally linked to the trade unions the primary functions of these Internal Commissions were to check upon the application of collective agreements, social security legislation and health and safety rules.

The Charter of Employees' Rights enacted in 1970 provides for the setting-up of Works Councils (*Rappresentanze Sindacali Aziendali*) composed of employees normally selected from members of the trade unions organizations and elected by the employees. The main functions of these bodies are, in addition to those of Internal Commissions, negotiating agreements at plant level, making proposals for the improvement of working methods, assisting in the improved functioning of social services, provided by the employer and com-

menting on draft regulations relating to production matters, holidays, working hours and the like.
To ensure that employees who are members of the Works Councils are not dismissed or transferred because of their union activities, special safeguards are established by law. Furthermore, employers are forbidden from doing anything which in any way could limit trade union activities or the right to strike.

D. Co-determination

Art. 46 of the Italian Constitution foresaw the introduction of co-determination, i.e. the right for employees to take part in the decision making process of business enterprises. However, as yet, no legislation giving effect to this Article has been made. In practice, however, it should be noted that the continuing extension of trade unions powers and influence in negotiating with the employers, in relation to productivity and the like, amounts, to some extent, to de facto co-determination.

E. Compulsory Profit-Sharing and Pension Schemes

There is no compulsory profit-sharing in Italy, although voluntary profit-sharing and similar schemes exist both on an individual basis and at company level.
The welfare of an employee in Italy is protected through an obligatory social security system which is based on the concept of insurance. The social security and welfare system provides benefits for disability, old age, death and unemployment. Compulsory insurance in respect of the above is provided for by means of special contributions and is administered by INPS (the National Social Security Institute). The employer is bound to insure the employee and pay contributions for him. Smaller contributions are paid by the employee. The obligation to pay contributions arises automatically on the engagement of an employee and lasts for the whole of his employment.
The employee is entitled to be paid a retirement pension at the age of 60 in the case of men and at the age of 55 in the case of women and the amount of such a pension is based on the payment of a percentage, varying in proportion to length of service, of the average salary paid to the employee during certain of the last years immediately before retirement. Private pension schemes are not common.
Under this heading it should also be mentioned that insurance against industrial accidents and disease is also obligatory. A separate contribution must be paid by the employer to another government agency, INAIL (National Industrial Accident Insurance Institute). From 1st January 1980, medical assistance is provided to an employee as well as to any resident through the new Italian National Health System.
Finally, without going into detail, it is of interest to note that insurance

against total or partial unemployment is also provided. Special benefits are available in the case of suspension of production or short-time working for reasons beyond the control of the employer. They are administered by the Cassa Integrazione Guadagni (Pay Supplementation Fund) run by INPS.

F. Residence-Work Permit for Non-residents

All foreigners living in Italy require a residence permit which is issued by the police authorities in the district where they live. Nationals of the EC countries are subject to no restriction on their taking employment and no work permit is required. They must simply provide the police authorities with a copy of their contract of employment and are issued with a residence permit for five years. In the case of non-EC nationals, the procedure is more complicated. In the first instance, the employer must obtain a permit from the labour authorities and such a permit is only granted where a particular need to employ the foreigner in question can be shown. Once this permit is granted, it is sent to the prospective employee who must then visit the Italian Consulate in his country of residence to obtain the necessary visa. On arrival in Italy he must then apply to the police authorities for a residence permit.
It is worthwhile noting that the non-observance of regulations regarding work permits for foreign employees amounts to a criminal offence for which the employer is liable.

V. BIBLIOGRAPHY

The Italian Legal System	Mauro Cappelletti	Stanford University Press, Stanford California, 1977
The Italian Civil Code	Translated by Mario Beltramo, Giovanni E. Longo and John Henry Merryman	Oceana Publications, Inc. Dobbs Ferry New York, 1969 and Supplement 1978.
Italian Company Law	Pietro Verrucoli	Oyez Publishing Ltd. London, 1977
Labor Relations and the Law in Italy and the United States	Mitchigan International Labor Studies	The University of Michigan, 1970

Luxemburg

Jacques Loesch

I. INTRODUCTION

1. The Grand-Duchy of Luxembourg is a small country, located almost in the centre of Western Europe.
It has a population of approximately 360.000 (Luxembourg City approximately 80.000).
It is an independent sovereign State, organized as a Constitutional Monarchy headed by a Heriditary Grand-Duke. Its political system is that of a Parliamentary Democracy.

2. Economically Luxembourg is a highly developed country and the per capita income is among the highest of Western Europe.
Its economic system is based on private and free enterprise which enjoys favourable conditions. Among others:
- there is a long established tradition of political and social stability, based on negotiation and consent;
- manpower is skilled and accustomed to high productivity;
- there is an excellent transportation system by road, rail, air, river navigation (Moselle);
- the access to the Administration is easy, even at the highest level;
- French and German are spoken fluently by almost everybody, and a great many people have also a good knowledge of English;
- there is a variety of incentives available for new enterprises and new investments.

During the last 10 years Luxembourg has become one of the large financial centres in Western Europe, with 110 banks, many of which are very prominent in international financial transactions.

3. Luxembourg has an economic and monetary union with Belgium. It is a member of Benelux and of the European Community and it is host to a number of European Institutions (European Court of Justice; European Court of Audit; European Investment Bank; Secretariat of European Parliament; several divisions of the European Commission).
Luxembourg is also a member of a great many international political institutions (United Nations; Nato, Council of Europe, etc.).

II. THE LEGAL FRAMEWORK

A. The Vehicle

1. THE WHOLLY-OWNED ENTERPRISE

1.a. THE BRANCH

1.a.(i) Setting-up – publication

1. Under Luxembourg law and practice the Luxembourg branch of a foreign company constitutes a secondary establishment of the foreign body permanently located at a fixed place within Luxembourg under the authority of a permanent representative who has the power to bind the branch and thereby the foreign body vis-à-vis third parties.

2. The statutes of the foreign company must be made public in Luxembourg. To that effect an up-to-date text must be:
- published in extenso in the Luxembourg Official Gazette ('Mémorial'). The text must be in either French or German. It may also be in English, but in that case a translation into one of these two languages must be added;
- the same documents must be lodged with the Registrar of the District Court in whose jurisdiction the branch is located (there are two jurisdictions in Luxembourg).

In order to achieve this, three copies of each document must be made available. They must be signed by a duly authorized person. The signature of the signatory need not be legalized.

3. The branch must be registered in the local Trade Register. This entry will be made upon presentation of a special request containing a summary description of the legal structure of the foreign company and of its branch, and the identification of the managers and representatives of the foreign company and the local branch respectively. Cost: 4.800,– Lfrs.

4. A corporate resolution must be taken by the competent corporate body of the foreign entity, resolving to establish a branch in Luxembourg, indicating the amount to be invested initially into the Luxembourg branch and designating the person or persons who will have power to validly bind the local branch. Any limitations to these powers should be specifically mentioned. This resolution must be publicized in the form indicated under (2) and (3) above.
If the foreign entity is not located within the EC, a capital duty ('droit d'apport') of 1% will be payable on the amount invested in the local branch.

5. Future amendments to the statutes and changes in the composition of the Board of Directors of the foreign entity as well as a transfer of the branch's

location in Luxembourg and a change of its representative must also be published in the way mentioned above.

6. Any acts, deeds, bills, letters, invoices, orders and other documents issued by the branch must state:
- the full denomination of the company and the specification of its legal form,
- the reference to its local branch with the complete address,
- the words 'Registre du Commerce' or their abreviation 'RC' accomplished by the indication of the location of the District Court of its registration and its registration number.

7. Besides penal sanctions any action brought before a Luxembourg Court by a company whose statutes have not been published in the 'Mémorial' as mentioned earlier may be dismissed.

1.a.(ii) Organization

– Management

A branch is managed by one or several representatives, either Luxembourg nationals or foreigners, with the powers granted to them by the foreign company.

– Liability

A branch is part of the foreign company and therefore directly binds it. The person entrusted with the management and the representation of the local branch is liable towards third parties as if it were managing a Luxembourg company.
As under Belgian law, directors of a Luxembourg company are liable not only for fraud but also for faults which they commit in the carrying out of their management duties. They are jointly and severally liable towards third parties for all damages resulting from an infringement of the company law or of the statutes of the company.

– Accounting – auditing

There are no specific requirements with respect to accounting and auditing of a branch. It is necessary and sufficient to comply with the general provisions of commercial law, according to which any business man must keep books and accounts as prescribed by sound commercial practice.
The foreign company having a branch in Luxembourg must publish its own annual accounts, but not separate accounts for the branch, in the same way as its statutes, i.e. in the 'Mémorial' and with the Registrar of the District Court. Failure to publish the annual accounts constitutes a criminal offence.

1.b. THE SUBSIDIARY

The Luxembourg company law is very similar to the Belgian company law. Consequently in many cases it will be sufficient to refer to the Belgian chapter of this book.

In Luxembourg, as in Belgium, two forms of business association are commonly used to establish a subsidiary:
- the 'private' limited company ('société à responsabilité limitée' – 'sarl'),
- the 'public' limited company ('société anonyme' – 'SA').

Both companies constitute legal bodies.

I. THE 'PRIVATE' LIMITED COMPANY ('SOCIETE A RESPONSABILITE LIMITEE' – 'SARL')

I.(i) Setting-up – publication

The establishment is made by a deed, containing the statutes, which must be executed before a notary public.

The company is formed for a limited or an unlimited duration. In the latter case, it is generally held that any member has the right to give notice of termination at any time subject to observing an appropriate delay.

The number of members must be at least two. Spouses may together establish a private limited company, subject to their marriage settlement not being modified thereby. The maximum number of members is 40. Both individuals and legal bodies may be members.

The object of the private limited company must not relate to insurance, finance or saving banks business.

The statutes must be published in extenso in the 'Mémorial' and lodged with the Registrar of the District Court in whose jurisdiction the company's seat is located.

The company must also be registered in the competent Trade Register.

Non-registration carries both penal and civil sanctions as is the case for branches (see above).

Any acts, deeds, bills, letters, invoices, orders and other documents issued by the company must state:
- its full denomination,
- the specification 'société à responsabilité limitée' fully spelled out,
- the complete address of its seat,
- the words 'Registre de Commerce' or their abreviation 'RC' accompanied by the indication of the location of the District Court of its registration, and its registration number.

I.(ii) Organization

I.(ii).a. Capital shares, debentures and transfer of shares

- Capital

  The minimum capital is 100.000,– Lfrs. or its equivalent in foreign currency. It must be fully subscribed and paid up and there may not be an authorized but unsubscribed capital.
- Shares, debentures

  The capital is divided into shares. All the shares must have the same par value, which must be of 500,– Lfrs. or multiples thereof or the corresponding amount in foreign currency. Each share confers equal rights as to voting and as to allocation of profits during the life of the company and on liquidation.

No preference shares and no non-capital shares may be issued.
All shares must be in registered form and are recorded in the register of members. Any member may inspect the said register.
The company may issue debentures and other similar debt instruments, but only on a purely private basis.

- Transfer of shares
  In principle the shares are not freely transferable. The law imposes certain minimum restrictions, which may be strengthened by the statutes. The transfer inter vivos or upon the decease of the owner to a non-member is subject to the approval of members representing at least three quarters of all the shares.
  However no agreement is required (unless the statutes provide otherwise) in case of transfer to members, to spouses and to certain heirs.
  Vis-à-vis the company and third parties a transfer must be accepted by the company in a notarial deed or, if made by private deed, it must be notified to the company by a bailiff.
  It must also be publicized in the same way as the statutes.

I.(ii).b. Management – representation

The company is administered by one or several managing directors ('gérants'), whether members or not.
Sometimes they are designated in the statutes: if that is not the case, they are designated by the members by a simple majority, unless the statutes provide for a higher majority.
The nomination is made for a limited or an unlimited period of time and must be publicized in the same way as the statutes.
Managing directors nominated in the statutes may not be revoked unless the statutes are amended, or provide for their revokal. Moreover, unless the statutes provide for the contrary, no managing director may be revoked without cause. Every managing director has the power to perform any acts necessary or useful for the accomplishment of the object and purpose of the company. This power covers all acts that are not expressly assigned by law to the decision of the members. The statutes may restrict the powers of the managing directors. However such restrictions do not prevail vis-à-vis third parties, even if they have been published, except that if there are two or more managing directors, the statutes may prescribe that they must act jointly.

I.(ii).c. Resolution of members

In principle resolutions are adopted by a general meeting of members. However, except if the articles so require, it is not necessary to hold a general meeting and resolutions may be adopted in writing if there are not more than 25 members.
In principle, resolutions must be adopted by members representing more than one half of the company's capital. If that quorum is not reached and if the statutes do not provide for the contrary, a second vote may be organized, at which resolutions are adopted by simple majority.
Special requirements as to quorum and majority are applicable in case of

amendment of the statutes and for the approval of a transfer of shares.
The shareholders, taking resolutions in general meeting or in writing, have no other powers than those entrusted to them by law, namely:

- election and revokal of the managing directors, and of the auditors if the company has auditors,
- approval of the transfer of shares,
- approval of the annual accounts and allocation of profits,
- amendment of the statutes, including capital increase or decrease and winding-up.

I.(ii).d. Liability of the managing director, of the parent company

The liability of the managing director vis-à-vis the company and vis-à-vis third parties is the same as that (one) of the members of the Board of Directors of a public limited company (see later).
In principle the parent company is not liable for the debts and commitments of its Luxembourg subsidiary.

I.(ii).e. Accounts, auditing, publication of accounts

- Accounts
  Private limited companies must prepare their accounts once a year which comprise the balance sheet and profit and loss account. There are no specific legal requirements as to the form and content of the accounts, except that the law prescribes that the amortizations deemed necessary must be made and that the balance must list separately the fixed assets, the current assets, the capital and reserves, the debentures, the secured and unsecured liabilities and the liabilities towards members.
  Out of the annual net profit 5% must be allocated to the legal reserve, until it reaches 10% of the nominal capital.
- Auditing
  The auditing by one or more auditors is only compulsory in case the private limited company has more than 25 members. The auditor may be designated in the statutes or by the members.
  The auditor has the same powers and responsibilities as the auditor of a public limited company. However, he may be elected for more than 6 years and he is not obliged to deposit shares by way of guarantee.
- Publication of accounts
  The private limited company is not obliged to publicize its annual accounts.

II. THE 'PUBLIC' LIMITED COMPANY ('SOCIETE ANONYME' – 'SA')

II.(i) Setting-up – publication

II.(i).a. Substantive conditions

The establishment of a public limited company requires the fulfilment of the following three conditions:

- There must be at least 7 shareholders who may be individuals or legal bodies.
- The initial capital must be fully subscribed.
- One fifth of each share must be paid up in cash or in kind. In case of capital contribution in kind, the shares issued against such a contribution are freely negotiable only ten days after the publication of the second annual accounts following their issue.

The company's duration may not exceed 30 years, but it may be renewed.

II.(i).b. Conditions of form

Like Belgian law, Luxembourg law recognizes two ways of incorporation: direct incorporation and incorporation through public subscription.

- Direct incorporation

  It is made by a deed containing the statutes, which must be executed before a notary public. The notary must certify the fulfilment of the three substantive conditions indicated above. As soon as the deed is signed, the funds contributed may be disposed of by the company.

  The statutes must contain:
  - the precise objects of the company;
  - the description of any contribution in kind, its valuation and the name of the contributor;
  - for any immovable property contributed in kind, a description of the transfers thereof made during the 5 years preceding the establishment;
  - mortgages or liens encumbering the immovable property contributed;
  - special advantages or privileges granted to the founders;
  - estimate of costs and expenses in relation to the establishment.

  The statutes must be published in the 'Mémorial' and lodged with the Registrar of the District Court in whose jurisdiction the company's seat is located.

  The company must also be registered with the competent Trade Register.

  Any acts must bear the same particulars as those of the 'sarl', except that the specification to be given on the company relates to 'société anonyme' (see above).

  Among shareholders the company exists as soon as the statutes are signed: vis-à-vis third parties it exists as from the date at which the statutes have been published.

- Incorporation by public subscription

  This procedure is very similar to the one used in Belgium (see Belgian chapter of this book).

- If one or more of the conditions imposed by law are not fulfilled, this does not mean that the company as such is null non-existent.

However, the founders and, in the case of capital increase, the directors are jointly and severally liable for all obligations contracted by the company until it has 7 shareholders, and for any part of the capital which has not been validly subscribed and for the payment of the subscription of up to one fifth. The law also provides that the founders are jointly and severally liable for all transactions performed on behalf of a company before its actual establishment, if such transactions have not been taken over by the company within two months following its establishment, or if the company has not come into existence within two years.

II.(ii) Organization

II.(ii).1. Capital, shares and transfer of shares, debentures

- Capital
  There is no minimum capital. The capital may be expressed in foreign currency.
  Besides the subscribed capital, there may be an authorized capital, i.e. a maximum amount of capital fixed by the statutes or by a resolution adopted by an extraordinary shareholders' meeting, within which the Board may from time to time issue additional shares.
  Unless the statutes or a shareholders' resolution provides for the contrary, in case of issue of new shares, existing shareholders have no preferential right to subscribe. However, if the new shares are issued publically, the Banking Control will require such a right to be recognized.
- Shares
  The share capital is divided into shares, which may have a par value or no par value.
  - All the shares must have the same value with a minimum of at least 50,– Lfrs. or its equivalent in foreign currency.
  - In addition to the shares representing the capital, the company may also issue shares which do not represent the capital, i.e. the assets or funds contributed to the company, ('parts bénéficiaires', 'parts de fondateur', etc.), the rights and privileges of which (financial rights, voting right) to be defined by the statutes.
  - The statutes may provide for several categories of shares with different financial rights and privileges.
  - As to their form, shares are either registered or bearer shares. The name of the owner of registered shares is entered into a shareholders' register kept at the seat of the company. A registered share is transferred by a corresponding entry made into the register. Holders of bearer shares can always request the conversion into registered shares, and vice-versa, unless the statutes do not permit the latter conversion.
    In certain cases shares must remain in registered form.
  - Shares entitle their owners to participate in the financial result of the company, either during its life-time (annual dividend) or upon winding-up (liquidation distribution).
- Transfer of shares
  In principle the shares are freely transferable unless the law, the statutes or an agreement among shareholders restrict the transferability.
  Bearer shares are transferred by delivery and registered shares by agreement between transferor and transferee to be entered into the shareholders' register.

- Debentures
  The company may issue privately or publicly any debentures or similar debt instruments. The company law defines the conditions of form and substance to be observed.

II.(ii).2. Management, representation

- Board of Directors
  The public limited company is administered by a Board of Directors, consisting of at least 3 members. The law does not fix any maximum number. The directors may be shareholders or not.
  They are appointed by the general meeting of shareholders for a period which may not exceed 6 years. They may at all times be re-elected and revoked by the general meeting with or without cause. Their appointment must be publicized in the same way as the statutes. Legal entities may also be appointed directors.
  As under Belgian law, certain persons are disqualified from becoming directors.
  In case of a vacancy between two shareholders' meetings the remaining directors and the auditor may, unless the statutes do not so permit, provisionally co-opt a new director, whose appointment must be confirmed by the next following general meeting.
  Directors may be remunerated if the statutes so provide. If they do not perform any other function within the company, they are not deemed to be employees, for purposes of labour law and social security.
  There must be pledged on behalf of each director that number of shares fixed by the statutes as a guarantee for the proper fulfilment of his duties. These shares must be in registered form.
  The Board of Directors as a body has the widest powers to perform all acts necessary or useful for the accomplishment of the company's objects. All powers not expressly assigned to the general meeting of shareholders by the company law or by the statutes fall within the competence of the Board of Directors.
  It represents the company vis-à-vis third parties.
- Representation
  The representation of a Luxembourg 'public' limited company is organized in principle in the same way as in Belgium.
  However, in comparison with the corresponding provisions of the Belgian law, the following particulars should be noted:
  a. The Board of Directors may not delegate all of its powers, be it to one or more of its own members or to third parties or to a committee or sub-committee; it may only delegate the day-to-day management. The question of knowing whether a given act or transaction does or does not fall within day-to-day management depends on circumstances and may differ from one case or company to another.
  b. The delegation by the Board of Directors of the day-to-day management to one or more of its own members is subject to the prior authorization of the general meeting of shareholders and to the Board annually accounting to the said meeting for the remuneration

granted to the delegate(s). In case to day-to-day management has been delegated by the Board, it cannot be restricted vis-à-vis third parties and thus concerns the entire day-to-day management.

c. As in Belgium, a specific proxy cannot cover the entire management or the entire conduct of the day-to-day business; it may only concern a specific act or transaction or a series of such acts or transactions.

d. Again as under Belgian law, the powers of representation vis-à-vis third parties of the Board of Directors and of the person or body entrusted with the day-to-day management respectively, may not be restricted. However, a statutory provision to the effect that a double signature is required is enforceable against third parties.

II.(ii).3. General meeting oj shareholaers

The general meeting of shareholders regularly constituted represents the entire body of shareholders. It consists of all shareholders who have complied with the conditions laid down by the statutes. Its resolutions validly adopted are binding on all shareholders.

A general meeting must be held at least once a year. The statutes must specify the exact date, hour and place of the annual meeting. Any other general meeting may be convened at any time by the Board of Directors or by the auditors. It must be convened upon the request of shareholders representing 20% of all shares issued.

Each holder of shares representing part of the company's capital has the right to vote. It is up to the statutes to determine to what extent a voting right is attached to shares which do not represent the capital ('parts bénéficiaires', 'parts de fondateur', etc.). The voting rights of all shares must be equal and there cannot be shares with multiple voting rights.

However, the voting power is limited as follows: no one may, either as shareholder or as proxy, vote for more than one fifth of the total number of the shares entitled to vote, or two fifths of the shares represented at the general meeting, whichever is the lowest. That limitation is not applicable at an extraordinary meeting of shareholders convened for the purpose of amending the statutes.

The procedure to be followed during a shareholders' meeting is laid down in the statutes; the range of provisions that they may contain on that point is extremely wide.

The powers of the general meeting are those which the company law and the statutes entrust to it, namely:

- election and revokal of the directors and the auditors,
- approval of the annual accounts and declaration of dividends,
- winding-up of the company and appointment of liquidators,
- extension of the company's life,
- increase or decrease of the share capital,
- merger, reorganization and, more generally, amendments to the statutes.

II.(ii).4. Liability of directors

As under Belgian law, the directors are not bound personally by the commit-

ments of the company, and their liability both towards the company and towards third parties is organized as it is under Belgian law (see: Belgian chapter of this book). The same applies as regards the absence in principle of any liability of the parent company.
However, there is one difference: in Luxembourg there is no such Act as the Belgian Act of 1978, according to which a director, former director or manager of a company can be held severally liable for a company's debts.

II.(ii).5. Accounts, auditing, publication of accounts

- Accounts
  Public limited companies must prepare annual accounts along the lines applicable to private limited companies (see above).
- Auditing
  A public limited company must be supervised by one or more auditors, whether shareholders or not, who need not be professionals. However banks must have an audit made by independant professionals.
  They are appointed by the general meeting of shareholders for a term not exceeding 6 years. The general meeting determines their number and their remuneration and it may re-elect them and revoke them at any time with or without cause. In case their number is reduced through death or otherwise by more than one half, the Board of Directors must call a general meeting forthwith, to fill the vacancies.
  There must be pledged on behalf of each auditor that number of shares fixed by the statutes as a guarantee for the proper fulfilment of his duties.
  The auditors have an unlimited right of supervision and inspection of all the company's business. They may examine, (without removing them) documents, books, minutes and correspondence.
  At the ordinary general meeting the auditors must report on their examinations and they can make any remarks and recommendations they think appropriate. In practice their report is always in writing.
- Publication of accounts
  The public limited company must file its annual accounts with the Registrar of the District Court within 15 days after their approval by the general meeting of shareholders. These accounts must also be published in the 'Mémorial'. The documents published and so filed must also indicate the name, first name, profession and domicile of each director and auditor and give particulars as to the appropriation of the annual net profit in accordance with the shareholders' resolutions. The obligation to file and publish the annual accounts lies with the Board of Directors. It is a criminal offence to fraudulently neglect to publish them.

III. CHECKLIST FOR ESTABLISHING A SUBSIDIARY IN THE FORM OF A 'PRIVATE' OR 'PUBLIC' LIMITED COMPANY

III.a. Formalities

- statutes enacted by a notary public before whom the founders must appear either in person or by proxy (which need not be legalized). In the case of a public limited company, evidence must be produced for the

notary that the amount to be contributed initially is freely available to the company;
- statutes published in extenso in the 'Mémorial' and lodged with the Registrar of the District Court in whose jurisdiction the company is located;
- entry in the Trade Register;
- application to the 'Ministère des Classes Moyennes' in order to obtain a permit to do business.

III.b. Cost
- 1% capital duty on the subscribed capital. In the case of a public limited company: no tax due on the authorized but unsubscribed capital. No stamp duty on shares or other securities issued;
- notary's fee: based on an official schedule and proportionate to the capital, e.g. for a capital of 10.000.000,– Lfrs. the fee will be 22.000,– Lfrs.
- cost of printing of statutes in the 'Mémorial': proportionate to the length of text; for an average size text in one language: approximately 25.000,– Lfrs.;
- entry in the Trade Register: 4.800,– Lfrs.;
- cost of permit to do business: 500,– Lfrs.

III.c. Timing
Once there is an agreement on the draft statutes, the enactment before the notary public and the publicity measures can be achieved within several days. It normally takes several weeks, sometimes even longer, to obtain the permit to do business.

III.d. General remark
Luxembourg law does not prescribe any conditions as to nationality or residence in respect of shareholders or members of any type of company, or of managers, directors, auditors, liquidators or branch representatives. In practice there is one exception: the Banking Control requires that in the case of a bank located in Luxembourg, its member of the Managing Board (in the case of a Luxembourg entity) or its local representative (in the case of a branch) actually resides in Luxembourg.

1.c. OTHER FORMS

Besides the two forms described above, Luxembourg company law, just as Belgian company law, recognizes other forms of companies. All of these forms are legal bodies.

1.c.(i) General partnership ('société en nom collectif')

The general partnership is formed between two or more persons with the aim to carry on business under a firm ('raison sociale'). It is established by private deed. The deed of establishment has to be published, by way of extract only, in the 'Mémorial' and lodged with the Registrar of the District Court. The partnership's firm may only contain the name of the partners. All partners are jointly and severally liable without limitation for all obligations entered into by the partnership.

1.c.(ii) Limited partnership ('société en commandite simple')

The limited partnership is formed between one or more partners without limited liability ('general partners' 'associés commandités') and one or more partners with limited liability ('limited, silent partners' – 'associés commanditaires') whose liability is limited to the amount of the funds contributed to the partnership.
It is not uncommon to have as a general partner a legal body, which generally is a private limited company, whose shareholders sometimes are the sole limited partners of the partnership ('GmbH & Co, KG'). The validity of such a set-up is recognized by Luxembourg commercial practice. Its attraction lies in that the general partner's liability is indirectly limited and in that, tax-wise, it is not subject to corporation tax (see section corporation tax).
The partnership's firm may contain the name of one or several general partners only, and it may not contain the name of any limited partner.
The limited partnership is managed solely by one or several general partners; the limited partner is not allowed to in any way participate in the management, were it by way of a proxy. He may only advise and supervise management.
The rules concerning the establishment and publications are the same as those applicable to the general partnership.

1.c.(iii) Partnership limited by shares ('société en commandite par actions')

As in Belgium, this form of company is now-a-days very seldom used. It consists of one or more general partners ('associés commandités') and of shareholders with limited liability ('actionnaires'), whose liability is limited to the amount of capital contributed to the partnership. It is a combination of a limited partnership and of a public limited company.
The firm of the partnership may contain only the name of one or more general partners. A special denomination may be added.
The partnership is managed solely by one or several general partners, to the exclusion of any shareholder.
The rights and duties of the shareholders are those of shareholders in a public limited company.
There must be a supervisory Board ('Conseil de Surveillance') of at least 3 members.
The rules concerning the establishment and publication are the same as those applicable to public limited companies.

1.c.(iv) Co-operative association ('société coopérative')

As in Belgium, this association consists of associates (members) whose number and contribution are variable. The liability of the associates (members) is either unlimited or limited, depending on their commitment. The assignment of shares to non-associates ('non-membres') is restricted.

1.c.(v) Non-commercial company ('société civile')

The non-commercial company also constitutes a legal body. However, it is not a commercial company, since its activity is limited to non-commercial transactions, such as: owning and administering real estate, mines, performing a non-commercial professional activity (e.g. chartered accountant). Its liabilities are divided among its members proportionately to their number, irrespective of the percentage of interest held by each one of them.

2. THE JOINT VENTURE

2.a. **The jointly owned company**

In Luxembourg as in Belgium, no statutory rules exist at the moment concerning the concepts of joint venture, participation, reciprocal participations, parent and subsidiary companies, and groups.

(i) Shareholders agreements

Agreements among shareholders relating to their rights and obligations as shareholders are rather common. In so far as they relate to the exercise of the voting right, they create a special problem, since, as under Belgian law, such agreements are in principle considered to be invalid. It is generally held that shareholders attending a shareholders' meeting must be completely free to form their opinion on the basis of the discussions at the meeting and the information received prior or during the meeting. However, certain agreements are valid, e.g. the agreement to consult each other before the general meeting in order to reach a collective opinion, or the agreement to vote in a certain way, if such an agreement is limited both in time and as to specific items or matters.

(ii) Minority rights

Again as in Belgium, the protection of minorities is not comprehensively organized under Luxembourg law.
The latter contains but a small number of provisions which, directly or indirectly, purport to protect the minorities:

- A minority of more than one third can veto any amendment to the Articles; if the form or purpose of the company is to be amended, the veto can be exercised by a minority of over 25%.
- The limitation of the voting power at ordinary general meetings has been described above.
- As also indicated above, the Board of Directors must convene a shareholders' meeting if requested by shareholders representing at least 20% of the stock; it is understood that a meeting so convened does not necessarily mean a favourable decision.
- According to a provision which is not frequently used, an investigatory action may be decided in Court at the request of a minority representing

20% of the stock. In that case the Commercial Court may appoint special auditors in order to verify the corporate books and documents. However, according to established case law, the Court will grant such an application only if there is clear evidence that there has been a serious lack of care in accounting procedures.
- In a public limited company having lost more than three quarters of its capital, a 25% minority has the right to resolve the winding-up and liquidation.

2.b. Consortia

Besides the forms dealt with in section 1, Luxembourg law, like Belgian law, recognizes the two forms of commercial partnership without legal personality described in the Belgian chapter of this book, namely the:
- 'association momentanée', and the
- 'association en participation'.

Both types of commercial partnership have the same characteristics as they have under Belgian law.

B. External Controls

1. EXCHANGE CONTROL

Luxembourg is linked to Belgium by a Treaty of Economic Union. Part of that Treaty is the foreign exchange control organized for common accounting and administered by a common administration, the 'Institut Belgo-Luxembourgeois du Change'. The system of control currently applied by that institute is described in the Belgian chapter of this book. It is therefore sufficient to state here that under present foreign exchange rules and regulations, foreign investment in Luxembourg and remittance of funds so invested, including the profit generated thereby, is extremely liberal and does not meet with any special obstacle.

2. TAKE-OVER CONTROLS, BANKING COMMISSIONER

The Luxembourg company law does not organize a specific control over take-overs, take-over bids or similar transactions.
However, a grand-ducal decree of 19th June, 1965, provides that any public exhibition, offer or sale of any kind of securities falls under the control and supervision of the Banking Control Commissioner ('Commissaire au Contrôle des Banques' – hereafter 'BCC').
To that effect any such operation, and in particular any public issue of shares or debentures or similar instruments must be reported to the BCC at least 15 days in advance. This notification must be accompanied by a file containing all relevant information on the issuer or offerer and on the proposed transaction. This information is commonly condensed in a Prospectus or similar

document. At present the information to be made available is very much in line with what is customary in other industrialised countries, and it closely follows the pattern on the EC directives and recommendations on the subject matter.
If the BCC is of the opinion that the proposed transaction is likely to disrupt the capital market or that the prospective subscribers may be misled, he may recommend the reduction of the offer or the postponement of the transaction and the amendment of the documentation. In case no consideration has been given to his recommendation, he may recommend to the Minister of Finance to forbid the proposed transaction during 3 months and the listing on the Luxembourg Stock Exchange of the securities concerned.
Although these various measures only consist in a postponement and not in a final prohibition, practice indicates that this is sufficient in many cases to definitely wreck any take-over bid or similar proposal. In addition the Luxembourg Stock Exchange has established a Code of Conduct which may be applicable to operations of this kind.

3. ANTI-TRUST

Luxembourg anti-trust law is embodied in the law of 17th June, 1970, on restrictive commercial practices ('loi du 17 juin 1970 concernant les pratiques commerciales restrictives').
That law purports to set-up within the territory of Luxembourg an anti-trust body of law corresponding to what articles 85 et 86 of the EEC Treaty aim at in relation to the trade between member states.
According to art. 1, all agreements between enterprises, decisions by associations of enterprises and concerted practices which have as their object or effect the prevention, restriction or distortion of competition and which adversely affect the general interest are the object of penal sanctions.
The same applies to the activities of one or more enterprises which commit an abuse of a dominant position on the market and thereby adversely affect the general interest.
There is an exemption for agreements between enterprises, decisions by associations of enterprises and concerted practices which result from the application of a legal provision or for which the parties concerned are in a position to evidence that they contribute to improve the production or the distribution of products or to promote the technical and economic progress and duly respect the consumers' interest.
A special commission on restrictive trade practices is given power to investigate any matter likely to fall under the Act.
The commission may advise the Minister of Economic Affairs either to abandon any further investigation, or to address to the parties concerned a warning or recommendation, or to totally or partially prohibit any measures or practices recognized as being contrary to the provision of art. 1 of the law.
An appeal against the Minister's decision may be lodged with the 'Conseil d'Etat, Comité du Contentieux'.
In case of infringement of any final decision of prohibition or injunction, there is a punishment by emprisonment or heavy fine.
The law of 1970 has already been applied on several occasions.

4. ENVIRONMENTAL CONTROLS

4.1. The law of 16th April, 1979, extensively deals with enterprises engaged in what the law describes as dangerous, unhealthy or inconvenient activities. It extensively applies broadly speaking, to any industrial or commercial enterprise, the existence or operating of which may create danger or inconvenience with respect to either security or salubrity or otherwise vis-à-vis the public, the environment and the personnel employed.
For the purpose of applying the numerous and detailed provisions of the law, enterprises are divided into three categories. Each enterprise to which the law applies must obtain a special 'non-inconvenience' certificate, to be issued, depending on the class to which it belongs, by either the 'bourgmestre' (mayor) or the Government after completion of an investigation procedure called 'commodo et incommodo'. Any transfer, extension or transformation of an enterprise is subject to a new permit. The permit may impose such restrictions and conditions as it deems necessary in order to fully protect anyone concerned by the law's aim.

4.2. According to the law of 29th July, 1965, on conserving nature and natural resources, it is unlawful to build any construction of whatever kind outside any agglomeration. An agglomeration in the sense of the law means at least 5 houses permanently used as human living accommodation and not separated by more than 100 metres. However, an exemption may be granted for setting-up industrial and commercial enterprises outside agglomerations, as defined by the law. According to a recent re-development plan, certain geographical areas of Luxembourg have been set aside as industrial zones.

4.3. The law of 16th May, 1929, deals with water pollution. A number of subsequent laws and decrees set up a whole body of law dealing with the subject matter.

4.4. The law of 21th June, 1976, aims at preventing pollution of the air and contains detailed provisions to that effect.

4.5. The law of 21th June, 1976, aims at preventing excessive noise. An additional decree of 13th February, 1979, contains a number of rules with respect to limiting the noise in the immediate vicinity of any industrial enterprise and building site.

4.6. The law of 12th June, 1937, imposes on each local community having 10.000 and more inhabitants the duty of having a general development project and plan, covering its entire territory. Such a project and plan will normally divide the whole territory of the local community in sections or zones. The setting-up of industrial enterprises is permissible only in those sections or zones set aside for that purpose, so that no industrial enterprises may be erected in residential sections or zones.

5. STATE MONOPOLIES

In Luxembourg state monopolies, either legal or de facto, exist in the following main areas:

- water and gas supply: through individual local communities or inter-communal bodies,

- electricity supply: through individual local communities and through a private company ('Cégédel') entrusted with the country-wide distribution on the basis of a state monopoly,
- post-office, telegraph and telephone: state monopoly,
- transportation:
  - railways: CFL monopoly,
  - road transportation of people and goods: CFL competing with private sector,
  - air transportation: private company, Luxair, entrusted with the transportation, which is international only, on the basis of a state monopoly,
- social insurance: state monopoly through several public bodies in all sectors: pension and retirement, family compensation, unemployment, illness and disablement, occupational accident and disease,
- financial sector: no monopoly, the state owned Savings Bank ('Caisse d'Epargne de l'Etat') competing with the private sector in the whole field of financial services,
- radio and television: through a private company, but on the basis of a state monopoly.

6. PERMIT TO DO BUSINESS

The Luxembourg Constitution guarantees the freedom of commerce and industry.
Under Luxembourg law, no consent whatsoever is required to form a company or to set-up a branch, nor is there a prior control thereof.
However, for purposes of administrative control, the law prescribes that anyone, individual or legal body, Luxembourg or foreign, must obtain a permit prior to engaging in any kind of commercial or industrial activity or in a wide range of other activities such as: architect, independent engineer, horticulturist, chartered accountant, patent agent, etc. Special laws govern protected professions or activities (e.g. chemist; etc.).
The operating of multiple branch or multiple store enterprises is either completely prohibited or strictly limited.
The permit to do business is delivered by the Government on the basis of an application to be supported by documentary evidence. The latter bears in particular on the professional and moral qualification of the applicant and, in case of a company, of its member of the Managing Board, managing director or representative. Any extension or modification of the purpose initially described is also subject to a specific authorization. In the case of banks or other financial institutions a minimum capital, as determined from time to time by decree, is a condition for obtaining the required permit. The permit is personal, non-assignable, and it may be revoked on serious grounds. Cost of permit: 500,– Lfrs. The total number of permits allowed is in no way limited.
Foreigners may obtain a permit, provided Luxembourg nationals enjoy similar rights in the foreign country concerned. That specific reciprocity condition is not any more applicable to nationals of other EC countries.
It is a criminal offence to actively engage in any kind of activity depending on the prior delivery of the permit to do so without having obtained it.

7. COMPULSORY WINDING UP

The Commercial Court may, at the request of the Public Prosecutor ('Procureur d'Etat') decide the compulsory dissolution and liquidation of any company which is in breach of the criminal law or which severely infringes the prescriptions of the company law.
This provision has been added to the company law by a recent Act (Act of 19th May, 1978). It is generally recognized that the Public Prosecutor will start an action to that effect only in cases where it appears that the violation of the law is a serious one.

III. TAXATION

General
As in all other developed countries, taxation in Luxembourg is embodied in numerous instruments of law and is of a highly complex character, subject in addition to frequent changes. The following lines therefore cannot possibly give more than a very general and extremely summarized view on the subject matter.

A. Corporate Income Tax

1. ENTITIES SUBJECT TO TAX

1.1. The following entities are subject to corporate income tax:
- Public limited companies
- Private limited companies
- Partnerships limited by shares
- Cooperative associations
- Certain other types of legal entities.

Not subject to corporation tax:
- General partnerships
- Limited partnerships
- Non-commercial companies ('sociétés civiles').

Income tax and other taxes are levied directly on their members.
'Holding companies' enjoy a special tax treatment (see hereafter under K).

1.2. Resident companies are subject to corporate income tax on their worldwide income, whereas non-resident companies are subject to corporate income tax on their Luxembourg income only.
A resident company is a company whose registered seat or actual place of management is located in Luxembourg.
A non-resident company is a company which does not have in Luxembourg its registered seat or actual place of management but which earns income from Luxembourg sources, e.g. through a 'permanent establishment' located in Luxembourg or through the activities of a permanent local representative.

2. COMPUTATION OF PROFITS

2.1. Income

2.1.1. In principle the taxable income is based on the company's accounts. The accounts must be prepared in accordance with sound accounting practice, without having to follow a strict scheme imposed by law.
The accounting period cannot exceed twelve months.

2.1.2. The taxable profit is the difference between the net asset value at the end of the accounting period and the net asset value on the last preceeding accounting date. Amounts taken out are added and amounts contributed are deducted.
No difference is made between distributed and undistributed profit, nor between operating profit and liquidation profit.
The tax profit also comprises director's fees and remunerations except if they are paid as compensation for day-to-day management.
Hidden profit distributions are treated as constructive dividends.

2.1.3. As regards valuations, the following may be said:

- the whole tax system is based on the minimum value principle;
- unrealized profits may not be included whilst unrealized losses must be accounted for;
- current assets and liabilities must be valued at cost or at the lower going concern value;
- fixed assets are valued at cost, but may be valued at the lower going-concern value; the going-concern value is the price which a purchaser of the entire business would allocate to the individual asset if he were to continue operating the business;
- for inventories, the first in first out principle is often applied; however the tax authorities also accept any other method consistently applied if it adequately reflects the tax payer situation;
- depreciation allowances are mandatory; the straight-line method of depreciation is generally used; however the declining balance method is permitted for tangible assets other than buildings: depreciation rates are not fixed by law: they are based on the useful life of each asset.

2.2. Capital gains/losses

Capital gains/losses are treated as operational gains/losses: there is no special capital gains' tax.

2.3. Exemptions

2.3.1. Dividends and other distributions of profits as well as all other income such as liquidation profits received by a resident company from another resident company are not taxable if the recipient company has owned directly and continously 25% or more of the shares of the distributing company for at least twelve months prior to the end of its financial year ('affiliation privilege'). The same exemption is granted for resident companies receiving such income from non-resident companies, provided the non-resident company is subject in its own country to a corporation tax similar to the Luxembourg one. This exemption is also granted if two or more resident companies own together at least 25% of the capital of a non-resident company and if one of the recipient companies owns more than 50% of the shares of the other recipient compan(y)(ies).

2.3.2. With respect to income from sources outside Luxembourg generated by a permanent establishment located abroad, there is a general foreign tax credit against Luxembourg income tax. The relevant tax provisions are highly technical and can, very briefly, be summarized as follows:

- Separate accounting records are kept for the foreign permanent establishment.
- The amount of foreign tax imposed on the foreign permanent establishment against Luxembourg income tax is limited by the amount of the Luxembourg corporation tax due on the income from foreign sources. The non-creditable portion of foreign taxes is deductible from income as an expense.
- The foreign taxes which may be credited against Luxembourg income tax must be similar to the Luxembourg corporation tax. There is no tax credit in Luxembourg for other foreign taxes.
- The foreign tax credit is principally calculated on a 'country by country' basis, i.e. for each country a subtotal of taxable income must be established.
- Losses incurred by the foreign permanent establishment may be carried forward for five years and may be credited against future positive income originating in the same country.
- The above provisions apply, whether or not there is a double tax treaty with the foreign country concerned, provided that where there is a treaty it must apply the tax credit and not the exemption method.

2.3.3. As regards income from foreign capital assets (essentially dividends; debt and bond interest) the tax-payer may opt for the so-called 'global method'. It consists in adding together all the corresponding net income accrued abroad, including that on which no foreign tax has been levied. The total amount of foreign tax paid on this income will be credited against the Luxembourg tax. However the setting off against Luxembourg tax will only be granted on foreign tax not exceeding a rate of 20%. The surplus is deductible as an expense. Moreover the total amount of Luxembourg tax credit is limited to 15% of the total amount of Luxembourg tax.

2.3.4. If a capital gain is realized when an asset is either destroyed by an act of God or is expropriated, taxation of such capital gain is deferred if the asset is replaced under certain conditions. In case of a voluntary conversion of a non-depreciable asset, taxation of the capital gain may also be deferred under similar conditions.

2.3.5. Reorganizations by merger or splitting of resident companies are tax exempt if all assets and liabilities are transferred at book value in exchange for shares to be allocated directly to the shareholders of the reorganized companies.

2.4. Deductible expenses

2.4.1. In principle all business expenses related to the company's activities are deductible.

2.4.2. Particulars:

- In principle debt interest is deductible regardless of its rate.
- Wages and salaries are deductible.
- Insurance premiums for property and for personal liability insurance are deductible; allocations to pension scheme reserves are deductible only if certain specific conditions are fulfilled.
- Lease payments are deductible.
- Corporation tax and net worth tax are not deductible; in the absence of a double taxation treaty, foreign taxes which cannot be credited against Luxembourg taxes are deductible as an expense item from income on which the foreign tax is levied; municipal business tax, tax on real estate and other taxes levied on a particular object are deductible.
- Reasonable amounts of travel and entertainment expenses are deductible if incurred in connection with the companies business.
- Formation and similar expenses are immediately deductible: in practice they are often written off over three to five years.
- A general provision for doubtful debtors is not allowed; however banks are permitted to make general provisions for doubtful debts at the rates of 1% and 1,5% respectively depending on the kind of debts concerned.
- Royalties for use of patents, trade-marks, etc., are deductible.

2.4.3. Non deductible expenses are:

- corporation tax, net worth tax, subscription tax, registration tax;
- remunerations and fees granted to directors (see above);
- charities, except limited amounts granted to specific Luxembourg institutions.

2.4.4. Operating losses incurred during the five preceding fiscal years are deductible and may be carried forward.

3. RATES OF TAX

3.1. Resident companies are subject to corporation tax at the following rates:

– If the taxable income is less than 400.000,– Lfrs.:	20%
– If the taxable income is between 400.000,– and 600.000,– Lfrs.:	80.000,– Lfrs. + 50% of excess over 400.000,– Lfrs.
– If the taxable income is between 600.000,– and 1.000.000,– Lfrs.:	30%
– If the taxable income is between	

1.000.000,– and 1.313.000,– Lfrs.:	300.000,– Lfrs. + 72% of excess over 1.000.000,– Lfrs.
– If the taxable income exceeds 1.312.000,– Lfrs.:	40%

On the basis of a law providing for temporarily funding an unemployment fund, an additional 1% is payable.

3.2. Non-resident companies are subject in principle to the same tax rates as resident companies, except that the actual tax rate is determined on the basis of worldwide income. This means that the lower tax rates are applicable only if the company's worldwide income is lower than 1.312.000,– Lfrs.

4. TAX CREDITS

Shareholders of companies subject to corporation tax are not entitled to any personal tax credit on the basis of the corporation tax paid by the company. On the contrary, on the dividends paid out they will suffer the 15% withholding tax, subject to any reduction thereof on the basis of double tax treaties.
In addition, resident shareholders will have to pay their personal income tax, according to the rate applicable, against which the 15% tax withheld at source will be credited.

5. TIMING OF PAYMENTS

Tax returns must be filed by 31st May of the calendar year following the company's accounting date. On request to the competent tax controller, an extension may be granted.
The tax administration is entitled to obtain full co-operation from the tax payer in order to properly assess the tax.
Taxes are payable in quarterly instalments on presumed taxable income as estimated by the tax controller.
If payment is not made, interest at the rate of 0,5% per month will be charged.
The statute of limitation is, in principle, 5 years. However it may be extended to 10 years in case of an additional assessment caused by an incomplete or inadequate tax return.

6. REVIEW AND APPEAL

The tax payer may apply to the Head of the Tax Administration ('Directeur de l'Administration des Contributions Directes et des Accises') to have the tax assessed by the tax controller reviewed.
An appeal against the decision of the Head of the Administration may be lodged with the 'Conceil d'Etat, Comité du Contentieux'. Neither an application for review nor an appeal constitute a stay of payment.

B. Withholding Taxes on Dividends, Interest, Royalties

1. The following categories of income are subject to withholding tax:
- dividends or other income from shares or participations, including profit sharing bonds;
- income received by the silent partner of a business enterprise;
- royalties on patents and royalties on literature and film rights paid to non-resident recipients.

The withholding tax on dividends does not apply if the debtor of capital income is a Luxembourg holding company or if it is a resident company whose share capital is owned for at least 25% by another resident company.
The withholding tax on interest paid on bonds, debentures and similar instruments has been totally abolished.

2. The income to be taken into account is the amount actually paid out.

3. The rates of withholding tax are the following ones:
- on dividends or profit sharing bonds: 15%; if the payer assumes final liability of payment, the rate is 17,65%,
- on patent royalties: 12%,
- on royalties on literature and film rights: 10%.

It is worth mentioning that in the case of royalties, the tax is to be withheld only if payment is made to a non-resident person.
In addition, the Tax Administration may request tax payable by non-residents to be withheld at source on any kind of Luxembourg income.

4. The effect of tax treaties is shown on the schedule of withholding taxes (see hereafter under J).

C. Registration and Stamp Duties

1. A registration tax ('droit d'apport') of 1% is payable on formation and on any capital increase by contributing additional funds. However that tax is not due if the capital is increased by incorporating retained earnings or surplus. It is not due either if the life of the company is extended. The tax is assessed on the amount of cash or on the market value of the assets in kind contributed. The same tax is due if a company located in a non EC country sets up a branch in Luxembourg.

2. There is no stamp or similar duty of any kind on securities issued by a Luxembourg company.

3. Apart from the corporation tax which may be due on the liquidation profit, no tax is payable on dissolution or liquidation, except a flat amount of Lfrs. 20.–.

4. On registration of certain deeds, a proportionate registration duty is payable. E.g. 0,6% on lease contracts; 0,24% on loan agreements.

5. The transfer of real estate property is subject to a registration duty at a rate of 6% (or 9% if the property is located on the territory of the Municipality of Luxembourg City) and an additional 1% for transcription in the property and mortgage register.

D. Individual Taxation

1. PERSONS SUBJECT TO TAX

1.1. Resident individuals are subject to income tax and to net worth tax on their worldwide income and net worth, whereas non-resident individuals are subject to income tax and to net worth tax on their Luxembourg income and Luxembourg net worth only.

1.2. A resident individual is a person who has in Luxembourg a domicile or a customary place of abode.
The domicile is a dwelling kept under circumstances which indicate that it will be maintained and used for residence/living.
A customary place of abode is deemed to be the place where an individual has lived continuously for a period of at least 6 months whether in one calendar year or not.

1.3. Husband and wife are jointly taxed if they are both residents and live together.

2. COMPUTATION OF INCOME

2.1. Income

2.1.1. Taxable income is sub-divided into 8 categories, being income from:
- trade or business,
- agriculture and forestry,
- independent professional services,
- employment,
- pensions or annuities,
- capital assets,
- letting or leasing,
- other sources as specified by law.

2.1.2. As to these various sources of income, it seems sufficient for the purpose of this chapter, to notice the following only:

(i) income from trade and business includes
- income from a commercial, industrial, mining or artisan activity,
- income from the sale or liquidation of such enterprises,
- income of whatever kind, including profit on transfer of shares, derived by a partner in a general partnership, a limited partnership, or a similar entity, and by a general partner in a partnership limited by shares.

(ii) income from independent professional services is the income earned by independent professionals, such as medical doctors, solicitors (attorneys), public notaries, public accountants, architects, experts, etc.
It includes allowances paid to Board members and auditors as compensation for their Board and supervisory functions.

(iii) income from employment includes any kind of remuneration such as salary, wage, bonus and any other benefit in cash or in kind derived from an occupation in a dependent status.
It also includes payment to Board members if such payment is made for compensation of day-to-day management or special services.
The tax on income of this category is basically withheld at source, subject to final assessment.

(iv) income from capital assets includes dividend and all form of interest on shares, bonds, loans, deposits, bank-accounts.
Several kinds of income belonging to this category are subject to withholding tax (see above).

(v) income from other specific sources includes:
- gains realised on the sale of a 'substantial participation', i.e. shareholder who either alone or who together with his wife and minor children owns more than 25% of the stock of a company,
- gains from 'speculative transactions' such as sale of movable property within 6 months of purchase,
- capital gains on the sale of land and buildings of the private patrimony, under certain conditions and with certain rebates.

2.1.3. Income is computed according to either the accrual method (income from trade or business, from agriculture and forestry, from independent professional activity) or the cash receipts and disbursment method (other categories of income).
As regards determination of taxable profit and valuation, the rules are in principle the same for personal income and corporation profit. They have been explained very briefly above.
For the taxation of individuals, the following might be added:
- Income from a foreign permanent establishment or from real estate property located abroad is taxable in its entire amount, unless exempted by a double tax treaty. The tax-payer may claim a foreign tax credit against his Luxembourg income tax (see above).
- The rental value of the tax-payer's private home, as computed on the standard value of such property, is added to his taxable income.

2.2. Capital gains

There is no specific capital gains tax. Capital gains are taxed only in limited cases (see above), and then in principle at the rate of all ordinary income, except for special tax rates and special rebates in cases specified by law.

2.3. Exemptions, deductions, rebates

2.3.1. Exemptions.

The most important tax exempt items worth mentioning are the following ones:

- allowances from the Luxembourg social security,
- under certain conditions: cash settlement by life insurance companies,
- under certain conditions: overtime salary, retirement, jubilee or dismissal allowances,
- travel and entertainment expenses reimbursed to staff, to the extent that they are substantiated by documentary evidence or do not exceed daily allowances such as laid down in official regulations.

2.3.2. Deductions, rebates.

- Deductible special expenses which are worth mentioning include:
- interest on debt, annuities,
- contributions or premium on all kinds of insurance, but only up to certain amounts which are determined in relation to the tax class (see later),
- compulsory contributions to the Luxembourg social security institutions,
- additional special deductions recognized by law or granted upon request in a number of cases defined by law,
- the first Lfrs. 40.000,– of interest for savings deposits and certain Luxembourg public bonds are tax free.

2.3.3. Non deductible expenses include:

- household and living expenses,
- personal income tax and net worth tax,
- charities, except limited amounts granted to specific Luxembourg institutions.

2.3.4. To the extent non-resident individuals have income from Luxembourg sources, they are taxed on such income. As regards expenses, they must prove the relationship of expenses to the taxable income in each category. Moreover they are not granted certain deductions.

3. RATES OF TAX

3.1. Taxable income is subject to a progressive income tax

Tax-payers are classified in 3 groups:

I. single persons without dependents,

II. married persons without dependents, single persons over 65 years, single persons with dependents.

III. persons entitled to dependent allowances (children under 21 either belonging to the household or mainly dependent on the taxpayer and children over 21 but under 25 studying or engaged in professional courses who are mainly dependent on the tax-payer).

The tax rates vary from 22 to 57%.

On the basis of a law providing for temporarily funding an unemployment fund, an additional 2.5% is payable.

3.2. Non-resident tax-payers pay income tax at the rate applicable to tax group II with a minimum rate of 15%.

3.3. On request individuals coming from abroad to establish their fiscal residence (see above) in Luxembourg may obtain a lump-sum tax for a maximum period of 10 years.

3.4. Individuals are also subject, according to circumstances, to the other taxes levied in Luxembourg (see later). These taxes are levied on individuals in the same way and at the same rates, except that individuals may be entitled to certain special rebates or deductions.

4. SUCCESSION DUTIES (ESTATES TAXES/GIFT TAXES)

4.1. Succession and inheritance duties

Succession assets are subject in Luxembourg to succession and inheritance duties under the following conditions:

- If the deceased has had his last domicile in Luxembourg, there is an unlimited liability. However real estate property located outside Luxembourg is exempted.
- If the deceased has not had his last domicile in Luxembourg, only real estate property located within Luxembourg is subject to duty.

In the case of unlimited liability, the duty is payable on net assets only, whereas in the case of limited liability, the tax is assessed on the gross value of real assets located in Luxembourg.

The tax rates are variable according to the relationship of the deceased to the heirs and to the value of the portion received by each heir:

- descendents, ascendents and surviving spouse with children: in general: nil,
- brothers and sisters: 6%,
- other or no relationship: 9 to 15%.

These basic rates are subject to sur-tax, depending on the values, the maximum rate being 48%.

In the case of limited liability, the rates are slightly different and there is no total exemption.

4.2. Gift taxes

In principle gifts must be made by notarial deed and are subject to registration duties.

The making of gifts may be restricted by the provisions of the Luxembourg Civil Code – to the extent it is applicable – as to the portions of the estate reserved for descendents and for the surviving spouse.

Gifts of movable property are subject to tax irrespective of the place of location of such property, if the donor is domiciled in Luxembourg. Gifts of real estate property located in Luxembourg are subject to tax, irrespective of the place of residence of the donor.

The tax rates vary according to the relationship of the donor and the donee between 1.8 and 14.4%.

The tax is assessed on the fair market value of the donated good.

E. Indirect Taxation

The essential tax to be mentioned under this heading is the VAT tax ('taxe sur la valeur ajoutée').
Since the basic principles of that tax are derived from the EC law on the subject matter, reference is made to the corresponding chapter of this book.
As regards Luxembourg, it seems sufficient to give the following brief information.

1. The VAT tax applies to:
- the delivery of goods and the rendering of service within Luxembourg by entrepreneurs,
- the importation of goods into Luxembourg.

2. Both the Luxembourg and the EC law contain detailed definitions of what is meant by 'delivery of goods', 'rendering of services within Luxembourg' and 'importation of goods'.

3. The tax is levied on the total amount payable or the total market value, excluding VAT itself.

4. The basic tax rate is 10%.
A reduced tax rate of 5% applies to certain goods and services:
- goods: sugar, motor fuel, water, gas, electricity, books, newspapers, a number of agricultural products,
- services: transportation of persons, independent professional services, other services related to cultural, scientific or educational purposes, agricultural services.

A special rate of 2% is applicable on certain food products and on pharmaceuticals.
There is no 0% rate.

5. Exemptions include:
- in general: export transactions and international transportation,
- in particular: a number of transactions such as: most banking services, including gold transactions, and certain financial transactions; leasing of real estate, except business machinery; services in relation to health.

6. The tax is payable by the entrepreneur delivering the goods or rendering the services. The entrepreneur may claim tax relief by means of an invoice for VAT charged by other entrepreneurs, as well as for VAT due or paid on goods imported for business purposes.

F. Incentives

Several laws provide for a variety of incentives, which may be summarized as follows:

1. Companies setting up new industrial enterprises may be granted a partial tax relief for a period not exceeding 8 years.

2. Two different types of tax credits are available for companies and individuals deriving income from business operations. They are granted only for investments in permanent establishments located in Luxembourg and are deducted from the income tax due for the tax year in which the investment is made. Unused credits can be carried forward for 4 years. The credits were made available for investments made until successive expiration dates. The dead-line currently applicable is 31st December, 1982:

- a 12% credit on the end-of-the-year increase in book-value of investment in tangible depreciable assets other than buildings.
  However assets acquired through transfer of a whole enterprise, second hand assets purchased in Luxembourg and isolated assets acquired gratuitously cannot be taken into account,
- a 2% and a 6% credit, applied on the cost of investments in tangible depreciable assets other than buildings and vehicles. These assets must be new and the depreciation rate taken must not exceed 25% per year. The rate of 6% is applied against the first Lfrs. 3.000.000,– of investments and the rate of 2% against any excess.

3. Public funds are available for making grants to banks and financial institutions which grant loans in favour of new investments in order to reduce the interest load on such loans. The actual interest rate charged to the borrower as a result of such grants may not be reduced to less than 3% and the grants may not be made for more than five years.

4. The Government may guarantee up to 50% of their total amount as to principal of and interest in any debts contracted for new investments.

5. Public funds are also available for granting a capital subsidy of up to 15% of the total amount of disbursments made for new investments.

6. The 'Société Nationale de Crédit et d'Investissement' has been set-up as a public body for the following purposes:

- to grant long and medium term loans in favour of new investments,
- to assist recognized banks in granting special credits in favour of small and medium size enterprises,
- to give similar assistance in view of export credits,
- to take participations in companies and enterprises whose registered seat and principal place of business is located in Luxembourg.

7. Other incentives are also available at EC level, such as:

- loans at reduced interest rate granted by the European Coal and Steel Community,
- allowances by the European Fund of Regional Development,
- loans by the European Investment Bank.

8. The Government and Municipalities are making considerable efforts in order to make available land suitable for industrial purposes, including con-

nections to public utilities systems, road access and complementary equipment work. In special cases they proceed with the construction of industrial buildings which will then either be sold or leased. They may also participate in the partial or total financing of a construction of business premisses.

G. Social Security Premiums

The premiums/contributions to the various social securities schemes operated in Luxembourg may be very briefly summarized as follows:

1. WORKERS

(i)	Retirement – invalidity pension:		
	Total premium/ contribution	Employer's share	Worker's share
	16%	8%	8%
(ii)	Health:		
	Total premium/ contribution	Employer's share	Worker's share
	8%	4%	4%
(iii)	Children allowances:		
	Total premium/ contribution	Employer's share	Worker's share
	variable between 1% and 2,8%	variable between 1% and 2,8%	–
(iv)	Unemployment fund:		
	Total premium/ contribution	Employer's share	Worker's share
	0,25%	0,25%	–
(v)	Occupational accident/disease:		
	Total premium/ contribution	Employer's share	Worker's share
	variable between 0,33% and 14,03% in relation to the risk of the employer's enterprise	variable between 0,33 and 14,03%	–

For all schemes there is a minimum and a maximum of wages, which, at 1th May, 1981, were Lfrs. 21.454,– and Lfrs. 85.816,– per month respectively.

2. EMPLOYEES

(i)	Retirement – invalidity pension:		
	Total premium/ contribution	Employer's share	Employee's share
	16%	8%	8%
(ii)	Health:		
	Total premium/ contribution	Employer's share	Employee's share
	4,5%	2,25%	2,25%
(iii)	Children allowances:		
	Total premium/ contribution	Employer's share	Employee's share
	1,45%	1,45%	–
(iv)	Unemployment fund:		
	Total premium/ contribution	Employer's share	Employee's share
	0,25%	0,25%	–
(v)	Occupational accident/disease:		
	Total premium/ contribution	Employer's share	Employee's share
	variable between 0,33% and 14,03% in relation to the risk of the employer's enterprise	variable between 0,33 and 14,03%	–

For all schemes there is a minimum and a maximum of salaries, which, at May 11, 1981, were the same as for workers.

H. Others

Several other taxes levied on companies should be mentioned.

1. SUBSCRIPTION TAX ('TAXE D'ABONNEMENT')

This tax is levied annually on shares and bonds issued by resident companies. It is assessed on the market value of such securities, as determined on the basis of the average prices at the stock exchange, or, if the securities are not listed on the basis of the intrinsic and financial values of the securities.
The tax rates are as follows:
- 0,18% for private limited companies
- 0,36% for public limited companies, partnerships limited by shares and cooperative associations.

The same tax is levied against a foreign company in respect of its local branch.

In that case the tax is assessed on that portion of its total securities which is deemed to be part of the local branch.

2. MUNICIPAL BUSINESS TAX ('IMPÔT COMMERCIAL COMMUNAL')

The municipal business tax ('impôt commercial communal') is levied by the Tax Administration for the benefit of the local communities. It is assessed on profit, on net assets and on the total payroll.

2.1. Municipal business tax on profit

This tax is assessed on the taxable profit for Corporation tax purposes. However certain items are added, such as: interest on long term debt salaries paid to staff owning at least 25% of the company's shares.
Other items are deducted, such as: the profit generated by a permanent establishment located abroad; an annual deduction of Lfrs. 200.000,–; losses of the preceding five years.
The basic tax rate is 4%. It is multiplied by a municipal factor which varies from one municipality to the other and which is frequently 2,5, thus making the effective tax rate 9,09% (since the municipal business tax is deductible from its own taxable basis).

2.2. Municipal business tax on net assets

This tax is assessed on the net asset value as assessed for the purpose of the net worth tax. However certain items are added such as: long term debts. Other items are deducted such as: net assets invested in a foreign permanent establishment located abroad.
The basic rate is 0,2%. It is multiplied by a municipal factor which is identical to that one applied for fixing the rate of the municipal tax on business profit (see above). If the applicable factor is 2,5, the effective tax rate will be 0,5%.

2.3. Tax on total payroll ('impôt sur le total des salaires')

The most important local community levy this tax.
It is assessed on the total gross amount of salaries and wages, including the employer's contribution to social security, paid by any company, the registered seat, operational head office or a branch of which is located on the territory of the municipality concerned.
The basic rate is 1,28‰. It is multiplied by a municipal factor which is usually 600, thus making the effective tax rate 0,768%.
Degressive deductions are applied to the taxable basis.

3. NET WORTH TAX ('IMPÔT SUR LA FORTUNE')

3.1. Both resident and non-resident companies are liable for the net worth tax. Since companies are taxed on their own net assets and their share-

holders are taxed on the market value of their shares, the company's net worth is ultimately subject to double taxation.
Resident companies are taxable upon their world wide net worth, except where assets located abroad are exempted by double tax treaties.
Non-resident companies are taxable on their net assets located in Luxembourg (real estate, net asset value of a permanent establishment).

3.2. The tax is assessed on any movable or immovable property, unless specifically exempted. The law deals in great detail with classifying all taxable assets into various categories and setting up detailed valuation principles.

3.3. In principle assessments are made every three years.
The tax is payable in four quarterly instalments.
The 'affilation privilege' also applies (see above).

3.4. The tax rate is 0,5% per year of the taxable net worth, with certain minimum amounts.

4. TAX ON REAL ESTATE ('IMPÔT FONCIER')

All Luxembourg Municipalities levy this tax.
It is assessed on the value of all real estate property located on the territory of the municipality concerned. For purposes of levying the tax, the value of each property is separately assessed by the Central Tax Administration, according to special criteria laid down in great detail by the law. The amounts thus obtained are generally substantially below current market value.
The basic tax rates are comprised between 7‰ and 10‰ of the value determined by the Administration as indicated above, depending on the nature and category of the property concerned. The basic rate is multiplied by municipal factors which vary from one municipality to the other and with the different types of real estate. These factors number between two hundred and three hundred and twenty.

5. WITHHOLDING TAX ON DIRECTORS' FEES

A special withholding tax applies to allowances paid to the directors or to the statutory auditors of Luxembourg companies. The tax is assessed on the gross compensation paid for the board or supervisory function. The tax is not payable on any remuneration paid for day-to-day management or for the performance of services to the company which are beyond the normal performance of the above board or supervisory functions.
The tax rate is 20% if the director or auditor is a resident recipient and pays the tax himself. If the company pays the tax on behalf of the resident recipient, the tax rate is 25%.
The special tax is not creditable against income tax, but is deductible as an income connected expense. The net amount is part of the normal taxable income and is therefore comprised in the resident's tax return.
As regards non resident recipients, the tax rate is 28,2% if the recipient bears the tax and if the gross amount is not in excess of Lfrs. 53.000.–.

The tax rate is 39,27% if the company bears the tax and if the gross amount is not in excess of Lfrs. 53.000.–.
In both cases there is no necessity for the recipient to file a tax return.
If the amount is in excess of Lfrs. 53.000,–, the non-resident recipient must file a personal tax return.

I. Double Tax Treaties

1. Ratified double tax treaties exist with the following countries:

Country	*Date of Signature*	*Date of Application*
Austria	October 18, 1962	January 1, 1961
Belgium	September 17, 1978	January 1, 1972
Brazil	November 8, 1978	January 1, 1981
France	April 1, 1958	January 1, 1957
	September 8, 1970	January 1, 1971
Germany	August 23, 1958	January 1, 1957
(Federal Rep.)	June 15, 1973	January 1, 1971
Ireland	January 14, 1972	January 1, 1968
The Netherlands	May 8, 1968	January 1, 1967
United Kingdom	May 24, 1967	January 1, 1966
	July 18, 1978	January 1, 1975
United States of America	December 18, 1962	January 1, 1964

2. Double tax treaties limited to air transportation exist with the following countries:

Country	*Date of Signature*	*Date of Application*
Ireland	April 29, 1975	January 1, 1973
USSR	June 6, 1975	June 6, 1975

3. Double tax treaties have been negotiated and are signed or initialed with the following countries:
- Denmark
- Italy
- Morocco
- Norway

4 Negotiations for the conclusion of a double tax treaty are currently engaged with the following countries:
– Finland
– Spain.

J. Schedule of Withholding Taxes

Recipient	*Dividends (portfolio)*[1] %	*Dividends (substantial holdings)*[2] %	*Royalties on patents* %
Non-resident companies and individuals:			
Non-Treaty	15	15	12
Treaty			
Austria	15	5	–[3]
Belgium	15	10	–
Brazil	15	15	–
France	15	5	–
Germany (Federal Republic)	15	10	5
Ireland	15	5	–
The Netherlands	15	2,5	–
United Kingdom	15	5	5
United States of America	7,5	5	–

1. Dividends paid by Luxembourg holding companies are not subject to any withholding tax.
2. A substantial holding is deemed to exist in:
a. Austria, France, Germany, Ireland, the Netherlands, the United Kingdom – where the recipient company holds at least 25% of the Luxembourg company's shares or voting power.
b. Belgium – where the recipient company holds a 25% investment or an investment valued Lfrs. 250 million at cost. Such investment may be held by several Belgian companies, provided one owns at least 50% of the shares of each one of the others.
c. United States – where the recipient company holds during the entire year (alone or with up to 3 other U.S. companies each holding at least 10% of the shares) 50% of the Luxembourg company's shares, provided a maximum of 25% of the gross income of the Luxembourg company originates from interest and dividends from non-group companies.
d. Brazil – where the recipient company holds at least 10% of the Luxembourg company's shares.

3. Royalties paid to Austria are taxable at 10% if the Austrian company owns more than 50% of the shares of the Luxembourg company.

K. Special Types of Companies

In Luxembourg, holding companies have a special tax status.

1. GENERAL

The Luxembourg Act of 31th July, 1929, defines a holding company as follows:

> 'Holding company means any Luxembourg company established exclusively for the purpose of acquiring holdings in whatever form in other Luxembourg, or foreign companies and administering as well as improving these holdings provided that the holding company undertakes no industrial activity and has no commercial establishment which is open to the public'.

'Holding company' as mentioned by this Act covers 'pure holding companies' only, to the exclusion of so-called 'mixed holding companies'. A mixed holding company in addition to acquiring holdings also engages in an industrial or commercial activity.

The prohibition against industrial activity does not mean that the holding company may not change its investments by disposals and acquisitions. This is regarded as the normal investment activity of a holding company and does not rank as industrial activity disqualifying the holding company from the definition.

2. THE LEGAL OBJECT OF HOLDING COMPANIES

2.1. The assets of a holding company normally comprise holdings of the share and loan capital of public bodies and private companies. There is no restriction for the place of incorporation of the entity in which the holding company has investments. Shareholdings will extend to ordinary shares, preference shares, founders' shares and similar securities. The investments may also include debentures, bonds and notes of States and Municipalities or of other public or private bodies corporate.

2.2. A holding company is frequently used as a closed-end or open-end investment company or investment trust. Furthermore, the fiscal law relating to holding companies also applies to 'open-end funds', organized on a mutual basis and administered by Luxembourg management companies having the status of holding companies. A detailed examination of the legal status and the taxation consequences for Luxembourg open-end funds is outside the scope of this chapter.

2.3. A holding company may not be in a general partnership ('société en nom collectif') nor be a general partner in either a limited partnership ('société en commandite simple') or in a partnership limited by shares ('société en commandite par actions'); nor may it be a silent partner in a limited partnership. However it may act as a silent partner, i.e. shareholder, in a partnership limited by shares.

2.4. With limited exceptions, a holding company is prohibited from directly owing real estate.

2.5. The portfolio of a holding company may include the ownership of patent rights. The holding company may not itself exploit patent rights in commercial activity and it may not either acquire a licence with a view to direct exploitation. It may administer its patent rights by granting licences for royalties or fees, and it is not necessary for the holding company to have an equity holding in its licencees. (In this connection it is interesting to note that to the extent that a deed of purchase or sale of a patent right or of a licencing contract, (either Luxembourg or foreign) is registered in Luxembourg, the rate payable on registration is Lfrs. 20,– only).

2.6. A holding company may not own a trading business, even if the management is conducted by some third party.
It may not either act as general agent or hold exclusive selling rights, or own industrial or commercial models or designs.
It may own a trademark only if the law of the country of registration permits that that trademark may be transferred without a simultaneous transfer of the industrial or commercial enterprise to whose products the mark relates.
It is not premitted to own copyright except in very exceptional cases.

2.7. While a holding company may administer its own investments, it may not administer the investments of third parties.

2.8. The power of holding companies to make loans and advances is limited. It may lend to a company in which it has a participation. If it complies with certain special conditions imposed on 'finance holding companies' ('holdings de financement') to be recognized as such by the competent Administration, it may also make loans and advances to companies which are part of the same group of companies as the holding company, even if the latter does not own a direct participation in the beneficiary of such a loan or advance. Loans and advances may only be made out of funds becoming available in the normal course of the investment activities or, in the case of a 'finance holding company', from an issue of loan capital. However, a holding company may not receive monies on deposit of third parties having no connection with the holding company solely with a view to making loans or advances to other parties.

2.9. A holding company may incur debts and other liabilities, but these must not exceed a sum equal to 3 times the amount subscribed on the share capital of the holding company. Debentures, bonds and similar instruments issued by the holding company do not rank as debts for the purpose of this limit. However, the amount of temporarily outstanding debentures and similar instruments of the holding company must not exceed a sum equal to 10 times the amount paid-up on its share capital.

3. THE LEGAL STATUS OF HOLDING COMPANIES

3.1. Under the definition of 'holding company' given above, only companies which have been organised in Luxembourg in pursuance of the Luxembourg law and which have their seat in Luxembourg qualify as such. Companies incorporated outside Luxembourg and their Luxembourg branches cannot qualify as holding companies within this definition.

3.2. The significance of qualification as a 'holding company' is limited exclusively to tax. In all other respects the status of the holding company is no different from that of other Luxembourg companies.
For various reasons both of a legal and a practical nature, most holding companies are organised in the form of a public limited company ('société anonyme' – 'SA') and very rarely indeed as a private limited company ('société à responsabilité limitée – sarl'). The essential features of either type of company have been described above.

3.3. Contrary to operating companies, a holding company does not need any permit.

4. TAXATION

4.1. In 1929 it was the purpose of Luxembourg legislation to eliminate double taxation, and thus to promote the concentration of capital within Luxembourg. To this end a tax system was introduced which is characterized by its extremely low rates, by the very simple method by which the tax is computed and by the liberal interpretation always accorded to this tax law by the Luxembourg Administration. Since its inception in 1929, the taxation of holding companies has virtually not changed.

4.2. On formation the 1% capital duty ('droit d'apport') is payable as it is on formation on any other company (see above).

4.3. There is only one annual tax, the 'taxe d'abonnement'. The rate is 0,20% with a minimum of Lfrs. 2.000,– per annum.
The tax is computed on the actual value of the holding company's own shares and other securities (debentures, bonds) and *not* on the investments held by it.
If the holding company's shares are quoted on a Stock Exchange, the tax is computed on the basis of the average of the prices quoted in the preceding calendar year. If the holding company's shares are unquoted, their actual value must be established by the company. This calculation is based upon the yield of the shares, that is to say upon the dividend paid. As long as the dividend is not in excess of 10%, the shares' value is deemed to be at par. If the dividend is higher, the tax will be assessed on 10 times the dividend, the tax rate always remaining at 0,20%. If the holding company makes high profits without paying dividend, the valuation of its shares remains at par, though by virtue of accumulated reserves their real value may have substantially increased.
The same tax is charged on debentures or bonds issued by the holding company. In this case also the tax is computed on the average of the

prices on the Stock Exchange if they are quoted; if not, except for special cases, the valuation will be at par.
The tax is payable in equal quarterly instalments.

4.4. The 'taxe d'abonnement' constitutes the only annual tax levied on holding companies. No other annual taxes are collected on such companies by the Luxembourg tax authorities. In particular Luxembourg tax authorities do not levy any:
(i) tax on dividends and interest respectively on shares and debentures of foreign companies held by Luxembourg holding companies. From Luxembourg dividends, 15% is deducted at source (see above),
(ii) tax on any other income (e.g. interest on loan) earned by the holding company,
(iii) tax on capital gains on the assets held by the holding company, unless such capital gains result in an increase of the dividend paid by the holding company above the 10% rate (see above),
(iv) tax on the dividends and interest paid by the holding company. In this regard neither the holding company nor its non-resident shareholders or bondholders are liable to tax, but shareholders or bondholders residing in Luxembourg are liable to normal income tax computed on all income from whatever source, including from dividends and interest paid by holding companies,
(v) tax on liquidation profit.
However it should be noted that all the double tax treaties concluded by Luxembourg with various foreign countries (see above) do not apply to holding companies insofar as they and the holders of shares or bonds are liable to the taxes regulated in these agreements.

4.5. Special regulations grant a still more favourable tax treatment to holding companies which, on formation or during their life-time, have acquired holdings in foreign companies amounting to Lfrs. 1.000 million or more or the equivalent in foreign currency. In brief, this treatment consists in replacing the 'taxe d'abonnement' by a single decreasing annual tax, the maximum of which is 3%, assessed jointly on the dividends paid on shares, the interest paid on debentures and the fees paid to non-resident directors with a minimum of Lfrs. 2.000.000.–.

IV. LABOUR ASPECTS

A. Principles of Law on Employment

1. GENERAL

1.1. Luxembourg law draws a basic distinction between employees and workers. An employee is a person of either sex whose work is exclusively or at least predominantly intellectual. A worker is a person of either sex whose work is essentially manual. Employment, either as employee or as worker, exists on the basis of individual contracts. Very frequently such contracts are concluded within the frame of collective bargaining agreements. In addition there may exist internal regulations within the enterprise concerned.

1.2. In principle men and women are entitled to equal remunerations for equal jobs.

1.3. Wages of workers are usually fixed at hourly rates and are payable at least twice a month. Salaries of employees are usually fixed at monthly rates and are payable at least once a month.

1.4. The portion of wages and salaries which is assignable or attachable is limited.

1.5. The law fixes minimum amounts of wages and salaries. At 1st May, 1981 this minimum amount was of Lfrs. 21.454,– per month.
For those having special professional qualifications, as defined by law, the above minimum is to be increased by 20%.
All wages and salaries, irrespective of their amount or of the position of the recipient, must be tied to the official cost of living index.

1.6. Elaborate legal provisions fix in great detail matters such as:
- maximum duration of daily and weekly work;
- duration of fully-paid legal holidays and vacations;
- conditions of work as to health and security.

2. EMPLOYEES

2.1. The employment contract between employer and employee may be either for a fixed duration or for an undetermined duration or for a probationary period. It must under all circumstances be made in writing in two signed copies. The contract must specify the nature and essential characteristics of the job, and it must state the contract's duration and the amount of the employee's remuneration, including, if applicable, the way in which it will be increased in the future, and it must state any complementary agreements between parties. Any provision which is less favourable for the employee than the prescriptions of the law is invalid.

2.2. The employment contract for a probationary period must specifically state that it is for a probationary period. If it does not do so, the employment is deemed to be final and for an undetermined duration, The duration of the probationary period varies from two to six months, depending on the basic formation of the employee and on his age.

2.3. Termination of the employment contract

(i) In case a fundamental change occurs in the employer's situation, such as death, sale or transfer of the enterprise, merger, reorganization, etc., the employment contract is not terminated and remains in existence between the new owner of the enterprise and the employees of his predecessor.

(ii) The contract entered into for a fixed duration automatically expires on the date set for its expiration. If the employee actually continues to work beyond the said date, a new employment contract for an undetermined duration is deemed to have come into existence.

(iii) The contract entered into for an undetermined duration may be terminated by either party giving notice to the other by registered mail, with a deferment. If the notice originates with the employer, the duration of the deferment is of two, four or six months, if the employee concerned has been employed by the employer for less than five years, less than ten years, or more than ten years respectively. In case the notice originates from the employee, the above deferments are reduced by one half. An employee absent for reason of illness or a woman absent for reason of pregnancy may not be dismissed.

(iv) In addition, the employer may at any time terminate any type of employment contract if the employee has committed a serious breach of law or of contract. The termination based on that cause must be notified by registered mail within three days and it must specify in detail the alleged grounds.

(v) In case an employment contract is terminated without the above conditions having been duly observed, the employer is liable for damages. If the employment contract was for an undetermined duration, the amount of damages is equal to the remuneration corresponding to the deferment which was not duly observed.
In addition, if an employee is dismissed and if he is not entitled to any retirement allowance payable by the public social security, the employer must pay an additional compensation, the amount of which is proportionate to the total period of services of the employee and is comprised between an amount equal to one and twelve monthly salaries, except if the dismissal occurs for serious breach of law or of contract. Finally, on receiving termination notice on any ground, the employee may request in writing the employer to specify the grounds of dismissal. If it is held that the dismissal occurred for illegitimate reasons or constitutes an act deemed to be economically and socially abnormal, the employer is liable for additional damages, the amount of which is fixed by the competent jurisdiction.

3. WORKERS

3.1. In principle the work contract is concluded in the same way as the employment contract (fixed duration; undetermined duration; probationary period). It may be made verbally, in which case it is deemed to be a firm contract for an undetermined duration. The probationary period must be expressed in weeks, and it may not exceed six weeks. Moreover, if not terminated by notice given with a deferment – such deferment comprise as many days as the probationary period has weeks – it is deemed to have been made from the beginning on as a firm contract for an undetermined duration.

3.2. Termination of the work contract.

(i) Any work contract automatically ceases when the worker reaches the age of sixty-five years or suffers a permanent disability entitling him to obtain the invalidity allowance payable by the public social security.

(ii) As for employees, a fundamental change in the employer's situation keeps in existence existing work contracts.

(iii) The contract entered into for a fixed duration automatically expires on the date set for its expiration.

(iv) The contract entered into for an undetermined duration may be terminated by either party giving notice to the other.
The notice given by the worker may be verbal or in writing and the duration of the deferment is of two weeks.
The notice given by the employer must be by registered mail and the duration of the deferment is of four, eight or twelve weeks, depending on whether the worker has been employed for less than five years, more than five years or more than ten years respectively. The right of dismissal is suspended for the same reasons as for employees. Even in case the deferment has been duly observed, the worker is entitled to a severance payment equal to one month, two months' or three months's salary if he has been occupied for between five and ten years, between ten and fifteen years, or more than fifteen years respectively.
Moreover, in those enterprises which have less than twenty workers, the employer may choose between paying the above compensation or extending the deferment to twelve, twenty or twenty-four weeks respectively, depending on the total duration of the worker's employment, as indicated above.

(v) Any work contract may be terminated at any time for serious breach of law or of contract, the procedure being similar to that one applicable in case of employees.

(vi) A dismissed worker may be entitled to additional compensation payment under conditions similar to those applying to employees (see above).

(vii) Special delays and procedures are applicable in case of collective dismissal i.e. dismissal of more than ten workers within less than thirty days. This also applies to employees.

4. Special provisions deal with the conditions under which the employment or work contract of an employees' or workers' delegate may be terminated (see later). In short, these rules consist in permitting notice of termination only in cases of serious breach of law or contract. Even in that case only the competent court may decide whether there is sufficient ground for severing the contract. Pending the court's decision the employer may only provisionally prevent the employee or worker concerned from actually continuing to perform his job, and it is up to the court to decide whether during that period the salary or wage is payable.

B. Labour Procedures

1. The Luxembourg Constitution guarantees the right to work and the freedom of association, including the formation and activities of trade unions.
There does not exist any special body of law organizing or otherwise govern-

ing trade-unions in general. Hence trade unions are organized on a contractual basis. Subject to what will be said later, they do not constitute corporate bodies or other bodies recognized by law; consequently they may neither sue nor be sued, except in limited cases.
In Luxembourg there are a number of trade unions for employers and for workers. There is no general and unique trade union representing the entire body of organized labour force. Trade unions play a dominant role in collective bargaining.

2. The collective bargaining agreement ('convention collective de travail') constitutes an agreement governing work relations and general conditions of work. It is entered into by one or several trade unions of workers or employees, or of both, on one hand, and one or several employers organizations, such as the Luxembourg Federation of Industrials, or even a single enterprise, on the other. Those professional associations which have an internal organization and have as their purpose to defend the professional interests of their members and to represent them are recognized as trade unions for the purpose of participating in collective bargaining. The ability to be a party to an agreement of that kind is measured by the large number of the members and the independence of the union.
The collective bargaining agreement must be made in writing, otherwise it is invalid. It must be filed with the competent administration, in specie the 'Inspection du Travail et des Mines'. It is applicable as from the date of such a filing. The Minister of Labour may refuse to accept the filing, but only on purely formal grounds. Once filed, it must also be publicized by posters affixed at the main doors of the place of work.

3. The collective bargaining agreement is binding on all persons having executed it or on whose behalf it has been executed, as well as on all other persons who adhere to it or accept it later on. In addition any such agreement which conforms to law may be declared applicable and enforceable on all employers and on all persons belonging to the profession for which it has been negotiated. This declaration of general appliance is made by a Governmental decree.

4. If the duly qualified representatives of the personnel of an enterprise or the trade unions so require, any employer is under an obligation to enter into collective bargaining negotiations with a view to forming an agreement. In case the employer refuses to negotiate, or in case no agreement can be reached, the law provides for a compulsory conciliation procedure. There may also be an arbitration procedure, either before or after a tentative conciliation. The law organizes in great detail the powers of the various conciliation and arbitration bodies and the procedures to be followed by them. It is sufficient to notice that in case the dispute is settled by an arbitration award, such an award is the equivalent of a collective bargaining agreement.
A professional strike is lawful in principle, but only after the conciliation and arbitration procedures have been tried unsuccessfully. It is worth mentioning that, due to this mechanism, there has not been any professional strike in Luxembourg for a great many years.

C. Works Council

In Luxembourg the representation of the labour force of an enterprise is vested in two bodies:

1. the 'délégation du personnel'
2. the 'comité mixte d'entreprise'.

1. DÉLÉGATION DU PERSONNEL

1.1. Each industrial, commercial or professional enterprise, including those owned by or depending on public bodies, which permanently gives occupation to at least 15 workers or 12 employees, must have a workers' or employees' delegation, or both.
As soon as the above minimum number of either category of personnel is reached, elections must be organized within the enterprise, so as to allow the personnel to choose their delegates, who will form the delegation.

1.2. The law fixes in great detail the composition of the delegation, which must be proportionate to the number of personnel, and the election procedure. If an enterprise comprises several sections or branches, there must be a delegation for each one of them, with a central delegation for the whole enterprise.

1.3. The main rights and prerogatives of the delegation may be summarized as follows:
- to safe keep and defend the common interests of the personnel in relation to working conditions, maintaining of jobs, security and social security, to the extent these do not fall within the competence of the 'comité mixte d'entreprise' (see later);
- to accept any complaint from any worker or employee and to try to find a solution through amicable settlement;
- to express its views as to the setting up and amendment of any internal regulations, and to supervise their implementation;
- to cooperate in the administration of any social fund set up by the employer;
- to cooperate in the setting up and implementation of the regulations applicable to apprentices;
- to assist in preventing labour accidents and professional illnesses.

1.4. In case the enterprise exists in the form of a public limited company, the Board of Directors or the management must, at least once a month, report in writing to the delegation on the economic and financial development of the enterprise. In case the enterprise is owned by an individual, he must from time to time inform the delegation on the activity and prospects of the enterprise.

1.5. As already indicated above, the members of the delegation enjoy a special protection as to dismissal.

2. COMITÉ MIXTE D'ENTREPRISE

Besides the 'délégation du personnel', there exists the 'comité mixte d'entreprise'. This is a body in which the employer and the personnel have equal representation.

2.1. Any enterprise located within Luxembourg and having given occupation to an average of at least 150 persons for three years must have a 'comité mixte'.
The number of members of that committee is proportionate to the number of personnel. The employer is free to designate his representatives as he wants. The representatives of the personnel are designated by the delegates, by secret ballot. They must be chosen from within the personnel occupied by the enterprise for more than one year. Only Luxembourg and EC citizens of age are eligible.
The total number of seats available for the personnel's representatives is divided among employees and workers according to special rules.

2.2. The 'comité mixte' has the following rights:
(i) the right to receive information and to express its views
(ii) the right to co-decide
(iii) the right to supervise.

(i) The right to receive information and to express its views, is organized in the following way:

- Every six months the employer must inform, (in writing) the 'comité mixte' on the economic and financial development of the enterprise and ask their views on the matter. To that effect he must submit a general report on the enterprise's activity, containing particulars on the global result of production and operations, the orders, the evolution of the structure and amount of the payroll, and the investments made. In addition, in the case of a public limited company, management must submit the annual balance and profit and loss account, the auditor's report and any other document made available to the shareholders, prior to submitting these documents to their general meeting.
- Once a year the employer must in the same way inform and ask for the views of the 'comité mixte' on the present and foreseeable need of manpower and on all measures relating to professional courses, improvement and re-education likely to be necessary for the enterprise's personnel.
- In addition, the 'comité mixte' has a general right to express any views as to any managerial decision of an economic or financial character which may decisively affect the enterprise' structure or the number of people it employs. In these matters the information to be supplied by the employer must in principle be prior to any decision taken, except if such an advanced information would impede management or endanger the implementation of a projected operation.

(ii) The 'comité mixte' must give its agreement on the following measures:

- Introducing or applying technical instruments aimed at measuring the behaviour and performance of any employed at his job.
- Introducing or changing measures relating to the health and the security

of the personnel and the prevention of occupational diseases.
- Setting up or amending general criteria in relation to selecting manpower, on hiring, on promoting, on displacing and on dismissing.
- Setting up or amending general criteria for the appreciation of manpower.
- Granting bonuses to any member of the personnel who, by his initiatives or proposals, or technical improvement, has contributed in a special way to the enterprise's wellbeing (this does not cover inventions and patents, nor does it limit the employer's exclusive prerogative to hire, promote, displace or dismiss individual members of the personnel).

(iii) The right to supervise consists in supervising the social funds and other facilities set up for the benefit of the personnel.

2.3. The personnel's representatives at the 'comité mixte' enjoy a special protection as to dismissal, which is similar to that one recognized for members of the delegation.

2.4. The law imposes on members of the 'comité mixte' and on their external advisers, who, under certain circumstances, may be called in, the duty to strictly observe the secrecy as to any confidential information which may have come to their knowledge. Any breach of that special duty carries penal sanctions.

D. Co-determination

1. The law of 6th May, 1974, which set up the 'comité mixte d'entreprise' also granted to the personnel of public limited companies the right to be represented at the board of directors and at the board of auditors.

2. The right so granted only applies within a public limited company which
- has its seat on Luxembourg territory and has given occupation within such territory to at least one thousand persons for a three years reference period, or
- having its seat on Luxembourg territory, comprises a shareholding of the Luxembourg Government of at least 25% or exercises its main activity on the basis of a concession (license, franchise) granted by the Luxembourg Government (e.g. Electricity Distribution Company Cegedel, Luxair, Radio Luxembourg – see above).

3. In those companies to which the first criterium is applicable, the personnel is entitled to three board members and the board must comprise a minimum of nine members.
In those companies to which the second criterium is applicable, there must be one board member per one hundred persons employed, without the total number of board members representing the personnel being less than three and more than one third of the total number of board members.

4. Contrary to the principle laid down in the company law, according to which directors and auditors are elected by shareholders, the directors repre-

senting the personnel are designated by the delegates of the personnel by way of election according to the principle of proportionate representation. They must in principle be chosen from among persons occupied within the company. However in the steel industry, trade unions operating nation-wide are entitled to designate three board members, who need not be employed by the enterprise, out of the total number allocated to the personnel. In order to be eligible an employee or worker of the enterprise must have been employed there for at least two years.

5. The Board members representing the personnel have the same rights, privileges and duties as all other board members, except that they need not deposit shares as a guarantee for the proper performance of their duties.

6. Board members representing the personnel may not belong simultaneously to more than two boards. Under no circumstances may they be board members of companies competing one with the other, nor may they be employed by another enterprise engaged in the same activity as that one to whose board they belong.

7. The board members representing the personnel enjoy a special protection as regards dismissal.

8. The representation of personnel at the board of auditors is organized in such a way that the board of directors must, by unanimous consent of all its members representing both shareholders and personnel, designate an independent public accountant as additional auditor.

E. Compulsory Profit Sharing and Pension Schemes

1. In Luxembourg there does not exist any compulsory profit sharing scheme. To the extent the personnel of an enterprise shares in its profits, this occurs on a purely voluntary basis. However the allocation of bonuses to the entire personnel, usually in the form of an extra one month salary or more, and of gifts to persons who have remained with the same employer for a long period, is widely practised.

2. For *workers* there exists a compulsory old age and invalidity pension scheme administered by a public entity.

2.1. All workers without distinction as to sex or nationality must participate in that scheme.
In case of permanent invalidity or occupational disability the worker is entitled to a pension provided he has been affiliated to the scheme for at least two hundred and seventy days.
At the age of sixty-five years he is entitled to a retirement or old age pension, provided he has been affiliated for at least thirteen hundred and fifty days. However an anticipated old age pension may be allocated from sixty-two years for a member who has been affiliated for at least

ten thousand eight hundred days, provided he ceases to exercise any professional activity.
No minimum affiliation duration is required in the case of invalidity due to occupational disability.
Membership of the system will not be maintained if during a period of two consecutive years the member does not reach a minimum of one hundred and sixty days of affiliation. However the rights so suspended will revive if thereafter a new membership period of at least one thousand eighty days is accomplished.

2.2. The old age or invalidity allocation comprises a fixed portion, assumed by the Government and the Municipalities, and a variable portion, proportionate to the total amount of contributions paid to the scheme.
Additional allocations are made in favour of children supported by the pensioner.
In case of permanent invalidity prior to the age of fifty-five years, a surplus allowance is granted until the age of fifty-five years.
No invalidity or old age pension may be lower than a certain minimum amount per month, which, as at 1st May, 1981 was of Lfrs. 21.454,–, provided the beneficiary has been a member of the scheme for at least nine thousand five hundred days.
Survivors of a deceased member are also entitled to certain allocations, provided the deceased has been a member of the scheme for at least two hundred and seventy days at the date of death and has maintained his rights without interruption, or had the benefit of an invalidity pension. The total amount of allocations granted to survivors may not exceed the amount which the deceased himself would have obtained had he survived.
The survivors comprise the widow or widower, minor children (the age of majority being eighteen years) disabled children without any age limit and children at school or in professional training, up to twenty-five years. Illegitimate and adoptive children are treated as if they were legitimate children.
In case a member of the scheme dies without leaving a widow or widower entitled to a pension allowance, certain next of kin are also entitled to pension allowances.

2.3. The rate of contribution is sixteen percent and must be paid one half by the employer and one half by the worker. It is assessed on the amount of wages, but there is a minimum and a maximum, which, as at 1st May, 1981, were of Lfrs. 21.454,– and 85.816,– respectively.
The part of the contribution to be borne by the worker must be withheld by the employer from the monthly wages.

3. For *employees* there also exists a compulsory old age and invalidity pension scheme administered by a public entity.

3.1. As regards affiliation and entitlement to allocations, the scheme is organized in a way very similar to that one existing for workers. It is therefore sufficient to notice the following differences:

– The minimum period of affiliation is twelve months in the case of death, sixty months in the case of old age pension and one hundred

and eighty months if the old age pension is to be paid before the age of sixty-five years.
- In order to be entitled to receive the fixed portion of the allocation, which is to be borne by the Government and the Municipalities, the beneficiary must in principle have had his residence in Luxembourg for at least one hundred and eighty months.
- In order to maintain his membership rights, the employee must remain affiliated with the scheme for an average period of eight months per year.

3.2. As for the workers' pension scheme, the rate of contribution is sixteen percent and is due one half by the employer and one half by the employee. It is assessed on the total amount of salary, including any additional remuneration in cash or in kind. There is also a minimum and a maximum, which, as at 1st May, 1981 is the same as for workers (see above). The part of the contribution to be borne by the employee must be withheld by the employer from the monthly salary but the public body administering the scheme may request the employee to personally pay his own contribution.

F. Residence/Work Permits for Aliens

1. RESIDENCE PERMIT

A basic distinction must be drawn between EC citizens and non EC citizens.

1.1. EC citizens who intend to reside in Luxembourg for more than three months with a view to carrying out a professional activity as wage earnier must obtain a residence permit from the competent Municipality. In order to obtain such a permit they must submit:
- the identification document which they used for entering Luxembourg;
- a certificate stating that they have undergone the medical examination to be passed within eight days of their arrival in Luxembourg;
- a document evidencing that they qualify for admission into Luxembourg under one of the categories established for EC citizens.

1.2. Non EC citizens who intend to reside in Luxembourg must obtain from the Luxembourg authorities an identification document for foreigners. In order to obtain that document they must evidence that:
- they have paid the corresponding duty;
- they have submitted their travel document (passport, identification card, etc.);
- they have undergone in Luxembourg the prescribed medical examination;
- they have obtained a work permit;
- they have a place to live in in Luxembourg;
- they have exhibited an excerpt of the 'casier judiciaire' or similar document, such as 'no police record'.

If all this is found satisfactory, they will receive a provisional permit of residence, the duration of which is limited to one year. After an administrative investigation has been made, the provisional permit will be replaced by a final one.

2. WORK PERMITS

2.1. In principle the hiring of non-Luxembourg wage earners is not free. It is in the hands of the Administration, which, alone, is entitled to recruit foreign wage earners, to find them a job and to control the conditions of their admission to work in Luxembourg. However the Administration may authorize individual employers or employers' organizations to recruit wage earners abroad. In practice this is not uncommon.
Special agreements for the recruitment of wage earners exist with Portugal and Yugoslavia. In addition the EC recruitment procedure is applicable in Luxembourg.

2.2. EC citizens do not need any work permit in Luxembourg.

2.3. As regards non EC citizens, they must obtain a work permit, to be delivered by the Luxembourg Minister of Labour, before being permitted to take up a job in Luxembourg. The same applies to non EC apprentices and trainees.
To that effect the employer must first declare the job vacancy to the Administration. If countersigned by the wage earner, this declaration constitutes an application to obtain a work permit. It must under all circumstances be made before the person concerned enters Luxembourg and takes up his job.
The Administration will thereupon issue a provisional work permit, unless the application is turned down.
The final work permit is issued by the Minister of Labour who, before issuing it, will give due consideration to the present situation and future prospect of the labour market. The delivery of the work permit may be made conditional upon passing a professional examination or test.
In practice, even non EC citizens have in general not met with special difficulties in securing work and residence permits in cases where the prospective employer could establish that he was specifically in need of these persons. This is particularly true in the sphere of certain services (banking, finance).

V. REFERENCE MATERIAL

In Luxembourg the law is embodied in a variety of instruments: Acts, decrees, etc., all in French. Their text is published in the Luxembourg Official Gazette – 'Mémorial'.
There are only very few reference books or booklets or articles in English. The author has drawn from the following:

- Tax Management, Foreign Income, edited by Leonard L. Silverstein, Business Operations in Luxembourg, by G. Kioes and E. Schmit;

- Corporate Taxation in Luxembourg, by Guy H. Urbin;
- Peronal Taxation in Luxembourg, by Guy H. Urbin, Comptoir de l'Edition Krippler & Cie sarl, Luxembourg;
- Double Taxation Relief in Luxembourg, by Jean Werner, Banque Générale du Luxembourg, Facts and Prospects;
- Luxembourg: Ideal Location for your Development Plans, Luxembourg Chamber of Commerce 1979.

The Netherlands

Paul M. Storm
Maarten J. Ellis

I. INTRODUCTION

Since about 1973 a number of factors have contributed to a substantial decrease in foreign investments for industrial purposes in The Netherlands. Those factors included high costs of labour, a very strong guilder, increasingly burdensome environmental and social legislation and practices and, of course, the general economic recession. Some of these factors, such as the high costs of labour and the strong currency, seem to be losing importance, at least compared with other European countries.
On the other hand, there have always been and still are a number of advantages in investing in The Netherlands. These include its strategic position in Europe and the high level of education and skill of its population. However, there is yet another reason why The Netherlands plays an important part in international business: it has quite attractive tax features. This does not apply to the investor who wishes to set up an industrial enterprise in The Netherlands (although there are incentives to allure him, see the part on Taxation, sub F) and even less to personal income tax (although there are some benefits for expatriates working in The Netherlands, see the part on Taxation, sub D, I, 1). But as a result of the happy interaction of an extensive network of favourable Double Taxation Treaties and the so-called participation exemption, The Netherlands offers an extremely favourable climate for holding companies. In addition, the combination of these Treaties and the total absence in The Netherlands of any withholding tax on interest or royalties appeals to the imagination of tax planners throughout the world seeking a country to locate a vehicle for loans (including Bonds Issues) or royalties.
In view of this particular tax situation the information in this chapter highlights, in some respects, the position for those who are contemplating the creation of a Dutch holding, financing or royalty company.

II. THE LEGAL FRAMEWORK

A. The Vehicle

1. THE WHOLLY-OWNED ENTERPRISE

1.a. THE BRANCH

As compared with a subsidiary, a branch is seldom used in The Netherlands. For various reasons one finds branches in banking, insurance and the oil and gas industry (exploration and production in the Dutch sector of the North Sea Continental Shelf).

Apart from the obvious lack of limited liability the branch has the inconvenience of lacking a clear profile from an organisational point of view. On the other hand, a branch is not subject to Dutch company law (e.g. the structure regime, see (ii) (b) below, and Directors' liability, see (ii) (d) below). However, a branch is subject to the provisions of the *Wet op de Ondernemingsraden* (Works Councils Act), at least to a certain extent (see IV, C below).

From the point of view of taxation the branch has certain advantages as well as certain disadvantages (see the section on Taxation, sub A.1 below). The pros and cons will have to be considered in each individual case, but in most instances the advantages of a branch do not outweigh those of a subsidiary.

A branch must be registered in the Trade Register. This involves the filing of certain data and documents (e.g. a certified copy of the Certificate of Incorporation and bye-laws or equivalent documents, a list of Directors and their powers and the capital) of the foreign company, as well as data concerning the manager(s) of the branch and the extent of his (their) authority. It should be noted that the branch is under a continuous obligation to file all data and documents about the foreign company which the company must under its own legislation file with the Trade Register (or equivalent register) at home or otherwise publish.

The initial as well as the annual fees to the Trade Register are computed on the basis of the capital employed in the branch (see (iii) (5) below).

There are no special rules about the liability of the managers of the branch. As long as they act within their authority as filed with the Trade Register, the company will be liable. The company may also be liable for torts committed by branch managers in the course of the performance of their duties.

There are no separate requirements as to the keeping of accounts, auditing and publication of accounts in respect of the branch. However, reference is made to what is written above about filing and disclosure in respect of the company itself.

1.b. THE SUBSIDIARY

Introductory remarks

Until 1971 there was only one kind of company limited by shares in The Netherlands: the *naamloze vennootschap* (NV, comparable with the SA, AG, SpA, A/S, plc). As a consequence of the first EEC Directive on Company Law the *besloten vennootschap met beperkte aansprakelijkheid* (BV, 'closed' company with limited liability, comparable with sàrl, GmbH, sarl, ApS, private company) was introduced. The BV is very similar to the NV, the only differences being that the BV's shares must be registered, that it cannot issue share certificates and that there are certain restrictions on the transferability of its shares which need not apply to the NV. For tax purposes NV and BV are treated identically. However, there is one aspect of the BV which has been of particular interest to the business world: with the implementation of the First Directive on Company Law an obligation to disclose annual accounts was introduced. This applied to all NVs but only to very few BVs. Consequently, some 45,000 NVs were converted into BVs. At about the same time the limited liability company gained, for various – mainly tax – reasons, enormous popularity and many new BVs were formed. As a result, there were about 160,000 BVs and only some 6,000 NVs by early 1981.

At that time the same differences between NV and BV still existed, but with the implementation of the Second and Fourth Directives the relationship between these two forms of company were to undergo substantial changes. The most important change will result from the implementation of the Fourth Directive. The Fourth Directive makes no distinction between NV and BV. The Dutch Bill to implement this Directive does not go that far, but the group of BVs which are more or less exempt from the requirements concerning accounts, auditing and disclosure is smaller than under the Dutch legislation of 1971. Consequently, there is a larger group of enterprises for which these requirements are no longer relevant in making the choice between NV and BV. Nevertheless, whatever exceptions to the requirements exist, they only apply to the BV and never to the NV. Some of these exceptions are quite significant (see below, (ii) (f)).

As set out in the chapter on European Company Law, the Second Directive applies to NVs only and so does the Dutch Act implementing this Directive. However, since Dutch company legislation has traditionally been rather weak on the protection of the company's capital, it was felt that on this point the law relating to the BV should also be improved. Consequently, on one of the last days of 1980 a Bill to that effect was introduced. On a number of points this Bill (hereafter: the Capital Bill) is simpler and less stringent than the one to implement the Second Directive. The Capital Bill is likely to be enacted by the end of 1982.

The Third Directive, which applies to NVs only, will be implemented in The Netherlands for NV and BV alike.

On balance, in particular for the purposes of a subsidiary the BV-form would seem to continue enjoying the preference over the NV-form which seems to become more and more reserved for companies having securities quoted on a Stock Exchange. If anything, the preference for the BV will become stronger as the two corporate forms grow further apart which to some extent is inevitable.

This is why, bearing in mind the purpose of this book, the information given below will be limited to the BV. It follows from the above that most of it will also apply to the NV.

(i) Setting-up a BV

A BV comes into existence at the moment its Deed of Incorporation is passed before a (civil law) notary by two or more[1] incorporators, provided a Declaration of No Objection has been given in respect of (and in fact stamped on) the draft Deed on behalf of the Minister of Justice[2,3]). This requirement of a

1. The Bill to Combat Abuse of Legal Entities (see (ii) (d) below) provides that henceforth NVs and BVs can be incorporated by a single incorporator.

2. The Act also allows for the Declaration of No Objection to be given on the Deed after it has been executed (in which case the company comes into existence upon the Declaration being given), but this happens very seldom in practice.

3. The Bill referred to in note 1 provides that the Declaration lapses if the Deed of Incorporation has not been passed within 3 months of the date of the Declaration.

Declaration of No Objection, which dates from the time the Monarch created a company by giving it a charter, is unique in Western Europe. In practice it is a benefit as well as, often, a serious nuisance. Until roughly the second half of the 1970s the Department of Justice, in examining the draft Deeds of Incorporation, mainly verified that they were in good shape from a legal point of view. In doing so the Department applied tests which in a number of cases went beyond the requirements of the Act. Many of these tests have been published under the name *'Departementale Richtlijnen'* (Departmental Directives). Being constantly reviewed, these Directives constitute a kind of informal supplement to the written law on companies which since 1976 has been included in Book 2 of the new Civil Code. The Department sometimes makes demands that are not at all supported by the law. In such cases there is usually little sense in appealing against the demands since an appeal (which could be lodged with the *Raad van State*, the Council of State) would cause an unacceptable delay. On balance, however, this aspect of the departmental supervision has had a beneficial effect in that the legal quality of Dutch Deeds of Incorporation is of a very high standard and claims that a company is null and void do not occur.

In the second half of the 1970s the Department has shifted the emphasis of its attention from the technical legal supervision (without, however, abandoning this) to 'the intentions (!) and antecedents of the persons who will determine or contribute to determining the policy of the company' so as to refuse the Declaration of No Objection if in view of those intentions and antecedents there is a serious danger that the company will be used for unlawful purposes or that its activities will prejudice its creditors. This has probably led to a reduction of the abuse of BVs for fraudulent purposes (mainly to avoid tax and social security contributions, especially in the building industry). On the other hand, it has led to an increase in paperwork (see the checklist below) and an unacceptable increase in delays. These delays, which have been as long as 6 months, constitute a serious drawback of the system. Fortunately, in the case of foreign investors the investigation into 'intentions' and antecedents is normally simplified and in really urgent cases the notary often succeeds in obtaining the Declaration of No Objection within a very short time. However, one cannot always count upon a co-operative attitude from all civil servants.

In this connection, it should be noted that the company's business can commence even before it has been incorporated. The Act provides explicitly, in accordance with art. 7 of the first Directive, that acts on behalf of the company to be incorporated (the 'BV i.o.', *in oprichting*) will create rights and obligations of the company if after its incorporation it ratifies such acts explicitly or implicitly. Failing such ratification those who acted will be personally and jointly liable for any loss suffered by the third party unless otherwise stipulated.

A Bill to Combat Abuse of Legal Entities introduced in Parliament in 1981 provides that, unless expressly stipulated otherwise, the persons acting on behalf of the BV i.o. will be jointly and severally liable until the BV has ratified the act. It also provides that those persons are jointly and severally liable for the loss if the BV, in spite of having ratified the act, fails to perform its obligations and they knew or should reasonably have known that the BV could not perform its obligations.

The Deed of Incorporation is a notarial Deed incorporating the Statutes of the company and containing special statements concerning the number of shares subscribed by each incorporator, any contributions other than in cash, and particulars about the members of the Managing Board and any Supervisory Directors named in the Deed.
Although upon incorporation there must be not less than two incorporators who must each subscribe at least one share, there is no requirement that there should be more than one shareholder. Consequently, in practice one of the incorporators is often a nominee who immediately after incorporation transfers the one share subscribed by him to the parent company. As mentioned in note 1 above, this practice can be abandoned as soon as the Act to Combat Abuse of Legal Entities has come into force.
As to the paying up of the shares, reference is made to the next paragraph sub (ii)(a).
The members of the Managing Board of the BV are under an obligation within one week of the incorporation to have the BV entered in the Trade Register and to file an authenticated copy of the Deed of Incorporation with the documents attached thereto (e.g. relating to the payment for the shares).
For this purpose two or more special forms must be filled in and signed by members of the Managing Board. The notary will normally file these forms. Until this obligation has been fulfilled, the minimum capital (fls 35,000)[4] has been paid up, and at least 10% (under the Capital Bill 25%) has been paid up on each share subscribed under the Deed of Incorporation, each member of the Managing Board shall be jointly liable with the BV for any act by which he binds the BV (under the Capital Bill for any act by which the BV is bound, by whomsoever). This liability is not extinguished by the said requirements subsequently being met.
During the life of the BV a number of facts must be entered in the Trade register as well: any appointment, resignation, dismissal or suspension of Directors[5] or persons having power to bind the BV, any amendments of the Statutes (which always require a resolution of the General Meeting of Shareholders, a notarial Deed and a Declaration of No Objection), any change in the subscribed and/or paid-up capital, change of address, as well as the dissolution and liquidation. If the BV must disclose its annual accounts it must do so by filing them with the Trade Register. With respect to each entry in the Trade Register a notice is published in the *Staatscourant* (Official Gazette). The (modest) costs involved are charged to the BV. The conditions laid down in the First Directive for a company to rely as against third parties on data so published (see the chapter on European Company Law) have been included in the *Handelsregisterwet* (Trade Register Act).

(ii) Organisation of the BV

(ii)(a) Capital and shares

Under Dutch law there are three different concepts of share capital: the authorized capital, the subscribed capital and the paid-up capital. The autho-

4. This figure may be increased for BV's to be newly incorporated in order to keep up with inflation.
5. Whenever the word 'Directors' is used, both the members of the Managing Board and the Supervisory Directors, if any, are meant.

rized capital must always be stated in the Statutes. There is no obligation whatsoever to issue shares up to the amount of the authorized capital. The Statutes may authorize some other organ (e.g. the Managing or Supervisory Board) than the General Meeting of Shareholders to issue shares up to the amount authorized. The Capital Bill brings no change in this respect. The subscribed capital must amount to not less than 20% of the authorized capital. It is not possible to issue more shares than the amount of the authorized capital allows. In order to exceed this amount the Statutes must be amended, which costs money and takes time. It is therefore advisable, in order to have a maximum of flexibility, to start with an authorized capital which is five times as high as the subscribed capital. Under present legislation not less than 10% of the par value of each share must be paid up. This is 25% under the Capital Bill. There are certain inconveniences attached to shares that have not been fully paid up. They must be registered and in principle each holder remains jointly liable for paying up, even after having transferred the shares. Therefore, unless there is a special reason for having partly paid-up shares (e.g. to grant one shareholder relatively more voting rights for his part of the paid-up equity, each share of the same par value carrying the same number of votes whether it has been fully paid up or not), it is advisable to fully pay up the shares.

In the event that there is not sufficient time to amend the Statutes in order to increase the authorized capital the BV could issue shares at a premium.

Under present law there is no statutory pre-emption right for the shareholders in the event of new shares being issued. The company's Statutes may provide that such a right exists. However, the Capital Bill provides for such a right (except in the case of preference shares and of an issue of shares to employees of the company or a group company), unless the company's Statutes provide otherwise.

Under present law the Statutes of a BV can provide that the BV may acquire its own shares up to 50% of the subscribed capital. Authority for such acquisitions is usually vested in the Managing Board, often subject to approval of the General Meeting or the Supervisory Board, if there is one. Under the Capital Bill the BV will still be allowed to acquire 50% of its own issued shares, but there are some additional requirements which are similar to the ones set forth in the Second Directive. The 50% will include the BV's shares held by its subsidiaries, which may only acquire the BV's shares to the extent that the BV may do so itself. The BV will not be permitted, with a view to the subscription or acquisition of its shares by other parties, to lend monies or to give any security. The same prohibition will apply to its subsidiaries.

The Capital Bill's provisions as to reduction of capital are rather similar to those of the Second Directive.

As under the present law, the Capital Bill provides that interim dividends may only be distributed to the extent that the net assets exceed the amount of the paid-up and called capital plus any reserves which may not be distributed. However, this need not be evidenced by any balance sheet drawn up prior to the distribution.

The Capital Bill also provides that as from 1st January of the fourth year after the Act has come into effect (probably 1-1-'86) BVs which existed when it came into effect must have an authorized, subscribed and paid-up capital of not less than fls 35,000, but the members of their Managing Boards will already be jointly liable with the BVs if their paid-up capital is less than fls 15,000 on 1st January of the second year after the Act has come into effect and less than fls 25,000 on 1st January of the third year. In addition, by 1st January of the fourth year at least 25% of the par value of each issued share must have been paid up.

It should be kept in mind that the provisions of the Capital Bill are of course subject to amendment in Parliament.

As to the shares, these must be registered (shares of an NV may also be bearer shares) and they must have a par value expressed in guilders. The usual par value is fls 1,000, but it can be as little as one guilder. It is not allowed for a BV to issue share certificates. A BV can issue to a shareholder an extract from its Register of Shareholders, but see below for the conclusiveness of such an extract.

Under present law the following general rules apply as to the payment for the shares. Payment is due immediately upon subscription of the shares (also if these are issued after incorporation). As stated above, each member of the Managing Board is jointly liable with the BV until (i.a.) at least 10% has been paid up on each share subscribed in the Deed of Incorporation. This does not apply to shares subscribed at a later stage. Apart from this liability there is no written rule as to the timing of the payment. Payments made on behalf of the BV prior to its incorporation can by way of ratification by the BV at the time of its incorporation be deemed to have been made for the shares subscribed upon incorporation. Payment may be made in cash (the Department of Justice requires this to be guilders) or in kind.

In the event of payment in kind for shares issued upon incorporation the contract relative to such payment must be mentioned in, and attached to, the Deed of Incorporation. The Department of Justice requires that it must appear from the contract in combination with the Deed that the value of the contribution in kind together with any remaining obligation to pay up equals at least the par value of the shares subscribed, which in fact means that any shortfall in the value of the contribution in kind at the time of the incorporation must be made good in cash.

In the event of payment in kind for shares issued after incorporation the contract concerned cannot validly be entered into unless the Managing Board has been expressly authorized by the General Meeting or the company's Statutes and the essence of the contract must be included in the notes to the accounts for the financial year during which it was entered into.

Under the Capital Bill a number of restrictions will be introduced which go even beyond the requirements of the Second Directive. The main rule is that payment must be made in cash if and to the extent payment in kind has not been stipulated. Payment in cash must be made in Dutch guilders.

As to payment for shares subscribed upon incorporation, reference is made to the checklist (item (iii) below). In the event of shares being issued after incorporation there are no special requirements as to payment in cash (except that it must be made in Dutch guilders). As to payment in kind for shares subscribed after incorporation, the requirements are rather similar to those applying when shares are subscribed upon incorporation. It should be noted that the auditor's[6] report may be dispensed with if the contribution is made by one or more Dutch or foreign (EC) companies which meet the requirements of the Fourth Directive on annual accounts and if a number of other (stringent) conditions are met (cf. art. 10, paragraph 4 Second Directive). After the fashion of the Second Directive (art. 11), the Capital Bill also contains similar requirements concerning the acquisition of assets from an incorporator within two years of the incorporation.

Payment in kind will have to be made forthwith after subscription or after a call for further payment. If the value of the contribution in kind at that moment is less than the par value of the shares or the amount called the balance will have to be paid in guilders, unless this balance has disappeared by the end of the financial year in which the contribution was made.

The BV and its incorporators or shareholders are at liberty to agree that a premium shall be paid on the shares, even after they have been issued and fully paid up.

The Statutes of a BV may provide for other shares than ordinary shares: preference shares and priority shares. These will be dealt with sub 2 below in the context of voting rights and the distribution of power in the company. In that part of this chapter we shall also briefly deal with *certificaten* (depository receipts for shares), *administratiekantoren*, etc..

As stated above, the Statutes of a BV must contain provisions restricting the transferability of shares. The Act allows a choice between two systems: either a system by which a shareholder wishing to dispose of his shares must offer them to the other shareholders or a system that requires the approval of an organ of the company (e.g. the General Meeting, the Managing Board, the Supervisory Board, the Meeting of Holders of Priority Shares) for any transfer.

It is important to note that shares can only be validly delivered by way of an instrument in writing[7] which must either be submitted to the BV (after which the BV must acknowledge the delivery) or served upon the BV. Although the BV is under an obligation to enter the transfer in its Register of Shareholders, such an entry is no requirement for the delivery and consequently this Register does not provide conclusive evidence as to the ownership of the BV's shares. An invalid delivery may invalidate subsequent resolutions passed at a General Meeting.

A BV may issue debentures (*obligaties*) which may carry all sorts of rights. There are no statutory provisions as to debentures. The rights of holders of debentures are determined by the documentation of the issue. If a BV issues debentures to bearer or if depository receipts to bearer for registered debentures issued by the BV are in circulation it must always disclose its annual accounts in full.

6. The audit must be carried out by a *'registeraccountant'* or by an *'accountant-administratieconsulent'*. The latter may only act if the law does not require that the BV's annual accounts be audited by a *'registeraccountant'* (see item (ii)(e) below).

7. Such an instrument of transfer is not the same as a purchase agreement although the two can be combined in one document.

(ii)(b) Management, representation, supervision

For most people from Anglo-Saxon and Latin countries the organisation of management and supervision of Dutch companies is difficult to understand. We shall therefore pay special attention to this point. What follows applies to NV and BV alike.

A Dutch company must have at least one Board: the *Directie* (in larger companies sometimes called *Raad van Bestuur*). We shall translate this Board as 'Managing Board', although 'Board of Management' is perhaps slightly more correct. Its members are called *'Directeuren'* or *'leden van de Raad van Bestuur'*. In order to avoid any confusion with the English 'Managing Director' we shall refer to them in English as 'members of the Managing Board'. When the Board is called *'Raad van Bestuur'* the company sometimes has a number of *'Directeuren'* who are not members of any Board and who are in fact only *'procuratiehouders'* (persons on whom certain powers to bind the company have been conferred) with a more impressive title. The title does not, therefore, warrant the existence of unlimited power to bind the company. In principle only members of the Managing Board have power to represent the company. In accordance with the First Directive, Dutch law provides that their powers can only be limited (vis-à-vis third parties) by a provision in the company's Statutes to the effect that the company can only be bound by one or more members acting either independently or jointly or jointly with one or more other persons (who need not be employed by the company). This limitation applies to the general power to represent the company, in whatever transaction. The powers of the Managing Board or any of its members cannot be validly restricted to e.g. dealings by which the company is bound up to a certain maximum amount. A member of the Managing Board, therefore, has either full power to bind the company or no power at all or only power to bind it jointly with another member or another person. If a member of the Managing Board acts without having power to do so the company will, generally speaking, not be bound. The members of the Managing Board can either jointly or individually authorize another person to act on their behalf and in so doing bind the company. The 'other person' could also be one of the members of the Managing Board who would otherwise have no power to individually bind the company. Of course, in such a case the authorisation must be given by two members who have authority to act jointly or by one member who can act alone.

Although in most cases each member of the Managing Board can individually bind the company, the underlying internal authority is in principle based on a resolution of the whole Managing Board, either explicitly or implicitly as a result of a distribution of functions among the members. In practice, a Managing Board very rarely passes formal resolutions and tax and other authorities do not normally require that any evidence of Board resolutions be produced. This can be different in the case of holding companies forming part of an international group (when foreign tax authorities require evidence of the Dutch company's 'substance').

There are no requirements as to nationality or residence of any member of the Managing Board. The minimum number of members is one. There is no maximum. The Statutes can provide for a minimum and/or a maximum. There is no age-limit for these members. They may be corporations.

Members of the Managing Board are in principle appointed, suspended and dismissed by the General Meeting of Shareholders. If there is a Supervisory Board they can usually also be suspended by that Board. All this is only different in the 'unmitigated structure regime' (see below). In companies with more than one shareholder one often finds 'oligarchic clauses'. These will be dealt with in the part on the joint venture.

Any Dutch company may have a two-tier Board system. Its Statutes may provide for a *Raad van Commissarissen* (Supervisory Board). Only in 'large companies' (also called 'structure companies') is such a system compulsory. The 'structure regime' is dealt with below. It should be emphasized, especially for Anglo-Saxon readers, that Supervisory Directors have no power to sign for and bind the company, except in very special circumstances, e.g. when there are no members of the Managing Board or when there is a conflict of interests between the company and one or more of these members. It is the duty of the Supervisory Directors to supervise the Managing Board and the general course of events in the company and the enterprise connected with it, as well as to give the Managing Board advice. In doing so they must let themselves be guided by the interests of the company and the enterprise connected with it. It is clear that these interests do not always coincide with those of the shareholders. The Statutes of many companies contain a list of decisions the Managing Board cannot take without the approval of the Supervisory Board. Such a list has only an effect internally between the company and the members of the Managing Board. The absence of such approval cannot be relied upon as against third parties.

Again there are no requirements as to nationality, residence or number of Supervisory Directors. The age-limit for Supervisory Directors is 72 years. They may also be corporations. In all companies other than 'structure companies' Supervisory Directors are in principle appointed by the General Meeting of Shareholders. However, the Statutes of such other companies may provide that not more than one third of their number may be appointed by others than the General Meeting.

'Structure regime'

The 'structure regime' was introduced in 1971 and it applies to 'large companies' which meet each of the following three conditions:

a. subscribed capital plus reserves (according to the balance sheet with explanatory notes) or not less than fls 10,000,000[8] ;
b. a Works Council instituted by virtue of a statutory obligation either with the company itself or with 'a legal entity of which it holds directly or indirectly for its own account not less than half of the shares' (hereafter called subsidiary); and
c. not less than 100 employees working in The Netherlands and employed by the company and its subsidiaries.

Large companies must have a Supervisory Board with specific powers. These powers are:

a. to appoint and dismiss the members of the Managing Board;
b. to determine the annual accounts;

8. This figure may be increased in order to keep up with inflation.

c. a number of decisions of the Managing Board are subject to the approval of the Supervisory Board.
These decisions include *inter alia*:
- issue, acquisition and redemption of the company's shares;
- permanent direct or indirect co-operation with another company or legal entity, and the discontinuation of such co-operation, if such co-operation or discontinuation is of fundamental significance;
- direct or indirect participation in the capital of another company to an extent of not less than 25% of the company's own subscribed capital plus reserves as shown on its balance sheet with explanatory notes, as well as a substantial alteration in the size of any such participation;
- investments requiring an amount of not less than 25% of the company's own subscribed capital plus reserves as shown on its balance sheet with explanatory notes;
- a proposal to amend the Statutes;
- termination of the employment of a substantial number of employees simultaneously or within a short period of time;
- substantial change in the circumstances of employment of a substantial number of employees.

The members of the Supervisory Board of a 'structure company' are co-opted (for a term of not more than 4 years) by the Supervisory Board itself. The General Meeting of Shareholders, the Works Council and the Managing Board have the right to recommend persons for co-optation. The General Meeting of Shareholders and the Works Council have the right to object to the appointment (co-optation) on the ground of the expectation that the nominee will be unfit for the performance of the duties of a Supervisory Director or that as a result of such an appointment the Supervisory Board will not be properly composed.
Notwithstanding such objection the Supervisory Board may take the appointment if, at the request of the Supervisory Board, the Social and Economic Council (see part on External Controls sub 2.2 (g)) declares the objection unfounded. There are special rules as to the dismissal of Supervisory Directors.
The system described above applies to companies which have filed for 3 consecutive years a statement to the effect that they meet all three conditions referred to above. Such a statement must be filed with the Trade Register within two months of the determination or approval by the General Meeting of the annual accounts which show that the condition as to the fls 10 million has been met.
There are certain exceptions for companies forming part of a group of companies and for holding companies, and a 'mitigated structure regime' applies to companies forming part of an international group and to certain joint venture companies. The wording of these exceptions and special rules is rather complicated. The structure regime does not apply to 'a company the activities of which are exclusively or almost exclusively confined to managing or financing legal entities with which it forms a group and its and their participations in other legal entities, provided the majority of its employees and of those of the legal entities with which it forms a group are employed outside The Nether-

lands'. The structure regime is mitigated if the Dutch company is a subsidiary of a (Dutch or foreign) legal entity of which the majority of the employees (including those employed by other companies of the same group) are employed outside The Netherlands, unless the majority of the employees of the subsidiary and the legal entity put together are employed in The Netherlands.[9] The mitigation is that it is not the Supervisory Board but the General Meeting of Shareholders which appoints the members of the Managing Board and determines the annual accounts. This mitigation was felt necessary in order to avoid complete loss of control by parent companies of the Dutch subsidiaries in their group.
Supervisory Directors appointed for an indefinite period of time prior to the date on which the structure regime comes into effect can remain in office until 4 years after that date.
It should be noted that the structure regime may well be changed in the next few years since the two major political parties seem to agree on the introduction of a tripartite Supervisory Board with one third employees' representatives directly elected by the employees, one third representatives of the shareholders and one third representing the 'public interest'.

(ii)(c) Shareholders' meetings
There is not much to say about the General Meeting of Shareholders of a wholly-owned subsidiary. It should be noted that such Meetings cannot validly be held outside The Netherlands. However, the Statutes may provide that the shareholders can validly adopt resolutions without any meeting being held. Such resolutions must be adopted unanimously and in writing. In order to make sure that all formalities are complied with it is advisable to instruct a Dutch lawyer to hold a General Meeting 'on paper' with a Power of Attorney from the shareholder.
The powers of the General Meeting are in practice rather limited, although the Statutes may confer some additional powers on it. In practice these powers are: to appoint, suspend and dismiss Supervisory Directors (except in 'structure companies'), and members of the Managing Board (except in 'unmitigated structure companies') to determine the annual account (except in 'unmitigated structure companies'), to declare dividends, to resolve upon the issue of shares (unless the Statutes provide otherwise), to amend the Statutes (which further requires a notarial Deed and a Declaration of No Objection) and to dissolve the company.
Questions of voting rights etc. will be briefly dealt with in the part on the joint venture and participations.

(ii)(d) Liability
There are some provisions in the new Civil Code (Book 2 on corporations) on liability of members of Managing and Supervisory Boards both to the company itself and to third parties. In addition, liability can be based on the general provision on tort. In this connection, members of Managing Boards have been held liable in tort in some cases where they knew that their companies would be unable to meet the obligations they incurred on their behalf. However, in

9. See for the mitigation for joint venture companies item 2.b (iv) below.

practice these provisions have very seldom been applied. There seems to be a great reluctance to even try to hold Directors personally liable. The Courts tend to test management and supervision only marginally and refuse to give the appearance of sitting in the chair of the manager. In this mild climate some cases of abuse of corporate vehicles for fraudulent purposes (especially in the contracting business) have occurred in recent years. The resulting political upheaval has prompted the Government to introduce three Bills, two of which[10] relate to personal liability of members of the Managing Board.

A Bill introduced in December 1980 is designed to secure the position of the tax collector and the institutions which collect social security and compulsory employee pension contributions. As soon as it has become apparent that a company will be unable to pay its debts it must inform the tax collector and the said institutions, failing which each member of its Managing Board will be personally and jointly liable unless he can demonstrate that failure to inform and to pay is not due to him. If the company has done its duty to inform the authorities the burden of proof shifts back and the Director will only be liable if it is demonstrated that he is to blame for the failure to pay the tax and contributions.

This liability will be extended to any person who is not a member of the Managing Board but who has determined or contributed to determining the company's policy as if he were such a member, as well as to individuals who are members of the Managing Board of another company which in turn is acting as a member of the Managing Board of the aforementioned company.

Apart from the matters referred to in section (i) above, the second Bill, the Bill to Combat Abuse of Legal Entities, mainly provides for stricter liability of the members of Managing and Supervisory Boards (and, if these in turn are legal entities, also of the members of their Managing Boards) in case the company has gone bankrupt. If they have not properly performed their task within a period of three years prior to the bankruptcy and if this is likely to have substantially contributed to the company going bankrupt they will be liable for the amount by which the company's debts exceed its assets. If the Managing Board has not met its statutory obligations as to the keeping of the company's books and publishing its accounts it will be deemed not to have properly performed its task and this will be presumed to have substantially contributed to the bankruptcy. The Court may under certain circumstances mitigate the amount for which liability exists and individual members of the Managing Board may exculpate themselves.

For the purposes of these provisions persons who have determined or contributed to determining the policy of the company as if they were members of the Managing Board will be treated as such members.

In addition, the so-called *actio Pauliana* will be extended in that there will be a rebuttable presumption that both parties to transactions between the company and members of its Managing or Supervisory Board or their family or associated companies (companies in the same group) knew that such transactions were prejudicial to the creditors, in which case the receiver in bankruptcy can invoke the nullity of such transactions.

10. The third Bill (which received Royal assent on 4-6-'81 but will not come into force until 1-7-'82) makes contractors liable for certain obligations of their sub-contractors.

It should be kept in mind that both above-mentioned Bills may well be amended in Parliament.

There is no general rule of Dutch law under which a parent company (or an individual sole shareholder) can be held liable for the debts of a subsidiary. However, in a few specific cases Courts have held (sole) shareholders liable and there is a considerable body of authoritative writing in support of liability in other cases as well. Like other aspects of the law on groups of companies, liability of parent companies (rather: dominating companies) is in the course of development in The Netherlands (see item (ii)(g) below).

(ii)(e) Accounts and auditing requirements

Although for many years the standard of the Dutch accountants' profession has been high, the law on companies' accounts was very rudimentary until 1971. In that year the Annual Accounts of Enterprises Act introduced a modern and flexible set of rules on the contents of the accounts of NV, BV and two other forms of enterprise. However, these rules, which were incorporated in Book 2 of the new Civil Code in 1976, are to be short-lived since in 1983 they will make way for the much more detailed provisions implementing the Fourth Directive. Since these provisions are likely to apply to all annual accounts to be determined or approved with respect to financial years which will commence after 31st December 1982 there seems to be little sense in dwelling on the old law.

In September 1980 the Bill to implement the Fourth Directive was introduced in Parliament. It follows the Directive rather closely and reference is therefore made to that Directive and to the chapter on European Company Law. However, the Bill deviates from the Directive on a number of points and some of these will be dealt with below.

Like the Directive, the Bill treats NV and BV in the same manner. However, the exceptions and mitigations for small and medium-sized companies (artt. 11 and 27) and the transitional provision as to exemption from the requirement that the accounts be audited (art. 55, para 2 sub e)) will apply to the BV only.

A BV which (together with its subsidiaries) meets at least two of the following requirements is a 'small BV':

a. the value of the assets according to the balance sheet with the notes to the accounts does not exceed fls 3 million;

b. the net turnover of the financial year concerned does not exceed fls 6 million;

c. the average number of employees during the financial year does not exceed 50.

A small BV may draw up condensed accounts which need not be audited.

A 'medium-sized BV' is a BV which is not a 'small BV' and which (together with its subsidiaries) meets two out of three requirements of a similar nature as those referred to for the small BV, but the figures are fls 12 million, fls 24 million and 250 respectively. The accounts of a medium-sized BV need not mention certain details (in particular relating to turnover), but they must be audited.

Until such time as the Government may determine (probably 30th July 1985) the accounts of a BV must only be audited if:

a. it has an issued capital of not less than fls 500,000, *or*
b. it is engaged in the banking or insurance business, *or*
c. the total of its assets according to the balance sheet and the notes to the accounts is not less than fls 8 million *and* the number of its employees (including those of its subsidiaries) is not less than 100.

It should be kept in mind that even if the accounts need not be audited they will still have to be published in the manner set out sub (ii) (f) below.

A subsidiary (NV or BV) forming part of a group whose group accounts are drawn up, audited and disclosed in accordance with the provisions of the Fourth Directive by a company established within the EC is (subject to certain conditions, including a public statement by that company of joint liability for all debts arising from transactions of the subsidiary) exempt from most of the provisions as to the contents of the accounts and from the audit (see art. 57 Fourth Directive, one of the transitional provisions in abeyance of the adoption of the Seventh Directive). This exemption does not apply if the subsidiary has issued bearer securities or if any of its securities are quoted on any stock exchange.

A Dutch company which has one or more subsidiaries must include consolidated group accounts in the notes to its accounts.

The Bill's provisions as to the contents of the annual accounts and the annual report as well as the further information to be added thereto are roughly the same as those of the Directive. The Bill follows the Directive in that it is based on historical cost accounting, but it explicitly allows departure therefrom in favour of the replacement value method or other methods which take account of current values. If the true and fair view is seriously prejudiced by valuation at historical cost a revaluation against current values is even mandatory. This rule, which could prejudice investment in The Netherlands, is controversial and may be amended. Subject to the foregoing, the Bill permits valuation of any 'participation' (as defined by the Bill[11]) at net asset value, which means according to the equity method.

It should be noted that the amounts must be expressed in Dutch guilders, except in group accounts provided consolidation on the basis of a foreign currency is justified by the international ramification of the group. The items of the accounts must be described in Dutch unless the General Meeting has prior to the beginning of the financial year decided to use another language and no shareholder has objected during that year. The same goes for the annual report which will have to be in writing.

Within 6 months of the end of the financial year the annual accounts must be determined by the General Meeting. There is no sanction if this period is exceeded[12]. In 'unmitigated structure companies' the accounts are determined by the Supervisory Board and subsequently approved by the General Meeting. Prior to being determined the accounts (i.e. the balance sheet, the profit and loss account and the notes to the accounts) must be signed by all members of the Managing and Supervisory Boards. In case any of their signatures is mis-

11. According to the Bill a company 'participates' in another company by providing it directly or indirectly with equity with a view to being permanently associated with that company in furtherance of its own activities. There is a rebuttable presumption that a 'participation' exists if the company, together with any company with which it forms part of a group, provides 20% or more of the equity of the other company.

12. But see item (ii)(f) as to the obligation to publish.

sing the reason must be stated. It should be kept in mind that as soon as possible after being determined the accounts must be submitted to the Works Council for discussion.

Under the Bill the auditor is no longer appointed but he is commissioned to audit the accounts. The commission may be for an indefinite number of succeeding annual accounts. The commission is given by the General Meeting and if it does not do so, by the Supervisory Board, failing which by the Board of Management.

The auditor must be a registered accountant or a person who has been admitted to practice by the Minister of Economic Affairs by virtue of a foreign certificate of qualification. It is also possible to commission a firm of registered accountants or of such admitted persons. In addition, *'accountants-administratieconsulenten'* (who have not had the same thorough training as registered accountants) will be qualified to audit the annual accounts of small and medium-sized BVs, provided they have passed a special exam.

The auditor reports to the Supervisory Board (if any) and the Board of Management.

Book 2 of the new Civil Code provides for a special procedure by which any interested party may demand that annual accounts which do not meet the requirements of the law be drawn up in accordance with directions ordered by the *'Ondernemingskamer'* (Enterprise Chamber) of the Amsterdam Court of Appeals.

(ii)(f) Publication of accounts

NVs must publish their full accounts without any exception, even if they are subsidiaries of another company which has published its accounts.

Until the Act to implement the Fourth Directive has come into force a BV does not have to publish its accounts, unless the total of its assets is not less than fls 8 million and it employs (together with its Dutch subsidiaries) at least 100 employees on the balance sheet date, in which case it must publish a condensed balance sheet with notes and the auditor's report. There is a total exemption from publication if the BV's accounts are consolidated in the published accounts of another Dutch company and if this company has publicly stated that it will be jointly liable for all debts arising from transactions of the BV. On the other hand, full publication is required if the BV is engaged in the business of banking or insurance or if it has issued bearer debentures.

What follows below will apply as soon as the Act to implement the Fourth Directive has come into effect.

The small BV (as defined in the previous section) must publish its condensed balance sheet with notes thereto.

The medium-sized BV (as defined in the previous section) must publish its profit and loss account in the somewhat condensed way in which it has to be drawn up and its balance sheet which for the purpose of publication may to some extent be simplified, as well as the notes to the accounts.

All other (large) BVs and any BV engaged in the business of banking or insurance must publish their full accounts.

A BV which forms part of a group whose group accounts are drawn up, audited and published in accordance with the provisions of the Fourth Directive by a company established within the EC is (subject to certain conditions, see the corresponding exemption in section (ii)(e) above) exempt from the obligation to publish its accounts. This is an important difference from the NV.

Publication is effected by filing a copy of the accounts (or, in the case of a small BV, the balance sheet and the notes thereto) with the Trade Register within 8 days after they have been determined (or, in the case of an 'unmitigated structure company', approved by the General Meeting).

If the accounts have not been determined and, if required, approved, within 7 months of the end of the financial year, then the Managing Board must forthwith publish them indicating that they have not been determined or approved. If the General Meeting has extended (by a maximum of 6 months) the statutory period of 5 months within which the Managing Board must draw up the accounts then the aforementioned obligation to publish starts two months after the end of the extended period.

The annual report (which must be in Dutch if it is to be published) and some other data (such as the destination of profits, the accounts of subsidiaries which have not been consolidated, and substantial losses and risks which have arisen after the end of the financial year) must be published in the same way. Some of these data may, instead of being published, be kept at the company's offices and copies must be made available to the public upon demand, provided this is published in the Trade Register.

The Trade Register causes the *Nederlandse Staatscourant* (the Official Gazette) to publish a very short announcement of every new entry.

Failure to comply with any obligation relating to publication as referred to above constitutes a criminal offence.

(ii)(g) Groups of companies

In Dutch law there is no general concept of groups of companies as there is in German law. In fact, it is felt in The Netherlands that it would perhaps be better not to work with a single concept of groups of companies but to create special provisions for different purposes, such as annual accounts, liability, protection of outside shareholders, etc.

However, since 1971 a number of statutory provisions have been introduced which take the existence of groups into account. These provisions relate mainly to the annual accounts (i.a. the exemption for subsidiaries (BVs) set out in section (ii)(f)), to the 'structure regime' (see section (ii)(b)) and, to some extent, to the revised Act on Works Councils (see IV, C).

Further provisions are being introduced with the Bill to implement the Second Directive, the Capital Bill, and in particular the Bill to implement the Fourth Directive. The latter Bill gives, for the first time, definitions of 'participation' (*deelneming*, see note 11), 'subsidiary' (*dochtermaatschappij*) and 'group company' (*groepsmaatschappij*).[13] In doing so it goes, of course, beyond the requirements of the Fourth Directive and anticipates the Seventh. The main elements of the German '*Konzernrecht*' (protection of creditors and outside shareholders, publication and '*Weisungen*' (binding directions given by the dominating company)) can hardly be found in express provisions of Dutch

13. It should be noted that the word '*maatschappij*' is broader than 'company' in that it covers any legal entity as well as limited and general partnerships.

law. As to protection of creditors, reference is made to item (ii)(d) *in fine*. However, reference is made to the exemptions for subsidiaries in item (ii)(e) above and the condition that there must be a public statement of joint liability made by another group company within the EC.
Outside (minority) shareholders are to some extent protected by the requirement that the relationships between a company, its shareholders and the members of its organs must be governed by reasonableness and equity and by the rule that decisions of the company's organs can be declared null and void on the ground of their being contrary to *inter alia* '*bona fides*'. Outside shareholders are also protected by the condition that, in order for the subsidiary to benefit from the exemptions referred to in items (ii)(e) and (f) above, all its shareholders must have given their consent to such exemptions.
In this connection mention should be made of the 'right of enquiry' which can be exercised by one or more shareholders or holders of depository receipts ('*certificaten*', see item 2.e) representing not less than 10% of the subscribed capital or a par value of not less than fls 500,000 and also by trade unions. They can request the Enterprise Chamber ('*Ondernemingskamer*') of the Court of Appeals in Amsterdam to order an enquiry into the affairs of a company if there are reasons to doubt that it is being properly managed. In the event that the enquiry produces evidence of mismanagement the Enterprise Chamber may make far-reaching orders, e.g. to dismiss members of the Managing and/or Supervisory Boards, to replace them with others, to nullify decisions and even to dissolve the company.
As to publication, reference is made to the exemptions for a BV forming part of a group (item (ii)(f) above), in particular the condition that a company in the group must have included that BV's accounts in its consolidated and published accounts.
Finally, as to '*Weisungen*', although Dutch company law is still in principle based on the independence of each company, legal writers, the Department of Justice and some case-law have recognised the authority of the parent company, subject to the requirements of *bona fides* vis-à-vis outside shareholders, to give general policy directions to its subsidiary, and to some extent, subject to further conditions, even to give ad hoc instructions.
The law on groups of companies is no doubt one of the areas of Dutch company law which will be the subject of interesting developments during the Eighties.

(iii) Checklist for the formation of a BV

1. Whom to approach?
Although the Deed of Incorporation of a BV must be passed before a (civil law) notary, in many cases the formation entails the need for legal advice on a variety of questions for which lawyers (*advocaten*) are usually better equipped. Most large lawfirms closely co-operate with notaries, and can therefore offer an integrated package of services. As to tax questions, it is assumed that the decision in which country to form a subsidiary is taken on the basis of tax advice. This can be obtained from a Dutch firm of tax consultants whose advice will be required on a more or less permanent basis throughout the life of the subsidiary. Dutch lawfirms do not normally advise on tax matters.

2. *Company law aspects*

Information and documents to be provided include in any event:

a. Proposed name, preferably with one or two alternatives. An enquiry will be made with all 35 Chambers of Commerce as to the availability of the names. This takes 5-15 days.

b. Corporate seat. The Statutes (part of the Deed of Incorporation) must mention a municipality in The Netherlands. The address need only be filed with the Trade Register after incorporation.

c. Objects. These are usually very short but very broad.

d. Share capital. Minimum subscribed and paid-up: fls 35,000.

e. Management. Will there be only a Managing Board or also a Supervisory Board?

f. Any restrictions of the powers of the members of the Managing Board (only dual signature system has external effect).

g. Financial year. First year can be long or short (e.g. if BV is formed on 1st May 1982 and financial year is same as calendar year, first one may end on 31-12-82 or on 31-12-83).

h. The incorporators. Until the Bill to Combat Abuse of Legal Entities is enacted there must be not less than two. They can be legal entities.

If non-Dutch legal entity:
supply full name, registered office or seat and latest annual accounts or letter from bank to the effect that the company has a good financial reputation.

If individual non-resident in The Netherlands:
supply full names, place and date of birth, nationality, private address as well as letter from bank as above

If Dutch legal entity:
questionnaire from Ministry of Justice must be filed, with extract from Trade Register and latest annual accounts.

If individual resident in The Netherlands:
questionnaire from Ministry of Justice must be filed State the number of shares to be subscribed by each incorporator upon incorporation.

i. The first members of the Managing Board and Supervisory Directors to be named in the Deed of Incorporation. Only one member of the Managing Board (no Supervisory Director) need be named in the Deed. Others can be appointed later. For information and documents to be supplied see under (h) above.

j. Payment of share capital.

1. Until the Capital Bill becomes law the position is as follows:
   Payment in cash: this is due immediately upon incorporation.
   Payment in kind: the contract relating to the contribution in kind must be mentioned in, and attached to, the Deed of Incorporation.
2. As soon as the Capital Bill becomes law:
   Payment in cash (this must be Dutch guilders): one or more Dutch banks or the Dutch postal giro service must have sent one or more than one statement to the notary to the effect that the money to be paid up on the shares subscribed upon incorporation is at the disposal of the BV immediately upon its incorporation. This means that the payment must be made prior to incorporation.

Payment in kind: inventory of all assets contributed must be signed by each incorporator and this as well as the auditor's report on the value of the assets must be attached to the Deed of Incorporation. Sums due from the BV (i.o) to the incorporator may be applied towards his subscription to the company's share capital. In that event the incorporator must furnish a description of the matter in respect of which the sums are due to him from the BV (i.o), together with a valuation by an auditor, and these documents must be attached to the Deed of Incorporation.

3. Consents required

None. However, the (draft) Deed of Incorporation requires a 'Declaration of No Objection' from the Department of Justice. The investment in the share capital of the BV must be reported to De Nederlandsche Bank NV. This is normally done by the BV when it receives payment for its shares through a Dutch bank. If no payment in cash is received a separate form must be filed with De Nedèrlandsche Bank NV.

There is no requirement as to debt/equity ratio, but for tax reasons such a ratio may be desirable.

4. Tax

Within one month of payment of the share capital the BV must file a form and pay capital tax at the rate of 1% of the capital paid (including any premium). Under certain conditions the capital tax is waived or reduced in cases of shares-for-shares or assets-for-shares transactions involving companies within the EC.

There is no tax on loan capital.

5. Costs

Advice given by the *advocaat* is charged for on the basis of time spent.

Notarial fees are charged on a scale depending on the size of the authorized capital. Since this scale gives only minimum fees notaries usually charge higher fees. For the formation of a BV with a minimal authorized capital (this could be fls 35,000, but it is usually 5 times fls 35,000 = 175,000) the fee will be between fls 2,400 and fls 3,000 (in 1982). In the case of an authorized capital of fls 500,000 the fee will be between fls 2,500 and fls 3,500. When fls 5 m., between fls 6,000 and fls 9,000. In most cases the amount of work is taken into account to arrive at a figure between these brackets. The disbursements (including a retribution to the Ministry of Justice of fls 150, costs of enquiry into availability of name, extra copies of Deed of Incorporation) will be close to fls 500.

The fee for initial registration in the Trade Register (including a surcharge for the Social and Economic Council) is charged in relation to the paid-up capital and the long-term debts of the BV and subject to annual changes.

For 1982 it was for

a capital of fls	35,000 ± fls	180
a capital of fls	100,000 ± fls	480
a capital of fls	1,000,000 ± fls	2,100

As of 1st January of the year following the registration there is an annual fee at half the rate of the initial fee.
After each filing with the Trade Register a publication in the Staatscourant (Official Gazette) follows. The costs are usually between fls 10 and fls 30. A translation of the Deed of Incorporation will cost between fls 1,000 and fls 2,000.

6. Time
Due to very considerable delays at the Ministry of Justice it may take up to 6 months to obtain the Declaration of No Objection. However, in really urgent cases (e.g. if the company must be used for a Bonds Issue) the delay may be reduced to less than a week. Of course the period does not start until the notary has received all data and has had time to prepare the draft Deed of Incorporation. It is advisable to make the enquiry as to the availability of the name (see 2.a. above) prior to submitting the draft Deed to the Ministry of Justice. Deciding upon the name and alternatives should therefore be first priority.

1.c. OTHER FORMS

Apart from the branch and the subsidiary (BV) there are no other legal forms used by foreign investors for a wholly-owned enterprise. Limited and general partnerships are sometimes used for joint ventures and will therefore be briefly dealt with in section 2 below.

2. THE JOINT VENTURE AND PARTICIPATIONS [14]

2.a. Introductory remarks

As in other countries, joint ventures may take all sorts of shape. They are often entered into by a simple contract without any company or partnership being created. There is a very large degree of contractual freedom which in such cases allows for an organization very similar to that of a company or partnership. However, for the larger joint ventures a BV or partnership is usually used. The choice between these two forms will often depend on tax considerations. The same considerations coupled with the desire to limit the partners' liability often call for a limited partnership between two Dutch subsidiaries of the (possibly foreign) partners as limited partners and a (very small) joint subsidiary as the general partner. In all cases where a company or partnership is used the partners will conclude a joint venture agreement (JVA) which will contain provisions supplementary to those of the Statutes of the vehicle. Some practical guidelines will be briefly set out below sub 2.b. to 2.d.
All foreign investment in The Netherlands does not occur by way of branches, subsidiaries or joint ventures. A foreign investor may acquire a participation in the share capital of a Dutch company (often an NV) without any JVA

14. In this context the term 'participation' is not confined to the definition given in 1.b (ii)(e) above.

being concluded with other shareholders. The participation may or may not be a first step towards a complete take-over. The foreign investor may come across certain peculiarities of Dutch company law and practice which he should know about. Some of these will be dealt with sub 2.e. below.

2.b. The jointly owned company

(i) This is probably the most common form of joint venture vehicle. Almost invariably a BV (and not an NV) will be used for the reasons set out in section 1.b. Dutch company law provides quite a variety of ways to organize the division of powers between the partners. The Statutes can provide for qualified majorities on any subject to be decided at General Meetings of Shareholders or in the Managing or Supervisory Boards.[15] They can prescribe a special quorum in each of these organs. Although shares without voting rights are not permitted voting rights can to some extent be limited and special shares (*'prioriteitsaandelen'*, priority shares) can carry special rights, e.g. to nominate candidates for either Board. Such nominations will be binding unless the General Meeting decides otherwise by a two thirds majority representing more than half the subscribed capital (and unless the company is a 'structure company'). Special rights can also be carried by other (classes of) shares and generally there is a large degree of freedom to attribute rights to different kinds of share. The Statutes may also contain intricate rules about the relationships between and the powers of the various organs of the company (in particular the requirement that the General Meeting and/or the Supervisory Board must approve certain important transactions to be entered into by the Managing Board). The Statutes of a BV must contain provisions restricting the transferability of the BV's shares. Such provisions are normally very detailed in the case of BVs which are not wholly-owned.

(ii) The provisions in the Statutes are usually supplemented by more or less detailed provisions in the JVA, e.g. on the number and appointment of members of the Managing and Supervisory Boards, on the issuing of additional shares, on deadlock situations, on the distribution of profits, etc.. All such and other customary provisions in JVAs are in principle perfectly legal under Dutch law which in principle permits voting agreements. Of course one should be aware that the European Commission has taken the view that in principle joint ventures fall within art. 85 EEC Treaty but they often qualify for an exemption under art. 85, paragraph 3.

(iii) As to minority rights, a distinction should be made between two categories. First, the genuine outsiders, i.e. shareholders in the joint venture company who are not parties to the JVA at all. Such outsiders are rare in joint ventures. As to their protection, reference is made to item 1.b. (ii) (g) above.

15. In joint venture companies one often finds a Supervisory Board as an additional means to divide the powers between the partners and to facilitate their supervision of the joint enterprise.

The second category of 'minority rights' is that of one or more partners who do not have a majority of the shares in the joint company. However, they cannot be regarded as minorities in the proper sense since they are not 'outsiders' and their position should be sufficiently secured in the JVA. Questions of alleged infringement of their 'minority rights' will therefore normally arise under the JVA which under Dutch law must be performed in good faith (*bona fide*) and which usually provides for settlement of disputes (often arbitration). It is not uncommon, especially in 50/50 joint ventures, for a third party or a Supervisory Director to be given one share by each partner so as to give him a casting vote in the event of deadlock between the partners.

(iv) The 'structure regime' (see item 1.b. (ii) (b) above) provides for certain exceptions in the case of joint venture companies. They are totally exempt from this regime if the majority of their shares are held by a number of companies, parties to a joint venture, which are themselves subject to the structure regime. The 'mitigated structure regime' applies to companies the majority of whose shares are held by (a) two or more companies which are parties to a joint venture and the majority of whose employees (including those of other group companies) are working outside The Netherlands or (b) by one or more such companies and one or more companies which are already subject to the regime or totally exempt on the ground that their parent(s) is (are) subject to the regime. The mitigation does not apply if the majority of the employees of the joint venture company and of the parties to the joint venture (including the companies of the groups to which they belong) put together are employed in The Netherlands.

(v) When setting up a joint venture in the form of a company or of a partnership one should not forget that if one of the partners has a Works Council in The Netherlands this Council must in most cases be consulted (with all the consequences thereof (see IV, C)) and also that the rules for the protection of employees in the Merger Code may apply (see B.2.2. (d)).

2.c. Consortia

There are no special rules of Dutch law relating to Consortia.

2.d. Other forms of joint venture

As stated above, joint ventures may also take the shape of a general or limited partnership (*vennootschap onder firma (vof)* and *commanditaire vennootschap* respectively). The drawback of partnerships is that they are not legal persons, which means that the liability of the general partners towards third parties is unlimited, and that the law on partnerships is rather scanty and obscure. On the other hand, the lack of legal personality, and therefore the transparency, may be beneficial from the point of view of taxation.
A partnership contract (also called 'Statutes') requires very careful drafting, in particular with respect to such matters as powers to act on behalf of the partnership, internal and external liability of the partners, continuation of the

partnership in the event of termination by one partner or accession of another, termination and liquidition. Of course some of these subjects could also be dealt with in the JVA which, in addition, will deal with the normal matters provided for in such a contract.
The partnership contract need not be passed before a notary; it need not be submitted to the Department of Justice for a Declaration of No Objection; there is no requirement as to minimum capitalisation; the law on annual accounts does not apply to partnerships (although they must keep books of accounts), and the 'structure regime' does not apply to them either[15a]. On the other hand, the Act on Works Councils does apply to partnerships employing not less than 100 employees and all partnerships must be registered in the Trade Register.

2.e. Participations

Anyone contemplating participation in a Dutch company (in particular an NV) should be aware of the fact that by acquiring a certain number of shares he can by no means be certain of acquiring a corresponding degree of power in the company. In some cases he cannot even acquire shares but only '*certificaten*' (depository receipts) of shares.
Corporate practice has invented a number of devices to concentrate power in the company in the hands of a small group of persons, often members of the Managing and/or Supervisory Boards. Such devices are often presented as a means of protecting the company against an unsolicited take-over bid.
One of the best known devices is the issuing of shares to a trustee ('*administratiekantoor*' in the form of a company (NV or BV) or a '*stichting*', foundation) which will then issue depository receipts for those shares to the public or, in the case of (family) BVs, to the persons who would otherwise be shareholders.[16] Thus the administratiekantoor itself becomes a shareholder of the company and can exercise all rights attached to the shares. The object of the exercise is that it exercises the voting rights in accordance with the wishes of the management of the company, but that it passes all financial benefits attached to the shares on to the holders of the corresponding depository receipts. The rights of the holders of such receipts are determined by the conditions of issue which may vary. Sometimes these conditions stipulate that the holders may exchange their *certificaten* for shares at any time, but often this is not the case since such *royeerbare certificaten* would afford little protection from influences by the General Meeting. Since 1976 the new Civil Code protects the holders of certificaten to some extent by giving them various rights, e.g. to attend and to speak (but not to vote) at General Meetings and to exercise the right of enquiry (see item 1.b (ii) (g)).
Depository receipts may even be officially quoted (e.g. *certificaten* Unilever), but it should be noted that the Amsterdam Stock Exchange makes the listing

15. However, this may change in the future. In 1981 the Committee on Company Law advised the Minister of Justice that general and limited partnerships which have NVs or BVs as general partners should be assimilated to subsidiaries of such NVs or BVs for the purposes of, *inter alia*, annual accounts and structure regime.
16. Of course the public or those persons can also exchange their shares for depository receipts or the company can do so after having acquired the shares.

of *certificaten* which cannot be exchanged for shares conditional upon (i.a.) the absolute independence of the administratiekantoor from the company which had issued the shares.
This condition prevents this device from being waterproof against aggressive take-overs. Other devices are therefore also used, often cumulatively. One such device is priority shares (see 2.b. (i) above) the existence and exact powers of which can be ascertained from the Statutes. The Statutes may also provide for the possibility of preference shares (*preferente aandelen*) being issued. These could be issued to some friendly company and only partly paid up, thus giving that company full voting power corresponding to the par value of the shares and diluting the shares of the would-be acquiror. However, in some Court cases this device has not proved successful where it was obvious that the company was not in need of new equity. It will also become less attractive as soon as measures are introduced to restrict the company purchasing its own shares and the minimum to be paid up on each share is increased from 10 per cent to 25 per cent (see 1.b (ii) (a) above). Another device is a provision in the Statutes that no shareholder (except the *administratiekantoor*) may own more than e.g. three shares. So far no device has been found which is considered to be completely watertight.

B. External Controls

1. EXCHANGE CONTROL REGULATIONS

1.1. In line with the open nature of the Dutch economy, exchange control regulations are very liberal. Since 1945 they have been based on the *Deviezenbesluit 1945* (Exchange Control Decree 1945), but on 1st May 1981 the *Wet financiële betrekkingen buitenland* (Foreign Financial Relations Act) came into effect. This change of legal basis has not brought about any significant change in the regulations themselves. Set out below is a brief summary of the regulations applying to foreign investments in The Netherlands and some related matters. It should be kept in mind that regulations may be changed, abolished or introduced at any time in the light of changing economic, financial or political circumstances.

1.2. *a. Dealings in and issues of shares* in Dutch or foreign companies are unrestricted. Subscription for and acquisition of shares in a Dutch company do not therefore require Dutch exchange control consent. However, capital investments by non-residents in The Netherlands and by residents abroad, as well as any changes which may occur, must be *reported* to De Nederlandsche Bank NV (DNB).
b. Loans or credits not involving bonds or other securities in guilders *from residents* (except, subject to certain conditions, authorized banks) *to non-residents* are unrestricted, unless they exceed fls 10 million in any one calendar year to the same non-resident, in which case consent is required.
c. As to the *raising of loans by residents from non-residents*, the following general rules apply.

Residents are allowed without specific consent to obtain from non-residents credits or loans totalling not more than fls 500,000 in any calendar year. They may also give guarantees or security to non-residents in connection with such credits or loans.
Credits or loans in excess of fls 500,000 per calendar year are in principle not allowed. However, there are certain exceptions. DNB will grant Dutch subsidiaries consent to borrow any amount from their foreign parents, provided no direct or indirect repayment is made during the first five years of the term of the loan. Subject to certain conditions, residents can obtain consent for raising loans from non-residents to finance oil and gas exploration and production in the Dutch sector of the North Sea Continental Shelf. Residents can obtain consent for other loans from non-residents, provided certain conditions as to maturity, average term, fixing of rate of interest, etc., are met.
d. Borrowing and lending through resident financing companies. For tax reasons Dutch companies are often used to raise funds abroad (whether or not by issuing bonds or notes) and to lend them to or invest them in non-resident companies in the same group. This requires consent which is granted as a matter of routine on condition that payments regarding these loans (except payments of interest) are not channelled through The Netherlands. Such financing companies must register with DNB and report regularly.
e. Direct guarantees, suretyships and other security given by residents on behalf of or to non-residents as security for financial credits are subject to consent. Such consent is granted if, and to the extent that, the liabilities undertaken by non-residents for which the security is given do not result in domestic credit restrictions being frustrated.
f. Payments by residents to non-residents as well as by non-residents to residents must in principle be effected *through an authorized bank*. For almost any such payment a DNB form must be filled in and filed with the bank concerned.
g. Residents are free to open bank accounts abroad, provided they *report* them to DNB. The same goes for any *settlements in current account with non-residents* and *settlements by way of intra-group clearing*. In the latter cases the Exchange Control Regulations Department of DNB should be contacted.
h. Transactions in connection with the international *supply of goods and services* are virtually unrestricted.
i. Obtaining exchange control consent usually takes *about 10 days*, but in urgent cases this can be reduced to one day.

2. MERGER CONTROLS

2.1. *No general control as to the consequences of a merger* exists in The Netherlands, neither from the point of view of anti-trust nor from a more general point of view (public interest, e.g. protection of employment or regional interests, prevention of undesirable foreign economic influence). There are, however, controls in some specified areas, such as banking and insurance. In 1977 the SER (see below) adopted a report recommending a general system of merger controls applying various criteria (competition, employment, regional policy), but at the beginning of 1982 no Bill to implement the recommendations had yet been introduced. The whole subject is still rather controversial.

2.2. *a.* Since 1970 there have been *rules on the procedural aspects of mergers.* These are laid down in the so-called Merger Code *(Fusiegedragsregels)*, the third version of which, dating from 1975, was still in force in 1982. The Code is designed to protect the interests of both shareholders and employees.
b. The *rules for the protection of shareholders* apply in principle only if a public offer for shares or convertible bonds is made, whether by a Dutch or a foreign offeror. Certain rules also apply if an offeror whose shares are quoted on the Amsterdam Stock Exchange makes a public offer for the shares of a foreign company.
c. The Boards of the companies involved in the preparation of a merger (including any foreign offeror!) must make public announcements in time to prevent the price of the shares from being influenced by rumours, but in any event as soon as the offer price has been fixed. Such announcements are usually drafted in joint consultation. In the event of an aggressive take-over bid being contemplated the offeror must invite the Board of the offeree for consultation prior to issuing any public announcement about the terms of the offer. A Notice of Offer with detailed information must be made available. The Notice must contain a statement to the effect that the same offer is made to all holders of the same kind of security. All Directors of each of the companies concerned must disclose to the Committee for Merger Affairs (see below) their holdings and dealings in the shares of the offeree company (and, in the event of a share for share transaction, also of the offeror) during the six months prior to the first public announcement.
There are a number of other more or less detailed provisions on, *inter alia*, further announcements, information to shareholders at General Meetings and the way in which a bid becomes unconditional. It is also forbidden (with the possibility of exemption) to acquire shares in the offeree on terms more favourable to the seller for a period of three years after the offer has become unconditional.
Copies of all documents published and announcements made must be sent to the Committee for Merger Affairs and to the Amsterdam Stock Exchange *(Vereniging voor de Effectenhandel).*
d. The *rules for the protection of employees* apply in the case of any merger (defined as the acquisition of direct or indirect control of the activities of an enterprise or a part thereof – this includes for example the creation of joint holding companies and of joint ventures) if at least one of the enterprises involved is established in The Netherlands and (whether or not together with any other Dutch enterprises with which it forms part of a group) employs not less than 100 employees. It should be noted that the Merger Code can be declared applicable to other enterprises by way of collective labour agreement. Thus, in the construction industry the number of employees is 75 instead of 100.
The rules for the protection of employees do not apply to mergers within the same group, nor to mergers 'outside the Netherlands jurisdiction'. It would require too much space to explain the meaning of this expression.

e. The Board of each enterprise involved is under an obligation to observe the rules for the protection of employees. No public announcements must be made until the trade unions (the rules contain provisions as to which trade unions are involved) have been informed of their contents.
The most important provision by far, and the most difficult one to apply, is that the trade unions must be informed 'as soon as the merger talks have reached a stage which justifies the expectation that agreement can be reached'. The trade unions must be given an explanation of the reasons for the merger, the anticipated social, economic and legal consequences and the measures envisaged in connection therewith. They must be given an opportunity to express their opinion of the merger in a discussion. During the discussion, consideration will in principle be given to such matters as the outline of measures to prevent, eliminate or reduce any consequences of the merger which are prejudicial to the employees, including financial compensation, and the basic principles of policy towards employees after the merger. There are fairly complicated rules about confidentiality and the lifting of it. In the event of an unsolicited take-over bid being contemplated the offeror must inform and discuss with the trade unions before fixing the price of his offer. He must inform the Board of the offeree company not less than 7 days prior to announcing or making the offer. In that event the offeree Board must also inform the trade unions forthwith and hold discussions with them. The Committee for Merger Affairs and the Ministry of Economic Affairs must be informed at the same time as the trade unions. These bodies will send out questionnaires which must be answered as soon as the merger has been completed.
f. The Merger Code is, like the English City Code on Take-overs and Mergers, a system of voluntary self-regulation, not a statutory enactment. However, this self-regulation is not entirely voluntary in that in the event of a breach the Committee for Merger Affairs may have recourse to public announcements or even public censure; the *Vereniging voor de Effectenhandel* has declared that in the event of public censure its members must refuse or discontinue any co-operation in the implementation of the offer. This has, in fact, happened only twice during the first 10 years of the Code's existence. With respect to observance of the rules for the protection of employees, the trade unions perform the function of watch-dogs, complaining to the Committee when they become aware of a breach. There have also been complaints against trade unions for breach of the secrecy provisions. Out of the 4,500 mergers dealt with in the first 10 years 225 breaches were reported and only 14 cases gave rise to public censure. It appears that in practice the Merger Code is now generally observed. Nevertheless, the SER, in its report of 1977, proposed that the procedural rules for mergers should be given a statutory basis. Until January 1982 no Bill had been submitted to Parliament.
g. One of the reasons for this proposal on the part of the SER was that it did not consider itself the appropriate body to issue general rules in this field and that it could not provide for effective sanctions. The SER (*Sociaal-Economische Raad*, Social and Economic Council) is a tripartite body consisting of equal numbers of representatives of trade unions, employers and the government. Instituted by an Act in 1950, the SER acts both as an advisory body to the government on social and economic matters and as the top institution in

the typically Dutch statutory organization of trade and industry (*publiekrechtelijke bedrijfsorganisatie*). This organization consists of a number of bodies instituted by Act of Parliament and in which certain powers which normally belong to central government are vested. There are two categories of such bodies: 'horizontal' bodies for certain branches of trade and industry (*bedrijfschappen*) and 'vertical' bodies for specific groups of products (*productschappen*). The *bedrijfschappen* comprise enterprises active in the same branch of industry, the *productschappen* comprise two or more kinds of enterprises in different fields of activity involving the same group of products. Composed of equal numbers of representatives of employees and employers, the corporations have certain regulatory powers in such fields as (for *productschappen*) economic relations between various stages of production or supply (including prices), collecting information and (for *bedrijfschappen*) enhancement of quality, rationalisation of enterprises, wages and other conditions of employment, training, administration, etc.

3. COMPETITION

3.1. The *Wet economische mededinging* (Act on Economic Competition), which dates from 1956, does not have a great influence on Dutch business. It is based on a system of combatting abuse rather than on prohibition. In principle, any '*mededingingsregeling*' (restrictive agreement) must be notified to the Minister of Economic Affairs, who registers it. However, certain categories of agreements which do not aim at dominating the market are exempted. The register is not open to inspection by the public. On 1st January 1981, 610 nationwide and 753 regional restrictive agreements were on the register. One may safely assume that there are quite a few which have not been registered. The Ministry investigates each restrictive agreement, applying the test of the public interest. The government can publish details of a restrictive agreement or declare it wholly or partially unenforceable (in which case it is forbidden to carry out the restrictive agreement), but in most cases the policy is 'informal', which means that if the Ministry finds that certain restrictive agreements or provisions thereof are contrary to the public interest, discussions will be held with the enterprises concerned. These discussions will nearly always result in some change. The only restrictive practice to which the Act is frequently applied is pricing. The parties to any restrictive agreement must report any changes in the prices they charge and this means in practice that they require consent for such changes. This system of price control comes in addition to the price controls under the *Prijzenwet* (Act on Prices) mentioned below. Since 1964 there is a general prohibition of collective resale price maintenance (with the possibility of exemptions). Individual resale price maintenance in respect of certain consumer durables has also been prohibited.

3.2. The government can also take action against dominant positions the effects of which are contrary to the public interest. In practice, dominant positions have seldom been attacked. In 1977, however, the government forced Hoffmann-La Roche BV to reduce its prices for valium and librium by 25% and 35% respectively on the ground that the company abused its dominant position on the Dutch market. In 1979 this decision was annulled by the competent administrative Court on the ground that the government could not reasonably have come to the conclusion that Hoffmann-La Roche BV occupied a dominant position on the market of tranquillizers.

3.3. In December 1977 a Bill was introduced in Parliament to amend the Act in relation to (horizontal) price fixing and to resale price maintenance, as well as to confer powers on the Minister of Economic Affairs to issue minimum price regulations. As to price fixing and resale price maintenance, initially a system of prohibition with possible authorizations was proposed. However, in an amended Bill submitted in 1981, the Government proposed a different system for price fixing. Price fixing will in principle be permitted, but it can be prohibited if it does not meet one of the conditions to be spelled out in the Act. In 1982 the Bill was still pending in the Lower House. At that time many important price fixing cartels had already been dismantled as a result of intervention by the EC Commission.

3.4. In January 1981 the government introduced a Bill to make the register of restrictive agreements open to public inspection. Not all such agreements need to be registered any longer. In principle only 'horizontal' restrictive agreements and (non-binding) practices which aim at dominating the market must be notified for registration and the Bill provides for the possibility of exempting certain groups of agreements and certain individual agreements. On the other hand, the Bill also authorizes the Government by way of Royal decree to require that certain 'vertical' agreements be included in the public register, in particular agreements between one supplier and several buyers relating to e.g. resale prices or exclusive supply and purchase. Notification will have to be made by any party within one month of the agreement coming into existence or being modified (or terminated). As long as the agreement has not been notified it will lack any binding force. Finally, reference is made to paragraph 2.1. above.

4. ENVIRONMENTAL CONTROLS

During the seventies a sizeable body of legislation for the protection of the environment was built up and there is more to come in the eighties, partly as a result of Directives of the EC. Even though the *Wet Algemene Bepalingen Milieuhygiëne* (Act containing general provisions on environmental control), which came into effect in 1980, coordinated and improved a number of procedures for applications, objections and appeals under 9 different Acts in this field, investors wishing to start industry of a kind which could have any impact on the environment will have to be prepared for long delays and complicated procedures. It is impossible in this context even to give an outline of all the Acts and regulations. The investor is advised to consult a lawyer specialized in this field.

5. STATE MONOPOLIES

The foreign investor is very unlikely to trespass on the domain of a State monopoly. There are only very few economic activities which have been reserved by law to the State or public corporations. These include the *Staatsbedrijf der Posterijen, Telegrafie en Telefonie* (including the postal giro service), the Mint and the Government Printing Office (but bank notes and stamps are printed by a private enterprise). In fact, central or local government have an important say in a number of industries, through shareholdings or otherwise: the production and distribution of (natural) gas, the railway system, public utilities, heavy chemicals (Dutch State Mines) etc.

6. OTHER CONTROLS

6.1. Investments

There are virtually no controls on investments as such. We refer to paragraph 1 above with respect to exchange control. New investments are encouraged to the extent permissible under the EEC Treaty. Reference is made to paragraph F of the chapter on Taxation.

6.2. Exercise of certain activities

There are restrictions on the exercise of certain activities, mainly in the retail trade and relatively small business.

a. Under the *Vestigingswet Detailhandel 1972* (Establishment of Retail Trade Act 1972) a licence to set up is required. In order to obtain such a licence, the applicant must demonstrate the necessary professional skills. In a number of trades, nationals of other Member States of the EC can rely on experience over a certain period of time.

b. Under the *Vestigingswet Bedrijven 1954* (Establishment of Businesses Act 1954) over 30 Royal Decrees have been issued, each covering a specific branch of business and prohibiting establishment unless certain requirements are met. These requirements relate only to credit-worthiness, knowledge of the business and professional skills. The Act provides that exemptions from the prohibitions must be given wherever necessary to comply with the provisions of any Directive of the EC, thus giving direct effect to such Directives.

c. Under the *Bedrijfsvergunningenwet 1954* (Business Licences Act 1954) the government may issue a Decree prohibiting the exercise of any activity in a specific branch of industry if, *inter alia*, there is serious overcapacity. Up to early 1982 this Act had been applied only twice.

d. There are also controls under legislation applying to specific branches of industry only. Thus the new *Wet toezicht kredietwezen* (Act on the Supervision of the Credit System) which came into effect in 1979 requires a licence for *banking* in The Netherlands and even for approaching the public with a view to commercially raising money below a certain amount (fls 100,000) per transaction (e.g. per bond) or acting as an intermediary in such a transaction. However, since 1st June 1981 an exemption applies if money is raised against an issue of securities which are to be officially quoted on a Stock

Exchange of one of the Member States of the EC. The Act provides for far-reaching controls on the exercise of the banking business and, since 1st June 1981, also of near-banking activities (the business of obtaining the disposal of funds withdrawable at two years' notice or more and of granting credits and making investments for one's own account).

e. In order to do business as a life assurance or other *insurance* company consent from the *Verzekeringskamer* (Insurance Supervisory Authority) is required (with certain advantages for EC nationals as a result of various Directives) and to be a broker or other intermediary in the insurance industry one must be registered with the SER (see paragraph 2.2. (g) above) after having demonstrated that one meets a number of requirements under the *Wet Assurantiebemiddeling*.

f. *Trading in securities* is in principle not subject to statutory controls. However, the majority of securities in which there is any regular trade are quoted on the Amsterdam Stock Exchange (ASE). In order to be admitted to trade at the ASE one must be a member of the *Vereniging voor de Effectenhandel* and to become a member one must meet certain requirements relating, *inter alia*, to professional skills, experience and capital. All partners of a firm or members of the Managing Board of a company which seeks membership must qualify as members.

g. The *Mijnwet continentaal plat* (Continental Shelf Mining Act) requires a licence for the reconnaissance, exploration and production of oil and natural gas and provides for state participation in the production thereof.

h. Road *transport* of goods and passengers and transport of goods by inland waterway are only permitted with a licence which can be refused if there is overcapacity. Air transport to, from or over The Netherlands may only be effected by licensed airlines. Such a licence is only granted to 'Dutch enterprises which have demonstrated that the majority of their capital and the effective management are in Dutch hands'. Vis-à-vis enterprises from other EC Member States this requirement is in our view contrary to the EEC Treaty (artt. 7 and 52 or 60).

i. Under the *In- en Uitvoerwet* the government can prohibit or restrict imports and exports. This Act is mainly applied to implement Common Market agricultural policy and its application in other areas is very considerably restricted by the EEC Treaty (Articles 30-36 and 110-116). The Act can also serve as a basis for sanctions against particular States, e.g. Rhodesia and, in May 1980, Iran. Since May 1980 the *Sanctiewet1977* (Sanctions Act 1977) can also be used for this purpose.

j. Finally, mention should be made of controls on prices and wages. Under the *Prijzenwet 1961* (Prices Act 1961) and some other Acts, the government can issue, and since the early seventies has issued price regulations, both general and for certain (groups of) products or services. These regulations aim at imposing maximum prices as a means of combatting inflation. There are also certain legislative provisions which allow for minimum prices to be fixed in order to reduce cut-throat price competition. Both kinds of price control are subject to limitations resulting from the EEC Treaty (art. 30).

k. Since the early Seventies wages have been controlled under the *Wet op de loonvorming* or under special Acts of Parliament. Reference is made to part IV of this chapter.

III. TAXATION

A. Corporation Tax

1. ENTITIES SUBJECT TO TAX

Dutch tax law draws a basic distinction between two categories of taxpayers; residents and non-residents. A non-individual taxpayer (entity) is deemed resident for purposes of corporation tax if it is managed from The Netherlands, and/or if it is incorporated in The Netherlands.
A resident entity is subject to corporate tax on all its income and gains if it is either a company with capital divided into shares (e.g. NV or BV) a co-operative society, an 'investment association' (*open beleggingsfonds*) or any of a number of Government-owned corporations. Although this group of taxpayers consists of many different types of entities, in the following paragraphs reference is made only to the BV (which is the most common type of company) as representing the entire group.
Other resident legal entities (such as foundations or associations) are subject to corporate income tax only if and to the extent they carry on business activities. Non-resident taxpayers include all legal entities and non-incorporated associations.
Partnerships, if their capital is not divided into shares (as defined for tax purposes) are not regarded as taxpayers. The partners are assessed directly on their share of the partnership's income and expenses.For example, a non-resident company participating in a partnership that carries on a business in The Netherlands for tax purposes is normally regarded as carrying on business in The Netherlands directly.
Resident taxpayers, to the extent taxable, are taxable on their worldwide profits including capital gains, regardless of source and regardless of remittance.
Non-resident taxpayers are taxable only on income arising from certain specified Dutch sources. In this context, the most important of these are:

a. profits arising from business carried on through a permanent establishment or a permanent agent in The Netherlands;
b. income arising from Dutch real estate;
c. interest arising from loans secured by mortgage on Dutch real estate;
d. dividends and interest derived from, and capital gains realized on the sale of shares in, Dutch resident companies if the recipient holds a 'substantial interest' (at least one-third of the outstanding shares), unless the shareholding can be regarded as a business asset;
e. profit derived from a participation in a Dutch business activity, otherwise than as a shareholder.

A Dutch resident company (and exceptionally, the Dutch branch of a non-resident company) together with one or more of its resident wholly-owned subsidiaries may elect to form a fiscal unit. The accounts of the companies involved are then consolidated for tax purposes. Certain conditions are imposed on the election relating mainly to carrying-forward of losses and valuation of assets.

The foreign investor, in determining the structure and form of his investment, would normally take the following tax considerations into account.
From the Dutch tax point of view, the following differences exist between investment through a Dutch resident company (normally a BV) or a branch or partnership:

- Only resident companies are subject to capital tax (see D. 1).
- Although corporate income tax rates are identical for resident and non-resident tax payers, profit distributions by a resident company are subject to dividend withholding tax (see B), while profit transfers from a branch or partnership are not.
- There is usually no Dutch tax on the sale or transfer of shares in a Dutch company, but there is tax on a gain realized or deemed realized on the sale or transfer of branch or partnership assets, or of participations in a partnership.
- Dutch companies are entitled to benefit from the Dutch unilateral rules on avoidance of double taxation and from tax treaties, while branches or partnerships are not.
- Dutch companies are, and branches or partnerships are not normally entitled to file a consolidated return with wholly-owned Dutch subsidiary companies.

In addition to these Dutch tax considerations, the investor will of course be guided by tax aspects existing in his own country of residence, e.g. the ability to deduct branch losses from domestic profits, or potential tax credit complications.

2. COMPUTATION OF PROFITS

2.a. Income

Taxable revenue includes all income and gains. The annual profit should be determined on an accrual basis in accordance with good business practice and along consistent lines.
There is no requirement that the tax accounts should equal the commercial accounts. Generally, conservative tax accounting methods are permitted.
For inventories the very conservative 'base stock' method is permitted. For depreciation, straight-line methods are usually applied.
'Goodwill' paid on the acquisition of a business is usually a depreciable asset, 'goodwill' paid on the acquisition of shares usually not. Distributions of profits and corporation tax are not deductible. Foreign profits taxes are only deductible if the relevant income is fully taxed without a credit or rebate for the foreign tax. There are some restrictions on the deductibility of payments made to 'substantial interest' shareholders who are members of the supervisory board.
Recognition of and providing for future inflation (e.g. in pensions) is not permitted.
Interest paid or accrued is deductible, except if it relates to loans that are used to acquire or capitalize foreign subsidiaries the dividends from which are exempt (see below, participation exemption).

Although there is no maximum debt-equity ratio under Dutch law, excessive capitalization by loans may be challenged by the revenue authorities. In cases where 'advance rulings' are obtained a maximum debt-equity ratio (of e.g., seven to one) is often stipulated as a condition for the ruling. Loans may be treated as capital if no interest is charged, and/or if they are subordinated, and/or if it is clear that the debtor will not be able to repay them.
Losses may be carried back two years and forward eight years. Losses incurred in the first six years of operation may be carried forward indefinitely.
Upon liquidation of a BV or a branch, it is deemed to have sold all its assets at fair market value and distributed the proceeds to its shareholders. The 'deemed' profit is subject to tax under the normal rules, and the distribution by a BV is subject to Dividend Tax.

2.b. Capital gains/losses

As noted above, capital gains are treated as ordinary income and are subject to full tax while losses are deductible.
By adopting conservative valuation methods, recognition of gains may often be deferred until realization, while losses may be recognised even before realization.

2.c. Exemptions, deductions, rebates

There are some important exceptions to the rules set out above. The most important of these are:

(i) Gains made on the disposal of a fixed asset may be credited to a 'replacement' reserve provided the asset is replaced within four years; the reserve is then applied to the acquisition cost.

(ii) Gifts to charities etc. are only deductible up to 6% of profits.

(iii) Until 1978, accelerated depreciation and investment allowances were available for investments in certain assets. These incentives have now been replaced by the WIR (see below, section F).

(iv) A very important feature of Dutch corporation tax is the participation exemption. This rule provides that dividends received, and capital gains realized, on shares of 'qualifying participations' are exempt from Corporation Tax.
A 'qualifying participation' is a shareholding of at least 5% in a Dutch company. A shareholding of at least 5% in a foreign company is a 'qualifying participation' if such a foreign company is subject to a tax on profits and the shareholding is not in the nature of a portfolio investment.
The exemption applies only if the shares have been held since the beginning of the recipient's bookyear. Losses suffered and amortizations charged on 'qualifying participations' are not deductible except if the subsidiary is liquidated. Expenses incurred in connection with foreign subsidiaries are not deductible.

(v) A tax-free roll-over is permitted where the entire business (or an independent part thereof) of the taxpayer is transferred to a company in exchange for shares in that company. Certain conditions are imposed.

(vi) Certain qualifying foreign source income is effectively exempt from tax. This exemption is granted through a tax rebate mechanism which is dealt with under paragraph 4. iv (tax credits).

2.d. Advance rulings

It has become common practice in The Netherlands to discuss certain tax aspects with the revenue authorities in advance and to agree on the tax treatment of certain companies and/or transactions. This is particularly useful if the investor's decision to invest in The Netherlands depends on certain tax consequences. These advance rulings usually are concerned with the interpretation of certain facts or the determination of the arms' length nature of certain intercompany transactions.
For example, frequent subjects for advanced rulings are
- whether a shareholding in a foreign subsidiary constitutes an exempt participation;
- what interest margin should be earned by a finance company established to borrow funds for onlending to affiliated companies;
- what margin should be earned by a company established to exploit industrial property rights within an affiliated group;
- the fees to be earned by a service company or branch established to render services of an administrative or auxiliary nature to affiliated companies.

Generally, no advance rulings are possible if the Dutch company or branch is engaged in selling activities, either as an agent or for its own account.

3. RATES OF TAX

The rates of corporation tax are as follows:

if profit is between		*tax on lower limit*		*% on excess*
fls	0 – 40,000	fls	0	45
	40,000 – 50,000		18,000	60
	50,000 and over		24,000	48

4. TAX CREDITS

For certain items of income that have been subject to tax and are included in the income which is subject to corporation tax, tax credits are granted. The most important of these are:
(i) a credit for Dutch dividend withholding tax. This is also granted if the dividends qualify for the participation exemption.
(ii) A credit for foreign withholding taxes on dividends, interest or royalties if such a credit is provided in the treaty or the unilateral measures for the avoidance of double taxation.
No credit is given in respect of dividends that qualify for the participa-

tion exemption. In most treaties, tax credits are provided for withholding taxes. In non-treaty situations, such credits are available only if the payer is resident in a listed developing country; the credit for dividend withholding tax is limited to 25%.

In all cases, the credits are limited to the Dutch tax applicable to the income; in computing this limit, the Revenue takes the view that expenses incurred in generating the income should be deducted from it. Unused credits may be carried forward for eight years. The taxpayer may elect to deduct the foreign withholding tax rather than credit it.

If the tax is not creditable, it may be deducted from income.

(iii) WIR. The system of investment grants introduced in 1978 is administered through the tax system: A grant takes the form of a tax reduction to the extent tax would otherwise be payable, and a cash grant for the remainder, if any. This is dealt with in more detail under section F.

(iv) Tax rebate (exemption) for certain foreign-source income. As indicated above, tax relief is granted in respect of certain categories of foreign-source income. This takes the form of a tax rebate which effectively constitutes an exemption of the income from corporation tax. The categories of income for which this relief is available may differ depending on whether a tax treaty applies.

Generally, the following categories are eligible:

a. profits attributable to a permanent establishment or permanent agent abroad;

b. income from, or gains on foreign real estate;

c. (in non-treaty situations, and under a few treaties) interest on a foreign mortgage.

In non-treaty situations, to be exempt, the income must have been subject to a tax abroad.

There are complex 'carry-over' provisions where foreign losses have been deducted from Dutch income and vice versa.

5. TIMING OF PAYMENTS

For resident taxpayers, the taxation year is the taxpayer's accounting year. The tax return is due usually within six months of the close of the preceeding accounting period. Extension can easily be obtained provided the taxpayer files an estimate of the taxable income for the previous year.

Preliminary assessments are then issued based on this estimate. The income tax liability is established by assessments. Resident taxpayers generally receive preliminary assessments during the current year; these assessments are usually established at 85% of the previous year's taxable profit and are payable in several instalments beginning at approximately the middle of the current year.

A further preliminary assessment is issued when the actual (estimated) profit figure is forwarded to Inland Revenue, and a final assessment when the Revenue has reviewed the tax return.

The Revenue must issue a final assessment within three years from the end of a taxable year plus the time, if any, for which an extension for filing the return is granted. However, reassessment is permitted within five years from the end of a taxable year (again, increased by extension time, if any) provided that a new fact has come to light which the Revenue could not be expected to know within the three-year period.

6. REVIEW AND APPEAL

If the taxpayer disagrees with a final assessment, he must file, within two months of the date of the assessment, a notice of objection with the inspector having jurisdiction.
The inspector will review the assessment and reduce or confirm it; the law does not provide a time limit for the inspector's decision.
If the taxpayer does not accept the inspector's decision he must appeal to the Appeals Court (*Gerechtshof*) within two months of the date of the inspector's decision. Court proceedings are comparatively informal; no representation by counsel is required. The taxpayer and Inland Revenue can appeal against the Court's decision by lodging an appeal with the High Court (*Hoge Raad*) within one month.
This Court reviews only questions of law, it accepts the Appeals Court's findings of fact.
Quite apart from this procedure, if the taxpayer considers himself the victim of double taxation in conflict with a tax treaty he may also invoke the 'competent authority' procedure which is provided in most double tax conventions (cf. art. 25 OECD-Model). No objection or appeal is possible against a preliminary assessment.
Under certain conditions, the Revenue may issue a notice of reassessment if the original assessment was too low or if no original assessment was issued. In such cases, the taxpayer must appeal directly to the Appeals Court.

B. Withholding Taxes on Dividend, Interest, Royalties

1. INCOME CATEGORIES SUBJECT TO WITHHOLDING TAX

Netherlands tax law knows three forms of withholding taxes: one is the Wages Tax (*loonbelasting*) which must be withheld from salaries and benefits paid to employees and directors; the second is the Lottery Tax and the third is the Dividend Tax (*Dividend Belasting*, based on the 1965 Dividend Tax Act).
Dividend tax must be withheld from all distributions, open or hidden, of profit and/or capital made by resident companies whose capital is divided into shares, and by investment associations. Only repayments of capital which are the result of a formal reduction of capital or the purchase by a company of its own shares are exempt; upon such a purchase, the excess of the purchase price over the paid-up capital is considered a dividend. The tax also applies to interest on profit-sharing bonds. The dividend tax does not apply to distributions of profit by branches of non-resident companies, nor to non-resident companies.

No dividend tax need be withheld if the recipient of the dividend is entitled to the participation exemption in respect of the dividend.
For resident recipients the tax is always creditable; for non-resident recipients the tax is usually a final tax, except where the recipient is subject to Dutch income or corporation tax.

Other than in respect of profit-sharing bonds, there is no withholding tax on interest. However, it should be noted that a non-resident may be subject to Dutch income tax on certain categories of interest received from Holland (notably, interest on a Dutch mortgage or interest paid by a company in which the recipient has a 'substantial interest').
There is no withholding tax on royalties, rentals, management fees, service fees, etc.

2. COMPUTATION OF TAXABLE AMOUNT

The taxable amount is the value of the net assets distributed. No deductions are permitted.

3. RATE OF TAX

The rate of dividend tax is 25%. This is often reduced to 15, 5 or even 0% if the recipient of the dividend is resident in a treaty country and files the appropriate return.
When expressed as a percentage of the net amount received by the shareholder, the rate of tax is $33\frac{1}{3}$%.

4. EFFECT OF TAX TREATIES

In all tax treaties, The Netherlands have agreed to reduce the dividend tax on dividends paid by Dutch companies to residents of the other country, on condition that the recipient submits an appropriate form (which usually must be certified by the Inland Revenue of the other country). The reduced rate is usually 15% if the recipient is an individual, or a company portfolio shareholder. If the recipient is a company owning 25% or more of the Dutch company's shares, the rate is often reduced to 5% or even 0%.
Further details are provided in the schedule of withholding taxes (see section J below).

C. *Individual Taxation*

1. INCOME TAX

1.a. Persons subject to tax

(i). *Resident individuals* are subject to tax on their worldwide income, regardless of source and remittance. For certain kinds of foreign source income that is subject to tax abroad (notably, income from employment exercised abroad, income from foreign real estate, business profits attributable to a foreign permanent establishment) a tax rebate is granted which is tantamount to an exemption, although the income is taken into consideration in determining the rate of tax ('exemption with progression').

(ii). *Non-resident individuals* are only taxable on certain specified categories of income from Dutch sources. This includes, inter alia, income attributable to employment exercised in The Netherlands, income from Netherlands real estate, business profits attributable to a Dutch permanent establishment and dividends, interest received from and capital gains realized on shares of a company in which the individual has a 'substantial interest' (roughly one-third of the shares).

(iii). *Expatriates* who are transferred to The Netherlands by their employer may be eligible for a special tax status. By administrative regulation (there is no statutory basis for this), for a period of up to five years, they are then regarded as non-resident taxpayers except in respect of their income from employment.
All income from employment is subject to Dutch tax but 'expatriates' may claim a standard deduction of 35% in respect of such income.

1.b. Computation of income

Income is computed on a cash basis[17] except business profits which must be computed on an accrual basis. The taxable year is the calendar-year.
Taxable income includes business profits, income from employment or other personal services, income from assets such as rent, interest, dividend, annuities, and capital gains on 'substantial interest' shares.
Deductible expenses include expenses incurred to earn taxable income, social security premiums, interest[18], annuities paid and within certain limits, gifts, medical and education expenses and support of dependent relatives. Resident taxpayers may claim a basic allowance (up to fls 12,000 for a married man). Non-resident taxpayers may claim such allowance only up to the amount of their taxable income from employment.

1.c. Rates of tax

The rates of tax are progressive, ranging from 17.5% on the first part to 72% on taxable income exceeding fls 200,000. A reduced rate of tax (between 20-54%) may apply to certain categories of non-recurring income. Capital gains on shareholdings constituting a substantial interest are taxed at a rate of 20%.

2. WAGES TAX

Taxable exployment income paid by a Dutch employer is subject to wages tax, withheld at source at the same rate as income tax. Usually, but not

17. Except prepaid interest which is only deductible within defined limits.
18. A Bill to limit the deductibility of interest has been introduced.

always, wages tax deducted can be credited against the ultimate income tax liability, any excess being refunded.

3. NET WEALTH TAX

Resident individuals are subject to an annual tax on the value of their net assets with a basic exemption of fls 48,000 (fls 96,000 for married men) which may be increased on certain conditions such as age, marital status and dependent children. The rate of tax is 0.8%; it is not deductible for purposes of income tax. To the extent the total of income tax and net wealth tax in a year would exceed 80%, the net wealth tax is waived. Non-resident individuals are subject to annual net wealth tax only in respect of 'Dutch assets' (including Dutch real estate and a Dutch permanent establishment). The rate of tax is 0.8%; they are not entitled to the basic exemption.
Expatriates are regarded as non-residents for purposes of this tax.

4. SUCCESSION DUTY/GIFT TAX

This is levied on estates left by, and gifts made by Dutch resident persons.
For purposes of this tax, all persons emigrating from The Netherlands are deemed to be resident until one year after their departure; if they are Dutch citizens, they are deemed resident until 10 years after their departure.
The rate of tax varies with the amount of the gift/estate and with the relationship to the donee/legatee.
For example, the maximum rate for transfers between spouses and children is 27%. The maximum rate for transfers to unrelated persons is 68%.

D. Registration and Stamp Duties

The following registration and stamp duties are significant for most business operations.

1. CAPITAL TAX

This is the Dutch version of the EC's tax on the issuance of capital (see, generally, chapter on the European Tax law). In conformity with the Directives, it is levied at a rate of 1% on the value of net assets contributed to a company upon the issuance of shares, or for no consideration.
The taxable amount may be reduced (even to zero) in the case of qualifying reorganizations or mergers involving other companies resident in the EC. The tax does not apply to branches of non-resident companies.

2. REAL ESTATE TRANSFER TAX

This tax is levied on the value of real estate that is transferred. The rate is 6%, levied on the fair market value of the real estate.

Exemptions apply in the case of multiple transfers occurring within a three-month period, and in certain qualifying 'assets for shares' transactions.
Under certain conditions, shares of a company whose assets consist mainly (70% or more) of Dutch real estate, are deemed to be Dutch real estate.
If such shares are transferred to an individual or entity owning or acquiring, directly or indirectly, more than one-third of the company's shares, real estate transfer tax is levied on the value of the 'underlying' real estate.

3. STOCK EXCHANGE TAX

This tax is due on the sale or purchase of negotiable securities (shares, bonds etc.) through a Dutch broker. The rate is 0.12% on the fair market value of the shares. It does not apply to new issues. By law, transfers of Dutch securities or the purchase or sale of foreign securities by a Dutch resident individual or entity must take place through a Dutch broker.
However, an exemption from this requirement can be obtained for transactions involving unquoted securities, that are executed outside the open market.

E. Indirect Taxation

1. VALUE ADDED TAX

Of the indirect taxes levied in The Netherlands the one of most general interest is the value added tax. This tax is levied according to the EC Directives (see, Chapter on European Tax Law) on most goods and services. The rate of the tax is 18%, with a 4% rate applying to foodstuffs, books, medical supplies and several other basic commodities and services.

2. OTHERS

Other indirect taxes include excise taxes (tobacco, wines, spirits, beer, other beverages, hydrocarbon, sugar), import duties, a special tax on passenger automobiles, etc. Not being of general interest, they are therefore outside the scope of this book.

F. Incentives

Until May, 1978 a system existed of stimulating investments through accelerated depreciation and investment allowances. In that month a system was introduced called the *Wet Investeringsrekening* (WIR) in which investment subsidies (referred to as WIR-premiums) are granted by way of a reduction of income or corporation tax payable, or a tax refund if the WIR premium exceeds the tax payable.

The WIR-system is extremely complex because it consists of a basic premium to which one or more of six special premiums may be added, because of detailed anti-abuse provisions and because of the interrelationship with SIR, a levy designed to offset the benefits of WIR for investments in certain regions. The following is therefore only a sketchy summary of the basic elements of WIR. Within certain limits the WIR-premiums may be increased or decreased by Royal Decree, and they may therefore be changed on very short notice.

Eligible investments:	*Basic WIR premiums (as of January 1982)*
new buildings (excluding homes)	14%
existing buildings (excluding homes)	8%
fixed installations in the open air	12%
ocean-going vessels	12%
airplanes	12%
other fixed assets	12%

The following *additional premiums* may be granted:

- small business premium (if total investment in a year is below fls 920,000: up to 6%
- development planning premium (moving business premises to a development area:): 15% or 7.5%
- special regional premium (for investments in a development area): 20% or 10%
- large projects premium (for creating additional employment): up to 4%. (In a 1980 judgment, the Court of Justice of the EC held that the large projects premium was in violation of art. 92 of the EC treaty).
- energy premium (for energy conservation or use or development of alternative resources): up to 15%
- environment premium for pollution prevention): up to 15%.

The total of all premiums (excluding large projects premiums) cannot exceed 50% (for buildings) or 40% (for installations).

If the asset is disposed of within a certain period (varying from 6 years to 18 years), a disposal levy is charged. The disposal levy is the lower of the premium received on investment or the premium percentage applied to the disposal proceeds.

G. *Social Security Premiums*

There are two categories of social insurances:
1. General insurances, applicable to every taxpayer
2. Insurances applicable only to employees.

In the case of employment, the premiums are partly borne by the employer.

1. GENERAL INSURANCES

The most important item is old age security and widow's/orphans pension (AOW/AWW).
The 1981 premium is 11.85% of taxable income, with a maximum premium of fls 5,776 p.a., which is withheld from employment income. The other premiums in this category are 9.9% of taxable income, with a maximum of fls 4,828 p.a., in the case of employment, they are borne by the employer.

2. EMPLOYEE INSURANCES

These include Health Insurance (ZW), Disability Insurance (WAO), Family Allowance (KWZ) and several others. Their combined rate in 1981 is approximately 21%, with certain maxima per employee. Of this the employee bears 5%, the employer 16%. These amounts exclude medical expenses insurance (compulsory for employees earning less than fls 42.300). The premium of 8.6% (max. fls. 3,100) is shared equally by employee and employer.
The combined effect of all insurances could be as much as 53% of the salary paid to an employee, of which 25% (max. fls. 12,200) is borne by the employee, and 28% (max. fls 13,100) is borne by the employer.

H. *Others*

1. SIR

Another important levy that can affect business operations is the Selective Investment Levy (SIR). This levy is intended as a disincentive for investments in certain overpopulated areas, mainly the Western provinces. It is imposed when a permit is obtained for the erection of a building, and upon the erection of open-air installations in one of the SIR-zones.
The rate of the levy is 13% for buildings and 8% for installations.
Although the levy should be seen in conjunction with the WIR (see above, section F), its terms and conditions do not necessarily run parallel to it, and situations may arise when the SIR-levy is not offset by a WIR-grant.

2. MUNICIPAL TAXATION

Municipalities levy some taxes and retributions on an annual level. The most important of these is the Real Property Tax which is levied annually on the value of real property owned and/or occupied by the taxpayer. The rate of these taxes is limited by statute; it varies for each municipality. The tax generally is not regarded as a significant cost factor.

3. ENVIRONMENTAL LEVIES

The Central Government, the provinces, municipalities and other public authorities are authorized to establish levies designed to cover the expense of protecting the environment.
A very complex framework of legislation has been developed in respect of pollution of surface water, air pollution, chemical and oil product waste. These laws are very technical in nature and fall outside the scope of this book. For certain industrial undertakings these levies can be quite significant.

4. EXTRACTIVE INDUSTRIES

Apart from the normal tax rules set out above, certain levies of a different nature apply to mining operations conducted on Netherlands territory on the Netherlands area of the North Sea Continental shelf. These range from bonuses, surface rentals, and royalties to compulsory state participation and a State profit share (which is a pseudo-tax). These levies are very substantial but in view of their very special nature are not dealt with in this book.

5. COMPULSORY EMPLOYEE PROFIT SHARING (VAD)

On several occasions in the past few years, the Government has introduced Bills to provide for compulsory employee profit sharing, known by its Dutch initials as VAD.
Although the scheme has some features in common with income tax, it has a totally different character, and is therefore included in the chapter on labour aspects (see IV, E).

I. List of Netherlands Double Taxation Agreements

Three categories of agreements are listed:
- agreements dealing with double taxation of income and capital (I + C)
- agreements dealing with double taxation of estates and inheritances (E + I)
- agreements dealing with shipping and air transport profits (S + A).

The dates noted are the dates of signing. The listing reflects the position as at January 1, 1982.

Argentina (S + A)		15- 1-1949
Australia (I + C)		17- 3-1976
Austria (I + C)		1- 9-1970
Belgium (I + C)		19-10-1970
Canada (I + C)		2- 4-1957
	am.	28-10-1959
	am.	3- 2-1965
China (Peoples Republic) (S + A)		14- 8-1975
Czechoslovakia (I + C)		4- 3-1974
Denmark (I + C)		20- 2-1975
	am.	22- 6-1966
Egypt (S + A)		15- 5-1957
Finland (I + C)		13- 3-1970
(E + I)		29- 3-1954
France (I + C)		16- 3-1973
German Federal Republic (I + C)		16- 6-1959
	am.	13- 3-1980
Greece (I + C) (not yet in force)		16- 7-1981
(S + A)		26- 7-1951
Hungary (I + C)		15-11-1938
Indonesia (I + C)		5- 3-1973
Irish Republic (I + C)		11- 2-1969
Israel (I + C)		2- 7-1973
(E + I)		9- 9-1974
Italy (I + C)		24- 1-1957
Japan (I + C)		3- 3-1970
(S + A)		26- 1-1933
Korea (I + C)		25-10-1978
Luxemburg (I + C)		8- 5-1968
Malawi (I + C)		15-10-1948
	ext. + am.	20-12-1962
	am.	7- 6-1969
Malta (I + C)		18- 5-1977
Morocco (I + C) (not yet in force)		12- 8-1977
Netherlands Antilles (I + C, E + I)		28-10-1964
New Zealand (I + C)		15-10-1980
Norway (I + C)		22- 9-1966
Poland (I + C)		20- 9-1979
Romania (I + C)		27- 3-1979
Singapore (I + C)		19- 2-1971
South Africa (I + C)		15- 3-1971
Spain (I + C)		16- 6-1971
Surinam (I + C)		25-11-1975
(S + A)		25-11-1975
Sweden (I + C)		12- 3-1968
(E + I)		25- 4-1952

Switzerland (I + C)		12-11-1951
	am.	22- 6-1966
(E + I)		12-11-1951
Thailand (I + C)		11- 9-1975
U.K. (I + C)		7-11-1980
(E + I)		11-12-1979
U.S.A. (I + C)		29- 4-1948
	am.	30-12-1965
(E + I)		15- 7-1969
Venezuela (S + A)		4- 1-1980
Zambia (I + C)		15-10-1948
	ext. + am.	20-12-1962
Zambia (I + C) (not yet in force)		19-12-1977
Zimbabwe (I + C)		15-10-1948
	ext. + am.	20-12-1962

J. Schedule of Withholding Taxes[19]

	On payments by a Netherlands company of			
	Dividends (normal rate)	*Dividends (to parent company)*[20]	*Interest*	*Royalties*
Recipient company is resident in:				
Non-treaty country	25%	25%	–	–
Belgium	15	5	–	–
Denmark	15	0	–	–
Canada	15	15/0[21]	–	–
France	15	5	–	–
W-Germany	15	10	–	–
Greece	15	5	–	–
Ireland	15	0	–	–
Italy	0	0	–	–
Japan	15	5	–	–
Luxembourg	15[22]	2,5[22]	–	–
Switzerland	15	0	–	–
U.K.	15	5	–	–
U.S.A.	15	5	–	–

19. This schedule is a summary only. It does not show special conditions that may apply.
20. Assuming a 100% parent company.
21. 0% rate only for international holding/finance companies.
22. Does not apply to Luxembourg holding companies.

K. *Special Types of Companies*

1. GENERAL

Although Dutch corporate and tax law, with one or two exceptions[23] do not award special tax status to any type of company, some categories of Dutch companies have become very popular and are frequent phenomena on the international tax scene, and some reference to them may be appropriate. It should be stressed that for corporate and tax law purposes, these companies are identical to other, 'regular' Dutch companies; they are identified by the very specific function they perform, usually within an affiliated group of companies.

The feature that such companies have in common is that they are established to exploit a combination of Dutch tax rules and/or Dutch tax treaties, that is attractive to investors from third countries.

2. HOLDING COMPANIES

As explained earlier, Dutch corporation tax under certain conditions exempts dividends received and capital gains realized on shares in qualifying participations. This applies to all corporate taxpayers, and it makes The Netherlands an attractive base for a holding company owning shares in one or more Dutch or foreign subsidiaries. Benefiting from The Netherlands tax treaty network, dividends can be paid by such subsidiaries to their Dutch intermediate parent with little or no withholding tax, and be reinvested from there without tax, corporate or exchange control complications.

The Dutch tax exemption for capital gains on such shares and the fact that under most Dutch tax treaties the right to tax such capital gains is restricted to the country of the shareholder guarantees the flexibility of unwinding the structure if this should become desirable. Since the Dutch holding company is fully taxed on all its other income, careful planning is often necessary to avoid unwanted taxation on e.g., exchange gains, interest, fees etc.

An advance tax ruling (see earlier under, A.2.d.) is often desirable to establish the exempt character of foreign participations. This is particularly true if the Dutch company has no business activity of its own: a prominent 1973 High Court decision (BNB 74/2) held that under these circumstances the participation exemption does not apply. Therefore, it may be advisable for the Dutch company to have some business income.

Expenses incurred by the Dutch company in connection with non-Dutch participations (e.g., interest on loans used to acquire the participations, capital tax paid in respect of capital increases used to acquire the participations), are not deductible. Losses incurred on the sale or transfer of a participation are

23. For example, so-called investment institutions (*beleggingsinstellingen*) which are exempt from tax if they distribute all their income.

not deductible, except if the participation is liquidated.
Dividends and other distributions of profits are subject to dividend withholding tax under the normal rules. There is no obligation in corporate or tax law to distribute any of the company's earnings.
A rather more sophisticated form of Dutch holding company is one where instead of holding subsidiaries, the company holds branches. Such a structure may have significant tax or legal advantages depending on the country where the activities are carried out, and that of the ultimate foreign investor.

3. FINANCE COMPANIES

These companies are set up to benefit from the fact that The Netherlands do not have a withholding tax on interest, while most Netherlands tax treaties reduce withholding taxes on interest paid to a Dutch resident company to a minimum level, often to zero.
Since the Dutch revenue authorities are usually willing to accept that the Dutch company need not earn more than a minimum spread between interest received and interest paid (a net margin of $\frac{1}{8}$% p.a. of the amount borrowed and on-lent, after deduction of all expenses, is usually sufficient), it is often possible to channel loan funds through a Netherlands company at minimum tax cost. Consequently, many international groups have set up Dutch finance companies in order to borrow e.g. in the Eurocurrency market and on-lend to affiliates in countries that would in the absence of a treaty, levy substantial withholding tax. As with holding companies, careful planning is essential to avoid tax on unplanned income such as exchange gains. The combination of a holding company with a financing activity may be quite attractive and is frequently arranged.
Finance companies should be careful not to violate Central Bank regulations for credit institutions and exchange control. Within these well-defined rules, however, there is little interference from the Central Bank.

IV. LABOUR ASPECTS

A. Principles of Law on Employment

1. INTRODUCTION

As in many countries enjoying the blessings of industrial civilization, labour law in The Netherlands has become a vast body of very complicated and ever changing rules which provide a very high degree of protection for the employee. Consequently, in this section no attempt is made to give a survey of the principles of the law on employment. This section is confined to a few practical notes which may be helpful to the foreign investor employing people in The Netherlands.

2. CONTRACT IN WRITING

Although much of Dutch labour law is mandatory and laid down in the Civil Code and other Acts of Parliament as well as in collective labour agreements (*collectieve arbeidsovereenkomsten, CAOs*) which apply in most branches of industry for personnel up to levels usually just below management (see IV. B), it is advisable for any employment agreement to be put in writing, if only in the form of a letter signed by both parties. Certain terms in favour of the employer must be laid down in writing, failing which they are deemed non existent. In addition, documentary evidence can be of vital importance in a dispute. Obviously a contract of employment of a secretary can be less elaborate than of a manager. Since labour laws differ the world over and mistakes may prove to be very costly it is advisable to consult a lawyer prior to taking any step in this field.

3. EQUAL TREATMENT OF MEN AND WOMEN

Directive 76/207 of the Council of the EC (dated 9th February 1976) has been implemented by the Act on Equal Treatment of Men and Women of 1st March 1980. The employer may not discriminate between men and women, by e.g. referring to the married or unmarried state or to family circumstances, in advertisements or in the negotiation of the employment contract, training, promotion or termination of the employment, nor in the conditions of employment. Any clause in the employment contract amounting to such discrimination is null and void. An Act of 20th March 1975 implementing the Council's Directive 75/117 of 10th February 1975 prohibits any discrimination as to remuneration.

4. PROBATIONARY PERIOD

Any stipulation to the effect that the probationary period is not equally long for both parties or is longer than 2 months is null and void. During the probationary period no period of notice need be observed, and no reason for discharge need be given. There is no probationary period unless it has been expressly agreed upon. It is advisable to do so in writing. It is not possible to renew or extend the probationary period. Therefore, if the employer feels a period longer than 2 months is necessary, he could employ the employee for a definite period, for example 6 months. During these 6 months dismissal is impossible (unless the employee has given an 'urgent cause for summary dismissal', see item 10 (a) below, but the agreement automatically ends after this period. Of course both parties can agree to continue the employment.

5. REMUNERATION

It should be noted that in recent years (including 1982) the Government has ordered that salaries may not be increased by more than a certain percentage.

These orders do not affect the freedom of parties to a new employment contract to negotiate any level of salary, subject to the statutory minimum wages for persons up to 23 years of age. Both employee and employer could benefit from a provision in the employment contract under which the employee is entitled to a fixed amount by way of reimbursement of general expenses (for which no voucher needs be shown). Neither employee nor employer pay any tax or social security contributions for this amount. The limits depend on the circumstances and the judgement of the tax inspector.

6. HOLIDAYS

The employee is entitled to annual holidays of at least three times the agreed number of working days per week. For juvenile employees (under 18) the holidays are four times the agreed number of working days per week.

7. HOLIDAY ALLOWANCE

Under the Act on Minimum Wages and Minimum Holiday Allowance the employee is entitled to a holiday allowance of 7.5% of his annual salary with a maximum of 7.5% of three times the statutory minimum salary (in 1982 about fls 2,000 per month for employees over 22 years of age), payable before the end of June each year and calculated on the salary earned during the 12 months to 31st May. In the case of staff whose annual salary is more than three times the statutory minimum, it is possible to make an agreement that their normal salary shall be deemed to include holiday allowance. It should be noted however that under several Collective Labour Agreements (CAOs) a higher holiday allowance must be paid. In practice the holiday allowance is very often 7.5% or more of the total annual salary even if this exceeds the statutory maximum. This allowance may be subject to limits imposed by the Government (e.g. fls 5,200 in 1982).

8. SICKNESS

In the event of sickness the employee is entitled to continuation of payment of his salary for a 'reasonably short period', the length of which depends upon various factors, such as duration of employment etc. This right has lost much of its significance since the introduction of the *'Ziektewet'* (Health Insurance Act) under which the employee is entitled to 80% of his salary (up to a certain maximum) from the third day of his illness for not longer than 52 weeks, and of the *'Wet Arbeidsongeschiktheid'* (WAO, Unfitness for Work Act) under which there is a (lower) benefit after expiry of the 52 weeks. After the 'reasonably short period' there is no statutory obligation for the employer to pay the difference between the benefit under the *Ziektewet* and the total salary, but in practice this is often done for some time (e.g. 6 months), particularly where senior staff are concerned. It is advisable for the employer to take out collective insurance to cover the risk of payment of the said difference to senior staff after, say, 6 months. See also under Termination sub 10 below.

9. NON-COMPETITION CLAUSE

A non-competition clause by which the employee is restricted in his activities after termination of the employment must be in writing. The employee must be not less than 18 years of age.

The *Kantonrechter* (the Judge who normally adjudicates on claims under employment contracts) may at the request of the employee wholly or partly set aside such a clause (e.g. reduce its period or geographical extent) on the ground that the restrictions on the employee are not justified by the interest of the employer.

The employer cannot invoke any rights under such a clause if he has wrongfully terminated the agreement.

The *Kantonrechter* always has power to reduce any liquidated damages agreed upon in advance in the event of breach by the employee. Should a non-competition clause be a serious obstacle for the employee in finding other work, the *Kantonrechter* may order the employer to pay the employee a compensation during the period the clause applies, unless the employee himself has wrongfully terminated his employment or has given cause for dismissal.

10. TERMINATION

Under Dutch Law, employment contracts, other than those entered into with a member of the Managing Board of an NV or BV, are subject to two different sets of statutory provisions as to termination. In addition, there are some special rules on collective dismissals (reduncancy). The law governing termination, which includes a good deal of case-law, is so intricate that legal advice is indispensable, even in seemingly clear-cut cases.

a. The first set of provisions relating to all contracts of employment, are to be found in the Civil Code. The Code provides that an employment contract made for an indefinite period of time may be terminated by either party giving notice to the other. The Code further provides that the period of notice shall be equal to the normal interval between successive dates of payment of salary, but not longer than six weeks.

However, the parties may agree in writing upon a longer or shorter period of notice, provided that such period does not exceed 6 months and is not shorter in respect of notice by the employer than notice by the employee. Subject to the foregoing, the period of notice to be given by the employer should be at least as many weeks as the number of years during which the contract of employment has been running since the employee came of age, with a maximum of 13 weeks, and the period of notice to be given by the employee should be at least as many weeks as the employment has lasted for periods of two full years since his coming of age, with a maximum of 6 weeks. The period of notice is further extended by one week for every full year during which the employee has been in the employment of the employer since his 45th birthday. This extension may add up to another 13 weeks.

Special rules exist in the event that the person to be dismissed is a member of the Works Council or of certain committees thereof. Such a person cannot be validly dismissed except for an urgent cause for summary dismissal or when the enterprise closes down. Someone who has at any time during the last two years been a member of the OR or any committee thereof or who is a member of a special committee of the Works Council or even a candidate for election to the Works Council cannot be dismissed without the approval of the *Kantonrechter* unless there is an urgent cause for summary dismissal or the enterprise closes down.

An employee cannot be dismissed during illness, unless he has been unfit for not less than two consecutive years.

It is prohibited to dismiss an employee because of his or her marriage or during her pregnancy or because she has given birth to a child. In the latter event the prohibition applies for 12 weeks after the confinement. Any clause in an employment contract to the effect that employment shall terminate in the event of marriage or because of pregnancy or confinement is null and void.

Under the Act on Equal Treatment of Men and Women referred to under para 3 the employee can claim that any dismissal is null and void on the ground that it was prompted by his or her invoking (in or out of Court) the law on equal treatment of the sexes. Such a claim must be made by a simple notice to the employer within two months of the dismissal.

Even supposing that all statutory provisions with respect to termination of the employment contract have been complied with, each of the parties (but in practice this means the employee) may nevertheless claim compensation where termination of the employment contract was patently unreasonable. Generally speaking, termination by the employer is deemed to be 'patently unreasonable' if no reason or false reasons are stated for the termination and whenever, having due regard to all provisions made in favour of the employee and the possibilities existing for him to find other suitable employment, the consequences of termination are unreasonably severe for the employee compared with the interests of the employer. It is this provision which provides the legal basis for the 'golden handshakes' which are nowadays almost invariably given if the employee does not leave of his own free will.

In the event of lay-off of a number of employees at the same time, the terms of dismissal (which usually include a 'golden handshake') are normally negotiated by trade-unions (see also paragraph (d) below).

It is important to note that the above provisions of the Civil Code do not apply if both parties agree upon the termination or if the other party has given an urgent cause justifying summary dismissal.

b. The second set of provisions relating to termination is a Royal Decree of 1945 which provides that neither party to an employment contract may give notice of termination to the other party without the prior approval of the Director of the local Regional Labour Office *(Gewestelijk Arbeidsbureau)*, unless the termination has been agreed upon by both parties or unless one of the parties should have given an urgent cause to the other party justifying summary dismissal (termination without notice). Such urgent causes given by the employee to the employer include all acts or qualities or any conduct of the employee as a result of which it could not be reasonably expected of the employer to continue the employment contract. The Courts seem increasingly reluctant to accept a cause as being urgent. Such a cause must in any event be communicated to the other party immediately, preferably both in writing and orally.

On the other hand, the Royal Decree does not apply to an employment contract which has been entered into for a definite period of time and where no notice of termination is required to terminate the contract at the expiration date.

However, if an employment contract has been made for a definite period of time but is continued after the expiration of that period, it is deemed to have been continued for the same period with a maximum of one year and notice will be required to terminate it at the expiration date. The provisions of the above-mentioned Royal Decree will therefore apply.

Any notice of termination given without the prior approval of the Regional Labour Office, where such approval is required, is null and void and the contract of employment remains in force notwithstanding the giving of such notice.

The Director of the Regional Labour Office acts in a quasi-judicial capacity in giving his decision to grant or refuse approval. The time-lag between the application for approval and the actual decision may be long and the procedure is often unsatisfactory because the parties are never heard at the same time and disputed facts are not resolved.

The Royal Decree does not apply to members of the Managing Board of an NV of BV.

c. The provisions of the Royal Decree of 1945 and those of the Civil Code apply concurrently. This means that the approval of the Regional Labour Office will not protect an employer against the consequences of a breach of the Civil Code. In such a case he will be liable for damages to the employee.

Conversely, termination of the employment contract with due observance of all the requirements of the Civil Code is nevertheless null and void and has no legal effect without the approval of the Regional Labour Office where such approval is required.

The provisions of the Civil Code do apply to Managing Directors of NVs and BVs.

Either party may request the Cantonal Judge to rescind the employment contract on the ground of a so-called 'serious cause'. This notion comprises the notion of urgent cause referred to above and also changes in circumstances that necessitate the termination of the employment contract on equity grounds. The Cantonal Judge's decision may make the approval of the Director of the Regional Labour Office as well as the observance of the rules with respect to the period of notice superfluous. The Cantonal Judge may award compensation to one of the parties (usually the employee) and the amount thereof is at his discretion. This renders the action somewhat aleatory for the employer, the more so since no appeal lies against the Cantonal Judge's decision.

All the above observations on termination do not apply during the probationary period (see 4 above).

d. In 1976 Parliament adopted an Act on the notification of the intention to dismiss not less than 20 employees within a period of 3 months. Such notice must be given to the trade unions that have members among the employees of the enterprise, as well as to the Director of the local Regional Labour Office. The notice must state the reason for the dismissal as well as various details. No notice is deemed to have been given until all data have been provided. The Director of the Regional Labour Office will not take any action on a request for approval to dismiss until one month after receipt of the notice has expired, until the Works Council (if there is one) has been consulted, and until consultations between the employer and the trade unions have started. Cf. the Council's Directive 75/129 of 17th February 1975 (see the chapter on European Social Law).

e. The Netherlands has been slow implementing Directive 77/187 on the safeguarding of employees' rights and benefits in the event of transfers of enterprises, businesses or parts of businesses. The implementing Act of 15th May 1981 came into effect on 27th July 1981. The Netherlands has made use of the option given in Article 3 of the Directive by providing that the transferor shall for one year after the transfer continue to be liable in respect of obligations which have arisen from the employment contract prior to the transfer (see the Chapter on European Social Law).

11. TRANSFER TO ANOTHER LOCATION

In groups of companies such transfers occur frequently. As far as Dutch labour law is concerned, it is fortunate that employees usually accept a transfer, since there is great uncertainty as to when the employer can impose one. There is generally less mobility among Dutch employees than, for example, among Americans and this is reflected in the law. It is advisable to stipulate expressly in the contract that the employer may transfer the employee to any (reasonable) location within the group.

12. APPLICABLE LAW

Even though most provisions of Dutch labour law are of a mandatory nature, it is possible to choose as the applicable law any other law which has a reasonable connection with the case. It is in any event advisable to make an express choice of law in the contract, if only to avoid uncertainties.
In the absence of any choice of law the following rules of Dutch private international law apply to an employment contract with international connecting factors:

a. in the event a certain country can be identified as the place where the work is usually done or, if the field of activity extends over more than one country, as the country where the employee has his base, then the contract is governed by the law of that country;

b. and if no such country can be identified, then the contract is governed by the law of the country where the employer is established;

c. both cases are subject to special circumstances which could entail that the law of another country ought to govern the contract.

Rule (a) and the proviso sub (c) also apply in the event of multinational enterprises and the fact that the employee receives his instructions from the head office does not of itself mean that the law of the country of the head office will apply. That law would, however, apply if the employee had been transferred from that country to a foreign establishment (whether a branch or a subsidiary).

It should be noted that the Royal Decree referred to in 10 (a) will be applied irrespective of the applicable law as long as the social and economic relations in The Netherlands, and in particular the Dutch labour market, are involved. This also means that even if Dutch law applies to the contract the Decree will not be applied if the above condition has not been met.

B. Labour Procedures

1. TRADE UNIONS

a. General

The right to form and join trade unions has not been specifically dealt with in Dutch law. This right is based on the freedom of association, laid down in art. 9 of the Constitution, and on the general rules relating to all associations, contained in artt. 26-52 of the Second Book of the new Civil Code.

These general rules entail the freedom to form trade unions without any governmental approval or regulation. The only formal requirements for obtaining incorporation and full legal competence are the embodying of the Statutes of the union in a notarial deed and the registration of the union with the Register of Associations kept at the local Chamber of Commerce. These formal requirements, however, apply to any and all associations.

In principle each worker is free whether or not to join a trade union. The closed shop, which can be stipulated in a collective bargaining agreement, is very exceptional in The Netherlands.

About forty percent of all workers and civil servants have joined a trade union. Trade unions are normally organised within one trade or branch of industry, e.g. unions of transport workers, unions of building and construction workers, unions of workers in the industry, unions of civil servants. Within one trade at least three unions used to operate next to each other, viz. a socialist union, a Roman Catholic union and a Protestant union. During the Seventies, however, the socialist and Roman Catholic unions have formed federations or even merged in order to create more powerful general unions, called Federation of Netherlands Trade Unions (FNV). As of 1st January 1982 the Roman Catholic Unions have completely merged into the FNV. The Protestant unions, which were the smaller ones compared to both other unions, have so far refused to join. Roman Catholic workers are increasingly joining the Protestant union so as not to have to submit to 'the predominantly socialist FNV'. The FNV-unions are by far the biggest unions. About 60% of all employees who are members of a trade union are members of an FNV-union.

b. Bill on Trade Union Activities in Enterprises

In March 1981 the Government introduced a Bill on trade union activities in enterprises. This Bill provides that an 'entrepreneur' must discuss with any trade union which has a certain minimum of members within his enterprise (3% of the employees, but at least 10 members) facilities for trade union activities. Such activities must include (unless otherwise agreed) at least:

- access to the enterprise for trade union officials who do not work there themselves;
- distribution of trade union papers and documents;
- collecting of trade union subscriptions;
- notification of trade union activities on notice-boards of the enterprise; and
- meetings of trade union members within the enterprise outside working hours.

The number of trade union workers per enterprise will depend upon the total number of its employees (one for 100 or less, a maximum of 10 for 12,000 or more). The trade union workers will benefit from special protection against dismissal. Both trade union workers and their unions will be able to sue the entrepreneur who does not meet his obligations under the future Act. The Bill is strongly opposed by employers' organisations. In January 1982 one could not predict whether, when or in what form the Bill would be passed.

2. COLLECTIVE BARGAINING

a. Organization and procedure

Employers or associations of employers who conclude collective labour agreements (CAOs) have to deal with the FNV-unions, the Protestant unions and often also with one or two unions of white collar workers. For in The Netherlands, unlike the situation in many other countries, a CAO is concluded between an employer or an association of employers on the one hand and three or four unions on the other. In such a situation all three or four unions have to agree to the CAO, which happens in most cases. It is obvious that the powerful FNV union plays a big role in the collective bargaining process. No employer or association of employers would conclude a separate CAO with a smaller union and leave out the FNV union. They would almost certainly be hit by a strike organised by the FNV union.

Although the percentage of employees who have joined a trade union is relatively low, the conditions of employment of about 80% of all employees are governed by CAOs. This is a result of three factors:

(i) The institution of collective bargaining has been well established in The

Netherlands (there is no obligation, however, for an employer to negotiate and to conclude CAOs, but he can scarcely avoid it – without the risk of strikes – if the union members among his employees are numerous).

(ii) The Collective Bargaining Act of 1927 obliges an employer who is bound by a CAO to apply all terms and conditions of the CAO to all his employees, regardless of whether or not they are union members.

(iii) In some instances the Minister of Social Affairs used his power to declare the terms and conditions of a CAO binding upon all employers and employees in a trade or branch of industry. This power is based on an Act of 1937 and may be exercised if the majority of the employers and employees of that trade or branch of industry are already bound by a CAO.

CAOs are legally enforceable contracts. As fas as the negotiations are concerned, the trade unions will first consult their members before presenting their demands to the employers. The normal procedure is that the trade unions aim at a tentative agreement with the employer(s). The tentative agreement will then be presented to the union members for their approval. Only after this approval will the CAO be concluded.

b. Strikes and lockouts

If the negotiations between the parties prove to be unsuccessful the trade unions may put extra pressure upon the employer(s) by announcing a strike. The right to strike has not been laid down in any Dutch Statute. It is, however, based on the European Social Charter as well as on case-law. Generally speaking, strikes are only legal if they are:

- organised by a trade union when a deadlock in the negotiations has occurred,
- announced in advance,
- not contrary to law or obligations under a CAO,
- not patently disproportionate to the object they seek to achieve,
- not patently reckless of the interests of the employer(s).

The lock-out, the counter-weapon of the employer(s) in industrial conflicts, has neither been laid down in any Statute nor dealt with in case-law. The reason is that lock-outs have only been applied by employers on very rare occasions long before the Second World War.

c. Government wage controls

To conclude this survey of collective bargaining it is necessary to point out the important role the Netherlands' Government plays in the fixing of wages. Although an Act of 1970 has left the determination of wages to the parties to CAOs, in times of recession the Government has intervened and set general limits on the determination of wages. This power is based on art. 10 of the Act of 1970 and is vested in the Minister of Social Affairs. In those years in which the Government has not intervened it will still try to influence the development of the wages, but now by means of a so called 'Central Arrangement' with the central organisations of employers' associations and trade

unions. Both the associations of employers and the trade unions are organized at national level in central organisations. Separate central organisations of trade unions exist for the FNV unions, Protestant unions and unions of white collar workers.
If a Central Arrangement can be agreed upon the result will be guidance on the acceptable limits to wage increases for the parties in their negotiations for CAOs. However, such a Central Arrangement has seldom been reached in recent years. In the absence of a Central Arrangement, the parties to the collective bargaining process are completely free to determine wages as long as the Government does not decide to intervene on the basis of art. 10 of the Act of 1970 by reason of a recession in the Dutch economy.

C. *Works Council*

1. INTRODUCTION

Ever since 1950 Dutch law has known Works Councils (*ondernemingsraden*, ORs; singular OR). The Act on Works Councils was amended in 1971 and very substantially amended again as soon afterwards as in 1979 after a fierce political battle. The new Act is a political compromise and therefore full of ambiguities and defects.
Under the Act an OR must be instituted in every enterprise which regularly employs not less than 100 people. However, in May 1981 the Upper House approved a Bill to change the Act again, this time to extend it in a slightly mitigated form to enterprises with between 35 and 100 employees. The Bill has meanwhile been given Royal assent and has come into effect on 1st May, 1982. The Act also contains provisions concerning enterprises with less than 35 but not less than 10 employees. See item C. 6 below. It has taken some time to bring the Act into effect since the Industrial Committees which administer the Act had to be expanded in order to be able to cope with the flow of new ORs to be created as a result of the new law.
Since the Act on ORs applies to 'enterprises' (*ondernemingen*) of any legal form, to those who own the enterprises ('entrepreneurs') and to 'managers' (*bestuurders*, i.e. those who directly exercise the highest authority in directing the work in the enterprise) rather than to companies, their shareholders and members of the Managing Boards of companies respectively, there is considerable uncertainty as to how it should be construed where an enterprise forms part of a group of companies.

2. ORGANIZATION

The minimum number of members of the OR is 7 and the maximum 25 (in enterprises with 7,000 employees or more). The members are elected by all employees who have been employed for not less than 6 months. Those eligible for election are persons who have been employed by the company for not less than a year. Trade unions may submit lists of candidates from among such employees. A *Centrale Ondernemingsraad* (COR) may and in some cases must be instituted if an entrepreneur has several enterprise with ORs. In addition for groups of such enterprises (e.g. various divisions) a group OR (GOR) may be instituted. The distribution of powers between OR, GOR and COR is somewhat vague, but in principle the COR and/or GOR deals with matters affecting all or a majority of the enterprises. On those matters the powers of the ORs pass to the COR or GOR. The members of a COR or GOR are elected by the members of the lower council from among their members, the hierarchy being that the COR is the highest and the ORs are the lowest councils with possible GORs in between. Any OR, GOR or COR may institute permanent or ad hoc committees.

Until 1979 the manager (or one of them) used to be a member of the OR and preside over it. Now the OR consists of elected employees only. In order to make up for the resulting lack of communication and consultation between management and OR the new Act provides for a so-called *'overlegvergadering'* (consultation meeting) which must be held if and when requested by either party and if required by the Act, but not less than 6 times per annum. The Act leaves it to entrepreneur and OR to agree who shall preside over these meetings. If no agreement is reached the manager and the Chairman of the OR will preside in turn.

At least twice a year the general course of events in the enterprise is discussed in such meetings. If the enterprise is run by a BV or NV, at least one of the Supervisory Directors must attend. If the BV or NV is a direct or indirect subsidiary of another company (this can be a foreign company and it is always the top holding company) then the Board members of that company or one or more representatives designated by them must attend. What was said in the previous two sentences does not apply if at least 5 enterprises with ORs are operated by the same entrepreneur.

The entrepreneur (i.e. in most cases the company) must allow the OR and its committees free use of all facilities he has available in his capacity of entrepreneur and which the OR and the committees reasonably need for the performance of their duty. In case of disagreement the *'bedrijfscommissie'* (Industrial Committee) (one of the more than 70 committees instituted by the Social and Economic Council to administer the Act per branch of industry and consisting of equal numbers (at least 3) of representatives of employers and employees) will decide. The costs of the OR are for the account of the entrepreneur. OR and entrepreneur may agree on a budget within which the OR may spend freely.

The OR and its committees may invite one or more experts to attend their meetings or to give advice in writing. The cost of consulting experts must be borne by the entrepreneur but only if he has been advised in advance. If he objects the *'bedrijfscommissie'* will decide. The cost of consulting other persons or of litigation can only be charged to the entrepreneur to the extent he agrees. The foregoing does not apply if a budget has been fixed.

3. POWERS

a. General

The OR has considerable powers, especially since 1979, in the following fields: co-decision, advice (consultation), information, and proposals and discussion. It should be noted that additional powers may be vested in the OR by collective labour agreements (CAOs).

b. Co-decision

The entrepreneur is required to seek the consent of the OR before taking a decision on a number of subject-matters (unless these are covered by a CAO). Included are such matters as pensions, profit sharing or savings schemes, regulation of rates of pay, working hours and holidays, arrangements in connection with safety, health or welfare at work, the introduction, amendment or abolition of rules on recruitment, dismissal and promotion, training and assessment of staff and dealing with complaints. The *'bedrijfscommissie'* decides at the request of the entrepreneur if the OR refuses to give consent. A decision taken without consent is null and void, but only if the OR invokes the nullity within one month of becoming aware that the decision is being carried out.

c. Consultation

The most important powers of the OR are in the field of consultation, particularly in connection with the new legal remedies given to the OR. Under the 1971 Act the entrepreneur already had to consult the OR on a number of important economic decisions, including the transfer of the enterprise or a part thereof, the establishment, acquisition or disposal of another enterprise, the co-operation with other enterprises, the discontinuation of or a substantial change in the activities of the enterprise or a substantial part thereof, merger, closure and substantial reorganisation. In 1979 the list was extended to include substantial investments for the enterprise, the raising of substantial loans, recruitment or borrowing of personnel in groups, the seeking of advice on any of the foregoing subjects from an expert outside the enterprise (which may well be within the group, e.g. from legal counsel of the parent company!) and also the appointment or dismissal of a *'bestuurder'* of the enterprise (this may be a Managing Director but also a manager of a branch). 'Important reasons' are no longer an excuse for the entrepreneur not consulting the OR on these matters. The OR must be consulted at such a time that its opinion can be of essential influence on the decision to be taken. The opinion is not given until an *'overlegvergadering'* has been held. The OR must also be consulted about the implementation of the decision.

d. Information

The 1979 Act has considerably increased the OR's right to receive information. At the beginning of each period of office of the OR (in principle 2 years)

the entrepreneur must inform (and after each change advise) the OR of such things as the names of all enterprises forming part of the same group, the channels of control, details of enterprises and institutions with which the enterprise has permanent relations which can be essential for the existence of the enterprise (e.g. banks giving a credit facility, large suppliers and customers), and the organisation of the enterprise with various details.
In addition, the entrepreneur must provide the OR at least twice a year with general data on the activities and performance of the enterprise over the past period and expectations for the period to come, in particular on the matters in respect of which he is obliged to consult the OR (see 3.c above) and on all investments at home and abroad. If the entrepreneur is obliged by law to prepare annual accounts (as in the case of all BVs and NVs) these must be submitted for discussion as soon as possible after they have been determined. If the annual accounts relate to more than one enterprise, the OR must be given data from which it can see to what extent its enterprise has contributed to the total results. If the entrepreneur forms part of a group of entrepreneurs he must give the OR data on the total results of the group. Long term plans and budgets must also be submitted.

e. Proposals

The OR may make proposals to the entrepreneur either at the *overlegvergadering* (consultation meeting) or otherwise on any matter concerning the enterprise. The entrepreneur must discuss such proposals and decide on them.

4. LEGAL REMEDIES

One of the most important changes relates to legal remedies concerning the OR's right to be consulted on important economic decisions (not the decision to appoint or dismiss a '*bestuurder*'; see item 1 above). If the entrepreneur's decision is not completely in accordance with the OR's opinion he must inform the OR why he has not followed their opinion, and must suspend implementation for one month from so informing them. The suspension lapses before the end of the month when the OR notifies the entrepreneur.
If the decision is not in accordance with the OR's opinion (which is deemed to include the case where the entrepreneur has omitted to consult the OR) or if new facts have come to light, the OR can during the said month appeal against the decision to the '*ondernemingskamer*' (Enterprise Chamber, OK) of the Court of Appeals in Amsterdam. The only ground of appeal is that after weighing the interests concerned the entrepreneur could not reasonably have come to his decision. The OK can, at the request of the OR, order the entrepreneur wholly or partially to withdraw his decision and to undo certain consequences thereof, and it can also enjoin the entrepreneur from doing any act in implementation of the decision. Such an order or injunction can, however, not affect rights acquired by third parties. The OK cannot order the OR to pay the costs of the appeal.
Any employee, the OR and its individual members can sue the entrepreneur for non-compliance with certain provisions of the Act. The *Kantonrechter* has

jurisdiction for any such petition, but it will not be adjudicated upon unless the petitioner has first invoked the mediation of the *'bedrijfscommissie'*. The *Kantonrechter* can also give orders or injunctions.

5. LEGAL PROTECTION

Reference is made to item A.10 (b) above with respect to the protection from dismissal of members of an OR (or COR or GOR) and its committees as well as of candidates for the OR.

6. THE ACT ON ORS IN SMALLER ENTERPRISES

Under the Act to extend the Act on Works Councils to enterprises with between 35 and 100 employees (see item C.1 above), the powers of the OR of such small enterprises are the same as those of ORs of larger enterprises, except that the entrepreneur is only obliged to consult the OR if and to the extent that an intended decision may lead to the redundancy or a substantial change in the work, employment conditions or employment environment of not less than a quarter of the persons employed in the enterprise.
The obligation for the entrepreneur to suspend the implementation of his decision (cf. item C.4 above) does not apply, except in the event of:
- the discontinuation of the activities of the enterprise or a substantial part thereof;
- a substantial reduction, expansion or other change in the activities of the enterprise; or
- a change of the location where the enterprise carries on its activities.

In enterprises with less than 35 but not less than 10 employees the entrepreneur must give all the employees an opportunity to meet with him at least twice a year and whenever a quarter of the workforce makes a reasoned request for such a meeting.
The employees must be given an opportunity to give their opinion on intended decisions of the same nature as those referred to above on which the entrepreneur must seek the opinion of the EC in companies with 35-100 employees.

D. Co-determination

Co-determination in the sense of influence of labour in the corporate structure rather than in the enterprise itself exists in the rather mild form set out in item II.A.1.b(ii) (b) under the heading 'Structure Regime'. Reference is made to that item.

E. *Compulsory Profit Sharing and Pension Schemes*

1. COMPULSORY PROFIT SHARING (VAD)

During the past few years the concept of compulsory employee profit sharing (known by the initials of its Dutch name *Vermogens Aanwas Deling* or VAD) has been the focus of political attention. Several proposals have been put forward and discussed; the first Bills were submitted to Parliament in 1978. They met with strong resistance from employer organizations as well as labour unions, and Parliamentary action was suspended.

In October 1980 the Government effectively reintroduced the proposals, this time combined in a single Bill which substantially amended the earlier proposals.

The current proposal may be summarized as follows:

- All entities subject to corporate income tax are also subject to VAD.
- The amount on which VAD is calculated (VAD-able amount) is determined by taking taxable income reduced by exempt foreign income, the amount of tax due for the year, and by a notional return on net worth. For this purpose, net worth is determined on the basis of the tax accounts, reduced by assets the income from which is exempt and increased by an inflation adjustment for certain assets. The notional return is established at 3 percentage points above the return on long-term state bonds.
- If the notional return on net worth exceeds the amount of taxable income less exempt foreign income and tax payable, the excess is designated as a return shortfall which can be carried forward for eight years.
- There are two separate VAD-levies: (a) the 'individual' VAD and (b) the 'collective' VAD. The proceeds of the collective VAD accrue to a national fund, the proceeds of the individual VAD accrue to the employees of the VAD-payer up to a certain maximum, the surplus going to the national fund.
- The rate of each VAD-levy is the lower of 12% of the VAD-able amount or 3% of taxable income less exempt foreign income.
- Both VAD-levies are deductible for corporate income tax purposes.
- VAD must be paid in the form of shares or VAD-certificates (see below). The individual VAD-levy may be paid in cash if the Works Council agrees, the collective VAD if the national fund agrees.
- VAD-certificates are defined as certificates entitling the holder to a claim on the company's assets of a fixed nominal amount. This claim is subordinated to other creditors and carries annual interest at 1.5 percentage points above the return on long-term state bonds (for the VAD-payer this amount is deductible for tax purposes). VAD-certificates are redeemable after 10 years at the option of the holder or the company.
- The individual VAD is distributed equally to all employees of the VAD-payer with a maximum per employee that is determined on the basis of social security legislation (for 1980 this would have been fls 1,847 per employee). If the total amount of individual VAD payable exceeds the maximum that can be allocated to all employees, the excess can be carried for-

ward for eight years (to offset shortfalls, if any, in that period) after which it must be paid to the fund. However, to the extent the individual VAD payable exceeds 15 times the maximum that can be allocated to all employees, it is payable to the fund immediately.

- The fund to which collective VAD (and individual VAD surpluses as determined above) must be paid, is to be managed by a Board consisting of 12 representatives of employee organizations and 8 Government representatives.
- All individuals employed in the Netherlands in a calendar year are entitled to a share in the VAD received by the fund in that year. This share may be redeemed after 10 years.
- The effective date of the VAD has been postponed. Originally it had been set at January 1, 1977 for the individual VAD and 1-1-78 for the collective VAD. If the current proposals are enacted before April 1982, they will take effect from January 1, 1981. If they are enacted between April 1982 and April 1983, the effective date will be January 1, 1982 and so on. In the present political-economic climate, the chances of enactment in the short term are remote.

2. PENSION SCHEMES

2.a. General Old Age Security

Within the framework of social security legislation, the *Algemene Ouderdoms Wet* (AOW) provides a compulsory old age insurance to all resident individuals and certain non-residents. Contributions are compulsory for insured individuals between 15 and 65 years of age and they are collected through the wages tax/income tax mechanism. Each year, an individual builds up 2% of the pension entitlement. Residents who emigrate may elect to contribute on a voluntary basis. Integrated with the AOW-scheme is a scheme insuring a pension for widows and orphans, known as the AWW.
The contributions of AOW/AWW are established at 12.4% of taxable income (with some corrections), with an annual ceiling of approx. fls 7,000 (in 1982). The pension entitlement begins at the age of 65. Individuals having built up full pension rights receive approximately fls 18,500 (married couple) or 12,900 (single person) in 1982.

2.b. Industrial Pension Schemes

In 1949, an Act concerning the compulsory participation in industrial pension funds was enacted. This enables the Social Affairs Minister to make it compulsory for individuals employed in certain branches of industry to participate in a pension fund set up for that industry. Such a Ministerial decision can only be made at the request of representatives of the particular branch. In other cases, participation in industrial pension funds is not compulsory on the basis of the law but on the basis of collective agreements (CAO's) that apply to certain branches of industry.
The contributions and pensions are different for each industrial pension fund,

as is the allocation of the contribution between employer and employee. There are currently approximately 80 industrial pension funds.

2.c. Pension Schemes for Professionals

For individuals exercising certain professions, compulsory pension schemes have been set up in a similar way as the industrial pension schemes mentioned above. These are, for example, general practitioners, notaries and medical specialists.

2.d. Pension Schemes for Civil Servants

For civil servants, a separate compulsory pension scheme has been established. It is funded in the *Algemeen Burgerlijk Pensioenfonds.*

2.e. Other Pension Schemes

Apart from the above compulsory pension schemes, each enterprise is of course free to establish a pension scheme for its own employees. According to the *Pensioen- en Spaarfondsen Wet* (PSW), the employer must fund such pension schemes with a life insurance company, the appropriate industrial pension fund or a pension fund for the enterprise itself (which must meet stringent criteria established by the PSW).
Other conditions applicable to such individual schemes are found in the Income and Wages Tax Acts containing certain parameters that must be met if the employer contributions by the fund are to be non-taxable, and the employee contributions deductible for tax purposes. As a general rule, a pension scheme is acceptable if it builds up per year of employment, 1.75% of final salary, with a credit for the AOW-entitlement. This would permit a pension of 70% of final salary after 40 years of employment. In certain cases, a higher annual percentage is permitted, notably for managerial/professional staff hired at a higher age.
The PSW is not applicable if the employee owns 10% or more of the shares of the company granting the pension rights.

2.f. Further Developments

Although a general employee pension scheme has been debated for some time, it is not expected to materialize in the near future. The VAD (see above) could be regarded as a step in this direction, but its adoption is uncertain.

F. Residence and Work Permits for Aliens

1. INTRODUCTION

As a result of the EEC Treaty and its implementing Regulations and Directives (see the Chapter on European Social Law) there is a very considerable difference in the treatment of EC nationals and others. This difference applies both to residence and to work permits. The law relating to aliens is rather complicated. Only a rough outline follows below.

2. EC NATIONALS

2a. Nationals of the Member States of the EC (as well as the members of their families) are in a privileged position [24], at least if they enter The Netherlands in order to work (either as employees or self-employed) or to receive any services there. They can enter the country on their (valid) passports. According to Dutch law they will have to apply for a *residence permit* with the local police of the municipality where they wish to establish themselves. If the alien is to be employed by a Dutch employer he will have to submit a statement from the employer to that effect. The permit can only be refused if the alien presents a danger to public order, national safety or public health (only a very limited number of diseases are included). If the alien is to be employed, the permit is given for a period at least as long as the envisaged duration of the work if this is more than 3 months and less than a year. If it is more than one year the permit is given for 5 years. If the work will last less than 3 months the permit will be for 3 months. Obtaining the permit will take one to three months. Self-employed EC nationals are given a permit for 5 years.

In principle, permits given for 5 years will be renewed for the same period each time. Renewal can only be refused and the permit can only be withdrawn on the grounds for refusal referred to above as well as on the ground that the permit was given or renewed on the basis of incorrect information.

As long as no decision has been given on an application for a permit or for a renewal thereof, the alien cannot be expelled.

The requirement of a residence permit is contrary to EEC law. This has been established by the European Court of Justice on several occasions. EC nationals, therefore, have a right to reside in The Netherlands for the period referred to above even if they have no permit.

It should be noted that no permit will be given until any probationary period agreed between employer and employee (under Dutch law for a maximum of two months) has expired.

2b. An EC national does not require a *work permit.*

3. OTHERS

3a. Nationals of other countries can also enter The Netherlands on their valid passports, but for a period up to 3 months (in some cases less). If such a national comes to The Netherlands in order to stay there for more than 3 months he must have a provisional residence permit for which he must apply with the Dutch Embassy in his country of residence. It may take

24. Nationals of Belgium and Luxembourg enjoy even more privileges.

two to three months to obtain such a provisional permit. Within 8 days of his arrival he must report to the local police and apply for a *residence permit*. The latter can also be done before he enters the country. The residence permit will not be given until an employment permit has been obtained from the Regional Labour Office (see below). The residence permit can be given on certain conditions and refused on the ground of public interest (which is very wide). It can be withdrawn on a number of grounds. The residence permit is given for a maximum period of one year, and can be renewed for periods of up to one year.

3b. With a view to gradually reducing the dependence of the Dutch economy on foreign workers, the Act on Work by Foreign Employees was introduced in 1979. Under this Act it is no longer the employee who must have a work permit but the employer who must have an *employment permit* in order to employ an alien who is not exempted (such as an EC national or someone who has been working in The Netherlands for three years). The employer who employs a foreigner without such a permit commits an offence.

Employer and employee must jointly apply for the permit which is given by the Minister of Social Affairs. The application must be made on a special form to be submitted to the Regional Labour Office. An application will be deemed not to have been filed until a residence permit has been obtained or applied for. A decision must be given within 30 days.

The employment permit will be refused if the 'permits limit' would be exceeded if it were granted. Such a limit must be established for any enterprise employing more than 20 employees for whom a permit is required. In establishing the limit, such things as the availability of appropriate accommodation will be taken into account.

The permit can be refused if there is a supply of labour for the work to which the application refers or if such supply can reasonably be expected. In practice this means that the permit can be refused if unemployed are registered as seeking the same kind of job.

There are some other grounds on which the permit can be refused or withdrawn. The Act provides for the possibility of objections to be raised with the Minister and of appeal to the Council of State.

V. REFERENCE MATERIAL

Literature in English

A. BUSINESS LAW GENERALLY

1. CCH Common Market Reports – Doing Business in Europe – Doing Business in The Netherlands, by Dutilh, van der Hoeven & Slager, W. Westbroek c.s., and Moret, Gudde Brinkman & Co. (Commerce Clearing House, Chicago, 1980). A 74 page survey.
2. Steven R. Schuit, Jan M. van der Beek and Bonne K. Raap, Dutch Business Law. Legal accounting and tax aspects of business in The Netherlands (Kluwer, Deventer, 1978). A book of 568 pages.
3. Netherlands Comparative Law Association, Introduction to Dutch Law for Foreign Lawyers (Kluwer, Deventer, 1978).
4. F.D. Rosendaal and B. Westendorp, Corporate and Tax Law in The Netherlands, Review of a Modern Common Market Law System, The International Lawyer, Fall 1980 and Winter 1981 issues.

B. COMPANY LAW[25]

1. P.J.W. de Brauw and H.H. Nauta, Chapter on The Netherlands in Company Law in Europe, edited by S.N. Frommel and J.H. Thompson (Kluwer, Deventer, 1975).
2. M.G. Chester and F.O.W. Vogelaar, English/Dutch Company Law, A Review for lawyers and businessmen in the light of EEC requirements (Kluwer-Harrap Handbooks, London, 1973).
3. Prof. J.M.M. Maeijer, A Modern European Company Law System, Commentary on the 1976 Dutch Legislation (Sijthoff & Noordhoff International Publishers, Alphen aan den Rijn, 1978).
4. S.W. van der Meer, Corporate Law of The Netherlands and of the Netherlands Antilles (W.E.J. Tjeenk Willink, Zwolle, 7th ed., 1979). A translation of the provisions on company law in the Dutch Civil Code (except those on annual accounts and the right of enquiry) and in the Netherlands Antilles Code of Commerce.
5. P. Meinhardt, Company Law in Europe, 3rd ed., 1981. Chapter on The Netherlands (Gower Publishing Company Ltd., Farnborough, England).
6. Prof. M. Rotondi (ed.), The Company Limited by Shares – An inquiry of comparative law, chapter on The Netherlands, pp. 1439-1477 (Kluwer, Deventer, 1974).
7. Prof. P. Sanders, Dutch Company Law (Oyez Publishers Ltd., London, 1977). Volume 6 of European Commercial Law Library.

25. Dutch company law has undergone changes in 1976 (incorporation in new Civil Code), 1978 (introduction of minimum capital) and 1981 (implemention Second Directive), and will be changed substantially in 1982 (capital of BV, implemention of Third (Merger) and Fourth (Annual Accounts) Directives, possibly anti-abuse legislation).

C. TAX LAW

1. European Taxation, Chapter on The Netherlands, published by the International Bureau of Fiscal Documentation, Amsterdam (loose-leaf).
2. The Taxation of Companies in Europe, Chapter on The Netherlands, same publisher as 1, also loose-leaf.
3. C. van Raad, Foreign Business Operations in The Netherlands (Tax Management) (Washington DC, 1976).
4. M.J. Ellis/D. Juch, The Participation Exemption in The Netherlands, 77 pages (Kluwer, Deventer, 1977).
5. S.N. Frommel, Taxation of Branches and Subsidiaries in Western Europe, Canada and the U.S.A. (1978).

D. SOCIAL LAW[26]

1. Prof. H.J. Bakels, Chapter on The Netherlands in International Encyclopaedia for Labour Law and Industrial Relations, ed. Prof. R. Blanpain (Kluwer, Deventer, loose-leaf).
2. W. Kolvenbach, Workers Participation in Europe, (Kluwer, Deventer, 1977, pp. 61-64).
3. Prof. P. Sanders, The Dutch Works Council, in Journal of Business Law, May 1980, pp. 229-234.

26. The Works Councils Act was substantially amended in 1979 and 1982.

Switzerland

Peter Forstmoser
Walter Meier

I. INTRODUCTION[1]

1. COMPANY LAW

1.a. Swiss Company Law has remained basically unchanged since 1936. It is a *very liberal law based upon classical concepts* and has not been influenced by modern tendencies to give power to third parties such as employees, labour unions or governmental agencies.
The law of the joint stock corporation ('Aktiengesellschaft' or 'AG'/'Société anonyme' or 'SA') is drafted very flexibly so that the form of the joint stock corporation can be adapted by by-laws and contracts to the specific purposes of the shareholders. In particular the Anglo-American One Board system can be provided for as well as the German system of a Managing and Supervisory Board.
A commission has recently been discussing the necessity of revising the law of the Swiss joint stock corporation. It is still an open question whether there will be changes, which in any case will not become effective before 1985 and will not change the basic concept of the present legislation.

1.b. Although there are several forms of business organizations in Switzerland the *joint stock corporation is virtually the only one used by foreign investors.* It is by far the form which is most preferred by Swiss investors and business men.
The joint stock corporation *serves the purposes of both the privately held as well as the publicly held entity.* While it is true that in Swiss law the limited liability company ('Gesellschaft mit beschränkter Haftung' or 'GmbH'/'Société à responsabilité limitée' or 'Sàrl') exists, it is rarely used. The joint stock corporation typically is used for the same purposes for which the limited liability company is used in the Federal Republic of Germany.
The overwhelming importance of the joint stock corporation is illustrated by the fact that today more than 100,000 joint stock corporations exist in Switzerland (compared to only about 2,000 in the Federal Republic of Germany), whereas only some 3,000 limited liability companies are registered in Switzerland.
The following survey therefore deals almost exclusively with the joint stock corporation.

1. The chapters on Legal Framework (II) and Labour Aspects (IV) except sections II.B.1 and IV.D have been contributed by Prof. Dr. Peter Forstmoser, the chapter on Taxation (III) and the sections on Exchange Control (II.B.1) and on Residence and Work Permits (IV.D.) by Dr. Walter Meier. Both authors are partners of the Zurich law firm Niederer Kraft & Frey.

2. TAXATION LAWS

2.a. Switzerland is a Federal state (Confederation) of 26 cantons (or half-cantons) and some 3,000 municipalities. In the past each canton has been fully sovereign. Today the cantons still enjoy a remarkable degree of political and fiscal sovereignty. Federalism and regional socio-cultural individualism continue to play an important role and therefore are a reality in Switzerland's everyday life.
The Swiss tax system is a mirror of Swiss federalism. The major taxes are levied at three levels of Government: Confederation, cantons and municipalities (in a few cantons even the districts are entitled to impose taxes). Unlike other federalistic countries, the cantonal and municipal income taxes ordinarily represent a heavier burden for the Swiss taxpayer than the Federal income tax.

2.b. Each canton has its own tax code with sometimes quite different rules on the determination of the tax base, exclusions, deductions, rates, and the like which enormously complicates the taxation system. Also within a specific canton the tax rates may vary considerably depending on the rate of the applicable municipal tax. The cantonal and municipal tax rates may periodically be adjusted to conform to budgetary needs.

2.c. A concrete project has been made formally to harmonize the Federal and cantonal tax codes (the rates and allowances would, however, remain at the discretion of each tax jurisdiction). Due to differing opinions on some issues and the relatively slow pace of the political and legislative process in Switzerland, it is difficult to predict whether and when this will be realized.

II. THE LEGAL FRAMEWORK

A. The Vehicle

1. THE WHOLLY-OWNED ENTERPRISE

1.a. THE BRANCH[2]

1.a.(i) Setting-up a branch of a foreign enterprise in Switzerland

1.a.(i)1. The registration of the *first* Swiss branch of a foreign company corresponds to the registration of a Swiss main office with regard to form and content.
This means that the *application* for registration must *contain the following information:*

- the date of the Articles of Association,
- the name and registered office of the company,

2. The survey deals only with Swiss branches of *non-resident* enterprises.

- the object and purpose of the company and its duration if the Articles of Association contain a provision referring to this point,
- the par-value of the share capital as stated in the Articles of Association, the amount paid in the par-value of each share,
- the classes of shares, whether registered or bearer shares, and any preferential rights benefiting a particular class of shares,
- the identity and value attributable to contributions in kind and the nature and value of any benefits attributed to the founders of the company,
- the manner in which the company is to be represented,
- the names, addresses and nationality of the members of the Board of Directors and the persons authorized to represent the company,
- the form in which the company's official statements are published and, if provided in the Articles of Association, the form in which communications are to be made by the Board of Directors to the shareholders. (Information regarding the form and publication of such official statements need not be given if the foreign law under which the company is formed does not require such provisions).

The application shall be *made by the Board of Directors* of the company. If The Board of Directors consists of more than one person, then the Chairman of the Board or his deputy and the Secretary or a second member of the Board of Directors must sign the application.

The application *must be accompanied by the following documents:*
- an excerpt from the Commercial Register in the district of the main office or – if there is no Commercial Register there – an official document (e.g. a 'Certificate of Good Standing') confirming the regular existence of the company (according to the law where the main office is situated). This document must imply that the company corresponds in substance to a Swiss joint stock corporation and that it is a legal entity according to the law at the place of its main office;
- if the document mentioned heretofore does not refer to the paid-in capital, then a notarized certification of the amount of the paid-in capital must be enclosed;
- a copy of the Articles of Association ('Statuten'/'statuts'), which must be certified by the Commercial Register at the place of the main office, by another governmental authority or by a notary public;
- the application must contain a notarized certification of the family names, first names, place of domicile and nationality (in case of Swiss citizens their place of citizenship) of all members of the Board of Directors or notarized excerpts from the minutes of the election of the Board;
- an excerpt of the minutes of the competent organ of the company authorizing the creation of the branch, specifying the person or persons authorized to represent the branch and approving the manner in which they will sign for it (individually or jointly);
- since a branch must, according to Swiss law, have a certain independence (competence to engage in its own business, its own management, separate accounts and recording), the Commercial Register usually requires some evidence in this regard;
- if the branch has no office of its own at the place of its location, then the

application shall indicate with whom it is domiciled at such location. In this case, a written confirmation by the person or company with which the branch shall be domiciled is requested.

If the documentation is in a foreign language, it must be *translated.* The translation should be certified by a sworn translator or by a private person who fully masters both languages.

The documents are to be *legalized* by a diplomatic representative of Switzerland or, in the case of countries which have adhered to the Convention Abolishing the Requirement of Legalization of Foreign Public Documents dated October 5, 1961, to be accomplished by a Certificate (Apostille).

1.a.(i)2. If the foreign Company already has a branch in Switzerland, then *further branches* must be registered in the *same way as branches of Swiss companies.*

This means that the *following information must be filed* with the Commercial Register for the canton or district in which the new branch is located:

- the legal nature, the name and the place or residence of the main office,
- the statement that the main office is registered in the Commercial Register at the place of its residence (provided that a Commercial Register exists at the place of such residence),
- the name and the place of residence of the branch,
- the nature of the business or the purpose of the company,
- special provisions which only apply to the branch,
- the persons authorized to represent the branch, together with any provisions limiting their signatory power to the scope of business of the branch (if such limitations exist) and their method of signing,
- the business address of the branch.

The formation of the new branch must also be registered in the Commercial Register at the place of the first branch.

1.a.(i)3. The *business name* of the Swiss branch of a foreign company must comply with the requirements of the applicable foreign law. In addition the name of the Swiss branch must comply with the Swiss law on business names. In particular misleading names and terms that serve only advertising purposes are prohibited. Territorial and regional additions are authorized as business designations only if they are justified by special circumstances.

Moreover, the company name of the branch must be clearly distinguishable from any company name already registered in Switzerland.

Basically, the branch must use the *same company name as that of the main office* and it must contain the location of the main office, the location of the branch and its specific designation as a branch. Further, branches may make additions to the company name if these additions apply only to the branch.

1.a.(ii) Organization of the branch of a foreign enterprise in Switzerland

1.a.(ii)1. A duly authorized *Swiss resident having authority to represent the Swiss branch* must be appointed. The authorized person need not be a Swiss citizen. The authorization implies ex lege all legal acts that may arise within the scope of the company's purpose. The authorization may be limited, however, to the scope of the branch office's business.

1.a.(ii)2. The registration of a branch confers *jurisdiction over the business activities of such branch* on the court of the branch's location in addition to the jurisdiction of the court where the main place of business is registered.
With regard to the branch's liabilities, the *Swiss branch is subject to Swiss bankruptcy proceedings* which have to be instituted at the registered location of the branch. However, divergent clauses in international treaties remain reserved, such as the one in the convention which Switzerland entered into with France in 1869 (Convention entre la Suisse et la France sur la compétence judiciaire et l'exécution des jugements en matière civile).
Bankruptcy proceedings at the location of the main office do not embrace the assets of the Swiss branch.

1.a.(ii)3. According to Swiss law, the *legal entity as a whole is liable* for legal acts as well as for damages for unlawful acts committed within the scope of the business of the branch.
Whether Directors are personally liable can be decided either according to the law governing the legal entity as such or according to Swiss law. According to Swiss law all Directors, managers or auditors are responsible to the company as well as to the individual shareholders and creditors of the company for any damages caused intentionally or negligently by a breach of their fiduciary duty. However, claims of shareholders and of the company's creditors are restricted or impossible as long as the company or its branch has not been declared bankrupt.

1.a.(ii)4. *Accounting* and *auditing* requirements must be in accordance with the law governing the company. No publication of accounts is required.

1.b. THE SUBSIDIARY

As mentioned before, no differentiation is made between the privately and publicly held company. For both of them the form of the joint stock corporation is used, although Swiss law provides also for the form of the limited liability company.

1.b.(i) Incorporation

1.b.(i)1. At the time of incorporation there must be at least *three shareholders* who have subscribed for the whole amount of share capital. (Immediately after registration, however, the shares can be held by only *one shareholder*).
The *minimum initial share capital* is 50,000 Swiss francs of which at least 20 percent or 20,000 Swiss francs (whichever is greater) must be deposited in an escrow account before the company can be incorporated.
The incorporation meeting takes place in the presence of a notary public. The company then must be *registered in the Commercial Register.*

1.b.(i)2. A special detailed *written report* must be issued by the founders if some or all of the shares are paid for by *contributions in kind.*
However, there is no requirement of an official or private appraisal of such contributions in kind; the philosophy of the law is that such contributions

should be made publicly known by reference in the Articles of Association and by the report, but that it is up to the creditors or potential shareholders to decide whether or not the value attributed to such contributions is adequate.

1.b.(i)3. The above mentioned rules apply to *incorporations in one act*. There are specific rules for *incorporations by successive subscriptions* which attempt better to protect the investing 'outside' shareholder. However, since virtually all incorporations take place in one act, these rules are rarely applicable. In fact in order to form a widely-held company, a bank or related company usually subscribes to all of the shares and then resells these shares to the ultimate shareholders. If this procedure is applied then the rules for incorporations by successive subscriptions need not be complied with.

1.b.(ii) Organization

1.b.(ii)1. Share capital and shares

Share capital

The share capital must be *fully subscribed before the incorporation* of the company. The capital may be increased subsequently by decisions of a General Meeting. Such increases require an amendment to the Articles of Association. The capital may also be decreased by decision of the General Meeting of shareholders, subject to detailed rules which ensure that such decreases may not be made to the detriment of creditors.

Shares

The shares must have a *par value of at least 100 Swiss francs.*
With regard to the transfer of shares, one can distinguish between *bearer shares* ('Inhaberaktien'/'actions au porteur' which are freely transferable by simple delivery; the holder of the share certificate is recognized as the owner of the share) and *registered shares*('Namenaktien'/'actions nominatives' which are transferable by endorsement and delivery of the title. The company must keep a shareholders' register in which all registered shares and their owners are recorded, and it will accept as registered shareholders only the persons registered as such).
The Articles of Association may provide that the *transfer* of registered shares is *subject to approval by the Board of Directors* or by the General Meeting of shareholders. Such approval can be refused for specific reasons (such as the buyer's nationality) or without disclosure of the reasons thereof. According to the practice of the Swiss Federal Court, the buyer of a registered share who is not registered has no voting right but remains entitled to dividends and liquidation proceeds.
Besides *ordinary shares* ('Stammaktien'/'actions ordinaires'), there may be *preference shares* ('Vorzugsaktien'/'actions privilégiées') which have priority in the distribution of dividends or liquidation proceeds and *voting shares* ('Stimmrechtsaktien'/'actions à droit de vote privilégié') which have increased voting power.

If the share capital is increased, shareholders are entitled to subscribe for new shares proportionally to their previous holding. This *pre-emptive right* can be excluded for overriding purposes. Share ownership by employees, for example, is acknowledged as such an overriding purpose.
Apart from shares, a Swiss corporation can provide for ownership participation in the form of *non-voting profit sharing certificates.* Although such certificates originally were intended to facilitate financial reorganizations (creditors would waive their claims on exchange for such certificates), they have become a widely used financial instrument intended to attract non-voting capital.
The legal provisions for the issue of such certificates are extremely flexible: There is no minimum par value nor any other specific restriction.

1.b.(ii)2. Organs of the joint stock corporation
There are three necessary organs of the company:
- the General Meetings of Shareholders,
- the Board of Directors,
- the Auditors.

1.b.(ii)3. The general meeting of shareholders
The General Meeting is called the *'Supreme Organ'* of the company. It is supreme, however, only to the extent that the most important powers are assigned to it and that it elects the two other organs. The General Meeting is not entitled to interfere with the specific tasks of the other two organs.
An *ordinary General Meeting* must be held every year and *Extraordinary Meetings* can be held whenever appropriate. There are no legal distinctions between ordinary and extraordinary Meetings.
The Meetings must be *called* by the Board of Directors at least *10 days in advance*, either by individual notice or by publication.
Basically, resolutions are passed and elections are held by an *absolute majority of the shares represented* at the meeting; there is no requirement of a minimum representation. Exceptions (qualified representation and qualified quora) do exist for important decisions, such as the amendment of the purpose clause, extension of the company's scope of business within its purpose, mergers, change of name, transfer of the company's legal domicile, etc.
Each shareholder can be *represented* at a General Meeting by a person of his choice. In the case of bearer shares, the bearer will qualify as the shareholder. In the case of registered shares, a written power of attorney is necessary.
Unlike German law, *banks are not restricted from representing shareholders* (Depotstimmrecht). In publicly held companies, the General Meetings are usually controlled by the votes represented by banks. The banks vote according to a Gentleman's Agreement and normally in favour of the proposals of the Board.

1.b.(ii)4. The board of directors
The Board of Directors is composed of *one or more members, all of whom must be shareholders.* It is generally accepted in Swiss legal doctrine, however, that Board members are only formal and not beneficial owners of their shares and that they *act in a fiduciary capacity.* In fact in most foreign con-

trolled Swiss companies lawyers, bankers and other businessmen act as Board members bound by a fiduciary relation to the foreign shareholder.

If the Board consists of a single member, it must be a *Swiss citizen resident in Switzerland.* If it is composed of more than one member, the majority must be Swiss citizens resident in Switzerland. (The Swiss Federal Council may grant exceptions to this rule for holding companies if the majority of the enterprises held are located in foreign countries).

The Board has the duty and power to *conduct the business of the company.* It is authorized to decide all matters which are not delegated or reserved to the General Meeting or other corporate bodies.

Meetings of the Board are convened as often as may be considered necessary by its chairman. Every member can require that such a Meeting shall be called.

If the corporation has different classes of shares, then each class has a right to at least one representative on the Board. This rule applies when legally different classes exist and not when minority groups merely have different interests.

Swiss law provides for only one Board whose Directors are jointly responsible for the management and representation of the company. However, the Articles of Association or other company regulations may authorize the General Meeting of shareholders or the Board of Directors to *delegate the management*, or any part thereof, and the representation of the company to one or more persons who are members of the Board of Directors (managing Directors) or to third persons who need not be shareholders (managers). This allows to create an organization similar either to the German system of 'Aufsichtsrat' and 'Vorstand' or to the American Board system.

1.b.(ii)5. Auditors

The General Meeting has to elect one or more Auditors who do not have to be shareholders.

The Auditors need not have any professional qualifications. A report by independent professional Auditors is required, however, for economically important corporations, and in practice virtually all of the large Swiss corporations are audited by bookkeeping experts.

The Auditors must conduct an examination to determine that the statement of profit and loss and the balance sheet agree with the books and that the business results and financial position as represented in the financial statements comply with the legal requirements. The courts are insisting more and more that the examination be not merely a formal one: According to the present court interpretations, the Auditors must also examine whether the statements are correct in substance or not. In particular, they are required to determine that the principal assets of the company exist and their stated value does not exceed their actual value as of the date of the balance sheet.

1.b.(ii)6. Accounting and publication of accounts

The *annual accounts* must be prepared according to generally recognized commercial principles. They must be expressed in Swiss francs.

Few specific provisions regulate the preparation of an AG's balance sheet and profit and loss statement. For example, contrary to German law, the Swiss law does not prescribe a scheme of how the annual statement should be broken down.

The informational value of the annual accounts of most of Swiss companies is impaired to a large degree by the possibility of creating and dissolving undisclosed reserves. The creation of undisclosed reserves by the management is allowed to the extent appropriate to ensure the continued prosperity of the company or to distribute dividends as equally as possible throughout the years.

The Board of Directors must submit to the General Meeting a *written annual report* on the company's financial position and the results of its activities. Since no specific rules exist to regulate the contents of such reports, they often do not provide any further information.

Except for banks, there is *no obligation whatsoever to inform the public.* Upon the request of a proven creditor, a company must disclose, however, its profit and loss statement and its balance sheet as approved by the company's shareholders.

1.b.(ii)7. Rights and duties of shareholders

A shareholder's *sole duty* to the company is to *pay for his shares* in full. A Swiss shareholder has typical shareholder *rights*, such as:

- the right to vote,
- the right to attend General Meetings and to discuss any topics on the Agenda,
- a (limited) right to information,
- the right to contest in court resolutions of the General Meeting (but not of the Board), if such resolutions are against the law or the Articles of Association,
- the right to hold Board Members, Management, Auditors, Founders and Liquidators liable for a breach of their fiduciary duties,
- the right to receive dividends,
- the pre-emptive right to purchase newly issued shares, and
- the right to a proportionate share of the proceeds upon liquidation.

Minority interests have little protection under Swiss law because the Supreme Court tends to give preference to the interest of the company which, according to the Court, is usually expressed in the decision of the majority.

It should be stressed that the *information available* to a minority shareholder is limited in Switzerland. He is not entitled to inspect the books or correspondence of the company and he can obtain specific information only to the extent that business secrets will not be divulged.

1.b.(ii)8. Groups of companies

No specific provisions for groups of companies exist in Swiss law; a company which belongs to a group is treated like an independent company.

1.b.(iii) Checklist for the establishment of a subsidiary

In order to achieve the incorporation of a Swiss subsidiary, the following checklist should be followed:

- canton and city of incorporation,

- name of the company,
- purpose clause of the Articles of Association (can be drafted in a rather broad way),
- amount of the subscribed and of the initial paid-up capital,
- nature of shares (registered or bearer shares), their number and nominal value,
- names, addresses and nationalities of Incorporators and original Shareholders with number of shares held,
- number, name, address and nationality of the members of the Board as well as of the Managers,
- number, name and address of the Auditors,
- duration of terms of office for members of the Board and Auditors,
- duration of the business year,
- authorized signatures for the company,
- will there be an active office in Switzerland and, if so, what activities will it engage in,
- residence and address of the company.

1.c. OTHER FORMS OF BUSINESS ORGANIZATIONS

1.c.(i) 'Numerus Clausus' of forms of organizations legally provided for

Swiss law provides a limited number of forms of organization for commercial as well as for noncommercial purposes:

- Einfache Gesellschaft / Société simple
- Kollektivgesellschaft / Société en nom collectif
- Kommanditgesellschaft / Société en commandite
- Aktiengesellschaft / Société anonyme
- Kommanditaktiengesellschaft / Société en commandite par actions
- Gesellschaft mit beschränkter Haftung / Société à responsabilité limitée
- Genossenschaft / Société coopérative
- Verein / Association.

1.c.(ii) Survey on the various forms

1.c.(ii)1. Partnership ('Einfache Gesellschaft'/'Société simple')

This is an extremely flexible form used for all kinds of commercial and noncommercial purposes of a rather simple or transitory character. It can be established and dissolved without any formalities and is not registered in the Commercial Register.

The Partnership (it creates less intensive relations between the partners than the British partnership) is not a legal entity. Every partner is personally liable for the obligations of the Partnership.

1.c.(ii)2. General commercial partnership ('Kollektivgesellschaft'/'Société en nom collectif')

The General Commercial Partnership is an organization suitable to carry on a commercial enterprise by two or more partners who must all be individuals.

The General Commercial Partnership (it corresponds more or less to the British partnership) can be established and dissolved without formalities but must be registered in the Commercial Register.
The General Commercial Partnership is not considered to be a legal entity, but treated as such to a certain degree in its relations to third parties: It has its own business name, can enter into contracts, can sue and be sued and owns assets in its own name. If such assets are not sufficient to cover its liabilities, each partner is personally liable.

1.c.(ii)3. Limited partnership ('Kommanditgesellschaft/ 'Société en commandite')

This is a modified form of the General Commercial Partnership in which one or more partners have limited liability (up to a specified amount recorded in the Commercial Register). These limited liability partners can be other than individuals such as legal entities. They have no duty or right to manage the Partnership.

1.c.(ii)4. Joint stock corporation ('Aktiengesellschaft', 'AG'/'Société anonyme', 'SA')

This form has been dealt with in some detail in section 1.2. heretofore. It is by far the most important form of doing business in Switzerland.

1.c.(ii)5. Partnership limited by shares ('Kommenditaktiengesellschaft'/ 'Société en commandite par actions')

This is a combination between the joint stock corporation and the General Commercial Partnership which is of no practical importance in Switzerland.

1.c.(ii)6. Limited liability company ('Gesellschaft mit beschränkter Haftung', 'GmbH'/'Société a responsabilité limitée', 'SARL')

This form has been created as the 'corporation of the small man'. It was copied from German law and introduced into Swiss law in 1936.
Its functions correspond (or should correspond) to the role of the private company or the close corporation.
Unlike the situation in the Federal Republic of Germany, the GmbH has extremely limited commercial importance in Switzerland where it is typical to establish a Joint Stock Corporation for small and one-man companies.

1.c.(ii)7. Cooperative association (Genossenschaft'/'Société cooperative')

This corporation is designed to achieve commercial benefits by the cooperation of its members.
Cooperative associations, in particular agricultural and consumer cooperatives, play an important role in Swiss economy. However, they are not a suitable instrument for a foreign investor.

1.c.(ii)8. Association ('Verein'/'Association')

The association is a legal entity designed for noncommercial purposes and legally limited to such purposes. Nevertheless, it plays an important role as a form of organization for professional organizations, workers' unions and cartels.

1.c.(ii)9. Investment fund ('Anlagefonds'/'Fonds d'Investissement')

It should be noted that a special law for investment funds exists which has the protection of investors as its exclusive goal. The law applies only to investment funds that are organized on a contractual basis, but not to investment clubs and similar groups.

2. THE JOINT VENTURE

2.a. THE JOINTLY-OWNED COMPANY

2.a.(i) Shareholder agreements

According to Swiss legal doctrine and court practice, shareholder agreements and in particular voting arrangements are *legal.* They do not bind the company, however, but only bind the shareholders that are parties to the agreement. Thus, votes cast in violation of a shareholder agreement must be recognized as valid by the company. The only remedy for the other parties to the agreement is to claim damages.

In practice various possibilities exist to ensure compliance with shareholders agreements such as penalty clauses and the deposit of the shares with a third person.

2.a.(ii) Minority rights

2.a.(ii)1. The Joint Stock Corporation is governed by *majority rules*: unless otherwise provided for by law or Articles of Association, the absolute majority of votes represented at a General Meeting of shareholders is sufficient to pass resolutions and determine elections.

The Supreme Court has upheld majority decisions even in cases in which the majority has disregarded legitimate interests of a minority.

The power of the majority is limited by certain vested rights (see section 2.a.(ii)2.) and by certain rights of minorities (see section 2.a.(iii)3).

2.a.(ii)2. The law specifies the following *vested rights* ('wohlerworbene Rechte'/'droits acquis') (those of which shareholders cannot be deprived without their consent): the right to take part in General Meetings of shareholders, voting rights, the right to contest an illegal decision of the General Meeting in court, right to dividends and to share in the liquidation proceeds. The Articles of Association can contain further vested rights.

2.a.(ii)3. *Minority rights* are contained in the provisions which require certain quora or a minimal representation of shares for decisions of the General Meeting of shareholders which are of specific importance (see section 1.b.(ii)3. heretofore).

Further minority rights are:

- the right of one or more shareholders representing at least one-tenth of the capital stock to require the calling of a General Meeting of stockholders,

- the right of shareholders representing at least one-fifth of the capital stock to request the dissolution of the company for valid reasons by a court ruling,
- a group of shareholders can also be entitled to a representative on the Board of Directors, see section 1.b.(ii)4. heretofore.

2.b. CONSORTIA

According to Swiss law, the partnership is *the* legal form for consortia. See section 1.c.(ii)1. heretofore.

2.c. OTHER FORMS

No legal provisions exist with regard to management contracts. Such contracts are not very common in Switzerland and to what degree they are valid has not fully been clarified by court decisions.

B. External Controls

1. EXCHANGE CONTROLS

1.a. Switzerland has traditionally been a *net exporter of capital* and it functions, at the same time, as a widely recognized international financial centre. In view of the generally low interest rates Switzerland has been confronted from time to time with the problem of shielding the country's limited financial resources against large borrowings by non-residents and upwards pressures on domestic interest rates. Therefore, Switzerland follows a firmly entrenched policy to control the more important channels for capital exports.
The *Federal Law on Banks and Savings Banks* of 1934/71 sets forth rules with respect to certain capital export transactions applicable, in principle, to banks and banklike finance companies. Subject to authorization are particularly placements of bond issues by nonresident borrowers exceeding 10 million francs and of note issues exceeding 3 million francs as well as the granting to non-residents of bank loans with maturities exceeding twelve months and with principal amounts of 10 million francs or more. The power of authorization is vested in the Swiss National Bank (Central Bank).

1.b. Since the early sixties with the currency turmoil and the downward pressure on the US dollar, however, Switzerland was increasingly confronted with the *opposite problem* of protecting its small-sized domestic economy and the Swiss franc against the destabilizing effects of *excessive capital inflows*. The enacted measures such as the investment ban, restrictions on the borrowing from non-residents, negative interest charges on deposits by non-residents, limitation on foreign exchange forward sales to non-residents have meanwhile gradually been abolished.
In case of new and heavy currency turbulences re-enactment of certain measures cannot be ruled out. The Swiss National Bank has now been equipped

with adequate policy instruments in the amended Federal Law on the Swiss National Bank of 1953/1978. However, Switzerland with its traditional adherence to the principle of *freedom of capital movements* will certainly follow a policy of restraint in enacting new regulatory measures.

1.c. For *banks* and *banklike finance companies* some regulations are applicable with respect to financial data reporting requirements. There are also certain controls on issues of capital, bonds and other securities by residents. In addition an *Agreement* was concluded in 1977 between the Swiss National Bank and the resident banks on the observance of care in accepting funds and on the practising of banking secrecy.

2. TAKE-OVER CONTROLS

Take-over controls do not exist in Swiss law. The introduction of a duty to register planned mergers with the Cartel Commission is presently being discussed, but a change of the present situation is rather unlikely.

3. ANTI-TRUST PROVISIONS

The Swiss Cartel law does not prohibit cartels as such but only certain abuses of cartelisation. It imposes far less restrictions than the anti-trust laws of the Federal Republic of Germany, the United Kingdom or the EC.
The cartel law is presently being revised. The new law (which will not become effective prior to 1983) is expected to be somewhat tougher, although, again, still based upon the concept that cartels as such are not illegal.

4. ENVIRONMENTAL CONTROLS AND STATE MONOPOLIES

No particularities can be mentioned with regard to these topics.

III. TAXATION

A. Corporation Tax

1. LEGAL ENTITIES SUBJECT TO TAX

1.a. Resident legal entities

Resident companies and other corporate bodies such as joint stock corporations ('Aktiengesellschaften' or 'AG'/'sociétés anonymes' or 'SA'), limited liability companies ('Gesellschaften mit beschränkter Haftung' or 'GmbH'/'sociétés à responsabilité limitée' or 'Sàrl') and limited partnerships with shares

('Kommandit-Aktiengesellschaften'/'sociétés en commandite par actions') and cooperative associations ('Genossenschaften'/'sociétés coopératives') are subject to the Federal, cantonal and municipal direct taxes on income and capital.

For purposes of the Federal direct tax, a company is considered ***resident*** if it has its 'seat' ('Sitz'/'siège'), in other words its place of registration in Switzerland (the place of registration must be set down in the Articles of Association and entered in the Commercial Register).

The cantonal tax laws provide for unlimited tax liability of a company ordinarily at the place of its registration (seat) or at the place where its effective management is located.

Under the ***intercantonal conflict of taxation rules***, a company is usually deemed to be resident in the canton where its activities are effectively and regularly carried on (place of effective management) notwithstanding its formal seat.

1.b. Non-resident legal entities

1.b.(ii). General rules

Generally, non-resident legal entities are subject to a *limited* Federal, cantonal and municipal *tax liability* with respect to income and capital attributable to a permanent establishment located in Switzerland (see section 1.b.(ii)); income and capital related to immovable property situated in Switzerland; interest from debts secured by Swiss-situs immovable property and some other less significant types of income.

For Federal tax purposes, a non-resident legal entity is treated in the same manner as the resident legal entity to which it is most similar in legal terms and factual structure.

Non-resident legal entities with neither economic ties to Switzerland nor income from Swiss sources as outlined above are not subject to Swiss taxes with the exception of dividends and certain interest payments arising in Switzerland liable to the Federal Anticipatory Tax (see section B).

1.b.(ii). Branches

Under the Federal tax rules a permanent establishment is a fixed place of business through which a qualitatively or quantitatively essential part of the business of the enterprise is carried on. The branch ('Zweigniederlassung'/'succursale') is a typical form of permanent establishment through which a non-resident exercises a business activity in Switzerland. It is ordinarily subject to Federal, cantonal and municipal taxes on income and capital ***attributable*** to the branch located in Switzerland.

On the Federal level, non-resident individuals and partnerships maintaining a branch in Switzerland are taxed under the rules governing the taxation of individuals. Non-resident legal entities with a branch in Switzerland are, as mentioned above, taxed in the same manner as the corresponding resident legal entity. The tax of the branch is, in principle, levied on that share of total income (capital) of the whole enterprise which corresponds to the ratio between the factors of the branch and the factors of the whole enterprise. This

'fractional allocation method' is identical to the method used to determine the income of a permanent establishment of a Swiss enterprise located abroad. Under this concept, a permanent establishment in Switzerland is basically treated as a part of the whole international enterprise. If the net income of the permanent establishment exceeds the income of the head office abroad, the amount taxable in Switzerland may not exceed the total income. Conversely, if the permanent establishment suffers a loss, a part of the total income of the enterprise may be attributed to the permanent establishment. In view of the problems related to the application of this method in the international context where the tax authority of one country is often unable to obtain complete and reliable data on the total income of an international enterprise, the Federal Tax Administration ('FTA') recommends the assessment authorities to apply, if necessary, the *objective method* under which the assessment is carried out on the basis of the results of the branch alone. The FTA has issued Guidelines for such assessments in its Circular Letter of June 1, 1960.
The cantonal statutory rules on the determination of the income (capital) from a Swiss permanent establishment of a non-resident are few; and the existing rules vary from canton to canton.

2. COMPUTATION OF PROFITS

2.a. Income and capital

Resident entities subject to the unlimited tax liability are, in principle, taxable on their *worldwide* income and net wealth. Income arising outside of Switzerland is taxed whether remitted to Switzerland or not. Within this all-inclusive income and net wealth concept only income and capital related to *immovable property* and *permanent establishments* located outside of Switzerland are exempted from taxation in Switzerland (for the tax treatment of holding companies, domiciliary companies etc. see section K).

For Federal tax purposes income derived from immovable property and from permanent establishments located outside of Switzerland is exempted by reducing the total tax due in the same proportion that the income from immovable property or the permanent establishment bears to the taxpayer's total income (exemption with progression). In practice the exemption is also granted by the cantonal tax jurisdictions; however, not all of the cantonal tax laws explicitly provide for this exemptions. Some cantons grant the exemption only upon proving that a tax has been paid in the country where the income was earned.
With the exception of the non-taxables outlined above, basically all of an entity's net income is treated as taxable business income. These principles also apply to the capital tax. After making appropriate adjustments, net income (capital) as shown in the financial statements constitutes taxable income (capital).
Consequently, *dividends* and *interest* received by resident entities must be included in the gross income like all other forms of investment income. In

some cases, however, special relief is granted to holding companies and other types of entities (see section K). A refund may be claimed with respect to the Anticipatory Tax withheld on Swiss source dividends and interest (see section B). Foreign source dividends and interest are generally includible in income net of foreign taxes. A credit is not available unless specifically provided for by a tax treaty (see section 4.b.).

2.b. Capital gains (losses)

On the Federal level, the income tax applies to capital gains arising from the sale of movable and immovable property in the same manner as to other income items.

Under the cantonal tax rules the taxation of capital gains varies widely. Capital gains derived from the alienation of immovable property are ordinarily taxed (i) by aggregating such gains with other income, (ii) by a special tax on immovable property gains, or (iii) by a capital gains tax. The rate often depends on the length of time the property has been owned.

The transfer of all or a majority of the shares of a *real estate company* is generally treated as the transfer of immovable property itself.

2.c. Exemptions and deductions

As a rule, the Federal and cantonal tax statutes permit deductions for ordinary and necessary business expenses. The deductibility of taxes paid and losses carried forward vary among the 27 taxing jurisdictions. On the Federal level a loss at the end of a two-year period (see section 5) can be *carried forward* to be set off against profits realised in the subsequent three two-year periods. In general, the cantonal treatment of losses is less generous (for instance, Zurich only permits a loss to be carried forward for two years).

The Swiss tax statutes do never allow a *loss carry-back*. In addition, losses of one entity may not be set off against profits of another entity.

Capital expenditures are deductible in the form of periodic depreciation charges. While *depreciation* for tax and book purposes need not conform, depreciation for tax purposes may not exceed that entered in the books. The straight-line and declining-balance methods are both accepted.

Normally, depreciation may not exceed the maximum rates fixed by the FTA, unless the taxpayer can justify application of a higher rate. The following examples for common assets apply to the *declining-balance* method and must be reduced by one-half when the straight-line method is used:

Commercial and bank buildings, department stores	4%
Hotels and restaurants	6%
Factories, industrial buildings and workshops	8%
Office and workshop furniture and equipment	25%
Manufacturing machinery and installations, vehicles of all types except motor vehicles	30%
Motor vehicles	40%
Intangibles (patents, trademarks and goodwill etc.)	40%
Office machines, computers	40%
Hand tools and small equipment	45%

(The aforementioned depreciation rates are valid for the computation of the Federal income tax for the tax years 1981 and 1982.)
Higher rates of depreciation may be allowed if assets are subject to excessive use.
Most cantons also accept the rates set forth by the FTA. In some cantons even slightly higher rates are tolerated.
Deductions are also normally allowed for bad debt reserves, inventory valuation reserves and certain other purposes.
In addition, a general deduction of not more than 5% of outstanding domestic receivables and 10% of foreign receivables at the end of the year may be allowed.
Although appropriate deductions for accounting purposes, some items may be *non-deductible* for tax purposes, such as payments to undisclosed persons, excessive compensation paid to corporate officers, disguised distribution of corporate profits and – in some cantons (for instance in the Canton of Zurich) – income and capital taxes paid or incurred.

3. RATES OF TAX

As pointed out in the introduction, corporate income and capital are subject to Federal, cantonal and municipal taxes. In general, the aggregate of the cantonal and municipal income and capital taxes is higher than the Federal income and capital tax.[3]

3.a. Income taxes

3.a.(i) Federal tax

The Federal tax on the net income of corporations and related legal entities (and branches) is levied at progressive rates on a *yield-intensity* basis. The yield is the percentage that taxable net income bears to the company's proportional or reference capital composed of the nominal share capital and reserves plus retained earnings.
The corporate tax rates are composed of a

a. basic rate of 3.63% on all net income;
b. additional tax of 3.63% on the portion of net income in excess of 4% of the reference capital;
c. second additional tax of 4.84% of the portion on net income in excess of 8% of the reference capital.
(The computation of the additional taxes is slightly different if capital is less than 50,000 francs).

The maximum rate, however, is 9.8% of the net income. It is reached when the company's net income equals or exceeds roughly 23% of its reference capital.

3. In 1978 the Federal tax on income and capital accounted for 21.9%, the cantonal tax for 41.8% and the municipal tax for 36.3% of the combined Federal, cantonal and municipal tax receipts.

3.a.(ii). Cantonal and municipal taxes

The widely varying computation of the *cantonal* corporate income taxes in the 26 cantonal tax jurisdictions can only be briefly summarized here. In most cantons the corporate income taxes are progressive within a fixed range. The tax is frequently computed based on the percentage that net income bears to taxable capital. Some cantons do not use a yield-intensity formula, but simply tax successive segments of income at graduated rates up to a maximum rate. Generally, multiples are then applied on the resulting rate. The multiples are subject to periodical adjustments.
The *municipal* tax is usually levied as a multiple of the cantonal tax rate, varying from municipality to municipality within a canton. As a rule of thumb, the maximum (combined cantonal and municipal) corporate income tax rate generally does not exceed 30%; in some cantons the maximum rate is considerably lower. Most municipalities also impose small additions to the rate for a *church tax.*

3.b. Capital taxes

3.b.(i). Federal capital taxes

The Federal tax on capital and reserves of corporations and related legal entities (and branches) is levied at the flat rate of 0.0825% (regardless whether any income is earned).

3.b.(ii). Cantonal and municipal taxes

The basic capital tax rates are ordinarily increased by both a cantonal and municipal multiple comparable to the income tax multiple. In most cantons the combined cantonal and municipal capital tax rate is considerably less than 1%.

3.c. Corporate tax incidences in some selected cantons

As an illustration of Switzerland's heterogeneity in the area of taxation, the following table shows the combined annual taxes (Federal, cantonal and municipal) of a joint stock corporation (located in the Canton's capital) with adjusted net income of 10,000, 25,000 and 50,000 francs and taxable capital and reserves of 100,000 francs (based on 1978 figures):

Canton	*10,000*	*25,000*	*50,000*
Zurich	2,432	9,529	18,935
Bern	3,145	7,752	15,292
Zug	1,957	6,053	11,892
Basel-City	2,671	7,387	14,256
Grisons	1,468	4,602	11,441
Geneva	2,079	7,513	16,006

(Source: Steuerbelastung in der Schweiz, 1979)

4. TAX CREDITS

In the Swiss tax system, there are basically only the two following types of tax credits available:

4.a. Credit for anticipatory tax withheld at source

The Anticipatory Tax withheld at source from the specified income items of a resident represents, as a general rule, a kind of advance payment on the income and net wealth taxes. The tax withheld may be credited against such taxes on condition that the claimant is the beneficial owner of the asset generating such income and that he reports such income. Amounts in excess are refunded (see also section B).

4.b. Lump-sum tax credit under a tax treaty

Basically, Swiss domestic tax laws do not provide for a foreign tax credit (except in a few cantons in cases of marginal importance). A tax credit is granted only if provided for explicitly by a tax treaty. The treaties concluded or revised since 1965 contain special provisions for the so-called *'Lump-Sum Tax Credit'* ('Pauschale Steueranrechnung'/'imputation forfaitaire d'impôt'). This credit covers, in principle, the non-refundable part of taxes withheld in the other contracting country on dividends, interest and royalties.
The 'Lump-Sum Tax Credit' is granted in a single amount for the Federal, cantonal and municipal taxes. Detailed rules focus particularly on the grossing-up of foreign source income, determination of the maximum creditable amount, method of computation, reduction of the tax credit by expenses, and treatment of holding and domiciliary companies (for details see Decree of the Federal Council of August 22, 1967 and related Regulations and (in summary form) Instructions DA-M issued by the FTA).
No lump-sum tax credit is obtainable under the treaties with Finland (1956), Norway (1956), Pakistan (1959/1962) and the United States (1951).

5. TIMING OF ASSESSMENT AND PAYMENTS

The computation and assessment periods on which Federal and cantonal taxes are based vary in length. For computing, assessing and paying taxes there are different periods to be taken into account:

- The term *'computation (or base) period (year)'* means the period (year) on whose income the tax is based;
- The term *'assessment period (year)'* means the period (year) for which the tax is levied. The tax is generally, but not always, imposed on the basis of the computation period (year) which immediately precedes the assessment period (year);
- The term *'payment period (year)'* means the year in which the tax is to be paid. It is either identical with the assessment period (years) or with the calendar year(s) immediately following the assessment period.

If the accounting year of a company is not the calendar year, the assessment is based on its accounting year(s).

5.a. Federal direct tax

The Federal tax is assessed for a period of *two successive calendar years* (assessment period) beginning with an odd numbered year and based on the average net income for the two preceding years (computation period). The Federal direct tax is due on March 1 following the end of each year of the assessment period. To illustrate the interaction of the three periods: The Federal direct tax for the year 1981 and the year 1982 is based on the average net income and capital of the years 1979 and 1980, and the resulting annual taxes are due on March 1, 1982, tax for 1981, and March 1, 1983, tax for 1983.

5.b. Cantonal and municipal taxes

The majority of cantons also use the bi-annual assessment. A group of cantons base the assessment of the income and capital taxes on a one-year period, but also on a preceding year basis. A few cantons now follow the concept of the current-year basis under which the computation year and assessment year are identical. Cantonal and municipal taxes are due at different dates varying from canton to canton.

6. REVIEW AND APPEAL

The heterogeneity of the Swiss tax laws is also reflected in the great variety of protest and appeal procedures. However, a certain harmony exists with respect to the basic principles.

6.a. Federal direct tax

A taxpayer dissatisfied with a final Federal tax assessment decision is entitled to file a *'protest'* ('Einsprache'/'réclamation') with the Federal tax assessment authority of the country of residence. The assessment authority's decision may again be challenged by an *'appeal'* ('Beschwerde'/'recours') with a cantonal judiciary appeal commission. A taxpayer who is still dissatisfied with that decision may file an *'administrative-law appeal'* ('Verwaltungsgerichtsbeschwerde'/ 'recours de droit administratif') with the Federal Court. In specific cases a petition may be filed for the extraordinary remedy of a *'revision'* with the authority that last dealt with the challenged decision (notwithstanding the level of the deciding instance).
The protest procedure is a part of the assessment procedure and constitutes an administrative act. The protest must be filed within 30 days. The review of the contested assessment notice is governed by the principle of an ex officio investigation. Filing a protest does not automatically stay payment of tax; but the taxpayer may request a stay of payment.

6.b. Cantonal and municipal tax

The structure of cantonal tax protest and appeal procedures is rather complex and varies from canton to canton with respect to the number of protests and appeals available and the legal nature of the review bodies. Some cantons have set up 'appeal commissions'; some cantons use their civil courts to deal with cantonal tax matters; and in other cantons administrative courts are used as the higher appeal bodies.
A taxpayer alleging violation of his constitutional rights (such as equality before the law or the prohibition against intercantonal double taxation) is entitled to challenge a cantonal tax decision before the Federal Court by means of a *'public law appeal'* ('Staatsrechtliche Beschwerde'/'recours de droit public').

B. Withholding Taxes on Dividends, Interest, Royalties and Other Income

1. INCOME CATEGORIES SUBJECT TO WITHHOLDING TAX

1.a. General

The *Federal Anticipatory Tax* ('Verrechnungssteuer'/'impôt anticipé') is the only withholding tax of general application in Switzerland. It is levied at the source and in anticipation of the income tax liability to be borne by the recipient on income from movable capital, lottery winnings, and insurance payments. The withholding of tax, however, does not relieve the taxpayer from reporting the income. For non-residents, it may constitute a final tax charge.

1.b. Income from movable capital

Income from the following sources is subject to the tax[4] : interest, rent, profit distributions and similar types of income derived from

- *bonds and debentures*, serial mortgage certificates, serial land charge notes and registered notes issued by a resident person;
- *shares* in resident joint stock corporations, limited liability companies and cooperative associations and participation certificates (bons de jouissance);
- *units* of an *investment* fund or other conglomerations of property of a

4. A Bill has been submitted to the Federal Parliament which would permit the levy of Anticipatory Tax on interest derived from fiduciary deposits ('Treuhandguthaben'/'avoirs fiduciaries') with resident banks and savings banks at a reduced rate of 5% (the term 'fiduciary deposit' means a deposit in connection with loans or similar debt-claims or a share in such debt-claims with non-residents placed or administered by a bank or savings bank in its own name but at the risk of and for the account of another person). The planned tax on fiduciary deposits has, however, become an object of a controversy as to its constitutionality and economic justification and it is uncertain whether it will be introduced at all.

similar nature issued by a resident person or by a Swiss resident jointly with a non-resident;
- *deposits* in resident banks and savings banks.

Consequently, interest paid by a debtor other than a bank on a current account or an individual's note is, in principle, not subject to the Anticipatory Tax.

The Federal Tax Administration has also set forth minimum and maximum interest rates for loans to and by the shareholder. Any interest payment outside the permissible range is deemed to be a disguised dividend and taxed accordingly.

Lottery winnings and (at reduced rates) insurance payments to Swiss residents are also subject to the Anticipatory Tax.

The Anticipatory Tax may be reclaimed by beneficially entitled Swiss residents upon reporting the income items from which the tax was withheld. Persons subject to limited tax liability (including domestic branches of non-residents) may, in principle, claim a refund up to the amount of Swiss taxes actually paid.

1.c. **Royalties**

As already mentioned, no withholding tax on royalties derived from Swiss sources and paid to a non-resident is levied on the Federal level.

2. RATES

Regular rate:	35%
Rates on pensions and annuities:	15%
Rate on other insurance payments:	8%

3. EFFECT OF TAX TREATIES

In the case of non-residents, the Anticipatory Tax is, in principle, a final tax charge. Only the beneficially entitled recipient resident in a country with which Switzerland has concluded a tax treaty may claim a full or partial refund under the treaty rules or the regulations (see schedule of withholding taxes in section J).

C. Stamp Duties

The Confederation levies Stamp Duties ('Stempelabgaben'/'droits de timbre') on certain securities, bills of exchange and similar documents (Stamp Duty Act of June 27, 1973, and the Regulations of December 3, 1973). There are three types of duties: the *Issue Stamp Duty* ('Emissionsabgabe'/'droit de timbre d'émission') the *Transfer Stamp Duty* ('Umsatzabgabe'/'droit de timbre de négociation'), and the duty on certain *Insurance Premiums*. The

Federal Stamp Duties also apply in the Principality of Liechtenstein. Some cantons impose stamp duties on legal documents, but these duties are insignificant.

1. ISSUE STAMP DUTY

The Issue Stamp Duty is an important consideration when establishing a company in Switzerland. It is levied at a rate of *3%* on the creation of participation rights (shares) or the increase of their par value with or without consideration such as shares and profit-sharing certificates of a resident joint stock corporation and limited liability company and of other types of shares. The duty is also imposed on voluntary capital contributions made by shareholders to the company and on the transfer of a majority shareholding in a 'shell company'.

A ***reduced rate*** of 1% is levied on the issuance of participation rights or the increase of their par value in connection with a merger, transformation or splitting of a company, and on the transfer of a non-resident company to Switzerland.

A 0.9% duty is levied on the issuance of ***investment fund units***.

Contributions in kind are measured by their actual market value.

Normally, voluntary capital contributions to a company are taxable only if made by a shareholder. In the event a shareholder waives his claims against the company to cover corporate losses, the Federal Tax Administration may waive the Issue Stamp Duty.

2. TRANSFER STAMP DUTY

The Transfer Stamp Duty applies to transfers of securities for consideration if one of the contracting parties or one of the intermediaries is a resident *'security dealer'* ('Effektenhändler'/'commerçant de titres').

Taxable securities include bonds, debentures, certificates of deposit, shares in a joint stock corporation and limited liability company, profit-sharing certificates, investment fund units, bills of exchange, promissory notes and other notes of any kind issued by a resident as well as certificates of participation in such securities. The sale of securities or their economic or functional counterparts issued by non-residents is also subject to the duty.

'Security dealers' as defined by the Stamp Duty Act are basically (1) individuals, legal entities and partnerships who are professionally engaged in the purchase and sale of securities; (2) companies managing investment funds and depositary banks; and (3) joint stock corporations, limited liability companies and cooperative associations whose primary statutory purpose is investing in other companies and whose statutory share capital is at least 500,000 Swiss francs or which have more than one-half of their assets, according to their most recent balance sheets, invested in taxable securities within the terms of the Stamp Duty Act (shares etc.) and which have assets aggregating at least one million francs.

The rates are 0.15% on securities issued by *residents* and 0.3% on those issued by *nonresidents* (except for certain securities at three months' date for which the rates are 0.1 respectively 0.2%). For certain transactions, only one-half of the applicable duty is payable (for instance for the conclusion of a transaction outside of Switzerland with a non-resident bank or stock exchange agent). Primary liability for the payment of the duty rests on the resident 'security dealer'.

The Stamp Duty Act also provides for several transactions which are *exempt* from the duty, such as the issuance of shares which are subject to the Issue Stamp Duty and the purchase of bills of exchange, notes, participation interests in a loan, etc. by banks for their own account.

The Stamp Duty Act is supplemented by detailed Regulations issued by the Federal Tax Administration.

D. Taxes on Individuals

(This chapter provides only a very brief summary.)

1. PERSONS SUBJECT TO TAX

All individuals having a residence ('Wohnsitz'/'domicile') in Switzerland are subject to the *unlimited Federal taxation* on worldwide income and net wealth. The same tax status applies to individuals with a habitual abode in Switzerland if they are gainfully employed or if they stay there – without earning any income – for 6 months or more or own and occupy a house there for 3 months or more. The only *exemptions* from the Federal taxation are income and capital related to immovable property and permanent establishments situated outside of Switserland and income and net wealth items exempted by virtue of a tax treaty.

Under the *cantonal* tax laws maintaining a habitual abode in connection with gainful employment normally subjects an individual to unlimited tax liability with respect to cantonal and municipal taxes. An individual who is not gainfully employed is subject to tax in most cantons after living there for 3 months.

In line with Swiss civil law, the tax laws are based on the principle of the *'family unit'* by aggregating the income of a married woman with that of her husband in whom all her fiscal rights and duties are vested (tax substitution).

2. COMPUTATION OF INCOME

2.a. Income

In principle, *all* gross income, whether received in cash or in kind, is subject to tax (except the aforementioned exemptions and, in some tax jurisdictions, capital gains). It includes earned income, income from the operation of a business, rental income, dividends, interest, annuities, pensions (private and social security) and all other retirement income. Certain annuity and retirement income is reduced by 20% or 40%, depending on the recipient's contribution to the cost.

The amount of exempted income and capital (except capital gains) is ordinarily taken into account when calculating the amount of tax on the remaining income and capital (exemption with progression).

Some cantons withhold taxes (Federal, cantonal and municipal) from *expatriates'* employment income. In other tax jurisdictions, however, the ordinary assessment procedure applies if income exceeds a certain amount, or its application may be requested subsequent to the withholding of the taxes.

Aliens residing in Switzerland who are not carrying on a lucrative activity may – on the Federal level and in some cantons – apply for the *lump-sum tax* ('Pauschalsteuer'/'impôt à forfait'). This is a special method of computing tax based on the taxpayer's living expenses, generally measured by the rental value of his living quarters and other visible types of expenditures incurred by the taxpayer and his dependants. Special rules cover Swiss source income and treaty favoured income. In addition some tax treaties contain 'anti-lump-sum tax' clauses.

2.b. Capital gains

The taxation of capital gains is one of the more complex aspects of the Swiss tax structure particularly because of the difficulty of defining the tax subject and the widely differing statutory patterns.

On the *Federal* level, capital gains realized by an individual in the normal course of managing his private fortune are, in principle, not treated as taxable income. However, capital gains realized on the alienation of movable and immovable property may be taxable if such gains result from the taxpayer's professional activity or a principal or accessory occupation, even if derived from causal and isolated transactions. The borderline between exempt and taxable capital gains can be a hairsbreadth.

The *cantonal* treatment of capital gains realised on private movable assets varies considerably. One group of cantons exempts them from taxation, other cantons include such gains in the ordinary income tax, and a third group taxes private capital gains separately from ordinary income. Finally, in 1971 one canton introduced the taxation of 'participation gains' levied on gains from the alienation and liquidation of corporate holding if the ownership interest of the taxpayer amounted to at least 20% of the paid-up capital or of the voting stock.

Capital gains realized on private *immovable property* are taxed in all cantons (partly also by the municipalities). The majority of cantons imposes a special immovable property gains tax on such gains ('Grundstückgewinnsteuer'/'impôt sur les gains immobiliers'). The tax rates usually depend on the amount of gain, the location of the property, and the length of time the seller has held the property.

2.c. Exemptions and deductions

All tax laws grant certain *exemptions* depending on the civil status of the taxpayer. For instance, for Federal tax purposes a married couple has an

allowance of 2,500 francs plus 1,200 francs for each child or dependant.
Each canton has different rules for itemized deductions. Generally, *deductions* are allowed up to a certain maximum amount for transportation expenses to and from work, the excess expenses with regard to meals not taken at home and insurance and compulsory old age insurance premiums. Maintenance expenses for immovable property and loan interest are also deductible.

3. RATES OF TAX

The *Federal* income tax is levied at graduated rates rising to a maximum rate of 11.5% (reached at an income of over 392,000 francs for married individuals). In addition to the Federal tax, a *cantonal* (and municipal) tax is imposed at graduated rates.
Church and *poll taxes* may also be levied. As in the case of corporations, the cantonal (and municipal) tax is generally a heavier burden on the individual than the Federal tax.
The *net-wealth* of an individual is not taxed on the Federal level, but all cantons (and municipalities) impose a capital tax at either a graduated or a flat rate.
The following table shows the *combined tax charge* (Federal, cantonal and municipal taxes) of a married employed couple without children with aggregate annual incomes of 50,000 and 100,000 francs and a net wealth of 500,000 francs residing in the capital of the following cantons:

Canton	*50,000*	*100,000*
Zurich	8,036	24,741
Bern	10,839	27,695
Zug	7,473	19,754
Basel-City	10,989	28,471
Grisons	9,339	24,123
Geneva	10,843	27,267

(Source: Steuerbelastung in der Schweiz, 1979).

4. SUCCESSION AND GIFT TAXES

No Federal succession or gift taxes are levied. Succession and gift taxes of various sorts are imposed, however, in all but one canton (Schwyz). Two cantons do not tax gifts (Lucerne and Solothurn). Most cantons levy an inheritance tax, others an estate tax or an estate and inheritance tax. Within a few cantons the municipalities also tax successions (Lucerne, Fribourg, Grisons and Vaud).
The rates, which vary from canton to canton, are progressive and graduated depending on the degree of relationship between deceased and heir (or legatee), the value of the inheritance or estate and, in some cantons, the net wealth of the beneficiary.

As a rule, the right to tax inheritances and estates belongs to the canton in which the *deceased* had his *last residence* at the time of his death; the residence of the beneficiary is not relevant. Immovable property is regularly taxable in the situs canton. With respect to gift taxes movable property is subject to tax in the canton where the *donor* is resident.
The tax rates may range from a few percentage points (next-of-kin) to as high as 60% (no blood relationship).
Some cantons grant a full or partial exemption from tax to surviving spouses and descendants. Two cantons (Geneva and Vaud) apply reduced rates on resident aliens in specific cases.
Switzerland has concluded *succession tax treaties* with Austria, Denmark, Finland, France, Germany (Federal Republic), the Netherlands, Norway, Sweden, the United Kingdom and the United States. However, some of the treaties do not provide full relief from double taxation.
In the absence of a treaty provision so providing, the deduction of or a credit for foreign succession taxes is not available (except in the Canton of Vaud which grants a deduction).

E. Indirect Taxation

The most significant indirect tax other than the Stamp Duties (see section C) is the *Federal Turnover Tax* ('Warenumsatzsteuer'/'impôt sur le chiffre d'affaires'). Introduced in 1941 as a temporary emergency measure to meet the budgetary deficit, it has developed into an important source of revenue for the Federal treasury, accounting for more than 25% of the total Federal fiscal revenue. The Turnover Tax is also levied in the Principality of Liechtenstein by the Swiss Federal Tax Administration; the Liechtenstein Government shares the revenues collected. The proposed *Value Added Tax* (which has been designed to offset the declining revenues from customs duties) was rejected in two popular compulsory referenda in 1977 and 1979.
The Turnover Tax is a single-stage sales tax on domestic turnover and on imports of movable goods. The standard rates are 5.6%[5] for ***retail deliveries*** and 8.4%[5] for *wholesale deliveries*. Services are not taxable. Certain goods such as food and foodstuffs, agricultural and medical supplies, newspapers and most books are exempt.
On domestic transactions only *'wholesalers'* ('Grossisten'/'grossistes') are liable for the Turnover Tax. Wholesalers are basically

1. producers with annual sales (including self-consumption) in excess of 35,000 francs;
2. dealers (merchants) with annual sales (including self-consumption) in excess of 35,000 francs provided that at least one half of the sales represent wholesale deliveries; and
3. dealers in used products (secondhand goods, etc.) with annual sales in excess of 35,000 francs whether or not the sales are wholesale deliveries.

All of the wholesalers must register with the Federal Tax Administration.

5. The rates will be increased to 6.2% and 9.3% respectively, as from October 1, 1982.

Other firms which are predominantly retailers may request permission to be registered as a wholesaler on a voluntary basis.
Generally, the Turnover Tax is paid by the last registered wholesaler making a sale to a non-registered company or to an individual. A wholesale sale to another registered purchaser is not taxable if the purchaser provides the seller with its registration number, unless the purchase is made for its own use. Similarly, if goods are manufactured for internal use, the manufacturer-user is subject to the Turnover Tax.
The Turnover Tax is territorially connected with deliveries which are exclusively domestic. Thus, the moment of the actual delivery is decisive. The nationality or residence of the wholesaler and the location of its head office, place of management or permanent establishment are immaterial. For Turnover Tax purposes, the territory of Switzerland means the Swiss customs area, including the Principality of Liechtenstein and Campione d'Italia, but excluding customs-free bonded warehouses and areas ('Zollausschlussgebiete'/'enclaves douanières'). Direct export deliveries are exempt. Exemption of a wholesaler's domestic delivery for export is, however, granted only upon satisfaction of specific requirements.
The taxpayer must file a quarterly return and pay the Turnover Tax within 30 days after the end of each quarter.

F. Incentives

Switzerland offers a relatively limited potential for investment in new manufacturing operations mainly because of its shortage of labour, high labour costs (in 1979 Switzerland was fifth among 14 major industrial nations), restrictions on the acquisition of real estate by non-residents and a restrictive policy in granting work permits to aliens.
Only few genuine tax incentives are obtainable. To eliminate undue intercantonal competition for new industrial enterprises and for other attractive taxpayers, a *Concordat* between all Swiss cantons was concluded in 1948. The Concordat prohibits the conclusion of tax agreements between cantons (and their political subdivisions) and taxpayers. However, tax reliefs are permitted for new industrial enterprises (for less than ten years) and public service enterprises and the lump-sum taxation of individuals (see section D 2.a) to the extent which such reliefs are statutorily authorized. Special tax rules designed for some types of companies are not considered as incentives within the terms of the Concordat (see section K).
The tax laws of some cantons provide tax reliefs for new industries if their settlement in the canton is economically and regionally desirable.
Incentives are, as a rule, only available for settling new industries in 'less developed' and usually remote areas. The extent of tax incentives is negotiated on a case by case basis.

G. *Social Security System*

1. The Swiss social security system is based on '*three pillars*': The 'Federal Old Age and Survivors Insurance' scheme provides the basic insurance. When enacted by the Federal Parliament, the second pillar will be a compulsory professional insurance plan. Finally, the third pillar is left to each individual (life insurance etc.).

2. The '*Federal* 'Old Age *and Survivors Insurance*' plan ('Alters- und Hinterbliebenenversicherung' or 'AHV'/'assurance-vieillesse et survivants' or 'AVS') is a compulsory national pension plan. In principle, all persons permanently resident or gainfully employed in Switzerland and Swiss citizens employed abroad by a Swiss employer are subject to the insurance plan. Aliens gainfully employed in Switzerland are required to participate unless their employment lasts less than three months and their salaries are paid by a non-resident employer (or unless the person enjoys tax immunity under international law). Aliens participating in a compulsory pension plan of another country may be exempted if the contributions payable under both pension plans would constitute an unreasonable burden for the insured. The 'Old Age and Survivors Insurance' is financed primarily from compulsory contributions from insured persons and from employers at a present aggregate rate of 8.4% of the participant's salary. Self-employed persons contribute 7.8% of their earned income.
The benefits provided by this insurance plan include pensions for men at 65 years of age and women at 62, widows pensions regardless of age if with dependent children or if at least 40 years old, and orphans pensions.
Whereas the old age pensions are determined with reference to a maximum salary (at present 37,800 francs), the contributions are not linked to a salary ceiling but levied on the whole salary (contributions paid on amounts exceeding 37,800 francs, therefore, have the character of a disguised tax).

3. In addition, there is a compulsory '*Federal Disability Insurance Plan*' ('Invalidenversicherung' or 'IV'/'assurance-invalidité' or 'AI') financed by a contribution equal to 1% of the salary and a obligatory '*Compensation Plan in favour of Persons in Compulsory Military Service*' ('Erwerbsersatzordnung für Wehrpflichtige'/'régime des allocations aux militaires'), supported by a contribution equal to 0.6% of the salary. Alien employees are also subject to these plans. Under both plans, half of the contribution must be paid by the employer.

4. Thus, the aggregate premium for the first pillar of insurance amounts to 10% of which one half must be paid by the employer. The total premium for self-employed persons is 9.4%.

5. Persons who are gainfully employed are also covered by a *compulsory unemployment insurance.*
One half of the contribution of 0.5%[6] (payable on a monthly salary of up to 3,900 francs) is again borne by the employer.

6. This contribution is reduced to 0.3% as from January 1, 1982.

H. Other Taxes and Duties

Historically, *indirect* taxes were levied by the Confederation and *direct* taxes by the cantons and the municipalities. With the adoption of the Federal income and capital taxes this rule ceased. But indirect taxes imposed by the political subdivisions have remained relatively insignificant.
The Confederation, cantons and municipalities do levy a variety of other taxes and duties such as taxes on certain alcoholic beverages, registration taxes, motor vehicle taxes, entertainment taxes, taxes on visitors, poll taxes and Military Service Exemption Tax. These levies are ordinarily of little importance for normal business operations.
The following two levies, however, may have a certain relevance for the business community:

1. IMMOVABLE PROPERTY TRANSFER TAXES

The cantons and some municipalities levy a tax or fee on the transfer of immovable property at rates usually not exceeding 3% of the purchase price of the fair market value of the property.
Subject to the tax or fee are also inter vivos transfers of the title to immovable property and transactions that are economically equivalent to such transfers whether or not any gain is obtained as a result of the transaction (therefore to be distinguished from the immovable property gains taxes as outlined in section A.2.b.). The transfer of shares in real estate companies does, in some cantons, also give rise to a liability for this tax.

2. CUSTOMS DUTIES

The power to levy import and export duties ('Zölle'/'droits de douane') is exclusively vested in the Confederation. Most of the customs duties are import duties. Export duties are levied only on calf rennet bags, ash and residues containing metals or metallic compounds and certain machining waste and scrap. The import duties are, as a rule, assessed on the basis of gross weight (including packing). A statistical fee is levied at the time of import clearance (3% of the amount of the Customs charges). The Constitution requires that the rates on imports of raw materials for industry and agriculture and the commodities necessary to life be as low as possible whereas articles of luxury be subject to the heaviest duties. The rates are set forth in detail in the 1959 Tariff Law which systematically specifies the items based on the Customs Cooperation Councils Nomenclature (CCCN).
With the participation of Switzerland in the *General Agreement on Tariffs and Trade (GATT)* and the *European Free Trade Association (EFTA)* and particularly with the conclusion of the Free Trade Convention with the *European Economic Community (EEC)* on July 22, 1972, the revenues derived from customs duties have substantially decreased (in 1979 they amounted to 23% of the total Federal fiscal revenues).

The Principality of Liechtenstein is a part of the customs territory of Switzerland by virtue of a treaty concluded in 1923. The Swiss customs territory does, on the other hand, not include bonded warehouses ('Zollfreilager'/'dépôts francs').

I. *Double Taxation Treaties*

1. LIST OF TAX TREATIES

Australia	income	28. 2.80
Austria	income and capital estates and inheritances	30. 1.74 30. 1.74
Belgium	income and capital	28. 8.78
Canada	income	20. 8.76
Denmark	income and capital estates and inheritances	23.11.73 23.11.73
Finland	income and capital estates and inheritances	27.12.56/27. 5.70 27.12.56
France	income and capital estates and inheritances	9. 9.66/ 3.12.69 23.12.53
Germany (Federal Republic)	income and capital estates and inheritances	11. 8.71/30.11.78 30.11.78
Hungary	income and capital	9. 4.81
Ireland	income and capital	8.11.66
Italy	income and capital frontier workers	9. 3.76/28. 4.78 3.10.74
Japan	income	19. 1.71
Korea (Republic)	income	12. 2.80
Malaysia	income	30.12.74
Netherlands	income and capital estates and inheritances	12.11.51/22. 6.66 12.11.51
New Zealand	income	6. 6.80
Norway	income and capital estates and inheritances	7.12.56 7.12.56
Pakistan	income	30.12.59/15. 6.62
Portugal	income and capital	26. 9.74
Sweden	income and capital estates and inheritances estate and inheritances	7. 5.65/ 7. 2.79 16.10.48 7. 2.79 (not yet in force)

Singapore	income and capital	25.11.75
South Africa	income	3. 7.67
Spain	income and capital	26. 4.66
Trinidad and Tobago	income	1. 2.73
United Kingdom	income	30. 9.54 (only for certain territories)
	income	8.12.77
	estates and inheritances	12. 6.56
United States of America	income	24. 5.51
	estates and inheritances	9. 7.51

2. SWISS DOMESTIC AND TREATY MEASURES AGAINST ABUSE OF TREATY BENEFITS[7]

2.a. In 1962, the Swiss Federal Council issued a *'Decree concerning Measures against the Improper Use of Tax Treaties concluded by the Confederation'* ('1962 Decree'). The rules set forth in the 1962 Decree are designed to curtail abuses that surface in connection with claiming treaty benefits in combination with preferential tax rules under domestic law.

The 1962 Decree enunciates the general rule that treaty advantages (relief from foreign taxes withheld at source) may not benefit persons who are *not entitled* thereto such as recipients that are not bona fide residents in Switzerland, or residing recipients that do not have a beneficial interest in the income, or recipients that are not liable for Swiss taxes.

In addition, the 1962 Decree bars *'abusive'* claims for tax treaty relief. A claim by a resident individual, entity or partnership is abusive if a substantial part of the treaty relief would directly or indirectly benefit persons not entitled to the treaty relief. Under this rule, the 1962 Decree prohibits any relief from foreign withholding taxes particularly if the resident recipient falls in one of the following categories:

- if more than *one half* of the treaty-favoured foreign income is used (directly or indirectly) to satisfy claims of persons not entitled to treaty benefits ('pass-through'-companies);
- if an entity substantially controlled by non-residents (by participation or in some other way) does not distribute yearly at least *25%* of the treaty-favoured gross income as dividends ('accumulation'-companies);
- if the interest-bearing credit account is greater than *six times* the amount of share capital (plus open reserves) or if debts bear interest exceeding the rates periodically fixed by the Federal Tax Administration;
- if a resident receives the income only on a *fiduciary* basis;
- if the treaty income benefits a *family foundation* controlled by non-residents;
- if the recipient is a *partnership* with a seat but without exercising a trade or business, in Switzerland.

7. For a detailed analysis in English see Walter Meier, Swiss Tax Treaty Anti-abuse Rules, Tax Planning International Review, Volume 8 (1981), No. 12, page 15 et seq.

2.b. The tax treaties concluded by Switzerland with Belgium, the Federal Republic of Germany, France and Italy contain similar ***anti-abuse clauses*** and, in addition, rules directed against companies enjoying cantonal (and municipal) preferential tax treatment. These treaty clauses apply equally to taxes withheld at source and levied by ordinary assessment in the other treaty country.

J. Schedule of Withholding Taxes

Dividends paid by a company which is a resident of Switzerland and certain categories of ***interest*** (see section B 1.b.) arising in Switzerland are subject to the Federal Anticipatory Tax at a rate of 35% withheld at source.
No Federal withholding tax is levied on ***royalties.***
The tax treaty relief and non-refundable Swiss taxes for residents of the following countries are listed below:

	Dividends		*Interest*	
	Relief	*Non-Refundable Tax*	*Relief*	*Non-Refundable Tax*
Belgium	20	15	25[8]	10[8]
Participation of at least 25%	25	10		
Canada	20	15	20[8]	15[8]
Denmark	35	0	35	0
France	30	5	25	10
Certain participations of at least 20%	20	15		
Germany (Federal Republic)	20[8]	15[8]	35[8]	0[8]
Greece[9]	0	35	0	35
Ireland	25	10	35	0
Participations of at least 25%	35	0		
Italy	20	15	22.5	12.5
Japan	20	15	25	10
Participations of at least 25%	25	10		
Luxembourg[9]	0	35	0	35
Netherlands	20	15	30	5
Participations of at least 25% (anti-abuse clause)	35	0		

8. For special cases see tax treaty rules.
9. No tax treaty concluded.

	Dividends		Interest	
	Relief	*Non-Refund-able Tax*	*Relief*	*Non-Refund-able Tax*
Norway	30	5	30	5
Portugal	20	15	25	10
Participations of at least 25%	25	10		
Spain	20	15	25	10
Participations of at least 25%	25	10		
United Kingdom	20	15	35	0
Participations of at least 25%	30	5		
United States of America	20	15	30	5
Participations of at least 95% (anti-abuse clause and additional requirements)	30	5		

K. Special Types of Companies

1. PARTICIPATION (HOLDING) COMPANIES

1.a. General

A participation (holding) company is, in a broader sense, a company that is holding substantial equity participations in other companies. Although there is no harmonized legal terminology in this regard, two types of participation companies are ordinarily distinguished:

– *Holding companies:* A company qualifies as a holding company – sometimes the term 'pure' holding company is used – when its exclusive or primary purpose is the holding and the administration of substantial equity participations in other (resident or non-resident) companies.
– *Mixed participation companies:* A mixed participation (or holding) company may be defined as one that owns substantial equity participations in other (resident or non-resident) companies, but that also carries on industrial, manufacturing or commercial operations. Both types of participation companies enjoy a special tax treatment which depends on the tax jurisdiction and the size of the investment in participations.

1.b. Federal direct tax

The *holding company* and the *mixed participation company* are entitled to a reduction of the income tax on that part of the income which is derived from qualified participations. To qualify for the *holding 'reduction'* pursuant to the Federal Direct Tax Act (art. 59), the recipient company must hold participa-

tions with a *'substantial influence'* ('massgebender Einfluss'/'influence déterminante'). A participation is deemed to be 'substantial' if, at the beginning of the tax liability, it amounts to at least 20% of the share capital or 2 million Swiss francs in the share capital of the distributing company.
The income tax payable by a *participation company* is reduced in the same proportion that its net income from qualified participations bears to its total gross income. Therefore, if the entire income of the participation company is derived from qualifying participations, in principle, no Federal income tax is payable. For operating companies which also hold substantial participations the total Federal income tax is reduced roughly in the same proportion that the income derived from qualifying participations bears to the total gross income.
Income from *qualifying participations* is basically dividends, stock dividends, extraordinary distributions such as bonuses, liquidation dividends and constructive dividends. Total gross income consists, as a general rule, of profits derived from the operational activity after deducting business expenses allocable exclusively to that activity, income from participations, interest, rent, royalties, commissions, capital gains, revaluation gains and other income.
No reduction is available for *capital tax* purposes.

1.c. Cantonal taxation

All cantons except one exempt the (pure) holding company from income taxation. Some cantonal tax laws require that the participations or the management of participations be 'exclusive'. Most cantons exempt holding companies from income taxation if the holding of participations is merely a 'primary' or 'predominant' purpose. The Zurich tax practice, for instance, requires that at least 75% of the income must be derived from qualified participations and at least 75% of the assets consist of such participations. Some cantons set forth lower minima.
Mixed participation companies under most cantonal tax laws enjoy identical or similar tax reductions as outlined above with respect to Federal tax purposes.
In a majority of cantons, a *capital tax* reduction is provided for holding companies and in some jurisdictions also for mixed participation companies.
The special tax treatment granted to holding and participation companies is primarily designed to avoid triple taxation of profits derived from participations (because the distributing company has already paid taxes on its net income, and another tax is charged to the ultimate shareholder). It is therefore inaccurate to refer to the 'holding exemption' or 'participation reduction' as a tax 'privilege'.

2. DOMICILIARY COMPANIES

A domiciliary company generally is defined as an interposed company that has merely its seat (place of registration) in one of the Swiss cantons but that does not engage in any trade or business within Switzerland.
Domiciliary companies are frequently used as a non-resident's legal entity to hold intangible assets such as patents, trademarks, copyrights, or securities, or

to own real property located outside Switzerland, or to engage in a business or to perform services exclusively outside this country.

On the *Federal* level, domiciliary companies are fully subject to the income and capital taxation like other companies (see section A). However, a number of *cantons* grant special treatment to domiciliary companies by which such entities are either exempt from cantonal (and municipal) income taxation or taxed only on a certain percentage of the income or at a reduced rate. Special treatment is normally denied if the company has its own office or its own staff in the canton, but a few cantons permit a limited office and staff to be present.

Some cantons permit domiciliary companies to carry on certain operations in Switzerland with the result that income derived from Swiss sources is normally taxed and non-Swiss income items are taxed at a reduced rate. Normally, the majority of the corporate stock of such a 'mixed company' must be held by non-residents and only a relatively small percentage of the overall income may be derived from Swiss sources for the special treatment to be available.

The cantonal *capital tax* is usually levied at a reduced rate.

Internationally, it is important to bear in mind that the *tax treaties* concluded by Switzerland with Belgium, France, the Federal Republic of Germany and Italy exclude Swiss companies controlled by non-residents from the treaty benefits on interest and royalties if such entities do not pay full cantonal and municipal taxes on such income derived from sources within the respective treaty country.

In addition, a number of countries have enacted domestic legal measures to nullify or penalize any tax benefits obtained by interposing or using such types of entities such as the *'Subpart F'-rules* in the United States and the *'Aussensteuergesetz'* in the Federal Republic of Germany.

3. SERVICE COMPANIES

The term 'service companies' is generally used for companies that do not exercise a commerical or industrial activity of their own but perform administrative, financial, marketing or auxiliary services or any other assistance for affiliated companies located outside Switzerland. Such a company may have its own staff and its own office facilities in Switzerland.

The service companies are subject to special rules with respect to the *computation* of the taxable net income. They are taxed on a minimum income equivalent to that which an independent company would earn under identical or similar circumstances. For *Federal* tax purposes, the taxable net income deemed to be derived from rendering such services amounts, as a rule, to at least one tenth of the total expenses incurred in connection with such service activities or to at least one sixth of the salaries paid by the service company. Under particular circumstances, the tax authorities may also determine a minimum net income. Additional income such as royalties or interest derived from investments has to be added to this minimum income (see Circular Letter issued by the Federal Tax Administration on June 1, 1960).

Some *cantons* request a higher minimum net profit ranging between 10 and 20% of the total expenses.

With respect to those cantons in which taxes are not a deductible expense, the taxes paid in the relevant fiscal year must be added to the minimum net income.

IV. LABOUR ASPECTS

A. Principles of the Law on Employment

1. As a rule an individual employment contract need not follow any particular form. However, certain provisions are valid only if agreed upon in writing (such as prohibitions against competition following termination of the employment relationship).
If the term of the employment contract is not for a fixed period of time, the first month is considered a probationary period, unless determined otherwise by agreement or a standard or collective employment contract.

2. No minimal salaries and wages are required by law. However, such standards have widely been agreed upon by collective bargaining.
According to Federal law, the employer must grant the employee at least two weeks vacation. The cantons can extend the minimum up to three weeks; and in practice three to four weeks vacation are standard.

3. If the employment relationship has been entered into for a fixed period of time, it terminates without notice upon the expiration of such a period.
If the relationship has not been entered into for a fixed period of time and if such a period is not evident from the purpose of the work, notice may be given by either of the contracting parties. Notice periods must not differ for the employer and the employee.
If an employment relationship has lasted less than one year and unless otherwise determined by agreement, standard or collective employment contract, it may be terminated effective at the end of the month following the date of notice. If the employment relationship has lasted more than one but less than ten years, the notice period is two months. After ten years of service, it is three months. However, the employer cannot terminate the employment relationship during compulsory Swiss military or civil defence service, during the first four weeks of the employee's inability to work due to illness or accident not caused by the employee's fault, during eight weeks before and after child-birth and in certain other cases.
For valid reasons both the employer and the employee may at any time terminate the employment relationship without notice. A valid reason is considered to be any circumstances under which the terminating party cannot in good faith be expected to continue the employment relationship.
Severance pay is due upon termination of the employment relationship only if the employee is at least fifty years of age and has been employed for twenty or more years. Even in this case the employer is not obliged to give severance pay if a personnel welfare institution must make future welfare payments which exceed the contributions to be made by the employee.

B. Labour Procedures

Many collective employment contracts have been concluded between employers or their associations on one side and employees' associations or labour unions on the other one. The provisions of such collective employment contracts concerning the entering into, the content and termination of the individual employment relationship are directly applicable to the employers and employees organized in the participating associations or labour unions. They may not be eliminated by stipulation unless the collective employment contract provides otherwise.
Under certain conditions both the Federal as well as cantonal governments can declare that the terms of a collective employment contract are applicable to all employers or employees of a business sector or profession even if they are not members of the contracting parties. This unusual power is not often used.

C. Works Council, Co-determination, Compulsory Profit Sharing and Pension Plans

1. No law requires the institution of works councils. However, works councils are often installed pursuant to collective employment contracts. The scope of their authority is usually limited to questions concerning the working conditions.

2. Although there has been some discussion, no scheme of compulsory co-determination exists in Switzerland. Some years ago two proposals for the introduction of co-determination were rejected in a public vote.

3. No compulsory profit-sharing schemes exist in Switzerland. Pension plans are not compulsory. However, they are typically provided by Swiss companies.

D. Residence and Work Permits[10]

1. The economic benefit resulting from the presence of non-resident enterprises through resident subsidiaries or branches in Switzerland is widely recognized. In view of the relatively high proportion of resident aliens (1979: 884,000 compared to a total population of 6,314,000). The Swiss Government is nonetheless under sociopolitical pressure to apply a restrictive policy in granting permits and to stabilize the number of resident aliens.

10. A Bill for a new 'Aliens Law' ('Ausländergesetz'/'Loi sur les étrangers') is pending before the Federal Parliament. Certain rules, particularly with respect to stay, residence and permanent residence are, therefore, subject to modifications.

2. Visitors *not engaged in a gainful employment* and staying not longer than three months or, in case of repeated visits, not longer than six months within one year in Switzerland do not need a permit. In case of an extension of a visit over these limitations, the visitor must apply for permission to prolong his stay.
Persons visiting Switzerland for *business* or other *lucrative purposes* must ordinarily apply for a permit if they stay in Switzerland eight days or longer within three months or, in case of repeated visits, thirty-two days or longer within one year. This permit is ordinarily obtainable without difficulty.

3. A more cumbersome procedure is applicable to aliens intending to exercise as *residents* a *lucrative activity* in Switzerland. The prospective employer must apply for a *work permit* ('Arbeitsbewilligung'/'permis de travail'). The system is based on regulations providing for cantonal and Federal quotas generally over a twelve-month period (as from November 1, 1979 7,000 respectively 3,000 permits). The permit policy is quantitatively restrictive but endeavours to make a qualitative improvement of the labour market. Apart from purely national aspects, there are several criteria for granting permits. One concerns management staff, qualified experts or employees with a key function inside a company whose presence in Switzerland is likely to create job opportunities for a considerable number of resident employees. Another important consideration for easier access of new enterprises is evidence that the establishment or expansion of operations be of significant cantonal or regional importance.
The regulations also provide for certain exceptions from applying for a regular residence permit. One relates to personnel that is employed In Switzerland for no longer than three months in one year, enabling non-resident companies to transfer temporarily key personnel to Switzerland for setting-up a Swiss subsidiary or branch or for control functions within Switzerland. Another exception covers additional residence permits for a period of up to twelve months with respect to executives or highly qualified experts of internationally integrated companies for specific purposes. Generally, an intensive job rotation is disadvantageous because of the necessity to undergo the permit procedure basically in each case (an entity has no basic right to a share of a given quota).

4. Upon granting of the work permit, the employer must apply for a *residence permit* ('Aufenthaltsbewilligung'/'permis de séjour') valid ordinarily for one year. The residence permit does not necessarily cover the employee's family.

5. A permit for *permanent residence* ('Niederlassungsbewilligung'/'permis d'établissement') is obtainable only after an extended stay in Switzerland (ordinarily ten years, for nationals of certain countries five years).

V. REFERENCE MATERIAL

1. *List of Abbreviations*

AG	Aktiengesellschaft (Joint Stock Corporation)
AHV	Alters- und Hinterbliebenenversicherung (Old Age and Survivors Insurance)
AI	Assurance-invalidité (Disability Insurance Plan)
AVS	Assurance-vieillesse et survivants (Old Age and Survivors Insurance)
FTA	Federal Tax Administration
GmbH	Gesellschaft mit beschränkter Haftung (Limited Liability Company)
IV	Invalidenversicherung (Disability Insurance Plan)
SA	Société anonyme (Joint Stock Corporation)
Sàrl	Société à responsabilité limitée (Limited Liability Company)

2. *Statutes*

- Obligationenrecht/Code des obligations, of March 30, 1911, as amended
- Wehrsteuerbeschluss/Arrêté concernant l'impôt pour la défense nationale, of December 9, 1940, as amended
- Bundesgesetz über die Verrechnungssteuer/Loi fédérale sur l'impôt anticipé, of October 13, 1965, as amended
- Bundesgesetz über die Stempelabgaben (StG/Loi fédérale sur les droits de timbre (LT), of June 27, 1973, as amended
- Bundesratsbeschluss betreffend Massnahmen gegen die ungerechtfertigte Inanspruchnahme von Doppelbesteuerungsabkommen des Bundes/Arrêté du conseil fédéral instituant des mesures contre l'utilisation sans cause légitime des conventions conclues par la Confédération en vue d'éviter les doubles impositions, of December 14, 1962, as amended.

Other statutes are referred to in the text.

3. *Bibliography*

- Taxation in Switzerland, World Tax Series, Harvard Law School, International Tax Program, Chicago 1976
- Swiss Contract Law (English Translation of Selected Official Texts), Swiss-American Chamber of Commerce, Zurich 1977
- Swiss Corporation Law (English Translation of Official Text), American Chamber of Commerce in Switzerland, Zurich 1974.

United Kingdom

N. Fox Bassett
S.J. Hood

I. INTRODUCTION

Anyone contemplating the United Kingdom ('UK') for some business enterprise, whether wholly-owned or in some form of joint venture, has the benefit of a well established system of law in the business field and one that has stood the test of experience for foreign and domestic enterprises alike. Much of the legislation on company law and taxation has developed over the last century alongside the common law evolved by the courts. The significant growth of legislation in the business field has, however, been a feature of modern times, developing to meet the changing needs and sophistication of business.

The constraints of size dictate that this Chapter concentrates largely on company, fiscal and labour law matters. It follows the structure and headings common to other chapters of this book. The legal position described in this Chapter is at 1st May 1981. The text does, however, take note of some further legislation in 1981, particularly the Companies Act 1981 and the Finance Act 1981.

The term 'United Kingdom' comprises England and Wales, Scotland and Northern Ireland, while the term 'Great Britain' refers to all parts of the UK except Northern Ireland. For all practical purposes the courts of the three countries in interpreting the laws apply the same principles, and the Appeal Committee of the House of Lords is the final court of appeal for all of the UK.

The company legislation of Great Britain is for the most part contained in the Companies Act 1948 as amended by the Companies Acts 1967, 1976, 1980 and 1981. The 1980 Act was passed in order, inter alia, to bring English law into line with the Second Directive on Company Law of the Council of the EEC. The Companies Act 1981 which received the Royal Assent on 30th October 1981, implements, inter alia, the EEC Fourth Directive on Company accounts. It is to come into effect progressively and is expected to be in force in its entirety by the end of April 1982. There are some minor variations in the application of the Companies Acts to Scotland. Northern Ireland has its own company legislation, which is almost identical with the 1948 Act and certain provisions of the 1980 Act.

Further company legislation is contained in Section 9 of the European Communities Act 1972. This section was intended to bring company law in Great Britain into conformity with the requirements of the First Directive on Company Law of the Council of the EEC. This Chapter does not deal with the other EEC Directives on Company Law.

Each of the countries of the UK has its own Companies Registry and Registrar in London, Cardiff, Edinburgh and in Belfast respectively.

The fiscal legislation enacted by the Parliament at Westminster applies throughout the UK, except that Northern Ireland has its own stamp duty legislation.

The Channel Islands and the Isle of Man, while subject to the overriding authority of the Crown and the UK Parliament, have their own legislatures and laws.

The exchange control legislation (although presently of no practical effect) applies uniformly throughout the UK, the Channel Islands and the Isle of Man.

It is a fundamental principle of the laws of the UK that a company on being incorporated under the Companies Acts acquires a legal personality distinct from its shareholders. None of the laws of the UK however attributes to a branch of a company a legal personality distinct from that of the company of which it forms part.

Although there are public companies (in which the general public participate as shareholders) and private companies, the private company is the vehicle which is selected by most foreign enterprises wishing to establish a separate entity in the UK, whether wholly owned or in a joint venture. Partnership (not enjoying separate legal personality) is not often the chosen vehicle, and there has not been any apparent need for the various alternative forms of vehicle to be found in some countries, like the Federal Republic of Germany, on the continent of Europe.

The question whether a foreign company proposing to extend its activities to the UK should operate through a branch or a subsidiary (assuming it is not engaging in a joint venture) will in many instances be determined by policy, commercial, and, not least, taxation considerations.

II. THE LEGAL FRAMEWORK

A. *The Vehicle*

1. THE WHOLLY-OWNED ENTERPRISE

1.a. THE BRANCH

1.a.(i) Establishment

As a general rule, no governmental consent is required for the establishment by a foreign company of a branch in the UK nor for the use of the company's name in connection with the branch. Special legislation may however apply to certain activities like banking and insurance. For example, the Banking Act 1979 is relevant in this context in the case of banking business.

The Registrar of Companies has, moreover, a discretion to prevent the use by a foreign company of its corporate name if it is a name which would not be registered were the company a UK company (see 'Subsidiary-Establishment' below). If the Registrar exercises his discretion the foreign company should adopt another name which will be treated as its name for all UK purposes. However, a company should always be aware of the risk of a 'passing off' action if its name resembles that of an existing company in the UK.

A foreign company which establishes a place of business within the UK is called in the company legislation an 'oversea company'.

The requirements referred to below in connection with UK companies, concerning the statement of directors' names on the company's stationery, apply also to any oversea company. The stationary must also state the country in which the company is incorporated and that the liability of the company is limited, if such is the case.

An oversea company having a branch in the UK must file certain particulars at the Companies Registry, including a copy of the company's constitution, an English translation, particulars of the directors and secretary, particulars of charges on UK property and the name and address of a person in the UK authorised to accept service of legal proceedings or notices.

1.a.(ii) Organization

– *Management and representation*

Whilst there is no legal requirement to appoint a branch manager or any officer for the branch, in practice a branch manager will usually be appointed. To enable the branch manager to evidence his authority to bind the company, it is common to grant him a power of attorney, which will set out the manager's powers to act on behalf of the company (and may contain restrictions and limitations). A special power of attorney may be essential for certain transactions e.g. to sign customs declarations on behalf of the branch.

The branch will usually need a bank account in the UK and to open such an account the bank will require a copy of the oversea company's constitution and certificate of incorporation and the directors of the oversea company will be required to pass a resolution regarding the operation of the account in the form required by the bank.

– *Liability*

Since the branch of a company has no legal status separate from that of the company, the company is liable for the debts and other contractual obligations of the branch and for its tortious and criminal acts. The acts of the branch are the acts of the company.

As mentioned above, an oversea company must file at the appropriate Companies Registry the name of a person authorised to accept service of process upon it. Even if this requirement is not complied with, under English rules of procedure a writ can be served upon a foreign company by posting or leaving it at any place of business maintained by the foreign company in England. Any judgment against the company can be enforced against the assets of the branch in the UK.

Persons dealing with a branch manager are entitled to assume that he has such powers to contract on behalf of the oversea company as a person in his position might be expected to have. Thus, the extent of his authority may vary according to the type, size and importance of the branch concerned. This apparent or ostensible authority would however in any case normally extend to

all day to day expenditure of the branch, the purchase of furniture and equipment for the branch and the engagement, payment and dismissal of staff.
The oversea company will not be allowed to deny the authority of a branch manager, acting within the scope of his implied authority, to bind his company by contract to another person who deals with the branch manager in good faith, even though the branch manager in fact, as a matter of internal company regulations, had no such authority. If the branch manager acted contrary to his instructions, that may give rise to a claim by the company against the branch manager, but it will be of no concern to the third party, so that the company will be obliged to honour the commitment, unless the third party knew the branch manager was acting without authority. It should be noted that the provisions of the European Communities Act, 1972 concerning ultra vires, to which we refer below, do not apply to branches of oversea companies.
Any foreign company carrying on business in the UK may be wound up by the court in certain circumstances. The winding-up will in practice be limited to the assets within the jurisdiction of the court. Foreign creditors are entitled to prove debts in such a winding-up in the same manner as UK creditors.

– *Accounts and auditing requirements*
Every oversea company must (subject to the exemptions and modifications referred to below) prepare accounts, in respect of an accounting reference period and, if the company is a holding company, it must also prepare group accounts in respect of that period. The first accounting reference period will begin on a date determined by the company which date must be no later than the date on which a place of business is established in Great Britain. The first accounting reference period must be longer than 6 months and not longer than 18 months. Subsequent accounting reference periods start at the end of the previous period and, unless the date is changed as provided for in the Companies Act 1976, run for a period of 12 months to the accounting reference date.
It is desirable that the branch appoints as auditors professional accountants with practical experience in dealing with the tax authorities on behalf of oversea companies and in operating any relevant Double Taxation Convention.

– *Publication of accounts*
The oversea company must in respect of each accounting reference period deliver to the Registrar of Companies within 13 months of the accounting reference date a copy of every balance sheet, account or other document prepared in respect of that period and, if such documents are in a language other than English, a certified translation into English must be annexed.
Although the accounts of an oversea company are required to be in such form and contain such particulars as would be required for a company incorporated in Great Britain (See subsidiary Establishment below), the Registrar has not in practice required strict compliance with these provisions. He will normally accept for filing accounts which have been prepared in accordance with the laws and practice of the country of incorporation of the oversea company. The Secretary of State now has power under the Companies Act 1981 to

exempt certain oversea companies from the strict accounting requirements or modify their application.

1.b. THE SUBSIDIARY

1.b.(i) Establishment

The procedure for the formation of a subsidiary of a non-resident company does not differ from the normal procedure for the formation of a UK company as outlined below.

The term 'subsidiary' is defined in the Companies Act 1948, but for present purposes it will be sufficient to say that a company will be a subsidiary of another company if that other company, the 'holding company', owns more than half of its equity capital or if the holding company is a member of it and controls the composition of its board of directors.

Before the proposed subsidiary can be incorporated, consideration must be given to choosing an appropriate name. A common practice is to choose the name of the foreign company with the addition of 'Limited' or '(UK) Limited'. Under the Companies Act 1980 public companies are required to include in their name the words 'public limited company' or simply the letters 'p.l.c.'. Under the Companies Act 1981, the Registrar still has a complete discretion to object to a name if it is considered to be the same as that of an existing Company. Certain names will only be allowed if the circumstances justify the use of such words. In choosing a name, it must furthermore always be appreciated that a name too like that of an existing company in the UK may give rise to a 'passing off' action.

Special provisions apply to banks and deposit-taking institutions under the Banking Act 1979.

In the past a company wishing to carry on business under a name other than its own name had to register such name at the Registry of Business Names, but this Registry is to be abolished under the Companies Act 1981.

There are five principal types of company in the UK, but a commercial or trading company is almost invariably a company limited by shares and registered under the Companies Acts. The liability of a shareholder in such a company is limited to the amount, if any, unpaid on his shares. A company limited by shares may be either a public or a private company.

Both public and private companies must have at least two shareholders. A private company need only have one director, whereas a public company must have at least two. In addition, a public company must (under the Companies Act 1980) have a minimum issued share capital of £ 50,000 of which at least 25% is paid up.

A subsidiary of a foreign company will normally be a private company, since in ordinary circumstances there would be no point in forming a public company unless it were intended to invite the public to participate in its shares. Any shareholder may hold his shares as nominee for any other person or company so that it is possible for all the shares in a company to be beneficially owned by a single person or company.

Under the Companies Act 1948, a private company was required by its articles of association to restrict the right to transfer its shares, to limit the number of members to 50 and to prohibit an invitation to the public to subscribe for its shares or debentures. Conversion to a public company was achieved by removal of one or more of these restrictions by special resolution.

Under the rationalisation of the Companies Act 1980 a company is private unless it fulfils the criteria for a public company, and thus the restrictions are no longer necessary in the articles as a matter of law. However, as a matter of practice, the restrictions will be kept in many cases. In particular, the restrictions on the offering of shares to the public may be retained as it is now an offence for a private company to offer its shares to the public.

In order to form a company certain documents, including the memorandum and articles of association, must be filed at the relevant Companies Registry which, if satisfied that the documents are in order will then issue the Certificate of Incorporation (its 'birth certificate'). This is conclusive and incontestable evidence that the company exists as a separate legal entity.

A statement of the first directors and secretary and registered office must also be filed when applying for registration. A signed consent to his appointment is required from each director and the secretary.

The European Communities Act 1972 provides that the Registrar of Companies shall publish notice of the issue of the Certificate of Incorporation in the London or, (in the case of Scottish companies), Edinburgh, Gazette.

The memorandum of association is the company's 'charter', specifying the objects for which the company is incorporated. Any act or transaction not within such objects is ultra vires the company and invalid. Subject to what is said in the following paragraph an ultra vires contract cannot be enforced against the company by any other party with knowledge that it was ultra vires. For this purpose, all persons having dealings with the company are deemed to have express knowledge of the company's objects, since the memorandum is open to public inspection at the Companies Registry.

The strict ultra vires doctrine was, however, modified, as from 1st January 1973, by the European Communities Act 1972 in favour of any 'person dealing with a company in good faith', and in respect of transactions 'decided on by the directors'. The intention is that, generally speaking, such a person will be entitled to assume that anything lawfully decided upon by the directors is within the capacity of the company and will not be bound to enquire further.

In general, the ultra vires doctrine will not be applied to prevent a trading company from doing anything which may fairly be regarded as being incidental to its specified objects. However, in practice, the lawyer who drafts the memorandum will make the objects as wide as he can so that every activity envisaged is expressly covered.

The memorandum must further state the amount of the company's share capital and its division into shares of a fixed amount.

The articles of association regulate the internal affairs of the Company. They are the company's 'statutes' and constitute a contract between the company and its shareholders, and between the shareholders inter se. The articles normally deal with such matters as the issue and transfer of shares, voting rights, the increase and reduction of share capital, shareholders' meetings, the appointment, removal, powers and duties of directors and the procedure for meetings of the board and the payment of dividends.

The relevant Companies Registry maintains a file, open to public inspection, for every registered company. All documents lodged by the company at the Registry are kept on this file. The company is obliged to file particulars on the happening of certain events, such as amendments to the memorandum or articles of association, a change in the directors or secretary, the address of the registered office, or an increase in the authorised capital.

Further, if a company incorporated in the UK creates a charge over its property, details must in nearly all cases be registered at the Companies Registry by the company or the creditor within 21 days. Such registration constitutes effective notice to the world of the existence of the charge in question. If the charge is not registered, it is void against a liquidator and creditors and when the charge becomes void the indebtedness secured by the charge is immediately repayable.

– *Accounts and auditing requirements*

Once every year, the company must file what is known as its 'annual return', which contains details of its directors, secretary and shareholders. The accounts of the company for each accounting period must also be filed together with the report of the directors and the report of the auditor on the accounts. The Companies Act 1976 specifies how accounting reference periods are to be fixed and altered, and provides severe penalties on directors personally as well as the company for failing to file any documents within the prescribed time limits.

There are detailed statutory requirements as to the information to be disclosed by a UK company in the annual accounts, which consist of the profit and loss account and the balance sheet. For instance, such information must include certain particulars of the remuneration of directors and employees.

The Companies Act 1981, as already indicated, implements the EEC Fourth Directive on company accounts. It also introduces less less onerous requirements as to the accounts to be filed for small and medium sized companies as defined in the Act (but excluding public companies or banking, insurance or certain shipping companies or members of a group including a company of one of those kinds).

There are also detailed statutory requirements as to the contents of the report of the directors. In Great Britain, subject to some exceptions, certain particulars must be given of turnover, the number of employees, the total of their remuneration, political or charitable gifts and exports.

Every UK company must normally have an auditor, who must not be an officer or employee of the company and must be an accountant or firm of accountants belonging to one of the professional bodies specified in the legislation. The auditor may, however, perform other accounting services for the company, such as the preparation of the company's annual accounts.

The auditor is required by the Companies Acts to make an annual report to the members of the company as to whether the annual accounts have been properly prepared in accordance with the Acts and as to whether in his opinion a true and fair view is given of the company's profit or loss and of its financial position at the date of the balance sheet.

The company legislation contains special provisions regarding the rights of auditors and their appointment and removal from office and, in particular, confers upon them rights of access to the company's books and papers. At every annual general meeting, a company must appoint an auditor or auditors to hold office from the conclusion of that meeting until the conclusion of the next annual general meeting.

If the retiring auditors are to continue to hold office, they must be expressly reappointed at each annual general meeting. If auditors resign, they are obliged to state whether there are any circumstances connected with their resignation which they consider should be brought to the attention of members or creditors and, if so, what they are. On resignation they are also entitled to requisition an extraordinary general meeting to consider circumstances leading to the resignation.

There is a duty on holding and subsidiary companies and the subsidiary company's auditors to obtain or provide information about a subsidiary required by the auditors of the holding company. Companies must keep and preserve proper accounting records for a period of 6 years.

The European Communities Act 1972 requires every company to have stated in all its business letters and order forms its place of registration, its number and the address of its registered office. Any reference to the amount of the share capital (which is not mandatory) must be to paid up share capital.

The Act also requires the Registrar of Companies to publish in the relevant governmental gazette notification to him of alterations in the memorandum or articles of association, amendments in the register of directors, the annual return, the location of the registered office, and any order for the winding up or dissolution of a company. A company shall not be entitled to rely against third parties on any such event if it has not been duly so notified by the Registrar of Companies at the material time or if it is not shown by the company to have been known at such time to the third party concerned. (A)[1]

1.b.(ii) Organization

– *Capital, shares, transfer*

As mentioned above, there is now (since the Companies Act 1980) a minimum issued capital requirement of £ 50,000 (of which at least 25% must be paid up) for a public company. There is no such requirement for a private company. Shares are always in registered form; a share certificate under the company's seal is prima facie evidence of title.

Shares in both public and private limited companies are usually either 'ordinary' or 'preference'. The holders of preference shares enjoy a right to receive dividends at a fixed percentage rate, before ordinary shareholders are entitled to a dividend. Dividends on preference shares are often cumulative, so that if no dividend is declared in one year, preference shareholders will be entitled to twice the fixed rate if a dividend is declared the next year, and so on. If desired for special situations (e.g. in joint ventures), various other different classes of shares are possible.

The articles of association normally provide that dividends shall be declared

1. Capital letters refer to works in the Bibliography.

by a general meeting of the shareholders but that they shall not exceed the amount recommended by the directors.

It is a basic principle that dividends may only be paid out of profits available for the purpose. These are defined in the Companies Act 1980 as the accumulated realised profits of a company so far as not previously utilised by distribution or capitalisation, less its accumulated realised losses, so far as not previously written off in a reduction or reorganisation of capital duly made. In the case of public companies, a distribution may only be made if the amount of net assets exceeds the aggregate of the paid up share capital and its undistributed reserves. Any distribution which is made may not reduce the amount of net assets to less than this aggregate.

The right to transfer shares in a private company may be restricted. This commonly takes the form of a provision in the articles that the directors may refuse to register a transfer of shares.

Transfers of shares are only effectively completed in law when registered in the register of members maintained by the company. Arrangements can however be made (e.g. by declarations of trust) for the beneficial interest in shares to be enjoyed by parties other than the registered shareholders although the company will not normally take note of this.

Shares in public or private company may not, in most cases, be alloted unless first offered to existing shareholders in proportion to their shareholding. This provision may be excluded by a private company in its articles of association. The directors of a public company may also be given authority, either in the Articles of Association or by special resolution of the company, to allot shares without observing such rights of pre-emption. Similar provisions apply in respect of shares held under an employee's share scheme.

Directors may not allot shares on behalf of a company unless they are authorised to do so either by the articles of association of by the company in general meeting. Any such authority must state the maximum amount of shares which may be so alloted, and must be renewed at least every five years.

The Companies Act 1981 has introduced a substantial change in company legislation in that it enables a company in future to purchase its own shares, including any redeemable shares which it may now issue, if authorized to do so by its articles of association. Certain conditions have to be met and particulars delivered to the Registrar of Companies, and provision is made for the maintenance of a company's capital reserves on redemption or purchase of its own shares.

– *Management, representation*

Articles of association usually confer upon the directors all the powers of the company not specially reserved to the shareholders by the memorandum and articles of association or by the Companies Acts. Thus the powers of managing and carrying on the company's business are normally vested in the directors. The directors usually have powers of delegation, and the conduct of day to day business is usually delegated to managing and executive directors or even to managers without seats on the board.

It should be noted, however, that the conferment of the title of managing director acts as a representation that the director so appointed has a wide power to bind the company in contract. It follows that the company may be

bound by contracts entered into by a managing director on behalf of the company, even though those contracts are outside the powers expressly conferred upon the managing director by the board of directors. The same applies, but to a more restricted degree, to other directors and employees.
It may in practice be possible to achieve some protection for the company by including restrictions on the powers of directors and employees in the company's articles of association.
Unless there are special provisions in the articles of association, or in a separate shareholders' agreement, shareholders holding more than 50% of the voting rights will have complete control of the power of appointing directors. A director may be removed from office by a resolution passed by a simple majority of the shareholders present and voting at a meeting, notwithstanding anything in the articles or any agreement between the director and the company. The director may however, be entitled to compensation if he is removed in breach of a contract of employment. It is often provided in the articles of association of a wholly-owned subsidiary of a foreign company that a shareholder or shareholders holding a specified percentage of the issued share capital for the time being may appoint and remove the directors by notice in writing, without the necessity of convening a shareholders' meeting for the purpose.
There is no statutory requirement that a director shall be a British subject or resident in the UK or that he shall hold any shares in the company. Nor need a director, as such, apply for a work permit.
With regard to company stationery, a company may choose to name either all (but not some) of its directors in its business letters, or to name none of them, except in the text of the letter or as signatory.
Meetings of the directors are usually held periodically. There is no requirement that such meetings shall be held in the UK, but (as indicated later in this Chapter) the place where the directors' meetings are held has been a crucial consideration in determining where the 'central management and control' of the company is exercised, and hence in which country the company is resident for tax purposes.
Normally each director present at a meeting of the board will have one vote on any resolution. Provision is often made for the chairman of the board to have a casting vote if votes are otherwise equal. There is, however, nothing to prevent different provisions from being made in the articles as in the case of some joint ventures. The articles of association frequently provide for the appointment of alternate directors to act in the absence of directors.
The directors are generally speaking agents of the company and, as such, stand in a fiduciary relationship to the company which gives rise to obligations of good faith similar to those owed by other fiduciaries.
It must be stressed that these duties are owed to the company and not to any particular shareholder. A director must exercise his powers bona fide for the benefit of the company as a whole, that is to say for the benefit of all the shareholders. This is so even if he is himself a shareholder or has been appointed by a particular shareholder or class of shareholders. The Companies Act 1980 also specifically requires the directors, when exercising their powers, to consider, inter alia, the interests of all the company's employees.
Directors must exercise their powers honestly and must not put themselves in

a position where their duties and interests are likely to conflict.They must not make a secret profit out of their position. Nor must they be interested in a contract with the company unless the articles of association otherwise provide. Articles normally permit directors to be interested in such contracts on condition that the director discloses his interest at a board meeting. Should a director fail to disclose his interest in a contract, it may be avoided by the company.

The provisions of the Companies Act 1948 in relation to loans to directors have been repealed and replaced by new more extensive provisions in the Companies Acts 1980 and 1981, which deal both with prohibition of certain loans and disclosure to the company of interests in certain other loans. The provisions extend to certain loans made by third parties to directors under arrangements with the company.

The duties of individual directors will normally depend on the terms agreed between them and the company. The duties of a managing director will clearly extend considerably further than the duties of a non-executive director, who will frequently do little more in connection with the company's affairs than attend and vote at board meetings.

The directors are liable in damages to the company for any breach of their duties and, as fiduciaries, are liable to account to the company for any of the company's property of which they have disposed for a purpose which is ultra vires the company.

Every company, whether public or private, must have a secretary. He will be responsible for seeing that all necessary corporate formalities are complied with and records, including minutes of meetings, kept.

Secretaries of public companies must be suitably qualified: the requirements as to qualification are specified in the Companies Act 1980.

– *Shareholders' meetings*

An annual general meeting of the company must be held every year, and extraordinary general meetings may be convened when necessary on giving the requisite notice.

A resolution of 75% of the shareholders present and voting at a meeting (a 'special resolution') is required to alter the company's objects or articles of association, or to reduce the share capital of the company (which however requires to be confirmed by the court) or for a members' voluntary winding-up. A simple majority of shareholders (an 'ordinary resolution') is required to increase or the company's share capital and generally for all matters, except the few by company law requiring a 75% majority or as may be specially provided otherwise in the articles of association.

– *Liability*

As a subsidiary is a separate legal entity, its parent company will not normally be liable for its obligations or otherwise be responsible for its activities. Only in exceptional circumstances (e.g. where the subsidiary is found to have been acting as agent for the parent company, or the parent company is guarantor for the subsidiary) will the parent company itself be liable.

The directors of a company will not be personally liable for acts or omissions in the course of their duties as directors of the company. They may, however, incur personal liability to third parties if they lack actual authority to bind the company. Their position vis-à-vis the company has been described (under 'Management and Representation' above).

Directors of a company may also be held personally liable for acts or defaults of the company contrary to law. Such personal liability is common in relation to company law offences.

In general, only the company itself (as distinct from its shareholders) is entitled to take proceedings against a director for breach of duty. This is because in most cases the director's unauthorised act can be ratified by the vote of a simple majority of company shareholders at a general meeting.

In the following cases individual shareholders may be entitled to take proceedings against directors for breach of duties owed to the company:

a. Where a director has acted illegally or ultra vires the company, since such action cannot be ratified by the company in general meeting;

b. Where what has been done amounts to a fraud on the minority of shareholders and those responsible for the fraud are in control of the company and are thereby benefited;

c. If the director's action is an action which can only be done validly or ratified by a 75% majority of shareholders.

In certain cases specified in the Companies Acts, the Department of Trade can take proceedings in the name of the company.

The company legislation provides for investigations to be made in certain circumstances by inspectors appointed by the Department of Trade. On the application of the company or of not less than 200 shareholders or of shareholders holding onetenth of the issued share capital, the Department of Trade may appoint an inspector or inspectors to investigate the affairs of a company and report on them. The Department of Trade must appoint an inspector if the court by order declares that an investigation is necessary.

The Department of Trade also has power on its own initiative to appoint an inspector in cases of suspected fraud, oppression of minority shareholders, misconduct of the management, or failure to give shareholders reasonable information as to the affairs of the company.

Where directors fraudulently permit trading to continue when they know that the company is insolvent, they may be prosecuted criminally and in such circumstances the courts have power to make them personally liable to creditors. They may also be disqualified for fixed periods from taking part in the promotion, formation or management and liquidation of a company.

The legislation has contained further special provisions for the protection of minority interests. For example, a reduction of capital has required the consent of the court which, on considering the application for consent, will have regard to the interests of creditors and minority shareholders. As already indicated (under 'Organisation-Capital, Shares, Transfer') a company will now, however, under the Companies Act 1981 be enabled to purchase its own shares subject to certain conditions.

Where there is more than one class of shareholders and the rights of a particular class are varied in pursuance of a clause in the articles of association, the court has a discretionary power to order a cancellation of the variation on the application of 15% of the shareholders affected by it. Similarly, 15% of the company's shareholders may apply to the court for the cancellation of an alteration in the company's objects.

Another example of protection of minority shareholders is the right of shareholders to petition the court for a compulsory winding-up order on the ground that it is just and equitable that the company should be wound up.

The Companies Act 1980 has improved the existing legislation for the protection of minority shareholders. A minority shareholder may now petition the court on the ground that the affairs of the company are being conducted in a manner unfairly prejudicial to some part of the company's members. The Court may make such order as it thinks fit. This may be a winding up order or an order, inter alia, to regulate the conduct of the company's affairs or require the purchase by the company or by other shareholders of the shares of the minority shareholders.

Protection is also afforded by the doctrine of 'fraud on the minority'. For example, the doctrine can be invoked where it can be shown that the majority shareholders have caused the articles of association to be altered in such a way as to constitute a fraud on the minority. Similarly the court will interfere where it can be shown that the company's property has been fraudulently taken and those who have taken it use their majority voting power to prevent the company from proceeding to recover the property.

– *Publication of accounts*

As mentioned above (under (i) Establishment), accounts must be published in respect of each accounting reference period of a UK company. In respect of a UK holding company, group accounts must be published, that is to say accounts incorporating the results and financial position of all that company's subsidiaries.

– *Group of companies*

A holding company controlling different companies in its group (rather than one company incorporating different business divisions) is the structure often preferred for the carrying on of different business.

The degree of autonomy given to each subsidiary will be a matter of choice in each case. Commercial and taxation considerations may influence the choice of structure, although special taxation provisions prevail as between companies in the same group. (See Section III below). As already indicated, companies in the same group will, as separate legal entities, not normally be liable for each other's liabilities. In practice, banks and other third parties may require cross-guarantees for certain transactions.

1.b.(iii) Checklist for establishing a subsidiary

	Action	*Time*	*Cost*
1.	Consider and select appropriate name		–
2.	Submit: (i) Memorandum of Association)	allow 3-4 weeks for issue	1% capital duty on issued

Action	*Time*	*Cost*
(ii) Articles of Association) (iii) Statement of capital) (iv) Statutory declaration of Compliance) (v) Details of registered office) (vi) Consent of directors and secretary to act) (vii) PUC form)	of Certificate of Incorporation	share capital paid or due and payable – £ 50 registration fee on submission of documents
3. Submit details of Accounting Reference Date	Submit within 6 months of incorporation	
4. Appoint auditors/ accountants	As soon as possible after incorporation	
5. Open bank account in name of company	As soon as possible after incorporation	–
6. Register with Customs and Excise for VAT	As soon as taxable turnover is reached (or before, where required)	–
7. Register with Inland Revenue for P.A.Y.E. (income tax on employees)	As soon as possible in consultation with accountants	–

1.c. OTHER FORMS

Representative office

Where no trading activity is contemplated, it is sometimes sufficient for a foreign company merely to have a representative office in the UK which will confine itself to forwarding business enquiries to the home office and answering enquiries. If such an office is established in the name of the company, its position will need to be carefully considered as it may well constitute a place of business and as such have to comply with the requirements for registration at the Companies Registry applicable to the branch of an oversea company (as set out under 1(a) 'the Branch' above). This may be so even if the activity within the UK is not such as to attract UK tax. Registration may, however, be avoided by establishing the office in the name of an individual describing himself as the representative of the company.

It should again be noted that the provisions concerning ultra vires contained in the European Communities Act 1972, to which we referred above, do not apply to branches of oversea companies.

The company limited by shares (the private company described above) is by far the most common form of establishment for foreign enterprises commencing a business venture in the UK, either wholly-owned or as a joint venture. There are other forms of company (e.g. a company limited by guarantee, an unlimited company, a statutory corporation, a company formed by Royal Charter) but their very specific roles are not relevant to this Chapter.

Non-resident company

It might be mentioned here that a UK private company is also considered a useful vehicle by foreign enterprises wishing to do business outside the UK. For this purpose, a company non-resident in the UK is established i.e. non-resident for UK taxation purposes and also (when it applied) exchange control purposes.

The company may be incorporated in the UK with limited liability and its capital may be denominated in any currency. The company will operate as an 'off-shore' company and, to qualify as a non-resident company and consequently bear no UK tax, it must be controlled from outside the UK, and must have no place of business in the UK and not trade within the UK or have other sources of UK income (see Section III 'Taxation' below).

Partnership

The only other form of business organisation worth mentioning briefly is partnership. The law of partnership is governed principally by the Partnership Act 1890. Under English law a partnership is not a separate legal entity from the partners although, for the purposes of the Partnership Act, persons who have entered into partnership with one another are collectively called a firm. In Scotland the position is different in that a firm is a legal person distinct from the partners.

As a form of business organisation the partnership is used principally by individuals, especially in the carrying on of a profession where the governing body of that profession forbids incorporation. However, it is not uncommon for companies to enter into partnership for some special taxation or other commercial reason, such as a wish to avoid disclosure of the annual accounts of a joint enterprise. Two limited companies, (one or both of which might be incorporated abroad), could enter into partnership for the purpose of carrying on a business in the United Kingdom. In this way a partnership would indirectly enjoy limited liability.

For a partnership to exist, there must be a business and there must be two or more persons carrying on that business. A partnership relationship arises from contract, express or implied. No formal act is required to constitute a partnership, but partners will normally enter into a partnership agreement which will govern such matters as the type of business to be carried on, the profit and loss sharing ratios, the provision of capital, the internal regulation of the partnership, the circumstances in which the partnership may be dissolved and the consequences thereof. To the extent that these matters are not specifically spelled out in a partnership agreement, or where no formal agreement is entered into, terms will be implied by the Partnership Act.

If the partnership carries on business under a firm name which is in any way different from the names of the partners, it has been necessary to register the firm name under the Registration of Business Names Act 1916. The purpose of this registration was to enable the public to make a search and ascertain the persons or companies behind a particular firm name. The Companies Act 1981 will abolish this Registry but it will require disclosure of certain information on all letter headings and other documents.

All the partners are jointly liable in contract, and jointly and severally liable in tort, for the acts and omissions of the partnership.

The law on agency applies as between a partner and the firm. The Partnership Act provides that every partner is an agent of the firm and his other partners for the purpose of the business of the partnership; and the acts of every partner who does any act for carrying on in the usual way business of the kind carried on by the firm of which he is a member, bind the firm and his partners. The position is only qualified if the partner so acting in fact had no authority and the person with whom he is dealing either knew that that was the case or did not know or believe him to be a partner.

In large partnerships the day to day management is frequently delegated to a committee of partners under the express provisions of the partnership agreement. However, this does not affect the ability of any partner to bind the firm as provided for in the Partnership Act.

There is no requirement to publish the accounts of a partnership, nor do partnership accounts need to be audited unless there are special statutory requirements applicable to particular professions or trades.

Another form of business organisation used occasionally is the limited partnership under the Limited Partnerships Act 1907. This form enables one or more partners to have limited liability provided, generally speaking, that they do not take any part in management of the business. The partner or partners who manage the business cannot enjoy limited liability and, in practice, it is generally only for special taxation considerations that an individual or company would consider entering into a limited partnership.

2. THE JOINT VENTURE

2.a. THE JOINTLY OWNED COMPANY

Subject to take-over controls (see 'External Controls', B.2 below), there are no restrictions on foreign companies or persons entering into joint ventures with English companies or persons by way of a jointly-owned company.
Such companies will take the same form as a private company (as described above under A.1.b. 'Subsidiary'), although the articles of association normally contain special provisions to meet the requirements of the joint venture. The joint venture company would usually be created as a new company for the purpose, but it could be adapted from an existing company, possibly already wholly-owned by the local participant.

2.a.(i) Shareholders' agreement

The parties to a joint venture will generally enter into a joint venture agreement. This will provide, inter alia, for the scope of the company's proposed activities; the proportion in which shares are to be held; the share capital; the name of the company; the financing policy; the duration of the joint venture; composition of the board of directors; limitations on the powers of the directors; dividend policy; accounting policy; publicity; any technical aid agreements and industrial property licences; competition provisions; personnel; and provisions relating to termination of the joint venture.
Many of these provisions will be reflected in the memorandum and articles of association, especially those concerning the board of directors and the issue and transfer of shares. For instance, in the case of 50-50 joint companies, it is often provided that the directors appointed by each of the co-owners of the company will collectively have one vote no matter how many attend a board meeting, so that the board of directors cannot act unless the co-owners are in agreement. If deadlock persists, so that it is impossible to administer the company's affairs, the court, on the application of one of the co-owners, may order that the company be wound up.
As between the company and its shareholders, the articles of association will determine their respective rights and obligations. However, a shareholders' agreement is enforceable between the parties to it, and the courts have a discretion to will grant an injunction or other relief to prevent a shareholder acting contrary to such agreement.
The advantage of placing many important provisions in the articles of association is that any act contrary to the articles should be ineffective, whereas an act contrary to the shareholders' agreement may be effective, although giving rise to a claim for damages. If, however, the wrongful act can be anticipated, it is possible that the party concerned may, as indicated above, be restrained by injunction beforehand.
In practice, parties are often content with many provisions being placed in the shareholders' agreement, particularly when they would not want to publicise in the articles of association any special arrangements for the running of the

company. There normally is no need for publication of the shareholders' agreement.

2.a.(ii) Minority Rights

These are described above under (A.1.b.(ii), 'Subsidiary Liability'), including the powers of the court to protect minority interests and in the last resort order the winding up of the company. In practice, the position of minority shareholders in a private company is not a particularly strong one, and it is preferable for the minority shareholders in a joint venture to negotiate special provisions either in the articles of association or in the joint venture agreement. It is common for certain major matters to be expressly reserved for decision by either the board of directors or the shareholders in such a way that the minority shareholder has, in effect, a right of veto. These matters would include such items as changing the business, raising further capital, transferring shares and transactions other than in the ordinary course of business. It is also important for the minority shareholder to have, if possible, certain circumstances defined where he can require termination of the joint venture and also the consequences to follow such termination.

2.b. CONSORTIA

Joint ventures in the form of consortia may be formed, usually for a limited period or for a specific purpose. They may be formed by more than the two parties who commonly form joint venture agreements. Examples are the consortia of industrial companies in related fields who may join together to obtain some major foreign construction contract(s); or the banks from different countries who join together in London to pool their skills for entry into fields of financial transactions that might not be open to them individually.
A consortium may be formed by agreement between the parties, without the creation of a new legal person such as the private company, usually the vehicle for joint ventures. Where no new entity is created, as in the case sometimes of industrial companies seeking a particular construction contract, one of the companies will act as main contractor to the customer and enter into sub-contracts with the other manufacturing companies and the design consultants and other necessary parties. In this way, the performance of the main contract by the consortia is achieved by a series of interrelated contracts, the aim of which will, in effect, be to share responsibility for performance of the main contract. Where, however, banks have entered into a consortium, it is usually achieved by establishing a new consortium company, again regulated by a shareholders' agreement.

2.c. OTHERS

Reference has already been made above (A.I.C. 'Other Forms') to the fact that a partnership is sometimes established, for special tax or commercial reasons, as the vehicle for an enterprise in the UK. The means of establishment and practical consequences are mentioned above. As already indicated, the establishment of a joint venture company is, however, the most usual course to follow, unless possibly only one project is envisaged by the parties and some form of consortia arrangements are considered adequate. Each case must, however, be examined in all its aspects to decide the best vehicle.

B. *External Controls*

1. EXCHANGE CONTROL

All Exchange Control restrictions have been removed by order of H.M. Treasury. However, the Exchange Control Act 1947, which provides for restrictions to be imposed, has not been repealed and restrictions could therefore be reimposed at short notice. The following is a summary of the restrictions which existed before such removal.

It was necessary to apply to the Exchange Control authority under the Exchange Control Act 1947, namely the Bank of England, for consent to issue the shares in a proposed subsidiary company to the non-resident parent company and to the provision of loan capital for the subsidiary, unless the parent company was resident in the sterling area.[2] The application was required to give details of the proposed activities of the company and the source of the funds out of which the company's share or loan capital was to be provided. Normally the consent could be obtained without difficulty, but usually only on the basis that both share and initial loan capital was provided from non-sterling sources.

Any further borrowing by the subsidiary also required Bank of England consent. Unlimited sterling borrowing in the UK by any UK company controlled by residents of member countries of the EEC was normally allowed.[3]

Such borrowing was also normally allowed for new expenditure in the so-called Special Development, Development and Intermediate Areas ('the Areas for Expansion') or in Northern Ireland by companies controlled by other non-residents.

Otherwise, the Bank's practice was to permit companies (other than companies such as financial, importing and distributing companies which normally do not employ many fixed assets) to borrow from UK sources for working capital requirements but to require that any other borrowing was provided from external sources. Non-sterling borrowing was normally required to be for a minimum period of two years. Where, however, a project was judged to be highly beneficial to the UK economy (for example because it may make a significant contribution to the balance of payments or provide employment in an Area for Expansion), the company concerned was usually permitted to raise monies in the UK as fixed capital.

If a company was to be formed jointly by a foreign enterprise and UK residents, it was usually stipulated that a proportion of borrowing would have to

2. The sterling area comprised the UK, the Channel Islands, the Isle of Man, the Republic of Ireland and Gibraltar.

3. This also applied to companies controlled by residents of countries removed from the sterling area in June 1972, known as the Overseas Sterling Area.

be from external sources, namely the proportion which the non-resident shareholding bears to the total issued share capital.

Consent was normally given for the following payments to the parent company:

a. the remission of dividends, subject to adequate provision being made for UK taxation and other liabilities;

b. the repatriation of the proceeds (including capital appreciation) of a sale or liquidation of the subsidiary;

c. reasonable payments of loan interest, patent and know-how royalties and for technical services;

d. reimbursement of salaries of personnel loaned to the subsidiary and of the cost of providing the subsidiary with the benefits of research carried out by the parent company;

e. reasonable commission for marketing services rendered.

Applications for certain of the above consents were normally made to the company's bank. All the principal banks were authorised agents of the Bank of England for such purpose.

Before the lifting of exchange control restrictions, a UK branch of a foreign company was treated for exchange control purposes as a separate legal entity from its head office and as resident in the UK. It was subject to the same restrictions as regards raising of capital and transfers of funds from the sterling area to the external account area countries as were applicable to companies resident in the UK.

2. TAKE-OVER CONTROLS

Under the provisions of the Fair Trading Act 1973, the Secretary of State may refer any takeover or merger to the Monopolies and Mergers Commission where either the value of the assets taken over exceeds £ 15 million, or as a result of the transaction at least 25% of goods or services of any description supplied in the UK are supplied by or to one and the same person or by or to the persons carrying on the enterprises involved in the takeover or merger. The Monopolies and Mergers Commission must report within 6 months. If it finds the takeover or merger to be against the public interest, the Secretary of State may, inter alia, order that the transaction be 'unwound'.

In practice, application is made at the outset of a transaction to the Office of Fair Trading for a clearance that the Secretary of State does not intend to refer it to the Commission. Although such a reference is not often made, and the Office of Fair Trading responds quickly in most cases, the legislation here should not be overlooked.

Where it is proposed to take over a public company (as distinct from a private company) resident in the United Kingdom, then it is often essential to comply with the requirements of the City Code on Take-overs and Mergers. The City Code does not have the force of law but it must be followed by persons wishing to have the facilities of the securities markets in the United Kingdom. The City Code covers items such as the information to be provided to shareholders, contents of announcements, responsibility of directors for statements, etc. The City Code does not apply where the offeree company is a private company.

The Industry Act 1975 contains some provisions enabling the Secretary of State to prevent control of manufacturing undertakings in the UK from passing to enterprises not resident in the UK. The power applies only where the undertakings are of special importance to the UK or part of it. It is believed that the power would only be used in exceptional circumstances and, as yet, it has not apparently been exercised.

3. ANTI-TRUST CONTROLS

In addition to EEC competition rules, which are of particular concern to joint ventures, the Competition Act 1980 provides for the control of anti-competitive practices, the Restrictive Trade Practices Act 1976 provides for the compulsory registration and justification of restrictive trading agreements and the Fair Trading Act 1973 provides further controls over trading practices.

In practice, this legislation is not likely to be so relevant at the stage of setting up the UK enterprise (except in the case of a joint venture) as in the subsequent trading practices of the enterprise.

4. ENVIRONMENTAL CONTROLS

Planning permission may be required for any 'development', which is defined by the Town and Country Planning Act 1971 as 'the carrying out of building, engineering, mining or other operations in, on, over or under land, or the making of any material change in the use of any buildings or other land'. Also, Building Regulations approval may be required for internal alterations which affect the structural soundness or sanitariness of a building.

There are also statutory provisions for the prevention and control of pollution of the environment, including the control of noise. Employers are required to provide a safe and healthy environment for employees at their place of work.

5. STATE MONOPOLIES

There are various state monopolies which operate to the exclusion of private enterprise – e.g. the Post Office, Electricity and Gas Boards.

6. OTHERS

Certain controls may be encountered in the case of establishing enterprises in some special fields like banking (particularly under the Banking Act 1979) and insurance (particularly under the Insurance Companies Act 1981), where there may be specific regulations to protect the public. There is also the new general legislation, in particular the Unfair Contract Terms Act 1977, affecting contract conditions which has increased in recent years, particularly to protect the consumer, and which must therefore be borne in mind when the new enterprise commences business in the UK.

III. TAXATION

A. Corporation Tax (B)

1. ENTITIES SUBJECT TO CORPORATION TAX

Corporation tax is charged on the profits of any corporate body (incorporated in any country) or unincorporated association which is resident in the UK or carries on a trade in the UK through a branch or agency. The term 'profits', for the purposes of corporation tax, includes both income profits and chargeable capital gains.

In the case of a UK resident company, corporation tax falls upon all of its profits, wherever they arise and whether or not they are remitted to the UK. In the case of a non-UK resident company, corporation tax is charged only on the income of any trade of the company carried on in the UK attributable to a branch or agency of the company here and on capital gains arising on the disposal of assets situated in the UK, which are used in or held for or were acquired for the purposes of the trade of that branch or agency.

A company's residence status is determined currently by the place where the central management and control of the company is exercised. If it is exercised in the UK the company is resident in the UK for tax purposes (although the law may be subject to change in this area). The words 'central management and control' refer to broad issues of organisation and policy, rather than to control of the day to day business operation. Generally, the company will be resident in the country where its board of directors meet to take decisions. If a company is UK resident, it may not normally cease to be UK resident or transfer any part of its trade or business to a non-UK resident without consent from H.M. Treasury.

Under UK domestic tax law, a trade is generally held to be carried on within the UK if contracts for the sale of goods or the rendering of services are made in the UK. However, this test is not conclusive, and cases may arise where contracts are made outside the UK, but other activities have been carried on in the UK, with the consequence that the trade will be regarded as carried on within the UK if it can be said that the profits of the trade in substance arise from the UK.

The position above may be modified by the terms of any relevant double taxation treaty. Most of the UK's double taxation treaties follow the broad pattern of the OECD Model Convention, which provides that tax will be paid in the UK only on such of the industrial or commercial profits that are attributable to a 'permanent establishment' through which the enterprise carries on its business in the UK.

The industrial and commercial profits attributable to a permanent establishment will be those profits which that establishment would be expected to make if it were a separate enterprise engaged in the same business activities under the same conditions and dealing at arm's length with its parent. In determining its profits, the actual expenses of the permanent establishment may be deducted, as may a proportion of the overheads and administrative

expenses of the head office, if the permanent establishment obtained any benefit from the services of that head office.
Loss relief, capital allowances, stock relief and other incentives available to trading companies (see F below) will normally also be available to a permanent establishment.
Where it is difficult to ascertain the taxable profits of a permanent establishment, the taxation authority, known as the Inland Revenue, will sometimes agree to charge tax on an estimated or notional amount of profits based on a percentage of turnover or expenses of the permanent establishment concerned.

2. COMPUTATION OF PROFITS FOR CORPORATION TAX PURPOSES

As mentioned above, corporation tax is charged on the total profits of a company, which consist of the aggregate of that company's taxable income and its chargeable capital gains.

2.a. Income profits

All categories of income profits are assessable to corporation tax, except dividends and other distributions received from UK resident companies (known as 'franked investment income').
All expenses of a revenue character wholly and exclusively incurred for the purposes of the company's trade (such as the remuneration of employees, social security contributions, rent of business premises and interest payable to a UK bank – including the UK branch of an overseas bank – but not dividends or other distributions of profits) are deductible from the trading income of a company for the purpose of calculating its liability to tax.
Charges made by a parent company for technical and other services rendered to its UK subsidiary will normally be allowed by the Revenue as a deductible expense, provided that such charges are not in excess of the open market rate for the services provided. The position with interest on inter group loans is more complex. In the case of loans provided to a UK company by a non-UK resident owning 75% or more of the UK company's share capital, interest will not be deductible from profits under UK domestic law. This position is, however, usually modified by the terms of any relevant double taxation treaty. As a matter of practice interest will generally be deductible where the debt to equity ratio of the UK company does not exceed 4:1.
In addition certain payments which, by UK domestic legislation, do not qualify as revenue expenditure, such as patent royalties, may also, subject to complex rules, be deductible from overall profits.
If the amount of expenses and charges in relation to a particular trade exceeds the profits of that trade in an accounting period, then in the case of a trading company, the excess can generally be utilised as a trading loss for taxation purposes.
Trading losses in an accounting period can be treated in two ways. First, the loss may be set against the company's profits (including capital gains) from any other source in the accounting period in which the losses accrued and in certain of the accounting periods preceding that period. Except where the

losses were generated by means of capital allowances (see below), losses may not be carried back beyond an accounting period ending in more than a timė equal to the length of the accounting period in which the more than a time equal to the length of the accounting period in which the loss was incurred. Losses due to capital allowances may be carried back three years. In both cases, however, losses may only be carried back to profits of preceeding years if the company was then carrying on the same trade. Secondly, the loss (or that part of it which remains unrelieved) may be carried forward indefinitely and set against the future trading income of the same trade.

2.b. Chargeable capital gains (C, D)

Gains accruing on the disposal of a capital asset are computed by deducting from the consideration received on the disposal of the asset, the aggregate of the acquisition cost, any capital expenses incurred in the enhancement of its value and any costs incurred on the disposal of the asset. Where, however, the transaction is not a bargain made at arm's length, the market value of the asset is substituted in general for the actual consideration received on its disposal. Transactions between 'connected persons' usually have the market value basis applied to them.

If a capital loss arises on a disposal (losses being calculated in the same manner as gains), that loss may be set-off against any chargeable gains realized in the same accounting period. Any excess of losses may then be carried forward (but not back) and set against capital gains in future accounting periods. Capital losses may not be set-off against other income.

There are provisions covering the disposal and replacement of certain specified classes of business assets, which provide for what is termed 'roll over' relief. The old assets are treated as disposed of without gain or loss so that no charge to tax arises. Roll over relief is available until any further assets are not replaced by other appropriate business assets.

Transfers of assets between UK resident companies, which are members of a group of companies, are deemed to be for a consideration giving rise to no gain or loss. This relief is not available where assets are transferred between UK resident and non-resident companies. Relief from corporation tax may also be available on chargeable gains realised, or deemed to be realised, in the course of a reconstruction, amalgamation or demerger of UK companies.

Only a fraction of a company's capital gains is taken into account in calculating its total profits for corporation tax purposes. The appropriate fraction is currently 15/26ths, which gives an effective rate of corporation tax on chargeable gains of 30%, the same as the rate of tax paid by individuals on such gains (see below).

A separate tax, known as Development Land Tax ('DLT'), is currently charged at the rate of 60% to the extent that any development value realised when an interest in land in the UK is disposed of, or when the development of land is commenced, exceeds £ 50,000. The computation of realised development value is complex but a charge generally arises only where land has increased in value due to its potential for development.

2.c. Capital allowances (E)

Certain allowances (known as capital allowances) are deductible from profits for tax purposes in respect of various types of capital expenditure (including plant and machinery and industrial buildings).

A 100% allowance in respect of the cost of plant and machinery is available to a company that purchases plant or machinery for the purposes of its trade. The allowance is usually taken for the whole expenditure in the year in which it is incurred. However, a company may disclaim any part of its 'first year allowance'. The part disclaimed will then be subject to an annual 25% 'writing down allowance' on a reducing balance basis.

Expenditure on the construction of an industrial building or structure which will be occupied for the purposes of certain trades will qualify for an 'initial allowance' of 75% and an annual writing down allowance of 4%. Where the building or structure is situated in an 'enterprise zone' (see F(e) below) an initial allowance of 100% of the capital cost of the construction of an industrial or a commercial building will be granted in the year in which that expenditure is incurred. The 100% initial allowance also applies to expenditure on 'small workshops' that is, industrial buildings with an internal floor space not exceeding 2,500 square feet.

Subject to certain anti-avoidance provisions, capital allowances can be set against the profits of the trade in respect of which they are available in full. Any surplus allowances will create a taxation loss in that trade which will be available for utilisation as explained in A2(a) above.

In the case of both plant and machinery and industrial buildings, the benefit of capital allowances previously given may be recovered by the Revenue in whole or in part, on the disposal, or deemed disposal, of the asset in question. This will occur, for example, if the asset is disposed of for more than the tax written down value.

2.d. Stock relief

The taxable profits of a company's trade in an accounting period will include any increase in the value of its trading stock over that period. By way of relief, a company may claim a deduction against its profits of an amount calculated by reference to percentage movements in a special index over the period of account reflecting the average price of stock. This relief, known as 'stock relief', may, however, be 'clawed back' from the company if the business ceases or the scale of its operations become small in comparison to its recent past. In such a case all the stock relief claimed over the previous 6 years will be brought into the charge to tax. Relief that has not been clawed back, however, may not be recovered if it is attributable to a period of account which ended six or more years before the period in which the recovery is sought. The first £ 2,000 of stock does not qualify for relief.

2.e. Close companies

Additional restrictions and rules apply for tax purposes to certain companies, known as close companies. A close company is a company which is under the control of five or fewer 'participators' or of any number of participators who are directors of that company. The terms 'participator' and 'control' have wide meanings. However, broadly the term 'participator' includes a person who has a share or interest in the capital, income or assets of the company. A company which is controlled by a company which is not a close company will not itself be a close company. Certain companies whose shares are quoted on a recognized stock exchange and in which the public have a substantial interest are also excluded from the definition of close company. The majority of the taxation disadvantages of close trading company status have been removed. The principal restrictions which remain are, in outline, the following:-

a. Subject to certain exceptions, if a close company distributes to its shareholders less than 100% of its investment income (as distinct from its trading income) the undistributed balance of that income may be apportioned among the company's participators according to their respective interests in the company. Any sum so apportioned to an individual must be included in his total income for income tax purposes. Income tax at the basic rate is treated as having been paid on the sum apportioned, but the individual remains liable to income tax at the higher rates and to the investment income surcharge.

b. The term 'distribution' has an extended meaning in the case of a close company with the result that certain benefits provided for participators are treated as distributions. Accordingly, they are not deductible from the profits of the company for tax purposes and advance corporation tax is payable in respect of those distributions.

The above is only a brief summary of the complex provisions relating to close companies. Careful consideration should be given to the precise terms of those provisions in any proposed transaction involving close companies to ensure that excessive tax liability does not arise.

3. RATES OF TAX

Under the imputation system of tax, corporation tax is charged at a single rate, assessed on the profits of accounting periods, whether distributed or not. This single rate is fixed in arrear and for the financial year 1980 (i.e. 1st April, 1980 - 31st March, 1981) is 52%.

When a company declares a dividend or otherwise makes a distribution of its profits it is required to make an advance payment of corporation tax (known as Advance Corporation Tax or 'ACT'). The rate of ACT for the financial year 1981 is 3/7 ths. Thus, if a company pays a dividend of £ 70 to a shareholder in that financial year, it must also account to the Inland Revenue for ACT of £ 30. An individual shareholder then receives a tax credit equal to the amount of the ACT (see further in A4 below).

ACT paid on distributions during an accounting period may, subject to certain limits, be set-off against the company's liability to corporation tax on its income profits (but not its chargeable capital gains) for that accounting period. In no case may a company set-off against its liability to corporation tax ACT exceeding an amount equal to the ACT that would have been payable if the company had made a distribution equal to the whole of the income charged to corporation tax in that accounting period. Surplus ACT which cannot be set against corporation tax of the period in which it is paid, may usually be carried back and set-off against tax paid in the preceeding two years or carried forward indefinitely against any future corporation tax liability.

The balance of corporation tax payable at this point is known as 'mainstream corporation tax'.

There is a special rate of corporation tax (currently 40% 'the small companies rate') for UK resident companies having profits which do not exceed £ 80,000. Where profits exceed £ 80,000 but do not exceed £ 200,000 the effective rate of tax progressively increases with the effect that, where profits exceed £ 200,000, the full rate of 52% is applicable. Thus, corporation tax on profits falling between these figures is payable at a marginal rate of 60%. Where, however, a company is associated with other companies, the figures of £ 80,000 and £ 200,000 respectively must be divided by one plus the number of those associated companies. Companies are associated if one has control of the other or each is controlled by a third company. A company may be associated with another even though it is not resident in the UK and trades entirely abroad. Thus, where a foreign company trades in the UK through a UK resident subsidiary, the availability of the small companies rate will be diminished.

4. TAX CREDITS

Where a distribution is made to a UK resident individual by a company in which he holds shares, it will carry with it a tax credit corresponding to the amount of ACT paid in respect of that distribution. The credit can be set off against the individual's liability to income tax at the basic rate in respect of the distribution. A UK resident company receiving a distribution from another UK resident company may set-off the tax credit against its own obligation to make an ACT payment on any distributions made by it in the same period.

A non-UK resident is generally not entitled to a UK tax credit in respect of dividend payments unless the relevant double taxation treaty so provides. For example, the treaties between the UK and Denmark, France, Ireland, Luxembourg and the Netherlands have been amended to enable such a credit to be given.

A more detailed examination of the tax treatment of distributions made by a UK company to non-UK residents is given in the Schedule of United Kingdom Double Taxation Agreements at J below.

5. TIMING OF PAYMENTS

Advance Corporate Income Tax is calculated by reference to distributions made in a company's accounting period. A return of distributions is made to the Inland Revenue within 14 days of the end of each 'return period' (usually quarterly). The ACT payable in respect of distributions made during the return period is due when the return is made.

Mainstream corporation tax is normally due 9 months after the end of the company's accounting period, or one month after the Inland Revenue issues an assessment, whichever is the later. If tax is not paid promptly, interest is charged currently at the rate of 12% per annum. Such interest payments are not deductible in computing profits for taxation purposes.

6. REVIEW AND APPEAL

The company has 30 days in which to appeal against an assessment issued by the Inland Revenue. Following the making of an appeal, the company's tax liability is usually determined by agreement with the Inland Revenue. If agreement cannot be reached, the liability is adjudicated by a tribunal of General or Special Commissioners of Income Tax. If either party disputes the Commissioner's decision, an appeal on a point of law only may be made to the High Court. Thereafter, further appeal may lie to the Court of Appeal and the House of Lords. There is no appeal from a finding of fact by the Commissioners (an incorrect finding of fact may in certain circumstances, however, amount to a question of law against which an appeal may be made).

B. Withholding Taxes on Dividends, Interest and Royalties

1. DIVIDENDS

As mentioned in A.3 above, when a company pays a dividend, the company must account to the Inland Revenue for Advance Corporation Tax at the rate of 3/7ths of the amount of that dividend. ACT is, however, not a withholding tax and can give rise to a tax credit (see 'Tax Credits' above and J below).

2. INTEREST

Where any yearly interest on money is paid by a company, or by any person to a person whose usual place of abode is outside the UK, the payer must deduct out of it a sum representing an amount equal to basic rate income tax thereon (currently 30%).
The requirement to make a deduction on account of income tax on the payment of yearly interest does not apply in the case of payments to and by banks in the ordinary course of their banking business in the UK.

3. ROYALTIES

Where any royalty or other sum is paid in respect of the use of a patent, the payer must similarly deduct from it a sum representing the basic rate of income tax thereon.

4. EFFECT OF TAX TREATIES

The requirements mentioned in B.1-3 may be modified by the provisions of any relevant double tax treaty. Thus, in certain cases, the rate of the deduction may be reduced or eliminated by the treaty. A Schedule of the applicable rates and an outline of any tax credit attaching to a dividend payment under the principal UK double taxation treaties is set out at J below. This Schedule is designed as only a broad guide, however, and reference in any particular case should always be made to the detailed provisions of the relevant treaty.

C. Registration and Stamp Duties

1. STAMP DUTY

Stamp duty is a tax payable on certain documents which pass title to property, the duty being assessed on the value of the assets transferred by the document. Duty is not paid, however, where assets, such as trading stock, merchandise and moveable plant and machinery, are transferred by delivery.
Transfers of assets between associated companies may not attract stamp duty if the transferor and transferee are related by a 90% shareholding and certain other conditions are satisfied. Relief from stamp duty may also be given in the case of transfers of assets as part of the amalgamation, reconstruction or demerger of a company or companies.
The rate of stamp duty is 2%. Reduced rates may apply to the transfer of certain assets whose value is less than £ 35,000. Transfers of marketable securities to non-UK residents bear duty at only 1%.

2. CAPITAL DUTY

Capital duty is charged at £ 1 per £ 100 or part hereof on certain transactions of involving company capital – principally the formation and increase in the capital of a limited company. Duty is charged on the actual value of assets contributed to the company. Relief from capital duty may be obtained on an issue of shares on the amalgamation, reconstruction or demerger of a company.

3. FEES ON REGISTRATION OF UK COMPANIES

On the registration of a new company in the UK, a fee of £ 50 is payable. Each year thereafter, a fee of £ 20 will be payable when the statutory annual return is filed.

D. Individual Taxation

1. INCOME TAX

An individual is subject to UK income tax in respect of:
(i) any income which accrues to him from a UK source irrespective of whether or not he is a resident of the UK; and
(ii) his worldwide income if he is resident in the UK, but subject to certain exceptions if he is either not domiciled or not ordinarily resident in the UK.
A person will normally be regarded as resident in the UK if he:
a. visits the UK for more than 182 days in a tax year; or
b. visits the UK for 90 days on average each tax year for a period of four consecutive tax years; or
c. has accomodation available for his use in the UK and he visits the UK at any time during the tax year. This rule does not apply, however, where the individual works full time outside the UK in an employment trade, profession or vocation and only performs incidental duties in the UK.
Ordinary residence broadly implies habitual residence in the ordinary course of an individual's life and may be contrasted with special, occasional or casual residence. In practice, if an individual has been resident in the UK for four consecutive years, he will also be regarded as being ordinarily resident in the UK in the fourth year. A person who comes to the UK to take up permanent residence or to work in the UK for at least three years may also be regarded as ordinarily resident in the UK from the date of his arrival in the UK.
Domicile means, briefly, the place which a person regards as his permanent home and is determined by an individual's actual presence in a country coupled with an intention of permanently residing there. A person coming to the UK to work for a branch or subsidiary of an overseas company will not usually be regarded as domiciled in the UK.

– UK source income

As mentioned above, all individuals are subject to UK tax on income which arises in the UK. A UK resident will be taxed on that income at the basic and, if applicable, the higher rates of tax. Unearned (or investment) income is also subject to the 'investment income surcharge' if it exceeds a certain amount in a tax year.
Where a person not domiciled in the UK is employed by an employer who is not resident in the UK, a deduction equal to one half of the amount of the emoluments, which are subject to UK taxation, is given. The deduction is reduced to 25%, if the individual has been resident in the UK in nine out of ten successive tax years.
A non-UK resident in receipt of UK source income may also be charged to income tax at the basic and higher rates and the investment income surcharge. (By Revenue concession interest paid on money deposited in a bank in the UK is, depending on the depositor's overall circumstances, not subject to tax).

– **Non-UK source income**

A UK resident is usually charged to UK income tax on non-UK source income which accrues to him whether or not it is received into the UK. An individual who, if a British subject, is not ordinarily resident or a person not domiciled in the UK is, however, only liable to tax on such income if it is brought into the UK.

2. COMPUTATION OF INCOME

2.a. Income

Taxable income is calculated by taking the net income of an individual from each source, and deducting therefrom the charges on income, personal allowances and other reliefs to which that individual is entitled in the tax year in question.
The most common charge against an individual's income is that in respect of payments of interest on a loan not exceeding £ 25,000 to purchase a house for the occupation of the individual. Interest on loans to purchase certain interests in close companies is also allowable as a charge.
A single person is entitled to a personal allowance of £ 1,375 for the tax year 1982/82 and a married man £ 2,145. A married man is also given an allowance of up to £ 1,375 in respect of any earned income of his wife in a tax year.
A tax year runs from 6th April to the following 5th April.

2.b. Capital gains tax

Gains realised by individuals resident or ordinarily resident in the UK during a tax year on the disposal of chargeable assets (wherever situated) are subject to capital gains tax. The gain is calculated in the same manner as for companies (see A2 above). No tax is charged on any gain arising on the disposal of an individual's only or main residence, or of movable physical property valued at less than £ 1,000. Where a person is not domiciled in the UK capital gains tax is only charged on the disposal of assets situate outside the UK if the gains are remitted to the UK.

3. RATES OF TAX

Income tax is charged for the tax year 1981/82 at the basic rate of 30% on the first £ 11,250 of an individuals taxable income. Thereafter, tax is charged at higher rates rising to 60% on taxable income in excess of £ 27,750. Investment income above £ 5,500 is also subject to tax at an additional rate of 15% (the 'investment income surcharge').
Capital gains tax is charged at a flat rate of 30%, but the first £ 3,000 of an individual's chargeable gains are exempt from tax.

4. SUCCESSION DUTIES

Capital Transfer Tax ('CTT') is charged generally on transfers of property or assets wherever situate by an individual which are either made as a gift by him during his lifetime or are deemed to be made on his death. If an individual is not domiciled in the UK, however, CTT is only chargeable on property situate in the UK.
The rates of CTT are progressive and are applied by reference to the cumulative total of the value of all the transferor's chargeable transfers in the previous ten years. The value of a transfer is taken to be the amount by which the value of the transferor's estate is reduced by reason of his having made the transfer in question.
A gift of property during a person's lifetime may also involve a charge to capital gains tax. Capital gains tax is not, however, chargeable on an individual's death.

E. Indirect Taxation

1. VALUE ADDED TAX (F)

In common with the other members of the EEC, the UK has adopted a value added tax ('VAT'). VAT is imposed on all supplies of goods and services in the UK by a taxable person in the course of a business and on all imports of goods, into the UK except where the goods or supplies are exempt supplies. VAT is generally levied at a standard rate of 15%, although a nil or zero rate applies to certain categories of goods or supplies. Exports of goods and services, for example, are usually zero-rated, as are food, books, newspapers and journals, sources of power, transport, the construction of buildings and clothing and footwear for children.
Exempt supplies are supplies of land, insurance, postal services, betting and gaming, finance, education and health services. A taxable person is defined as a person who makes taxable supplies in excess of £ 15,000 per year*. Such a person is required to register for VAT purposes and to charge VAT on all supplies made or treated as made by him. A taxable person may also reclaim VAT paid by him on supplies to him for the purposes of his business. However, a taxable person who makes any exempt supplies of goods or services may not be able to reclaim all the VAT he has paid to his suppliers.

2. CAR TAX

This is a separate tax payable (in addition to VAT) on new locally made and imported motor cars and motor cycles at the rate of 10% of the wholesale value of the car or motor cycle.

F. Incentives

In addition to the other reliefs mentioned elsewhere (i.e. capital allowances at A.2 (c); and stock relief at A.2 (d)), substantial grants and other kinds of financial assistance are available to companies from government sources. It should be noted that with the abolition of exchange control on 24th October 1979 there is no restriction on the repatriation of profits to non-UK investors.

1. SELECTIVE FINANCIAL ASSISTANCE FOR PROJECTS IN THE NATIONAL INTEREST

This assistance, usually in the form of loans or interest relief grants, is available on a discretionary basis where such assistance is likely to benefit the economy and where it is in the national interest. Such assistance has previously been granted to aid specific sectors of industry and to promote the development or expansion of industrial capacity in general.

2. REGIONAL INCENTIVES (G)

Government assistance is available for areas (known as Assisted Areas) suffering from problems of unemployment and economic imbalance. The most important kinds of regional incentives in the Assisted Areas are as follows: –

(i) Cash grants are available towards capital expenditure incurred in the provision of new buildings, adaptations of existing buildings and new machinery and plant. The grant is generally confined to the manufacturing business.

(ii) Discretionary assistance may be given to projects which will improve employment prospects. The assistance usually takes the form of loans at commercial rates of interest.

(iii) Grants towards employee costs are available where employers transfer key workers into an Assisted Area. The grant may include travelling, removal and settling-in costs.

(iv) Assistance from EEC funds in the form of grants is not generally directly available to private industry, but the European Investment Bank will lend up to 40% of the cost of projects in Assisted Areas for certain modernisation schemes and projects of common interest to several member states. Loans are also available from the European Coal and Steel Community for projects in the coal and steel industries and for re-employment of redundant workers from these industries.

(v) The Regional Development Agencies and the National Enterprise Board may offer assistance usually in the form of loans or equity participation, to private industry on a discretionary basis.

(vi) Companies in certain Assisted Areas are given preferential treatment in tenders for government and public contracts.

3. EMPLOYMENT GRANTS

A number of special schemes operate to mitigate the effects of unemployment. These generally apply to the employment and training of young workers, deferral of redundancies and labour intensive projects.

4. SPECIALISED INDUSTRIES

Special incentive schemes operate in a number of industries, in particular agriculture and fisheries, offshore supplies and services, research and development, mineral exploitation, transport and small or rural projects.

5. ENTERPRISE ZONES

To attract industries and employment to certain areas of the UK, parts of the UK have been designated as 'enterprise zones' by the Secretary of State. Enterprise zones are at present located in Clydebank, Inner Belfast, Lower Swansea Valley, Speke, Isle of Dogs in East London, parts of Newcastle and Gateshead and parts of Salford Docks and Trafford Park in Manchester.

G. *Social Security Premiums (H)*

The UK has an extensive social security system, which is financed out of national insurance contributions paid by employers and employees. Employers only contribute if they are UK resident or have a place of business in the UK. When an employee comes to work in the UK from abroad, social security contributions must be paid from the commencement of his employment or long-term residence. Contributions are generally related to earnings. The rates of contribution in respect of all employees in the UK are currently as follows:

	Employee	*Employer*
standard rate	7.75%	13.7%
	(of earnings up to £ 200 per week – no contribution if earnings do not exceed £ 27 per week).	
contracted-out rate – i.e. employee has	7.75%	13.7%
	(of earnings up to £ 27 per week)	
elected not to take part in the state	5.25%	9.2%
pension scheme	(of earnings between £ 27 and £ 200 per week).	

Contributions are also paid, at different rates, by self-employed persons.

H. Other Imposts: PAYE and Rates

1. PAYE

PAYE is the abbreviation for 'Pay As You Earn', which is the system by which an employer deducts income tax from the pay of his employees and accounts for it to the Inland Revenue. The employer must remit the sums so deducted to the Revenue following each tax month. If the employer fails to deduct sufficient tax he remains liable to the Revenue for the amount which should have been deducted. The employer has no general right of recovery against the employee.

2. RATES

Rates are a property tax levied by local government authorities at varying rates on the value of land or real property owned or occupied by companies or individuals to finance local authority services.

I. List of United Kingdom Double Taxation Agreements

Antigua:	Arrangement of 19 December 1947 Amending Agreement of 5 March 1968
Argentina:	Agreement of 28 July 1949 (Shipping and Air transport profits)
Australia:	Agreement of 7 December 1967 Amending Protocol of 29 January 1980
Austria:	Convention of 30 April 1969 Protocol of 17 November 1977
Bangladesh:	Convention of 8 August 1979
Barbados:	Agreement of 26 March 1970 Amending Protocol of 18 September 1973
Belgium:	Convention of 29 August 1967
Belize:	Arrangement of 19 December 1947 Amending Arrangement of 8 April 1968 Amending Supplementary Arrangement of 12 December 1973
Botswana:	Agreement of 5 October 1977
Brazil:	Agreement of 29 December 1967 (Shipping and Air transport profits)
Brunei:	Arrangement of 8 December 1950 Amending Arrangement of 4 March 1968 Ammending Supplementary Arrangement of 12 December 1973.

Burma:	Agreement of 13 March 1950
	Supplementary Protocol of 4 April 1951
Canada:	Agreement of 12 December 1966
	Convention of 8 September 1978
	Protocol of 14 April 1980
Cyprus:	Convention of 20 June 1974
	Protocol of 2 April 1980
Denmark:	Convention of 11 November 1980
Dominica:	Arrangement of 4 March 1949
	Amending Agreement of 7 March 1968
Egypt:	Convention of 25 April 1977
Ethiopia:	Agreement of 1 February 1977 (Air transport profits)
Falkland Islands:	Arrangement of 4 March 1949
	Amending Arrangement of 8 April 1968
	Amending Supplementary Arrangement of 18 December 1974
Faroe Islands:	Danish Convention of 27 March 1950
	Extension of 31 October 1960
	Danish Amending Supplementary Protocol of 18 December 1968
	Extension of 27 November 1970
	Danish Amending Supplementary Protocol of 8 February 1973
	Extension of 7 March 1975
Fiji:	Convention of 21 November 1975
Finland:	Convention of 17 July 1969
	Amending Protocol of 17 May 1973
	Amending Protocol of 16 November 1979
France:	Convention of 22 May 1968
	Amending Supplementary Protocol of 14 May 1973
Gambia:	Convention of 20 May 1980*
German Federal Republic:	Convention of 26 November 1964
	Amending Protocol of 23 March 1970
Ghana:	Convention of 29 November 1977
Greece:	Convention of 25 June 1953
Grenada:	Arrangement of 4 March 1949
	Amending Agreement of 25 July 1968
Guernsey:	Arrangement of 24 June 1952
Hungary:	Convention of 28 November 1977
Iceland:	Agreement of 27 April 1928 (Shipping profits)
Indonesia:	Agreement of 13 March 1974
Iran:	Agreement of 21 December 1960 (Air transport profits)
Irish Republic:	Convention of 2 June 1976
	Amending Protocol of 28 October 1976
Isle of Man:	Arrangement of 29 July 1955
Israel:	Convention of 26 September 1962

	Amending Protocol of 20 April 1970
Italy:	Convention of 4 July 1960
	Exchange of Notes of 4 July 1960
	Amending Protocol of 28 April 1969
Jamaica:	Agreement of 16 March 1973
Japan:	Convention of 10 February 1969
	Exchange of Notes of 10 February 1969
	Amending Protocol of 14 February 1980
Jersey:	Arrangement of 24 June 1952
Jordan:	Agreement of 6 March 1978
	(Shipping and air transport profits)
Kenya:	Agreement of 31 July 1973
	Amending Protocol of 20 January 1976
	Exchange of Notes of 8 February 1977
Kiribati and Tuvalu:	Arrangement of 10 May 1950
	Amending Arrangement of 4 March 1968
	Amending Supplementary Arrangement of 25 July 1974
Korea:	Convention of 21 April 1977
	Protocol of 21 April 1977
Lebanon:	Agreement of 26 February 1964
	(Shipping and air transport profits)
Lesotho:	Arrangement of 25 November 1949
	Amending Agreement of 3 July 1968
Luxembourg:	Convention of 24 May 1967
	Amending Protocol of 18 July 1978
Malawi:	Agreement of 25 November 1955
	Amending Agreement of 1 April 1964
	Amending Agreement of 2 April 1968
	Supplementary amending Agreement of 10 February 1978
Malaysia:	Agreement of 30 March 1973
	Amending Protocol of 30 March 1973
Malta:	Arrangement of 28 March 1962
	Amending Agreement of 29 November 1974
Mauritius:	Arrangement of 8 August 1947
Montserrat:	Arrangement of 19 December 1947
	Amending Arrangement of 8 April 1968
Netherlands:	Convention of 7 November 1980
Netherland Antilles:	Dutch Convention of 31 October 1967
	Extension of 24 July 1970
New Zealand:	Agreement of 13 June 1966
	Protocol of 25 March 1980
Norway:	Convention of 22 January 1969
	Amending Protocol of 23 June 1977
	Second amending Protocol of 29 March 1978
	Exchange of Notes of 5 May 1978
	Third amending Protocol of 16 October 1979
	Fourth amending Protocol of 16 October 1979
	Fifth amending Protocol of 30 September 1980*

Pakistan:	Agreement of 24 April 1961
Philippines:	Convention of 10 June 1976
Poland:	Convention of 16 December 1976
Portugal:	Convention of 27 March 1968
Romania:	Convention of 18 September 1975 Exchange of Notes of 3 February 1976
St. Christopher (St. Kitts) & Nevis:	Arrangement of 19 December 1947
St. Lucia:	Arrangement of 4 March 1949 Amending Agreement of 5 April 1968
St. Vincent:	Arrangement of 4 March 1949 Amending Agreement of 1 April 1968
Seychelles:	Arrangement of 8 August 1947 Amending Arrangement of 18 March 1969 Amending Supplementary Arrangement of 25 July 1974
Sierra Leone:	Arrangement of 19 December 1947 Amending Agreement of 18 March 1968
Singapore:	Agreement of 1 December 1966 Amending Protocol of 21 July 1975 Exchange of Notes of 27 December 1975 Exchange of Notes of 12 March 1976 Exchange of Notes of 23 July 1977
Solomon Islands:	Arrangement of 10 May 1950 Amending Arrangement of 8 April 1968 Amending Supplementary Arrangement of 25 July 1974
South Africa:	Convention of 21 November 1968
South West Africa (Namibia):	S. African Convention of 28 May 1962 Extension of 8 August 1962 S. African Amending Protocol of 14 June 1967 Extension of 14 June 1967
Spain:	Convention of 21 October 1975
Sri Lanka:	Convention of 21 June 1979 Exchange of Notes of 13 February 1980
Sudan:	Convention of 8 March 1975
Swaziland:	Agreement of 26 November 1968
Sweden:	Convention of 28 July 1960 Amending Supplementary Protocol of 27 June 1968 Amending Supplementary Protocol of 27 September 1973 Amending Supplementary Protocol of 6 June 1979
Switzerland:	Convention of 8 December 1977
Trinidad & Tobago:	Agreement of 29 December 1966 Amending Protocol of 10 December 1969 Supplementary Protocol of 15 November 1971
Uganda:	Arrangement of 24 June 1952
Union of Soviet	Agreement of 3 May 1974

Socialist Republics:	(Air transport profits and employees)
United States of America:	Convention of 31 December 1975 Exchange of Notes of 13 April 1976 Amending Protocol of 26 August 1976 Amending Protocol of 31 March 1977 Amending Protocol of 15 March 1979
Venezuela:	Agreement of 8 March 1978
Zaire:	Agreement of 11 October 1976 (Shipping and air transport profits)
Zambia:	Convention of 22 March 1972
Zimbabwe:	Agreement of 25 November 1955 Amending Agreement of 23 July 1964

The list is up-to-date 27 May 1981.

J. Schedule of United Kingdom Withholding Taxes on Interest and Royalty Payments and Tax Treatment of Dividends

	Interest	*Royalties*	*Dividends*
Antigua	*	Nil	Nil A
Australia	10%	10%	15% B, D
Austria	Nil	Nil or 10%	15% B, C, D
Bangladesh	7½ or 10%	10%	10% or 15% F
Barbados	15%	15%	15% B, C, D
Belgium	15%	Nil	Nil A
Belize	*	Nil	15% B, C, D
Botswana	15%	15%	15% B, C, D
Brunei	*	Nil	15% B, C, D
Burma	*	Nil	Nil A
Canada	15%	Nil or 10%	15% B, C, D

* Indicates the Agreement or Protocol is not yet in force.

	Interest	*Royalties*	*Dividends*
Cyprus (5)	10%	Nil or 5%	15% B, C, D
Denmark	Nil	Nil	5% or 15% B, E
Dominica	*	Nil	Nil A
Egypt	15%	15%	20% F
Falkland Islands	*	Nil	15% B, C, D
Faroe Islands	Nil	Nil	15% B, C, D
Fiji	10%	Nil or 15%	15% B, C, D
Finland	Nil	Nil	5% or 15% B, D, E
France	10%	Nil	15% B, C, D
Gambia	15%	12½%	15% B, C, D
German Federal Republic	Nil	Nil	Nil A
Ghana	15%	15%	15% B, C, D
Greece	Nil	Nil	X
Grenada	*	Nil	Nil A
Guernsey	*	+	X
Hungary	Nil	Nil	5% or 15% F
Indonesia	10% or 15%	10%	15% B, C
Irish Republic	Nil	Nil	15% B, C, D
Isle of Man	*	+	X
Israel	15%	15%	Nil A
Italy	*(1)	Nil	Nil A
Jamaica	12½%	10%	15% B, C
Japan	10%	10%	15% B, C

	Interest	*Royalties*	*Dividends*
Jersey	*	+	X
Kenya	15%	15%	15% B, C, D
Kiribati and Tuvalu	*	Nil	15% B, C, D
Korea	10% or 15%	10% or 15%	15% B, C
Lesotho	*	Nil	Nil A
Luxembourg	Nil	5%	5% or 15% B, E
Malawi	Nil (2)	Nil (2)	15% B, C, D
Malaysia	15%	15%	15% B, C, D
Malta	*	Nil	15% B, C
Mauritius	*	Nil	Nil A
Montserrat	*	Nil	Nil A
Netherlands	Nil	Nil	5% or 10% B, D, E
Netherlands Antilles	Nil	Nil	Nil A
New Zealand	*	15%	15% B, D
Norway	Nil	Nil	5% or 15% B, D, E
Pakistan	*(3)	Nil	Nil A
Philippines	10% or 15%	15% or 25%	25% B, C
Poland	Nil	10%	15% B, C
Portugal	10%	5%	Nil A
Romania	10%	10% or 15%	15% B, C
St. Christopher & St. Nevis (St. Kitts)	*	Nil	Nil A
St. Lucia	*	Nil	Nil A

	Interest	Royalties	Dividends
St. Vincent	*	Nil	Nil A
Seychelles	*	Nil	15% B, C, D
Sierra Leone	*	Nil	Nil A
Singapore	15%	15%	15% B, C, D
Solomon Islands	*	Nil	15% B, C, D
South Africa	10%	Nil	Nil A
South West Africa	*(4)	Nil or 5%	Nil A
Spain	12%	10%	15% B, C, D
Sri Lanka	10%	Nil or 10%	15% F
Sudan	15%	10%	15% B, C, D
Swaziland	*	Nil	Nil A
Sweden	Nil	Nil	5% or 15% B, D, E
Switzerland	Nil	Nil	5% or 15% B, E
Trinidad and Tobago	10%	Nil or 10%	Nil A
Uganda	*	Nil	Nil A
United States of America	Nil	Nil	5% or 15% B, D, E
Zambia	10%	10%	Nil A

The notes at the end of the Schedule must be referred to in any case under consideration.
Schedule J comprises only those countries with which the UK has a comprehensive Agreement.
The rates of tax are those applicable to payments from the UK to residents of the other state.
The Notes below form an integral part of the Schedule and both should be read in conjunction with the relevant passages on United Kingdom domestic tax legislation. The Schedule is up to date to 27 May 1981.

Notes

* No interest Article. UK domestic legislation is applicable.

(1) Interest Article does not cover existing taxes.
(2) Interest and royalty Article provides that exemption from taxation is not applicable if the recipient company owns 50% or more of the paying company.
(3) Interest Article does not provide for exemption to taxation or reduced rates.
(4) Interest Article is not applicable to payments from the UK to a resident of the other state.
(5) Interest, royalty and dividend Articles do not apply to residents who enjoy special fiscal benefits under provisions of Cyprus legislation.
\+ No royalty Article.
X No dividend Article.
A. There is no provision for payment of the tax credit (or any part thereof) which would be available to a UK resident shareholder. The Article does not now apply to dividends payable to a resident of the other state.
B. A resident of the other state who receives a dividend from a UK resident company, provided he is the beneficial owner of that dividend, is entitled to the tax credit available to a UK resident and to the payment of any excess of that credit over his liability to UK tax. Tax is charged at the rate of 15% on the aggregate of the amount of the dividend and the tax credit.
C. A tax credit is not available where the beneficial owner of the dividend is a company which either alone or together with one or more associated companies controls directly or indirectly at least 10%* of the voting power of the company paying the dividend.
D. If the beneficial owner of the dividend, being a resident of the other state, owns at least 10% or more of the class of shares in respect of which the dividend is paid then relief under the Article is not available to the extent to which the dividend can have been paid only out of profits which the company paying the dividend earned or other income which is received in a period ending 12 months or more before the relevant date. The term 'relevant date' means the date on which the beneficial owner of the dividend became the owner of 10% or more of the class of shares in question. Such provision is not applicable if the beneficial owner of the dividend shows that the shares were acquired for bona fide commercial reasons and not primarily for the purpose of securing the benefit of the Article.
E. Where the beneficial owner of the dividend, being a resident of the other state, is a company, which either alone or together with one or more associated companies controls, directly or indirectly, at least 10% of the voting power of the paying company, that company is entitled to a tax credit equal to one half of the tax credit that would have been available to a resident of the UK and to the payment of any excess over its liability to UK tax. Tax is charged at the rate of 5% on the aggregate of the amount of the dividend and the available tax credit.
F. Dividend Article does not provide for payment of the tax credit available to a UK resident (or any part thereof). However, it is understood that in practice no additional tax will be charged under the Article in the UK on a payment of a dividend to a resident of the other state.

* NB 20% with regard to Switzerland.

IV. LABOUR ASPECTS

A. *Principles of Law on Employment*

An employer in the United Kingdom is generally speaking free to employ any person for a particular position so long as the employer does not discriminate on the grounds of either race or sex.

An employment contract may be either oral or in writing although there has been a statutory requirement since 1972 (now contained in the Employment Protection (Consolidation) Act 1978) for the employer to provide an employee within 13 weeks of the commencement of employment with a statement of his terms and conditions of employment. This statement should specify among other things the commencement date (including whether the employment is continuous from employment with another employer), hours of work, remuneration, holidays, sickness pay, grievance procedure and a disciplinary procedure. The statement is not the contract itself, although it is, of course, good evidence of the terms of the contract.

Formal employment contracts in writing are more commonly used for senior employees, or those fulfilling special roles, than for employees generally. These are normally adopted when the employer and employee desire to provide for a service period of a number of years. In the case of directors, the Companies Act 1980 now effectively prohibits a period exceeding five years if the company is not free within that period to terminate the employment by notice, unless such period has been approved first by the company in general meeting of the shareholders.

Employees have a number of rights and duties but, within the scope of this chapter only the rights concerning an employee's security will be considered. Fundamentally there are two rights in this context: first, the right not to be wrongfully dismissed and second, the right not to be unfairly dismissed.

– WRONGFUL DISMISSAL

A claim for wrongful dismissal is a claim for breach of the employment contract by virtue of the failure of the employer to give any notice of termination of the employment or insufficient notice.

The proper period of notice is either the period agreed as a term of the contract between the employer and the employee or 'reasonable notice', a concept implied by the common law. The period of 'reasonable notice' depends upon the nature of the employment and its duration but, in any event, it can never be less than the minimum periods enacted by Parliament in 1972 which are now detailed in Section 49 of the Employment Protection (Consolidation) Act 1978 namely:

a. 4 weeks to 2 years employment – 1 week's notice

b. 2 years to 12 years employment – 1 week's notice for each year of continuous employment

c. 12 years or more – not less than 12 week's notice.

A claim for wrongful dismissal is presented in the ordinary courts and the remedy is damaged. The employee is obliged, following the breach of contract, to endeavour to mitigate his loss by finding suitable alternative employment. If an employee fails to mitigate his loss in this way, the damages awarded to him may be reduced.

– UNFAIR DISMISSAL

Until 1971 employees in the UK only enjoyed the right not to be wrongfully dismissed. As will be seen from the above, it is a limited remedy and, in order to provide additional protection to employees, the right not to be unfairly dismissed was introduced by Parliament in 1971. The provisions relating to it are now enshrined in the Employment Protection (Consolidation) Act 1978 as amended by the Employment Act 1980.
Subject to certain exceptions, an employee who has been continuously employed for a minimum period of 52 weeks enjoys the right not to be unfairly dismissed. A claim of unfair dismissal is presented to an Industrial Tribunal. If the employee can establish to the satisfaction of the Tribunal that his dismissal was unfair within the meaning of the statute he may be awarded compensation up to a maximum, currently £ 16,910.

– REDUNDANCY

In the above context it is also necessary to have regard to the law relating to redundancy, now also part of the Employment Protection (Consolidation) Act 1978. The legal definition of redundancy is narrower than the ordinary understanding of the term. It occurs when the dismissal arises because the employer ceases or intends to cease to carry on the business for which the employee was employed or in the place where the employee was employed or, alternatively, because the employer's requirements for employees of the particular kind in the place where the employee have ceased or diminished or can be expected to cease or diminish.
Where the circumstances surrounding a dismissal fall precisely within the terms of the definition, an employer may be able to avoid a claim for unfair dismissal. However, to do so, the employer must show both that his reliance on redundancy as a reason for dismissal was reasonable in all the circumstances and that he followed the correct procedures.
The employer must first ensure that his selection of a particular employee for redundancy is fair. If, as is now common in practice, the employer has an agreed procedure for dealing with redundancies, he must show that this has been followed. If there is no agreed procedure, the employer will usually be expected to operate a first in, last out, system. If he does not, he will have to justify his reasons for selecting a particular employee for dismissal. As is the case with unfair dismissal, the employer should also consult in good time with the employee concerned, ascertain his opinions and give him due warning of what is to happen. The employer should also try to find suitable alternative employment for the employee, either in the business in which the employee

is employed or in an associated undertaking. This latter point may be particularly relevant in the common situation of a business closing down in a particular place.

If the employer has failed in any of the above respects he may be unable to rely on redundancy as a fair reason for dismissal before an Industrial Tribunal. If this happens, he will have to make the normal payments of compensation to the employee. If the employer does succeed in his reliance on redundancy, he must generally make a redundancy payment to the employee. These payments are now governed by the 1978 Act and are calculated by reference to age and length of service. To qualify, the employee must have had two years' continuous employment, and the redundancy payment will be subject to a maximum, currently £ 3,900.

All employers make an annual contribution to a national fund, out of which they are partially reimbursed when a redundancy is made. The employer is currently entitled to a rebate of 41% from the State.

In addition to the procedures which an employer should follow to avoid a claim by his employee for unfair dismissal, the employer is, in certain circumstances, required to notify and consult with any recognised independent trade union and the Department of Employment. Failure to do so will result in a 'protective award' being made against him, and these are penal rather than compensatory in nature and may be large. The employer should notify where it is intended to dismiss more than 10 employees en bloc at the same place within 30 days, or more than 100 en bloc within 90 days. The Protective award may be up to 30 days pay for each employee in the former case and up to 90 days pay in the latter if there is a failure to consult.

New Regulations came into force in 1981, which provide that, where an undertaking is transferred, the employees contracts of employment are also transferred and these Regulations provide, amongst other things, for consultation with recognised trade unions. Hitherto, transfers could be arranged in such a way as to break continuity and leave the transferor with responsibility for making redundancy payments.

B. Labour Procedures

There are many different types of workers' organisations of which trades unions are the most important. In order to be a trades union, the organisation must consist wholly of mainly of workers, and must be an organisation whose principal purposes include the regulation of relations between those workers and employers or employers' associations.

A distinction is also made between those trade unions which are, and those which are not, independent trade unions. In order to be an independent trade union, the organisation must, in addition to the definition specified above, not be under the control of an employer or group of employers. A trade union must be independent in practice in order for it to carry out the functions generally expected of a trade union in the UK.

To secure independence it is necessary for a trade union to obtain a Certificate of Independence under the Employment Protection Act 1975. The necessary prerequisites are laid down in this statute and it may be assumed that most trade unions which an employer is likely to negotiate with in practice will be independent.

An independent trade union must be recognised by the employer for the purposes of collective bargaining before a system of collective bargaining is operated. Many unions are recognised by several employers for collective bargaining purposes.

A system of collective bargaining is now well established particularly in the larger and more important industries. A collective agreement made between an employer and a trades union is not legally enforceable unless it is expressly stated to be so. Legal effect is however usually given to agreements reached between employer and a trades union by incorporating, expressly or by implication, the substantive terms of the collective agreement, as to hours, wages and other conditions of employment, into the individual contracts of employment which are binding as between employer and employee.

C. *Works Councils*

In some West European countries, particularly Germany, works councils have been established under legislation to create a measure of compulsory industrial democracy. There has been no such approach in the UK and formal works councils of the European model do not exist. It is erroneous, however, to suggest that there is no worker participation in UK industry, because it exists in various forms and is increasing. The most important development below board level has been the extension of the scope of collective bargaining referred to above.

Collective bargaining is central to UK industrial relations, and the scope of collective bargaining is widening. Trade unions are no longer concentrating exclusively on questions of wages and conditions, and there are now a number of other areas where some trade unions are already in substantive negotiations with management. These areas include provision of facilities for trade union representatives amongst the workforce, manpower planning, job and income security, and the disclosure of information. Recent legislation such as the Employment Protection Act 1975 and the Health and Safety at Work etc. Act 1974 gave legislative backing to specific extension of collective bargaining.

Although the question has been the subject of considerable public debate, there is at present no legislation on industrial democracy (i.e. worker participation on company boards), and it would seem that in the UK the extension of collective bargaining is the principal means whereby employees may increase their say in company decision making.

D. *Pension Schemes*

There is a state pension scheme in the UK to which all employed and self-employed contribute by means of national insurance contributions. By virtue of the Social Security Pensions Act 1975, the state scheme pension payable is divided into two components, the basic component and the additional component. The basic component is the rate of state retirement pension for the time being in force; the additional component is earnings related and is payable in respect of the insured person's 20 best years of earnings, earnings being revalued for each year of the employee's working life in line with subsequent inflation.

National insurance contributions are payable both by employers and employees, and are payable on earnings up to a maximum of 7 times the current annual rate of State retirement pension. This has the effect that the percentage of final earnings received as pension is higher for lower paid than for higher paid workers.

It is possible for the additional component of the state pension scheme to be provided for employees out of their company's private pension scheme, if that pension scheme can satisfy the stringent requirements for contracting-out of the state pension scheme.

Private pension schemes have been common in the United Kingdom for very many years. Indeed pension schemes enjoy attractive tax advantages, and almost all employers of any size have their own schemes. To achieve the available tax advantages, schemes must be exempt approved by the Inland Revenue under the discretionary powers given under the Finance Act 1970. The Superannuation Funds Office of the Inland Revenue issues extremely lengthy and detailed guide-lines as to the benefits which can be provided for employees. The vast majority of pension schemes are funded in advance. The guide-lines are designed, in the interests of employees, to ensure no underfunding and equally, in the interests of preventing unfair tax advantages, to ensure no overfunding.

The maximum benefits allowed by the discretionary rules are generous, but very few schemes provide the maximum benefits allowed. For example the maximum pension allowed on retirement is two-thirds of final pay, part of which can be commuted for a lump sum of a maximum of 1½ times final pay. A pension can be inflation-proofed and guaranteed for five years. On the death of a pensioner, a pension of two-thirds of his pension can be given to his widow and/or minor children. On death in service, a pension can be paid to an employee's widow of two-thirds of the pension which he would have received had he remained in service until retirement age at his pay at the time of his death; also a lump sum can be paid of four times his pay.

As has been indicated above, pension schemes enjoy attractive tax benefits. Contributions both by employers and employees are deductible for tax purposes, and the income of pension schemes (e.g. earned by the pension fund from its investments) is entirely free of tax. Lump sums paid to members or their families are normally free of tax, and pensions are considered as earned, rather than unearned, income and thus not subject to the investment income surcharge.

E. Compulsory Profit Sharing

There are no compulsory profit sharing schemes in the UK, although voluntary schemes do exist and are actively encouraged. The Finance Act 1978 contains provisions giving income tax relief to participants in certain profit sharing schemes. Taxation benefits are only available if the profit sharing scheme in question has been approved by the Inland Revenue under the 1978 Act.

The Finance Act 1980 enlarged upon these provisions and broadened their scope to include relief for savings-related share option schemes for employees. A company operating an approved scheme makes an allocation of funds for the purposes of the scheme to the trustees of the scheme. The idea behind the legislation is that employees and directors should, through their own investment, share in the profits of the company of group for which they work.

The trustees use the funds allocated to them to subscribe or purchase shares in the company which established the scheme or in an associated company. The shares are then earmarked for the employees and directors who participate in the scheme, and a participant will not normally be allowed to deal with his shares in any way within 5 years of their appropriation to him.

Certain requirements must be satisfied if the approval of the Inland Revenue is to be obtained namely:—

1. The trust must be set up in the UK.
2. All persons who have been for five years full time employees or directors of the company operating the scheme must be eligible to participate in the scheme on 'similar terms'.
3. Participants must be employees or directors of the company operating the scheme at the time when the shares are appropriated to them or within the previous 18 months.
4. Only certain kinds of shares may be acquired under an approved profit sharing scheme.
5. If the ordinary share capital of the company whose shares are to be acquired under the scheme is divided into two or more classes, then shares appropriated to participants must not be the shares of the class the majority of which have been acquired under profit sharing or other share incentive or share option schemes.

F. Overseas personnel (I)

If a foreigner wishes to take up residence in the UK, permission must be obtained from the Home Office. If he wishes to work in the UK, his employer must obtain a work permit from the Department of Employment. In practice, there is usually no problem over any work permit required for the managing director of a subsidiary or the chief representative of a branch of a foreign company. Application should be made as early as possible in advance of arrival.

Normally there is no difficulty in obtaining work permits for senior executives or necessary technical experts who, immediately before coming to the UK, are in the employment of the foreign company or one of its associated companies. It is in the clerical and secretarial grades of employment that difficulty will be experienced.

A number of significant changes have recently been made in the arrangements for the issuing of work permits which reflect the level of unemployment in the UK, the need to protect resident workers, and, in addition,the requirement to allow those from the EEC who wish to work in the UK to do so. The position as from the 1st January 1980 is that:–

1. Except as provided in the immigration rules, any person, other than EEC nationals, subject to immigration control, coming to work in the UK is required to have a work permit. Permits are issued for employment in Great Britain by the Department of Employment, and for employment in Northern Ireland by the Department of Manpower Services.
2. The prospective employer must apply to the Department of Employment for a work permit for a named overseas worker and for a specific job. The permit will be issued for an initial period not exceeding 12 months. Only workers between 23 and 54 years of age are eligible for permits. A permit will not be issued if suitable resident labour is available to fill the post.
3. In general an application for a work permit will only be considered if the vacancy is in an occupation which necessarily requires a worker having specified professional and executive qualifications. When applying for the permit, a prospective employer must satisfy the Department of Employment that a genuine vacancy exists, that no suitable resident labour is available and that he has made adequate efforts to find a worker from that source and from the EEC. The employer is expected to notify the vacancy to the nearest employment office and to allow four weeks for a suitable worker to be found. He is also expected to advertise the vacancy in the press or appropriate trade and professional journals, and to undertake to pay the travelling expenses of any worker resident in this country who comes from a distance for a pre-arranged interview or to take up employment.
4. The holder of a work permit is not permanently restricted to the particular job for which the permit was issued, but he will be expected to remain in the same occupation and will require the consent of the Department of Employment for any change of job and for any promotion. A change or promotion will only be approved if the new job satisfies the relevant conditions for the issue of a permit to a person overseas.

V. BIBLIOGRAPHY

Booklets

A. 'Notes for the Guidance of Registered Companies' published by the Department of Trade.
B. 'Corporation Tax' (I.R. 18) issued by the Board of Inland Revenue.
C. 'Capital Gains Tax' (CGT 8) issued by the Board of Inland Revenue.

D. 'Capital Gains Tax – Development gains from Land and First Letting charges' (CGT 10) issued by the Board of Inland Revenue.

E. Four pamphlets issued by the Board of Inland Revenue:
Income Tax and Corporation Tax Capital Allowances, on
Machinery or Plant (CA1),
Industrial Buildings (CA2),
Agricultural or Forestry Buildings and Works (CA3),
Allowances for Scientific Research (CA4).

F. 'Value Added Tax' – General Guide (Notice No. 700) published by HM Customs and Excise.

G. 'Incentives for Industry' published by the Department of Industry.

H. 'National Insurance Contributions' (Leaflet NP 15) published by the Department of Health and Social Security.

I. 'Employment of overseas workers in the UK from 1st January 1980'.
(1) Training and work experience OW21.
(2) Work permits for workers from countries other than EEC member states and Gibralter OW5.

Availability of above booklets (as amended or replaced from time to time):–

A. Department of Trade
Companies House,
55-71 City Road,
London,
EC1Y 1BB

B, C }
D, E } Board of Inland Revenue,
Somerset House, London, WC2

F Board of Customs and Excise,
King's Beam House,
Mark Lane,
London, EC3

G. Department of Industry,
Millbank Tower,
Millbank,
London,
SW1P 4QU

H. Department of Health and Social Security,
Alexander Fleming House,
Elephant and Castle,
London, SE1

I. Department of Employment,
8 St. James's Square,
London, SW1

Text Books

COMPANIES:

Buckley, The Companies Acts, Butterworths, 14th Edition 1981.
Gore-Browne, Companies, Jordans, 43rd edition 1977, loose-leaf.
Gower, Priciples of Modern Company Law, Sweet and Maxwell, 4th ed. 1979, Suppl. 1981.
Palmer, Company law, Stevens & Sons, 22nd edition 1976 volumes 1, 2 and 3 (loose-leaf).

TAX:

Butterworth's Orange and Yellow Tax Handbooks, published annually.
Pinson, Revenue Law, Sweet and Maxwell, 14th edition, 1981.
Simon's Taxes, Butterworths, Vols A-I, loose-leaf.
Wheatcroft and Whiteman, Capital Gains Tax, Sweet and Maxwell, 3rd edition 1981.
Whiteman and Wheatcroft, Income Tax, Sweet and Maxwell, 2nd edition, 1976. Supplements 1980 and 1981.
Bramwell, Taxation of Companies, Sweet and Maxwell, 2nd edition 1979.
De Voil, Value Added Tax, Butterworths, Loose-leaf.

LABOUR LAW:

Hepple and O'Higgins - Encyclopaedia of Labour Relations, Sweet & Maxwell, 1972, 3 vols, loose-leaf.
Harvey, Industrial Relations, and Employment Law, Butterworths, loose-leaf.

* New edition in 2 vols due August 1981.

GPSR Compliance

The European Union's (EU) General Product Safety Regulation (GPSR) is a set of rules that requires consumer products to be safe and our obligations to ensure this.

If you have any concerns about our products, you can contact us on ProductSafety@springernature.com

In case Publisher is established outside the EU, the EU authorized representative is:

Springer Nature Customer Service Center GmbH
Europaplatz 3
69115 Heidelberg, Germany

Batch number: 10824476

Printed by Printforce, the Netherlands